SAINT BRIDGET OF SWEDEN

SAINT BRIDGET IN ECSTASY
from the carved wooden statue in the Vadstena Chapel

SAINT BRIDGET
OF SWEDEN

by
JOHANNES JØRGENSEN

Translated from the Danish by
INGEBORG LUND

VOLUME I
(1303-1349)

*Amodo reputaberis non solum sponsa mea, sed
etiam monacha et mater in Watsteno.*

BRIDGET'S *Revelationes* VII, 31

'Thou shalt not only be counted my bride,
but also a nun and mother in Vadstena.'

CHRIST TO BRIDGET

LONGMANS GREEN AND CO
LONDON · NEW YORK · TORONTO

LONGMANS, GREEN AND CO LTD
6 & 7 CLIFFORD STREET LONDON W I

ALSO AT MELBOURNE AND CAPE TOWN

LONGMANS, GREEN AND CO INC
55 FIFTH AVENUE NEW YORK 3

LONGMANS, GREEN AND CO
215 VICTORIA STREET TORONTO I

ORIENT LONGMANS LTD
BOMBAY CALCUTTA MADRAS

First published 1954

NIHIL OBSTAT: DANIEL DUIVESTEIJN, S.T.D.
Censor deputatus
IMPRIMATUR: E. MORROGH BERNARD, *Vic. Gen.*
WESTMONASTERII, *die 24a Martii, 1954.*

IN MEMORIAM

K. FR. KARLÉN
*'The Watchman by the grave of
Saint Bridget'*
1819–1903

ERIK IHRFORS
'Monk Erik'
1846–1929

TRANSLATOR'S NOTE

In Swedish the letter a with a circle above it—å—is pronounced like the English a in au or aw, but a little more closed.

The a with a diæresis above it—ä—is pronounced like the English e in best.

The letter o with a diæresis—ö—is pronounced approximately like eu in French, *e.g.* heure; the final e in all words is always pronounced, forming a separate syllable. Example: Dovre, in Dovre Fell. It is approximately like the French e in le, ce, but more open.

The word 'ur,' primeval, is pronounced like 'oor' in 'moor.'

The letter i is pronounced like ee in English, *e.g.* keep, and the final e as above, forming a separate syllable.

PREFACE

AMONG my papers there is a small leaf which has lain there for nearly twenty years now. A small leaf which is the draft of a title-page—Johannes Jørgensen: *Saint Bridget of Vadstena*, Copenhagen, 1923. Nearly twenty years have gone by since then, and only now can I write the preface to the book about Saint Bridget—and only to the first part.

Yet I began early to think of this work. During a winter sojourn in Rome in 1899–1900 I visited those places in the Eternal City where the memory of the Swedish saint is still living; the church on the Piazza Farnese which at that time belonged to the Polish Carmelite nuns; the room where she died in the convent next to it; San Paolo fuori le Mura where the Crucifix had spoken to her; San Sebastiano in the Via Appia; the three churches that were dedicated to her favourite saint, Saint Laurence (of Lund!); San Lorenzo in Damaso, with the oratory where the angel dictated *Sermo angelicus* to her; San Lorenzo fuori le Mura, to which she and Karin made so many pilgrimages, notwithstanding the perils of the road; San Lorenzo in Panisperna, outside the convent door of which the mistress of Ulfåsa had once sat begging. . . . On the basis of these pilgrimages then, and a little reading (Hammerich, Brinkmann, Madame de Flavigny and, of course, Verner von Heidenstam), I wrote in my book *Pictures of Roman Saints* (Copenhagen, 1902) a chapter of about fifty pages entitled 'Saint Bridget.' The small work was noticed in Bridget's own country—'its descriptions are particularly applicable to educational purposes' it was said. I had perhaps not thought of that.

But I continued to think of Bridget and in the summer of 1902 I came for the first time to Vadstena. The journey was made from Falkenberg, where I was having a summer holiday with my family, and my wife came with me—enduring the torments of sea-sickness on the crossing from Hjo to Hästholmen. Together we explored the ruins of the monastery in Alvastra, where Otto Frödin had not yet begun his excavations; we climbed the Omberg, wandered across Stocklyckeäng, and from Hjässan looked out across the *trolska** Vättern. In Vadstena we called upon old Father Karlén, 'the watchman over Saint Bridget's grave,' and with him paid a visit also to *den där unga arkivarien*,† Eric

* 'Eerie' is perhaps the nearest word.
† 'That young keeper of the archives.'

ix

Ihrfors, who was then scarcely sixty years old, while Karlén was eighty! Karlén died in the following year, but almost twenty years later I could still call upon the indefatigable old scholar, whose copious library now stands in the room in which I am working, and which has been of invaluable help to me. I have dedicated my book to the memory of those two old friends.

The years passed—years at home and years in exile. The books of exile were written: the book about Francis of Assisi, the book about Catherine of Siena. Then the First World War came, and the period after the war. But one day in 1920 it was clear to me that the book about Saint Bridget was to be written. The studies for it began and the study journeys—from Finsta to Naples and from the Bay of Biscay to Jaffa. In the summer of 1921 I sat in the Royal Library in Stockholm, guided by Oscar Wieselgren, and came again to Alvastra where I was received by Otto Frödin. In the following year I stood by the Jordan, I knelt in the grotto of the Nativity in Bethlehem and by Christ's empty tomb. Then I went to my home in Assisi to begin the book about Saint Bridget of Vadstena. And in 1923—I thought—it was to see the light. . . .

Perhaps a word about the title of the book would not be out of the way. One says Saint Francis *of Assisi*, Saint Catherine *of Siena*, because these two saints were born, respectively, in Assisi and Siena. But Bridget, daughter of Birger, was *not* born in Vadstena. No one, as yet, has ever thought of calling her 'Bridget of Finsta': in France she is called 'Sainte Brigitte de Suède,' in England 'Saint Bridget of Sweden.' Bridget was not from Vadstena—but she is '*of* Vadstena,' as one says of a queen: Queen of Denmark, Queen of Sweden. Vadstena is Bridget's kingdom—this very day she sits on her throne in the coat of arms of the town. . . .

Years passed. Other work, more pressing, came in the way. To state it briefly, I had to live. And one cannot live on the study of the *Revelations* of Saint Bridget. A university Professor can do so—a writer who has to make his living by his pen cannot. I realized that so great and difficult a task as a biography of Saint Bridget could not be achieved, unless for a couple of years I could put all other work to one side. And that I could not do.

So the years passed—and one day, to my own great wonder, I found that I had reached the span of years allotted to man by the Psalmist.

Preface

But on that very day a call came to me from Sweden—Swedish friends would bestow upon me the peace necessary for my work.

To these Swedish friends I therefore send my thanks to-day. First and above all to you, Harald Schiller, who never despaired, never gave up, but persevered in your action of helping. And to you, Andreas Lindblom, who guided my first steps on the road of research of Bridgettine places and were a faithful friend down the years. I must thank Isaac Collijn, who so willingly placed the results of his researches at my disposal, and Oscar Wieselgren, who received me in 1938 at the Royal Library in Stockholm with the same helpfulness as in 1921. Nor had Otto Frödin in Alvastra lost faith in me, when I came to him and had not got further in my work than I had seventeen years earlier.

There is also a small circle of Danish friends who have kept faithful and to whom I am indebted for moral and material support. The Carlsberg Fund twice showed me confidence in giving me help to undertake journeys for the purpose of study, and giving me support finally to write the book; I tender my thanks to the director of the Carlsberg Fund, Professor Johannes Pedersen, and remember gratefully his predecessor, Professor A. B. Drachmann. The Catholic Bishop of Sweden, Dr. Johannes Erik Müller, has been untiring in showing me good will and giving me assistance. And I am indebted to the Bridgettine scholar, Pastor S. Nordmark, in Vadstena for much valuable information.

And then there is a big 'I thank you' to be said to Saint Bridget's daughters in Vadstena, in the Home of Rest by the shores of Lake Vättern and in the shadow of *blåa kyrkan*. With them I found a place in which to work, which could not have been imagined better. From the chapel next to my studio the clear voices came in to me singing Bridget's hymns—*Ave, maris stella* and *Rosa rorans bonitatem*. And if I looked up from the paper, my glance went out between the white trunks of the birches across the blue lake, or, when the 'sleepless waters of Vättern' were bound by frost, out across the white desert of ice towards the coast of West Gothland, blue-toned in the distance. On dark autumn evenings I saw Charles's Wain high up in the heavens, and its shaft of stars pointed down to the star I call mine of old. One night the northern lights stood in a flaming arch over the lake and heralded winter. But even in the blackest nights the lighthouse at Fiuk flashed its light—opened and shut, opened and shut, opened. . . .

I thank you, Mother Elisabeth, down yonder in Rome, because for so long you gave me shelter. I thank you, Mother Reginalda; I thank you, Mother Ansgaria and all the sisters—*Iddio vi paghi*, as we say when we speak the dear Roman tongue, 'May God repay you!'

But there is no end to my thanskgiving! For must I not also thank the town of Vadstena, the citizens of Vadstena! Year in, year out, they have seen me walking in the streets and lanes of the town and wandering along the roads of East Gothland: to Quisberg and to 'Rismarken,' to Strå and to Börstad, to Fivelstad and Orlunda and Hagebyhöga (dear names!). Still it was said that 'that Danish professor' was writing a book about Saint Bridget—and the years passed, and the book did not come. But they still believed in me, they still showed me courtesy, amiability, kindness, all of it *on credit*. The keeper of the archives, Dr. Sten Engström, treated me like a colleague in historical research, and you, Harold Thorngren, the writer with the greatest local knowledge, took me up to Granby Hill, where the pilgrims took off their shoes to walk barefoot down to the holy city. And last, but not least, I thank my wife, who for my sake became a resident of Vadstena and stood by my side with word and deed and, most of all, simply by being with me.

In my treatment of so exhaustive and so difficult a subject as Bridget I have thought myself justified, here and there, in working out in detail that which is only indicated in the original sources. I hope, however, that I have kept faithfully to the advice once given by Leo XIII concerning all historical research: *ne quid non veri audeat, ne quid veri non audeat*, 'not to dare to tell an untruth, not to dare keep back a truth.' God has no use for our lies, and the light of truth can never be too bright.

And so I close with the words written by a nun in Vadstena half a thousand years ago on the last page of her book: Bidhen och för den, som thetta skriptade—hon hafde godan vilian ok littla maktena, ok ey är godt at tagha mera än til är. (MS. A. 78, Stockh.).

JOHANNES JØRGENSEN

Vadstena. The Feast of St. Catherine of Sweden, 1941.

CONTENTS

BOOK I

THE LAND MOST NORTHERLY IN THE WORLD

Wi ärum nordast i wärldiæne hwar altidh bläs kalt nordan wädhir.

Revelationes iii. 31

Ego sum quasi avis illa quæ . . . nihil vult bibere nisi sanguinem purum cordis.

Christus (Extrav. cap. 50)

'I am like that bird which will drink nothing but pure heart's blood'

BRIDGET was born in the country 'which lies most northerly in the world, and beyond that there is no country where men can live. The sun is seldom seen here and always the cold north wind blows.' But though the country lay furthest to the north, it still belonged to Europe—and 'Europe is the empire of Rome, all that which is north and west of Rome—and there is true Christendom.' Northernmost in the world, but within the borders of the Roman Empire, which means within Christian civilization.(1)

Although the Middle Ages had no modern means of communication, Europe was united, was one body. This oneness was the work of the Catholic Church and had been achieved by the struggle of centuries against the powers that wanted to break the common faith with its common culture. After Arianism had died out, and after Mohammedanism had been driven back, Europe was for some centuries one in faith, one in customs and morals, one in civilization. A cosmopolitan spirit with a wide outlook was developed in this period; the whole of Europe was open to the genius and the saint. The sixteenth century had not yet set up its religious boundaries, the nineteenth its national frontiers and the twentieth its racial ones. Civilization was catholic, that is, common, general.

This must be borne in mind in order to grasp the international character and cosmopolitan destinies of the great mediæval personalities. Contemplate, for instance, the life of Saint Thomas Aquinas. He is born in South Italy, at the castle of Roccasecca near Aquino. He studies first under the Benedictines of Monte Cassino, later at the University of Naples; there he enters the Dominican Order. By way of Paris he then goes to Cologne where he studies under Albertus Magnus, who was a Swabian, and who had attended the Universities of Bologna and Padua and later became a professor in Paris. Thither Thomas follows him and becomes a doctor of theology on the same day as another famous Italian, the Franciscan, Bonaventura of Bagnorea. He now teaches theology in Paris, but after only three years he leaves the French capital because the Pope calls him to Rome. In company with the latter he lives successively in Orvieto, Anagni, Viterbo and Perugia. Then he becomes the head of the Dominican school in Rome, finally works at the University of Naples and dies of malaria on the way to the second Council of Lyons in 1274, in the Cistercian monastery of Fossanuova in the Pontine Marshes.

One of the fairest dreams of the nineteenth century was the thought of a United States of Europe. The twentieth century attempted to create a League of Nations, and failed. But at a given point of time Europe was not far from having realized this ideal. From Iceland to Sicily, from the Atlantic to the Danube, there was then a common faith, a common Church, a common art, common customs and a common language understood and spoken by all educated persons, and which our own times have tried in vain to replace by a miserable substitute. At that time Europe was well on the way to creating a general civilization.

It is therefore impossible to understand the men and women of those times without turning away from the definitely national mode of thought of the present day, and identifying oneself with the mediæval outlook.

In order to understand the men and women of those times one must therefore withdraw entirely from the specifically national mode of thought of the present day, and identify oneself with the European viewpoint of the Middle Ages. This applies in fullest measure also to the mediæval *North*—to the personalities who left their mark there during the five centuries when the three Scandinavian kingdoms were Catholic.

There is the same cosmopolitan stamp on their great mediæval men as on a Thomas Aquinas or an Albertus Magnus. Far away Rome was the spiritual centre of Denmark—hence wide spaces and an open horizon. Denmark (to speak of one's own country, though the same held good of Norway and Sweden)—Denmark was not a small enclosed duckpond, in which spiritual life stagnated; it was an open briny inlet in constant communication with the great European currents. Danish kings, a Canute the Great, an Erik Aye-good, went on pilgrimage to Rome, to Jerusalem; the reforming influence is felt in the letter which King Canute wrote home to England in 1027. Valdemar the Great comes forward and is of importance at a French Church Council. Absalon, Saxo, Anders Suneson return from Paris, having attained the highest degree of European culture; young Danes have their own college at the Sorbonne.

And at home these 'Europeans' do not encounter any stiff-necked, provincial opposition; Church and King vie with one another in placing them on the most exalted seats in the kingdom. The day had not yet dawned when Tycho Brahe had to go to Prague, Niels Steensen to Florence. The monastic orders were continually introducing new movements into northern intellectual life: after the Benedictines came the reforms from Cluny, after the Cluniacs the Cistercians, later on the Mendicant Friars—the grey ones of Saint Francis, the black of Saint Dominic and the White Friars of Carmel.

Regarded from that European fellowship of culture, it will be understood that persons of a southern origin often came to play an important part among Scandinavian people, and *vice versa*. Two Italian monks, Lanfranc and Anselm, come to the French monastery of Bec and thence pass on successively to the archdiocese of Canterbury. An Englishman, Stephen Harding, becomes, as third abbot of Citeaux, the real organizer of the order of Saint Bernard. The Frenchman, William, canon of St. Geneviève in Paris, reforms monastic life in Denmark. A Finnish bishop journeys to Avignon with a message and a letter from a noble lady in Sweden, and with the object of making peace between France and England. A Swedish ecclesiastic, Bishop Nicholas Ragwaldi, is sent by the Church Council in Basle to Arras in Flanders to mediate between France and Burgundy. Catholicism made the whole of Europe the sphere of action of the individual eminent spirit, and this must be borne in mind when trying to understand how a Swedish widow in the fourteenth century could become one of the most influential personalities of her time. On such a background alone can a figure like Bridget's be imagined and realized.

II

Men of the Middle Ages had, moreover, another great advantage over those of our own times: *they knew what was the purpose of existence.* Dante knew it, Bridget knew it; here is the earth, below us is hell, above us heaven; it is our task so to live that we avoid hell and attain heaven. Life is not a riddle, the world is not a mystery. The earth is not a grain of sand in the infinity of the universe—it is the very centre of existence. When a man of the Middle Ages lifts his eyes to gaze up into the starlit nights he does not stare up into an infinite world space with so many degrees of cold in the stratosphere and with distances of millions of light years. No chilling breath of doubt blows against him from the bottomless depths. Man is not a miserable creeping thing in a remote corner of the astronomic universe, not planetary 'vermin,' as modern voluptuous love of self-abasement delights to call it. Man is created in the image of God for everlasting life and everlasting bliss, or (and this is a deeper tragedy than the mere dread of annihilation) for everlasting death and everlasting damnation. Such are the conditions—whether you accept them or no—there *are* no others. When time has ceased to be, when both hands of the clock point to twelve and the weights have reached the bottom, eternity begins. In all the cemeteries all over Christendom the graves will open, the gravestones will be pushed aside (we see it in the pictures of the old painters) and the dead will rise and go forth to judgment. In the clouds of heaven sits the Judge, He who once hung on the Cross, but who has now come back to judge the living and the dead. From His mouth issue the lily and the sword—the lily on the right, the sword on the left. And to those on the right are spoken the words: 'Come to Me, ye blessed of My Father, and possess the kingdom which has been prepared for you from the foundation of the world.' But to those on the left the words are: 'Depart from me, ye cursed!' It is for man, then, to take care to be on the right side, for the saga of the human race on earth is at an end, there is no longer any choice. As on the first day of creation, 'God separates light from darkness.' Henceforth there are only two worlds, two eternal cities—the city of God, *Civitas Dei*, and 'the city full of torment.' Either—or!

'Does it not make them sad in heaven to see those in hell in that woeful torment?' asks the disciple of his wise master in the old book. And the master answers: 'Not more than we when we see fish lying in the water, but they rejoice all the more that they are not in it themselves. They are not sad, even though a father should see his son there, or a sister her brother, or a wife her husband.' 'Do they who are in heaven not pray a little then for those who are in hell?' asks the disciple again. 'No,' answers the master, 'they do not pray for them, for it is against the will of God to pray for them.'(1)

Such are the spiritual conditions by which men of the Middle Ages lived. Only against this background of the everlasting joys of heaven and the everlasting torments of damnation can a figure like that of Bridget be imagined or realized.

III

In Snorre Sturlason's version of the Battle of Svold he describes how Danes, Swedes and Northmen advance against the Long Worm. Of the Danes, Olaf Tryggvason says: 'We are not afraid of *them*—for never have the Danes shown courage.' Of the Swedes he says: 'It is better for them to sit at home and lick the blood from the bowls of their sacrifices than to march against the Worm under our weapons!' But of his fellow-countryman, Earl Erik, and his troops, the king says: 'From them we may look for sharper fighting, for they are Northmen like us.'

It is Henrik Schück who applies these words of the Norse hero-king as the starting-point of his characterization of the Swedish national spirit. The Swedish author deducts this peculiarity from the natural conditions of the country.(1)

> The Sweden of former times was an extensive, thinly populated country, in which the towns were separated from each other by vast forests and desolate tracts of land. The peasant lived in isolation with his family in a *stuga* on the borders of the forest—it was but rarely that he came into contact with the world outside, when he went to the Thing or a lonely wanderer stopped at his door. Otherwise he went about alone on the borders of the dark and solemn pine forest. This seclusion from the world, the lack of sun and light during the greater part of the year, of necessity exercised a great influence upon him. An Italian can be superstitious or bigoted, but he is not religious like a northerner, who spends half his life in darkness or dusk.

It is perhaps for that reason, Schück thinks, that Scania, in its comparatively southern situation, has not provided suitable soil for strong religious movements, while these (*e.g.* Læstadianism) are to be found in Norrland. (As the descriptions by Harry Sjöman indicate, this is also the case with Småland, thickly wooded and thinly populated in comparison with the part of Sweden that surrounds it.)

The influence of natural environment has perhaps been overrated here. Though the northerner has the long dark winter, he has in compensation the 'white nights' of summer. Lorenzo di Medici's *Maggiolata* is more ingenious, but there is not more joy of life in it than in the Dala peasant's tramping round the maypole. 'To-day is the first of May! To-day is the first of May, May, May—to-day is the first of May!' Not everything in Sweden is overshadowed by the pine forests. The sunshine plays merrily over the silvery trunks of the birch trees, and their light green foliage waves in the wind like the hair of a dryad. No people has a greater love of colour than the Swedish—the art of Carl Larsson shows it. And in Denmark, far away from the 'black out' of the pine forest, the Danish lover walks with his splendidly tall girl under the light green beeches; but on a path in the woods they meet Soeren Kierkegaard, pondering over his father's terrible secret, and Grundtvig, who cannot yet listen to 'the talking of the little birds,' because he hears only 'the thunder of the Law from above: Die, or do what a sinner cannot do.' Ingemann's gentle evening songs are not the only expression of Danish religious feeling, still less are they of most consequence.

It is true, though, that even in pagan times Sweden was the greatest of the three northern nations; no heathen temple could in fame and magnificence approach that of Frey in Uppsala. When the Catholic Church came into the country—late, later than in Denmark and Norway—the Swedes were slow to accept the new Faith but, having accepted it, they became all the more zealous. It was the same with Lutheranism; once the 'pure Gospel' had penetrated the country, Sweden became the strongest bulwark of Protestantism (as Spain on the extreme outpost of the Continent became that of Catholicism). It was no theatrical gesture, but the expression of deep religious feeling, when Gustavus Adolphus, before the Battle of Breitenfeld, lifted his sword to heaven and prayed. Nor was it a woman's whim when the daughter of the same Gustavus Adolphus gave up her throne and kingdom and returned to the Christianity of Saint Bridget. And in the nineteenth, indeed in the twentieth, century the State Church of Sweden still emphatically maintains that it possesses the *Apostolic Succession*, the valid consecration of bishops inherited from the Roman Church—an interest and an anxiety which in Denmark have been swept aside on the part of the clergy with a remark that the Swedes 'did not seem to be very well acquainted with *the Danish smile*'—for which one might in this connection venture to be thankful!

In the beginning of the present century a movement could therefore be started, without a smile, under the slogan, 'the people of Sweden, the people of God!' And it was the archbishop of Sweden, not of any other Protestant country, who took the words *ut omnes unum*, 'that all may become one,' as a motto for guidance in the effort to bring about the union of the Christian Churches.

Moreover, who is not aware of the part which religious problems have played in Swedish literature of the present day? Who does not know Selma Lagerløf's *Jerusalem, The Miracles of Antichrist, Christ Legends*—the Christian feeling, Christian consciousness, permeating all her work? August Strindberg too, the author of *The Red Room* and later on the disciple of Swedenborg, who wanted to die with the Bible on his breast, and on his grave wished only for a rude wooden cross with the inscription *Ave crux, spes unica*! August Strindberg, the internationalist, and Erik Axel Karlfeldt, the poet who sang of his own Sweden, whose most beautiful poetry is inspired by the Biblical pictures painted by devout peasants in Dalarne, the most Swedish part of Sweden. When one thinks of this, and of much else, one understands that Saint Bridget could not have come forth from any other country in the North, and that her personality and her work are expressions of that which lies deepest in the soul of Sweden—the foundation of granite on which Sweden stands.

IV

In the thirty-first year of His becoming Man, on the first of May, Christ began to preach, and this was the beginning of the apostolic life. . . . And in the year of the Lord 845, Saint Ansgar, who was archbishop in Hamburg, preached the gospel of Christ to the Swedes and Danes, and one hundred and forty-five years later, in the year of the Lord 1008, the kingdom of Sweden was converted to Christianity by Saint Sigfred, who was archbishop of York, and in his time Olof, who was also called 'Skotkonung,' was king of Sweden. He was baptized by the same holy Sigfred in West Gothland, at Husaby near Kindaberg; he was the first Christian king of Sweden.(1)

The story of the first introduction of Christianity into Sweden can hardly be written more concisely than it has been written here in the old monastic chronicle with its modest title *Historiske Antegnelser fra Aaret 845 til Aaret 1445*. Perhaps it was written by a Grey Friar in the Franciscan monastery in Stockholm—this is indicated by his rather elaborate account *ad annum* 1223 of how the Franciscan rule was approved in that year by Pope Honorius III; he even knows that this rule was composed by four persons, viz. Francis of Assisi himself, his friend the Cardinal of Ostia, later Gregory IX, the Cardinal's chaplain Reginald, who later became pope under the name of Alexander III, and Brother Cæsarius of Speier. In the list of collaborators the name of Reginald is a new one; the Swedish chronicler may be right. Moreover, he also knows that the papal approval of the rule was given on 1 December (but whether it is also right that 'Christ Jesus began to preach on the first of May' in His 'thirty-first year' must be left unsettled).

In all his conciseness the old Grey Friar gives a correct account of how Sweden first became Christian.(2) It is well known how Saint Ansgar set out on a mission journey from Hedeby in Denmark to Sweden, how he and his companion, Vidmar, were attacked and plundered by pirates, how, also, after many difficulties they reached Birka (Björkö) where the Swedish king, Bjørn, received them with kindness, and where his chief man on the island, Hergeir or Heriger consented to be baptized, and on his own land built a church, the oldest in Uppland, nay, in all Sweden. As yet, however, Christianity was but a frail and tiny plant, which only with difficulty took root in the Swedish granite. Ansgar's successor, Gautbert, had to flee the country and for seven years no Catholic priest showed his face in Sweden; it was not until Ansgar's second mission journey that he and his fellow Benedictine, Rimbert, were allowed to preach. After Ansgar's death in 865 most of a century and a half had to pass before a Christian missionary again began to labour in the country. It was King Olof, 'Skotkonung,' who, about the year 1006, sent word to King Ethelred in England, begging him to send one of the messengers of Christianity to Sweden. The priest who undertook this task was Sigfred (archbishop, according to the legend) of York, and with him came his sister's three sons, of whom one was called Unaman and was ordained; the second was a deacon and his name was Vinaman, and the third, Suneman, was a sub-deacon. Småland became the scene of Sigfred's first labours; later he went northwards and King Olof was baptized at Husaby near Kindaberg (Kinnekulle), where in olden times there was a holy well. This was a great victory for Sigfred, but meanwhile his three nephews down in Småland had fared ill.

While the holy father Sigfred was with the king [says the legend], his three nephews remained in Växiö, where he had built a church of wood, and they preached there and were of great use to the people. But inasmuch as they spoke not the tongue of the country, they had taken some men of the people to be with them, and to take counsel of them. And they felt so great a trust in these men that they opened all their stores to them, and showed them all their costly treasure, dishes of silver and bowls of silver. And when the men saw all this the devil put into their hearts that they should kill the three holy men. And in the night they went in where the holy men slept and dragged them out, and beheaded them all three. And they took the three severed heads and laid them in a vessel and tied it to a stone which was so big and heavy that two oxen could hardly drag it. Then they sank the vessel in a lake beside the church. But they took the bodies and tied a rope about the feet and dragged them to a place where not even the wild animals could come, and where the sun never shone [according to tradition on Mount Gilboga near Växiö]. And they piled up a great mound of stones over the holy bodies and hoped that their misdeed would remain hidden. But God willed that His servants should be glorified. And ravens came and screamed over the place where the bodies lay, and at night a light from heaven shone over them. But the devil rejoiced exceedingly over the death of the three men of God, and brought great unrest into the young congregation. . . . And when Saint Sigfred heard that his sister's sons had been murdered, he thanked God, who had saved them from this evil world and given them the martyr's crown.(3)

Saint Sigfred continued his missionary labours alone, but without making much headway. Many of those who had been baptized fell away and but few replaced them; he seemed to preach in vain and in vain were his penances, his long prayers and his vigils in the cold church. One night the man of God went out of the church, down to the little lake nearby. It was dark around him and there was darkness in his soul. Every fighter for the cause of the spirit has met with such an hour, when all one has done seems to have failed, and all one's efforts seem to be only a delusion, or (still worse) a presumption. In such hours it is not Simeon's joyful *Nunc dimittis* that rings in the soul— 'Lord, now lettest Thou thy servant depart in peace'—but it is the plaint of the prophet when he sat under the juniper tree in the wilderness: 'Lord, it is enough, take away my life, for I am not better than my fathers.'(4)

An angel was sent to the prophet in the desert, with bread that gave him strength to travel the long way he still had to go before he reached Horeb, the mount of God. For the missionary in the midst of the heathen land of Sweden the light of hope arose,

> like three fair candles in the middle of the lake, shining like three stars. They came from the east and drew nearer and nearer to land, and when they were not far from the shore the servant of God took off his shoes and gladly went out to them in the water. But when he came quite near the lights vanished and he found a vessel with three heads and a big stone tied to it. He took the vessel and guided it in to land. There he laid all the three heads on his knees and wept over them, saying: 'May God avenge!' A voice from one of the heads then answered: 'It will be avenged.' The second said: 'When?' The third answered: 'On the children's children.' It was indeed a great miracle that lights should appear on a stormy lake, and a still greater miracle that heads which had been severed so long since should have tongue and speech in their mouths. By these signs the servant of God gained new strength to serve Him, so that no toil was too great for him, but he went about in Sweden preaching, baptizing and building churches and ordaining priests. After having brought many souls to the Lord, Saint Sigfred came back to Växiö and lived there a long time until he had reached the fullness of his years and of a surety entered into the joys of heaven. And in Växiö he lies buried.(5)

It was two other Englishmen who carried on the work of Saint Sigfred, Saint David, whom Saint Sigfred sent to Västmanland, and Saint Eskil. Saint David was a Benedictine (like Ansgar and like Rimbert), Saint Eskil a bishop. It is related of Saint David that when he was old and could no longer see very well, it happened once that he stepped into a church where it was rather dark and only a single sunray came in. Saint David drew off his gloves before taking holy water, and thinking that the sunbeam was a pole or a railing he hung his gloves upon it. When he came home he missed his gloves and sent his servant to the church to fetch them. And behold! the servant found them; they were still hanging on the sunbeam! (6) Of Saint Eskil it is told that in his youth he received from God the same command as Abraham (and later Bridget): 'Get thee out of thy country and from thy kindred,' and that he left his own civilized country of Britain and came to the heathen Sweden of the eleventh century, 'with the conviction' (which was also that of Bridget) 'that the further he journeyed for the love of God from his own country, the nearer would he come to heaven.' With him Christianity in Sweden won its first martyr. At first Eskil had only laboured in *Landet sunnan skog*, the land south of the great border forests, Tiveden (between Vänern and Vättern) and Kolmården (from Vättern out to the Baltic). The real heathen country though was *Landet norden skog*, 'the land north of the forest'—Uppland with the largest temple in the north, the temple of Frey in Uppsala; in its rich splendour it was perhaps an imitation of the churches which the *Varangs* had seen in Byzantium. Adam of Bremen, who died in 1076, says that it was still standing in his time. The Christian king, Inge, had attempted to get it closed, with the result that he was banished and had to flee to West Gothland, and that the people of Uppland 'chose for their king an idolater named Sven, who was justly called "Blood Sven," because he allowed his subjects to drink the blood of the animals that had been offered to the idols, and himself ate of the flesh of the sacrificial animals.'

Not only in Uppsala but also in Strängnäs did the worship of heathen gods now flourish again, and when Saint Eskil, in June 1080, made his appearance to preach conversion at a great sacrifice, he met with a martyr's death. Eskimas is still celebrated in Sweden on the twelfth of June, and round the grave of the martyr bishop arose the town of Eskilstuna.

As long as Uppland had not been conquered for Christianity the victory over heathenism had not been gained. And as in Norway, as in Denmark, it was with the blood of a martyr king that the Swedes were christened. It was King Erik who was at last to confirm the work of Ansgar. 'As his first object,' the legend tells us, 'he set himself to build churches and to enrich and extend the service. Above all he gave his care to the church of Uppsala, of which earlier kings had laid the foundation and which they had begun building, but he completed it with mighty and costly stonework.'

In this church, dedicated to the Holy Trinity, King Erik was hearing the prayers of the Church and Mass on Ascension Day, 18 May 1160, when word was brought to him that an enemy host, led by Henrik Magnusson, son of the Danish king, was advancing and that they would do best to take up arms and go to meet them. 'Then the king answered: "Let me hear the service of this great feast to the end in peace. I have hope in God that what may still be lacking for us of this service we shall hear elsewhere." Having said this he commended himself to the will of God, made the sign of the Holy Cross, put on his armour, together with his men, and though they were but few, like men they met the enemy. But the enemy came up against them and aimed their weapons most against the king, and striking him to the ground they pierced him wound upon wound, sorely tormenting him though he was half dead, and at last they struck off his head. And in the place where his blood was shed a spring gushed forth and is still to be found to this day.

'But when the enemy had departed a few of the king's men, who had not been killed, took his body and bore it to the house of a poor widow who lived nearby. And this poor widow who lived in the house was blind, and she touched the holy king's body with her hand, and stroked her eyes with his blood, and immediately she could see, and praised God in His holy martyr, Saint Erik. . . . Now this holy King Erik suffered death in the year of the Lord 1160 on the eighteenth day of the month of May, when Alexander III was pope in Rome, and Our Lord Jesus Christ ruled in heaven: to Him be praise, honour and glory, world without end.'(7)

Only four years after the martyr death of Erik, Sweden was proclaimed an independent province of the Church by the same Alexander III, and the Cistercian monk, Stephen, from the monastery of Alvastra, founded by King Sverker in East Gothland in about 1140, became archbishop of Sweden with a see in that same Uppsala—later called Old Uppsala—where the heathen temple had stood.(8) After King Erik's wooden church had been destroyed by fire in the year 1215, it was resolved to build a new one in a more suitable place, that is, at Fyris Aa, on a height directly opposite the trading place of Östra Aros. All earlier Catholic churches in Sweden had been of modest dimensions, but for the new cathedral on 'the mount of the Lord' (*Mons Domini*) a site of over a hundred yards was laid out. The work on the new cathedral was begun under Archbishop Laurentius, a Franciscan from the Grey Friars' monastery in Enköping, and in January 1273 it was so far advanced that the relics of Saint Erik could be brought thither from

Old Uppsala. The day appointed was not Ersmas Day, the day of King Erik's death, 18 May, but that day in winter (24 January) when the great Disting Fair, a heritage from the Disarblot (sacrifice), was held in Uppsala. On that day people gathered together from all over Sweden: from Ångermanland merchants who brought good, home-woven linen, from Helsingeland and Jämtland peasants who offered linen, furs and game birds for sale. The people of Uppland brought the skins of foxes. King Valdemar himself, the son of Birger, came with an imposing retinue; in honour of the martyr king he granted the cathedral a water-mill in Spånga and four marks' worth of land in Husby.(9)

Like so many saints of the Middle Ages Saint Erik was never officially canonized. But in a papal letter, dated Anagni, 23 October 1256, Alexander IV promises an indulgence of forty days to those who devoutly visit the blessed martyr's tomb in Uppsala; in it the expression *beatus* is used of him. Likewise in a papal letter from Clement IV, ten years later.

Meanwhile Ersmas Day on 18 May was not forgotten. Every year on that day the casket containing the saint's relics was carried in a great procession to its old place and brought back again in the evening. In Sweden it is just about the time, near the middle of May, when the fields begin to look green, and the clouds of incense passed over the sprouting grain like a benediction. It is the dangerous season when 'the three ice-saints' (Servatus, Pancras, Boniface, 12 to 14 May) followed by Saint Sophia (in Germany *die böse Sophia*) can work so much havoc among the young growth. But 'Erik gives ears' (to the corn). And many miracles happened at his grave. 'So help me God and Saint Erik the King,' became the most solemn oath. King Erik's banner, the red cross on a golden ground, became the standard of the kingdom of Sweden. Uppsala, where the temple of Frey had stood, became the city of Saint Erik, and from there Christian law went forth over the land. In the older West Gothland law (of 1240) it is said:

'*Svear äga Konung att taga ock så vråka*'—the Swedes have the right to elect a king [on Mora Stones] or to reject him. When the king had been elected, the Upplanders were the first who took the oath of allegiance and he swore them peace. Then those who had sworn accompanied the king to Strängnäs where the people of Södermanland received him, took the oath and went with the king to the monastery of Krokek in Kolmården, where they were met by the East Goths. The latter acclaimed the king and went with him as far as the middle of the great forest of Holaveden, where the people of Småland had assembled. The Smålanders now accompanied the king to Junabäk (Jönköping), whence the West Gothlanders accompanied him to

Ramundaboda. From here, the Närkingers to Uphofra Bridge, where the great high road passes the river Arboga. Then the peasants in Västmanland through their country to Östens Bridge over the river Sag, where the Upplanders were waiting to take the king back to Uppsala. 'Then has the king entered lawfully into possession of land and realm . . . then has he ridden along Eric's road.'(10)

Now followed the crowning of the king in Uppsala, performed by the archbishop and the bishops under him. The coat of arms of Uppland justly bears the golden orb of the realm.

Uppland was the seat of the monarchy and from Uppland was issued law. The first lawgiver of the land that we are told of was Viger Spa, 'heathen in a heathen time.' The *flockar* or collected laws written by him grew antiquated, however, and became partly useless after the introduction of Christianity. Uppland had originally consisted of the three kingdoms (Fjärdhundraland in the west, Tiundaland in the middle, Attundaland in the east), and Tiundaland—around Sigtuna and Uppsala with Fyrisvold and Mora Eng—had always been the most important. Its kings were said to have descended from Frey himself. And so it was from the peasants of this country that a wish came for a new law suited to the times, Viger Spa's code of laws containing 'much that was not quite just, much that was obscurely expressed, and to which it was hard to submit.'(11) In order to obtain a new and better law they now turned—it was about the close of the thirteenth century—to the law-man in Tiundaland, Birger Persson of Finsta Gaard.

In the beginning, the law-man in the social order taken over from heathendom was only *primus inter pares*. When the peasants assembled at the Thing to pass judgments on the complaints brought before them, the law-man was he who knew the law and read it out—perhaps because he was the only one who could read. The Thing therefore began by the law-man repeating the law from memory; in Iceland he was therefore called the law-saying man. 'Now shall all men go to the Thing and hear our Law Saga. Let those who are present hear it and tell it to them who sit at home,' are the opening words of the Småland and the Östgota law. Gradually the law-man became not only he who knew and spoke the law—he had also to *lagh göma, i.e.* know how similar cases had been judged on earlier occasions, as well as *lagh yrkia, i.e.* to propose suggestions for judgments, which were then approved or rejected by the Thing.(12)

Now the Uppland law was not written by Birger Persson alone; as collaborators he had a whole circle of the best men in the country.

Their names have been recorded: the knights Röd Keldsson, Bengt Bosson and Ulf Langmansson; the peasants Hagbard of Söderby, Anders of Forkarby, Torsten of Sandbro and many others. But the lawman's best coadjutor was without any doubt the dean of the cathedral in Uppsala, Master Andreas And.

It is law for a *Christian* country that these good men write to take the place of old Viger Spa's heathen *flockar* or collections of laws. The foreword to the law therefore begins by a reminder of 'the time when God sent law by Moses,' who was 'the first law-man.' It says further, that 'the law shall be the honour of the just and wise, but shall chastise the wrong-doers and the unwise.' 'If all men were just no law would be needed.'

The law is divided into several sections (*balkar*), and each of these sections ends: *Nu är tald ärfda balken . . . nu är tald jordabalken,* 'now the law on inheritance has been spoken . . . now the law on land has been spoken'—the law being still proclaimed by word of mouth. The greatest innovation was the church *balka*, which had been unknown in heathen times; now it came first, even before the king's *balka*. But it is the king who is the centre of everything; it is his right to rule the country, either himself or through his feudal lords; it is he who gives power to the judges elected at the Thing to judge (*dom i händer*); it is, of course, he who calls to arms and leads the army. As in the Danish law of King Valdemar, the principle is that *land skall med lag bygges ock ej med våldsverk, ty land står väl då lag följes.* * It is evident that the peasants had an active share in the making of the law: 'No one must lack land, all shall have earth who have come from the earth.' But it is still more evident that a new spirit has come into the country; the possession of land is not the highest good. *Gud låte os så till jord trå, att vi måtte himmelriket få,* it says—'God lets us so desire land that we may obtain heaven'—with a phrase that reminds one of the prayer of the Church on the third Sunday after Pentecost: that 'we may so pass through the good things of this life that we may not lose those of life everlasting.'(13) In the *balka* of inheritance it says: 'May God so let us divide the inheritance, that we may inherit the kingdom of heaven.' A new age has arisen: 'no one shall sacrifice to idols, and no one shall believe in groves and stones.' Thraldom is abolished: 'for Christ was sold and then redeemed all Christians.' The last *balka* (*tingmålabalken*) contains regulations about peace (church peace, Thing

* 'The land shall be built upon the law and not upon violence, for the state of a land is best when the law is followed.'

peace, women's peace) and concludes: 'This is said of peace. May God give peace to all who come hither with the will to peace, to be here and to fare forth from here. Peace be to our king, our land and law-man, and to all those who have listened to the saying of the law.' It is the *peace of Christ* that is pronounced here over the land, as the bishop pronounces it when he turns from the altar to the people: *Pax vobis!* 'Peace be unto you!'

Birger Persson's Uppland law was confirmed by King Birger Magnusson in 1295, in *octava sancti Stephani* (2 January). A few years later the law-man's daughter, Saint Bridget, was born at Finsta Gaard.(14)

V

'In the midst of Sweden lies Uppland, where dwells many a fine man,' says the old chronicler Messenius.(1) And one of the 'finest men' about the year 1300 was without any doubt the law-man Birger Persson of Finsta. Birger's father Peder was law-man in Tiundaland, his grandfather, Anders of Mohammar, is said to have descended on the male side from the Christian King Sverker in East Gothland. There is a greater possibility that Birger belonged to the Ängel family—at any rate he had on his coat of arms two lowered angel's wings. Through his first wife, Kristina John's daughter (*d.* 1295), daughter of the knight John Elofsson, Birger was connected with the pious Ingrid Elof's daughter, who in 1270 founded the convent in Skenninge; she was the sister of his father-in-law. It is known of this Ingrid that at first she was attached to the gay court of King Valdemar Birgersson and Queen Sophia, that later she had a religious awakening (it may have been through the Dominican of the monastery at Skenninge, Petrus de Dacia, known for his love of Kristina of Stommeln), that she made a pilgrimage to the Holy Land, and on her return founded the convent of nuns mentioned above.(2) By his second wife, Ingeborg Bengt's daughter, Birger married into the Folkunga family; Ingeborg's father, Bengt Månsson (Magnusson) of Ulfåsa, the law-man in East Gothland, was the son of a nephew of Birger Earl.

Finsta Gaard [says an old description] lies in Uppland, in the jurisdiction of Aska, and the parish of Skederid, about eight miles to the east, a little to the south of Uppsala . . . the country, full of small lakes and streams, is thickly covered with conifers, yet it is not unsuitable as arable land. The neighbouring lake of Björken has pleasing shores—from its north-eastern end a stream flows past the house, between low hills, where aspen and alder, birch and fir grow amongst each other. In heathen times it was a sacrificial grove, numerous cromlechs, runic stones, barrows, and stone erections are memorials thereof.(3)

Nothing is now left of Finsta Gaard. And if you try to visualize Birger Persson's home, you must abandon all imaginary pictures drawn from French *châteaux* or German *schloss* strongholds. The great homesteads in the Uppland of the Middle Ages consisted of a collection of wooden houses enclosed within a wall of earth and round a house or tower of stone. On an island in the Mälar, for instance, remnants of the small fortress of Gröneborg have been preserved. The 'keep' is surrounded by two earth walls or ramparts with a moat between; the inner rampart having had oaken palisades. There is a gate in the ramparts and a bridge over the moat. In the middle of the inner square lies *kärnan* or the 'keep,' a tower built of grey stone; round this *kärna*, or keep, would stand the wooden houses.(4)

In the parish of Länna, south of Norrtälja, lies Penningby, one of the best preserved strongholds of the Middle Ages. It is mentioned as early as 1339, so that it is not much younger than Finsta. The castle stands on a sloping field by the shores of a small lake and consists of an almost rectangular middle building with two corner towers, from the embrasures of which the whole range of walls could be attacked. The towers contain—like the church tower in Bjälbo—only one room in each story, the light coming through deep and narrow slits in the walls. Between the towers stands the main building, also in two stories. Through each story there is a vaulted passage, and on either side of this there are two or three rooms with barrel-shaped ceilings and with narrow slits in the thick walls. Up above there would probably be one more story of wood, with a lofty hall and balconies. A chapel generally formed part of the stronghold—at any rate there was one at Finsta.(5)

In our own times there are not even ruins of the childhood home of Saint Bridget. On its site now stands a fairly new country house, built in the second half of the eighteenth century. A few wall fragments can be seen near Skederid church—a horseshoe-shaped stone rampart with an opening to the south-east, and another rampart of large blocks outside it. There is no doubt, however, that they had nothing to do with the old Finsta. On the other hand, the iron pump, which on a day in July twenty years ago (alas!) was shown to my friend Andreas Lindblom and myself as 'Saint Bridget's well,' may have stood in the right place. In any case the huge boulders under the whispering ash trees in the garden must certainly have been Bridget's contemporaries.(6) The wood is here as it was then: ash and maple and birches with silvery trunks, and dark spruce firs. A wood-pigeon coos for a moment, is again silent—'so must Bridget have heard the wood-pigeon cooing.'

Later we follow the little stream running past the house down to the lake, *Björkan*. The clover-green meadows stretch away to the reeds bordering the lake. There is a scent of clover and goose-grass, a cow-bell is tinkling a little way off. The sky is blue over the quiet green country; on a hill a little way off stands Skederid church, Bridget's parish church—Skiädarghi is mentioned as early as 1317.

We walk out to the shore of the lake. Wild duck fly up from the reeds; close to the shore the water is quite covered with water plantain —pond weed, explains a peasant who comes up to have a chat. On the other side of the lake there is a wood of birch trees with white trunks and a wood of dark spruce. Everywhere it is quiet and lonely under the mild, blue sky.

VI

Six hundred years ago it was not so quiet and lonely here by the shores of Lake Björka. All over Sweden there was at that time unrest—'wolf-time'—the clash of arms and the din of battle. Swede fought against Swede and the lord of Finsta stood in the midst of the strife.

About the middle of the thirteenth century the family of Saint Erik became extinct. The last descendant of the saintly king, Erik Eriksson, surnamed Läspe, was proclaimed king at the age of only six years. When he was grown up he had to contend with rebellious nobles, and lived for a time in exile with his mother's father, Valdemar the Victor, in Denmark, and only came back (in 1234) thanks to his queen, Katerina, who was of the powerful family of the Folkungs.

The Folkungs were East Gothlanders, descended from Folke the Fat who (about 1100) was married to Ingeborg, daughter of Saint Canute the King. The family seat was Bjälbo Gaard, not far from Skenninge. The rhymed chronicle relates of King Erik Läspe's sister Ingeborg, that the king 'gave her an East Gothland husband—Birger Earl, the people called him—he was born in Bjälbo, and was an earl before he died.' Birger did in fact become an earl before he died—and more than an earl, the actual ruler of Sweden. It is related of his mother,

Ingrid Ylfva, that when she was on her death-bed she said that so long
as her head was erect, the family of the Folkungs would not die out.
She was therefore buried in a pillar in the porch of Bjälbo church,
standing up (like Clemenceau in his grave in Vendée). It is true that
when, at a later date, the porch was pulled down, no erect skeleton was
found walled up in a pillar. But the largest bell in the church tower is
still called 'Ingrid Ylfva's bell,' and it bears the inscription: *Dock,
Ylfva, som mig skänkt,* låt ej ditt hufvud luta, *fast fjender vårt land med
list og våld omsluta,* 'Yet Ylfva, who didst bestow me, *let not thy head
stoop,* even though foes encompass our land with craft and might.'(1)
In the coat of arms of the Folkungs there is a lion *statant*, and Bridget,
daughter of the Folkungs, did not bow her head before anyone; she
always stood erect.

On his marriage to the sister of Erik Läspe, Birger became the
king's earl, and after Erik's death the guardian of his son, Valdemar,
who became king in name. During Birger's rule the mediæval feudal
system was at length introduced into Sweden; following the European
model, Birger gave large portions of the land in fief to his younger
sons, Erik and Magnus (who was given the title of 'Duke of the Svear'
—it is the first time this title occurs in Sweden). Together they then
formed that 'duke's party,' which after the death of Birger rose in open
rebellion against the elder brother and defeated him in the forest of
Tiveden (1275). In the same year, after the death of Erik, Valdemar
of his own free will gave up his right to the crown and was now succeeded by Magnus, so beloved by the people and called by them
Magnus *Ladulås*,* because he put an end to the time-honoured bad
custom by which the nobles made free of the peasants' barns and took
what they found there. In return he ordered that in each town there
should be a *rättere*, that is, an innkeeper, from whom travellers could
purchase 'food and ale, and hay and corn for their horses.'

It was Magnus Ladulås who, following the example of the great
Europe outside, created an upper class of the nobility, the knights, who
in return for their service in war were exempt from taxation; the clergy
too were to enjoy the same exemption from taxes (*frälse*, the church
privilege of 1281). New religious houses were founded, and in one of
them, the church of the Grey Friars in Stockholm, Magnus Ladulås
found his last resting-place. He died during a sojourn at Visingsö in

---

* Ladulås, *i.e.* 'Barndoor lock,' the surname given Magnus by the peasants
because he allowed them to lock the doors of their barns against the aggressiveness
of the nobles.

Vättern, on 18 December 1290, and the monastery journal of Stockholm relates that the peasants, in grateful remembrance of his having put locks on their barns, carried his coffin on their shoulders all the long way to Stockholm.(2)

Magnus Ladulås left three sons of minor age, Birger, Erik and Valdemar. The situation of the previous generation was repeated. This time also, the younger sons, 'the dukes,' rose up against their elder brother. In 1293 Erik, 'duke of the Svears,' and Valdemar, Duke of Finland, attacked the king in his castle of Håtuna and took him prisoner (*Håtunaleken*). After four years of captivity the king regained his liberty, but on very humiliating terms. In order to get revenge he invited his two brothers to a Christmas feast at the castle of Nyköping. The two brothers came and were received with great hospitality, but in the middle of the night (between the 10th and 11th of December 1317) the king's men burst in upon them with swords and torches and put them in prison. Christmas in the North in olden times often ended in tragedy—a Dane is reminded of Knud Lavard. King Birger had his brothers brought before him in chains: 'Do you remember the Håtuna game?' he cried to them. 'This game is not going to be merrier!' The two dukes were thrown into the dungeon of the castle, and when Birger left Nyköping he threw the keys of the dungeon into the river. It was said among the people that the dukes were starved to death. But their death did not remain unavenged—their friends among the nobility raised an army from among the people against the treacherous king. In Uppland Birger Persson sent a 'stick' message 'from *Granne* to the nearest *Granne*.'* West Gothland, Småland, also arose; the king's strongest fortress of Stegeborg was taken. Birger fled to his brother-in-law, Erik Menved, in Denmark and died there in 1321.

But when the people at midsummer mustered at the Thing at Mora Stones (1319), the ruler of the kingdom, Mats Kettilmundssön, stepped forth, carrying Duke Erik's three-year-old son, Magnus, on his arm and the people acclaimed the child as King of Sweden. At Master Mats Kettilmundssön's side stood Sir Birger Persson of Finsta.

* A message sent by means of a short stick of iron or wood, sometimes furnished with a cleft into which a message could be pushed. The quotation: 'from a neighbour to the nearest neighbour,' is from an old ballad about a Scotsman named Zinklar (no doubt the Norwegian version of Sinclair), who with a band of freebooters invaded Norway but came to a disastrous end, because of the prompt action of the Norwegians in sending the 'stick' message. [Trans.]

VII

In the night when Saint Bridget was born, the parish priest of the nearest parish church was praying devoutly, when he saw as it were a bright cloud, and in the cloud sat a virgin holding a book in her hand. He marvelled greatly what this might mean. Then the virgin said to him: 'A daughter has been born to Master Birger, and her wondrous voice shall be heard all over the world.'(1)

It was not the parish priest of Skederid who, on a night in June 1303, had this vision. It was Master Bengt of the neighbouring Rasbo, an eminent ecclesiastic, who became bishop of Åbo in 1321, where he died in 1338, and where he lies buried in the chancel of Åbo cathedral. Bridget was her mother's seventh child. Only two of her brothers and sisters grew to maturity; her brother Israel, who became law-man in Uppland after his father, but died fairly young on a crusade in Finland (1351), and her sister Katerina, who was married to Bridget's brother-in-law, Magnus Gudmarsson, and died so late as 1390, after having been twice married.

God showed His protecting hand over Bridget even before she came into the world. 'It befell, at the time when her mother was carrying her in her womb, that she, with several others, suffered shipwreck on a rock in the sea. Many men and women were drowned. But a chieftain of the land,' the old chronicler of her life relates, 'carried her to land with much toil and labour. And the next night there appeared to her a man in shining raiment who said to her: "Thou wert saved now from death because of the good thou bearest within thee. Bring it up therefore in the love of God, for God has given it to thee." '(2) This shipwreck seems to have taken place off Öland, and it is believed that it was the king's brother, Duke Erik, who was that brave 'chieftain of the land' who saved Bridget while yet unborn. At the town of Kläppinge on Öland, where a ness juts out into the sea, a stone cross still standing is said to have been raised by Bridget: here sailors were wont to pray for a fair wind and a good voyage across the gulf of Bothnia.

At first it did not seem as if the prophecy uttered at Bridget's birth was to be fulfilled, for until her third year little Bridget remained dumb. But suddenly the gift of speech broke out, and then she spoke 'more perfectly than it is usual for children of that age to speak.'

Bridget then grew up at Finsta Gaard. 'And now it must be told that her mother, the Lady Ingeborg, had seven children, three sons and four daughters. Her first son was named Peder, the second Bengt, the third Israel; her first daughter Ingrid, the second Margretha, the third

Karin (Katerina), the fourth was the dear Mother Saint Bridget' we are told by Margareta, Claus' daughter.(3)

The original accounts have nothing but good to tell of Bridget's parents. In the old Swedish biography (which is a translation of the Latin *Vita* by the confessors Petrus of Skenninge and Petrus of Alvastra) we read: 'Sancta Bridget was of very honourable race and birth . . . she was born of pious parents of high rank, who were zealous in all just works and in keeping the law of God. . . . Her father and grandfather, and his father before him, each in their own time, fared forth on pilgrimage to Jerusalem, and to the places of other holy men, namely Saint James and other saints, and it had not been heard of before, that men so rich and great should go so long a way to the furthest ends of the world, to see and do honour to the places where Christ had lived a life of the body.' Bridget's mother, too, 'was of a very honourable house, for her father was of royal kindred. He laid the groundwork under many churches and gave lands to many churches and convents. His wife too was very devout, yet she hid her devotion and appeared before the world attired as became her station.'(4) When a somewhat too zealous nun rebuked her for this, thinking that such fine raiment was not becoming to a lady so well reputed for piety as the lady of Finsta, the same scandalized sister in religion received a forcible reminder of that place in the Gospel, which says: 'Judge not, that ye be not judged, for with what judgment you judge, you shall be judged, and with what measure you mete, it shall be measured to you again.' As everyone knows who has frequented the circles which are particularly called 'pious,' the above-mentioned text is one of the least popular of the commandments and precepts of the Gospel—at the present day as in the fourteenth century. And it is by no means always, rather is it extremely rare, that heaven takes the trouble to rebuke the pious scandalized one, such as befell for the sake of Bridget's maternal grandmother. 'In the same night there appeared to the nun a righteous person (*quædam persona miræ pulchritudinis*) who said to her: "Why hast thou despised my handmaid and said that she was proud, which is not true. But thou shalt know this, that from her shall come forth a daughter, by whom I will do great things in the world, and so much grace will I give her, that all men shall marvel at her, yea, even my friends shall wonder." '(5)

Here the manuscript for the process of canonization has a small note in the margin: it says *Nota Monasterium Sko*. Bridget's grandmother must therefore already have been interested in this famous convent of

Cistercian nuns, which her father rebuilt after the fire in 1297. So at least Margareta, daughter of Claus, relates. This is disputed, however, in Edvard Ortved's great work on the Cistercian Order and its monasteries and convents in the north.* As far as Sir Birger is concerned, his benefactions to the Cistercian religious houses were quite inconsiderable, when it is remembered that he was the most powerful man of his time. Twenty marks, which he bequeathed to Sko in 1326, while the other houses of the Order received only three each, was all he had given. His wives, Kristina, daughter of John, and Ingeborg, daughter of Bengt, bequeathed to Sko ten and five marks respectively.(6)

When a choice has to be made between a scholar who has made a special study of the subject, like the Danish historian, and a short note in the family chronicle of Margareta, daughter of Claus, it is difficult to arrive at a decision. It is true that the chronicle in question was written a hundred years after the event, but as abbess in the convent of Vadstena from 1440 to 1486 the authoress would have had access to documents no longer available. If Birger Persson really did rebuild the convent of Sko after the fire, he may have thought that he had done enough. A more weighty argument is to be found in Ortved's further remark, that in not a single letter of indulgence of that period is such a fire mentioned, and it was a general rule for an indulgence to be promised for the rebuilding of churches and religious houses. In any case, the church was consecrated on 28 August 1300.

To Margareta, daughter of Claus, is due also the well-known story of Sigrid the Fair (whose name by a confusion in the bull of canonization has become the name of Bridget's mother).

Bridget's mother's father was Sir Bengt, law-man, he was brother to the king who was then ruling the kingdom [read: *Birger Earl*]. He took to wife a noble and beautiful maiden named Sigrid, daughter of a great and noble house, and yet not of so great and mighty a race as he, wherefore the king his brother showed him much ill-will and in mockery sent him a robe, woven half of cloth of gold and half of wadmal, to signify that he had brought dishonour to their house. But Sir Bengt had that part broidered all over with gold and pearls, and adorned with such precious gems that it was made more costly than the other part. After this the king declared him an outlaw and sent word that he would attack him; when Sir Bengt learned this he bade the Lady Sigfrid attire herself in her finest garments and receive the king with all grace, and himself fled into the forest.

There is about Swedish women something that can only be described by the word used by the Swedes themselves—*tjusig*. A Swedish *flicka* is seldom *bildschön* like a German *Mädchen*; she is not *bella* like a

* *Cistercierordenen og dens Klostre I Norden, II.*

black-haired, dark-eyed Italian *ragazza*, but with her fair fluffy hair, her snub nose and her big blue eyes, she is just that which the word expresses—*förtjusande, i.e.* confusing, and (another term which always comes back to the lips of a Swede when speaking of a young girl)—*så söt*. And to this the wonderful Swedish language with its twittering rhythm, its clear ringing vowels—and then, if Sigrid the Fair, like the maiden in the Danish folk-song, stood in the courtyard of the castle, 'slender like a willow wand, holding a cup of gold in each hand'—well, what wonder if the angry brother dismounted quickly from his horse and came up to his beautiful sister-in-law (perhaps in his haste he stumbled over his spurs?), fervently to embrace and kiss her. 'Truly, dear sister, had not my brother wedded you, I would have done so.'

A messenger was then sent to the fugitive in the forest to tell him that the danger was over, and that he was free to come back, and there was great feasting at Ulfåsa.(7)

On this wise in the days of the Old Covenant had fair Esther appeased King Ahasuerus and turned away his wrath from her people [is the comment of Margareta, daughter of Claus, on this incident]. Now it must be told that this Lady Sigrid left three daughters: the first was the Lady Ramborg; she is buried in the convent of Risaberga. Her husband was Sir Erengisle; he rests in Svanshals where their stone house stood aforetime and the church stands now.(8) And that worthy gentleman, her husband, when at the point of death, revealed that the honest lady was as good a virgin when he died as she was when she came to him.... The Lady Sigrid's second daughter was named Ingrid [erroneously for Katherina] 'and dwelt at Aspanäs: she was a good and God-fearing lady in whose care our dear Mother was placed after her mother's death.'

Ingeborg Bengt's daughter died as late as 1314. Little Bridget was still to spend eleven years at Finsta under the careful guidance of her pious mother.

VIII

As a matter of course the daughter of Birger Persson received the best education that could be provided in the fourteenth century, and in 'the most northerly land in the world.' The learned dean of the cathedral in Uppsala, Andreas And, was a friend of the house—it has been conjectured that he (as also that Mats Kettilmundssön, likewise a friend of Sir Birger) was the author of the work *Um Styrilsi Kununga ok Höfdinga*, a kind of political ethics. The original of this work, which was almost certainly written about the middle of the fourteenth century, is a treatise by Egidius Romanus, *De regimine principum*; the Swedish author may have become acquainted with it during a period of study abroad in the south, *e.g.* in Paris, where Andreas And had just founded *Domus Uppsalensis*, a well-arranged college for Swedish students of theology. The thoughts expressed in this work are a foundation for the mediæval outlook on life, to such a degree that there is good reason to study it in connection with the spiritual equipment of the life of Bridget, the law-man's daughter. The thoughts in this work are like the very air she breathed, the pure air of Christian law.

It starts with the assumption of the Christian faith: man is one of God's creatures, and man's place in creation is 'midway between angels and animals. In common with angels he has life and reason, with animals' life and a body. In his reason and spirit he is like angels, in his body and his bodily things he resembles unclean and worldly animals.'(1)

It is perhaps the first time in the literature of the world that this definition of man appears—*half animal and half angel*. Here is Goethe's thought already: '*Zwei Seelen wohnen, ach, in unsrer Brust.*' And as a result of this there are three possibilities open to man—to be wholly angel, wholly animal, or that which is half-way between the two, and which a later age calls the human.

First there is the *angelic life*—'and that life is lived by people living a pure life, those who have renounced all worldly goods and all worldly desire and all bodily pleasure, and even their own will, and seek for naught but to serve God at all times with a pure life and have naught in their minds but godly and spiritual things. This life has its own rules and laws, wherever houses of such pure life are found, whence they cannot depart.'

Then comes the opposite of this *vita angelica*, the highest known to the Middle Ages: 'another manner of living is, like the wild animals, not to think of anything but to eat and drink and sleep and to follow all bodily desire. This life has neither rule nor law nor direction.'

But between these two extremes lies the *via media*, which is by no means mediocrity, but 'the right life in this world.' And this life is led by those (and they are the most) 'who live in just wedlock and live on the goods which they have justly earned and by honest work. This manner of living gives a good conscience, and it shall be the manner of living of the common people.

'And these "common people" are best ruled by one man—for so say "all wise masters," that it is better for the people to have a king who rules alone, who governs the land and guides it to peace and safety and union between man and man, rather than several shall rule and govern.' The old author is *not* a democrat, although he is well aware of what can be said for the government by the people—'that several wise men can more speedily find what is right than a single one.' Yes, he admits, 'provided they all have one intent and one will,' but how often does one see that? It is quite right that when a ship has to be launched, it takes several men to haul it from the slips—but if there is not *one* who commands and steers, the whole thing will only lead to shouting 'ahoy, ahoy!'

One must rule, but this one *has his superiors*. We read further:

> Now a king must know that he is not only a man, even more than a man, but that he is less than God. Because he is man, he must live justly and like a man, but because he has been given more power by God than other men, he must serve God better than others and live a more just and manlike life than all other men. For he is God's steward in this world, appointed to judge and punish and torment men of evil deeds and chastise them for their ill-doings, and to honour and guard and help good men, who live in virtue and worthy of men and at peace with their fellow-men. And for himself he must live in great fear of God and in all that he does beware of the enmity of God and of God's vengeance, if he do aught that is displeasing to God or the friends or servants of God.

And this is not only Christian doctrine, but 'the wise Master Aristotle' admonished the great king Alexander with the same exhortation, 'that he should never do aught that he knew would be displeasing to God.'

The steward of God in this world—that was indeed how Bridget was to consider a king. With this measure she was to measure a Magnus Smek, an Albrecht of Mecklenburg, a Valdemar Atterdag. A king who was no longer God's steward was therefore no longer a true king. Aristotle had already said this very subtly, and Andreas And—or whoever it was—had repeated it. It is not enough, says the wise master of antiquity, that a king carries pious words on his lips, but is not God-fearing in his actions. (The word 'God-fearing' has unfortunately, in modern phraseology, become restricted to mean about the same as that one goes to church. It meant something quite different in the Middle Ages, which is shown by the synonym 'dread of God.' It meant that one *dreaded displeasing God*, and to displease God was the same as being unjust to one's neighbour. One feared God, because one knew that the time would come when one was to stand before His face and be judged by Him. How many modern people still believe this and act according to this belief? *Dies iræ* is an item on a concert programme—for how many is it more than that? The fear of God, so Aristotle taught his royal pupil, must be shown in the king's acts and in all his conduct.

'For the people are quick to see whether the king dreads the almighty God or no. And if they find from his deeds that he really honours and obeys God, then the people will honour and obey him as their king and chief. But if the king's or chief's deeds are found to be evil and ungodly, then this king is unworthy, and the common people will not obey him.' This is not only a fact verified by the old politician, but it is just and right that it should be so. God's commandments are above the king's commandments. 'If a king despise the right of God and offends against the law of God with his deeds of violence and the laws that he makes, then shall his might and honour be despised and quickly perish.'

How often, later, was Bridget to hurl out this threat—and see it fulfilled!

Perhaps it was chiefly because of the great authority possessed by the name of the Stagirite in the Middle Ages that the author of *Um Styrilsi Kununga* quoted him. He might have found the same political ethics closer at hand in a book which about the time of Saint Francis of Assisi, *i.e.* about 1220-30, was written somewhere in the north of Norway and bore a title similar to that of the Swedish treatise— *Konungs skuggsjà*, 'the king's mirror.' (Titles with 'mirror' were common at that time. I need only recall *Speculum virginum*, for the use of maidens of the nobility, and *Speculum perfectionis*, in which Franciscans of the fourteenth century could contemplate what they ought to be like and were not.) The unknown author was an ecclesiastic; the work was intended to be a kind of instruction on statecraft, with a section for each of the four states of the realm (king, ecclesiastic, merchant, peasant). Only the sections about the king and the merchant were completed before the author's death; that about the king was the most important, hence it had given the book its name. 'It is fully as much the duty of the king,' it says, 'daily to watch over the observance of the holy laws and the justice of the judgments that have been pronounced, as it is the duty of the bishop to provide for the performance of the Holy Mass and all the prayers of the holy office. . . . There are many who believe that kingly dignity has been ordained that it may give the right to pleasure and unrestrained enjoyment, according to the desire of each one.' This is an error—it is quite the opposite, so that '*the king must always be under the yoke of God*, and daily must he bear a heavy burden in all the care he has for the well-being of the people.'(3).

This is a northern conception of kingly dignity and kingly duty. Bridget was not to think differently.

IX

Little Brita grew up in the northerly air of Finsta, and in a Christian atmosphere. We do not know much about her going to school; her teachers probably consisted only of her mother and the castle chaplain. We may venture to think, however, that when little Brita had once learned to read she would be given lessons from one of the most widely used text-books, the *Lucidarius* (from the two words *lux*, light, and *dare*, to give—therefore, the Giver of Light).

This book was originally written in German, at the request of Henry the Lion, Duke of Brunswick (1129–95), the great adversary of Barbarossa, who was zealous for the enlightenment of his people. It is said that four of the Duke's chaplains were set to work on the book, which was based on four of the most eminent scientific works of the early Middle Ages.(1) Like the Norse *King's Mirror*, the book is written in the form of a dialogue between a disciple eager for knowledge and a 'wise master.'

The first question, then, which the disciple puts to the master is this: 'Tell me first something about God, good Master. What is God, and how are we to understand Him, though we may not see Him?'

Tell us something about God. In our times, too—more than ever, perhaps, in our times—this question is addressed to the sages of our days. Tell us something about God; we are so much in need of it! Our pious mothers taught us to fold our hands and pray to our Father who is in heaven—but the heavens are darkened to us now by the smoke of burning cities, and in despair we ask ourselves whether it is by the will of our Father that bombs fall to the ground. As a grown-up woman, as a young widow, Bridget herself was to contend with the demons of doubt when riding from Alvastra to Vadstena, and was rapt in her vision of the monk storming heaven on his ladder, like a hostile warrior about to storm a castle and raising his ladder against its walls. But as yet Bridget was only little Brita and she piously accepted all that the text-book told her: 'God is the good whence comes all that is good in all created things. Because He is Himself the very highest good, which is so perfectly good that all that is created in heaven and on earth can never fully understand His goodness and thank Him for it. Consider, then, how good it is to be with Him for those who so will live here on earth, that they may be the nearer to Him in heaven.'(2)

This is plain speaking. God is the highest good, and man is created that he may share in that good. God Himself has shown us the way,

when He became man and 'took manhood from the Virgin Mary.'
Only the Son of God became man, the two other Persons in the Holy
Trinity only helped Him in it, 'so as we see two men helping a third
to clothe himself, and yet it is himself who puts on the clothes.' But
the manhood of Christ 'was like a window that lights up the world.
For He suffered hunger and thirst and other pains for this: to be an
example for us to follow. He suffered death, for nothing has so much
power to draw man to the love of God as the death of God, for thereby
He showed how much He loved us. And if we do not love Him in
return we do Him a great wrong.'

The thought that *we do God a wrong* in not loving Him in return
is one to which Bridget was to come back again and again. In a revelation, she even hears Christ reproaching a soul which is lost with the
wrong which the soul *does Him*, Christ, by being condemned, when
Christ has suffered so bitterly to save that soul, and now has to see that
He has suffered in vain. Bridget was to see that the window which gave
light to the world was also to shine through the dark forest of existence, 'like the candle which a mother places in the window for the son
whose homecoming she is awaiting.'

Little Brita could not be in any doubt about the purpose of life.
One had to travel along the road and try to reach everlasting joy with
God. And the best thing would be to get as near to God as possible.
But in order to attain such heights one would have to be a saint—like
Saint Erik in Uppsala, or like Saint Botvid, Saint David, Saint Eskil—
or like Saint Elin of Skövde. At an early age little Brita must have
heard of Saint Erik's tomb; her parents had their family burial-place
and chapel there, and Hammerich is probably not far wrong when
describing the journey of the family from Finsta to the Christmas week
in the cathedral at Uppsala.

Christmas morning with smooth roads, bells ringing in a long train of
sledges, each with its pine torch, coming out of the forest and hastening away
to the brightly lighted church. Here, among the soaring Gothic pillars within
it, everything spoke to little Brita of Saint Erik, his shrine with gold and
precious stones, the tapestries in which his holy deeds and his martyr's death
were pictured . . . and the antiphony in honour of Saint Erik sung by the
canons sounded more perfect than anywhere else in the kingdom:

> *Ave, martyr pretiose,*
> *Miles Christi gloriose,*
> *Ave, regum gloria!*
> *O Erice, rex Svecorum,*
> *posce nobis peccatorum*
> *veniam et gaudia!*(3)

But Saint Erik was a man, a king. The holy bishops and martyrs, too, were men—was there not in Sweden, then, also a woman who had merited the name of saint, and who might serve a little girl better as a model? Yes, there was one indeed. Her name was Helena or Elin, from Skövde in West Gothland, and Bishop Brynolf of Skara, who was himself a holy man, had written the story of her life. It is scarcely to be imagined that no one in Finsta had ever heard tell of Saint Elin. West Gothland was not so far away, and Bishop Brynolf of Skara was the son of one of the great men of Sweden, the powerful West Gothland law-man, Algot. Before the cathedral of Uppsala was built, the cathedral in Skara was the largest in the country; it had a cathedral chapter of eleven canons. Brynolf had studied in Paris and was the author of several Latin poetical works: an office in honour of Saint Eskil, another to the glory of the Blessed Virgin, one to that of the Crown of Thorns, and then there was that in honour of Elin of Skövde, as well as the legend about her.(4) There must have been talk about her by the fireside in the long winter evenings at Finsta, when the flames crackled on the open hearth and the snowstorm howled about the corners of the house, vying with the wolves in the big forests.

Now it was related in the legend that Saint Elin's parents came of great families, and that from her childhood she was trained in the law of the Lord. But when she had reached the age of marriage she was, according to the custom of the land, betrothed to a man whom she consented to wed, as Sara consented to wed Tobias. And God bestowed upon her the faithfulness of Leah and the grace and beauty of Rachel, so that even her body was a picture of her soul. Like Esther she found favour in the eyes of all men, and by her pure life she did honour to her noble birth.

But later, when her husband was dead and both her age and the state of her fortunes led her to think of a new marriage, she was drawn to a union with God in a marriage of the spirit, rather than submit herself to carnal pleasure, which always begins with joy but ends in sorrow. She resolved to enter upon the heavy path of widowhood and to follow in the steps of Judith, serving God by prayer and fasting, and like holy Job her door was ever open to the wayfarer, and the poor received warmth from the wool of her sheep. She loved the glory of the house of God, and out of her own purse she paid for the building of a large part of the church in Skövde, where her holy body now rests.(5)

It is further related that a persecution arose among the still heathen population (Elin of Skövde lived about the year 1150), against the pious widow. To escape from this she went on a pilgrimage to Jerusalem; like her great patron, Saint Helen, the mother of Constantine the Great, 'to see the tomb of the Lord, and the places where He had suffered.' But when she came back to Skövde the hatred against her flared up afresh, and one day when she was on her way to the church in the neighbouring Götene, which was to be consecrated on that very day, 'some of her blood-thirsty enemies threw themselves upon her and dyed their swords in the blood of the just one.' This happened on I August. Her body was found by a boy who was guide to a blind man. The boy saw what seemed to him to be a light in a bush by the wayside and found that the light came from one of the fingers of the saint, which the murderers had cut off, and on which she wore the ring that she had brought home from the Holy Land. The sight of the blind man was restored when he touched his eyes with the ring, and when the body was brought to Skövde, and they who carried it stopped to rest on the way, a spring gushed forth at the place. Many other wonderful things happened later, so that Pope Alexander III, at the entreaty of Bishop Stefan of Uppsala, wrote her name in the golden holy book of the saints.(6)

It is permissible to imagine that Bridget, daughter of the Uppland law-man, would be acquainted with the legend about Elin, daughter of the law-man of Vestgöta. Marriage was good, but widowhood was better—one would be more free to serve God and set out on a pilgrimage, to see the land of Saint James, and go 'to Jerusalem to see the tomb of the Lord and the places where He had suffered.' Best of all, of course, was the state of virginity—that was plain to read, for instance, in the book called *The Virgins' Mirror, Speculum virginum*.

It is true that Bridget did not make acquaintance with this step until her sojourn in Alvastra between 1346 and 1349. But the thoughts expressed in the book were an utterance of the possibilities afforded to women as understood at that time. *The Virgins' Mirror* is composed in the form of a dialogue; this time between a woman, Theodora, and a 'wise master' named Peregrinus. It was written about 1100 by an unknown monk in the abbey of Hirsau in the present Württemberg.(7) Here Theodora is told that only thirty per cent. of married women have a prospect of getting to heaven, widows sixty per cent., but virgins one hundred per cent. In Bridget's process of canonization Prior Petrus relates that one day in Alvastra he read aloud to Bridget from the *Speculum virginum* (in Latin; the Old-Swedish version edited by Geete, dating from the close of the fifteenth century, having been

translated by Mats Larsson, monk of Vadstena, between 1472 and
1486). During the reading Bridget was rapt in ecstasy and exclaimed
when she awoke: 'I heard a voice say to me: "Virginity merits the
crown, widowhood draws the soul near to God, marriage does not
shut out from heaven." '(8)

Virginitas meretur coronam—while to marriage is only conceded the
modest testimony that 'it does not shut out from heaven.' Virginity
merits the crown—and what a crown! That of which it is said in the
hymn: *Jesu, corona virginum!* Is it not conceivable that little Brita, who,
after having overcome the first years of dumbness, was evidently an
unusually intelligent child, may have accompanied her mother on
one of the visits of the latter to the Cistercian nuns in the convent at
Sko? May it not be imagined that the visit would take place on the
occasion of the festival that is always held when a new sister takes the
veil? And if little Brita was there we can be certain that she would ask
her mother about all the strange things that she saw there. She would
hear a young woman speak the significant words, answer with the
'I will,' which is binding like the vow of marriage; she would see the
priest standing with the Sacred Host in his hand and asking the kneeling
maiden: 'Dost thou promise to serve God in obedience, chastity and
poverty to the end of thy life?' She would hear the low-toned answer:
'I do, I promise it,' and she would see the priest lift up the Host and
answer: 'Then, in the name of God, I promise thee life everlasting.'
And the singing of the nuns would be heard behind the grille, infinitely
gentle and persuasive: *Veni, sponsa Christi, et accipe coronam*, 'Come,
bride of Christ, and receive the bridal wreath.' . . .

> Now when Bridget was seven years old, she saw one night facing her bed an
> altar, and a lady in shining raiment sitting on the altar and holding a crown in
> her hand said to her: 'Oh, Bridget come hither!' When she came up to her the
> lady said: 'Will you have this crown?' She said that she would. Then the lady
> put the crown on her head, so that she distinctly felt the ring of the crown on
> her brow. And immediately the vision vanished, but it never faded from her
> memory.

Perhaps in that hour Bridget already felt that 'she would die
rather than enter into wedlock.'(9)

X

It was at Finsta in Uppland and it was Quinquagesima Sunday in the
year of the Lord 1314. The severe Swedish winter was at its height—
a *Varga* winter! The snow lay in thick drifts on the roads and made the

forests impassable. Hart and roe cut themselves so that they bled on the ice-crust, which after many days froze over the snow in the ringing cold nights, and in the blue moonlight the hare sat, with long quivering ears, munching in the cabbage gardens. The night before Quinquagesima there had been a snowstorm; in the castle yard the men were hard at work clearing away the snow by the light of red torches before the most important doors. In particular before the castle chapel, to which a broad path was made, for Brother Algot from Skara, of the Order of Preachers, was to preach at the early Mass, and it was to be expected that everybody in the castle who possibly could would come to hear him. Towards five o'clock the snow had been cleared away and now Sir Birger, the Lady Ingeborg and the little eleven-year-old Bridget came out of the house. Wrapped in furs against the chill air of the morning they walked quickly across the courtyard and disappeared into the lighted chapel where the retainers of the castle were soon all assembled. When the Mass began, the chapel was full to the very door. In the first row Sir Birger, the Lady Ingeborg and their young daughter knelt in the carved benches. Sir Birger had only on the previous Friday made his confession to Brother Algot—'on Fridays I will so make ready,' he used to say, 'that I may be ready on the other days to bear what it shall please God that I must bear.'(1)

The priest was now standing before the altar, saying the Introit in a low voice: *Esto mihi in Deum protectorem,* 'Be Thou unto me a God, a protector, and a place of refuge, to save me: and for Thy name's sake Thou wilt lead me, and nourish me.'

It was very quiet in the little chapel at Finsta. Outside, silence reigned—the snow was silent and the air was still; not a sound came from the forests. The wolves had gone to rest, and no human beings were abroad. In all the great land of Sweden there was silence and snow on this dark morning of Quinquagesima Sunday in the year 1314.

Brother Algot now turned away from the altar, holding the Gospel book in his hands. The deacon stood behind him with a candle in a candlestick, so that he could see to read. Everyone made the sign of the cross towards Brother Algot on brow, lips and breast to hear the Holy Gospel—*in nomine Patris, et Filii et Spiritus Sancti.* . . .

Brother Algot read:

At that time: Jesus took unto him the twelve, and said to them, Behold, we go up to Jerusalem, and all things shall be accomplished which were written by the prophets concerning the Son of Man: for he shall be delivered to the Gentiles, and shall be mocked, and scourged, and spit upon; and after they

I

have scourged him, they will put him to death; and the third day he shall rise again. And they understood none of these things.

Brother Algot was silent for a moment and gave back the book to the deacon. Meanwhile the people were settling themselves in the benches. Then the preaching friar began to interpret the Word, according to the rule of his Order, in which it is one of the chief tasks.

First, that the time is drawing near, when Our Lord will suffer pain, and that He foretells it to us in this holy reading. To-day, then, the hour is come in which all Christians must surely call to mind that they are born again in the precious blood of the Son of God, wherefore they must serve Him in more godly wise and with greater abstinence. For, as Saint Paul saith: They that are Christ's have crucified their flesh to keep from vice and concupiscence.

But, it is sad to tell, so many do that which is all against this, for most of all at this season they fill themselves with sumptuous food and overmuch drink at feasts and now work more evil than they are able to atone through a whole year. The more bitterly they have been redeemed, the worse do they live, and the more wantonly do they sin. More gladly and willingly do they behold worldly things than the torments and death of Our Lord and the rose-red of His wounds. But if they do not come to other ways they shall speedily be condemned together with those who parted His garments among them and cast lots for them. Our Lord died for our souls, to the end that we should preserve them from all uncleanness. Which they do not who have given themselves up to all worldly pleasure in food and drink, and in dancing and idle talk and other sins of the tongue.

The next that we must mark is that Jesus took His disciples with Him and made known to them His passion. This was for a sign that they who are true disciples of Jesus, should follow Him perfectly in abstinence in a hard life. For as Our Lord says: Whosoever does not take up his cross—that is, hard duty for the betterment of sinners—he cannot be my disciple. And they, who would rather seek places of carousals and drunkenness, than they would think of God's torment and His love and other good works, they are like disciples of the rich man who burned in the flames of hell. The rich man begged for a drop of water to cool his tongue, which had tasted so much pleasant food and sweet drink, and spoken so many idle words and evil reports at drinking feasts, and he did not receive that drop of water for which he begged. He, therefore, who does not refrain himself from surfeit in food and drink, ought to think of the torments of the rich man in hell; he had as great poverty there as he had had plenty in the world here. Let therefore each one take heed to himself, whom he follows and loves. The beloved Saint Bernard justly says: He who loves the world more than God, unchastity more than purity, gluttony more than fasting, follows the devil and enters with him into everlasting torment.

The third matter that we should mark is what Jesus says about His passion, that He should be given up to the heathen, and be mocked and scourged and spit upon and at last be killed. Now as Our Lord Jesus Christ at that time suffered such bodily pains, so is He now mocked and tormented in spirit, even

though He can no longer suffer or be saddened. He is betrayed and given up
to the heathen when godless people, who yield themselves up to the desires
of the world and the flesh, do violence to His Holy Church. Next Jesus is
mocked and despised, when His priests fail His ignorant and common people
by their evil living. The judgment of God shall be heard upon them: 'Where
is the flock that was entrusted to thee, where is my chosen people? Thou
didst teach those under thee by evil example, therefore shall the torments of
all those who followed thy evil ways be added to thy own torments.' Next
Jesus is scourged when His poor are oppressed with injustice, like the people
of God by the servants of Pharaoh. And it is written of those who afflict the
poor of God: Our Lord will tread down hard-hearted men, those who
chastised the people in their wrath. Saint Augustine says: Why is a hard-
hearted man proud? Of him God makes a rod wherewith He chastises His son,
but when the chastisement is over He throws the rod into the fire. Jesus is spit
upon when just men are scorned, as Saint Augustine also says: To spit Jesus in
the face is to scorn the just of God in this world and to fling words of scorn
against them like spittle. Jesus is slain when love is quenched in a man. For,
says Saint Augustine, nothing is fairer before the face of God than the virtue
of loving-kindness, and nothing gives more joy to the devil than the quench-
ing of love.

But because the love of God is quenched in many souls Jesus is now
scorned in spirit as He was aforetime in the body. He is kicked and buffeted
in the back when men are feared and honoured more than God and there is
no one who cares aught for righteousness. Men strike Him on the mouth
when they hear His commandments but say: 'Let us do what pleases us in the
world, we shall not in any wise reach heaven!' This is the same as striking our
dear Lord in the face, for if it had been the will of God that we should all be
lost in everlasting torment, He had not created us, neither redeemed us so
bitterly. Therefore must all men now learn that He is just, that He rewards
even the least good and punishes even the least evil, and that in His mercy He
shapes us anew according to the image of His adorable life, to be formed in
likeness to Him, the only true, wise and holy God, to whom be glory and
praise, honour and thanksgiving for ever and ever.(2)

Brother Algot's sermon was ended. He now turned again to the
altar, his big, bright and shaven skull shining white above the purple
chasuble of the Mass. With uplifted arms and outspread hands he began
again to pray; the murmur of his voice could be heard all over the
chapel. Deeper and deeper fell the quiet under the low roof, all heads
were bowed lower and lower. By her mother's side knelt Bridget, her
face hidden in her hands—only at the words, uttered in a low voice, *Qui
pridie*, 'Our Lord Jesus, in the night He was betrayed,' did she look up
for a moment, and then she saw Brother Algot standing with his arms
stretched out wide in the form of a cross. A little after she again glanced
up, but then he had lowered his arms and stood like other priests.

In the evening, after that same Quinquagesima Sunday, Bridget could not fall asleep. No lamp was burning in her room, but outside the night was bright with snow, and a faint grey light came in through the narrow window. She could distinguish the little kneeling-stool, where she used every evening to kneel down and say her prayers, and the crucifix hanging above it.

Then, suddenly, she could see nothing but the crucifix. It grew so big, so real, so alive. She saw distinctly all the crimson weals of the scourging on the poor, thin arms of the Crucified, the ugly, yellow splashes of spittle sticking to His beautiful beard and on His pale cheeks. The drops of blood, trickling down from under the crown of thorns and dripping into His eyes that were sore with weeping, and blinding them. She saw it all, and it was so mournful a sight that her heart came near to breaking with grief and pity and anger.

'Oh, my dearest Lord, who has ill-treated You so?' she asked, hardly knowing that she was speaking; her heart was beating violently in her breast.

Then the Crucified opened His blue, almost frozen lips, and a voice that was sad like the moaning of the wind in the reeds by the shore of the lake answered softly:

'All they who forget Me and despise My love.'

Of a sudden it seemed as though a brightness was extinguished in the room. The light was grey as before, and Bridget could hardly distinguish the kneeling-stool and the crucifix. But she did not fall asleep, her little heart kept hammering in her breast; she heard its dull thudding in the deep stillness of the night, and it was as though each beat drove hard nails into her soul. She could not stay in bed; with bare feet she jumped out on the cold floor and fell on her knees before the cross. Then she said a prayer which seemed to be uttered from within her:

O Lord God, forgive me my sins for the sake of Thy bitter pain and for Thy love of the race of man. O Lord Jesus Christ, who wast taken captive by the Jews, have mercy upon me. O Lord Jesus Christ, who stoodest bound to the stake, have mercy upon me. O Lord Jesus Christ, who wast without guilt and was judged by hard-hearted men, have mercy upon me. O Lord Jesus Christ, who wast robbed of Thy garments and clad in the raiment of mockery, have mercy upon me. O Lord Jesus Christ, Thou who wast so cruelly torn that Thy bones could be seen and there was not a whole spot upon Thee, have mercy upon me. O Lord Jesus Christ, Thou who wast stretched upon the Cross, as a bird of prey is stretched with four nails upon the door of a barn, have mercy upon me!

Christ *is* a bird of prey. Like an eagle He struck that night into the young heart of Bridget.(3)

XI

Praise be to Thee, Lord, for our sister, bodily death, whom no living creature shall escape. Woe to them who die in mortal sin. But blessed are they who live according to Thy holy will, for the second death has not power to do them harm.

So had the saint of Assisi, into whose Third Order Bridget was later to enter, sung on his death-bed, down yonder on the plain at Portiuncula, in the hut made of branches, where he lay awaiting a visit of that Guest, of whom Dante says that 'no one willingly opens the door to her.' Francesco had not only opened the door to her, he had even bid her welcome. It was on an October evening in 1226, the swallows were circling over the roof of the hut of poverty, and twittering, as if they would follow, singing, the soul of the dying man to Paradise. Many had since then learned of the saint of Assisi to bid death welcome—not to hear the knocking at the door like the hard knocks of a bony hand, but like the gentle tapping of a friend, who pushes the door slightly ajar and asks: 'May I come in?' Among those who felt like this was Bridget's mother. Only a few lines about her last illness and death are to be found in the legend: the Lady Ingeborg, 'who was perfect in many virtues, fell ill and foretold her death some days before she died. When she saw her husband and the others weeping and mourning she said: "Why do you mourn? Long enough have I lived here on the earth. There is more cause now for rejoicing, because I have been called to a mighty Lord." After that she blessed her husband and the children and fell asleep in God.'(1) Margareta, daughter of Claus, further relates: 'This lady lived well, and so she is with God. . . . And after Saint Bridget had come to years of discretion and to a true knowledge of God, it came to pass once that the Blessed Virgin came to her and brought with her the soul of the Lady Ingeborg, and the Virgin Mary spoke to the soul and said: "Oh, daughter, lovest thou thy daughter Bridget?" The soul answered: "Oh, blessed Lady, thou knowest how it is with us, if she loves God, she is dear to me, if she loves not God, then is she hateful and evil in my sight."'(2) The body of the Lady Ingeborg was carried to the chapel of Saint Catherine and Saint Nicholas in the cathedral of Uppsala—the canons received two hundred marks in silver as an offering for Masses for her soul.

Birger Persson remained at Finsta with the three youngest children, the only ones now living: Bridget, Catherine and little Israel. Sir Birger kept the two little ones at home. But he decided to send Bridget, who would soon be a big girl, and whose education and upbringing he did not think he was able to carry on himself, to his sister-in-law, that is, the sister of Bridget's mother, Katherine, daughter of Bengt, and married to the law-man in East Gothland, Knut Jonsson of the family of the Blå. In this way Bridget came for the first time to that part of Sweden in which she was to spend her youth and live until, as a mature woman, she left her native country for ever.

Andreas Lindblom writes:

> Then came a sunny morning at harvest time. It had frozen during the night, the leaves were falling and falling. It was but lately that a distinguished company of travellers had knelt in the cathedral of Linköping and recommended themselves to the protection of Our Lady for the last part of the road. The candles gleamed in the limestone grey obscurity of the nave, the windows began to take on a bluish tone from the first light of dawn outside, the chisel strokes of the Gothlandic and English masons re-echoed under the vaultings —were they never to finish their work? It had now been going on for years.

And now they ride out, through Slaka and Gammelkil. In the morning sun the riders see before them the wide, fertile country of East Gothland; large boulders stand up in the brown soil of the ploughed fields, here and there a small wood, pine and fir and birch mixed; in the woods of spruce fir there are large rings of mushrooms in the places where the witches have danced, and the maple trees glow like a golden flame. The peasants' houses are grey roofed with turf, much larger than those at home, for the East Gothland peasants have always built better than the Upplanders.

The company consists of the constable of the kingdom, the lawman of East Gothland, Knut Jonsson, and his wife Katherine, daughter of Bengt. A little girl is riding between them, half hidden by the high saddle; it is the daughter of Katherine's sister, Bridget, daughter of Birger. It has been decided in the family council at Finsta that the eleven-year-old, slightly delicate girl is to go with her aunt and her husband to their home at Aspanäs by the lake Sommen.

The day is advancing, the shadows are beginning to lengthen. They pass through large forests; the armed horsemen look warily about them; scouts are sent on ahead to find out whether the road is safe. For it is in the year 1314, half-way between *Håtunalegen* and the banquet at Nyköping. For the time being there is peace and reconciliation between the brothers, but the dukes know that the king is planning revenge. It is true that Sir Knut Jonsson is the king's man, but not five years are to pass ere he takes his share in raising the standard of revolt.

Then the forest opens out; they look out over a broad sheet of water, shining like mother of pearl in the evening light—Sommen! A halt is made at the church town, Malexander, which consists of a few wooden booths, an inn and a priest's house standing round the wooden church, which is tarred and shingle-roofed. On the opposite shore of the lake there is a glimpse of a castle—Aspanäs. The horizon is closed in by large forests rising bluish against it; it is the beginning of thickly wooded Småland. One of the company lights a fire on the shore; another beacon is lit over at Aspanäs—it is the ferryman's answer, and soon the boat comes over and takes the travellers home.(3)

From one great house Bridget has come to another, for her aunt's husband, the law-man Knut Jonsson, is not in any way inferior to Birger Persson. Together with other lords and good men serving the realm he had, at this very harvest season, been called by the king to Söderköping, where the Council of the Realm had signed, on the feast of Saint Dionysius (3 October), an assurance in which they swore fealty to the king, and after his death to support with all their might his queen and his heirs. Knut Jonsson was then still constable but soon after resigned office, perhaps that he might be able to remain neutral in the fight again breaking out between the king and the dukes. Later, however, Knut Jonsson became a member of the regency, having guardianship over young Magnus Eriksson. He continued being law-man—the oldest copy of the East Gothland law, a beautifully ornamented manuscript on parchment, was written out at his expense. But the law is older than he; he is not, like Birger, the author of the law.

His wife, the Lady Katherine, whose father, Bengt Magnusson of Ulfåsa, had been law-man in East Gothland before her husband, was educated according to the best standards of her time. She was Godfearing; she had not in her seal, as she was entitled to have, the crest of the Folkungs, but an image of the Blessed Virgin.(4) Her principles in the bringing up of children were those prevalent at the time—the rod was always ready to hand.

That the couple at Aspanäs had a friendly disposition towards the Church and religious houses can be seen, *inter alia*, from their having, on 22 September 1345, bequeathed several properties to the cathedral of Linköping, besides money, valuables, vestments and other equipment to several monasteries and ecclesiastical houses, *e.g.* to the Dominican monastery, the House of the Holy Spirit and the hospital in Skenninge, as also to several churches—the church of Malexander thus receiving six marks.

Knut Jonsson's house was not, any more than was Finsta, a strong-hold in mediæval Gothic, such as may be seen on the banks of the Rhine and in the Tyrol. There was nothing romantic about these old manor houses. Memories of childhood awaken in Bridget when she speaks, in a revelation, of the various houses that must form part of a well-arranged manor. Finsta and Aspanäs were both such blocks of buildings; the 'big room,' the bedrooms, work rooms, kitchen, maidens' bower, houses for the servants, besides barns, stables and all kinds of outhouses. They were built in a square round a big courtyard with a well in the middle and closed in by a strong gate—a Danish peasant farm is to this day built in the same way. There would also be a chapel, and therefore a chaplain. A farm bailiff was the overseer of the work on the lands when the master was away.(5)

For two years little Brita now lived here at Aspanäs with her aunt and her cousins. On Sundays and holy-days they were ferried by the farm servants across to the little grey church at Malexander—the boats on the lake have the same peculiar shape as those of the Middle Ages (*Sommarskep*). The parish priest may have been that Master Lambertus to whom Knut Jonsson bequeathed three marks.

In the long winter evenings they all assembled in the work room, by the flaming and crackling fire in the chimney. Here the women worked at weaving and sewing or carding wool, while the men carved with their sheath knives or other useful implements and one of the maids would sing an old ballad, or an old woman recount legends and stories. There was plenty to relate there, on the shores of Lake Som-men, close up to the wooded mountains. One could tell of the *Ur-Ko** which made its home by the steep wall of rock, the *Ur-berg*. The 'ur-cow' is a descendant of Audhumbla, a figure in Norse mythology. With its huge cloven hoofs it kicks open the hole which is now the lake, but a mountain giant catches it and shuts it up inside the fell. For fodder the ur-cow is given a cowhide, of which it eats one hair every Christmas Eve. When all the hairs are eaten up the cow escapes and destroys the whole countryside. Round about in the neigh-bourhood there are many small round lakes and ponds—footprints of the cow's forelegs where it stood kicking! In the lake itself there are dangerous powers—every year they demanded a human life as sacrifice, and no winter passed without one or another, who had ventured out on the ice where it was not safe, sinking and disappearing. It happened one year that the lake had not received its tribute, and near the end of

* Ur—pronounced Oor.

the winter a terrible shout could be heard from it: 'The time is up and no one has come!' A man who heard the shout became as though bewitched by it, went out on the ice and was dragged down.(6)

In her own home Bridget had heard many similar stories about what the Swedes, with a sinister-sounding word, call *schrock*—all the supernatural, with which it is best to have no dealings. In the forest lives the forest lady or *skogsrået*, in the lake *sjörået*, in the stream sits the *Nökke* playing his harp. The mountains are the homes of the trolls; the elves dance on the meadows; the underground creatures, the 'Tomts,' corresponding perhaps to the brownies, even venture into the houses. It was the *sjörå* that sang to Gustav Vasa's son, Magnus, as he sat by the window in the castle of Vadstena and saw the moonlight gleaming in the waves of Lake Vättern—like a singing woman the *sjörå* rose up from the moonlit water and spread out her white arms towards him—and the unhappy prince threw himself out to embrace her. The *skogrå*, too, sings; the lonely knight riding through *tiomila skog* (ten-mile forest) 'while all the others are sleeping,' often hears beautiful singing far, far away in the forest—it is the forest lady singing. But beware of following the singing, for 'where the forest lady has walked all the flowers are scorched away and she leaves a smell of sulphur behind her.'(7)

Eerie, too, are the *Mylings*. They are the souls of the little children whom their mothers have born in secret and killed directly after their birth. Never were they baptized, their mothers hid them in heathen soil. You can hear them screaming at night in the fields: 'Mother, come and feed me!' One peasant, hearing the cry, went out and dug up the poor little body to lay it to rest in consecrated ground. After that time the crying ceased. Perhaps Bridget was thinking of these poor little ones when she grieved at the fate of the children who were born too soon—like the *Mylings* they had never 'enjoyed the sweetness of their mother's breast or the warmth of her bosom.'(8)

All this and much more of the same kind was talked about—or whispered, for fear that some of the evil powers might hear and be offended—down in the servants' room by the flaming winter fire in the chimney. Perhaps there was also a discussion on how one should protect oneself against these creatures from the realm of darkness. They were most powerful at midsummer, when the witches flew to Blåkulla to acclaim their lord and master, whose name it were better not to speak —he was referred to only as *That One*. Then the midsummer beacons were lit, and on all the doors of the homestead it was advisable to write the names of the three Wise Men, or only their initials C., M., B. (Caspar, Melchior, Balthasar); then no witch could come in. Putting the herb called houseleek under the rafters kept away witches and other evil troll folk. There were also certain holy wells, whose waters were good to drink, or one might sacrifice to the elves—they are not evil. You pour a little fresh milk into the hollows of the big stones lying here and there in the woods, called elf-querns, and they will give help in return. If a witch has caused illness in anyone it will help to melt lead over the sick person: three times for *Sjörå*, for *Skogsrå* and for *Gårdsrå* (another name for the tomt). But a little gold scraped from a wedding ring must be mixed with it, and then you must say . . .

The talk ceased when the Lady Katherine came into the room, for she did not approve of this superstitious chatter. (Bridget too, later, became a decided opponent of all superstition.) Aunt Karin was on the watch to prevent all this talk of the servants' room from finding an entrance into the young soul that was entrusted to her care, and she resolved to be very vigilant. And sure enough, one evening, when the Lady Katherine like a good housewife was going on her last round to see that the fire was covered with ashes and all candles and lamps had been put out, she found little Bridget kneeling on her bare knees beside her bed. In case of need, the strict lady carried a birch rod on her nightly round. 'What does this mean, Brita?' she exclaimed. 'Have the maids taught you some of their crazy incantations?' The birch rod was already raised. But little Brita looked up at her with big blue eyes: 'I only got out of bed to praise Him who is always near me and always ready to help me!' 'And who is that, if one may be allowed to ask?' The big blue eyes looked straight into her aunt's face, and her voice grew a little husky with emotion: 'It is Jesus Christ who was crucified for our sakes and *whom I have seen*!' 'Then the rod broke into little pieces,' says the old story of Bridget's life.

Bridget might well be in need of having Someone near who could help her. For though she did not believe in the *Skogsrå* or the *Sjörå*, in the elves or the tomts, there was *one* whose terrible reality she could not doubt, who had power to cast souls into hell. She knew that a single little sin might bring her soul into danger—and one evening she had played far too merrily with cousins and friends and said her evening prayers with less devotion than usual. And he was there at once, the vile and malignant enemy of God and human souls. He had a hundred hands and feet and all the hands were curved claws, and all the claws were stretched out to seize Bridget and drag her with him down to everlasting damnation. Then, in her terror of death, she threw herself upon her bed and cried to her Friend and Protector, the Crucified— and behind her she heard the Evil One hissing: 'When He does not give me leave, I cannot do you any harm!'

And so the years passed—two years. Bridget flourished at Aspanäs, grew big and strong; *era da marito*, as it is said in realistic Italian, she was of marriageable age. In the Middle Ages women were married very young; Saint Elisabeth of Thuringia, who has so many features in common with Bridget, was married at the age of only fourteen, to the landgrave Ludwig of Thuringia. In her biography we are told that she entered unwillingly into matrimony, but consented to it, 'not to yield to the lust of the flesh, but to obey her father's behest and to bear children to serve God.'(9)

Bridget's education was drawing towards its close. She was taught all the accomplishments of a young girl of the nobility. Together with the other maidens she sat in the maidens' bower—the folk-song describes it: 'Three maidens are sitting in bowers, two of them are winding threads of gold.' At Aspanäs, too, threads of gold were used in making costly, gold-embroidered garments; perhaps little Brita was working at her trousseau. One day she was alone at her work, and yet not alone, for when her Aunt Karin came in she saw by her niece's side a lady she did not know, and who was helping the young girl. The strange lady vanished when the Lady Katherine came in. 'Who was that?' she asked Bridget in surprise. Bridget looked up astonished: 'No one has been here, Aunt Karin!' The Lady Katherine did not say anything, but had her own thoughts about it. And later, those to whom the Lady Katherine showed the finished work were agreed that it was so beautiful and done with so much skill that it was impossible it could have been done by so young a girl, almost a child. The Lady Katherine did in fact put it away and preserved it as if it had been a relic.(10)

Perhaps it was on that day that the Lady Katherine sought out Bridget to bring her the message which had long been expected—that Sir Birger had promised his two daughters in marriage to young Sir Ulf Gudmarsson and his brother Magnus, sons of the law-man in West Gothland, of a family just as noble as the house of Finsta. It may have been on that day, or on another. But on whatever day it was, the evening of that day would see Bridget praying more earnestly than was her wont, and kneeling before the crucifix she would shed the bitterest tears she would ever shed in all her life. Like Saint Elin she knew what marriage was—'it begins in joy but ends in sorrow'; she was, herself, many years later, from her own experience to warn against 'the sweet joy of the flesh, which at last tastes like venom and ends in affliction.'(11) Now she was herself delivered up to that sweet joy! Her Aunt Katherine could speak only in terms of praise of Bridget's future husband; he too was quite young, only eighteen. Yet, though he be ever so good and worthy, he was not that Bridegroom of whom it is sung in the hymn: *Jesu, corona virginum.* . . . Bridget fell down on her bed sobbing: 'Better to die than to be a bride!'

BOOK II

ULFÅSA

Virginitas meretur coronam, viduitas appropinquat Deo, conjugium non excludit a cælo.

Virginity merits the crown, widowhood draws near to God, matrimony does not exclude from heaven.

Bridget

Thæt livernit havir thæt folk, som liuir i rættu hionalaghi.

UM STYRILSI KUNUNGA

I

A KING's son loved a maiden 'and presented her with gilded shoes and a golden girdle, a gold ring on her finger and a crown on her head.'(1)

Young Ulf Gudmarsson was not the son of a king but almost as good, and he loved Brita, daughter of Birger. He had given her a golden girdle and gilded shoes; his gold ring shone upon her finger, slender as a child's, and he had placed the bridal crown upon her head. And now she was sitting in that room at Ulfåsa, where they were to sleep so sweetly under the blue coverlets. She was sitting there now on that September evening in the year 1316, and waiting. And while she waited her thoughts went back to all that had happened during these last months.

It began with the evening when she had wept so bitterly. The next morning Aunt Karin had seen little Brita's tear-swollen eyes and had asked and asked until at last she had been told everything; in other spiritual matters, too, Bridget had confided in the Lady Katherine.(2) And the kind aunt had comforted her little niece as well as she could and reasoned with her. Matrimony was a holy sacrament, one of the seven means of grace of the Church; marriage was a good state and well-pleasing to God; it was not everyone who could follow the example of Aunt Ramborg at Svanshals. . . .

And then things had taken their course, as they should according to old usage and custom. First Birger Persson had come to Aspanäs to fetch his daughter home. It would be a hard parting for Bridget—the parting after two quiet, peaceful years under the not too severe rule of Aunt Karin, the farewell to the cousins and friends, farewell to the view over the blue lake, farewell to the house and garden, farewell to the little grey church at Malexander on the red, sandy beach. And above all, above all, to the room where she had slept so sweetly and kept such devout vigils—but if she came back to it one day, she would no longer be a maiden; she would have lost the crown of virginity. . . .

The road was the same as that of two years before and, as then, it was harvest time. The fir trees in the forest whispered softly or boomed with the deep notes of an organ, the birches stood with golden veils over the silvery trunks, the maple trees shone like golden candles, here and there an ant-hill raised its brown, pointed tent, far away in the depth of the woods old women and young girls went about plucking berries or gathering mushrooms. The horses trod softly on the thick carpet of fallen fir needles or in the deep moss. It was late in the year— no birds were singing, but the woodpecker hammered eagerly at a tree trunk and suddenly a wood-pigeon chimed in with its strangely threatening cooing. At a place where there was a clearing the travellers stopped; everyone dismounted and it was good to stretch one's legs. Then the provisions for the journey were unpacked, some moss-grown stones and an old tree stub could be used as seats. A cloak was spread out for Bridget to sit on, the moss being already damp after the heavy dew of the last few nights. And here they sat eating the good bread and drinking home-brewed ale with it out of tankards, and above their heads went the whispering of the forest, falling, rising, again falling. Far away was the great world, there they were fighting and murdering —here in the forest there was peace! Why can we not stay here, build ourselves a little *stuga* in the midst of the forest—*beata solitudo*. . . . But this was only dreaming. The reality was that Sir Birger gave the signal for starting again; they had to be at home before sunset, and the sun sets early in September.

Then, after two years' absence, there was the sight of the childhood home again—a home where the mother was missing. But Sister Karin ran to meet her big sister and helped her to dismount. 'And is *that* Israel? How big you have grown!' Bridget too had grown taller, quite a grown-up lady. . . .

The days sped away and the weeks too, with preparations for the great family feast, the marriage of the two daughters of Birger with the two sons of Gudmar. Everywhere the house was decked out with sprays of fir and the russet and golden foliage of autumn, and the last flowers. The kitchen was the scene of great activity; big tables were set out and arranged in the festal hall for the guests, out in the court-yard for the servants and the peasants.

Finally the great day comes. Yonder from the fir forest could be heard early in the morning the merry blast of horns, and now the wedding company from Ulfåsa comes riding in to fetch the bride. According to an old custom, they must first ask for safe conduct before they ride up to the house and promise that they have no evil intent. Their word is believed, but for the sake of safety they must hand over their weapons, and the saddles are taken off their horses and hidden away. This being done Sir Birger steps forth and asks what is the errand of the young men. Well, it is this, that Sir Ulf asks for the well-born maiden Bridget in marriage, and Sir Magnus asks for the hand of her sister. Sir Birger gives his consent, the horses of the two sisters are brought out, and then comes the parting from the home of their childhood, the ride out into a new world. . . . Sir Birger himself goes with his daughters to their new homes. For Bridget this new home is Ulfåsa.(3)

There too is great feasting, 'for here there is joy and no sorrow, and here shall the marriage be,' says the old song. By her father's hand, in the presence of friends and kinsfolk 'unto the third degree,' Bridget steps forth, wearing the golden crown, the girdle and the gilded shoes. And Sir Birger makes the marriage speech to Ulf(4): 'So I give thee this my daughter to honour and wife and to the half of thy bed, of locks and keys, of every third penny and all the right which is hers after the law of King Erik and of Uppland.' . . . But first, over in the chapel, her hands and Ulf's hands had been joined together under the blessed stole of the priest, the two rings had been blessed, and Ulf had placed the ring upon her finger. Then the priest had pronounced the blessing on Bridget. 'Lord, look in mercy upon this Thine handmaid now that she is to enter into matrimony. Let the yoke she is to bear be a yoke of love and peace. . . . Make her loved by her husband like Rachel, wise like Rebecca, full of days and ever faithful like Sarah . . . the God of Abraham, the God of Isaac and the God of Jacob be with you! May He pour the fullness of His blessing upon you, and may you see your children's children unto the third and fourth generations and in the time to come possess the life that is never to end. . . .'

In this blessing there was a word which had awakened a memory in Bridget—the name *Sara*, the daughter of Raguel, who married the young Tobias, and who on the wedding evening said to the bridegroom: 'We are children of holy parents—let us not come together like the heathen, which have not more understanding than horses and mules.' And Tobias did according to the wish of Sara, and they lived like brother and sister until the day when they understood that now they should come together to beget children and bring them up to the glory of God. . . .

Sara, daughter of Raguel, had lived in the days of the old covenant, but the new covenant had not altered a jot or a tittle of that which was pleasing to God. What was there not to be read in the book about Saint Cecilia?

A proud maiden was named Cecilia, she always carried the Gospel of Our Lord hidden in her bosom, and neither day nor night did she cease from praying. But a young man named Valerianus was filled with great love toward her and made ready for a marriage feast. Saint Cecilia wore a hairshirt next to her body but outwardly she was clad in raiment of cloth of gold. And her parents and her bridegroom loved her so much that she dared not tell them that she served Christ Jesus. At length the day of the marriage came, and while they sang the wedding songs and kept festival she sang in her heart to the glory of Our Lord and said: 'Lord, keep my heart and my body undefiled, that I be not polluted!' And at length it was night and Saint Cecilia went in secret with her bridegroom and spoke thus to him: 'Oh, sweetest and dearest young man, there is somewhat that I must tell thee, if thou wilt promise to fulfill that which I shall ask of thee.' Valerianus promised gladly. Then she said: 'I have for lover an Angel of God who guards my body. And if He learns that thou wilt draw near to me with unclean love He will be so wrath that He will take thy young life. But if He sees that thou lovest me with a pure love, so that I continue to be a maiden, He will love thee also and show thee His grace' And Valerianus yielded to the will of his devout bride, and she led him to Urbanus who was bishop in Rome; he was baptized and they lived together in chastity like brother and sister, and were both counted worthy to receive the crown of martyrdom.(5)

The crown of virginity, the crown of martyrdom—compared to them what was a bridal crown worth? Bridget took it off and placed it on the *prie-dieu* before the crucifix. Now downstairs they were singing the hymn to Saint Anne:

> Sancta Anna, grandmother of Christ,
> thou wilt help us, we know it for sure,
> that in holy matrimony all
> may do God's will, both night and day.(6)

'God's will night and day'—Bridget wished for nothing else. But what *was* God's will for her and Ulf? 'Saint Anne, you who became the mother of the mother of Christ and conceived the Holy Virgin, not of the desire of the flesh, but because it was the holy will of God—Saint Joachim, you who became the father of Mary, though all lust of the flesh was dead in you, because it was the holy will of God that that virgin should be born, from whom the salvation of the world was to come, pray for me, pray for us!'(7)

Then the door opened. It was Ulf. Bridget rose from the *prie-dieu* and went towards him. He took her into his arms and sought her lips. She laid her head confidingly close to his heart, looked up at him just as confidingly with her big blue eyes and said: 'Oh, sweetest and dearest Ulf, there is something I will beg of you; do you promise me to grant it?'

I

II

When Saint Martin of Tours (who died in the year 400)—one of the saints so greatly revered in the Middle Ages, and to whom we who live here in the North owe our thanks for roast goose on Saint Martin's Eve—travelled about his diocese on his visits of inspection, there was one parable which he was wont to use in his sermons. It was at Whitsuntide that he set out on his circuits, when nature was arrayed in her fairest attire of spring flowers. Now the road went over fertile fields, where the cows lay chewing the cud in the tall grass or stood lowing that they wanted to be milked; now the bishop and his retinue rode through dark forests of oak trees, where the swine wallowed in the mire of the morasses, grunting and gulping; now the path led across meadows bright with all the flowers of spring. 'Look,' said Saint Martin, 'so it is also in the world of men. Marriage—it is like a fertile field, where useful creatures are born, thrive, grow, multiply, all to the glory of God. Immorality—that is the filthy swamp in which human beings, who are like unclean animals, wallow and find their pleasure. And then there are the green meadows of virginity, full of brightly coloured and sweet-smelling flowers!'(1)

Not otherwise was Christ to speak to Bridget a thousand years later. 'Ordinary, honourable matrimony [*communis laudabilis status*] is pleasing to Me. Moses, who led My people out of the thraldom of Egypt, was married. Peter was called to be an apostle while his wife was still living. Judith found grace in My eyes by her widowhood. But John, who was a virgin, pleased Me most, and I gave My mother into his care. For because he lived like the angels he deserved to be the guardian of chastity.'(2)

Ulf had promised his little Brita to live 'like the angels' with her. 'For a whole year they lived together in a state of virginity,' we are told in the two accounts of the life of Bridget written by her confessors. Catherine, who has heard it from her mother, knows that Ulf had not known any other woman before Bridget, and knows that the period of abstinence lasted 'two years or thereabouts.' 'And constantly they prayed to God that if they came together carnally, He would grant them children who might serve Him and never displease Him. And when they resolved later to come together they prayed each time beforehand to God that they might not sin thereby, and that He might grant them issue, ready always to serve Him. And that, although they were both young,' Katherine adds.(3)

For about two years Ulf and Bridget lived together like brother and sister, until they had between them firmly grounded a communion of hearts strong enough to bear the union of passion. And this sacrifice to God of the first fruits of their marriage worked a constant blessing of their whole life, a blessing for peace and for good, heart-felt love. It was not the fire of straw of the senses that burned on their hearth, and it was therefore warm and bright and safe in their house.(3a)

Then three years after the wedding of Ulf and Bridget a little girl was born at Ulfåsa. It must have been in 1319 or 1320. The little girl was given the name of Mereta. Soon afterwards came a son, Karl, and again a son, Birger. The next daughter, Catherine, who was to become her mother's helper and friend, was born in 1331 or 1332. Two boys, Bengt and Gudmar, came into the world after Karin; they both died quite small. Then there were the daughters, Ingeborg and Cecilia, the last.

Thus in the course of twenty years Bridget bore to her husband eight children, four sons and four daughters. In the fourteenth century this was not considered unseemly; the French system had not yet been invented, although attempts at it were not lacking—more than once Bridget speaks of bad women who by means of certain medicines procure the destruction of their issue. But the excesses had not yet attained those easily accessible means by which continence is imitated in our times. For it cannot be *asceticism* that makes so many modern marriages barren. No, but the devil is the bitter enemy of *all* life, from Jesus in the manger to the child in the cradle. And in every child he sees a germ of Jesus.(4)

Once Bridget had accepted marriage, she lived her married life to the full. And the plan of her life had been given her in a Christian text, that which is read in the Mass for 'a holy woman who was neither a virgin nor a martyr'—and yet a holy woman? Yes, we read this in the Book of Proverbs:

> Who shall find a valiant woman? The price of her is as of things brought from afar off, and from the uttermost coasts. The heart of her husband trusteth in her, and he shall have no need of spoils. She will render him good and not evil all the days of her life. She hath sought wool and flax, and hath wrought by the counsel of her hands: she is like the merchant's ship, she bringeth her bread from afar: and she hath risen in the night, and given a prey to her household, and victuals to her maidens: she hath considered a field, and bought it; with the fruit of her hands she hath planted a vineyard. She hath girded her loins with strength, and hath strengthened her arm. She hath tasted and seen that her traffic is good; her lamp shall not be put out in the night.

She hath put out her hand to strong things, and her fingers have taken hold of the spindle. She hath opened her hand to the needy, and stretched out her hands to the poor. She shall not fear for her house in the cold of snow; for all her domestics are clothed with double garments. She hath made for herself clothing of tapestry, fine linen and purple is her covering. Her husband is honourable in the gates, when he sitteth among the senators of the land. She made fine linen and sold it, and delivered a girdle to the Chanaanite. Strength and beauty are her clothing: and she shall laugh in the latter day. She hath opened her mouth to wisdom and the law of clemency is on her tongue: she hath looked well to the paths of her house, and hath not eaten her bread idle. Her children rose up and called her blessed; her husband, and he praised her. Many daughters have gathered riches; thou hast surpassed them all. Favour is deceitful, and beauty is vain; the woman that feareth the Lord, she shall be praised.(4a)

This programme was thoroughly carried out. 'She hated idleness,' says the old chronicle of the life of Bridget,

and was always busy with some useful work. Sometimes she sat with her handmaidens and sewed Mass vestments and other things of that kind, serving the honour and worship of God. Sometimes she worked for the use and good of a fellow Christian. Sometimes she read the lives of holy men and the Bible, which she had caused to be translated for her into Swedish. Sometimes she heard Mass and divine service and a sermon. And sometimes she went to convents and cathedrals to beg indulgences and hear the sermons of wise priests, and then she would go on foot. . . . She gave many and rich alms and was a mild and careful mother for the sick and poor, and she caused a large house to be built for the needs of sick and poor people, and often she served them herself very humbly, and washed their feet and kissed them.(5) If there were old garments to be mended—and that would often happen among the clients of the house—Bridget herself set to work, darning and patching.(6) No task was too mean for her, when it was a question of those of whom it is said in the Gospel: 'What ye have done for one of these the least of My brethren, ye have done for Me.'

But this was only one side of Bridget's activity, only one of her many fields of action. The young mistress of Ulfåsa was also a capable housewife. Here and there we look as through a chink in a door or a keyhole at the clever and busy housewife who is occupied all day upstairs and downstairs, indoors and out. She is there when bread is being baked—'the dough must be kneaded thoroughly, whatever the kind of bread it has to be: fine bread for the family, coarse bread for the servants or biscuits for the dogs.'(7) She is present when ale is being brewed—good, strong home-brewed ale; when it ferments it froths and foams and you must let the foam settle and not put your nose in above the foaming beverage, for then it will only make you sneeze. Bridget is also acquainted with the distilling of spirits—she had seen how the spirits bubbled up, rose and sank in the cauldron and its tubes and pipes.(8) She knows how to make cheese(9); and as she did not do any washing herself, she would look after her washerwomen. She would stand there when there was a big washing at Ulfåsa and she would see the washerwomen rinsing the clothes down on the beach, but they had to take care that the wave beats did not take the clothes away out in the lake.(10) She would peep into the smithy at the farm, for there must have been a smithy at Ulf Gudmarsson's farm, such as there was at Finsta. She would hear the puffing of the bellows, see the iron glowing in the forge and take shape on the anvil under the strong blows of the smith's hammer.(11) She would visit the potter at his turning wheel and the glassmaker at his furnace, long before Orrefors beautiful glass was made in Sweden.(12) She would stand beside the water-mill, see the pent-up water foaming down when the floodgate was withdrawn— and within the mill the great querns would begin to grind, the cogs of the wheels would begin to work into each other, the millstones turning, and now the first flour would come out between the stones, white and pure and smelling of all the health of summer.(13) And of course she would attend to her garden—with joy she would see how a sprout could make its way through the hard soil, nay, even push aside the stone which happened to be lying over it and would hinder its growth upwards to the light. And if she saw the sky darkening and the waters of the lake growing menacingly black under a sudden gust of wind, she would hasten to bind up the young plants with a stick and tie up the tiny shoots so that they would not be broken.(14)

For her servants, Bridget was a solicitous housewife and a watchful mistress. She tolerated no others in her service than modest handmaidens and young men. It should not be possible for anything evil to be said of the household at Ulfåsa. Still more did this watchfulness apply to her children. 'She brought them up with much care and taught them to do nothing that was displeasing to God, and entrusted them to pious and learned men, by whom they could be trained in everything that was good,' says the *Vita* composed by the confessors. So particular was the pious lady that when one of the sons—probably it would be the always flighty Karl—had transgressed one of the strict fasting commandments of the time, she wept bitter tears over it. As for herself, she fasted on bread and water on the vigil before a number of the feasts of the Church (all the feasts of Our Lady, Trinity, Corpus Christi, Saint John's Day, Michaelmas on 29 September, Saint Laurence on 10 August, Saint Olaf, Saint Eric and still others).(15) And it was just on the eve of Saint John, Midsummer Eve, next to Christmas the most Swedish of all popular feasts, that the children from Ulfåsa had joined in the dancing round the maypole. And when you dance you get warm, and when you get warm you get thirsty, and yonder under the oaks round the green meadow where the dancing is going on a wandering innkeeper has just set up a table. . . . Not a proper table, only two or three planks laid across a couple of trestles—and he pours out ale, good brown ale, from an anker lying on the table. . . . There is a crowd round the table, tankards are filled, are emptied, are filled again; the young squire from Ulfåsa has been dancing and is thirsty—the ale tastes good, nor is a rusk to eat with it to be despised. . . . There is still dancing like that every Midsummer Eve to this very day, this very year—one young fellow or another perhaps gets a *Pilsen* or a '*Pilo*' more than is good for him. But probably it happens but rarely that a mother weeps so bitterly over it as Bridget did, so that Saint John the Baptist himself had to come down from heaven to comfort her. Later on she was to express herself very sternly about the drinking so common in Sweden in her time.(16)

Bridget did not take her children to dances, but she liked to take them with her on her visits to the sick. Catherine remembers well, she relates in the Process of Canonization,

> how Mother took me and my sisters with her when she visited the hospitals which she had caused to be built [*fecit reparari*, perhaps only repaired], and without disgust she bound up their wounds and sores with her own hands. . . . And when Mother was reproached with taking us little girls with her, and that we might be infected from the stench of the sick people, she answered that she took us with her just while we were still small, so that we might learn at an early age to serve God in His poor and sick. . . . And already, while Father was still living, and later when Mother was a widow, she did not sit down to table without having given twelve poor people to eat, and every Friday she washed their feet herself. And every year Mother sent clothes to many poor people, and sent alms to many convents round about the country, while she provided dowries for young girls who wished to be married, and others she helped to enter convents. And she visited harlots' houses, and if any of the girls there wanted to leave Mother taught them how to do penance, and for those who wished to enter into matrimony she found a husband and out of her own means she provided a dowry for them. Altogether Mother helped all who had a hard life, whether they were poor, sinners, pilgrims, orphans or widows—to all of them she was the most gentle, most compassionate mother.(17)

Petrus Olai, the sub-prior of Alvastra, gives the same testimony about his penitent as Catherine about her mother. He knows, furthermore, that it was at the family seat itself of Ulfåsa (in villa sua de Wluasa) that the hospital stood, in which Bridget without fear of infection nursed the sick and eased their sufferings (Petrus counts up *scabies*, skin diseases, *ulcera*, boils, *vulnera*, sores, and speaks of *sanies*, suppurations). And when Bridget had got the young women sinners out of their evil surroundings she took them to her own home and kept them there for a time, for fear of possible relapses. She made use of this period of trial to examine the natural aptitudes of her young guests. If there were any who could think of entering a convent she undertook to place them, perhaps, in the convent at Sko, which was under special obligation to Bridget's father, or the convents at Vreta and Riseberga situated nearer to Ulfåsa, all of them belonging to the Order of Saint Bernard. For the others she found husbands—the handsome dowry given by Bridget no doubt having a share in the bridegroom's being willing to overlook the somewhat damaged past of the bride.

Her husband, too, her own dear Ulf, whom she had gradually come to love like 'her own heart'(18) had a place under Bridget's motherly wings. The first thing was that the worthy landowner, such as Ulf was (in education he was greatly inferior to his father-in-law) *learned to read*. Bridget must certainly have been his teacher, and she seems to have been pleased with her rather oldish pupil. Once he was able to read he made great progress by himself: 'he accustomed himself to say those daily offices and prayers which were to the glory of God and all the saints'—and thus he followed the example of his pious spouse and fulfilled the duty of the tertiaries of the Franciscan Order of saying daily the Little Office of Our Lady.(19) Besides this he studied 'the books which are concerned with law and justice.' In the year 1330 he became law-man in Närike; two years earlier he had been knighted. For the education of her sons Bridget sought a tutor and found him in the young scholastic of Skenninge, Niels Hermansson (*b.* 1326). Later, when in Rome, Bridget was to study Latin with great diligence—she had learnt the rudiments by taking part in the lessons given to her children by Niels Hermansson. The latter went to France later in order to study, took his doctor's degree, *utriusque juris*, returned to Sweden, became a canon in Uppsala, later on archdeacon in Linköping, and finally archbishop in the same place (1374).(20) He lived to see the mother of his pupils canonized a saint, and, deeply affected by the memories of the years he had lived at Ulfåsa, he wrote the hymn which was later to be sung in her honour in all Bridgettine convents, and which begins, *Rosa, rorans bonitatem,* 'Rose, thou whose dew—and whose scent—is goodness!' No doubt roses bloomed in the garden at Ulfåsa, and on beautiful summer mornings the young tutor would stoop over them and inhale their scent. The fresh, as it were, cool scent of a newly opened rose is in kinship with goodness—as the fragrance of the lily stupefies conscience, and the scent of the jasmine incites to voluptuousness. There would be a spiritual scent of roses about the young mistress of Ulfåsa.

Niels Hermansson, however, was too young to become of importance in Bridget's spiritual development. She found a real guide and director of souls in one of the canons of Linköping Cathedral, Master Matthias, *Magister in sacra pagina* (D.D.) of the University of Paris. Of the five great high schools (Paris, Bologna, Montpellier, Cologne, Oxford) Paris was the most frequented. The chief subjects there were philosophy (Aristotle and Thomas Aquinas) and canonical law; civil law was studied at Orléans, where Nicolaus Hermanni was later to take his doctor's degree. A complete course (philosophy and theology) took fifteen whole years.(21) The preparatory studies could be done at home. In each of the provinces of the Dominican Order there was a *studium provinciale*—in 1237 such a *studium* had already been set up in the province of Götaland; Svealand had one in Sigtuna.(22)

The Bible became Master Matthias' chief interest. In Paris he would be able to hear lectures on the Bible by the Jewish convert Nicolaus of Lyra (*d.* 1340). On his return to Sweden he displayed no slight literary activity in Latin, compiling, among other things, a collection of edifying stories (*exempla*) from the Bible, from the Church Fathers, from legends and folk-lore, arranged alphabetically and intended as a help to parish priests in need of subjects for sermons. Another work, *Homo conditus*, is a popular guide in Christian knowledge. For Bridget, Master Matthias acquired most importance by procuring for her 'a Swedish Bible,' her most precious treasure. He compiled in Latin, besides an interpretation of the Apocalypse—that book which in the fourteenth century engaged the attention of and disquieted so many souls—a concordance to the Bible in three volumes, which is now lost, as well as —and the most important—a translation of the Pentateuch. This translation has been preserved to us and is, properly speaking, an adaptation rather than a literal version of the text of the Vulgate. Which is not to be deplored—'here is something other and more than a mere translation, here we see before us a highly gifted Swedish writer.'(23) One need only read the very first verses of Genesis as reproduced by Master

Matthias: 'In the beginning God created heaven and earth, not of Himself as the Father begot the Son, not of another matter as a smith makes an axe. The earth was then still void, empty and dark; void, because nothing grew upon it; empty, because neither man nor beast had been created; dark, because there were neither sun nor stars.'

In this way Bridget read the Bible.

It was not only for this that she was indebted to Master Matthias. He also told her about his pilgrimages, not only in Europe, where he had visited Treves and venerated the relics brought thither by Queen Helena, but also in the Holy Land, where he saw, with an allusion to Swedish politics of the time which is almost a pun, that 'Pors grows higher than in Halland.'(24) Here it is as though one already heard notes from Bridget's fiddle, when one reads the judgment passed by Matthias, himself an ecclesiastic, on certain of the priests of the time:

> The physicians of the body should be ashamed of their name, so long as they have not yet learned the virtue of herbs. Much more should they be ashamed who would be physicians of souls and do not know the commandments of Our Lord and the Holy Scriptures. And yet the wounds of the soul are both more hidden and more harmful than those of the body. But they will not take any burden upon themselves. Like the knights they have horses and fine houses, but they do not like to wear cuirass or breastplate. Like well-born ladies they have warm, fair raiment, but know naught of the pains they suffer in child-bearing nor of other sicknesses. With the men of the cloister they have solace and salvation [exemption from taxation], but they will not fast and obey like them. They will eat and drink with the peasants, and that much better than they, but they will not plough with them.(25)

Later, but with far more drastic language, Bridget was to rebuke the uncleanness of the 'accursed priests.'

But the greatest importance of Master Matthias lay, perhaps, in the fact that through him Bridget became acquainted with the intellectual Europe of the time. During his years of study in France he must have come into contact with all the stirring of spiritual life, and become acquainted with the currents of both orthodox and heretical trends of thought. Often he had visitations of harassing doubts—once 'it seemed to him as if all the heretics stood before him and said, as if with one mouth: "We are the truth!" ' (26) During such assaults Bridget came to the aid of her teacher with her prayers. Together they studied the Apocalypse. As it had often happened in the history of the Church, so it was now, during the Babylonian captivity of the Pope, that an expectation pervaded Christendom that the last days were drawing near.

A 'wise master,' of the name of Miltetus had from Toledo sent out an encyclical

> to all faithful servants of Christ, wheresoever they might live. For the sake of the salvation of mankind we counsel you, that ye all straightway confess in the year of the Lord 1357, because of those things which shall come to pass in that year. First the sun shall go into the sign of the moon, which sign is exceeding hot, and the moon shall then be darkened. And the planets shall war against each other. Great afflictions shall at that time visit the earth, the slaying of men and many other disasters, and the sea shall pass up over the firm land and fill up four times more room than in the days of the deluge. . . . Strange signs will be seen on land and sea, manifold terrors and earthquakes shall come, and many towns shall be laid waste. . . . And at last on the seventh day in the month of August at the third hour the sun shall rise, red as blood. By its exceeding great fire and heat many houses, built of wood or having roofs of wood, will catch fire. In that third hour there will be great shedding of blood, most of all in the land of France, and later town will be set against town and country against country, but great numbers of Saracens will be converted by the preaching of the Gospel. And later lightning and thunder will come over the earth and terrors of other kinds, the like of which few men have ever seen. . . . We therefore counsel each and all to prepare themselves to die and to be good Christians. . . . All this is the prophecy of the Sybil, she who has said that after the year 1357 there shall be strange things to behold.(27)

Another prophecy was attributed to Saint Hieronimus, the hermit of Bethlehem; in 'honest books of the Jews' he is said to have found

> fifteen signs which shall be fifteen days before the Day of Judgment, namely these: On the first day the sea shall rise up thirty feet higher than the highest mountains and shall stand like a wall. The next day it shall sink so that it can hardly be seen. On the third day all the great and strange beasts of the deep shall roar and howl terribly up against heaven. On the fourth day the sea and all waters shall burn. On the fifth day herbs and trees shall stand bedewed with blood. On the sixth day all buildings shall fall. On the seventh day all rocks shall fall against each other and be broken asunder. On the eighth day the whole earth shall fall to pieces. On the ninth day the earth shall be made level. On the tenth day men shall go out of their hiding places and be like madmen and not be able to speak to each other. On the eleventh day the bones of dead men shall rise up from their graves. On the twelfth day the stars shall fall. On the thirteenth day all living men shall die, so that they may arise with those who have died before them. On the fourteenth day the earth shall burn. On the fifteenth day there shall be a new heaven and a new earth and all men shall stand before the judgment of God.(28)

Master Matthias would be acquainted with these or similar prophecies. In his commentary on the Bible he maintains Saint Augustine's doctrine of the seven ages of the world and Bridget took it up after him. The seventh and last began with the coming of Christ, so that we are now really living in the last times. Among the great cataclysms announcing the day of doom, there is also this, that forty days before that day the *rainbow* (the sign of hope, given to Noah after the Deluge) will no longer be seen. The Jews shall be converted, they shall no longer 'chew the Holy Scriptures like chaff,' but find the kernel, 'as they shall know the true faith and invoke Mary and her Son.' Antichrist shall be a Jew, of the tribe of Dan (Joshua xix. 47–8); he shall rule for three years and a half. His chastener will be Lucifer himself, and Christ will slay him with one word: 'Die!' Yet they who sinned with him will still be given forty days in which to repent and confess.(29)

Petrus Olai of Alvastra has justly called Master Matthias *docturus sponsam Christi*, 'he who was to teach the bride of Christ' (that is, Bridget). It was to him that she owed her knowledge of the Holy Scriptures, it was he who introduced her to her spiritual contemporaries, it was he who gave her an outlook beyond the borders of Uppland and East Gothland, nay, of Sweden. Many years later in Rome, when she received news from home of the death of her old tutor, she might well exclaim: 'Happy art thou, Master Matthias, for now thou enterest into the wisdom that never ends.'(30)

III

The years passed. The spring came to Ulfåsa and the birches stood arrayed in delicate, pale green foliage against the black firs. It was harvest time about Ulfåsa, and the foliage of the birches hung like jewels of gold on the dark ground of the conifers. In its simplicity the winter brought its snow one year after the other, and the summer came with its white nights and was not ashamed because they looked as they did last year. The blackbird sang at sunset in the long summer evenings, and redbreast and yellow-hammer, titmouse and shrike, gathered every Christmas about the sheaf in the courtyard of Ulfåsa.

And so life went on from day to day—nowadays one would call it the life of country gentlemen. Instead of croquet, tennis and badminton there were jousts and tournaments; instead of motoring there was hunting of bear and elk; instead of the radio, a couple of wandering minstrels, strolling people carrying a fiddle or a drum. Perhaps there are guests staying in the house, a number of relatives among them— above all old Birger Persson, who has come down from Finsta; the couple from Aspanäs; the Lady Karin and Sir Knut Jonsson; Bridget's sister with her husband, Magnus Gudmarsson; Bridget's brother

Israel; Aunt Ramborg from Svanshals; the marshal Sir Mats Kettilmundssön; the constable of the kingdom, Gustav Tuneson, married to
Ulf's sister; young Sir Eggert von Kyren, who cannot take his eyes off
the fair Karin; a chance guest or two. They sit down to a well-covered
table; ale and wine are poured into the big, silver-mounted horns,
which are emptied and filled up again. 'Is this a cow horn, this thing?'
asks a guest. 'It seems to me to be larger than those we have in this
country.' 'Yes, but it is not a horn, it is a *claw*, a claw of a griffin, an
animal that lives in the land of India.' 'Is it not rather on the island of
Taprobanes that the griffin lives?' someone asks, perhaps. But no, on
the island of Taprobanes there are no fearsome beasts, for it lies next
to Paradise, where every year there are two winters and two summers,
and there is growth both in winter and summer. . . . 'No, these
griffins live in the Indian land—griffins and dragons . . . they keep
guard over the mountains of silver and the mountains of gold, so that
no one can come near to those mountains. . . . And these griffins
have claws as big as the horns of a cow or an ox here in Sweden, and of
such a claw this drinking-horn is made—your health, good Sir!'(1)

They all empty their horns, which are refilled. It is good wine,
from the Rhineland or from France. The faces get flushed; all are talking at the same time. Now the gentlemen are beginning to talk politics
—*Håtunaleken, Nyköping*, dangerous, inflammable words fly to and
fro across the table. And what is going to happen about young King
Magnus—his mother, the Lady Ingeborg, is now staying at Varberg
with that Dane—yes, what do you think of it, Sir Mats? You remember, it was you who carried him on your arm, that day at Mora Stones.

If it was really Sir Mats Kettilmundssön who wrote *Um Styrilsi
Kununga** we know what he thought of that kind of noisy symposia.

Aristotle says that each member has its own use—the eye is for seeing, the ear
for hearing and the tongue is made for two things, partly it must convey the
speech of man, and partly it must turn over the food in his mouth and convey
it down to his throat. But the tongue cannot do these two things at the same
time—you cannot speak with food in your mouth, for, as it is written: he
who will work at two things at the same time does neither of them well.
This is further proved by other reasons, that when men eat and drink their
blood is heated by much and strong drink, and then they say much which is
neither courteous nor useful. Wise and good men have therefore always said
that for kings and chiefs it is more seemly to speak little, and rather to have
players and singers who can entertain their guests, so that they do not sin
by uttering useless words.(2)

* *The Ruling of Kings.*

Bridget is of the same opinion as the wise old statesman; perhaps they glance at each other and shrug their shoulders a little superciliously at the blustering fellows about them. The silver-mounted horns and the heavy tankards are set down with a thundering noise on the table—'the custom in Sweden' against which Bridget was later to warn her eldest son. It would have been better to have a little singing and jesting. . . .

Bridget looks about her in the festive hall. It has grown late; the candles in their sconces along the wall are burning low, one or another here and there flickers and goes out. With her delicate sense of smell Bridget is aware of the smoke from the reeking candles. . . . But what is that? Is not somebody standing down there, a long way down the hall . . . a strange figure? Is it a strolling player, a juggler who has heard the sounds of merriment, and who has thought that perhaps he might be able to earn a few pence? In any case it is One who has not been invited, yet who has after all come in. . . .

Now He advances a few steps up the hall—no one seems to notice His presence. . . . And now, a little light from a candle falls upon Him and Bridget *sees* who it is—knows Him by the Crown of Thorns, —and by the eyes, which are blinded by blood and tears, and which look at her with such infinite sadness. . . .(3)

IV

When her husband was away, she kept vigil nearly every night in pious prayers and tears, and spared not her body, but chastised it with genuflections and the discipline. And she took her rest in a bed which was more than commonly hard.(1)

In the Process of Canonization Karin testifies that this bed was nothing but a bag of straw, laid on the stone floor, without any mattress or pillow, and the covering quilt was only a bearskin; later on, in Rome, Karin used to get up when her mother slept and slip a pillow under her hips. And she lay there fully dressed.(2)

It was different, of course, when Ulf was at home. Then the couple slept in the big, new canopied bed, which Bridget had caused a capable joiner to make, and which was something beyond the usual. But Bridget did not sleep in it with a good conscience. Had she not, one day when she stood admiring it, got such a blow on her head that she could hardly move, and had she not heard a Voice—the Voice which she knew so well, but which, alas! she had not listened to of late, and the Voice said: 'I hung on the Cross, and had not where to lay my head, and you want to be so grand and to rest so softly'? Then Bridget burst into tears, and as often as she could she lay on the floor with only the bag of straw under her and the bearskin over her.(3) Even in the coldest Swedish *varga* winter Bridget slept like this, and when anyone wondered at it she answered that by the grace of God she felt so great an inner warmth that the outer cold did not mean anything to her.(4) Saint Elisabeth of Thuringia practised the same penance; even when her husband was at home she got up and lay down to sleep on the rug beside the bed. When her faithful handmaid Isentrud remonstrated with her Elisabeth answered: 'It is in order to do violence to my flesh that I remove myself like this from my beloved husband' (*avellor a predilectio marito meo*). Often the young landgravine got up to pray—she had so many prayers to say. Then she would kneel beside the bed, and her husband would lie and faithfully hold one of her hands, her dear little hand, which he had so often taken to his lips and which he now held fast until he fell asleep.(5) Assuredly the good, worthy Ulf would willingly have done the same, if his dear Brita had wished it. . . .

Bridget's fasting gave occasion to a great deal of talk—she had to rearrange it when, for social reasons, she could not practise it, by imposing certain restrictions upon herself at table. It would look as if she had a great deal of food on her plate, but it was the same piece of meat she kept toying with. Wine would be served all round the table, but in the silver goblet of the mistress of the house there was only water. Nor did she ever leave the table so satisfied that she could not have eaten a little more. When she was bidden to a feast with the great persons of the world, and one sumptuous dish was served after another, she partook only of two dishes; in those days of coarse eating, it was almost scandalously little. And what she drank was not very much either—'she thought of how bitter a cup Christ had drunk for us on the Cross.'(6) Once her throat had grown so dry from sheer thirst that she could not speak, and Master Matthias, as her confessor, had to order her to drink.(7)

Bridget's life became more and more a realization of the Pauline programme: 'they that are Christ's, have crucified their flesh, with the vices and concupiscences' (Gal. v. 24). As a Franciscan tertiary she wore the girdle with three knots round her waist, but she pulled it so tightly that it hurt and caused her sores. Her body had enjoyed many delights. In spite of all her fasting Bridget, too, had found pleasure in a good table and a cool drink; and in Ulf's arms she had tasted a woman's deep joys. Now her tongue was to be punished for what it had sinned by evil speech, by calumny, by mockery. (As in the twentieth century, so there were in the fourteenth 'luncheon chats,' which were not exactly inspired by love of one's neighbour.) There is a root called gentian, which gives a bitter taste to the tongue when you chew it. Bridget accustomed herself to having it always in her mouth—her breath actually smelt of it! The tongue was to be punished, and her arms—the beautiful, round arms, of which as a bride she had been so proud, and which Ulf had so often kissed—*they* were to do penance too. Every Friday evening Bridget bared them, took the wax candle burning before the crucifix and held it aslant, so that the burning wax dripped down on the beautiful white flesh and burned blisters in it. And Bridget did not give the sores time to heal; when they were on the way to doing so, she scratched them open with one of her nails—like the Apostle she wanted to bear on her body wounds in remembrance of the wounds of Christ.(8) In the midst of the pain, in the midst of the suffering, the words of prayer rose to her lips:

> Thou true and living Son of God, and Son of the Virgin, who of Thy own free will didst allow Thy hands and feet to be pierced, and didst suffer so great bitterness for the health of my soul, grant, O most sweet Jesus Christ, to enter into my heart, and there to be consumed with burning love. I beseech, O most adorable Redeemer, for the sake of the nails and the spear which were withdrawn from Thy dead body, and from Thy so sorely wounded heart, to withdraw from my heart the desire of all things that offend Thee. Amen.(9)

V

And so life went on. Children were born: Karl and Birger, Bengt and Gudmar, names which had precedents in the family, Märta, Karin, Ingeborg and Cecilia. When Bridget was pregnant with Cecilia, Märta was already preparing to become a bride.

But before this, old Sir Birger of Finsta had died. In the year 1321 he had followed the custom of his fathers and made the pilgrimage to Compostella—in any case he came to Avignon, with the intention of going on to the Holy Land, but he gave it up and returned home.(1) And indeed there was enough for him to do there.

On the last day in May the exiled King Birger had died in Denmark. During the minority of King Magnus Eriksson the two kingdoms of Sweden and Norway were to be governed by the respective Councils of the Realm of the two countries, under the rule of the Lord High

Constable. It was soon evident, however, that the real regent was the king's mother, the Duchess Ingeborg, and a crowd of fortune-hunters soon gathered about her, coming both from abroad and from her own country, and seeking the favour of the young woman—and with an eye on her two crowns. The successful wooer was a Danish knight, Sir Knud Porse, to whom was entrusted the command of the strategically important castle of Varberg—and here he and the Duchess Ingeborg lived together for several years before (in 1327) they decided to enter into the bonds of matrimony.

Although there was peace between Denmark and the other two Scandinavian kingdoms, Knud Porse was thinking of making a lightning attack, in July 1321, on Scania. The attack was to be supported by Duke Heinrich of Mecklenburg, and in order to confirm the league it was decided that the Duke's son, Albrecht, was to be betrothed to Ingeborg's four-year-old daughter, Euphemia. Nothing came of the occupation, however, for the Swedish Council of the Realm heard of the matter. On 20 July 1322, thirty-five of the good men of the kingdom assembled at Skara: the archbishop, two bishops, three other ecclesiastical gentlemen, twenty-five knights and esquires, among them Birger Persson, newly returned from his pilgrimage. At this meeting the good men of the kingdom resolved to keep faithfully together, inviolably to serve the king, Magnus, who was not yet six years old, and honourably to have a care of the rule of the kingdom until he attained his majority. None of the members of the league were, without the consent of the whole council, to enter into any communication with the Duchess Ingeborg or keep up any communication previously entered into, 'in particular not when it was a question of obtaining for her greater power or share in the government than Swedish queens and duchesses have had hitherto.'(2) In February 1326 peace was made between the Council of the Realm and Duchess Ingeborg. Knud Porse was condemned to leave the country and he died some years after (1330).

Simultaneously with this conflict at home Sweden had been at war with Russia, which at this time, as it did six hundred years later, invaded Finland, attacked Viborg, but (in Nöteborg) had to agree to a peace by which the border between the two kingdoms was fixed at Systerbäck—of interest also in our own times.

In the period of peace following upon this, old Sir Birger at Finsta closed his tired eyes. He died one of the richest men in Sweden; in his will there is mention of twenty-two estates left to his heirs. As there were only three, and Bridget inherited a fourth of this landed property, she became one of the richest women in the country.(3) Birger Persson died at Easter time, more precisely on 25 March 1328, and, according to the accounts still preserved, the funeral, with the Masses and alms belonging to it, cost 275 marks, corresponding to more than 16,000 Kroner.* Among the items of funeral expenses are mentioned red wine, white French wine, Rhenish wine, sugar, almonds, rice, oil and several kinds of spices.(4)

On the occasion of his last pilgrimage Birger Persson had obtained, at the papal court of Avignon, the grant of indulgences of fourteen bishops for his friends, the murdered dukes.(5) He would no doubt also think in good time of the peace of his own soul. And in the cathedral of Uppsala, in the chapel of Saint Nicholas and Saint Catherine, the pious Lady Ingeborg awaited her husband. Wherever the funeral procession advanced on its way, in Sigtuna, Botvidskirke, Stockholm, all the bells were tolling with a dull, monotonous sound, as when nails are hammered into a coffin. Slowly the funeral train passed through the streets of Uppsala, across the cathedral bridge up to the 'Mount of the Lord,' *Mons Domini*, where Etienne de Bonneuil's French cathedral reared its Gothic towers. In front of the coffin (perhaps it was carried by peasants from Finsta, as the coffin of Magnus Ladulås was carried from Vissingsö) rode a knight in full armour, with the sword and shield of the deceased, but the point of the sword turned down and the shield hung on his back. After the coffin, came the great funeral train; all the clergy of the church, from archbishop downwards, kinsmen of the deceased and kinsfolk of kinsmen, great men from the whole kingdom. The flames of the candles flickered and fluttered in the vernal breeze, incense rose from the swinging censers, the canons intoned the hymn *Miserere*, 'Lord, have mercy upon me!' Then the procession passed in through the portal with the statue of Saint Erik, the main portal. (The other two were dedicated to Saint Olof—he looked towards the north, towards Trondhjem—and Saint Lars—was he thinking, perhaps, of his church in Lund, or did his thoughts take a further flight, to Rome and San Lorenzo in Damaso, next to the cardinal's palace, where Bridget was to live later and every morning receive the visit of an angel?) Slowly the procession advanced up through the church, past the chapel of the Holy Souls, where a gathering of pilgrims, votaries of Saint Erik, were praying for their dead, and further up to the chapel of Saint Nicholas and Saint Catherine.

* See note 7, Chapter V, page 272.

In the fourteenth century this chapel was the burial-place of several of the great families of Sweden. Here too the house of Finsta had chosen its last resting-place. And now the stone in the floor had been removed and the Lady Ingeborg's coffin could be seen down below; and by her side there was room for another—one who for the last time had left Finsta Gaard and would never more return to it.

The coffin was set down on the floor beside the open grave, and the priest walked round it, sprinkling it with holy water and enveloping it in a cloud of incense. All stood silent, the only sound to be heard was the jingling of the chains of the thuribles. Then the canons, who were standing round the grave, again began to sing. Slowly the voices rose, chanting the Latin song: *Libera me, Domine, de morte æterna, in die illa tremenda.* . . . 'Deliver me, O Lord, from everlasting death, on that terrible day.' . . . Bridget read the text in one of the big choral books lying open on the lectern in the middle of the chancel: *Tremens factus sum ego, et timeo, dum discussio venerit atque ventura ira*—yea, there is indeed reason to dread, when that which happened in secret shall be revealed in the light, and the soul shall stand naked before God and give an account of all that in which the flesh has transgressed. . . . *Dies iræ, dies illa*, that day of wrath, when heaven and earth shall be moved, and He, who hung upon the Cross, shall come again and judge the world with fire. . . .

Then all the threatening voices fell silent, only a single one was raised: *Kyrie eleison* . . . *Pater noster* . . . And then all the workmen came up and laid the stone over the grave—the artistically chiselled stone of Flemish workmanship, of black marble, quarried in the rocks between Dinant and Namur. A skilled master stonemason down in Flanders had carved out the pictures—Sir Birger in knight's armour, the Lady Ingeborg in the robes of a knight's lady, and round the edge the smaller figures of the children of the couple: Peter, Bengt and Israel, Ingrid, Margareta and Bridget. And the children, the three still living, stood by the grave, and in the black marble with light strokes they saw their own pictures and read the inscription running round the tombstone: *Hic jacet nobilis miles dominus Birgerus Petri Filius Legifer V plandiarum—orate pro nobis—et ejus uxor domina Ingeburgis cum filiis eorum qvorum animæ reqviescant in pace.* ('Here lies the noble knight Sir Birger Persson, law-man of Uppland, and his wife Ingeborg—pray for us—and for their children, may their souls rest in peace.') To this grave the body of Israel Birgersson was brought when he had died in Riga in 1351. But for Bridget the shrine of a saint was prepared—she did not know it as she stood there looking at the small relief bearing her own name: *B I R G I T T A*. Or had she already a glimpse of the saint's halo which was later to surround her own head?(6)

The stone was laid over the grave and farewells were said to all the friends and kinsfolk who had come. Then Ulf went in to the clerk of the cathedral and arranged the payment which came to forty marks in money for the building fund of the church, forty marks for the decoration of the chancel besides a separate amount for an 'anniversary Mass' for all time.(7)

Meanwhile Bridget prayed for a long time at the shrine of Saint Erik, at the altars of Saint Anna, Saint Botvid, Saint Olof, Ulf joined, too, in a Paternoster, when the business matters had been concluded, or a couple of Ave Marias on his rosary. Then they rode home together through the woods, now showing the green of spring. Perhaps they talked about the building going on at home at Ulfåsa; the furniture had been renewed, and the house had been rebuilt. Certainly they would talk about the children—'I do hope Karl has not been getting into mischief again,' says Bridget with anxiety. 'Now you are always so strict, Brita!' growls Ulf good-naturedly. 'He is a lively child, and there is no harm in that, and he is a funny little chap. . . .'

Bridget is silent—perhaps she is chewing that piece of bitter gentian root she has in her mouth.

VI

Throughout twenty years Bridget's life was centred in Ulfåsa, and Östergötland was her world. Though as a native of Uppland she could not proudly say: 'I am an East Gothlander, thank God!' Yet it was as if the poet of the Linköping bishop's chronicle, writing two hundred years later, had spoken from her heart when he sang:

> Blessed be God at every hour
> Who on East Gothland hath His grace bestowed,
> For the good of the soul and for worldly needs,
> The gift of the true and Christian faith,
> With honour of bishops and cathedral fane,
> With wise men skilled in all manner of art,
> With trusty knights who will ever defend the right;
> With forests and lakes and rushing streams,
> With leaping deer and swimming fish,

With all manner of trees, both oak and lime,
With marten and lynx, with stag and hind,
With ore in the hills, copper, iron and steel,
With courtiers who find their weapons there,
With modest maidens and goodly wives,
As good as the queens of other lands,
With cattle and sheep and horses big,
With country folk who welcome a guest,
With towns and cities and manners fair,
That honour give to this favoured land.

The chronicle next reckons up all those who have had a 'bishop's power' in the see of Linköping, from Herbertus to Johannes XXIV, Lincopensis, *i.e.* Hans Brask. Of all of them it says:

The good they did upon the earth
May God reward them in heaven above,
And for his death and grievous pain
May He grant to them His grace,
Likewise to all of Christian faith,
Who Linköping's peace have not disturbed,
Nor on her freedom have laid their chains,
The freedom bestowed by princes and kings,
And all who for East Gothland strive,
On them be the grace of God and of Holy Church,
May they all in heaven be crowned,
And there, before the face of God rejoice,
To this may all say Amen.(1)

Bridget was connected with Linköping and its cathedral through Nicolaus Hermanni and especially through Master Matthias. Nor was Skenninge to be despised, for it was Saint Ingrid's town with the Dominican monastery and with the House of the Holy Spirit, in which Bridget perhaps took lessons in nursing the sick, and the master of which, Petrus Olai, was later to become one of her confessors and to go with her to Rome. And then there was, a little to the east of Ulfåsa by the small Lake Roxen, the oldest Cistercian convent in the country, that of Vreta. It was here that Bridget's grandson's, Karl Karlsson's little daughter Bridget, was placed after her father's death (in 1398) 'to learn to read.' Here she fell ill, only eight years old, and when she lay dying (Margareta daughter of Claus relates) Saint Bridget appeared to her and reminded her of a sin which she had not confessed: 'When you were to have your mantle and your crown you could not sleep at night for joy!' It seems that the little girl was clothed on her death-bed in the habit of the novices: the mantle, that is the long cloak reaching to the ground worn by the Cistercian nuns, and a wreath or crown of roses, myrtle or rosemary as a sign that she was now the Bride of Christ. Perhaps little Brita had plumed herself on being able to wear the same habit as the real nuns—at any rate she sent for the priest and made a fresh confession. But Saint Bridget was not only the stern teacher, she was also a kind great-grandmother. For when the fever-stricken little girl lay wishing for strawberries, and those who attended to her said, perhaps rather brusquely, that it was impossible to have them because it was between Christmas and Candlemas, little Brita answered: 'Go out to the earth mound lying here outside the convent and scratch away the snow; there you will find some. Mother Bridget, who was here with me just now, has told me so.' 'And they went out and found that in truth it was as the maiden had said, and never had they known that there had been strawberries before in this place. After that the maiden died and was carried hither [to Vadstena] and lies here together with other children of Saint Bridget.'(2)

After Ulf had become law-man in Närike in 1330, the family also formed connections with this province, the smallest of the four surrounding Lake Vättern (Östergötland, Småland, Vestergötland, Närike). In the division of the inheritance from Sir Birger, Bridget had received as her share a good deal of landed property in the country lying north-west of Lake Vättern, among others 'the huts which Sir Birger owned in the iron hill in the Svin forest.' It is an old tradition, to which Verner von Heidenstam has given an artistic form in *Pilgrimage of Saint Bridget*, that on the hammer-shaped ness, projecting out into the Vättern from the coast of Närike, Ulf Gudmarsson laid out a farm which was called Ulfshammer (now Olshammer) after him, 'and to the north of the homestead his wife, the Lady Bridget, daughter of Birger, built a wooden church.' In the course of time the church has been rebuilt, cherry trees and lilacs in bloom have covered the windows, but outside the church door there is still to this day a stone lying on which the stern lady stood up when mounting her horse.(3)

Another local tradition has it that when Bridget wanted to go home from Olshammer to Ulfåsa she took the shortest road. First she rode along the shore to the village of Hinstorp, where a 'Santa Brita's lime' is still standing, and continued then *straight across the lake*—without going the long way round north of the Vättern.

This ride across the lake is, however, only half legendary. For from the coast at Hinstorp a reef or sandbank goes out into the lake, known to the Vättern sailors as the 'Hinstorp reef,' and easily recognized by the breaking of the waves over it. On this reef one can walk—or ride—a good way out into the lake, and that is just what Bridget did. Then, when the water rose too high, the horse would begin to swim.(4) On sunny days, preferably about the time of the feast of Saint Bridget, in the beginning of October, when a bright streak of light appears across the blue lake, the people on the shores of Lake Vättern still call it a 'Brittväg.'

At home in Ulfåsa, too, by the waters of Boren, strange tales were told of the mistress of the house. Now what was it on that day when Sir Ulf sailed alone across to Kristberg on the other side of the lake, and when he was on the way home the boat capsized and he was nearly drowned? (*Se noyer dans les lacs suédois est chose fréquente*, we are told by Madame de Flavigny, as if it was something peculiar to Swedish lakes!) But on the shore the Lady Bridget was kneeling in prayer, and Sir Ulf was saved.

> And what was that about the church in Ekebyborna? Sir Ulf had promised God to build a church in thanksgiving for being saved, but he did not know where it should stand. Then the Lady Bridget took a sprig of oak and threw it up into the air, and where it fell the church was built.... But this cannot be true, for the church at Ekebyborna stood there long before Sir Ulf and the Lady Bridget came here. But the beautiful chalice that we have has been founded by the master and mistress of Ulfåsa—and up in the tower the Lady Bridget has her oratory.(5)

And so the talk went on about the young mistress of Ulfåsa. In being conscientious she went to extremes! Once she happened to ride into a field of rye, just when the corn was in florescence, and the horse trod upon a few stalks of corn. The Lady Brita rode on a short way—then her conscience accused her and she went back to repair the damage. She dismounted and straightened up the downtrodden corn, and it grew better than all the rest in the field. . . . Ah, yes, she was scrupulous to extremes. How was it about that woman who had sneezed in church—over at Olshammar, wasn't it?—and the Lady Brita had forgotten to say, 'God bless you!' She was already a good way on the road home when it occurred to her—and, upon my word, didn't she go back, just open the church door and say, 'God bless you!' She was already that Bridget who was later to be driven by the spirit to confess three times a day—*Saint* Bridget, whose tender conscience had continually to be relieved and healed by the soothing unguent of grace.

VII

Magnus Eriksson attained his majority (1332) and took the government into his own hands. Mats Kettilmundssön had already died in 1326, Birger Persson in 1328; younger men took their places as the king's advisers. The young knight, Ulf Gudmarsson, who in 1330 had become law-man in Närike, was one of them.

And now it devolved on these good men of the realm to find a consort for the young king. According to custom they looked abroad. Our own Valdemar the Victor first sought as his bride a Bohemian princess, later a Portuguese. (One wonders what language these royal couples really spoke to one another? Latin, perhaps—but then almost certainly with very different accents: here a Danish, there a Bohemian, there a Portuguese pronunciation of the ever young verb *amare*! Or Greek, like Sigurd Jorsalafar?) The great men of Sweden turned their glances to the rich, industrious and highly civilized Flanders. In Namur, where the waters of the two rivers, Sambre and Meuse, famous in the World War of 1914, unite, lived Count Jean and his second wife, daughter of Philip of Artois, and little Blanche, one of his nine children, was just the right age. The Swedish legates who came a-wooing on behalf of Magnus received the consent of Count Jean, and carried off Blanche de Namur to that kingdom which is the most northerly in the world—'beyond it no man can live!' 'From far countries did she come,' Blanche de Namur! King Magnus awaited her in Varberg, as King Valdemar awaited Queen Dagmar in Ribe.*

The marriage took place in the autumn of 1335. In the beginning of the same year King Magnus had ridden his Erik's progress. In Skara he proclaimed an edict by which the Uppland law forbidding the buying and selling of thralls was extended to be in force also in West Gothland and Värmland. 'To the glory of God and the Virgin Mary' as also for the peace of his father's and grandfather's souls, the young king ordained that no child born of a Christian father and mother might be called a thrall, 'for in as much as God delivered us from heathendom He has made us all free.'

It is almost word for word Birger Persson's thought, as it is expressed in the Uppland law. No wonder then that it was Birger Persson's daughter who was entrusted with the education of the very young queen. In July 1336 Magnus and Blanche were crowned with

---

* Pronounced Reebé. In Danish and Swedish, the letter 'i' is pronounced like 'e' in 'dene,' and the final e is slightly accented.

great splendour in Stockholm; on that occasion the king was knighted by his brother-in-law, Albrecht of Mecklenburg, who in the same year had celebrated his marriage, already arranged in 1321, with the king's sister Euphemia.

But with this royal marriage Bridget's happy times at Ulfåsa came to an end. A good time, a happy time it had been. Bridget was what the Swedes call *et duktigt fruntimmer*, a capable woman. Her nature was *action*—she was one of those who must always be doing something or other. Her religiosity was *active*, whether it was a question of carrying on the Christian fight against one's own self or caring for the suffering limbs of the body of Christ.

A wife according to the words of the Scriptures, according to the commandments of the Church and in the grace of the sacraments, this Bridget was to Ulf—'she did well by him and wrought him no evil all the days of his life.' She knew the duties that marriage laid upon her— 'it is seemly for the bride to be ready when the bridegroom desires to hold a marriage, so that she is arrayed in comely attire and clean . . . the bride shall do the will of the bridegroom . . . and she must share in his work that she may rest all the more safely with him . . . with a crown on her head and a jewel on her breast she must wait for the bridegroom to say "Come." . . . No one cares to kiss a pale mouth,' Bridget knows, but her own lips would be red and warm when they met Ulf's 'in godly love and mutual affection and the blending of the flesh so that the blood of love may become fruit in the body of the bride.' In such a marriage the husband says to his wife: 'My rest is thy rest, my comfort, thy comfort!' And his wife answers him: 'Thou givest me bread by thy work, thou warmest me at thy breast, thou givest me joy by thy loving words, I will therefore rather die than be parted from thee.'(1)

Bridget had known marriage in all its depth and fullness. She knew the deep surrender with which woman yields up her body for a sacrifice, *a victim*, if need be, on the altar of life. She had also known the jesting and tender dalliance of love, the fluttering play of the little cupids round the stern image of Aphrodite, when the lover or the bride playfully hides from each other. Even on her deathbed Bridget still remembers these moments.(2)

But when the sun had risen Bridget was also a wife, a wife who could sit at her husband's side when he sat bent over his law books. She knows just as well as Ulf, perhaps even better, what they say about the rules of purchase, sale, property; she is well acquainted with the three legal systems then in force: canonical law, imperial law, the law built on the customs of the people.(3) And never yet had Bridget been made to feel that by her marriage she had come under a system of law which gave a married woman a lower position than was the case at home in Uppland. And this it was—the peasant of East Gothland has full rights over his wife, as he has over his servants, 'yet he may not chastise her in the church or in the ale-room (!). And if he does chastise her, so that she gets open wounds—that is, wounds which require "balm, bindings, linen and healing linen"—or blemishes, he shall not be fined.'

Never did it come to such a pass between Ulf and Bridget. Yet he once caused her a wound which needed more than balm, bindings and linen to heal. 'When Saint Bridget's eldest daughter, who was named Mereta, had come to a lawful age,' Margareta, daughter of Claus, relates, 'her father gave her to a mighty man named Sigvid Ribbing; he was a very hard and cruel man and is that robber of whom is spoken in *revelacionibus*.'

But in *revelacionibus* is said (the words are put in the mouth of Christ, and He speaks to Mary):

> Oh, my Mother, why dost thou pray for mercy on this robber? He has committed three robberies. First he robbed from my angels and elect, for he took away from them the souls of many men and women who should have been given into their care, as with thoughtless words and evil deeds and bad example he beguiled others to evil things. . . . Next he robbed the bodies of many people as he divided the soul from the body, before the hour of their natural death had come, and killed them in his wrath. In the third place he robbed many innocent people of their possessions and laid unbearable taxes upon poor and miserable people.(4)

The third accusation would assuredly not be that which would weigh least in Bridget's judgment on her daughter's future husband. Her scrupulous and sensitive conscience was not adjusted only to personal faults. Like Queen Dagmar she *could* reproach herself with having laced her silk sleeves on a Sunday—but she was also like the Danish queen in 'coming to the help of the poor peasant.' Again and again she reproaches both gentlemen of the nobility and ecclesiastics, bishops and cardinals, kings and popes, with laying heavy burdens on the shoulders of the common people, while they do not themselves touch them with a finger. Bridget's Christianity is not only a religion of mercy, the ambulance which follows the army and gathers up the wounded, the Samaritan who looks after the victims of the robber. It is that which has in later times been called *social* Christianity—the kingdom of God is to come *also on the earth*. Bridget by no means denies that God is merciful, on the contrary, she points it out again and again. But—and it is a great *but*—He is merciful only to those who repent. With Bridget there is no such thing as 'sinning in relying on grace'—each and every one gets that which is due to him. . . . 'How can anyone be with me who does not work for me, but rather against me?' says Christ. And about the robber it was thus that 'from the hour of his birth he grew up to do the works of the devil.'

And it was to such a man that Bridget had now to give her eldest daughter, her Märta! In vain did Ulf explain to her that Sir Sigvid Ribbing, whom he had met at the gathering of the great men in Kalmar in 1332, was a good match—'he is the guardian of the Duchess Ingeborg's sons, who are still under age, and live in Halland, in Varberg Castle.' Bridget's standard for people in general, and for sons-in-law in particular, was a different one. 'To begin with, Sir Sigvid is a climber, in the next place he is notorious for his lewdness, in the third he is so arrogant that he respects nobody. That is the kind of man to whom you will give our daughter!'(5)

Three years later Bridget found that she was right in her anxious misgivings. There were no longer any bridal songs, but only weeping and woe: Sir Sigvid's days were but few, his children brought him no joy, others seized the riches he had scraped together 'for he would not grow better.' But it was all hidden from Ulf's eyes, and Bridget discovered to her horror that she did not possess any lawful means of preventing this marriage. For according to the law of East Gothland it was the *husband alone* who gave the daughter in marriage. It was not so at home in Uppland; there the mother could put in a word, and a weighty word equally as good as her husband's. But Bridget was no longer under her father's jurisdiction.

At the same time she was with child, the eighth which Ulf had given her. She had stretched out her arms to him with the others in pride and joy—but now? In any case she would not, within so short a period of her confinement, put in an appearance at this wedding.

Ulf reasoned with her, tried to convince her, begged her—threatened perhaps—it was all in vain. Everything glanced off Bridget's stern resolve. 'You will have to make ready for the wedding without me . . . and as to what the Ribbings think—what the whole family thinks—what everyone here in Linköping and in Uppsala and in Stockholm thinks—it does not matter in the least to me!' A door banged, Ulf left her; soon after she heard his voice in the hall, where he gave orders about the silken tapestries from the East that were to adorn the walls, about the flowers to be strewn on the floor—she heard how angry he was, she knew, too, how unhappy he was—never before had there been an angry word between them. . . . But no, Brita would not give in; Brita was right; she saw what that stupid Ulf could not see—that it would be the ruin of Märta, in time and perhaps also in eternity, to go to the bridal chair with this scoundrel . . . wrath mounted up in Bridget's soul, her heart beat in great, hard beats—quite beside herself she threw herself upon her knees before the crucifix in her oratory: 'Lord, I cannot bear this!'

And then she felt not only the violent beats of her own heart, but below it a tiny heart was beating—a little heart beating so quietly, almost anxiously. . . . And she heard a tiny voice saying: 'Mother, Mother, do not kill me—for if you die now, I must die too! And I want so much to live, so very much!'

Then Bridget stood up and put on her dress for the wedding and entered the large room where the guests had already begun to whisper about the absence of the mistress of the house. Without a word she went up to Ulf, placed herself by his side and took his hand.

But not many days after Bridget was labouring with child and could not bring forth. It was her eighth child, and Bridget was small and slightly built. 'And the women who watched over her had no hope that she would be able to live. But then they saw someone like a human being clad in a silken robe come hastily in and stand by her bed and touch all her limbs. And at once, as this person went out, the Lady Bridget gave birth to the child without pain, so that all the women standing near her, wondered exceedingly. For there was no doubt that this person was the Mother of God, Mary, who also herself said to her: 'When you were in the pains of death in childbed I went in to you and helped you, it therefore behoves you to love me much, and that you strive for your children to become my children!'(6)

It was a daughter who thus came into the world through the aid of the Blessed Virgin; she was given the name of Cecilia. On 12 March 1399, she died in the convent of Vadstena after having been placed first in the Dominican convent of Skenninge, whence her brother Karl removed her, and she made two marriages, one with Lorenz Jogansson, King Magnus Eriksson's court physician, and a second one with Sir Bengt Philipsson. She was in danger of losing a long and rich life when from her mother's womb she sent forth her prayer: 'Dearest mother, do not kill me!' In our own days there are plenty of unborn children who send forth the same prayer and who are *not* heard.(7)

VIII

Bridget was a reader. Long before such an accomplishment had become general she would sit stooping over the Holy Scriptures, as did, about five hundred years later, the disciples of Rosenius in Småland, those whom Harry Sjöman has described in his narratives; and like the lay preachers who wandered faithfully from one 'red room' in the large forests of Tiveden to another, and with John the Baptist proclaimed that the kingdom of God was near.(1)

Bridget read the Bible, that is to say, she read the Old Testament, which she had herself caused to be 'turned to Swedish.' And she brought the Bible to others—one of the gifts she took with her to the wedding of King Magnus and Blanche of Namur was a Bible like her own. The marriage took place in 1335, the coronation in 1336; and we know that King Magnus Eriksson, in about 1340, possessed *unum grossum librum biblie in swenico*. This 'great Bible book in Swedish' can have been none other than Master Matthias' translation of the Pentateuch, and who could have brought the young couple such a wedding gift other than Bridget ?

There can hardly be any doubt that Bridget felt at home in the world of the five books of Moses.(2) The thunder of Sinai rolls, near or remote, also in her message to mankind. Now and then one may feel tempted to ask oneself what acquaintance the great seeress had with the *Christian* half of the Bible, beyond what mediæval art proclaimed with so much sweetness or with such blood-dripping realism: the birth of Christ, the passion and death of Christ upon the Cross; Bethlehem and Calvary? And that question can especially become insistent: Did she ever read the Sermon on the Mount?

It is clear that as soon as Bridget had advanced so far in her studies of Latin that she could understand the text of the Mass, she would, with the same eagerness and interest as devout Catholics in the twentieth century, follow the priest's prayers and readings. She would not, like modern churchgoers, possess a handsomely bound *Missel* or *Paroissien* or Schott's *Messbuch* with gilt edges. But we can be sure that she would ask her confessors to explain the Holy Gospel to her, if she found it difficult to follow it—perhaps because the priest read it in far too low a voice, or because his pronunciation of Latin was not like that to which she was accustomed. On going through the Missal it will be found that passages of the Sermon on the Mount are read as the Gospel on the following holy days: Matt. vi. 16–21, on Ash Wednesday; Matt. v.

43–vi. 4, Friday after Ash Wednesday; Matt. v. 20–4, 5th Sunday after Pentecost; Matt. vii. 15–21, 7th Sunday after Pentecost; Matt. vi. 24–33, 14th Sunday after Pentecost. If to this are added the Gospel for the Feast of All Saints, Matt. v. 1–13, and the texts for other feasts which were already celebrated in Bridget's time (the martyrs Cosmas and Damian, the Church Fathers Ambrose and Augustine, Bernard of Clairvaux), we get a Sermon on the Mount comprising the following passages: Matt. v. 1–24, v. 43–vi. 4, vi. 16–21, vi. 24–33, vii. 15–21, Luke vi. 17–23, and (on the feast of Saint Bartholomew, the Apostle) Luke vi. 12–19. Bridget would know, then, the eight beatitudes; she would know that when the salt has lost its savour it is good for nothing but to be cast out, and to be trodden on by men. She had sensed the commandment, that very hard commandment: 'Love your enemies, bless them that curse you.' She who gave so much in alms had learnt that alms must be given in secret, and that fasting, too, and other good deeds must be done in secret. She, who was one of the richest women in Sweden, knew the commandment about laying up treasure in heaven, not on the earth, and all through her teaching there is a *leitmotif*: *despicere terrena amare coelestia*, 'for where thy treasure is, there will thy heart be also.' And when she saw titmice and chaffinches darting from bush to bush—'they sow not, neither do they reap nor gather into barns'—she understood that so must also the true friends of God do.(3) And the roses in the garden at Ulfåsa, the red roses to whom Nicolaus Hermanni was to liken herself—they stand there and open their petals to the sun, and close them before the dew falls at night, and their perfume is so pure and chaste, and 'not even Solomon in all his glory was arrayed like one of them.' It had been said to them of old time: 'Go to the ant and learn wisdom.' Bridget had stood out there in the spruce forest by one of the great ant-hills, had watched the little brown insects swarming in countless numbers, seen them dragging and toiling, moving the eggs from the ground floor up to the attics and down again to the cellar. In broad columns they march across the path, to some place or other, whence they return like a victorious army, laden with booty; and then there is one that falls down dead just at the entrance, and a couple of others come up, take the burden from the fallen one, and leave him lying there, just as he thought he had reached the goal—what profit has he now of all his labour under the sun, and all the vexation of his heart?(4) 'Seek first the kingdom of God and His righteousness.' The kingdom of God is sought in solitude, as when Jesus went up on the mountain to pray and spent the night in prayer to

God. 'The kingdom of God is preached by those who are called there-to, the twelve, who were chosen from the company of the seventy-two disciples, and the first of them was Simon whom He also called Peter.' From the Gospel on the feast of Saints Peter and Paul, Bridget knew that it was to him that the Lord had given the keys of the kingdom of heaven; whatsoever Peter shall bind upon earth, it shall be bound also in heaven; and whatsoever he shall loose upon earth, it shall be loosed also in heaven. But not everyone who calls himself an apostle, or who calls himself by the name of Peter and sits in his chair is really so—'beware of false prophets, who come to you in sheep's clothing, but inwardly they are ravening wolves. By their fruits ye shall know them. Does one gather grapes from thorns or figs from thistles? But every tree that beareth not good fruit shall be cut down and cast into the fire.' Bridget was to feel herself called to lay the axe to the root of many an unfruitful tree and give it up to the everlasting fire. . . .

Meanwhile, for the present it was her task to be teacher and gover-ness to young Blanche de Namur and a good aunt (in the Swedish sense of the word) to her youthful relative and king, Magnus. Gladly she spread her motherly wings over the royal couple too. Ulf stayed at home at Ulfåsa; the youngest children were still small, Catherine was not more than five years old, little Cecilia only two. Bridget knew they were in good hands; she could devote herself entirely to her activities at the castle of Stockholm.

The king was still young, *puerilis est*, it is said of him in one of Bridget's revelations. In him she saw a soft and willing clay from which her strong woman's hands could shape the image she had in view for the *ideal Christian king*, a Scandinavian parallel to the French *bon signour Looys, roy de France*, of whom Joinville relates that he would rather that strangers should come and rule well over France, than that his own son should rule over it badly.(5)

Bridget was two years old when the seneschal, the master of Join-ville, began, at the age of eighty, to write down his memoirs of his beloved master and king (*d.* 25 August 1270). Joinville had heard of Norway. When he was on a crusade with Saint Louis in the East certain knights came to the army and related that 'their ship was built in the kingdom of Noroe which is the outermost in the world.'(6) And among many other things which these Christian descendants of the heathen Vikings could relate was also that 'in the land of Noroe the nights are so short in the summer that it is just as light when evening comes as when the day dawns.'

So much did the biographer of Saint Louis know about Bridget's country (in the Bull of Canonization 'Norway' is also used to designate Sweden-Norway). Did Bridget know anything about the French saint-king? Blanche was the name of the young Swedish queen, and Saint Louis' stern mother was also called Blanche. It was she who would rather see her son dead than that he should commit a mortal sin, and who watched so jealously over him and his lovely wife, Margaret, that the two young people had to make use of the craftiest ruses to be able to get together at all when the stern mother-in-law was in the house.(7) But in the ring which was taken from the king's finger after his death, three names were engraved: *Dieu—France—Marguerite*, with the addition, *hors de cet anneau nul amour*. This the Spanish Blanca had not been able to prevent.

Blanche de Castile—Blanche de Namur. . . . And what was contained in that costly casket of ivory which Blanche de Namur had brought with her to Sweden, and which Bridget had seen standing in one of the corridors of the castle, dusty and neglected? A light issued from it to Bridget's soul, a voice spoke to her heart—the casket was a reliquary and contained relics of several saints, but in particular of Saint Louis of France! Blanche willingly ceded the casket to the pious mistress of her household, and Bridget placed it on the altar in the castle chapel.(8)

Bridget knew, then, who Saint Louis was—who, by the way, could help knowing it, not one hundred years after his death? Joinville's book about him came out in 1309. Blanche de Namur, who brought the relics of Saint Louis with her, may also have possessed this biography, one of the most famous literary works of the time, in her travelling box. In any case the legend about him could be read in Jacopo de Voragine's *Golden Legend*.(9) In that he was described as the perfect pattern of a Christian king, such as he appeared to the Middle Ages, and as the people of those days looked up to him.

Joinville's book, which is written on the basis of the personal companionship of many years, by no means disavows this ideal picture. The author has divided it into two parts. 'In the first part is related how King Louis lived according to the commandments of God and the Church and the welfare of his kingdom. The second part tells of his warfares and his great deeds. And inasmuch as it is written: Seek first the kingdom of God, and all these things shall be added unto you, so I have first written that which is for the advancement of the soul and for a good rule of the people and the land.' In contrast to the general practice Joinville begins his book with that which usually comes after the biography proper, the so-called *exempla virtutum.*

At the head of the king's daily agenda are the duties towards God, *Dieu premier servi*, as Jeanne d'Arc was to say later. 'Every day he heard the Divine Office [Matins and Lauds] being sung, then he heard a Low Mass, and after that the High Mass for the day. After the midday meal he rested upon his bed, and after having slept he said, together with one of his chaplains, the office for the dead in his private room and then heard Vespers. In the evening he heard Compline.'

As is known, Saint Louis was a member of the Third Order of Saint Francis, hence these various prayers in the course of the day. Yet with all these prayers he did not neglect his royal duty—a fresco by Maurice Denis presents him sitting under the big oak in the wood near Vincennes and dispensing justice.

After Mass he went out into the wood and sat down with his back against a big oak and bade us all sit down. And all who had any complaint to make came thither, and there was no servant of the law to hinder them.

In the evening he was the good father of the family.

Before he lay down to sleep he bade his children come and told them about good kings and emperors and what they had done, and said that they should take such men as an example. He also told them about bad rulers, who by their loose living, their love of robbery and their miserliness had lost their kingdoms. 'And this I tell you that you may beware and keep from all such deeds, that God may not be wrath with you!' He made them read the Little Office of Our Lady, the same that he said as a tertiary of Saint Francis—'and made them persevere in it, so that they might be used to it when some day they had a country themselves to rule over.'

A strange bringing up of princes and princesses, was it not? But they knew no better in those days. Even our own Christian IV knew something about *Regnum firmat pietas.* . . .

And the French king did still many other strange things. Like so many pious great men he had the custom, on Holy Thursday, of inviting twelve poor persons and washing their feet. The Pope does it to this day, the Emperor Franz Joseph did it. Joinville honestly relates that he (like Peter in the Gospel) thought this washing of the feet was too much of a good thing. When the king asked him whether he practised this pious exercise at home in his own castle, as a work of humility and charity, Joinville, always sincere, answered that he could never think of doing so, *les piez de ces vilains ne laverai je jà* (i.e. *jamais*). He then received a very forcible reprimand from the king. 'He said to me,'

Joinville relates, 'that I should not be ashamed of doing what God Himself had done. Besides, even the King of England washes the feet of
twelve lepers and kisses them.'

Of no use to mention what Joinville relates about the other good
works of Louis, of alms, founding of monasteries and convents (nearly
a score of them, belonging to the most varied Orders, are mentioned—
it was enough to apply to the king and say that a house was desired).

> Outside Paris he built a house for the blind and had a chapel erected so that
> they could hear the divine service . . . and he had another house built, also
> outside Paris, on the road to Saint Denis, and in it he placed a large number of
> women, who because of poverty had given themselves up to an immoral life,
> and he gave each of them 400 livres in interest for a living [a yearly income
> corresponding to about 10,000 francs], and ordered that every woman should
> be received who desired to live in chastity.

But it was not enough for the pious king to give money for these
charitable purposes, he also took a personal interest in them.

> Wherever he came in the kingdom, he ordered that six poor persons were to
> be received daily in his house and to be served with bread, wine, meat or
> fish. . . . It often happened that the king himself served the table and carved
> the meat and placed it before them, and when they left he gave them money
> with his own hand. And if it was a great feast day the king did not eat until
> he had served the dinner for his poor people.(10)

As I have already said—but it will bear repeating—*the Christianity
of the Middle Ages was a social Christianity*, wholly inspired by the
twenty-fifth chapter of the Gospel of Saint Matthew: 'As long as you
did it to one of these my least brethren, you did it to me.' After having
served the poor the king and his courtiers sat down to the table with a
good conscience, and they were served 'both roundly and plenteously'
(*largement et habandonnement*), says Joinville. And there are still to be
found, in a world otherwise de-christianized, people who are of the
same mind as Saint Louis. I know of a family of the Roman nobility
who one day had as their guest a foreign prince of the Church. A
'round and plenteous' dinner was served, so round and plenteous that
the ecclesiastic felt scandalized and found that he ought to express a
criticism. He did it by taking off his crimson cardinal's gloves and
putting them in the glass which the servant was just going to fill for
him with good Frascati wine, and to this gesture he added (in Latin) a
scripture text: *Quod super est, date pauperibus*—that which seemed to
him to be too much on the richly covered table ought to be given to
the poor! There was a painful silence; everyone looked towards the
old *principe* who was giving the feast. And in an Italian which sounded

I   6

like Latin the prince said: 'Your Eminence can safely continue dining—
in this house we do not sit down to table *until the poor have been served*!'

The admonitions and advice with which King Louis on his death-
bed commended the kingdom to his son were as spoken from Bridget's
heart. In his testament he says:

> Maintain good morals and root out bad ones. Do not demand too much of
> thy people, do not burden it with taxes and imposts, unless thou art in very
> great need.... Have a care that thou hast good and honest men, ecclesiastics or
> seculars, who are not full of the greed of gain, and speak often with them.
> Avoid and flee from the company of wicked men.... When thou hast to
> administer justice be unbending and do not swerve either to the right or the
> left, but lend a willing ear to the complaints of the poor.... Beware of
> beginning a war against Christian men ... and if a strife breaks out among
> thy subjects make peace as speedily as thou canst.... The offices of the Church
> thou must give to good persons who live honourably ... and have a care to
> have good sheriffs and governors, and make a search into the manner of living
> of those who are in thy house.

Finally, all these rules and counsels are anchored in that in which the
whole of life was anchored in the Middle Ages:

> Go often to confession and choose for thyself a confessor who has wisdom
> to teach thee what thou must do and what thou must avoid—and who has
> courage to rebuke thee for thy misdeeds. Hear Holy Mass with devotion;
> pray, not only with thy lips, but from thy heart, and mostly so after the
> consecration, hearken willingly to the Word of God.... And may the Holy
> Trinity and all the saints preserve thee from all evil, and may God give
> thee His grace always to do His will and to honour Him here on earth that
> thou and I, after this earthly life, may meet Him and praise Him for ever
> and ever.(12)

More than six hundred years have gone by since a squeaky goose-
quill slowly printed these words on parchment and wrote the date under
them: 'This was written in the year of grace 1309 in the month of
October.' And no document rattled down on a typewriter has ever
reached up to the same heights of the spirit. But it was up to such
heights that Bridget would guide Magnus Eriksson, the young king.

IX

> Inasmuch as this king of Sweden humbly asks, how he shall live justly and
> wisely in the rule of his kingdom, I will make known to him ten things which
> he must do.(1)

These words are to be found at the beginning of that book to which
Alphonso of Jæn later gave the title of *Liber Cœlestis Imperatoris ad*

Reges, 'the message of the heavenly emperor to the kings of the earth,' that mirror of kings which Bridget held up to King Magnus. A law for kings which, like the law that was given to Moses, contains ten commandments.

The very first is that the king must dismiss the bad advisers he has and engage good ones. On her arrival at the court, Bridget seems to have found the new royal couple surrounded by sycophants and climbers, and her first action was to expel this generation of vipers from the royal castle. Of the good counsellors it is said in another place in *himerikis keysara book*, the book of the heavenly emperor, that they must be two in number, and they shall be *like two mothers* to the king, *thy han är barnlikin*, for he is childlike. Saint Francis of Assisi also used this word 'mother'—in the rule which he wrote for the brethren in the hermitages, that one half of the hermits must serve the others 'like mothers,' in order to be served themselves the next day in the same manner. *Scribo tibi sicut mater*, he writes in his letter to Brother Leone. One of these friends of the childlike king must now give him 'milk and bread,' and from the other he is to receive 'wine and the means of healing.' The first of these two symbolical gifts signifies that the king is to learn of his motherly friend

> in what things he errs and sins, and how he is to make good these transgressions, and how he is to repent of them and thus win the forgiveness of God who has been angry with him. From the other friend he is to obtain wisdom and judgment to administer justice and counsel, and help in dealing with cases which have become difficult to solve and are obscure, and wisdom to rule and defend his kingdom.

Bridget felt herself called to be a motherly friend of this kind to the inexperienced king and his still more childlike bride. First and foremost she would put in order the religious life of the young couple, and in particular she thought of the king. Like herself and Ulf he must pray daily the Little Office of the Blessed Virgin Mary, yet, when he has to preside in court, he may be dispensed from a part of the office. Likewise he must daily hear two Low Masses or one High Mass. Five times in the day (of twenty-four hours) he must with sorrow remember and think of the five wounds of Christ. It is a matter of course that as a Catholic he must observe the long fast, but further he is recommended to fast on the eve of the feasts of the Blessed Virgin and the great feasts of the saints. On Fridays there must be only fish on the table, on Saturdays only dishes made with milk. On Fridays he must also humbly remember Christ's washing of the feet of the Apostles, the king (like Saint

Louis) washing the feet of thirteen poor persons and with his own hands giving them food and a coin. Yet the king shall be dispensed from this when he is on a journey.(2)

From the religious, the obligation now passes over to the domain of justice. 'Every Friday, when the king is sitting quietly at home, may all men make ready and trust in his "on that day hearing the complaints of the common people and of his subjects and servants."' It is the oak in the forest of Vincennes which is transplanted to Swedish soil. 'And the king shall require accounts from his sheriffs and lieges and those who gather in the taxes.' He must give good wages to his servants but not be unjust to any, 'for it well becomes a king to command in moderation and to reward men who work in his service with love. The king may also give his gifts to foreigners living peaceably in his kingdom. Yet in such a manner that his own men are not neglected.'(3)

It is true that these counsels and rules of life for King Magnus, together with many others, occur in revelations which are usually dated as after 1344 (by Ingvar Andersson as after 1342), and Bridget had already come to Stockholm as mistress of the household in 1335-6. But it may safely be concluded that long before these thoughts took shape in writing they would have been living in Bridget's mind and have been decisive for her conduct. Among other things, this must apply to the exact directions about the king's costume and about the days when he ought to wear the crown. The people rejoice when they see the king in his splendour, his 'honourable and courtly attire,' and he must place the crown on his head on the birthday of Christ, 'which ignorant people call Yule,' on the thirteenth day (the feast of the Three Holy Kings), on Holy Thursday, Easter Day, the feast of Pentecost, the Assumption of Mary (15 August), the Exaltation of the Holy Cross (14 September) and the feast of All Saints.

In the ninth and tenth commandments Bridget returns to the king's duties towards his people. He must not rule and judge according to his own pleasure, but justly, according to the law of God—and he must not be idle but active; he must certainly concern himself with all the matters put before him, for it is not becoming that he should receive a big appanage and not do any work. Still less must his rule be marked by injustice and cruelty. Everything is again summed up in the religious obligation, in the duty towards God, the duty that keeps everything in its place, as the sun's attraction keeps the earth in its orbit. 'In his deeds let the king show himself worthy of the name of king, in humbling himself before God. For the higher the king is exalted above others, the humbler must he be before God, *from whom comes all power.*' This the rulers in the Middle Ages knew; *omnis potestas a Deo.* Even the emperor of the Holy Roman Empire *deutscher Nation* had a superior. The feudal system asserted itself right into the supernatural, the king was but the vassal of God. There was a heavenly emperor above the earthly one—the justice or injustice of this world is not ultimately decisive. There is always a possibility of an appeal to the highest instance, to a supreme court where Jesus Christ was the Judge, the Apostles assessors, the Blessed Virgin counsel for the defence, the devil the public prosecutor. And at this supreme court sentence was passed with inexorable justice—'I am so just,' God says to Bridget, 'that I will not be unjust even to the devil.' As in the Book of Job, the devil therefore appears to Bridget in the heavenly supreme court.

> There was a day when the sons of God came to present themselves before the Lord, and Satan came also among them to present himself before the Lord. And the Lord said unto Satan: 'From whence comest thou?' and Satan answered the Lord: 'From going to and fro in the earth, and walking up and down in it.'(4)

Goethe was thinking of this when he made Mephistopheles present himself before the throne of God, and on leaving say: 'I am rather glad to see the Old One from time to time.' God and Satan are enemies, nor is Bridget in any doubt about it. But the relationship between them is *de puissance à puissance.* For the innermost essence of God is justice. His device might be *suum cuique.* Every man shall have his due, and heaven acknowledges the claims of hell when they are found to be justified. There is no reason to be afraid—or there *is* reason to be afraid: Justice has the last word in the world.

X

Two years after the wedding of Magnus Eriksson and Blanche de Namur their first son came into the world, and it was Bridget who had the honour of holding him in her arms at his baptism. Her influence on the young royal couple seems at that time to have been very great (1337). Magnus, especially, willingly heeded the counsels of his kinswoman*; it might even be said of him as of Saint Erik that he was 'instant in prayer,' *assiduus in orationibus.* This at last reached such a

---

* The kinship is rather distant. Bridget's maternal grandfather, Bengt Magnusson, was the son of Birger Jarl's brother. But blood is always thicker than water—and in the Middle Ages race and family were of great importance.

point that Bridget had to restrain his too excessive zeal. He said, indeed, all the numerous prayers and psalms that she had prescribed for him, but without attention and interior recollection, so that all his piety was only a waste of time, nay, worse than that, neglect of more important duties. For while this reading of prayers was going on people could not get access to the king, and those who sought him in order to get their rights had to leave, their business unperformed.(1)

There was also something else of which Bridget did not approve. After the birth of the two first children (Erik 1337, Hakon 1339) Magnus had taken it into his head that he would live in continence with his wife. It is true such a marriage (Saint Joseph's wedlock) was one of the ideals of the time—Bridget's aunt, Ramborg, had lived in this way, and Bridget herself would gladly have done the same; the marriage of her second daughter, Karin, to young Eggert von Kyren, was like a life between brother and sister. But it was another matter concerning Magnus and Blanche, and Bridget did not approve at all of their resolve. Blanche, she says, has come to this far country of Sweden in order to 'bear fruit,' both spiritually and physically. The unquestionable good that matrimony is can, of course, be exchanged with advantage for a higher one, the earthly for the heavenly. But the motive must be *caritas Dei*. In Magnus and Blanche, however, the motives that assert themselves are of less value—*he* makes such a serious resolution in exaggerated religious zeal and with a certain thoughtlessness, *she* in order to please her husband, and especially in order not to have any more children. As the experienced woman Bridget is, she therefore advises the young couple to refrain from their ill-advised resolve and to return to their married life.(2) Apart from this she is not, after the first enthusiasm at the valuable gift that she had rejoiced to receive from Blanche, very pleased with the young queen who had been brought up to French ideas and customs. Blanche was frivolous and loose in her talk, and was very anxious to please and gain friends in her new country. (Here again the question occurs: What language did Blanche speak in Sweden? Latin with a French accent, or Swedish with a slight foreign accent?) She is not always in the mood to hear *verba Dei* and that which is good for the soul, nor to exercise the deeds of charity towards her neighbour. Blanche must take the holy women of the Scriptures for her models, Judith, Esther, the Blessed Virgin herself, and learn from the terrible fate of Jezebel that pride goes before a fall.

Bridget seems to have preached to rather deaf ears, at any rate so far as Magnus was concerned. His attempt at matrimonial continence led to the sinister result (if it is possible to believe *Revelationes*) that he succumbed to unnatural vice.(3) And he sinned gravely against the first of Bridget's admonitions: instead of attending to what wise and well-intentioned advisers said, he took a favourite whom he exalted above everyone and placed above all others, and whom he 'loved with all his heart more than himself' (one has a glimpse of an unnatural relationship), 'and who even made him hate his own son.'(4)

Although Bridget lived in full historical daylight, and archives and libraries contain ample information about the important personalities of her time, there has been a great deal of hesitation on the question of identifying that 'servant of the devil' of whom Bridget says that 'because of his family he was of low rank,' and she therefore admonishes the king to let him stay where he belongs. And if Magnus does not take this advice he will be afflicted with aches and pains from the crown of his head to the soles of his feet, until he says in his torment: 'Have mercy upon me, Mary, for I goaded thee to anger!' In the insurgent writings of the Swedish nobles against King Magnus from 1365 to 1371 the *servus diaboli* is mentioned by name: 'That servant of the devil was Sir Bengt Algotsson, whom the king made a duke against the will of God and of His Mother, and against the laws of the land and of its advisers.'(5) But Bengt Algotsson became an esquire in 1350, a knight in 1351, councillor of the realm in 1352 and Duke of Southern Halland at the earliest in 1353. Long before that Bridget was in Rome.

In any case, it was evident to Bridget that the evil enemy was busy at the court of Magnus and Blanca. There was much piety in the young capital of Sweden (Stockholm is mentioned for the first time in 1252). Magnus Ladulås had already in 1286 bestowed Riddarholmen on the Grey Friars, and in their church he was laid to rest. Since 1335 the Dominicans had their monastery in Svartmannagatan; the Poor Clares lived beside St. Clare's Church. The hermits of the Order of Pope Celestino V had settled on Fågelö in the Mälar.(6) At the corner of Tyske Brinken and Svartmannagatan stood a church dedicated to the great German seeress, Saint Gertrude of Helffta. There was indeed much piety in Stockholm, there was much piety in the land of Sweden.

Bridget stood one evening alone on the highest pinnacle of the tower of the castle and looked out. Down below, under her feet, were the three holms or islets on which the city had from the first begun to be built (and which were the cause of the Latin name in the plural: *Holmiæ*). On the other side of the stream lay the big sandbank, Malmen, on which a little building had already been begun; on *Sudhra-Malm*, too, there were some houses. Bridget stood alone up there on the tower, and it was night. But not one of the bright summer nights of the north, when the sea lies like a golden green sheet of glass out towards a golden red horizon. Across a dark sky the storm drove heavy, threatening clouds—only now and then could a glimpse of the moon be seen.

Bridget thought of her fatherland, of Sweden. Like a pure and clear summer sky the kingdom of Sweden ought to be, a kingdom of peace and justice. God had created many glorious lands on the earth, 'and among them one called Sweden.' Good champions you will find there, chivalry and brave heroes, who could well stand up to fight against Didrik of Bern himself.(7) It was so once—it is not so any more. The women of Sweden have left the 'old, honourable manners' of their country and have begun to adopt foreign dress; they lace themselves and show themselves in tightly fitting clothes in order to excite the desire of men.(8) Not only have the relics of Saint Louis come into the country with Queen Blanche, but also the *Fables of the God of Love*, the Breton romances, which instead of *l'Amour de Dieu* praise *le dieu de l'Amour*. Beside the casket of enamel from Limoges, containing the saint's relics, there may also have been in Blanca's box a copy of *Flores et Blanzaflor*, which was just at that time being translated, first into Norwegian, later into Swedish; or a copy of the poem about Aucassin and Nicolette, that loving couple who did not care about getting into God's heaven where there were none but tiresome saints, but would rather go to hell—

> there, where the gallant priests go, and the handsome knights who have died in tourney or in noble warfare, and where they will meet again the beautiful ladies who have been their *douces amies* on the earth, and where there is gold and silver and ermine and costly pelt, and where the harp players are, and the mountebanks and the kings and princes of the earth.(9)

Bridget stood gazing out into the night, listening. Now the bells were ringing for matins yonder at St. Clare's Church—the Poor Clares would be going into the choir. Other bells were answering— the Black Friars, the Grey Friars at Riddarholmen; perhaps she also heard the faint ringing from the hermitage at Fågelö. . . .

But from the big hall below in the castle arose the sound of merry singing and the playing of stringed instruments, and at this late hour King Magnus and Queen Blanca were still sitting at table. . . . 'Empty pleasure and shouting voices,' such is the world's happiness. 'Three devils rule in this land,' Bridget murmurs to herself, 'the first is drunkenness, the second voluptuousness.' She pauses for a moment, then she says under her breath, as if she were afraid of being heard: 'But the third demon is worse than all others: it excites men to unnatural intercourse with men.'(10)

Now the noise is growing a little quieter down below; only one voice can be heard—it is perhaps a wandering minstrel singing about 'Ivan the Lion Knight' or another of the ballads which Queen Euphemia of Norway has caused to be translated, and which are called the Euphemia ballads.(11) Euphemia of Norway was dead—may she rest in peace! Bridget was thinking of another Euphemia, King Magnus Eriksson's sister, whose wedding was celebrated in the same year that the king was crowned . . . she was married to the German, Albrecht of Mecklenburg, that fox . . . and she herself was as smooth and slimy as a snake and as a viper . . . and court vipers like these have now the ear of the king and queen.(12)

Bridget looks up, looks at the moon, which is just now sailing out between the dark driving clouds, silvery white with such a soft light . . . she thinks of the queen, Blanca, 'the white one.' Like a silvery white moon she was to shine over the land of Sweden, and the king was to be like the sun by her side . . . but now the sun has become as black as coal, and the moon has fallen into a great deep. . . .

It is growing darker about the lonely woman on the tower of the royal castle. A big black cloud, looking like a dragon, is opening its mouth as if to swallow the moon . . . and with its tail it will kill all the people on the earth, so that nothing is left but reptiles and creeping worms which devour the crops of the fields. . . . With horror Bridget sees them squirming . . . like maggots squirming in a corpse.(13)

XI

But when King Olav came from the east over Kjölen and went westwards down from the mountain, so that the land looked lower towards the west, land was seen in that direction. Many went before the king, and many came after him. He rode where there was room about him; he was quiet and did not speak with others. He rode a long while during the day in such a manner that he looked little about him. Then the bishop rode up to him and asked what he was thinking of, since he was so quiet; for the king was ever glad and talked much with his men on the journey, and so he made all those who were with him glad. Then the king answered earnestly: 'Strange things have appeared to me for a while. I was looking now over Norway, when I saw the mountain in the west. It came into my mind then that I had been glad many a day in this land. Then I had the vision that I looked out over the whole of Trondhjem, and then over the whole of Norway, and the longer this vision was before my eyes, the wider I looked until I looked out over the whole world, over both land and sea. I knew well the places I had seen before and now saw again, and just as plainly I saw the places which I had not seen before, and some of which I had heard tell, both built and unbuilt, as wide as the world.' The bishop then said that this vision was holy and very strange.(1)

Three hundred years later Bridget, daughter of Birger, stood in the same place where the hero and saint of Norway had looked out over the circle of the whole earth—*heimskringla*, in Snorre's words. They were on the way to the Olsok Feast in Nidaros, a journey of thirty-five days. Ulf and their escort had travelled part of the way on horse-back, but Bridget, whose body was strong 'like a young colt,' and whose will was like a bird that longs for the distant roads,(2) would not give way to any ease. If one is a pilgrim, one *is* a pilgrim!

It was at some time in the years between 1339 and 1341 that Bridget had for a while shaken the worldliness of the court off her feet and together with Ulf had taken a staff in her hand. It was their intention to make a pilgrimage to the shrine of another of the three holy kings of the North, to the martyr brother of Saint Erik in the cathedral at the mouth of the river Nid. The road was long and wearisome—it was that *via montanorum* which Olaus Magnus had drawn on his map of the North, and which he describes thus:

> From Jämtland the people of the country and strangers on a journey in the summer travel by a cheerless and dangerous road over these high mountains . . . while in winter they can make their course where they please, by short cuts and paths, over frozen marshes, tarns and streams. For these widespread fells, the like of which can scarcely be found in Europe, have on the eastern side as it were gates or openings in the hard granite . . . when you get into the openings you feel, in the summer too, such a cold striking from the fell sides, that if the travellers are not provided with clothes of several thicknesses, as in the winter, they expose themselves to almost unavoidable danger.

The old Swede, who in his Roman exile was so well informed about everything at home in that fatherland which had banished him, was no doubt here thinking about the narrow mountain pass called Skurdalsporten, through which the road went from Jämtland to Nidaros.(3) Saint Staffan, the apostle of Jämtland and Hälsingeland, had baptized many heathens in the neighbouring Skurdal lake. And by the pass was still standing 'the stone in the green valley,' which Saint Staffan is said to have raised himself, and in the granite of which he had inscribed in runes these prophetic verses:

When Swedes take up outlandish manners
and the land loses its erstwhile honour
the stone will still stand in the green vale.

Churches will be turned into prison houses,
the worship of God will lose its fair light
the stone will still stand in the green vale.

Rogues and rascals will have thriven,
the good and the old will be driven,
the stone will still stand in the green vale.

Olaus Magnus knew nothing about this stone, and perhaps it was raised at a much later time. But if it stood there in Bridget's time, and she passed that way, she would be able with a full heart to repeat its words. That 'Swedes took up outlandish manners' was just what she had to complain of at the court in Stockholm, where the king's good old advisers could no longer gain a hearing, while rogues and rascals flourished. And she could also repeat the words of the refrain—there was still hope for Sweden—'the stone was still standing in the green vale.'

And so Bridget went confidently on, along the road by which Saint Olav had travelled. Where he had rested on his journey the pilgrims rested too. There were inns by the roadside, and in the big forests there were 'souls' houses'—hostels built by pious people as a penance for the souls of their departed kinsfolk. In many places there were also holy wells, where crutches and staves had been left to bear witness to miracles that had happened.(4)

Bridget and her escort were almost certainly not alone on this pilgrimage, for Saint Olav was among those saints who were best known and most venerated in Sweden. 'When Erik gives corn, Olav gives cake'; this old saying joined the two saint-kings together like two gods of fertility. On 18 May, Erik's Mass, the corn is beginning to ripen and at Olav's Mass, 29 July, it is ripe for harvest.

You would think [says a Swedish historian] that Saint Erik would have been more venerated in our country than his Norwegian confrère, Saint Olaf. This is by no means the case, rather the reverse. The memorials of an Olaf cult in Sweden are overwhelming, compared to the relatively few testimonies to the Erik cult, and it is no exaggeration to assert that Saint Olaf is the most popular figure of a saint of the Middle Ages in Sweden. . . . The anniversary day of his feast came at a time inviting to festivity, at the height of summer, when the crops were to be harvested. In many places the feast of Saint Olaf was therefore kept as a great harvest festival, where the peasants gathered together and drank to the memory of the good king.(5)

As so often happened, the Christian saint took over the place which had been filled by a heathen god. The bearded King Olaf with his axe became the successor of Freir and Thor. As in heathen times Freir's image was carried round the fields to bless the crops, so was now a statue of Saint Olaf. He was also introduced instead of Thor: the old city of Thorshälla has in its coat of arms Saint Olaf standing on a ship—probably an allusion to the ballad of the marvellous sailing match between 'Saint Olaf and his brother,' in which King Olaf came in first, although he had a poorer ship. And that it is 'so good to rest in Trondhjem,' has been the experience of many a Swedish pilgrim.

And the North was the very place in which it was good that a great saint kept guard, at the extreme borders of the Christian realm. For what could you read in the Norwegian *Mirror of Kings*? 'One angel was more beautiful than all the others, and he was therefore called Lucifer; he was made a chief over many angels, and a great number of angels stood in awe of him in service and friendship. In pride he stood up against God and spoke thus: "Why must we submit to serving God, seeing that we have strength enough, beauty enough, and that we are strong in numbers?" And Lucifer disappeared from God with all his followers and said: "Now I will raise for myself a throne like that which God has in the northern part of the world." And he disappeared with all his followers towards the north.'(6) As it has been said by the prophet: 'Out of the north an evil shall break forth upon all the inhabitants of the land.'(7)

The pilgrims' road led over the wide moors and through the wildernesses. Over the Dovre Fell there was much traffic from Trondhjem; often people fell there by the wayside and could not go on. 'There I had soul houses built and gave land besides,' King Eystein boasts, at the beginning of the twelfth century. In some ways these soul houses were like the hospices of the present day. These houses belonged to all and stood on ground that was common to all, and all had a right to them; this was the Christian communism of the Middle Ages. The Norse law of the Gulathing mentions these soul houses and gives regulations for the sojourn in them. If many people come to a soul house and there is room for all of them and their luggage, all is well. But if there is not room for all of them to sit down because of the luggage, then it must be carried outside. Everyone has a right to stay three nights, and provided other guests do not come the stay can be extended. There is no host and no attendance; each one must serve himself, fetch fuel, carry water, cook food.

Bridget and Ulf were thirty-five days on their journey. There is nothing remarkable about this. In those days a journey from Nidaros to Uppsala took at least three weeks. The Italian traveller Quirini, going against his will to Norway and shipwrecked, took fifty-three days from Trondhjem to Vadstena.(8) In an old Danish guide for travellers to Rome it is stated that a journey from Hedeby to the Alps took three weeks, stopping, of course, on the way. The pilgrims to Nidaros would also break their journey here and there, to rest and bait their horses. In most cases there would be a chapel by the hostel as at Granby Hill, from which the pilgrims had their first sight of Vadstena and took off their shoes to walk the last mile barefoot. All might be in need of the chapel and the inn—but there was also a smithy for those who made the pilgrimage on horseback, and whose steed may have lost a shoe on the way.(9)

The pilgrims from Ulfåsa, then, are sitting one evening in one of the soul rooms up yonder on the Dovre Fell. There are other pilgrims there, too, and the luggage has been carried outside. Although it is midsummer it is cold up there on the wilds in the evening; a fire is lit on the hearth, the door is shut to the white night—it is like a winter evening, and no one would be surprised if the gale began to shake the house and the wolves to howl. . . . Nearest the fire sits an old Norseman. He has come from Lysekloster, the monastery near Bergen. They are Cistercians there, as in Alvastra, and is that not where Olav Aasteson lies buried?

The old man looks up, and instead of answering he begins to sing. Slow, long-drawn, solemn notes, as of an organ, or as when the Alp horn is heard among the fells. Do we Swedes understand him? He is singing in Norse. It is the old ballad about Olav Aasteson—the young man who lay down to sleep on Christmas Eve and fell into such a long sleep that he did not wake up until the Feast of the Three Kings, when people were going to church. He has had such a strange dream, his soul has been away on a queer journey in the beyond. He must needs tell others about it; he saddles his horse and rides to the church. The priest is standing before the altar but Olav sits down on a bench in the porch and begins to sing:

> I raised me up toward the sky
> And downward to black bog of hell
> I have seen some of hot hell
> And a part of heaven . . .

for the moon is shining and the roads are so white, the moon-white roads, out, far out, towards the horizon.

The old man sings on:

> I have come across blest waters
> and through deep dales—
> I hear the murmur of the waters
> but I do not see them,
> they are streams under the ground . . .

and the moon shines and the roads are so white. . . .

It is the silent kingdom of death that Olav Aasteson is riding through: 'my horse did not neigh, my dog did not bark, the birds of the morning did not twitter.' The road led over a plain, overgrown with thorns that tore rents in his scarlet cloak. Then he came to the Gjallar bridge, and only the just can pass across it:

> No one can pass over the Gjallar bridge
> Who judges with injustice. . . .

Bridget listens and understands. That is so, that is so! The song continues: Olav Aasteson comes through the valleys of hell, 'where the ice burned blue,' he sees Paradise far away, 'the light is shining over fair lands,' but first he must stand forth to judgment—in the clouds of heaven the judgment will be passed.

The old man goes on singing untiringly, one or two among the Norse pilgrims join in the refrain, 'there shall the judgment be passed.' And in the clouds of heaven the two armies meet—from the north comes the devil, disguised as an old greybeard (perhaps his name was Odin once)(9); from the south come the armies of light, led by him who in the Mass for the Dead is called *signifer sanctus Michael*, God's standard-bearer on the white horse.

He is called 'soul Michael,' for when he puts the trumpet to his lips 'all souls shall go forth to judgment.' And the trumpet is the *ultima tuba*. The old man's voice rises like the tones of the Alp horn, and it is as though the whole house is trembling: 'and then all the sinful souls trembled like aspen leaves in the wind, and the souls there could not but weep over their sins.' For it is hot in hell, hotter than the mind of man can conceive—Olav Aasteson saw a cauldron with boiling, bubbling tar, and small pieces of a priest's back were boiling in it. . . . But at last come the beatitudes of the Sermon on the Mount:

Blessed are they who have given shoes to the poor, the thorns in the hedge shall not prick them; blessed are they who have given bread to the poor, they need not fear the hounds of hell; blessed are they who have clothed the poor, they shall not be giddy when they cross the Gjallar bridge—for truth speaks for itself on the day of doom

are the words of the last refrain.

The old singer falls silent. The pilgrims lie down to rest on the sleeping benches against the walls of the room. Soon they are all asleep, Ulf joining in the snoring chorus of the others. Only Bridget is awake; her thoughts go to King Magnus. 'No one can pass over the Gjallar bridge who judges with injustice.' The trumpet sounds in Bridget's soul—judgment is at hand, judgment on King Magnus and Queen Blanca, judgment on courtiers and knights, judgment on priests and monks, judgment on bishops and archbishops and on the Pope himself. For against the Chair in Rome, on which the successor of Peter was to sit, and which rested on the four posts of humility, obedience, justice and mercy, a new chair had been set up on the banks of the Rhône, and its posts are pride, stubbornness, avarice and injustice.(10) There is not one who is just, not one. Judgment is drawing near.

But then Bridget remembers what she had read once about a vision which a pious monk had in Clairvaux in France, in the monastery of St. Bernard. It seemed to him that he saw Christ sitting on His throne, ready to judge the world, and by His side stood Saint Michael, with the trumpet to his lips. Christ bade him blow the trumpet twice as a sign that the Day of Judgment was at hand and the sound was so loud that the world trembled in its foundations. And if he had blown the trumpet a third time the world would have perished. But then the Blessed Mother of the Lord stood forth before the throne of her Son and pointed down to the earth. And down there in a beam of light lay Clairvaux, where the white monks prayed and worked and expiated the sins of the world. And the third trumpet did not sound.*

But two hundred years had gone by now and the sacred fire no longer burned with so clear a flame. Worldliness and luxurious living had taken the highest seats in the rich abbeys. The scales on which lay

---

* The same thought is the subject of one of Benozzo Gozzoli's frescoes in Montefalco. Christ is sitting on the seat of judgment and in His raised hand He is holding a spear with a glowing point which He will hurl upon the earth. But before Him kneels the Blessed Virgin, who points down to Saint Francis of Assisi and Saint Dominic, who meet in front of the church of St. John Lateran and give each other the kiss of brothers. An inscription below the fresco says: *Quando Beata Virgo ostendit Christo beatum Franciscum et beatum Dominicum pro reparatione mundi.* ('The Blessed Virgin shows Christ Saint Francis and Saint Dominic for the salvation of the world.') Gozzoli lived from 1420 till 1497.

the sins of mankind were by far the heavier; new, heavy weights of penance and prayer would have to be laid in the other scales. . . .

Ulf and Bridget, then, at length reached Nidaros and knelt by the tomb of the saint. A few years earlier a fire had devastated the cathedral, but the casket containing the saint's relics had not become a prey to the flames. And when Bridget rose up from her prayer she knew what God demanded of her. At home in Sweden, Ulf and she were to found a convent for the salvation of the land from the coming wrath.

XII

Saint James, brother of Saint John the Evangelist, went from the land of the Jews to Spain to preach, but he did not succeed in doing much good there, for the people in that land were very stubborn. At that time nine disciples came to him in Spain; two of them he left behind in Spain, and with the seven others he went back to Judæa.(1)

This we can read in the 'Old Saga of Saint James.' Furthermore, it relates how the Apostle disputes with 'a sorcerer named Hermogenes,' and converts him as well as a disciple of his named Philatus. This provokes the wrath of 'Abiater, the bishop in Judæa,' who lays a rope about the neck of James and takes him to King Herod, with the request that he may be condemned to death. This is done and James is taken to the place of execution by 'a Jewish clerk' named Josias. On the way the Apostle heals a crippled beggar, upon which Josias falls down at the feet of James and begs of him that he may be made a Christian. James baptizes him and both now suffer martyrdom. This takes place in Jerusalem, 'on the feast of Our Lady before Easter.' Then, in the night, the disciples of the Apostle come and take his body and embark with it on a ship which takes them to Spain. 'The angel of God steered to a harbour in the land of Galicia, where there reigned a queen named Ulvhild, that is, in Latin, *Lupa*.' The disciples carry the body ashore and lay it 'on the first stone they happen to find, and the stone yielded to his bones like wax to a seal.' And this came to pass 'eight days before the beginning of the month of August,' *i.e.* on the feast of Saint James, 25 July.

The disciples now proceed to the queen of the country, 'who had such a mind as her name implied,' and ask for a grave for the body of the saint. She tries in various ways to get rid of them, among others by sending them to her neighbour, the King of Portugal, who was said to be 'a cruel man,' in the hope that he will have them murdered. This hope fails, the disciples return unscathed, nay, they have even converted the cruel man to Christianity. Ulvhild now promises to grant the disciples' request, but she does not really mean to do so. She proposes that the Christian missionaries shall let the matter be decided by a miracle. 'Go out into my pasture,' she says, 'choose there two oxen, yoke them to a cart, place your holy body upon the cart and give the oxen two strokes with the whip. At the place where they stop of themselves the soil shall be yours.'(2)

This way of challenging the judgment of God was not uncommon in the Middle Ages. On the occasion when *il Volto Santo*, the picture of Christ which Joseph of Arimathea had carved in wood, had arrived at the Italian coast on a ship without sails and oars from Jaffa, and the miraculous picture had been found, both the seaport of Luna and the town of Lucca, further inland, claimed the right to own it. The picture was placed upon a cart drawn by two young oxen which had never been under a yoke, and to the grief of all the inhabitants of Luna the oxen took the road up to Lucca.*

Queen Lupa's oxen now appear, when the disciples come out to them, to be 'savage and mad bulls' (perhaps kept ready for a *corrida*), and directly the Christians approached them they

began to roar terribly, to stamp on the ground with their forefeet, and with lowered heads and horns outstretched they rushed upon the disciples. The latter fell on their knees and implored the help of God and Saint James. Their prayer was heard, for when they rose up from prayer and made the sign of the cross over the furious animals, behold, these came up to the disciples as meek as lambs, and the disciples laid the yoke upon their necks and harnessed them to a cart and took them down to the shore, where they had left the body of their master.

So the bulls disappoint the cruel queen's bloodthirsty hopes as thoroughly as the King of Portugal, for 'without a driver they went along the straight road and did not stop until they had reached the queen's hall. Then the queen was converted to the Christian faith, and had a church made of her hall, and had Sanctum Jacobum laid to rest there.'(3)

* The picture is still preserved to this very day in a special chapel (*tempietto*) in the cathedral of Lucca. It is a *Cristo velato*, of the period before that of the nude crucifixes, with a king's crown on the head. Only the face can be seen—hence *il Volto Santo*, in French *le Saint Vou*. Erik Aye-Good would kneel before this picture, which was known to him at home—'Saint Helper' in Kiplev is none other than *il Volto Santo*. A similar legend is connected with the little chapel of San Rufinello d'Arce near Assisi.

At the harbour of Padron the pilgrims could see for themselves the big stone (*la Santa Cueva*), on which the body of Saint James had rested, with a depression as of a human body. But this does not explain the name Compostella (*campus stellæ*). Another old author gives the explanation.

The Apostle died in the year 44. His disciples were already, in the first Christian century, preaching the Gospel all over Spain, and small Christian communities arose here and there in the Iberian peninsula. Two of the disciples, Athanasius and Theodorus, remained in Galicia and there suffered martyrdom.

Then came Diocletian's persecution. In a single month twenty-two thousand Christians suffered martyrdom in Spain. The Christians in Galicia then wished to bring the bodies of Saint James and his two disciples to a place of safety and carried them at night up on a mountain where they deposited them in a cave, the entrance to which was concealed by thorn-bushes and brambles. Years passed, centuries passed. At the foot of this mountain there lived, in 813, a hermit who often saw, as it were, stars gleaming up above the summit of the mountain. There was, in particular, a star bigger than all of them, standing fixed in the same place. The bishop of Iria Flavia, Theodomirus, was informed; with all his ecclesiastics he went at midnight up the mountain and there beheld the star standing over the entrance to a cave. After spending a night in prayer he said Mass there in the morning, and then in the grotto they found the bodies of the three martyrs. Athanasius and Theodorus in smaller graves, and in the largest grave Saint James. By his side lay a sword, the sword by which he had suffered martyrdom, the sword that San Jago el Matamoro was later to wield against the Moors. By his other side lay a staff, the staff of his long apostolic wanderings—the pilgrim's staff which thousands upon thousands of pilgrims from all over the world were to take in their hands to go to the place where the star had appeared—*campus stellæ*, Compostella.(3)

In the Middle Ages there were three great places of pilgrimage to which Christendom resorted, as in our own times to Lourdes. They were designated by three Latin words: *Deus, Angelus, Homo*. By *Deus* (God) they meant the tomb of Christ in Jerusalem, *il Santo Sepolcro*, sometimes briefly *il Sepolcro*, the tomb above all tombs. *Angelus* (the angel) meant Monte Gargano on the east coast of Italy where the Archangel Michael was said to have appeared once in the fifth century—the same Michael from whom Castel Sant' Angelo in Rome has received its name. (Mont Saint Michel is a Norman imitation of the Italian shrine.) Our forefathers knew 'Mikkelsborg' very well—Bridget also found her way to it later. Finally, the word *Homo* (man) was understood to mean above all the tombs of the Apostles in Rome, and after them the tomb of Saint James in Compostella.(4)

In Bridget's family the pilgrimage to Compostella was almost a tradition. It is related of Birger Persson that he and his father and his grandfather and great-grandfather had all made pilgrimages 'to Jerusalem and to many other holy places,' or, as it is expressed elsewhere, 'with great pains he visited the places of holy men, namely of Saint James and other saints.'(5)

Bridget had the longing for a pilgrimage in her blood, and it was not long before she and Ulf again took up their staff and set out. This time the goal of their journey was to be the land of Saint James; Bridget would not be unfaithful to the family tradition. Soon she and Ulf would have been married for twenty-five years—in 1341 they would be able to celebrate their silver wedding! What could be more reasonable, then, than to celebrate it by a pilgrimage?

Many things, however, had to be put in order first. In May 1340, Ulf still held office as a member of the king's council of twelve. Meanwhile, in the period between May 1341 and March 1343, his name does not appear on any official document; he must therefore have begun his vacation.(6) None of the children went with them on the journey. Birger and Karl, the two big boys, probably stayed at home at Ulfåsa.(7) Gudmar died quite young at school in Stockholm, probably already in 1338. The Dominican nuns in Skenninge took charge of the six- or seven-year-old Cecilia. Karin and Ingeborg were placed in a convent school with the Cistercian nuns in Riseberga. On 29 March 1341— that is, shortly before the departure—Ulf and Bridget issued a diploma in which it is stated that: 'We have devoted our beloved daughter Ingeborg to fight for God,' that is, to become a nun. As a dowry she receives a manor in the district of Vartofta in West Gothland, a hamlet and a water-mill with the reservation that their daughter is to receive for life seven marks yearly of the income for her own use and the convent the remainder, but after her death the whole. Ingeborg received the habit early but died young, and her body was taken to Vadstena. In the chronicle of Margareta daughter of Claus it is said of her: 'She was given to the convent of Risaberga and lived there a godly life, and now without doubt she is in heaven with God Himself and is believed to be a saint, for God works many miracles by her grave for those who come thither and call for her help.'(8) She died while Bridget was in Rome. 'Oh, Lord Jesus Christ,' the mother exclaimed with joy, 'I bless Thee, because Thou hast called her before the world could ensnare her.' And she arose at once and went into the chapel, and those who stood outside heard her sighing and weeping much, and they said to each other: 'She is weeping over her daughter.' Then Christ appeared to her and said: 'Woman, why weepest thou?' But she answered: 'Lord, I do not weep because my daughter is dead, I rejoice much more, for if she had lived longer, she would also have to account to Thee for more. But I weep because I did not at the time bring her up according to Thy commandments, and because I gave her examples of pride, and because I did not chastise her as I should have done when she erred.' Then Christ answered:

> Every mother who weeps because her daughter errs against the command-ments of God and who teaches her as well as she can according to her conscience is a true mother, she is a mother of tears, and her daughter is God's daughter for the sake of her mother. But the mother who rejoices that her daughter knows how to demean herself in the world and takes no thought of how she lives, if only she can be honoured and respected in the world and by the world, such a mother is no mother but a stepmother. And for the sake of thy love and for thy good will thy daughter has now been crowned in heaven with the crown of glory.(9)

One beautiful morning, then, probably in the beginning of June 1341, they set out on their great journey. The road goes south, first to Skenninge (a visit to the House of the Holy Spirit, to Master Petrus), then out across the wide, fertile plain of East Gothland, where the standing corn is green, and the many churches raise their white towers —Hagebyhöga, Fivelstad, Orlunda, further away Örberga, Källstad, Roglösa, Väversunda. The countryside is dotted over with churches; more than one of them owes its existence to the Folkungs. Bridget's aunt at Svanhals and her husband Erengisle gave one of their manors to be broken up in order to build a church with the stones.(10)

The road goes through Bjälbo—Bridget would no doubt think of her ancestor, the great earl, and of Ingrid Ylfva, who would not even in death bend her proud head. From the church tower in Svanhals (which would not then have had a swan as a weather vane) she would be able to look out over the reed-bordered shores of Lake Tåkern— and were the swans which now, at the present day, in their thousands populate the Tåkern waters already there in those times? Beyond Lake Tåkern she could see the Omberg raise its long, wooded ridge. A church tower or two gleams white over yonder—Rök, Heda. . . . But the goal of the day's journey is hidden behind the slopes of the Omberg—the monastery of Alvastra, where Ulf and Bridget will leave

behind little Bengt in the care of the white monks of the Order of
Saint Bernard, as they had in Skenninge left little Cecilia with the
Sisters in the convent of Saint Ingrid. . . .

But on the day when Bridget rode through the gate of the monastery of Alvastra she decided her own and her husband's fate.

XIII

. . . *Ad te clamamus, exules filii Evæ, gementes et flentes in hac lacrymarum
valle.* . . . 'To thee do we cry, poor banished children of Eve, mourning
and weeping in this vale of tears. . . .'

It is in the monastery church in Alvastra, the monks are singing
Compline. Outside, it is a bright June evening, and a thrush is singing
its clear evening song from a tree in the cloister-garth. Within, in the
chancel of the church, the white monks are chanting the last office of
the day.*

Down in the semi-darkness of the church Bridget and Ulf are listening, with little Bengt by their sides. Yes, they are right, those white
monks up there in the chancel—we are all the banished children of Eve
here on this earth, which is nothing but a vale of tears. 'The wilderness
of thistles in the vale of tears,' was what the first monks who had come
here from France had called Alvastra. The monastery chronicle relates
of this:

When our venerable Father [Saint Bernard] desired to harvest some fruit also
among the people of the North, he sent, at the prayer of a pious woman, the
Queen of Sweden, a company of brethren to these regions. When the monks
and lay brothers, who were chosen to teach these rough and untamed nations
religion and discipline, were stricken with exceeding grief and earnestly
begged that they might not be sent to strange and barbarous regions, the holy
Abbot answered them: 'Beloved brethren, why do ye grieve my soul with
unreasonable tears and prayers? In this matter I do not follow my own will,
but the will of God, which we must all obey.' And before the holy man there
was just then standing a large basin of bronze, which it was the custom of the
priests to use when washing their hands during the Mass. As he spoke the last

---

* The Divine Office or Hours was the name given in the Middle Ages to the
psalms and prayers which the monks were under obligation to chant at certain
hours. *Matins,* early in the morning, followed by *Lauds*; *Prime* at daybreak; *Terce*
at nine o'clock, before High Mass; *Sext* at noon; *None* at the ninth hour, that is, at
three o'clock, finally *Vespers,* evensong, and *Compline,* the nocturnal song. Each
office concludes with an *antiphon,* which varies with the season of the year; from
Trinity to Advent it is the *Salve Regina,* written by the monk Herman the Lame
in Reichenau (1013–54). Easter fell on 8 April in 1341.

words the man of God struck so hard a blow at this basin that a dent was made in the metal. The brethren selected for Sweden understand the miracle and give way, like the bronze. An abbot, twelve choir monks and several lay brothers were selected, and 'provided with the liturgical books prescribed, with vestments and chalices . . . they set out on the long and extremely difficult journey.' As food for the journey they receive from Bernard a loaf which he has blessed—eleven years after it was still as fresh as if it had been newly baked!(1)

'At the prayer of a pious woman,' Saint Bernard had sent his monks to the North. This 'pious woman' (as she had to be called in the official ecclesiastical style) was King Sverker's queen Ulvhild, one of the most sinister female figures of the twelfth century. Her first husband, King Inge, 'was poisoned [in 1125] in Vreta by an evil drink,' after which she married the Danish king Niels and incited her stepson Magnus to the murder of Knud Lavard. Her third marriage was with King Sverker the elder, and in order to atone for her sins she now prevails upon her husband to found the monastery in Alvastra, and her son Karl to found the convent in Vreta (Alvastra about 1140, Vreta 1162).

Saint Bernard's Order was in those days the leading one in Europe. Its real founder was Abbot Robert of the monastery of Molesmes in Burgundy, who with twenty-one of his monks left his abbey to live according to the rule of Saint Benedict with greater perfection else-where. He did not need to seek far, for in the trackless forests and swampy dales of the Côte d'Or, at this day still trackless and swampy, he found what he sought: Citeaux, with its Latin name *Cistercium*, from which the whole Order took its name. Robert of Molesmes is known only to church historians; the great man of the Order was Bernard. It was only when he, the young nobleman of Fontaine-lez-Dijon, then only twenty-one years old, with over thirty younger and older companions of like mind entered Citeaux and soon after (in 1015) became abbot in a new monastery (Clairvaux, 'the bright valley'—the place had previously been called 'the valley of wormwood'), that the Cistercian Order became what Robert and his English successor, Stephen Harding, had intended, a great movement of reform in the monastic world and in Christendom.(2)

Before Saint Bernard's delegates had come so far, Queen Ulvhild had died. King Sverker then bestowed upon them the site which she had, on her marriage, received as a wedding gift, and which was called Alvastra.(3) Here, under the southward-facing slopes of the Omberg, King Sverker had built his royal manor; here he had erected his domes-tic chapel; here was also the place of execution (*rätterplats*), belonging to the manor of a man of rank in the Middle Ages, which was the visible sign of his rights as a master and of his authority as lord of the manor.

This place of execution was used, at any rate, in one case which is historically known. Good King Sverker was murdered in the very night of Christmas, as he was on his way to the midnight Mass, and the murderer was one of his own servants, his groom. The faithless servant was seized and received his punishment—and it was terrible, though not more than was usual in the Middle Ages (and than those punishments in hell which Bridget was to describe later in her revelations). The sinner was hanged by a rope over a cauldron full of boiling lead. The bell in the adjacent church was rung three times; at the first ringing the murderer was lowered in the seething metal to the ankles, at the second to the knees, at the third ringing to the waist. But then the rope burst, and the miserable creature fell down into the bubbling metal and died.

When Bridget and Ulf came to Alvastra, King Sverker, who had died in the fame of sanctity, had long since lain buried in the monastery church, 'under a big stone, in front by the largest altar in the chancel.'(5) But like the modern tourist the pilgrims from Ulfåsa would quite certainly visit the chapel dedicated to Blessed Sverker (the remains of which have again seen the light of day, like the ruins of the monastery, through Otto Frödin's patient and persevering labours during a quarter of a century). Perhaps Ulf was already then thinking of seeking here a refuge for his remaining years and a resting-place under a gravestone like King Sverker's. How long the stay in Alvastra lasted we do not know. Perhaps Ulf and Bridget had to wait for their travelling companion, a monk named Svenung, from the Cistercian monastery of Varnhem. He had to go to Cîteaux to give a report to the General of the Order, and arrived there in January 1342. Perhaps they had to wait for their pilgrim habits to be finished, if Verner von Heidenstam is right in supposing that they were made by Peter, the tailor in the monastery. (But the great Swedish poet is not right in saying that the mussel shells rattled on the cloaks of the pilgrims. 'Saint Ib's shell,' as it was called in Denmark, was not a thing that the pilgrims brought with them from home; it was a thing they found on the shore at Compostella and took home with them as a sign that they had been there. Besides, the pilgrim journey described by Heidenstam was not concerned with the country of Saint James at all, but with Rome.) (6)

The day of parting came and it was hard, because it was a parting from little Bengt, who had to remain behind alone. I remember such a bitter parting myself, from Charlottenlund in Denmark. . . . I had received a grant which pledged me to a journey and my wife and the younger children came with me—it was not the first time that a couple of them had been in Italy. 'When *I* go to Rome . . .' my little daughter of seven would say self-consciously, as if it was something she did fairly frequently. But her older brother could not come too; he was too big this time, and had to stay with strangers in Denmark and attend to his lessons. He realized it quite well himself and was brave until the last minute. But when the train glided away from the platform and he saw all the dear faces in the carriage window, and saw all the hands waving good-bye, he understood that it was serious and ran alongside the train, crying: 'Take me with you, take me with you!'

Bridget and Ulf would have such moments as these when they rode through the monastery gates of Alvastra one morning in June, and little Bengt stood crying in the porch of the monastery beside one of the kind, bearded lay brothers and saw his father and mother and their escort disappear on the road up to Heda church.

Perhaps the company of pilgrims even made a halt at Heda, perhaps little Bengt's mother wept the bitter tears of parting before the statue of the Mother of Jesus, whom Verner of Heidenstam, five hundred years later, was to greet as the 'Queen of Heaven.'

XIV

In the Middle Ages three pilgrim roads led from the north to the south; the east road, by way of Gothland to Russia, through Russia to Byzantium, from Byzantium to Jerusalem; the west road, which followed the old route of the viking marches along the coast of Europe to the North Sea and the Atlantic into the Mediterranean; finally the south road, also called the 'road to Rome,' or the 'road of the people' (*Thiodvegr*), through Germany and Switzerland to Rome, through Germany, France and Spain to 'Saint James' land.' It was by this last road that Bridget and Ulf travelled with Svenung and the rest of their companions.

The first part of the journey was accomplished by sea. From Kalmar they sailed in the lee of the long bulwark of Öland (perhaps Bridget saluted the cross on Kläpping Ness, which she had caused to be erected in memory of her mother's miraculous rescue from distress at sea, the rescue to which she owed her own life!). Then the Swedish pilgrims landed at one of the German Baltic ports, probably Stralsund,(1) and going straight across Germany they reached Kölnisburg, where Die Pfaffenstrasse, the road along the sacred river Rhine, begins. The two mighty towers of Cologne Cathedral had not yet been raised (they can be seen for miles across the country, as you can see across the plain of the Beauce in France, Charles Péguy's plain, the towers of Chartres against the horizon—and if you know what Chartres means in French art and French spirit, there is a sudden silence in the motor bus). The chancel, though, was already there, built in the *French* style (that which was later called *Gothic*), and in the chapel to the left of the chancel were preserved the relics of the three holy kings, Caspar, Melchior, Balthasar, the mighty three whose mere initials, C., M., B., written on the door of a house, were a protection against witches and trolls. From their far-off homeland, to which they had gone from Bethlehem 'by another way,' not to meet Herod again, their bodies had, at some time in the tenth century, been brought by pious travellers to Byzantium; from Byzantium they had been taken to the Church of St. Eustorgio in Milan; and after Frederick Barbarossa had seized and plundered the capital of Lombardy in 1162 (in Carducci's poem the hatred of Italy against the violent usurper is still glowing), Rainald von Dassel, archbishop of Cologne (in Carducci *un vescovo scomunicato*), obtained the relics and brought them home, where they arrived on 23 July 1164, and were laid in a casket of precious goldsmith's art in Cologne. Bridget knew nothing about all this, nor did she know anything about those great men of intellect who had carried on their work at the University of Cologne, Albertus Magnus, Master Eckart, or had studied under those great teachers, Tauler and Suso.(2) Hammerich supposes, but probably erroneously, that Bridget would have been influenced by German mysticism—she uses the expression *amici Dei*, 'friends of God,' like the mystics use the word *Gottesfreunde*, but is that sufficient proof?(3)

From the Rhine, Bridget and her little company of pilgrims now advance to the second great river of Europe, the Rhône, which they must follow to get to the Mediterranean and then to Spain. The road seems to have gone by way of Aix, in their case, no doubt, in order to pray by the grave of another royal saint; for in the octagonal chapel by the cathedral Charlemagne lay buried, and in mediæval opinion he, too, was a saint. Had he not converted the obstinate Saxons to the Christian faith, as Saint Olav had converted the Norsemen, and Saint Erik the Finns?

As the next stage on Bridget's pilgrim journey Tarascon is mentioned. But of Avignon there is not a word. What was the reason for

Bridget passing the Pope's door? For there he was, the Vicegerent of Christ, an exile from Rome, whether he happened to be Benedict XII (1334–42) or Clement VI, to whom Bridget was soon to speak so severely. Perhaps when the Swedish pilgrims passed by it was just in the interregnum—Benedict XII died on 25 April 1342; Clement VI did not ascend the throne until 19 May, but by that time Bridget was no doubt home again in Sweden. In any case it seems strange that the pilgrims should have been content to contemplate in passing the newly erected papal palace on Rocher des Doms; it is as though one would in our own times go to Rome and look up at the Vatican without going inside! Twenty years earlier (October 1321) Bridget's own father had been in the city of the Popes, on the way to Compostella, as she was now. Bridget had heard enough about life in the new Babylon from him.

Not many miles south of Avignon lies Tarascon, and there Bridget made a halt. For here rested in her saint's shrine none less than Saint Martha, Martha of Bethany, sister of Lazarus and Mary Magdalene, she to whom the Lord had said that she was troubled about too many things.

But how had this come about? It is a long way from Bethany to the little town of Tarascon by the Rhône. But not farther than for Lazarus to Marseilles, and for Mary Magdalene to Saint Maximin. The sceptical Monseigneur Duchesne did not believe in these Provençal traditions,(4) but at home in Sweden Bridget had already read how it had all happened.

One of the seventy-two disciples of the Lord was named Maximinus, and into his care Peter had given Mary Magdalene. By enemies of God he was brought upon a ship without steersmen and rudder and food, and with him Lazarus and Mary Magdalene and Martha their sister, and Marthella her handmaiden and Alidonius, who was the man born blind to whom Jesus had restored sight, and several other Christians with them. And by God's help they came safely across the Great Sea to Marsilia. And as no one would give them shelter they found a hiding-hole by a temple to an idol in that country. But when Mary Magdalene saw the people coming thither to sacrifice she stood up in the midst of them with her bright and gentle face and preached to them with an eloquent tongue and bade them turn away from devils and know the true God, Jesus Christ. All were amazed at her bright face and her words of wisdom and her good speech, and it was not a wonder that such words came from the lips of her who had aforetime kissed the feet of Our Lord.(5)

It is further related how the heathen 'governor of the country' and his wife come to the temple to sacrifice that their marriage may be blessed with offspring. Magdalene converts them and their prayer is heard—in due time a child is born to them. They forget, however, to show gratitude to the Christians who have prayed for them, and Magdalene then turns to the governor's lady: 'Ye are so rich, how, then, can ye let those who serve God hunger and suffer cold?' The lady promises to speak with her husband, but when she has to do so, her courage fails her, for 'he is hard and not kind.' A renewed request to the wife of the wealthy official is likewise without any result.

But then Mary Magdalene appeared by the bed where they were both lying, and she was wrathful and terrible, and her face glowed as if the whole house was on fire, and she spoke to them in this wise: 'Are you asleep, you robber, you limb on the body of your father the devil, by the side of your viper of a wife who would not bring you my message! Are you asleep, with your belly filled up with all kinds of food and letting the servants of God perish of hunger and cold and thirst! Here you are in your palace, wrapped in coverlets of silk and down, and know not that the friends of God are lying shelterless outside, but little you care. But this cannot go on, and soon you will be made to feel the vengeance and wrath of God!

The vision vanishes, and the governor and his wife lie there in their fine bed, 'trembling with fear . . . and immediately they send for all the Christians to be brought to them, and clothe and feed them.' Not only this, 'but in Marseilles all temples to idols are pulled down and Christian churches built.'

With the same fearless frankness and the same holy anger Bridget was to speak later to mightier men than the Governor of Provence, and to more poisonous vipers and adders than his lady. Ardently did she wish to pray at the grave of such a woman apostle. But *Saint Maximin*, where Magdalene lay buried, was still far away—and before they met Magdalene the pilgrims met her sister Martha on their way along the banks of the Rhône, at Tarascon where she lay buried.

She, too, had been an apostle of Christ. The legend relates that during the first century of the Christian era the town of Tarascon suffered under the visitations of a terrible dragon, which no spear or sword could kill. But alone and unarmed Saint Martha went out to it in the forest, made the sign of the cross against the fearsome beast, went up to it and bound it with her girdle. Like an obedient dog the monster now followed the saint back to the town and lived there henceforth as peaceably as the wolf in Gubbio. At this very day this miracle is still remembered in the little town of Provence. On the saint's feast day, 29 July, a great procession goes through the streets of Tarascon, the most beautiful (and most virtuous) maiden, clad in white, leads by a golden ribbon a cardboard monster, which is so large that two men can hide inside it. The monster moves on wheels and behind it has a tail which is movable and which the men inside move from side to side, like a dragon beating its tail. The children shriek with joy—'but don't get too near the tail, *la Tarasque*' (as the beast is called) 'can knock you over with one blow. . . .'

The Swedish pilgrims may have stood in the street in Tarascon on 29 July and seen *la Tarasque* rolling by. They may also have made the pilgrimage to *les Saintes Maries* away near the Mediterranean, at the place where Mary Magdalene landed, according to another tradition, accompanied by Mary, the mother of James, and Salome; they had all three stood together at the foot of the Cross, and all three went into exile together.(6) One thing Ulf and Bridget would not omit to do, after having prayed in the Gothic Church of Saint Maximin, where the holy brother and sister from Bethany had found their last resting-place beneath the high altar, they climbed up that mountain where the great sinner had during long years done penance for her past, and to the summit of which angels bore her when it was time for her to say her prayers. . . .

After all temples to idols had been pulled down in Marseilles and Christian churches built, the Christian people there chose Lazarus for their bishop. From there he went to the town of Aquæ [Aix in Provence] and by preaching and signs he turned all the people from their errors to the Christian faith and there made Maximinus a bishop. Later, Mary Magdalene felt so great a longing for heaven that she searched and found a desolate place where there was no water and nothing grew, and there was nothing to sustain the life of the body. There Mary Magdalene lived for thirty years without anyone knowing of it, by the grace of God alone, without any bodily food, by the singing of angels and the joy of the soul in God. Seven times every day the angels lifted her high up in the air towards heaven, so that she heard the sweet singing of angels and felt heavenly joy.(7)

The mountain of which the legend speaks is La Sainte Baume, twelve and a half miles from Saint Maximin (the name is a corruption of the Provençal Santo Balmo, 'the holy grotto'). It is the ridge of a height rather than a mountain, and is seven and a half miles long, with an average elevation of close to three thousand feet. With its steep walls of rock this long ridge reminds one of Der Rosengarten at Bozen, and in the Middle Ages it was better known than the tourist-crowded mountain in the Dolomites is at the present day. The grotto, in which Mary of Magdala did penance, is situated twenty-six hundred feet above the wooded plain at the foot of the rock—a zigzag road winds up over the almost perpendicular stone wall. Three hundred and fifty feet still higher up is *le Saint Pilon*, that 'holy summit,' to which *magna peccatrix*, the great erstwhile sinner, was lifted in ecstasy by the angels.(8)

As early as the fifth century the Benedictines of the Abbey of Saint Victor in Marseilles had founded a small monastery here. Gradually La Sainte Baume became one of the great places of pilgrimage in the Middle Ages. The much travelled and industrious Franciscan writer, Fra Salimbene da Parma, visited it in 1248 and said that in 'the holy grotto' three altars had been set up for the sake of the great number of pilgrims. In 1295 Boniface VIII transferred the shrine to the Dominicans, at first with only two priests and two lay brothers, but in 1337 King Robert of Naples, Duke of Provence (father of that Giovanna who was later to cause Bridget so much grief), saw to it that the number was doubled.

In the furthest recess of the huge rock cave, into which the sun penetrates only at midsummer, and the water drips everlastingly from the raw, low ceiling of rock down over the rough floor of big, flat grey stones, Mary Magdalene had her bed—it was a slab of stone like that of Francis of Assisi on Mont' Alverna. No one was permitted to step on the stone, which was surrounded by a triple iron grating. But one could pray, while leaning one's forehead against the cold iron rails, and one could read the inscription: *Locus pœnitentiæ* and a verse of the Psalms of David: *Adorabimus in loco ubi steterunt pedes ejus.*(9) Before this grating Bridget knelt and prayed. How her heart would have leapt for joy, 'as if a child moved within her,' if she had known that a generation later Gregory XI was to kneel here and utter his last prayer on the soil of France, ere he obeyed the command of Catherine of Siena, which was also that of Bridget, and returned to Rome.(10)

From the grotto the pilgrims then climb up to le Saint Pilon. The road leads them first through a beech wood (the beech grows here, on these heights, as on Mont' Alverna, in spite of the southerly latitude). Then the wood comes to an end and one is on the bare, stony mountain; farther ahead the road goes between two grey rocks, as through a pass, straight into the blue sky. A modern pilgrim relates:

We go through the pass, we come from the northern slope of the mountain ridge, with its view over green woods and green fields, over to the south side. And it is like coming from northern Europe to the East. We are on a plateau of whitish grey stone, on which the sun burns. There are no trees, no shrubs —but the spaces between the stones are full of flowers: yellow *potentilla*, white saxifrage, blue salvia, violet thyme and some blue flowers which in Provence are called *zenōbi*—in shape and size like our pink bindweed (that which in the pious centuries in Denmark was called 'Our Lady's smock sleeves'), but a blue as sky-blue as Our Lady's cloak. Whence had all these flowers come, up here in this wilderness? 'Well,' says the guide of the pilgrims, 'when Mary Magdalene came here, she combed her golden hair. And it was full of flower seeds from the Holy Land, and they flew out over the stony wilderness and germinated there!'

Then we reach the little chapel on the top, standing there and looking down. Deep down below us there is a vast, bare or wooded hilly landscape, away in the distance low mountain ridges in a haze and further off shining white promontories out to the blue sea—the Mediterranean! Not a human dwelling to be seen, not a sound of wheels and not a wisp of smoke from a hearth or a fire. A lonely white road winds onwards across the desert.

A prayer in the chapel. And then we sit down on the warm rocks outside. Flies are buzzing down about the fragrant flowers. A bird is twittering a little way off behind the stones and falls silent again. And overwhelmed by the grandeur of the landscape we understand that up here, in this desert quiet, Mary Magdalene *had* to come from the gloomy grotto down below. She had to come up here to get courage to live on under the everlasting dripping of water from the roof of the rock in the grotto of penance. Up here she had to come to be reminded of the wilderness of Judæa, where the Baptist had preached and Jesus had been baptized, and to see in the distance the blue sea whose waves were even now rolling in on the shores of Tyre and Sidon.(11)

Across the same blue sea Bridget was to sail to Mary Magdalene's Holy Land. From this height she saw it for the first time.

XV

Brother Svenung is kneeling before the tomb of Saint James. Beneath the ciborium on the altar there is a statue of the Apostle, majestically enthroned, like that outside by the portal to the church called the 'portal of honour.' He is clad like a pilgrim, but his pilgrim cloak is of silver. He has no pilgrim staff; it is kept in the sacristy in a silver sheath —Jesus Himself gave him the staff when He said: 'Go out into the whole world.' The pilgrims are allowed to touch it when they leave.

Brother Svenung is longing to go home. The Spanish climate does not suit him—it is now the height of summer, according to the Spanish saying, 'six months of hell'; the sunshine scorches his Scandinavian eyes with its white fire. And then the food—*olla podrida*, or whatever it is called—everything fried and roasted in oil; and then the wine, the strong, dark red, Spanish wine—perhaps he has drunk a little too much of it. . . . But it was not *that* wine he was to drink of. . . . What was it the Lady Bridget had spoken of so beautifully that day at dinner?

God [she said], is like a great master who owns a vineyard and keeps wine
for sale. First he gives this wine to his friends and kinsfolk to taste. Next,
when he wants to sell the wine, he sends his servants out into the street to
cry: 'We have tasted the wine and it is good—come and drink, everyone who
cares!' But the wine is that sweetness which is above every sweetness, and
I have given it to my friends, to them who will hear the words I have to
say.(1)

But the words which God has to say and the words which come from
the lips of the Lady Bridget are often so stern. She judges harshly and
severely, not only King Magnus at home but also the kings in France
and England who are now at war (save the mark!). And above all,
above all, how did she speak of priests? In days gone by there had been
good priests, said the Lady Bridget. In their purse they had five pieces
of gold: understanding to discern between good and evil, holy wisdom,
chastity, moderation and perseverance in everything good. But nowadays it is no longer so. With the five pieces of gold these bad shepherds
had bought a woman's body, and if only they could satisfy their desire
for it they cared little about their flock and let the wolves ravage the
sheep. To these bad priests Christ Himself is only a sheep from which
they get their living—its wool gives them clothes, its milk nourishment. The priests are like that fruit of the rose, the hip—outwardly it
is clad in purple, but inwardly it is full of prickly uncleanness. All the
commandments of God and the Church have been gathered by them
into one: 'Come hither, give your money!' And the priests' sack is
never full.(2)

Thus spoke the Lady Bridget of the priests, nay, of bishops; even
of the Holy Father himself. Just as frankly did she speak of the King of
France and the King of England:

They are like two wild beasts! One of them is greedy to swallow everything
it can get, and the more it eats the hungrier it gets, and its hunger is never
satisfied. The other animal wants to exalt itself above all men and to rule over
them. Each of the two animals tries to swallow the heart of the other. The
terrible voices of these animals is heard far and wide across the world, and
their voice and cry is this: 'Take gold and the riches of the world, and do not
spare the blood of Christian men!'(3)

It was true, it was all far too true, but by what right did the Lady
Bridget speak like this? She said that when she came home she would
send both kings a message and admonish them to make peace. Whence
did she get the courage, and by what authority could she, Bridget,
daughter of Birger of Finsta, married to Ulf Gudmarsson of Ulfåsa,
make her will known here in the land of Saint James? The Spaniards

cannot even understand us Swedes, and we cannot understand them
and their strange, hard speech; they even distort the name of Saint James
and call him 'San Chiago'—Brother Svenung tries to pronounce it
like them, but he does not succeed in emitting the hard, aspirated 'J'
which the Spaniards have inherited from the Arabs.

Then he looks up at the statue over the tomb, and suddenly *he does
not see it any more*—nor does he see the pillars and vaultings of the church
—but a great light shines before him. In the light there is a figure of a
woman, crowned with seven crowns, one above the other like a tiara,
and when he looks at it more intently he sees that the woman with the
seven crowns on her head is *none other than the Lady Bridget*.

But above the woman, who is Bridget, there is a sun which is
darkened. And there is a voice which says:

> The sun, that thou seest darkened, is the King of Sweden—he has shone like
> the sun, but now he shall be despised by all men. And the seven crowns upon
> the head of the woman are the sevenfold graces of the Holy Spirit, which
> shall be given her. But this shall be a sign to thee, that from this moment thou
> shalt be well, and that thou shalt come home and be advanced to a greater
> position than thou now hast.

The vision vanished. Brother Svenung stood up and was well. And
he came home to Sweden and became Abbot of the monastery of
Varnhem.(4)

XVI

Then the homeward journey began from Compostella, at first probably in the direction of Citeaux, where Brother Svenung had to place
before the General of the Order a dispute between the monastery of
Varnhem and another Cistercian house in the diocese of Skara, Gudhem, a daughter monastery, by the way, of Varnhem. After a last parting prayer to Saint James, the Swedish pilgrims left the church through
the north door, La Porte de France. In the large square round the
beautiful fountain it was just as lively as at the fair of Saint Olav at
home in Skenninge—here were offered for sale pilgrim cloaks, belts,
shoes, pilgrim staves of the same pattern as Saint James' in the church,
travelling flasks with good Spanish sherry, bags with all kinds of
powder and spicy herbs, which it would be good to have at hand in
case of sickness. And, above all, there was a brisk sale of Saint James'
shells which were sown on to the cloak, the hat, or, almost the most important, the bread bag. For there were plenty of thieves and robbers on

the pilgrim roads, but even the most graceless wretch of a bandit would not dare to lay hands on bread that was under the protection of Saint James. Had not Saint Iago only last year shown his power when he came to the aid of the Christians against the Saracens in the great battle on the plain called Bucera, between the city called Carife and that which is called Sicera?

There the kings of Spain and Portugal, who were both Christians, fought against five heathen kings, of whom one was king of Granada and another king of Tunis. The kings of Spain and Portugal had between them eighteen thousand knights, but the five heathen kings and a woman named Mathuga had sixteen thousand knights and the woman alone had ten thousand knights in her army. And about the third hour the heathens pushed their ships off from the land, so that none might flee away upon them, and the Christians were put to flight. Then Saint James appeared to the Christians and gave them great courage. And they turned again against the enemy and began to defend themselves bravely, and gained the victory and slew countless enemies.(1)

Saint James gave the Christians victory, and to all who made a pilgrimage to his tomb he gave his strong protection.

In the year one thousand and eighty after the torments of Our Lord, a German and his son set forth on a pilgrimage to Saint James. On the way they visited a city called Toulouse. The host in the inn there made the German drunk, and while he slept the host put a silver cup in his sack. The next day the host and his servants ran after them and accused them of theft. But they boldly said they would submit to judgment if the stolen thing was found among their goods, and the judgment was that one of them should be hanged and the host should have all the money they had for their journey. The father said he would take the place of the son and the son would take the place of his father, and they strove long as to who should be hanged. At last the son was hanged and the father went forth on his journey to Saint James. Six and thirty days after the son had been hanged the father came back to the gallows and wept and mourned. Then the son spoke to the father: 'Sweet father, do not weep; never has it been so well with me as here by Saint James, who keeps me up with his hand under my feet.' Then the father was comforted and ran into the city and told it, and all the people came out of the city and found the pilgrim's son unharmed and alive, and they loosed him and hanged the liar.(2)

This legend about Saint James supporting the feet of the young man unjustly hanged was known all over the Catholic world in the Middle Ages. I have myself seen an artistic representation of it in the chapel of the hostel for pilgrims founded in Assisi in 1431. In this painting the artist, Pier Antonio da Foligno, called Mezzastri, has added a conclusion to the

I

story, not to be found in the Swedish chronicle of miracles. On the right of the fresco you see the miracle itself, the young man hanging in the gallows, and at the foot of the gallows Saint James kneeling. He has his pilgrim staff under his right arm, and holds his left hand flat under the feet of the hanged man. In the background you see a town with walls and towers on the banks of a river—Toulouse on the Garonne. A couple of inquisitive citizens are looking on and beside them, talking with the executioner and his assistant, stands the pilgrim's father, easily distinguished by the mussel shell on his hat, and next to him a woman, evidently his wife (not mentioned in the Swedish chronicle). On the left of the fresco you see the pilgrim and his wife, who have been admitted to the presence of the judge. The latter happens to be sitting just then at a richly decked table—you see handsome decanters of wine, a small, round loaf in front of each place (the judge is entertaining guests, or is it his family?), and as a *pièce de résistance* a couple of roasted chickens. You are in the Italy of the fifteenth century —the architecture is that of the Renaissance, a tame monkey is sitting on the floor gnawing scraps, a page is holding the judge's hat and sword. At one end of the table stand the pilgrim and his wife, relating the wonderful story and demanding their son to be set free from the gallows. You are in fifteenth-century Italy, the judge is an enlightened man, a humanist, a sceptic. 'My good man,' he is saying, 'you are mad! What you are telling me is just as impossible as if that roasted chicken could crow and fly away.' But hardly are the rash words out of his mouth when the wonder he has demanded happens: both the roasted fowls jump up, flap their wings, crow and fly out of the window. The sceptical gentleman cannot do other than follow the example given him by the vanished repast. *El podestate non tardò niente, andò alle forche, e seco una gran gente,* it is said in an Italian poem of the same period as the fresco—'the judge did not tarry a moment, but went out to the gallows and much people with him!'

It was my friend Alexandre Masseron of Brest, well known for his Franciscan research, who one day in the Cappella dei Pellegrini explained this fresco of Mezzastris to me.

No doubt it was the usual road that the Swedish pilgrims chose for the homeward journey. At Monte San Marco they saw for the last time the towers of Compostella. The highest chain of the Pyrenees was generally crossed at Ostabat, where there was an old cross set up by Charlemagne when making a pilgrimage to Saint James. The road then led to Roncesvalles, where Ogier the Dane had fought and Roland had blown his horn, Olifant; in the church in Roncesvalles they saw the rock which Roland had split in two with a single stroke of his sword, Durendal. After that came the country of the Basques, weird-looking people wearing black cloaks, each with a bundle of arrows in his hands and a horn hanging round his neck. They spoke a language which was neither Spanish nor French—the pilgrims only knew that they called wine *ardum*, water *aric*, bread *orgui*.(3)

If Ulf and Bridget came by the same road as Brother Svenung they would pass through the land of Burgundy, the good wine of which may have been a temptation to the worthy Ulf. For he had pledged himself, on the whole pilgrimage, not to drink between meals. But at dinner he may have indemnified himself, especially if the little company of Swedish pilgrims called a halt at Beaune, whose Burgundy, in particular that from the vineyards of the old hospital, is one of the most famous of the red wines of France. From Beaune the road goes towards the north to Dijon—and at Dijon stands the castle of Fontaine, where Saint Bernard saw the light of day in the year of the Lord 1091, and which is to this day a place of pilgrimage. Through the midst of Dijon flows a small river, the Ouche—if you follow it by the road to Paris, you pass three other shrines: Notre Dame d'Étang, on a wooded height above the village of Velars, Notre Dame de Lanteney, where the mother of Saint Louis is said to have prayed, lonely forest chapels on rocky summits in the desolate mountains of the Côte d'Or. Up in a steep rockside a cave opens out towards the valley—it is the grotto of the hermit Tebsima, he came from the East. But down in the valley lies the Cistercian abbey of La Bussière—here you can rest and be well received by the white monks as you can at home in Alvastra. And everywhere Bridget would be the leader, small and active, walking in advance of all the others, with the same short, brisk steps, which are to this day characteristic of Swedish women.(4)

Svenung remained behind in Cîteaux, where he probably spent the winter. Ulf and Bridget continued northwards—or rather towards the north-west, for we find them again in the Flemish town of Arras (famous for its looms and the woven rugs which are therefore called Arazzi in Italian). It was not exactly the straight road home to Sweden —except in so far as it was their intention to embark at Deventer, where pilgrims from the north often landed. Or had Ulf to bring a message from Queen Blanca to her family in Namur? In any case it seems that in the Flemish city it was known who the distinguished strangers were, for they were not allowed to stay long in the modest hostelry in the

Rue des Lombards, at which they had put up. One of the canons at the
cathedral invited them to stay with him, on a hill above the city
(*Colline de Baudimont*), in a house of such distinction that Louis XI put
up there in 1477.(5)

Meanwhile the Swedish couple had hardly been installed in the
house of the hospitable canon when Ulf had to go to bed. The exertions of the journey had been too much for him—he was only human,
he was not carried on the wings of the spirit like Bridget, but dashed
his foot against every stone on the road. And now his foot was tired—
'Little Brita, I cannot go on!' A physician was sent for—and after him
came a priest. It was even the bishop of the city himself, an Italian,
Andrea Ghini, Bishop of Arras and Tournai. Two priests came with
him, bearing lighted candles, and the Canon, whose guests Ulf and
Bridget were, carried under a cloth a silver vessel containing the Extreme Unction. . . .

In the Middle Ages the greatest shrine in Arras was *la Chapelle du
Saint Cierge*. In it a candle burned before an image of Our Lady and
when a few drops of melted wax from the candle were dropped on a
sick person he or she recovered. A couple of burning drops—Bridget
knew how it hurt! Perhaps she tried the remedy on herself first—or
it may have been that she did not know anything about the chapel and
the candle.(6)

But she prayed—prayed. . . . Ulf must not die—he must not die
now. . . . He was not ready to be brought to judgment. . . . Bridget
saw the priest touch the lips of the sick man with the blessed unction, she
heard his words: 'May the Lord forgive thee all that thou hast sinned
with thy mouth'—and that was not a little—'in being immoderate
in food and drink and in ill-timed jests and merriment.' The priest
anointed Ulf's hands—'May the Lord forgive thee all that thou hast
sinned by wanton touch'—and anointed his loins: 'May the Lord
forgive thee all that thou hast sinned by the desire of the flesh' . . .
penance had to be done for all of it.

Then the bishop and the priests left. There was a faint odour of extinguished candles and smoking wicks left in the room. Dusk was
falling.

Bridget knelt by Ulf's bed. She knew what Extreme Unction
meant—it was not only a preparation for the grave, it was also a way
back to life—'Is any man sick among you? Let him bring in the priests
of the church, and let them pray over him, anointing him with oil
in the name of the Lord, and the prayer of faith shall save the sick man.'

Was not that how the bishop had prayed—and was it not the Apostle James, exactly he, who had written these words?

Bridget carefully wiped away the sweat from Ulf's brow—the warm sweat of fever, not yet the cold one of death. 'Ulf,' she called softly to him, 'Ulf.' 'Yes, little Brita.' 'Ulf, do you remember our wedding night, when I had a prayer to ask of you—do you remember what it was? Yes, you remember . . . and now I ask the same thing of you: on all our pilgrim journey we have lived together, not like man and wife, in the desire of the flesh—but like brother and sister. Shall not we go on doing so—when you are well again too? For I *know* that you will get well. The prayer of faith shall save thee, for so has our dear Saint James of Compostella said. And now, when we get home, we will live together in chastity to the end of our days. . . . Will you do that, my own Ulf, my sweetest, dearest husband—will you, Ulf?'

'Yes, little Brita!'(7)

XVII

Ulf has fallen asleep—Bridget is watching by his bedside. The night is drawing near, one of the servants of the Canon comes in with a candle and places it in a niche in the wall. Bridget sits down in front of the candle, to prevent the light from falling on the sick man, and takes up a book which she had bought in Compostella and has since then always carried about with her: Saint Bernard's *Liber de modo bene vivendi*, the book on the manner of right living, written by him at the request of his sister, *quem composuit ad instanciem sororis sue*, as written on one of the first pages of the book.

Bridget read—a little slowly, she was not yet very advanced in Latin, but knew enough to understand it.

> This book [says the Prologue] is a mirror in which the soul can see its stains and learn what is pleasing to God and what displeases Him. Read this book again and again and you will learn how you must love God and your neighbour, despise what is earthly and transient, striving after the everlasting and heavenly, enduring for Christ's sake the adversities of this world and despising its prosperity and enticements, thanking God in sickness, not taking pride in good health, not becoming presumptuous in good fortune nor downcast in trials.(1)

The evening wore into night, the candle burnt down, Bridget read on. She read of the different ways in which one can fear God—

the purely human way when one fears temporal punishment for sin and therefore does not sin; this is a poor fear of God. The fear of the thrall, *timor servilis*, is not much better, but only does what is good in order to escape hell, not because one loves God. The true fear of God is the son's fear of offending the father—and from this fear follows the love of God 'as one may use a linen thread to draw a silken thread into the eye of a needle.' (The parable was exactly suited to a housewife like Bridget.)(2)

Still Bridget read on—of 'the love that casts out fear.' It bids us love our neighbour as our self—what does that mean? That is to say, that we wish for our neighbour the same that we wish for ourselves, namely that he may be good and go to heaven. In this wise we ought also to love those who are nearest to us, if they are good and serve God, but if it is not so, then there are others who are nearer to us, those who are united with us, not by ties of blood but by communion in love of God—'for holier is the union of hearts than the copulation of bodies.'(3)

Copula corporum, 'the mingling of bodies,' as Bridget expresses it— yes, she had given Ulf eight children, and she had loved him 'as her own heart.' But she had ever had the aversion of a virgin soul against the lust of the flesh 'in which there is naught but evil odour' (Sigrid Undset writes in the same fearless and pure-hearted way about that which concerns the flesh).(4) And now, here by Ulf's bedside in the foreign country, she was listening to the voice calling to her 'from the dust to the regions of higher spirits.' Bridget reads the words of Saint Bernard *ad sororem*:

And now I admonish thee that thou covet no longer that which is of the world. Let it be a chastisement to thee to live long, let it be thy desire to leave the world. Receive not any earthly consolation, but let all thy desire be towards Christ, thy lover. Let health or sickness be of no account to thee, let the wounds of love pierce thee through, so that thou mayest say, like the bride in the Canticle: 'Love hath wounded me!' Love Him, dearest sister, in this life, so that He may find thee worthy to be loved with the Father and the Holy Spirit in the life everlasting. Amen.(5)

The candle had burned down in the socket, now it flared up for the last time and went out. The snuff still glowed a short while, then it went out too. But it did not grow dark about Bridget—for suddenly a great light shone about her and filled the whole room. And in the midst of the light she beheld a figure, a man, to whom it seemed to her that she ought to know—where had she seen him? Yes, now she remembered—it was in Nidaros—in one of the niches in the huge façade of the Gothic cathedral—he stood there, a stone saint, robed like a bishop—but with both hands before him on his breast he held his bearded head with the mitre—it was Saint Dionysius, the councillor of Athens, disciple of Saint Paul, bishop in Paris, martyr under the Roman emperor Domitian. . . .

Then did Domicianus send a sheriff named Fescennius from Rome to France to have all Christians slain who would not worship idols. And Fescennius found Dionysius in Paris, where he preached, and had him seized and straitly bound with the others who were with him. And twelve soldiers were chosen to scourge Dionysius and his companions and afterwards to bind them with heavy fetters and throw them into the dungeon until the next day. But on the second day in the morning Fescennius had Dionysius roasted on hot coals above a grid-iron. But Dionysius sang in praise of God with a verse of the psalm that says: *Ignitum eloquium tuum vehementer, et servus tuus dilexit illud*, which is in our tongue: 'Burning is Thy word, O God, and thy servant hath delight in it!' Afterwards they threw Dionysius before ravening beasts that they might swallow him alive, but Dionysius made the sign of the Cross over the lion and immediately it became meek as a lamb. Then Dionysius was thrown into a burning furnace, but the fire died about him. Afterwards Dionysius was crucified and long did he suffer upon the cross, but he was taken down alive and locked into the dungeon with many other Christians. But when Dionysius said Mass the next morning and gave the Christians the body of the Lord, Our Lord Jesus Christ came and took Himself out of his hand and gave to him, saying: 'Take this, my dear friend, for thy reward is exceeding great in heaven.' Then he was taken before the heathen judge and beheaded with an axe before the temple of Mercury. And the body of Saint Dionysius rose up and seized his head with both hands and walked with a guard of angels and a heavenly light about him two miles from the place of the beheading, which is now called the mount of martyrs, to the city where he now rests, and which is called Sandinis [Saint Denis]. And so sweet a singing of angels was heard that many heathen became Christians for the sake of this wonder.(6)

Bridget had read about Saint Dionysius in his saga, she had seen his statue on the cathedral above the tomb of Saint Olav—now he was standing before her, shining with everlasting life and the bearded head with the mitre set upon his shoulders; his mouth opened and he spoke to her:

I am Dionysius, who came from Rome to this part of France to preach the word of God. And because thou hast always had a devotion to me, I have taken thee under my protection. And I say to thee that thou shalt come to Rome and to Jerusalem, and by thee God will be made known to the world. And I will always help thee and stand by thee, and this shall be a sign to thee, that thy husband shall not die of this sickness.

Then the light went out—the vision vanished. Bridget was sitting in the dark room by Ulf's sickbed. But she felt as if large gates had been thrown open for her to a new and greater world. She suddenly remembered that at one place in the wild Spanish mountains they had, on their homeward journey, passed by a stone on which there was inscribed only one word: HIERVSALEM. She knew what it meant, that here was the road to Rome, which was later called the road of palms, the road which via Rome led to Jerusalem and to the palms in Abraham's garden by the Jordan—those who came to it had the right to pluck a palm branch and to sew it on to their cloaks.

Bridget, too, was to wander along that road, as so many in Sweden had done before her—she too was to come home with palms from the groves of palm trees in Jericho, as she had now come home with Saint James' shells from Compostella. . . .

But what had Saint Dionysius meant when he said: 'I foretell thee that by thee God shall be made known in the world?' Was God still unknown then—thirteen hundred years after the birth of Our Lord?(7)

BOOK III

ALVASTRA

Longe a Deo est anima cui hæc miserabilis vita dulcis est.

BERNARD OF CLAIRVAUX

Far from God is the soul that finds this miserable life sweet.

Quarante ans est un âge terrible, c'est l'âge où l'on devient ce qu'on est.

CHARLES PÉGUY

ONE fine morning the pilgrims from the land of Saint James came back to Alvastra. Perhaps, as at their departure, little Bengt was standing beside one of the lay brothers at the monastery gate and watching the travellers come down from Heda church. Brother Svenung was not with them—he had remained behind in Citeaux to have an important matter settled: it was that affair about the Abbess in Gudhem, who had without leave moved with all her nuns up to Rackeby. . . . At the head of the train came Mother Brita, with short, rapid steps as usual—then came Father Ulf, riding, and the others of the company. But how pale Ulf looks—Bengt discovers it as the pilgrims draw nearer—'and how big you have grown, little Bengt,' say Father and Mother as with one mouth and kiss the boy. 'Are you going to stay here now a little while?' Bengt asks—he is playing with the Saint Ib shells on Mother Brita's cloak and bread bag. 'Shall I get such things, too, when I am big?' he asks. 'I will go to the land of Saint James, too, as you have done.' 'Yes and as your grandfather did, and his father and grandfather before him!'

But now Abbot Ragvald comes out and receives his guests. Together they go into the parlour—there is a great deal to tell. Bridget takes the lead, tells about Tarascon, about Saint Maximin and *La Sainte Baume*. 'But Avignon? But the Pope? Why did you pass his door?' Bridget evades the question, speaks instead of the terrible war that is devastating France. If only one could do something? There is one who might mediate, and only one, the Vicar of Christ (in 1340 as in 1940)—if only he would. . . .

The Abbot touches the silver cross on the chain over his white habit. 'If *He* would help!' he says. 'Without Him princes rule in vain.' Then he turns to Ulf who is sitting silent—he is tired after the journey, weak after his illness, needs his bed. 'For the present you are the guests of the monastery,' the Abbot declares and rises.

A day or two later Bridget travels on—alone—and this time on horseback. Ulf stays behind in the monastery with his son.(1)

Bridget rides towards the north followed by her retinue. She was at Mass this morning in the monastery church—very early, Ulf and Bengt were both still sleeping. Up in the chancel, behind the altar, the monks were kneeling, wrapped in their big, white cuculla—the tonsured heads were bowed deeply over the prayer desk when the sacred Host was lifted up—the shining crowns of their heads gleamed in the light from the lamp in the middle of the chancel. The lay brothers' places are on the benches in front of the altar; their habits brown almost like those of the Franciscans, but with a leather belt round their waists instead of a rope. There was one of them whom Bridget particularly noticed—old Brother Gerekinus—it was said of him that when the priest lifted up the sacred Host he saw in the priest's hands not the round white wafer, but a little living Child—the Child Jesus of Bethlehem. For Jesus *was* present there in the Host, truly, really, actually present—as He had been in the days of His flesh, when He walked on the roads in Galilee and in the streets of Jerusalem. . . .

The road led along the Omberg, it was the old Erik's Gata, which, continuing from Alvastra by way of Skenninge, Vreta, Linköping, Norrköping, Nyköping, Mariefred, Torshälla, led to Uppsala. Perhaps in Skenninge Bridget visited her old friend Master Petrus at the House of the Holy Spirit (there would be a great deal to relate and talk about). In Linköping she would surely look up Master Matthias—there would be still more to discuss with him. And at Botvidskyrka on Rogö in the Mälar she stopped to rest. Where the church now stood the pious priest Henrik had found the body of Saint Botvid—a bird flew alongside the ship on which the priest and his companions had set out to look for Botvid—the sailors wanted to catch the bird but Henrik forbade them to touch it, 'for I am hoping that it has been sent to us as a guide.' And so indeed it was, when the men wanted to row in another direction than the right one, the bird showed them the right way by its flight. 'But when they had at last reached the island where the body of Blessed Botvid rested, the bird flew away from the ship to the island and perched on a tree. There it settled and broke forth into singing so sweetly that the men forgot to row for sheer delight at melody so sweet.'(2)

Then it is related further how the body of the saint was found under the tree, and the bird, having performed its errand, 'steered its flight towards the stars and was never again seen by anyone.' But a spring gushed forth where the blood of the saint flowed out, 'and great fear and trembling came upon all the heathen in Sweden, most of all upon those in the halls of feasting, where they danced and fought with knives, for they found no healing unless they were baptized and called upon the name of Botvid.'(3)

Bridget, too, would surely call upon the name of Botvid there—

and behold, he came when she called! Like Dionysius in Arras, Botvid appears to her where she is praying earnestly and is 'almost beside herself,' and he speaks to her: 'I and other saints have gained for you the grace of God that you shall see and hear spiritual things and the spirit of God shall inflame your soul!'(4)

It was the same message as in Arras—an annunciation of a great vocation that was to be entrusted to her. As yet, though, everything was still like clouds on the horizon that are constantly changing in shape. It was a reality when Bridget and her retinue came riding home to Ulfåsa. The road led along Lakes Roxen and Boren—on the right, soon after you have left Linköping, you see the convent of Vreta —then there is the church in Klockrika, the church in Lönsås, the church in Fornåsa, all the thriving and pious white churches of East Gothland. At last, above the woods at the shore of Boren, the spire of the church at Ekebyborna comes into view—on the other side of the lake is the spire of the church at Kristberg—then comes the watch-tower at Ulfåsa—Bridget is at home. . . . The two big boys, Karl and Birger, come running out to meet their mother—'but where is Father?'

II

Perhaps this is the right place for the discussion of the visions and revelations of Saint Bridget. Is the psychiatrist right when speaking of hallucinations, of schizophrenia (the division of a personality), is the historian of literature right, who in revelation simply sees a literary form of which the writers of the Middle Ages availed themselves in order to give weight to their words? The *Divina Commedia* has of course never been considered to be anything but a poetical composition—it was only the old women in Ravenna who believed that the professor, a stranger whom they had seen in the streets, had such a brown face because he had been scorched on his wandering through the city full of lamentation. But what is to be said about writings like *Tundalus*, like the *Revelation of the Soul of Guido*? Tundalus is an Irish knight, a real child of the world like those whom Bridget describes in her revelations and whom she sees condemned to everlasting hell. 'Rarely and then only under necessity did he enter a church. He could never be troubled with poor people, but found pleasure in buffoons and jesters, and on these he delighted to bestow his gifts.'(1) He dies in the midst of a feast which he is giving for his friends—'when he stretched out his hand to take the first bite his hand stiffened so that he could not raise it to his mouth, and he cried aloud: "I am dying!" And immediately his body fell to the ground.' It is a scene like that in *Everyman*—'the servants come rushing in. The food is taken from the tables, the knights shout, the guests weep. The body is laid on the floor, all the bells ring, priests, monks and clerks come in, the whole city and the common people mourn and grieve at the sudden death of so noble a knight.' The death occurs on a Wednesday, but the funeral does not take place immediately, 'for a little warmth can still be felt about the heart. . . . And on the Saturday, as the clock struck ten, the spirit returned, and he opened his eyes.' Tundalus now desires to make his confession and to receive Holy Communion, and 'when he had received the most precious sacrament of the Body of God and tasted a little of the wine that is given after it, he lifted up his voice.'(2)

And now Tundalus describes his experiences during the three days beyond the grave. The soul wanted to return to its accustomed life on earth, to the dear and familiar joys, but could not enter into the body. And round about it there was a countless host of devils, roaring like lions and shouting and screaming to the soul, saying: 'Let us sing the song of death to this wretched soul, for it is the daughter of death, fuel for the unquenchable fire, the friend of darkness and the enemy of light.' And they gnashed their teeth at the soul and said:

Look, you miserable soul, here is the people you loved and chose, and with which you shall enter into hell and burn everlastingly like us, for you have loved all shameful deeds like us. Where are now all your display and your boasting, why are you not lying with your concubines, where is all your vain pleasure, your ornaments of roses, your retinue of servants, your great power to oppress others? Why are you not glancing at your mistresses, why are you not stepping lightly on their fair feet? Why do you not speak haughty words, and why do you not imagine false and treacherous counsels, as you did in your life of sinful luxury!

Yet on the brink of despair the sinful soul is saved. A 'brightest star' appears to him—it is his guardian angel who approaches him and greets him (in Latin): *Ave Thundale, qvid agis?* The soul—which has hitherto been sitting on its dead body—rises reverently and salutes the angel as his 'dearest father.' 'Yea,' says the messenger from the realm of light, 'now you call me dearest father, but aforetime you never thought of me! I was near to you from the hour when you were born, and enjoined upon you everything good, but' (and here the angel points to the most hideous devil) 'you preferred to listen to all the evil counsels which *that one* gave you—now you can receive your reward from him!'

But justice was tempered with mercy, and the angel conducts Tundalus, as Virgil conducts Dante through the realms of darkness to the coast of everlasting light. The road leads through a fearsome valley and across a narrow bridge (*Gjallarbru* in the Norse dream ballad, 'that bridge which no one can cross 'who pronounces false judgments.') Over the 'fearsome valley' there is as it were an iron lid, 'and on that lid countless souls were tormented, roasted and burnt, until there was nothing left of them but the fat that is left on a frying pan.' But this fat is sifted through the thick iron lid, 'like wax through linen' and rises again to the same torment. 'Here they are tormented who have killed parents, brothers or kinsfolk,' the angel explains.

Then the soul and his guide come to another valley—'it was quite black, so that the soul could not see the bottom, but he heard the sound of sulphur streams flowing down there, and the shouting and screaming of the miserable souls being tormented, and the stench of sulphur fumes and of the corrupted bodies burning surpassed all the torment the soul had yet seen.' And over the valley there was a bridge, from one mountain to another—a mile long, but not broader than a foot, and across that bridge no one could walk except holy men (here the bridge is not only *Gjallarbru*, it is also that keen and sharp sword-blade, which, according to the Mohammedan faith will be stretched on the day of judgment from Mount Moriah to the Mount of Olives, across the vale of Hinnom). 'From that bridge the soul saw countless souls fall down —only one came across, a priest who was a pilgrim.'(3)

Meanwhile *Tundalus* and *The Revelation of the Soul of Guido* are both literature—edifying literature, written 'that Christian men and women, and especially monks and nuns may take good heed of their lives and bear in mind that just as the smallest good deed is not without a reward in the kingdom of honour, so neither is the smallest sin left unrequited in the torment,' as Jöns Budde expresses it in his Epilogue to the translation of *Tundalus*. It is not Jöns Budde himself who has come back from the kingdom of death to relate what he has seen. Both Tundalus of Ireland and Guido of Italy have only a poetical existence—like the Knights of the Round Table in The Quest of the Holy Grail.

In the case of Bridget it is quite another matter. She is at home both in this world and the next. She writes about that which she has seen in her visions, heard in her revelations—about that which God will tell mankind 'now in the misery of this ageing world'—*in tot senescentis mundi miseriis*, as Alphonsus of Jaen says in his Preface to the eighth book of *Revelationes*.(4) It is the work of a life, the literary achievement of a generation—from the day when the widow of forty at Ulfåsa for the first time, in fear and trembling, seized her pen to write down on paper what the spirit spoke to her—to the trembling handwriting of an old woman on the last piece of parchment in Francesca Papazuri's house down yonder in Rome. The work of a life, the work of a human being—is it also the work of God?

From the very beginning Christianity is a religion of visions and revelations—modern man (and a modern Christian!) must come to terms with it. The New Testament leaves no room for doubt about it. After the death of Jesus on the Cross comes His Resurrection, and after the Resurrection the disciples during 'the forty days' meet their risen Lord and Master again and again. In Emmaus two disciples sit at table with Him, on the lake of Tiberias the Apostles see Him standing on the shore, and when they reach land He has prepared the meal which is so familiar to them—fish, roasted over a fire, with bread to eat with it. After the Ascension this communion between here and hereafter still continues. At the moment of his death Stephen sees heaven open and Jesus standing at the right hand of God—outside Damascus Saul is surrounded by a blinding light and hears a voice like thunder: 'I am Jesus whom thou persecutest!' Behind the thin veil of phenomena true reality is ever present, and the veil breaks in visions and revelations. With Stephen and Paul, a Francis of Assisi, a Catherine of Siena, a Jeanne d'Arc, in our own times a Don Bosco, see heaven open and hear 'unutterable words.' 'But whether they are in the body or out of the body they know not—God knoweth.' And what they speak or write in this state of ecstasy are not the words of man, but words *inspired* by God. The prophets of the Old Dispensation already said: 'So saith the Lord God of hosts'—they did not say: 'Thus do I say—Isaiah (or Jeremiah)!'

For everything which under a modern term can be called inspiration contains an element of ecstasy. The poet or artist who is working intensely feels himself raised above the demands of the body, quite absorbed in his work—and the work is done with ease, without hindrance or constraint, as if a power outside himself, another personality, were really doing the work. 'I am but an instrument, the Master plays upon me,' a Danish poet has said. Bridget calls herself 'God's fiddle,' the stringed instrument of God, only that He is not (as in Holger Drachmann) Apollo, but the God of Christianity.(5) But how much of the music does not depend on the building and sounding-board of the instrument, on the quality of the strings? Alien notes can intrude upon the heavenly ones, if the string is not of gold—or if the gold is alloyed with a less precious metal.

And this was so in the case of many of the revelations and visions in which Christianity, notably of the Middle Ages, was so rich. But the earthly instrument can also produce a fuller and more beautiful tone in its duet with a heavenly violinist. A very beautiful example of this is to be found in Henry Suso, the gentle mystic of the shores of Lake Constance. In many of his visions 'there can be no doubt that it is his own higher nature that breaks out in this way. . . . The purity of the heavenly visions, the sweetness of the songs, everything that impresses one so profoundly in his writings, what is it all but the hidden poet and singer in himself?'(6)

God speaks by the lips of Bridget, with Bridget's voice, in the language of Bridget. And that is not all. In a revelation dating from the last part of her life, Christ says to her: 'I am like a joiner who goes out into the woods and fetches wood, and brings it home, and from it carves a fair picture which he adorns with colours. . . . But his friends see the picture and find that it can be adorned with colours still more beautiful, and they adorn it with their colours and paint it over.' This parable is now explained as applying to Bridget's revelations. The heavenly wood-carver 'has felled a tree in the wood of God'—these are the words He has spoken to Bridget. But she has not always been able to understand or present what she feels—she therefore wrote down the words again and again, until she arrived at the right understanding. The Spirit of God sometimes leaves even His best friends to themselves, and they must therefore seek help from others—of late especially from the former Bishop of Jaen, the Spaniard Alphonsus. It fell to him (and Bridget's other ecclesiastical helpers) to complete the work, in putting the revelations into a literary form, adorning them and painting them. And in this task they must also see that nothing offends against Catholic orthodoxy.(7)

So that what we find in Bridget's revelations is a divine message—such as Bridget understands and reproduces it—and as her secretaries commit it to writing, 'according to the grace that is granted to them' and in the colours that seem to them (and to her) the most beautiful.

III

Ulf Gudmarsson is lying ill in the guest-house at Alvastra. At his bedside sits Bridget with little Bengt, now a boy of eight. Little by little

Ulf had resigned all his dignities and offices. In March 1343, he is still mentioned as law-man, later his duties are entrusted to a certain 'Lid-hinvard Holmgerson, upon whom the judicial duties of the law-man of Närike now rest.' And at the diet in November of the same year Ulf is once more present. But that is the end, henceforth he is only *Ulpho, frater ab extra.*(1) And some months after he was lying on a bed of pain, as once in Arras. But no rescuing angel appeared, it was death, irrevocable death. Again the priest was standing by his couch, probably Abbot Ragvald himself, attended by his monks—again the sick man was anointed with the oil of salvation, again the prayer of faith as-cended, but not to rescue. '*Proficiscere*, depart, Christian soul, from this world,' said the priest. 'We commend to Thee, O Lord, the soul of Thy servant Ulf. We beseech Thee to own this Thy servant, who has not been created by strange gods but by Thee, the true and living God. Let him come before Thy face, Lord, remember not his past mis-deeds nor any of those excesses he has fallen into through the violence of passion or corruption. Though he sinned yet he never denied Thee, Father, Son and Holy Spirit, but believed in Thee and faithfully wor-shipped Thee, the Creator of all things.'(2)

Ne memineris iniquitatem ejus antiquarum et ebrietatum. . . . Bridget heard the words and earnestly repeated them. Perhaps she laid a par-ticular stress on the word *ebrietatum*—indeed, might God forgive her dear Ulf all the long hours he had spent in sitting with good friends and carrying on useless and worldly talk, when the ale and wine went to his head. . . . Ulf would also be thinking of it—his lips were faintly moving: *In manus tuas, Domine*—'Into Thy hands . . .'

But why are the dying man's hands getting so restless now? Why is he fumbling with them over the sheet? ('Many dying people do that,' whispers the Abbot to Bridget.) There is something Ulf wants to do—what is it? Now Bridget sees it—he has taken the ring off his finger—the ring of the day when, so many years ago, they plighted their troth to each other. . . .

Ulf is now seeking Bridget's right hand. . . . With fingers already cold in death he takes hold of his wife's warm, living hand—and slowly puts the ring on her finger. . . . 'Little Brita, I have loved you so much!'

Then the dying man again folds his hands in prayer. The lips are slightly apart—not another word shall they speak, after this has been said. One of the monks takes a mirror and holds it to Ulf's mouth—the breath of life no longer bedews it. 'Sir Ulf Gudmarsson is dead,'

I

says Abbot Ragvald solemnly. A brother goes out quietly, and soon
after the tolling of the death knell can be heard from the church.
Another brother leads away the loudly weeping and inconsolable
Bengt. Bridget kneels motionless by her husband's body. Her face is
like white stone, but no tears well up from her eyes. Then she slowly
takes the ring off her finger and puts it back on the breast of the dead
man.(3)

IV

Bridget was at home again at Ulfåsa. The journey from Alvastra had
been severe, it was the Swedish *varga* winter at the end of February and
the beginning of March. Bengt was therefore left behind in Alvastra
with the white monks and the brown lay brothers. With the coming
of spring Bridget would return to him and to the grave in the right
nave of the monastery church. From Abbot Ragvald she had obtained
permission to live in a small house lying not far from the monastery.
This was a quite special favour—in 1193 the General Chapter of the
Cistercian Order had ordained that 'if women came into an abbey with
the abbot's leave he was to be immediately dismissed,' and in 1257
another General Chapter had severely censured 'the abuse which had
crept in in some places, that secular persons live near the churchyard of
the monastery or the infirmary.'(1) Nevertheless the mistress of Ulfåsa
had obtained permission—which, however, was by no means approved
by everyone in the monastery. There was, for instance, old Brother
Gerekinus, a very holy man. Never, during all the many years, had he
set foot outside the fences of the monastery, but day and night he spent
in prayer and had received the gift of grace that in spirit he nearly
always beheld the nine choirs of angels, cherubim, seraphim, thrones,
dominions, princedoms and powers, of archangels and angels. 'What
are all these new-fangled inventions?' the old man muttered in his beard.
'It is against the holy rule of our Order that a woman' (and a woman
only just over forty at that) 'should live here beside the monastery and
be allowed to go in and out of the church, which lay folk are otherwise
not allowed to do!' Brother Gerekinus, however, soon changed his
mind, for a voice from heaven spoke to him and said: 'This woman is
one of the friends of God, and she has come hither that on the Omberg
she may gather herbs from which healing may be prepared even for
those who live beyond the seas and in the uttermost parts of the earth.'
With his own eyes the old brother now received confirmation that the

voice he had heard spoke the truth—once, when Bridget was praying in the monastery church, he saw her lifted up by invisible forces into the air, and a flash, as of lightning, issuing from her mouth. And again the voice spoke to him:

> This is the woman who is to come from the country furthest to the north and who shall preach wisdom to countless nations. And this shall be a sign to you, that she shall foretell you the hour of your death, and you shall rejoice at her coming and at her words, for you shall be taken away that you may not see the tribulation with which the Lord will visit this house.(3)

Bridget herself had had her doubts concerning her installation in Alvastra. But had she not read in her Bible how David in a case of need satisfied his hunger with the showbread in the Temple, which no one but the priests dared touch? God is above all the rules of an Order, and the exception only confirms the rule. A voice from above strengthened Bridget in this thought. 'I permit you,' she heard the voice of God, 'to live for a time near that monastery, not because it is my will to abolish the rule or introduce new customs, but in order that the work I will entrust to you may thrive better in a holy place.'(4) Here the reading of the Holy Scriptures has taken the form of a revelation. And the words 'for a time' show that Bridget from the very beginning thought of the sojourn at Alvastra as something temporary—a preparation for the great mission which had already been foretold her in Arras, and by which God would make Himself known to the world.

But first Bridget had to set her house in order. Alphonsus of Jaen writes in the Preface to the eighth book of *Revelationes* about Bridget, that after the death of her husband 'she wished to live in poverty and imitate Christ who was poor and in some way to walk in His footsteps.' It is *the Franciscan ideal* she now wishes to realize. 'Of all her property she only kept what was necessary for herself to live simply and dress modestly. She divided everything else that she possessed among her children and the poor.'(5)

At Ulfåsa Karl stayed on—like his father he was law-man in Närike. A year before Ulf's death, that is in 1343, Karin had been married to Eggert (Edgard) von Kyren. Ingeborg was a nun in Riseberga, Bengt would probably become a monk in Alvastra. Cecilia, as yet only ten years old, was with the Dominican nuns in Skenninge, 'but had no vocation,' thought her brother Karl, who did, in fact, later take her out of the convent and get her married. Little by little the bonds were loosened which kept Bridget tied.

And so she was sitting alone by the fire one evening at Ulfåsa. Outside it was winter, the severe Swedish winter, round the farm buildings the wolves were roving and howling, they smelt the animals in the stables. But in the hall the fire was crackling in the open hearth. Bridget sat gazing into the flames.

And suddenly it seemed to her that she was not looking at an earthly fire. In the midst of the flames—was that not a human figure, a man?—*Ulf!* He had come once more, then, to Ulfåsa to bid her farewell! She called his name into the flames and asked: 'How are you faring?'

From the fire came the answer: 'The judgment upon me was severe, but now mercy is drawing near. In five things I have sinned most: first because I was too fond of Karl and found amusements in his pranks and did not check and chastise him in time.(6) Next there was a widow, that you know of, of whom I bought those things but forgot to pay her. But now she will come to-morrow to Ulfåsa; it is I who am sending her, and you will not fail to pay her what she asks, for she does not ask too much. The third is that I carelessly promised a certain man to stand by him in all his undertakings, and this promise made him bolder, so that he defied the king and the law. The fourth is that I exercised myself in throwing the lance and other knightly arts, more that I might show how well I could do it than because it was of any use. The fifth is that I was far too severe with him of whom you know, and who was doomed to exile—he *was* guilty but I could have shown him more mercy.'

No greater were the sins which Ulf Gudmarsson had to expiate in the cleansing fires of purgatory. 'Oh, happy soul!' Bridget had to exclaim, 'now tell me also what has been your greatest help to gain salvation, and what I can do that you may soon be released.'

'There were six things,' said the figure in the flames, 'that availed me most to my good. First, that I had all my life kept my Friday confession. The second that when I sat in judgment I never judged for gift or favour, but tried every cause with much care, and if I should have passed a wrong judgment I was ready to correct it. The third is—but you know that yourself—that I followed the counsel of my father confessor and had no communion with you from the time when the embryo that you carried had gained a living soul.(7) The fourth is that when I or my men were guests in other houses we did not burden the poor, and that I did not borrow money without knowing how I was to pay it back. The fifth is that on the way to the land of Saint James

I would not drink save at meals and thus I atoned for much idle talk and too much drinking. The sixth is that I chose honest men to pay my debts, and so that I would not get into more debt I gave back the king my office and my fief before I died. And now I have come well through the judgment and am sure of my soul being saved, only I do not know when. But as I have now been permitted to beg help for my soul, I beg of you that for a whole year you will have Masses said in honour of Our Lady, for the angels, for All Saints and before all things in honour of the Passion of Our Lord, for I hope that He will soon deliver me. And have an open hand for the poor; give away my drinking vessels and my horses, I have sinned enough with them! And if you can spare one or two of the cups for chalices, it will be for the good of my soul. But my estates you can with a quiet mind leave to our sons—my conscience does not reproach me with anything on that point—I have neither gained any of them unjustly nor kept or wished to keep what had come unjustly into our inheritance.'(8)

Bridget awakes from her vision, looks about her in the empty hall. The fire has burnt down—only embers are left—in the golden glow it seems as though buildings are forming, castles, palaces—for a moment they stand there, shining, then they fall apart and only ashes are left. . . . *Cuncta sublunaria cineres*, as I read once over the marble chimney piece in an old Italian palazzo—'everything under the moon is but ashes'— the thought might be Bridget's.

The lonely mistress of Ulfåsa carefully shovels the embers on the hearth together and covers them with ashes—one must 'have a care of light and fire.' From a ring in the wall she takes the burning deal stick, the feeble light of which is all that lights up the hall, and goes into her bedroom. There it stands, the large costly bed, which she had caused to be made in the days of her pride—and with which Jesus Himself had reproached her. In the days of pride—and in the days of carnality. . . . Here she had stood, washed and adorned, behind the curtain of the bed, waiting for Ulf, who had already lain down, to call her. . . . Here she had yielded herself to the pleasures of the flesh 'which are nothing but a foul smell' . . . but now it was all over and would never return— the hard sack of straw was for all time to be her resting-place.(9)

Bridget knelt down by the bed and said the prayer she had said so often while Ulf was living: 'My Lord Jesus Christ, Thou true God! Thou art my creator, my Redeemer and my Judge! I confess that I have sinned greatly against Thy commandments, but with Thy grace I will become better. Lord, I mourn before Thee over my heart, of how it is created! It seems to me as if there is in my heart a poison bladder, and through the heart there are two thorns, and round about it there is a membrane which presses and pains me sorely. My dear Lord and God, that which has now to be done is impossible to me without Thy help. I therefore pray for the sake of all the humility which Thou didst reveal to the world, tear away the membrane of pride about my heart and enfold it in its stead in the humility which Thou hast possessed from all eternity in Thy divinity. My Lord and God, I pray to Thee: because Thy Head was crowned with thorns, tear out the thorn that is in my heart and which is carnal love of my husband, of my children, my friends and kinsfolk and give me instead holy love of the good of the souls of my Christian kindred. I pray to Thee, dear Lord, because Thy blessed Hands and Feet were torn by the nails, tear out of my heart the thorn which is desire of the world, and place in its stead the desire to serve Thee. My dear Lord and God I pray for the sake of all Thy sacred heart didst suffer when Thou didst die upon the Cross, and all Thy limbs were cold, and Thy breast was pierced after death—tear asunder the bladder of poison in my heart.'(10)

Then, from Christ the Judge Bridget turns to His gentle Mother Mary, whom she was later so often to greet as 'Star of the Sea.' 'Blessed art thou, O Queen of Heaven, who dost not despise any sinner who with all his heart invokes thee. Hear me, though I am not worthy to open my lips to speak to thee. I know that if I am not supported by thy help I cannot guide myself, for my body is like an untamed foal, and if a bridle is not placed in its mouth it will run away to the pastures where it is wont to graze. And my will is like a bird which follows the fleeting thoughts and would fly far, far away. I therefore pray to thee, that a bridle may be laid upon my body, so that it can only fly thither where it can fulfil the will of thy Son. And lay a bond upon the bird of my will, that it may not fly further away than it pleases thy dear Son!'(11)

V

It was in the chapel at Ulfåsa—one morning in March. It was at the height of winter, the snow was lying in thick drifts, and more and more snow was falling—thickly and softly in large, white flakes. Pelle, the farm cat, sat on the steps and tried to catch these white butterflies—and when he had seized one he looked in surprise at his paw, where there was nothing but water.

It was winter—and it was the season of Lent—as it was that time so many years ago at Finsta. It was the time when it is written in the Holy Gospel that Jesus, going up to Jerusalem, took the twelve disciples apart, and said to them: 'Behold we go up to Jerusalem, and all that has been written of me shall be fulfilled. For I shall be delivered up to the chief priests and they shall condemn me to death, and shall deliver me to the Gentiles to be mocked and scourged, and to be slain by the death on the Cross.'

Bridget was alone in the chapel, again she said one of the prayers with which she had been inspired already while Ulf was still living, 'one day when she was uplifted in her soul and a prayer of exceeding beauty was given to her about the pains of Christ and His wounds, and afterwards she never forgot it but said it every single day.'(1)

The words of the prayer were these:

Glory be to Thee, O God, one God in three Persons, Father, Son and Holy Spirit.

Glory be to Thee, my Lord Jesus Christ, Son of God, who by the Father was sent into the body of a Virgin and dwelt and lived in her womb, until the hour came when Thou wast born of her and suffered Thyself to be tended by her hands, and to be wrapped in swaddling clothes and laid in a manger and to be nourished by her milk.

Glory be to Thee, my Lord Jesus Christ, who suffered Thyself to be circumcised and called Jesus, to let the kings come to Thee and to be presented in the Temple.

Glory be to Thee, my Lord Jesus Christ, who wast subject and obedient to Thy Mother and Thy Foster Father, and Thou didst advance in years and grace.

Glory be to Thee, my Lord Jesus Christ, who didst submit to be baptized by Thy servant John, and didst Thyself work many signs and preach, and revealed and proved that Thou art true God, and wouldst fulfil the words of the prophet and redeem the souls of men by Thy death.

Glory and praise be to Thee, my Lord Jesus Christ, who fasted so that Thou wast hungry, and wouldst be tempted by Thy enemy, whom Thou couldst drive away by a word.

Glory be to Thee, my Lord Jesus Christ, who didst foretell Thy death and at the Last Supper didst consecrate Thy precious Body and gave it to Thy disciples in remembrance of Thee and after that didst in humility wash their feet.

Glory be to Thee, my Lord Jesus Christ, who didst sweat blood, when Thou wast in an agony of death, but Thou didst not give up Thy work of redemption, but revealed Thy love for us, the work of Thy hands.

In her prayer Bridget walked in the *Via Crucis*, as so many pious souls have walked in it before and after her, and in which she was herself to walk one day in the streets of Jerusalem—from the *Ecce Homo* arch by the Roman fortress of Antonia to the Place of a Skull outside the walls of the town and to the empty Tomb. She heard the cries of the people: 'Give us Barabbas!' and the wild shriek: 'Crucify Him! Crucify Him!' She sees the Nazarene stumbling through the main street of the town with the cross on the thin Rabbi shoulders, she sees Him fastened naked to the terrible tree—the hands and feet are pulled into place with ropes, pierced with iron nails and then the strokes of the hammer are heard (those hammer strokes which are still, two thousand years later, re-echoing in the souls of men—and woe, if they did not re-echo any longer!). Bridget sees the whole of the terrible martyrdom of God, when He descended among men and would live among the sinister race of Adam—she stands with Mary at Golgotha and sings with her, no longer a *Magnificat*, but a *Stabat Mater*.

> Praised be Thou, my Lord Jesus Christ, because Thy face grew pale, when Thy blood flowed out, because Thine eyes closed, Thy tongue was parched with thirst, Thy mouth was moistened with so bitter a drink! Praised be Thou for the wounds of Thy head, for Thy hair and beard, for Thy whole scourgèd body! With Thy skin lacerated by the thorns, with veins and sinews cut asunder, thus didst Thou hang on the Cross waiting for death, O most beloved Lord!

On an earlier occasion I have raised the question whether Bridget was acquainted with the Sermon on the Mount. In the Middle Ages it was undoubtedly not—as it is to modern Christians, especially Protestants, and to the disciples of Gandhi and Tolstoi—the great programme preached by Christ, His message to mankind. In the Middle Ages—from Bernard of Clairvaux to Francis of Assisi, to Jacopone da Todi and to Matthias Grünewald—the Gospel was really identical with the story of the Passion. A prayer like Bridget's is the Scandinavian counterpart of Bernard's *Salve, caput cruentatum*, 'Hail, despisèd Head!' If Bridget's acquaintance with the Sermon on the Mount was but slight, she had penetrated all the more profoundly into the story of the Passion—the Saga of the Passion of God, of the Crucifixion of God, the Death of God. The death of *God*—for to Bridget there was no doubt of Biblical criticism or rationalism—that Human Being, that Man, that Jew thirty-three years old, who was crucified and suffered death under Pontius Pilate—was no other than *God Himself*.

And then it came to pass, there in the chapel in the lonely house on the shores of Lake Boren, that *God Himself* spoke to Bridget. Like Saint Paul, or like the Apostle Saint John on the island of Patmos, she was 'rapt in spirit.' Like the disciples on Mount Tabor she beheld 'a bright cloud, and a voice coming out of the cloud,' and the Voice said: 'Woman, hear me!' But Bridget feared greatly and thought it was a delusion; she sought the priest and made her confession to him, and the next morning she went to Holy Communion.(2)

Three times Bridget has this experience—and the Voice which comes from the bright cloud repeats the same words. But the third time Bridget sees One like a Son of Man in the cloud, and the Son of Man speaks to her:

> Fear not [He says], I am the Creator of all things, who speaks to thee. And I will speak to thee, not only for thy own sake, but for the salvation of others. And I say to thee, that thou shalt be My bride, and it shall be through thee that I will speak to the world. Thou shalt hear and see spiritual things, and My spirit shall come upon thee and remain with thee until death.

Bridget gazed overwhelmed into the light. Could this be possible? She, the widow of Ulf Gudmarsson, the mother of Karl and Birger and Märta and Karin and Gudmar and Bengt—she—Bridget, daughter of Birger of Finsta, the Bride of God? But she could not mistake the words—*thu skalt wara min brudh.* . . .

The Bride of God—yes, but—that was—that was the Blessed Virgin, that was Mary—*filia Dei Patris, mater Dei filii, sponsa Spiritus Sancti,* as Master Matthias had taught her—'the Daughter of God the Father, the Mother of God the Son, the Spouse of the Holy Spirit.' . . . Bridget was filled with dread. . . .

But He who spoke to her out of the light had read her thoughts. 'Go to Master Matthias,' were His words, 'he is learned in spiritual things, and is able to discern between the spirit that is from above and that which comes from him who in the dawn of time fell from heaven like lightning because of his pride.'

The Voice fell silent, the light was extinguished. Bridget was alone again in the chapel at Ulfåsa. But in her heart she felt as if something alive was moving, turning hither and thither—as once the embryo had moved in her womb. And then she knew that she had conceived again, that the old Bridget was dead, and that a new Bridget had come into being in her heart.(3)

VI

'Go to Master Matthias, he is learned in spiritual things and knows how to discern between the spirits.'

Bridget broke up from Ulfåsa—the last, final breaking-up—and in

Linköping she looked up her old faithful, spiritual guide. He had had to fight hard with the demons of doubt, 'the spiritual hosts of evil under heaven,' as Saint Paul says. When he sat alone in his study behind the grey stone mountain of the cathedral, and the memories of his youth in France came back to him—Paris and Orléans, the talks with learned doctors, with rabbis from Spain and muftis from the East, all the apostles of false doctrines and the disciples of heresy—they stood then like roaring lions about his soul to devour it.

We are the truth [was the cry that met him on every side], we who come from the high school of Averroes in Bagdad, we who have been to the courts of love of Provence, who are disciples of *la gaya scienza*, we, who robed in *il benito*, were tied to the stake, and the fire was lit around us, and we burned like howling and screaming torches, and our ashes were strewn to the four winds. But the wind spread them out over the world like seeds that came up everywhere where the soil was good, for the spirit cannot be burnt up, the spirit is immortal. . . .(1)

Bridget, then, was sitting as so often before, at the feet of Master Matthias and repeating the words that had come to her from heaven. 'I say to thee, that thou shalt be my bride and my messenger to mankind,(2) and thou shalt hear and see spiritual things, and my spirit shall remain with thee until death.' And she hands him a sheet of parchment on which she has written down, in her regular, continuous writing the first of those messages to the world which God will entrust her to bring. Master Matthias takes the sheet and reads:

The devil sinned in three ways—in pride, for I had created him beautiful; in covetousness, for he would not only be equal to Me, but be above Me; in concupiscence, for he found so much pleasure in My glory, that if it had been possible for him he would have slain me that he might reign in My stead. He was therefore thrust down from heaven and filled the whole world with these three sins, and ravished the whole race of mankind. Therefore it was that I took upon me the form of a man and came into the world, that by My humility I might destroy his pride, by My poverty drive out his covetousness, and I suffered the bitter pains of the Cross that I might uproot his evil concupiscence and by My heart's blood open heaven to man, who has been driven out of it by his sins, if only he will with all his might strive to help in this work.(3)

Master Matthias reads slowly and carefully. Now he looks up. 'Yes,' he says, 'this is the common teaching of our Holy Church. The devil is the prince of this world, and in Christ alone is there salvation for sinful mankind. Why do these words cause you trouble, Lady Bridget?'

But she signs to him that he must read on. And again his glance follows the written page. What he has read was only the Introduction, now comes the message proper which Bridget has to bring—she who was later to call herself 'a runner in the service of a great master.'(4) Christ speaks through the spirit of the bride to *the people of Sweden* and advances His complaint.

But now men and women are sinning in the kingdom of Sweden, and most of all those who are of the class of courtiers and knights, as the devil once sinned. For they take pride in their beautiful bodies which I have given them. They strive after the riches which I have not willed to give them. Thus they fall into hideous desires, that if it were possible they would rather kill me than renounce their concupiscence, and they pay no heed to the terrible judgment which will come upon them for their sins. The bodies of which they are so proud shall therefore be cut down by sword and lance and axe. The beautiful bodies in which they take pride shall be torn asunder and devoured by wild animals and birds. The possessions which they have gathered against my will shall be seized by others and they themselves shall hunger. Because of their abominable concupiscence they displease my Father so much that He will never find them worthy to behold His countenance. And because, if they could, they would fain kill Me, they shall be given into the hands of the devil and they shall be slain by him in hell with an everlasting death.

Master Matthias again pauses. Of course—the Lady Bridget has lived at court, has seen much of which he knows nothing, both at Finsta and at Ulfåsa. The son-in-law Sigvid Ribbing was a downright robber, neither was the eldest son, Karl, a good child of God. Plenty of faults can be found with King Magnus and Queen Blanca, as Master Matthias knows. But he knows, too, that there is such a thing as false zeal, and that it is pious people especially who can be too eager in judging others. He thinks of the Pharisee in the Temple and of that other Pharisee who condemned Mary Magdalene. And such zeal is not of God, for charity does not judge.(5)

Bridget sits motionless at the feet of Master Matthias, with downcast eyes, a little figure clad in mourning. He reads on, and a light seems to be dawning in his mind.

This judgment [says Christ], I would long since have caused to come upon the kingdom of Sweden, if I had not in the land certain friends who by their prayers move me to mercy. But the time will come when I will take these friends to myself, so that they may not see all the woe that shall come upon the kingdom. . . . And because the kings, the princes and the priests have not willed to know me, notwithstanding all the good I have done them, I will now gather the poor and the sick, children and those who are in sore distress to fill up the holes in my army, from which those others have fled.(6)

Master Matthias lets the parchment sink to his knee. The last words in what he has read are very obscure—what is meant by saying 'that God will gather the poor and the distressed to create from them a new army to fight in God's cause'—is it, perhaps, the Lady Bridget's intention to erect a new, large hospital, larger than that at Ulfåsa? Or does she intend to found a convent?

'I command you to look up,' says Master Matthias (for Bridget never directed her glance at anyone without the permission of her father confessor). But when she raises her pale face to look at him, he sees that the big blue eyes are full of tears. And with a voice broken by weeping she murmurs: 'The judgment which I have to proclaim is hard, but so long as there is a breath of life in a human being the way to heaven is open to him. Christ says that if the kingdom of Sweden will repent he will alter His judgment.'(7)

Master Matthias stands up, and Bridget does so too. 'Go back to Alvastra, my daughter, and stay there until you receive a message to go elsewhere.' When the old Bible theologian is again alone he murmurs to himself (in Latin, as he usually does from old habit): *Stupor et mirabilia audita sunt in terra nostra*—'Strange things have been heard in our land.' Then he goes to his reading desk and stands there, where his dear Bible is always lying open—it is the chapter about the prophet Elijah on Mount Horeb that Master Matthias is reading:

And he came thither unto a cave and lodged there in the night and behold, the word of the Lord came to him, and he said unto him, What doest thou here, Elijah? And he said, I have been very zealous for the Lord God of hosts: for the children of Israel have forsaken thy covenant; they have thrown down thine altars and slain thy prophets with the sword: and I, even I only, am left; and they seek my life to take it away. And the voice said, Go forth, and stand upon the mount before the face of the Lord. And behold, a great and strong wind rent the mountains and brake in pieces the rocks before the Lord, but the Lord was not in the wind: and after the wind an earthquake, but the Lord was not in the earthquake: and after the earthquake a fire: but the Lord was not in the fire: and after the fire a still small voice and therein was the Lord! *Sibilus lenitatis divinæ misericordiæ*—the still small voice of divine mercy.(8)

VII

Bridget rode towards the south—by the familiar road by way of Skenninge and Bjälbo. In Skenninge the usual visit to her old friend Petrus Olai in the House of the Holy Spirit, and in Bjälbo—well, there Ingrid Ylfva's body stands as before, walled up in the bell-tower, with a head which is never to be bowed to anyone. Then the Omberg raises its long wooded ridge beyond the waters of Lake Tåkern, where the swans breed in the rushes and reeds of the shore, and there is Svanshals, where Aunt Ramborg lived, and then there are the white churches in Rök and Heda, and at last, sheltering under the southward slopes of the Omberg, the low buildings of the monastery and the high Gothic church. Bridget is at home.

No great changes have taken place during her absence. Ulf's grave is in the right nave—covered by a common stone slab.(1) In the monastery school Bengt sat with bowed head over his Latin grammar, which Bridget had once herself studied in Niels Hermansson's time. He was looking poorly, tall and overgrown, not a boy any longer. Would he take the great step, she wondered? Old Brother Gerekinus, Bridget's special friend, had grown very frail, the time left to him could not be very long. Ragvald was still the Abbot, Thordo was the Prior, the Sub-prior was a certain Petrus Olai, a man of about Bridget's age (born in 1307). It may have been the likeness of names with Petrus Olai in Skenninge, but it is certain that Bridget quickly found a friend in him and made him her father confessor.

Before long he also became her secretary. She needed one. When the ecstasy came upon her she was often unable to write, she could only dictate (like Saint Catherine of Siena). At first a monk named Nicholas had helped her—through Bridget's intercession he was, as a reward, enabled to remain fasting the whole of Christmas night until the first Mass, which had hitherto been impossible for him.(2) For some reason or other, however, Bridget preferred Petrus Olai, but the Sub-prior was not particularly willing. In the Process of Canonization he writes about it himself:

> When the Lady Bridget began to live in Alvastra, in the year of the Lord 1346, it came to pass that God in His plenty inspired her with visions and divine revelations, not while she slept, but while she was awake and at prayer. Her body was as it was otherwise, but she was rapt and caught away from the senses of the body in ecstasy and spiritual contemplation.(3)

No doubt Petrus Olai was acquainted with several of these revelations of Bridget's, which Brother Nicholas had written down. He must at least have known what had happened to the previous Prior of the monastery, who had had the temerity, for gifts and favours, to inter a distinguished gentleman who had died excommunicated, in consecrated ground. Incidentally the same Prior had the bad habit of swearing odiously—always he had the devil's name on his lips. Bridget had been present at the interment, and she had hardly heard the Prior read the last words at the grave, when she was caught away in spirit and heard the following words:

The Prior has done as he pleased and has now held this funeral. But he shall know this, that the next one to be buried here from the church will be himself. For he has sinned against God the Father, who has forbidden respect of persons and honouring the rich more than the poor. For a little filthy lucre this Prior has shown honour to a man who ought not to be honoured, and has laid a miserable wretch to rest among the worthy. Next he has sinned against me, the Son of God, who have said: He who despises you, despises me. For he has honoured him, whom my Holy Church bade him hold in contempt. But there is still mercy for his soul, save that he must not any more utter the name of the Evil One.(4)

This message was given to the Prior, he came to himself, repented and died, as Bridget had foretold, only four days after.

One morning, then, Bridget came to Petrus Olai with a revelation concerning himself. Christ had spoken to His 'new bride' and these were the words: 'Tell the Sub-prior, Brother Petrus, from me that I am like a master whose sons are kept in severe confinement. He has sent out his messengers that they may set free the captives and warn others against falling into the hands of enemies in the belief that they are friends. Thus have I, God, many sons, namely the Christians who are kept in captivity by the devil, and lying in heavy chains. For love of them I send them my words, spoken by a woman. But do thou, Brother Petrus, give ear to this woman, and write down in Latin all the words that she will speak to thee in my name. And I say to thee, that for every letter thou shalt write thou shalt receive, not gold or silver, but a treasure which moth and rust cannot consume.'

Bridget departed. Petrus sat alone in his cell thinking about what she had told him. Was *he*, a little Sub-prior in a monastery far away in the north, in a country where the darkness is greatest, was he to be worthy to write down what Christ, what God Himself, would speak to the world through the mistress of Ulfåsa? Why had not the choice fallen upon another of her ecclesiastical friends—on Petrus Olai in Skenninge or, which would seem to have been the most reasonable, on the learned Master Matthias in Linköping, doctor of theology, with a master's degree in the Holy Scriptures? Petrus Olai went over to the church—he had to pray. It had often happened that the Prince of Darkness had spoken with the tongue of an angel. . . .

Petrus was alone in the church, it was towards evening, in an interval between two of the divine offices. And hardly had he thought out that doubt--'perhaps it is all only a delusion of the devil'—than he received such a mighty blow that he fell to the ground. There the other monks found him lying when they came into the choir to sing Compline. He was lifted up and carried into his cell, and lay there half the night—he could not move, could not speak, but his mind was awake. . . .

And then it occurred to him that perhaps he was being punished for having doubted the Lady Bridget. 'If this be so,' he said to himself, 'then forgive me, Lord. Behold, I am ready. I will obey and write down every word Thou sendest me through her.' At the same instant he was well and went without hesitation to Bridget's house and promised to be her helper. And Bridget said to him: 'Get boldly to work, and know for sure, that at the words you shall hear from my mouth the mighty shall be humbled and they who think they are wise shall be silenced.'(5)

At once Petrus began to write down and translate all the visions and revelations which the Lady Bridget told him—'but some were also written by Master Petrus who was her confessor when I was not present,' the Sub-prior concludes in 1380 his testimony of this great experience of his life. 'And at the command of Christ I followed her and was with her for thirty years until her death.'

As of Petrus Olai it could be said of all Bridget's friends, they were faithful to her until death, and beyond death.

VIII

Bridget's sojourn in Alvastra lasted only four years, from 1345 to 1349. During this short period she exercised an activity so comprehensive that it is hardly to be understood how it could be done in the time. Nothing is strange to her, nothing is indifferent, she feels everywhere that she has been called to speak and to intervene. The doubt of her vocation has been overcome, with Petrus Olai at her side she feels secure. Her great working day has dawned, and the field of her labours is the world. Sweden is to be born again spiritually, peace is to be made between the two great kingdoms in the West which are destroying each other in a senseless war. The Pope, the Vicegerent of Christ, must be brought back from the castle in Avignon, where she would not set foot, to Rome which mourns him like a widow. One day the Blessed Virgin appears to Bridget.

My Son calls thee His bride [says Mary], so I call thee my Son's wife. God and I have grown old in the hearts of men, no one cares about us. Like an old married couple who set their son's wife to busy herself and work in the houses and on the farms, so we will now through thee make known our will to our friends and to all the world.(1)

No one could understand this better than Bridget. The whole world was simply given her as a *new Ulfåsa*, infinitely bigger than the old, and there she was to work like the capable young daughter-in-law, the new mistress of the house, now that the old master and mistress had retired. But like an obedient daughter she was always to ask first—not to do anything of her own accord. Even if she would like to go on a pilgrimage she was to ask leave first.(2) She knew, too, how little she was *of herself*—once, when Master Matthias, after having become convinced of the genuineness of her revelations, had praised her from the pulpit, she was very unhappy and begged him not to do it again. 'I am only an ant in the sight of God,' said Bridget. 'If a great lord sends a poor messenger boy with a message to his friends, that is nothing to praise the boy for, is it?' When Master Matthias argued that the good example ought to be made known, and that Bridget's various virtues might serve as edification and imitation for others, the saint answered: 'My ship is still on the sea—do not praise me until I have reached port!'(3) Saint Francis of Assisi once gave a similar answer: 'Do not praise me—it may happen yet, that I go and bring children into the world!'

Charity begins at home—Bridget, too, knew this. The first thing to be done was to work in Sweden, for Sweden. For matters were in a bad way in Sweden. 'Thou must know,' said Christ one day to His bride, 'that three devils rule in this kingdom. One of them is fire and flame, he rules over gluttons and guzzlers; the second one is diabolical and rules over the soul; the third is more horrible than the others for it excites men to unnatural pleasures.'(4)

And Bridget had three demons at the very closest quarters here in Alvastra. That prior, who dared to bury an excommunicated person in consecrated ground—in him, too, three unclean spirits had held sway.

The first dwells in his secret members, the second in his heart, the third in his mouth. The first inspires him with unclean thoughts, which fill him more and more, as water fills a leaky ship. The second is like a worm in an apple, which devours the good will and leaves only desire for the things of this world, so that he dares to enter the church like a man without a heart, an apple without a core. And the third devil sits on his lips like an archer at an embrasure and shoots out sharp and bitter words that are like wounding arrows. Therefore shall he be condemned to the lake of burning pitch like a lecherous harlot, to have all his limbs cut asunder like a traitor and as he who has despised his Master to everlasting shame.(5)

Bridget, though, had also consoling experiences in Alvastra. Petrus Olai was her friend, though really under compulsion by that heavenly chastisement. She found other, entirely voluntary friends among the lay brothers, these humble workmen of the monastery, whose broad shoulders are the foundation of the whole building. The friend of my youth, the painter, Jan Verkade, now long since Father Willibrord, O.S.B., in Beuron, and I used to find amusement together at a passage in Father Sebastian von Oer's book, more well-intentioned than well written, *Ein Tag im Kloster*. The author describes how the monks are assembled in the refectory for the common meal—the Abbot, with the gold cross on his breast, at his special table, the guests (if there are any) at a place of honour in the middle of the room, and in front of the long tables on either side of the room the reverend fathers in their black habits, clean shaven and with the fine double ring of the tonsure through the carefully closely cropped hair. 'But who are these bearded figures in the background of the room?' asks the author, and gives himself an answer, which I *must* quote in German, or it will not have the right effect: *Das sind die lb. Laienbrüder*—'They are the dear lay brothers'—the adjective is not written out in full—they are not *die lieben Laienbrüder*, he cannot afford to spend so much space on them —they are only *lb*. . . .

But what monastery guest must not thank exactly these *lb*. lay brothers for perhaps the best hours during his stay? My thoughts turn to Mont' Alverno, to Fra Fortunato in the guest house and to Fra Achille who wandered about to the lonely farms up in the mountains, to which no doctor came, and brought medicine and comfort for the sick and some words of God into the bargain. My thoughts turn to Assisi, to Fra Eusebio in Santa Chiara and to Brother Wendelin down in San Damiano on their unwearying walk round church and cloister to say always the same to always other tourists: 'this is the body of Santa Chiara—the grave was found again in the year . . .'—'this is Santa Chiara's garden—here she grew only three kinds of flowers: roses, lilies, violets—the rose of love, the purity of the lily, the violet of humility'—'*Non clamor, sed amor* as you can read it here in the chancel —not many big words but quiet goodness pleases God' . . . the tourists go and come, year out and year in, mostly at Easter time and in October, to the feast of San Francesco, most of them include that as one of the many, numerous experiences of the journey—you do not neglect San Damiano, but neither do you neglect the latest Greta Garbo film— in a little while both will have been forgotten, 'Gone with the Wind.'

. . . But years after it may happen that a young Swedish painter sits at his soldier's post of guard somewhere out on the skerried coast thinking about his life, about his future. And suddenly the words from far away in Italy sound to him like a motto—'Yes, that is the point, *non clamor, sed amor*.' And he owes this motto, not to any priest and not to any professor, but to a *lieber Laienbrüder* down yonder in the little church in far distant Umbria. . . .

One of Bridget's friends in Alvastra was the janitor, Brother Petrus. For three years he had suffered from caries in one leg, so that marrow was always oozing out, but in his sufferings 'he was very sensible, and had nearly always Jesus in his heart and on his lips, and prayed: "Jesus, Thou most gracious God, have mercy upon me!"' When death was drawing near and the other brethren asked him which he would like best, to die or to get well, his answer was: 'I have only one wish: my God, who loves me and who has redeemed me. I have beheld Him in spirit, and so great a joy is this vision to me, that if I had to go on living in my sufferings a hundred years yet, I would gladly do it.' In this joy he fell asleep. But when Bridget was praying for his soul Christ appeared to her and said: 'Brother Petrus could neither read nor write, but from this day he is wiser than Solomon and owns the treasure which shall never be wasted and the crown he never shall lose.'

Bridget's first secretary, Brother Nicholas, had busied himself a great deal with the sick janitor, had visited him and nursed him. Christ therefore sent him the following message by Bridget: 'For the sake of the kindness he has shown Brother Petrus, I will give him strength for spiritual work, a blessed death and a waking up in the bosom of Lazarus.'(6)

In Alvastra as at Ulfåsa Bridget went often to visit the sick. There was one brother who had been bedridden for three years and who suffered also from great trouble of conscience. No confessor had been able to help him, but with her keen insight Bridget divined the cause of his distress—he had become a monk without really having had a vocation to the life, only for the sake of being provided for. (Such things happen! An Italian friend told me a spiteful story about a peasant who took his half-grown son round behind a monastery, to the kitchen side. It was not a fast day, and a delicious smell of frying came from the open window of the monastery kitchen. 'Can you smell it? That is how they live every day there!' says the peasant to his son. And they go round and knock at the main door. . . .) Never had the sick brother had the courage to confess that the whole of his monastic life from the first hour had been built upon a lie. When he went to confession he had only added that in this confession he included all sins, 'both those which he had confessed and those which he had not confessed, thinking that in this way he had put his account in order. Otherwise he was a good monk like the others, conscientious in fulfilling his duties, indeed being considered a holy man. Bridget spoke to him as no one else could have done, and in tears the sick man exclaimed: "Blessed be God, who has sent you to me—*now I will tell the truth!*" And he was given that peace which fills the soul when everything has been said, the peace that passes all understanding.'(7)

'He did not live long afterwards,' as it said with an almost constant phrase in the accounts of Bridget's care of souls in Alvastra. She usually comes 'in the last watch of the night.' In this way she also came to another monk whom by her prayers she had delivered from his doubts about the Sacrament of the Altar, and who had always been grieved because he had never been to the Holy Land—his superiors would not permit it. Then, on his deathbed, he was caught up in spirit and saw all the holy places exactly as those who had been there had seen them, and to whom he described what he had seen. *Et exultans in Domino defunctus est*—'and he fell asleep, rejoicing in the Lord.'(8) (Who dies in our times *exultans in Domino*? One dies, sitting in a bombing plane which has caught fire—and if, in the midst of the flames, one rejoices at anything, it is that one has made a direct hit and achieved irreparable destruction.)

Then one day near the end of July Bridget stood by the deathbed of her old friend Gerekinus. She had foretold him the day long before —had told him that God would take him away in good time, so that he should not see the disasters that were soon to come upon Sweden.(9) And now he was dying—perhaps he was waiting for a visit from the Blessed Virgin. It was she who had once helped him when he had been set to the work in the bakery, which he could not do at all. But fortunately there was a picture of Our Lady on the wall—to that Brother Gerekinus appealed, saying: 'Dearest Lady, you see that this kind of work does not suit me at all!' And Mary answered: 'No—just you go over to the church and pray, then I will attend to the baking—I was used to it at home in Nazareth.' And so it was done, only the other brothers working in the bakery did not know that it was the Blessed Virgin who had assumed the form of Brother Gerekinus.(10)

But this time the old Brother had another vision. It seemed to him that he saw a golden writing, and the writing was in three letters: P.O.T. He understood then what the writing meant, and with a loud voice he cried: 'Come, Brother Petrus, come, Brother Olaf, come, Brother Thordo.' And with this cry he passed away in the sleep of death. But on that day, a week after, Brother Petrus, Brother Olaf and Brother Thordo also lay buried in their graves.

IX

Now there was a Brother who found it hard to believe in the grace that had been bestowed upon the Lady Bridget. In a vision this Brother beheld a fire descending from heaven upon her. And as he wondered and thought it was an illusion, he fell asleep again and distinctly heard a voice saying twice: 'No one can keep this fire from going forth. For with my might I will send this fire out to the east and west, to the north and south, and many shall be enkindled by it.' But after this that Brother received faith in the visions and defended them and lived like a good religious of his Order until his death.(1)

Indeed to east and west, to north and south, was that message which Bridget had to bring to go forth. That was why the words which had been revealed to her had to be translated into Latin, the language of the world. She was not only sent out to the people of Sweden and Gothland—she had other sheep which were not of this fold, but which she had to gather together and lead to the one Shepherd.

First, however, a path must be cleared in the Swedish forest. Bridget knew it well—the dangerous forest land of Tiveden, the 'land above the forest' and the 'land south of the forest.' Robbers lay in ambush there; before the traveller ventured to go into the forest he made his confession and went to Holy Communion in the chapel of the Holy Cross by Husbyfjol (the present Borensberg) or to the Brothers of Saint Anthony in Ramundaboda. There is an old road called the 'Monks' Ladder' from Ramundaboda to Olshammer—Bridget would often walk along it.(2)

In a spiritual sense the world was such a dangerous ten mile forest road.

I came to the wild forest as a pilgrim [said Christ to Bridget]. But before I came forth there was a voice that cried: 'Now is the axe ready! He is come who shall clear the way and pull up by the roots all that withstands Him.' I laboured from the rising of the sun until its setting, that is, from when I became man until I died the death of the Cross for the redemption of mankind. I had to flee to the desert because of Herod who hated me, I was tempted by the devils, I was hated by men, I did many kinds of work, I ate and drank and fulfilled all the other needs of the body to show that I was really man. And afterwards when I cleared the path to heaven and pulled up the bushes that stood in the way, I was stung by sharp thorns, and rude iron nails wounded my hands and feet, and I was struck on my face and my teeth.

And thus I went forth in the wild forest of this world, in misery and labour and prepared the way in my blood and the sweat of my toil. This world must truly be called a wild forest, for all virtue was choked, and there was only one path that all men walked in, the damned to hell and the good to desolate darkness.(3) I came therefore like a pilgrim and laboured to prepare the way that leads to the kingdom of heaven. And when my friends saw how much travail it cost me, and yet how gladly I went to my labours, there were many who came with me for a long while.

But now that voice is gone that cried, 'Be ready!' And most have left my path, and bushes and thorns have again sprung up. The road to hell is open and wide, and the greater number walk in it. Yet *my* road is not quite forgotten—I have a few friends, but they fly like little birds timidly from bush to bush, and are ashamed to serve me. For now they all find their joy and happiness in following the path of the world.(4)

The world. Of the three enemies which a Christian has to fight against—the world, the flesh and the devil—Bridget believed the world to be the most dangerous. The flesh can be chastised and tamed, she knew this from rude experience; angels stood guard against demons, and the priest raises his hand in blessing, preparing holy water as a protection against the powers of evil. But worldliness is the direct denial of the words of the Apostle:

Love not the world, nor the things which are in the world. If any man love the world, the charity of the Father is not in him. For all that is in the world is the concupiscence of the flesh, and the concupiscence of the eyes, and the pride of life, which is not of the Father, but is of the world. And the world passeth away and the concupiscence thereof: but he that doeth the will of God, abideth for ever.

Bridget had no other message to bring.

Blessed are they who have not seen me and yet have believed [Christ says to her]. Likewise blessed are they who now believe my words and act according to them. Because my way has grown narrow, and the path of the world is wide and broad, I am now crying in the wilderness to my friends, that they must uproot the thorns and thistles and prepare the way for those who will walk in it. And like a mother who sees her erring son returning home and hastens to meet him with a light, so that he can see the path, and runs towards him with joy and embraces him, so shall I run to meet my friends and enlighten their hearts and souls with divine wisdom and take them into my arms in that kingdom where there is no heaven above and no earth below, and nothing but the face of God, and where there is no food or drink, but everlasting bliss. But the way to hell is open to the wicked, they shall enter into it and shall never come out. Honour and joy shall be taken from them and they shall be filled with everlasting misery and dishonour. Therefore do I now speak these words so that they who have turned away from me may return to me and know me, their Creator, whom they have forgotten.

'What do the proud ladies say in thy kingdom?' the Blessed Virgin one day asks Bridget. The proud Swedish ladies—'saddle of silver and bridle of gold, so do the Swedish ladies ride,' it is said in the old Danish folk-song (even then Sweden was already the land of greater wealth). 'I am myself one of them,' Bridget has to answer—there was blood of the Folkungs in her veins—'and I am ashamed to speak!' Besides, the Blessed Virgin knew, more than Bridget, about the grand ladies in Stockholm, and here and there in the castles of the knights. But the Blessed Virgin insists, she wants to have exactly Bridget's impressions. *Et ego respondi*, it is said in the text—'and so I answered' (one of the few occasions on which Bridget uses the pronoun of the first person— otherwise she is denoted as *sponsa*, 'the bride,' or as *illa quæ astat*, 'she who stands there,' that is to see and hear). And now she relates to her heavenly friend some of the experiences she has had at court and else- where in the kingdom. It is hopeless to speak to these ladies about humility and renunciation, about voluntary poverty. 'Fudge,' they say snappishly, 'our fathers and forefathers left us great possessions and gave us a good education—why should we not live like them? Our mothers sat in velvet and silk among the greatest ladies of the land, they had many servants and brought us up with honour—why should we not teach our daughters the same lesson, live in joy and be buried with great honour?'

This is the gospel of worldliness, concentrated in a few words—to have plenty of money, enjoy life, become honoured and esteemed and have a fine funeral—there is no room on the programme for what im- mediately precedes the funeral, and is necessary before it can be effected —what can a human being wish for more? What can a châtelaine of the fourteenth century—or the wife of a commercial magnate of the twentieth—desire more of existence? It is not a life in sin—there are no transgressions of the penal law in this manner of life. It is a com- fortable life—you have a husband of whom you are fond, and from whom you get a little dog, you have fine clothes, a home furnished in good style, you have friends and acquaintances to whose little dinners you like to go (and on the way home you do not leave either the friends or the dinner enough honour to cover a dessert plate). You go to the cinema, you have a wireless, play badminton, spend your holidays in your summer house, bathing, flirting, taking part in the great jazz dance of life . . . everybody lives like that, so why not we? And if we have to be judged so strictly, we are, after all, properly and honourably married, whether at a registry office or in a church. We are respectable people, Lady Bridget!

'Respectable married people,' says Saint Bridget. 'I think I will put a question mark after that.' It is true that marriage in the Catholic Church is one of the seven sacraments. It is true that where a man and woman come together in holy fear to beget children to the glory of God, Christ is present there as 'the third party in the contract.' But in how many marriages is that the case? Bridget had been present at many weddings, and her keen glance had seen through the young couple when, radiant with joy, they went up towards the altar. For what was the happiness they were seeking—what had brought them together? Bridget knew it and was not afraid of saying so. He is in love with the girl like a rat with a sweet cheese—or is it because she has money?—or is it sheer carnal desire, animal craving as in horses and bulls?—or is it in order to get into a great family and have children who will from their birth get a good place in the struggle of life for bread and honour? And the bride, oh well, she is proud of her fine clothes and is looking forward to the wedding feast, where she is to have the place of honour and wear the bridal crown, and there will be an abundance of food, ale and wine will not be wanting, and there will be singing and the playing of instruments, and shouting and carousals, and 'much joy and no sorrow, for this is the wedding feast.'

> But when such a couple step forth to my altar, and they are told there that they shall be one soul and one heart, my heart flees from them, for in their minds there is nothing but carnal desire. The fire that burns in them is not of God, for they covet only the flesh that the worms will devour. They come together without the blessing of God the Father, without the love of Christ, without the comfort of the Holy Ghost. And when they step forth to the bed my spirit recoils from them and the unclean spirit draws near to them, and such a couple shall never behold my face if they do not repent and are converted.

As a contrast Bridget now describes the couple who are after the heart of God. Not external beauty, but the inner being is here the object of love; there is no looking for riches, a needful subsistence suffices; scurrilous talk and ribald jests are not heard; there is no idle visiting of friends and relations, the friendship of God is sufficient; clothing and conduct are marked by humility; children are to come, but only because God wills it, and they are brought up to the glory of God. Such a couple shall be filled with the Holy Spirit and shall be ardent with the love of God, 'and I, the One and Triune, Father, Son and Holy Ghost, shall be with them, wherever they stand and sit or walk.'(6)

But of such wedded couples there are but few—Bridget's daughter Karin and her husband realized the ideal, nay, went beyond it. Of by far the most it is true what Mary said of the Swedish ladies—'whoever thinks and acts in this way goes on the straight path to hell.' Why? Because they have forgotten the Son of Mary.

He who was the creator of all things lived from His birth until His death in humility, and never did He wear the raiment of pride upon His shoulders. But the women of Sweden do not think of Him, they do not look upon His pale, bleeding countenance, they care not that He hung upon the Cross and had to hear Himself despised and mocked, nor have they any compassion with Him for the shameful death He took upon Himself. They have forgotten that He gave up His spirit in the place where thieves and robbers were punished, and that I, the being He loved most on the earth, was present and had to behold it.

'I was present—*and had to behold it.*' In these simple words we hear the whole bitter plaint of the Mother's heart—that *Planctus beatæ Mariæ Virginis,* which re-echoed under the vaults of the churches of the Middle Ages, but which were silenced by the Renaissance and the Reformation. 'Now there stood by the cross of Jesus, his mother' . . .

'But let him, who joins in the dance of this world, look upon my grief and mourn with me, for all the joy of the earth has passed away from me. And he shall give up the joys of the world.'(7)

X

Jerusalem and Babylon, in Saint Augustine the city of God and the city of the world, the two banners in Saint Ignatius of Loyola, always the same dualism (until the contrast of Louis Veuillot: *Parfum de Rome, Odeur de Paris*), always that 'Either-Or' which was Kierkegaard's cross. With Bridget it is *the two roads*—leading to *the two treasure chests.* The mistress of Ulfåsa was well acquainted with treasure chests, those big, heavy chests of hard oak, with iron bindings on the lid, and having in the skilfully ornamented scutcheons a big key of wrought iron, which added a good deal to the weight of the housewife's bunch of keys.

One of these two chests is full of burdens as heavy as lead and surrounded by a fence of barbed wire—but these burdens are only heavy to begin with, later on they become as light as a feather, and the barbed wire, on which one scratched oneself at first, till one bled, does not scratch any more. It is to this chest that all those come who deny themselves and disdain their own will, and this is the right road. When man sees the torment of Christ and His love, he will not do his own will and pleasure, but withstand them with all his power and strength, and will rather go on to higher things. And although this road is somewhat heavy at first, he who walks in it will be glad after a time, so that what seemed to him before unbearable, later on becomes the very easiest, and that it is indeed true that the yoke and service of God is good and sweet.(1)

In the other chest there are precious stones and gold and drink, that seems to be sweet and fragrant, but the gold is only dirt, and the sweet drink is poison. For death will come and the body grow feeble, and the marrow without strength, and the gold and precious stones of no more value than dirt. And the drink of the world seems to be pleasing, but when one has drunk it the heart grows heavy and the mind is befogged (Bridget had seen it so many times!), and the body is shrivelled up and withers like grass. Then, when death comes, that pleasing drink will be bitter like wormwood. But man is led by his own will and desire to this chest and these riches.

And now Bridget sees three people coming to the place where the road divides—and she sees a man standing at the parting of the ways and saying to them: 'This is the road which leads to life, and that is the road which leads to death.' And if any ask who that man is, He tells them His name: *Ego sum creator omnium*, 'I am the creator of all things.'(2) That this Creator exists—why, it is known from the reasonable order of the visible world. For there cannot be a man who does not understand that there must be a God, 'when he beholds how the earth bears fruit and heaven gives rain, and the trees grow green and blossom, and every animal remains in its shape, and the heavenly bodies serve mankind.' And if this proof of the existence of God—the old cosmological proof—is not enough, then the great signs of Christ and of all holy men must in any wise be a proof, 'for who can wake up the dead, give sight to the blind, drive out devils from men except God?'

This is what the man at the parting of the ways had to say to the three men. Bridget now heard the three men's answers.

The first says: 'In truth, it sounds reasonable, it may be right. Let us see whether it is so.' These are the people who have nothing against religion, who even find that it may be useful, or who go to church because that is the custom. 'Such people are in a very dangerous position,' says Christ to Bridget. 'They will not give up their own will, but will also do my will. They want to serve two masters—but when they are called away from here they will be rewarded by the master they have served best.'

The second of the three is the absolute unbeliever. 'It is all false what that man at the parting of the ways talks of, and his Bible is nothing but lies from beginning to end.' This is plain speaking, and the answer is just as unmistakable: 'He who speaks thus shall never see my face,' God declares.

The third is the man who, so to speak, believes, but does not live according to his belief. 'We know full well that God exists, but we do not care. It is all the same to us!' Such people enjoy the gifts of God—the sun shines upon them, the earth produces its crops to nourish them, they willingly accept everything from the hands of the Lord. This great ingratitude shall be punished with everlasting torment, for they have despised their benefactor.

They are but few who do not drink of the wine cups of the world. But these few are the dearly loved friends of God.(3)

Here the boundary line is made as distinct as possible—there the world and perdition, here the renunciation of the world and salvation. There is but one road—to separate oneself from the world, that world which is the enemy of God. 'I am like a king who has been banished from his country,' Christ complains to His bride. 'A robber is ruling in His place and the rightful King is entirely forgotten and neglected and despised. He is counted as less than a dog, nay, it seems as if none but He is despised. . . . It was my will to establish my kingdom in man, which was also my right, because I have both created man and redeemed him. But man has broken his oath of fealty to me, and has dishonoured his covenant of baptism, and violated and despised my laws. He loves to do his own will and despises my will. But he glorifies the devil, that evil robber, and to him he has given his faith. He is a robber, for he robs me of the souls whom I have ransomed with my blood.'(4)

Now how can this agree with the belief in the omnipotence of God? Bridget receives the answer at once—and the answer is characteristic of her and of the whole of her strictly law-bound conception of the eternal verities. The devil—the robber—is by no means the strongest—God has power to destroy him by a mere word of His mouth.

That which prevents God from doing so is the very *essence* of God—God is justice. . . . 'And though all the saints should ask it of me,' says Christ to Bridget, 'I would do nothing against justice.' And because man uses his free will to despise the commandments of God and desert to the devil's camp, it is just that man should taste the tyranny of the devil.

'I have created all things for the sake of man,' God makes complaint to His bride. 'I have made all things subject to him, but he loves everything but Me and hates nothing but Me.' Man prizes more the honour of the world, though it is but like the surf of the sea—or like the waves of Lake Vättern, when it thunders against the coast at Alvastra and is dissolved in foam—than in the everlasting glory and the blessedness that shall never end. God created the devil good—but now he can only be used as the headsman to whom the guilty souls are delivered up, so that they may receive their punishment. (Francis of Assisi also looked upon the demons as God's *gestaldi*, whose task it was to execute His judgments.) Yet God still hopes in man. 'Although I am now so despised,' He says, ' I am still so merciful, that whosoever humbles himself and prays for pardon, I will forgive him all his transgressions and deliver him from the evil robber. But he who persists in his contempt of me shall be visited by my justice, so that they who hear of it shall tremble, and they upon whom the punishment falls shall say: Woe to us that we were ever begotten and born. Woe to us that we have stirred up the Lord of the earth to wrath!'(5)

The thunders of Sinai can be heard again and the blast of the trumpet of the last day. And the demand which Bridget is to make of the world on behalf of God, is now directed to herself. 'Thou becamest Mine,' says Christ, 'when after the death of thy husband thou didst give up thyself into My hands and thoughtest of how thou couldst become poor for My sake. Thy heart was before as cold as steel, only a small spark of love for Me glowed in its depths. But when death robbed thee of thy mate whom thou didst love in the flesh above all other things, that little spark fell as though upon a mountain of brimstone and enkindled the mountain, for the honour and delight of the world may well be likened to a mountain of brimstone which burns with the blue flames of hell and has an evil smell.' For Bridget nought else of the world is now left but the wounds which have burnt her and the evil smell which has left a trace in her memory.

But thou, my bride, whom I have chosen, and with whom I speak in the spirit, love me with thy whole heart! Love me more than son or daughter, or parents or any other being, for I who created thee, of love for thee did not spare any of my members from torment. And rather than lose thy soul I would, if it were possible, submit myself to be crucified again. Make thy humility like unto mine, for I, the king of glory and of the angels, was robed in poor garments, had to stand stooping by the pillar when I was scourged, and with my own ears heard all the words of contempt and mockery. Prefer also my will to thine, for my Mother, who has the right to command thee [for Bridget is the wife of the Son], would, from first to last, nought but what I would. If thou doest this thy heart shall be in my heart and shall be enkindled with love of me; even as dry wood is easily enkindled by the fire, so shall thy soul be filled with me, and I shall be in thee, so that all temporal things shall become bitter to thee, and all the delights of the flesh like poison.

For the sake of God Bridget shall despise all things, not only honours and riches, but also children and kinsfolk; if she fears being despised she must bear in mind that God Himself has walked in the same path; if she finds it hard to bear the burden of work and the weight of sickness she must bear in mind that it is a terrible thing to burn in everlasting fire.

But Bridget must not be afraid—her Bridegroom will care for her, she shall not lack anything. It is seemly that a bride shall be clean and fittingly attired. This will be so, when Bridget always bears in mind her sins and bears the memory of the benefits of God as an ornament upon her breast.

Then comes the great promise of the Bridegroom to the bride—when she has worked faithfully in fellowship with Him she shall also rest with Him.

Thou shalt rest in the arms of my Godhead, where there is not carnal pleasure but the joy and delight of the spirit. The soul that rejoices thus, is filled within and without with joy and thinks and desires nought but the joy it has. Love also me alone, and thou shalt have all that is needful for thee, and thou shalt have it to overflowing. Is it not written, that the oil in the widow's cruse shall not fail, until the day that the Lord sendeth rain upon the earth, as the prophet said? I am the true prophet and if thou believest my words and dost act according to them oil and joy and rejoicing shall be without end for ever and ever.(6)

XI

Like softly played organ music heard from a church in the night, so the lament of Christ over the world resounds in Bridget's soul. Her joy is for ever gone—how can anyone smile and laugh who sees the distress of God (*Not Gottes*, the distress of God, is the name of a little old chapel outside Coblenz), that bitter death and torment, which is

now scarcely given a thought except by the few, and in England once
only meant a careless oath, of which the original meaning was forgotten by those who uttered it in the expression: 'Sdeath' or 'zounds,'
happily now fallen into disuse?

'My beehives in heaven are empty,' Bridget one day hears her
Bridegroom complain. The bees, that is the Christians, no longer
bring the honey of good deeds to the heavenly hives, but think only of
gathering the sweetness of this world for themselves. When God stoops
over the world and listens, a humming as of humble bees arises towards
Him. 'The humble bee flies low down along the earth and hums
hoarsely'—it has not the quivering humming of the bees as if it were
humming on a silver string—so does God hear the voice of the worldly
man: 'If only I can have my own way and do as I like, I do not care
what may happen later.' 'I will gladly let God keep His Paradise, if
only I may keep my Gurre.'* Neither the love of God—the suffering
and the Cross—nor the wrath of God—death and the judgment—makes
any impression upon them. And because this is so, God sees from His
heaven the souls sinking down into the yawning abyss of hell—like snow
falling upon the ground.(1)

But how can it have gone so far, after thirteen centuries of Christianity? Bridget might well ask. After twenty centuries of Christianity
we have still more reason to ask such a question! We have consoled
ourselves with the thought that at any rate Christianity had in earlier
times had a period of flourishing, during those ten centuries which
Léon Bloy called the millennium, from Augustine to Francis of Assisi,
that time when 'the churches knelt in their robes of stone' along the
banks of the rivers of France and Germany, in that Middle Age between ancient and modern heathendom, which the romantic style of
writing history called *les siècles de la Foi*. At least *so* much! But no—as
in our times so in the fourteenth century 'the world was de-christianized
more and more.'

Bridget asks—and Bridget gets an answer. 'From the beginning,'
Christ says to her, 'I chose three men, to whom I entrusted three tasks.
First I chose the priest; he was to proclaim my name with his voice and
reveal me through his acts. Next I chose the knight; he was to venture
his life for my friends and be ready to go into battle for me. Last I chose

* Gurre—pronounced *Goor-re* (the *e* as in the French *le*) was a castle belonging
to Valdemar, surnamed *Goor* (Another Day), King of Denmark from 1340
to 1375. The castle of Gurre, long since a ruin, was situated in the north of
Sealand.—[*Trans.*]

the peasant; he was to labour with his hands and feed the other two by his work.' These are the three estates of the Middle Ages, the clergy, the nobility and the peasants. All would be well in Christianity if each of them did their duty. But that is not the case—at any rate not in Sweden, which Bridget knows, and most likely not in other countries —she has suspected it on her travels. And now she hears the judgment of God on 'the three men' which means the three classes of society:

> The first, who is the priest, has become like a leper, and is dumb. For every-one who comes to him to find virtue and good morals flees away with a sad face and will not draw near to him because of the covetousness and pride that afflict him like a leprosy. He who goes to the priest finds that he does not say anything about the glory of God, but talks all the more loudly in praise of himself. How, then, shall the way to the sweetness of heaven be found when he, who ought to lead the way, is unable to do so, and how shall the way be known when he has become like one who is dumb, and cannot speak or cry?

So poor is the state of the priests. That of the soldiers is no better—in the first revelation of Master Matthias' Prologue the words of chastisement are already spoken against the nobility, the knights. 'He who ought to be a guard and protection for us has become fearful, and the deeds that he does are done to gain worldly honour.' And the peasant—he is like the beast that is called an ass, he stands with his head bent over the ground, he has but little faith and but a poor hope of gaining heaven, but his mouth is always open, and he is always eating. 'Oh, my friends,' are Christ's last words to Bridget, 'how shall the bottomless abyss be filled up, and how shall the heavenly hives be filled with honey?' The answer is heard: 'There shall come one whose voice shall be blithe like a song in the forest!'(2)

This voice—could it not be Bridget's? Even if it were, it would have to be so loud that it could be heard not only by the little grey peasant ploughing the field, not only by the knights in their castles and by the priest in his house, and by the bishop in his palace, but the voice was to be heard by the kings and emperors of the earth, whether they were called Magnus or Philip or Edward—nay, it was to reach even him who sits by the banks of the Rhône but who should be sitting in the Chair of Peter in Rome.

XII

For the popes had resided in Rome since 1305. As French historians have called to our attention, it was by no means anything new in the annals of the Church that the successor of Saint Peter resided outside

Rome. During the half century preceding the 'Babylonian captivity' the Eternal City did not see much of the Vicegerent of Christ upon earth. Innocent IV (1243–54) is elected pope at Anagni, is only a short time in Rome, flees from Frederick II in 1244 to Lyons, where he remains for seven years, and when at last he returns to Italy, it is to take up his residence in peaceful Umbria, afterwards in Naples, where he dies. Alexander IV (1254–61) stays by preference in Anagni and dies in Viterbo. The Frenchman, Urban IV (1261–4), resides in Viterbo, Montefiascone and Orvieto; these three towns also shelter within their walls his successor and fellow-countryman, Clement IV (1265–8), who, moreover, lives in Perugia and Assisi. Not one of the documents issued by this Pope is dated Rome. Gregory X (1271–6) leaves Rome to go by way of Orvieto to Lyons, where he convokes the fourteenth Œcumenical Council. When, finally, he again thinks of returning, the journey proceeds slowly, not to say reluctantly—with sojourns on the way at Orange, Beaucaire, Valence, Vienne; passing through Switzerland he crosses the Alps and dies in Arezzo. John XXI (1276–7) is elected, lives and dies in Viterbo; his successor, Nicholas III (1277–80) lives partly in the Lateran, partly in Sutri and Viterbo. Martin IV (1281–5) is elected in Viterbo 'where the Roman court resided' and spends his pontificate in Tuscany and Umbria. Honorius IV (1285–7) is one of the few popes of that time who liked Rome; he sets up his house at Santa Sabina on the Aventine, and in the summer is out at Tivoli. Nicholas IV (1288–92) is elected in Rome but prefers to stay in Rieti and Orvieto. Bonifacius VIII (1294–1303) often resorts from Rome to Anagni, Orvieto and Velletri. His successor Benedict XI (1303–4) stays, after his election, only five months in Rome, and has the intention of transferring the Papal Chair to Lombardy but dies in Perugia.

It was therefore absolutely nothing new that happened when Bertrand de Got, Archbishop of Bordeaux, after having been elected Pope (5 June 1304) and having taken the name of Clement V, had himself crowned in Lyons and established his residence in Gascony, or when his successor, John XXII (the Frenchman Jacques d'Euse), settled in 1309 in Avignon, where he had formerly been bishop.*

* The following were the Popes during whose reigns Bridget lived: Bonifacius VIII, *d.* 11/10 1303, Benedict XI (Benedictine, canonized among the saints of the Order) 22/10 1303–7/7 1304; Clement V 5/6 1304–14/4 1314; John XXII 7/8 1316–4/12 1334; Benedict XII (Cistercian) 20/12 1334–25/4 1342; Clement VI (Benedictine) 7/7 1342–6/12 1352; Innocent VI 18/12 1352–12/9 1362; Urban V (Benedictine, canonized among the saints of the Order) 28/9 1362–19/12 1370; Gregory XI 30/12 1370 [–27/3 1378].

It is under Clement V that the name of *Babylon* is flung for the first time against the exiled Roman Church. In the thirteenth century the great prophet of Calabria, Joachim de Fiore, had proclaimed his prophecies of the coming of a new age—after the ages of the Father and the Son the time of the Holy Spirit was now approaching. The reformation of the Church—the hope of all saints and the dream of all heretics —was drawing near, there was to be a judgment on all those who in the name of Christ had gathered for themselves unrighteous mammon. These visions and thoughts found a fertile soil in the extreme wing of the Franciscans, in Ubertino of Casale (1239 to about 1325), Pietro Giovanni Olivi and Angelo Clareno (1260-1337). For a zealous son of Saint Francis there might be good reason to feel scandalized when he saw the Vicegerent of Christ leaving over a million florins! During his ten years' pontificate Clement V had scraped together this pretty penny; from his testament it appeared that he had lent the French and English kings 320,000 florins with which to make war upon each other; and he bestowed 200,000 guilders upon his sorrowing relatives. Even a man like Petrarch, who was not really an enemy of filthy lucre, lifted up his voice and branded in immortal verse

the greedy Babylon, whose bags are so full of the wrath of God and are so stuffed with vices that they are near to bursting. The gods it has chosen for itself are Venus and Bacchus. Everlasting life is regarded as a fable, nothing is true, nothing is holy. Neither faith nor charity is found there, neither religion nor virtue. A source of grief, a school of error, a temple of heresy, is that false, guilt-laden Babylon, which once was called Rome. . . . In chaste and humble poverty wert thou founded. Now, oh! shameless harlot, thou liftest up thy horns against those who founded thee. . . . And such a city has become the capital of the world!(1)

For it was that. People of the twentieth century can only with difficulty form any idea of what the Pope meant when Bridget was living. And that applies perhaps exactly to the popes in Avignon more than to any earlier ones. Neither the Roman Emperor *deutscher Nation* nor the French King could compare with the Vicegerent of Christ in prestige and wealth. No worldly potentate kept so great a court as he.

First and above all the Pope had to provide for his family—nepotism is not an Italian invention, at any rate Italians have not taken out a patent for it. So there were the Pope's brothers, nephews, sisters-in-law and nieces—they had the privilege of being allowed to wear fur of ermine, and to dress in silk and adorn themselves with gold and silver. Next came the servants—first the Pope's guard of knights and esquires, all of noble family. In the year 1320 the esquires alone numbered a little over one hundred. The doors and gates to the great papal palace on the *Rocher des Doms* had to be guarded—there were various grades of porters—of the first, second and third class—and there were night watchmen, seventy-two in number, who were at the same time warders of the papal prison.

Then came the Pope's ecclesiastical household. His private chapel was served by about thirty chaplains, whose duty is was to get up when the bell rang 'Master Jacob, Master Jacob,' to sing Matins and to say Mass at dawn. Besides these there was another group of chaplains, more closely attached to the Pope—the difference, however, consisted mainly in their receiving a salary of 200 florins a year, the former only 100.(2)

And now come the papal chamberlains—they appeared at audiences and on other solemn occasions, laid the Pope's stole about his neck, attired him in his cope, placed the mitre on his head, in processions carried the two ostrich feather *flabelli* beside the *sedia gestatoria*.

The kitchen regions were very populous. At the head was the *administrator coquinæ*; it was he who ruled over the expenses for the kitchen. Under him he had a staff of clerks who kept the accounts. There were two kitchens, a large and a small one—in the small one only soup was made (Italian *brodo*, the cooks there being for that reason called *brodarii*). At the table bread, salt, cheese, fruit was brought round, no one helped himself; before the wine was poured out for the Pope and his household it was tasted by a specially trusted servant. The papal cellar contained the best wines that Burgundy and Provence, that Spain and the Rhineland could supply.

The papal stables, too, were well stocked, both with horses and mules—and over them presided three marshals (as is well known all later brilliant marshals under Napoleon and other rulers are descended from those *marahscalhs* who groomed a royal or imperial mare) and under the command of the marshals there was a crowd of footmen, muleteers, donkey drivers and coachmen. A special position was occupied by the so-called *cursores*, the papal postmen, whose business it was to bring out papal letters, to fasten papal bulls on the church doors, to summon ecclesiastics who had offended to report themselves in Avignon. There was still quite a number of other officials—one who had to look after the porcelain, another who had charge of the weapons, a third of the wax for the papal seal—and finally an army of bell-ringers (it was not without reason that Avignon was called *la ville sonnante*), of

I

water-carriers, of washerwomen. Nor were a physician and a barber lacking—and from the time of Benedict XII there was an *elemosiniero segreto*, an ecclesiastic who in the Pope's name distributed alms without saying from whom they came, according to the saying: 'Let not thy right hand know what thy left hand doeth.'

Altogether the papal household consisted of from three to four hundred persons. In addition there was the staff of the ecclesiastical administration, with all its various officials—first and foremost the *Camera Apostolica*, the Ministry of Finance. To this belonged the Papal Mint, where five ecclesiastics and twenty-eight workmen found employment. Next came the Papal Chancery, with a number of different offices (in one of them seventy to eighty clerks had the work of making fair copies of the papal bulls, in another the bulls were endorsed with the papal seal, in a third they were entered on the register). When the various papal courts, with their officials and clerks, are added to these, it is easy to understand that large incomes would be required.

For it was not apostolic poverty that prevailed in Avignon. Not only the Pope, but also the cardinals kept house on a large scale. 'Instead of apostles walking barefoot, you now see oriental satraps, riding on horses with cloth of gold saddle-cloths, bridles of gold and soon they are probably also shod with gold. If you did not know better you would think they were kings of Persia to whom you would have to kneel, and whom you would not dare to approach with empty hands.'(3) Nor was this done—the testaments of the right reverend gentlemen bear witness to this. Cardinal Hugues Roger, son of a small landowner of the French nobility, left at his death in 1364, 150,000 golden guilders in ready money, outstanding claims amounting to 6,000 guilders, while the executors receive 20,000 for their trouble— altogether one million modern francs in gold. Some part of the wealth of the cardinals comes from the gifts bestowed by every pope after his election upon those members of the Sacred College who voted for him in the Conclave—thus John XXII bestows upon his electors the round sum of 100,000 guilders, Clement VI gives about the same, Innocent VI 75,000; Urban V is more sparing, he distributes only a small *pourboire* (40,000 florins). In addition to these perquisites there were the fixed incomes—first and foremost half of the regular income of the Holy See, that is, the ordinary and extraordinary church tax, the incomes of the Italian Papal State, and of the county of Avignon. Also of the rent which all bishops had to pay at the obligatory visit to the Pope every five years, and of which the cardinals had the right to receive half (*ad limina*, 'at the threshold,' namely to the churches of Saint Peter and Saint Paul in Rome—the visit was now paid in Avignon). Finally the Pope, on the anniversary of his election, always distributed magnificent gifts to the members of the College—victuals, wines and also hard cash.

Life in Avignon was not cheap—most goods had to be imported. Gold brocade for the priestly vestments came from Venice, nay, even from distant Damascus. Silk, which was also continually required, was imported from Tuscany, cloth from Flanders, as well as linen. Every spring and every autumn new clothes were served out to the whole of the papal household, a winter coat cost from eight to twelve guilders. In the big palace on the *Rocher des Doms* the cold is severe on winter days when the bleak north wind sweeps down through the valley of the Rhône. It is no wonder that the papal account books contain records of large purchases of furs—Clement VI on a single occasion bought one thousand ermine skins for a fur cloak, a fur cap, fur hood, and even nine birettas (the square headdress worn by priests).

Nor were the expenses for food and drink slight, and good appetites were the rule. On 22 November 1324, John XXII gave a wedding dinner for his niece, Jeanne de Trian, who was married to Sieur Guichard of Poitiers. The food consumed on this occasion consisted of 4,000 loaves, 8¾ oxen, 55¼ sheep, 8 pigs, 4 wild boar, 200 capons, 630 fowls, 580 partridges, 270 rabbits, 37 ducks, 50 pigeons, 4 heron, 2 pheasants, 2 peacocks, 292 small birds of various kinds, 3,000 eggs, but only 2,000 pounds of apples, pears and other fruit. With this was drunk 11 hogsheads of wine. We do not know how many were present on this occasion. But we know what it cost the same Pope to give for another of his nieces, Bernarde de Via—70,000 gold francs. It would probably be one of these nieces, or daughters of one of them, who stuck a gold pin into Saint Catherine of Siena's foot to test whether her ecstasy was genuine!

The cardinals, too, gave great feasts. An Italian traveller was present when his fellow-countryman, Annibale Ceccano, had invited Clement VI to dinner.

There were nine 'courses' (*vivande*), and each course included three dishes—altogether twenty-seven dishes [he relates]. One 'course,' for instance, consisted of a gigantic piece of pastry work in the shape of a fortress, in which there was a roasted deer, a roasted wild boar, besides hares and rabbits. . . . After the fifth course a fountain was brought in, and it had a column with five pipes from which ran five kinds of wine. The border of the fountain was garnished with various kinds of game birds. Between the seventh and eighth courses there was a tournament, and after the meal was ended there was a concert. Two trees were brought in as dessert, one was of silver and was garnished with apples, pears, figs, peaches and grapes, the other was green like a bay tree, and among the leaves hung candied fruits of various colours. The wines had come from Provence, from La Rochelle, from Beaune and from the Rhine. When it was all quite finished the master of the kitchen and his thirty cooks performed a comic dance, after which the Pope retired to his rooms, while we remained sitting over the wine.(4)

This was not the end of the feast, however. Later in the day, probably after a thoroughly good after-dinner nap, the distinguished gentlemen would put in an appearance in order to be present at what Englishmen call a practical joke. Across the river Sorgue, a tributary of the Rhône, and to this day, as in Bridget's time, working a number of water-mills, while the thunder of its rushing waters fills the quiet streets in the lower town, a temporary wooden bridge had been built to give admission to the place where the festivities of the afternoon were to take place. A gay company of burghers, priests and monks walked out on the bridge, but got an unexpected ducking when the bridge, as planned beforehand, burst and they all fell into the river, to the great amusement of the Pope and the cardinals who were looking on from the cardinals' palace up above.

Of course life was not all made up of feasting and gaiety at the court in Avignon. But that was what strangers had noticed most. And there was a great number of persons who had business with the Pope, or who looked for work and profit in the new Rome. Not only all kinds of fortune hunters, thieves, usurers, girls of undoubted amiability; not only Italian bankers and money-changers; not only Tuscan painters and French architects swarm in a motley crowd through the narrow (and ill-smelling) streets, but also envoys from distant potentates—such as, in 1338, an embassy of sixteen men from the Khan over all Tartars; in 1340, after the Battle of Tarifa, a train of Spanish knights with twenty-four banners which had been taken from the Moors. And the kings came themselves. Under Urban V the King of Cyprus could shake hands with King Valdemar of Denmark.* In 1365 the Emperor Charles himself made his entry into the papal city. All these exalted personages were received with the *nopces et festins* due to them

---

* In the papal account books for the years 1363-4, there is an entry of the expenses for the reception of Valdemar Atterdag in Pont-de-Sorgue (the suburb on the tributary river Sorgue), and a bill is entered which the landlord in Pont-de-Sorgue had sent, in 25/2/1364, to the Exchequer. In this bill are mentioned bread, wine, oil, figs, spices, onions consumed by the king and his retinue, besides oats for the horses and fuel for the kitchens and the king's rooms. (Ellen Jørgensen: *Valdemar Atterdag*, Copenhagen, 1911, Note 2.)

and made return with princely gifts (like Sigurd Jorsalafar in Mykla-gaard).* Then, when the Norseman was again sitting at home by the evening fire in the gloomy raftered room and hearing the snow sweeping round the corners, and the storm howling like the wolves, he would tell his hearers about the sunny country far away in the south, about the city where the bells were always ringing for some feast, and where the Vicegerent of Christ lived every day in splendour and happiness.

Bridget's own father had been in Avignon, on his way to Compostella, during his great pilgrim journey in 1321-2. It was John XXII who was Pope then—the same who by the bull of 12 November 1323 (*cum inter nonnullos*) had condemned the doctrine of the Franciscan Spirituals about the poverty of Christ, for which four Franciscans in 1318, of the above-named strict school, had to suffer death at the stake in Marseilles.

When Bridget twenty years later herself made the pilgrimage to Compostella she passed Avignon by. She knew about it, she did not need to see what was going on in the new Babylon.

Yet there was something into which neither Birger Persson nor other guests and visitors to Avignon obtained an insight—the generous care for the poor and the well-organized nursing of the sick in the papal city. It was actually John XXII who created in Avignon that large institute for the support of the needy in the town, called, by a name borrowed from Italy, *la Pagnotta*. (A *pagnotta* is a large round loaf of the size of a Swedish 'limpa'—the classic alms loaf which can be seen on frescoes being distributed to the poor at some convent door or other.)

This *Pagnotta* was managed by three Cistercians, who undertook the necessary purchases of bread, wine, meat and vegetables, while they also ordered clothes and footwear for the poor from the tailors and shoemakers of the town. Accurate accounts were kept, and at the end of every quarter the bill was handed in at the papal exchequer. Soup was served daily, and a meat course, or on days of fasting fish and eggs. There must have been much poverty in Avignon, for on an average 30,000 loaves were distributed per week.

The papal budget of charity, however, was far from exhausted with *la Pagnotta*. Medicine was provided for the hospitals, young girls without a dowry were given one so that they could marry instead of joining the ranks of the loose-living women of the city. Students who could

* Sigurd Jorsalafar. King of Norway 1108-30. At the head of a pilgrimage to the Holy Land in 1107. Hence the surname Jorsalafar—the 'farer' to Jerusalem. Myklegaard—the old Scandinavian name for Constantinople.

not afford to study were given scholarships. Altogether the alms of John XXII amounted to the not inconsiderable sum of 16,000 florins per annum (according to French currency before 1914, 1,200,000 francs).

The popes in Avignon were not sparing either in the sums they spent on art. Urban V paid for the beautiful ciborium in the Lateran with the sum of 30,000 florins. It was he too who caused Giovanni Bartolo to execute the two silver and jewelled busts of the Apostles Peter and Paul for the same altar.(5)

But Bridget knew nothing about all this. Nor would she perhaps have approved of so much money being spent on art.

XIII

God commanded Saint Bridget to go to the king. She said that she did not know what she had to say. God gave her this answer: 'Open thy mouth and it shall be given thee what thou shalt speak.' And immediately when she came to the king, it was given to her from God, not only what she was to say to the king, but many other things that were to come to pass.(1)

Bridget had not let King Magnus out of her sight. Through her brother Israel she was well informed, and her two eldest sons, Karl and Birger, were frequently at court. She was needed there—'empty joy and shouting voices'(2) were the watchword of the day, but out in the country the tax-gatherers went about laying intolerable burdens upon God's poor, common people. The three devils kept on ruling the land —pride, gluttony, lechery. Bridget had given a warning and she had received an answer: 'God is merciful, He will do us no harm. Our time here on earth is so short, let us have a merry day!' Sweden is the most northerly land in the world, 'and the cold north wind is always blowing,' one needs a strong drink to cheer one up. Bridget knows that there are other countries in the world, sunny countries where the wind blows softly from the south, and she had tried to tell her fellow-countrymen about them. But that only irritates them, and they beg her to leave them in peace with that sort of talk. 'We are quite content with things as they are,' they say. 'We have our pleasures which you shall not take away from us. We like sitting a long time at table and having a jolly time over a good tankard of beer or a beaker of wine, and we have no inclination whatever to give up what we have, which is something we can take and handle, to go on a journey into that country of sunshine on which you waste so much talk, and which perhaps does not exist at all!'(3)

But everything comes to an end, and so does God's patience. Ere long Christ will have come over the Swedes, 'with sword and lance and great wrath.' In vain do they take comfort in His longanimity, and, like merry students, sing *Gaudeamus igitur*. 'I shall come upon them,' the Lord repeats, 'and shall spare none! I shall plough the field with my wrath and pull up bushes and trees by the roots. Where a thousand people lived barely a hundred will be left. The houses shall stand desolate and the birds of prey shall come and find meat for their claws,' says the Lord.

As always with Bridget there is a great silence after the storm and the earthquake, and in that silence the quiet whispering of God's mercy can be heard. 'If the people of Sweden will begin to clothe themselves humbly and modestly, be moderate in their drinking and curb their sensual desires, my wrath shall be softened.' This message is meant also for the king, 'he must apply himself to justice, he must not impose taxes without the consent of the people, and not deprive any of their lawful possessions. He must listen to the counsel given him by God-fearing people, and in atonement of all wherein he has transgressed he must build a convent in honour of the Mother of God in the place which will be shown him.'(4)

A new convent, nay, even a new Order; that was the task that had been laid upon Bridget to counterbalance the worldliness and to atone for the sins which her keen eye had seen in Sweden. She would create a new army of warriors of God and gather them to fight under a banner as red as blood and bearing on the front a picture of the Cross of Christ, but on the back Mary, the gentle Mother of Mercy, was to stand with open arms. She knew already where the convent was to stand. Was there not, a little to the north of the Omberg, by an inlet of Lake Vättern, a property called *Vadstena*, belonging to King Magnus?

What *was* Vadstena then in the middle of the fourteenth century? Bridget, returning home from Ulfshammer across Lake Vättern, must more than once have landed at this natural harbour, which is formed by the Nässjö land on the west and the little peninsula of Tycklingen to-wards the north-east.* In this cove or inlet people had settled already in the Bronze Age. The name Vadstena is formed of the words *vatn*, water, and *stenar*, stones, that is, the stones by the water—perhaps the stones for a mole like the present pier, perhaps (and more likely) a stone-built house by the water (in Antwerp the old castle is still called *het Steen*,

---

* Between Vadstena and Motala is shown a spring, 'the spring of Saint Bridget,' from which she is said to have drunk on the way home to Ulfåsa.

the stone). The first time Vadstena is mentioned is in a document of 27 October 1268, and it is concerned with an estate of this name belonging to Birger Jarl's brother Elavus. The house then belonged to the Folkungs—in 1306 Duke Erik, Birger Persson's friend, lived there and in 1313 King Birger Magnusson. The estate was not under the Crown but was 'independent property,' *i.e.* a family estate. There was a fairly large area of land attached to the property, so that, practically, it comprised the whole of that country on which lies the present Vadstena as well as the suburb of Kung's Starby. There was also land belonging to the estate beyond this area, besides water-mills in the adjacent Motala stream. As was natural, smaller houses were gradually built around the stone house, most of them probably of wood; artisans settled there, tradesmen came from the neighbouring Skenninge and did business with the people of the manor house and the inhabitants of the town. At the manor house there was a chapel, but soon it became too small, and in 1346 the town got its parish church, probably situated in the same place as the later Saint Per's church (of which only the tower is left now—'the red tower').(5)

Vadstena belonged to King Magnus—yet he was not the real owner. Behind his small figure rose another, bigger, more sinister—Bridget had seen him in her waking visions. 'It seemed to the bride of God that she was in a large room where much people had come together. And the Virgin Mary said to the King of Heaven: 'My Son, give me this place, Vadstena.' Then the devil stepped forward at once and said:

This place is mine, and I own it by a threefold right. In the first place it was I who inspired those who founded the town with the will to build here, and those who were the masters of the work of building were my servants and friends. Secondly, this is the place of wrath and punishment, and my friends here chastised without mercy those who were subject to them and therefore the lord of punishment and the chief of wrath is the master here and the place is mine. Thirdly, this town has been mine for many years, and where my will is obeyed there is my seat.(6)

From these words it is clear that there had been a stronghold at Vadstena, and that in this stronghold there was a prison, where the lords of the castle punished their subjects with unjustly severe punishments. Possibly there had also been a place of execution, or that in heathen times sacrifices were made to idols.(7)

But this is only one of the reasons why a convent had to be built in this place to atone here for the sins committed against justice and charity. Sin has stuck to the very stones of which the castle is built—

for it has been erected with the mammon of injustice. Again and again
Bridget returns to this thought—there is no blessing on goods which
one does not possess justly. Then Mary said to the Judge: 'My Son, I
ask thee, what is justice, then? If someone had robbed another of his
goods and money, and besides compelled that other to work for him,
and to build a house with the money which had been stolen from him,
whose, then, is that house?' Our Lord answered: 'My dear Mother, in
what is right he owns the house who owned the money and did the
work.' Bridget's social programme is here distinctly evident—the real
owner of the castle is not the harsh lord of the stronghold who has acquired money by laying heavy taxes upon his peasants and afterwards
set his bailiffs to whip them into dragging stones to the castle and to build
it with walls and towers and dungeons, where they can be made to sit
if they will not do as they are told. The building belongs to the workers,
the lord of the castle is only a usurper. 'My Son,' says Mary, 'if a headsman took possession of another man's house and the owner of the
house came, what then?' The answer is, of course: the headsman must
yield place to the master of the house—and to the mistress of the house,
the gentle Mother of mercy.

Afterwards the Judge said to Mary: 'This city shall be thine! Because the tears
and weeping of unhappy people have been heard in this city, and their
misery has cried to me and has come to my ears, so shall now the voice of
them who praise thee ascend to heaven from here. And because this place has
been one of punishment and a burden to the land, so shall my friends now
gather here and cry to me for mercy and compassion and for the forgiveness
of sins for the living and the dead, and they shall pray for the welfare of this
kingdom.'

In Bridget's sensitive mind, however, a doubt arises—can she with
a good conscience spend on that convent, which she intends to establish, so large and handsome a house as the castle? Does it not go against
monastic humility? Her doubt is dissolved by a reference to a place in
the Bible—after the fall of Jericho the Israelites took possession of the
city and set up their homes in it. 'For as much as this house has been
built with the sweat of poor people to satisfy the vanity of the rich,
it is right that my friends shall live in it and use all that was only too
abundant and served to encourage pride, in humility and serving for
their use.' The finished buildings could therefore remain standing and
only 'be altered for what was most needed.'(8)

But even for such alterations money was required. Bridget's own
fortune did not suffice, besides she had had to give her children their

inheritance. Before his death Ulf had bestowed a couple of farms on Vadstena, but that was not enough. Bridget would therefore suggest to King Magnus that he should levy a tax with a view to the establishment of the convent. Abraham was willing to offer up his son, the noble lords and good men of Sweden must also prove themselves ready to make a sacrifice. Christ says to Bridget: 'It is my wish that the lords of the land shall build a convent to the honour of my Mother, that the sins of the realm may be lessened. I ask the poor people too to share in the work and to show their good will as far as they are able.' The coin of the tax must be carefully reckoned according to the means of each. For an unmarried man or woman who is of age one penny each. Married couples to pay jointly two pennies. If they have children who are over sixteen, then for each of them likewise one penny. Priests, religious and all who are in service to others are exempt from tax. And this tax shall be called Our Lady's Penny.

XIV

Bridget then set out to go to Stockholm and her road took her by way of Vadstena. She went to the king's house—as was her custom. And there it came to pass 'when she was caught away in spirit and in ardent prayer had a spiritual vision' that a man and woman of the very fairest statures appeared to her, and a voice said to her: 'These two, whom thou seest, are Jesus Christ and His Mother, who now appear to thee as they were when they lived in the world. But what their bodies are now in heaven it is impossible for thee to see.'(1)

Bridget was a great admirer of physical beauty. She would have only handsome people about her as servants—later she bitterly reproached herself for this. We have from her hand a prayer to the Blessed Virgin which is a hymn of praise to Mary's beauty. The hair of the Blessed Virgin was bright like sunshine, her face more purely white than the moon, her eyebrows like sunbeams, her eyes gleam like stars, her lips are red like the rose, her throat, her back, her arms are lily white, her breast is like the purest gold. This external beauty, however, is a symbol to Bridget, it is a sign of the purity of the soul—beauty therefore fills the ugly with horror over their own hideousness and forces them with repentance into imploring eternal beauty for mercy. 'I have wasted my life in countless sins, I have loved my friends and kinsfolk with carnal love, with the desires of my life I have injured my soul! But now I repent of all of it with all my heart and gladly will I do better and never again do what is evil—help me to do this, thou pure Virgin Mary!'(2)

It was the *beauty of God* that was revealed to Bridget during the ecstasy in the castle of Vadstena. Mary stood there, radiant like the sunbeams, looking at Bridget with eyes like stars. And Christ opened His mouth and spoke—between the red lips Bridget saw His white teeth. 'Glory be to Thy teeth,' she prayed silently, 'for every time Thou dost chew with them what Thou hast Thyself created.'(3)

Christ spoke to Bridget about the new vineyard that he would plant. First He spoke about the vineyards He had planted in earlier times—'for a long time they produced the very best wine.' But it happened as in the Gospel—the *Enemy* came and planted his wild vine, and it grew up and choked the good vines. The master of the vineyard sent out his servants to attend to the vine, and they came back and said that the fence was broken down and the gate unhinged, that the watchmen were asleep and had allowed thieves to force their way in, that moles had been at work so that the roots of the vines were exposed, that the vine plants had withered and the grapes were blown down and were lying on the ground and getting trampled underfoot. The destruction was great—so great that the only thing that could be done was to leave the old vine to its fate and to start afresh. 'There is no one who arouses my wrath like man,' Christ exclaims. 'They are the only creatures who will never do as I tell them! All other beings obey my commandments.'

Yet He will try once more to plant a vineyard in the poorly fertile soil of the earth, that did best in growing thorns and thistles.

I will plant a new vineyard, from which many other vineyards shall arise. I will send watchmen who will not sleep in the night. I will fence it round with my love. I will let the roots of the vine, which are the good will of men, grow so deep that the devil, that mole, cannot scratch them up. I will let the vine plants flourish and make their grapes sweet. And thou, Bridget, shalt plant the young vines, but have a care to put them in a good place, sheltered from cold and frost, protected from heat and drought. Stand firm therefore and love Me with all Thy heart. Flee from pride, live in humility. Guard thy lips and all thy members in My honour. Obey My commandments. Examine thy conscience every hour whether thou hast sinned and in how much. If thou fallest then rise again immediately. Take no heed of the honour or friendship of the world—thou hast Me. And if thou givest Me all thy love, everything that is of the world will become bitter like wormwood to thee.(4)

Now follows the rule of the Order that Bridget has to found.

From the very first it is established that the Order is founded 'to the glory of my most beloved Mother,' and that it is to be chiefly an *Order for women—per mulieres primum et principaliter*, that is, first and above all an *order of nuns*. It is therefore reasonable that it is to be governed by an Abbess—'from whom all necessary things, such as the habit of the Order, bed and bedclothes and implements for work are to be expected,' and without whose advice and permission nothing may be done.

It is not quite correct that the religious house founded by Bridget is sometimes called a double convent, and the Order which issued from Vadstena as a double Order. Such Orders, which comprised both monks and nuns, had existed in the first Christian centuries in the East and on the Iberian peninsula. About the year 600 they were also to be found in Ireland, and under the influence of the Irish missionaries double convents were founded in Gaul (Poitiers) and South Germany (Merano, Chiemsee with Herren-Chiemsee and Frauen-Chiemsee, though they are on two islands separated by the lake). In the twelfth century double convents arose in England too (the Gilbertines) and in France (the Fontevraldenses).

The last-mentioned Order was founded in 1116 by Robert d'Arbrissel. Both the men's and the women's convents were subject to an Abbess, who in her turn represented the Blessed Virgin, to whom the whole Order was dedicated. It is possible that on her journey through France, Bridget may have heard some mention of the Fontevraldenses, and even have visited one of their convents.(5) But the mistress of Ulfåsa needed no model when she founded her Order. In her marriage it was *she* who had been the ruler and guide, and that had only been for the good of Ulf. And in heaven—why, was not Mary the Queen there, and was not her Son glad and willing to do what His Mother wished? 'Blessed be thou, dearest Mother, Lady of the angels, Queen over all spirits,' Bridget had heard Christ say to the Blessed Virgin in a revelation.

> Thy words are sweet to me like the best wine, they enter into my heart and make me rejoice, as thy milk once entered into my body and gave strength to all my members. Blessed be thy mouth and thy lips, whence words of mercy go forth to miserable sinners. It is said and sung of thee that thou art the Mother of mercy, and in truth thou art. Thou seest the need of mankind and thou bendest my heart to compassion. Ask me therefore for what thou wilt and thou shalt not ask in vain.(6)

As in heaven, so also upon earth. A convent for nuns alone is unthinkable—women can pray, they can sing, they can perform the seven bodily and the seven spiritual acts of mercy. But women cannot say Mass, cannot hear confessions, or administer the other sacraments. Priests are necessary ; next to the convent for nuns there must be not a monastery but a *house for priests*. And just as the nuns must have lay sisters to help them, so these priests must have lay brothers. An ecclesiastic who has to attend to the duties of his vocation, to study and write, cannot bake bread or brew ale. (Incidentally Bridget reserved, in her rule, the brewing of ale for the nuns. Was she afraid that the monks would make the ale too strong?) From personal experience Bridget knew what support a man could give—she needed only to think of Master Matthias or now, in Alvastra, of Petrus Olai. A convent of nuns had to have a priest's house (*curia*, not *monasterium* or *conventus*) beside it—but in both houses it was to be the Abbess who had the last word. This was to be clearly expressed, even purely in the matter of numbers—in every convent of her Order the nuns were to be in the majority.

In the first days of her conversion Bridget had already seen in spirit what such a convent should be like. Everything was to bear the mark of purity, the house is not to be built as the proud children of the world build. The first wall is to be called justice, the second wisdom, the third God's protection, the fourth God's mercy and *i thesse wägghin är nadhinna portir*—(the 'portal of the forgiveness of sins,' by which the pilgrims were to enter when the *blåa kyrkan* was at length standing complete by the shore of Lake Vättern). The roof of the house was to be moderately high, the windows clear, so that God's sun could shine into it, and there was to be a strong wall between men and women. 'For even though I be able to preserve and protect from sin without a wall, yet for the sake of the world and for fear of the craft of the devil, I will that there shall be a wall between both houses,' saith the Lord.(7)

This wall comes back in the twelfth chapter of the final rule of the Order.

There shall be sixty sisters and not more. They shall have priests who shall say Mass daily and recite the Divine Office daily, according to the custom of the cathedral in that country in which the convents of this Order are established. And they shall be completely separated from the sisters and have a house for themselves in which they shall live, and from the house they shall have an entrance to the church. And they shall have a lower choir, but the choir of the sisters shall be up above under the roof, yet so that they can see the Mass and hear the Divine Office. These priests shall be thirteen in number, after the thirteen apostles, of which the thirteenth, Saint Paul, did not work least. Then there shall be four deacons, who can be priests if they so desire it. They signify the four great doctors of the Church: Ambrose, Augustine, Jerome and Gregory. Next there shall be eight laymen who shall serve the priests. Altogether that makes sixty sisters, thirteen priests, four deacons and eight servants, which is the same number as the thirteen apostles and the seventy-two disciples.(8)

The rule contains in all twenty-eight chapters, which all bear witness to Bridget's careful and accurate mind as a housewife, and to her great conscientiousness. There are instructions as to what the bed is to be like, and how the nuns are to be dressed. There must be straw in the bottom of the bedstead and there must be two woollen blankets to cover them with and two pillows but no sheet. The sisters must not suffer from cold, they are to have two undergowns of white wadmal (two—because of washing), a gown of coarse wadmal and a cloak or mantle, the sleeves of which 'must not reach further than to the end of the middle finger.' The sisters must also have an outer garment, and in the winter it must be lined with fur, though not of an expensive kind, but of lamb or sheep. They are also allowed to line the garment with skin. But the outer garment must not come nearer to the ground than twice the distance between the thumb and the little finger when the hand is stretched out, and it shall be fastened across the breast 'with a wooden button.' It is Franciscan poverty; similar regulations can be found with the Poor Clares.

The headdress has always been that domain in which the various foundresses of Orders have had the greatest possibility of creating something characteristic. One need only think of the big white wings of the Sisters of Saint Vincent, of the goffered frills about the face of other Sisters—like the feathery wreath of a barn owl. For her Sisters Bridget created one of the most beautiful coifs in existence. First there is to be 'a wimple, going up under the chin and about the cheeks so that the face is partly hidden. And the end of the wimple shall be fastened at the back of the neck with a pin. Over this wimple is to be laid a veil of black linen; it shall be fastened with three pins, so that it cannot fall off: one in front, two beside the ears.' This does not yet deviate from the rather general type of a nun's veil. But here comes the new part—and the new is an expression of Bridget's fundamental religious feeling, that which she expressed in the words *Amor meus crucifixus est*, 'He whom I love has been crucified.' The description continues: 'Then a crown of white linen is placed over the veil, and on this crown are to be sewn five small pieces of red cloth like five drops of blood—the first over the forehead, the second at the back of the neck, the third and fourth by the ears, the fifth on the top of the head, as on the middle of a cross. . . . This crown shall be worn by widows as well as virgins'— and it signifies the Crown of Thorns of Christ.(9)

Now comes a number of regulations which do not differ very much from the content of the rules of other Orders. There are regulations for the order of divine service; a Mass in honour of Mary must be said daily, and the *Salve Regina*, taken over from the Cistercians, has to be sung. There are rules for monastic silence, for fasting, for contact with the outside world. No layfolk or ecclesiastics can be allowed to enter the convent of nuns. Talks with layfolk only on Sundays and on the great feasts of saints, and then through the grille in the parlour. This grille may be opened, however, when the visitor is a relative or they are 'decorous friends.' 'But if a Sister does not open the grille, a greater reward is promised her in heaven.'

Then come regulations about fasting, which lasts nearly all the year round. Strict fast is kept from Advent till Christmas and during the long fast which has already begun on Quadragesima Sunday. From Friday after Ascension until Whitsuntide and from the 14th until the 29th September the fast is milder (fish and milk dishes), likewise from All Saints till Advent. Fasting on bread and water has to be kept on the vigils of the four feasts of Mary (2/2, 25/3, 15/8, 8/9), of the feasts of the Apostles, of the feast of John the Baptist, of Saint John the Evangelist *ante portam latinam* (6 May), of Saint Michael, All Saints and the feast of Corpus Christi. The sick and the old, however, are exempted from this rather severe régime, like those who are of delicate health and who would not be able to do their work if they had to fast. Bridget is always reasonable and considerate when it is a question of making demands upon others. On herself alone does she make the 'ideal demand' (like Ibsen's Brand). On herself—and then on her whom she thinks must be soul of her soul, because she is flesh of her flesh, blood of her blood—Karin. . . .

Like the good housewife she is, Bridget has even fixed the bill of fare for a week in the intervals, short as they are, between the times of fasting. And in this she is not particular—there is meat on the table on Sunday, Monday, Tuesday and Thursday, on the three other days of the week fish and milk dishes. Christ Himself says to Bridget: 'It is good to fast on bread and water but it is not the highest good. The highest good is *charity*, that is, the love of God and man. You can get into heaven without fasting on bread and water—"but there is no salvation without *charity*." The Pharisees fasted—but were whited sepulchres, full of unrighteousness.' Not so in Bridget's convent—besides, we are not living any longer in the first enthusiasm of the early Christian age, and Sweden is not an Egyptian desert with palm trees and a spring next to the hermit's hut in the oasis. 'These are other times, we have to live in cold regions, and besides, the hearts are tepid and the body frail. Even when the fast is the very strictest—on bread and water—it shall therefore be permitted to give a relish to the dry bread with a few vegetables, and to use the water, which is so cold and sharp to drink, for the brewing of ale.'(10)

Bridget is inspired in chapter after chapter. She feels as though a casket with costly jewels and precious stones is being emptied on to the table before her, and she takes one jewel after the other to insert it in the crown of the Queen of Heaven. She need not write them down, she sees them so clearly before her that when she visits Master Matthias in Linköping on her way to Stockholm she can repeat the whole rule to him, word for word, so that he can write it down, and that although several days have passed.(11)

Incidentally, however, the new vineyard which Bridget had been appointed to found, was not to differ essentially from the old vineyards, whose only fault was that they were old and therefore decayed. Bridget by no means talked like Francis of Assisi—'Do not talk to me about the rule of Saint Benedict or Saint Augustine—what I want is something entirely new which has never been seen before'—namely the absolute, literal, reckless fulfilment of the commandment of the Gospel not to have two coats, or shoes upon one's feet, but to wander barefoot through the world like a poor minstrel of God. On the contrary, Bridget was very willing that those rules of the earlier founders of Orders should be taken over when they could be useful to her own Order. And as to poverty, she was of the Benedictine view that they might 'possess what is needful and useful, nothing in abundance, everything in humility, not in pride.'(12) Now and then she can make use of the Franciscan words about the body 'Brother ass'—but she knows from her life at Ulfåsa that if a horse has to work it must have enough to eat and drink, and would not that also apply to asses?

The convent that Bridget intends to build must therefore have a firm foundation, it must rest safely in the good, fertile soil of East Gothland. For each of the sixty Sisters must bring with her a yearly income large enough to secure her 'bread and ale.' It is the same system as that of a cathedral chapter, where each canon has his prebend. In Bridget's Order, too, the prebends are to be hereditary, and in this way it will be possible to admit women without a dowry. With her customary sense of justice and integrity she keeps a strict watch to see that no unrighteous mammon is to be found in the economic foundations of the convent, for then the house could not stand.

Of course it is not enough that daily bread is secured in this basic capital; a nun cannot live on bread alone, any more than anyone else. Bridget counts on gifts to meet the other expenses of the house (clothes, repairs, etc.) and to replenish the larder. These gifts too must come from an honest source—in every case that occurs there must be an investigation as to whether the money has been honestly earned. If this is proved the gift is received and the giver is included in the prayers of the convent. If it is doubtful whether the money is honestly earned and the evidence is contradictory the money must not be received, *not even in a case of necessity*—but the good will of the giver must be rewarded with intercession. If a gift fulfils all conditions, and the convent is not at the moment in need of it, the giver is referred to other worthy and needy objects of charity—poor churches, for instance.

Conscientious accounts must be kept of all incomes, both regular and irregular. All Saints' Eve is term day, a balance sheet is drawn up and what is left over of victuals from the end of the financial year is distributed on All Souls' Day to the poor—a somewhat unusual application of a surplus. If it is found, however, that there will *not* be provisions enough for the following year, a deduction may be made from the surplus of the year expired, though only what is most necessary.

The convent must be poor, though still more so the Sisters. A nun may not even call a thimble her own. The nun who sins by possessing something personal is liable to strict punishment—on the Thursday when the Chapter is held* she must fast on bread and water and kiss the floor on which the other Sisters have trodden. Not until the next day after Evensong is she permitted again to enter the choir to pray and sing with the others. If a Sister dies in this sin the Abbess must, in the presence of all the others, cry: 'This one allowed the devil to let her sin exceedingly against God and the vows of her Order.'(13)

The Abbess must take great care not to make terms with the demands of poverty—'as fire comes of a spark, condemnation arises from private ownership.'(14) And she must keep a strict watch when

---

* The Chapter, *i.e.* the weekly meetings at which the Sisters accuse themselves of possible transgressions of the rule, a kind of public confession of sins. At the beginning of the meeting a chapter of the rule is read, hence the name. The room in which the 'Chapter' is held is, for the same reason, called the Chapter Room.

there is a talk of building—Bridget knows this temptation to erect beautiful houses and warns against it. If the Abbess goes in for erecting handsome monastic buildings and big, beautiful churches 'it shall be reckoned to her as just as great a sin as if she had purposely robbed my poor people of food and clothes,' says Christ.(15) In this Bridget is of the same mind as Francis of Assisi.

No one ought therefore to be admitted to the convent who has not the spirit of poverty, but who only enters in order to be provided for. The motive which leads a young girl to seek admittance must therefore be carefully examined. The door is by no means opened wide but only ajar, and in the chink of the door a pair of critical eyes take a look at the young lady who has knocked, and she is sent away and told to come back in three months. If she then applies again she is told to come again in a month or two. In this way she is put off for a whole year—and this is necessary as there is no year of probation in the convent. Then it is explained to her what the life is that she is entering upon—to despise the world, to forget kinsfolk and friends, to live a hard and austere life, and that for the rest of her life, for twenty, thirty, forty years—never anything but this, and no other end to it than death, no other door leading out but the door leading to the cemetery.

Now if this prospect does not frighten her the Bishop is sent for. He ascertains that the young woman is over eighteen years of age, and standing in the church door he then puts a number of questions to her, while she is still standing outside. Is she free? Has she promised anyone marriage? Is she not excommunicated? 'Yes.' 'No.' 'No.' Yes, but it is not the trials of the world, or a disappointment in love, is it, that has driven her to the door of the convent? Or has she, perhaps, incurred debts which she cannot pay, and which she will now try to evade? All inadmissible motives are placed before the young girl, but none of them is among her reasons. (The idea of going into a convent because of a broken heart is one that still haunts the imagination of many old aunts.) There is no other reason, she says, but 'only the one, an ardent love of Christ.'

Then she is permitted to follow this, her love, and to enter the church. 'Before her must be carried a red banner, on which a picture of My Passion is painted on one side, and the image of My Mother on the other,' says Christ. The new bride of Christ must of the Crucified learn patience and poverty, and of the image of Mary she must learn purity and humility. Two candles, together with the banner, shall be carried before her by two clerks and they shall burn the whole time during the singing of Mass. But the Mass is a bridal Mass, and during the Mass the Bishop blesses the betrothal ring which he afterwards places on the finger of the young woman, saying: 'I dedicate thee to be the bride of God and to be His to own for ever.' And the bride vows to keep the rule of the Order to the end of her life and to love no one higher than her heavenly Bridegroom.(16)

Next the Bishop clothes the new Sister in the habit of the Order, and after she has received Holy Communion during the Mass she is taken to the door leading from the church into the convent. There the Abbess and all the Sisters await her, and standing beside the Abbess there is a bier with a little earth upon it—it is the bier upon which she will one day be carried out through this door by which she is now entering. Then the door is closed after her and she is taken to her cell. 'But during the first week she is not to be kept under any restraint.'(17)

Bridget hears it all in spirit and she sees the church—that church which she intends shall be 'of simple work, humble and strong.' The architectural ideal of the Cistercians is also hers. 'When the church is built so that there is room enough, and the walls are so strong that no storm can overthrow them, and the roof so well laid that the rain cannot come in, it is enough. For God is more pleased with a humble heart in a humble church than with high walls where the body may well be present but the heart is outside.' 'Nothing shall be drawn or painted upon the walls of the church but the Cross of Christ and pictures of the saints. For often it happens that those who come into the church give their minds more to seeing what is drawn and painted on the walls, than of thinking of the benefits of God.' 'There shall be no cunning carving on doors, windows or seats . . . the glass windows must not be coloured, they must be only white or yellow.'(18)

This last prohibition is also Cistercian. The statute book of the Order of 1152 had prohibited stained window panes. The General Chapter of 1240 ordains in the same spirit the removal or whitewashing of multicoloured altar pictures. In the statute of Abbot Stephen (1109–1133) it is said that 'in the house of God there must not be anything that might look like superfluity or that might destroy poverty, that shield of the virtues,' and everything that is to be used at the divine service must therefore be altogether simple: 'no Cross of precious metal, only a wooden cross on the altar, no embroideries on the altar linen or on the church vestments.'(19)

Bridget intends to have thirteen altars in her church, so that there is one for each of the thirteen priests. There must be a chalice for each of the altars, though there must be two for the high altar. Besides this two pairs of cruets, two pairs of candlesticks, three thuribles (one for every day, two for feast days), one ciborium. These sacred vessels must be of precious metal, but otherwise there must be nothing of silver or gold within church or convent—unless perhaps for a reliquary. Poverty must also be observed concerning books—the nuns must have the books required for singing the Divine Office 'but by no means any more.' The priests, on the other hand, may have all the books necessary for their studies. And every Sunday they must interpret the Gospel in the mother tongue.

That which is most surprising to a modern Catholic in Bridget's rule is the ordinance about Holy Communion. Since Pius X, more exactly since 1905, daily Communion has become daily Bread, not only for nuns in convents and for particularly devout ladies and gentlemen who have obtained the permission of their confessors, but for all who are conscious of being in the state of grace and are in need of help from above. Bridget's rule prescribes Holy Communion only on Christmas Day, Holy Thursday, Easter Day, Whitsunday and certain other great feast days. If any of the nuns should feel drawn to a more frequent reception of the Sacrament, she was to be permitted to receive it every Saturday.(20) When one considers how often Bridget herself confessed —even several times a day—it is perhaps still stranger that confession was restricted to 'at least three times a year.' Out of the thirteen priests the Abbess chooses one for Confessor General, in his turn he chooses from the twelve other priests the confessors required at the great concourse of pilgrims. All the Brothers must obey the Confessor General, and he must obey the Abbess, for 'she is the head of the convent' as the Blessed Virgin was the Queen of the Apostles on the earth; the Abbess sits in her place.(21)

The confession and communion of the Sisters did not take place in the church, to which they were not admitted, but beside the windows or apertures still to be seen in the north wall of the 'blue church' of Vadstena—that is, the wall facing towards the convent. Outside these apertures there must have been a building, or at any rate a roof under which the nuns at confession might be sheltered from the weather. Inside, in the chancel, there are five cells with a bench built into the wall, where the confessor would sit by the window of the hatch outside which the penitent knelt. Through this window the nuns also received Communion—'and these windows must be so broad that the Body of God and the Chalice can pass conveniently.'(22) This is not intended to mean Communion under both forms. Even if this was not expressly forbidden until 1415 by the Council of Constance, double communion had already been abolished in 1261 by the Cistercians, whose rite Bridget followed most faithfully.(23) The 'chalice' mentioned here is the cup of wine mingled with water, which the priest who celebrates Mass also receives after his Communion (the so-called ablution). This cup was formerly also handed to the laity after Communion, and the custom has not been quite abandoned—in the Cathedral in Assisi the twelve old people, who, on Holy Thursday, at the washing of the feet, represent the twelve Apostles, receive a drink of wine after their Communion so that they may be better able to swallow the Host.

Besides these windows which, as we have seen, only serve for the administration of the Sacraments, there must, in the wall between the two convents, be another window, at which the Sisters can speak with the priests or Brothers, and 'there must be a wheel in the wall,' *i.e.* a revolving disc, by the aid of which one thing or another can be sent in from the Sisters to the Brothers or vice versa. No Sister may sit alone at this window (where, by the way, she cannot be seen), another Sister must always be present. Priests have admission to the convent only when a Sister is to receive the Sacraments, and 'when a Sister is dead, all the priests and Brothers enter while singing and praying and bear her body to the grave.'(24) In order that the Sisters may not forget the day when this will come to pass for them, there is in the convent in a certain place a grave which is always open. To this the Sisters must go every day that God permits them to see, when they have sung Terce (at nine o'clock in the morning), and the Abbess shall take a little earth and cast it into the grave and all shall pray the *De profundis*. At the door from the convent to the church there shall always stand a bier with a little earth lying upon it—as if it had just been used.(25)

The ceremonies prescribed for the ordination of the priests and other Brothers is like that of the dedication of the nuns. They are ordained by the Bishop, but instead of the ring they receive only a pressure of the hand and the blessing that goes with it, and instead of the veil the Bishop lays his hand upon their hands with the same words that he uses in blessing the veil. The place of the crown is taken by the tonsure, also used in other convents. The thirteen priests are to have cloaks of grey wadmal like their habits, and a cross of red cloth, with a small white disc in the middle of the cross, must be sewn on the left side of the cloaks—the symbol of the Cross of the Passion and the white Host. But the four deacons must on their cloaks have a white circle with four red strips of cloth shaped like a tongue—the symbol of the four great Fathers of the Church who spoke with the fiery tongues of the Holy Ghost. Like the Sisters, the Brothers are also introduced into the Brothers' house, 'from which they may never go out except to the church.'(26)

> My Mother [said Christ to Bridget] divided the day into three parts—one in which she praised God with her lips, one in which she served Him with her hands, one in which she gave to her body its needful sustenance. The Sisters, too, labour with their hands, when they are not in choir or reading or receiving instruction. I laboured too when I was on earth, and My Apostles laboured. But the work of the Sisters is not to be for their own use and benefit but for the benefit of God or of the poor.(27)

Of the highest value in the sight of God, however, is prayer, the Divine Office, the Psalter, the Psalms of David, which the Church has taken over from the Temple of the Old Covenant. The praises of the Psalter are the keys of Heaven and the gates of Paradise . . . the songs of the Psalter sanctify the body, adorn the soul, draw hither the angels, drive away the devil, *scrape the sinners clean* (note the concrete expression about absolution). 'The Psalter increases the faith of the Christian, illuminates like the sun, cleanses like water, extinguishes all inordinate desire, raises the love of God in the heart. They who love the singing of psalms cannot sin.'(28) It is Bridget's confessor, Master Petrus of Skenninge, who writes these words in the Preface to the Bridgettine Office composed by him, and the words are spoken from Bridget's heart. Because this is so the singing of psalms shall never fall silent in the church that she will build on the shores of Lake Vättern—the holy songs shall without ceasing ascend to the throne of the Judge and ward off His wrath. All the sins of Sweden shall be scraped off, all inordinate desire extinguished, the three devils that rule the people of Sweden shall be driven out and King Magnus shall shine like a sun of righteousness, and Queen Blanca give light like the gentle moon of mercy. . . .

> But in a very short space of time all the articles of this rule were said to me by Jesus Christ, and to me it was all, not like words written on paper, but I understood them one by one and with the help of the grace of Christ I hid them all in my memory. And when the vision was ended my heart was filled with so much warmth and rejoicing that nothing more could find an entrance into it, if I was to go on living, for it would have burst with joy. For many days my heart was so filled to overflowing, like an inflated sack, and it continued until I could tell it all to a pious friend of God, who wrote all of it down as quickly as possible. But when all was written down my heart and my body grew slow as they were before.(29)

XV

Then one day Bridget was again standing before King Magnus in the castle of Stockholm. In her hand she holds a roll of parchment—the rule which Christ has revealed to her. With the words still burning in her heart she had hastened from Vadstena to Alvastra, and Prior Petrus had carefully written down word for word what she told him, and afterwards, with equally great care, translated everything into Latin. In Linköping she had called upon her old friend, Master Matthias, and he had read the manuscript through and had not found anything to remark upon it. And now she was standing here before the king to tell him the word of God.

There was a great deal with which she could reproach Magnus. There were great contrasts between the two characters—he was timid ('the heart of a hare'), afraid to displease anyone, easily yielding to the advice of others, amiable in word and deed—hence the nickname *Smek,* 'the caressing prince.' She, as a woman, certain of always being right, inflexible in her will, strict in her demands, with a deep aversion from everything belonging to 'the world.' Between the two no compromise was possible—one had to command, the other to obey. And it would be Magnus who had to obey. Really he ought to listen to reason and value the grace that had been given him, that in his kingdom there was a woman to whom God spoke without ceasing, whom he therefore could trust, and whose advice he simply ought to follow. Nothing could be more straightforward.(1)

But Magnus wanted to follow his own ideas, or rather, those of his bad advisers. And whither had they led him? He had wanted to help the Holsteiners in their fight against Valdemar Atterdag—and how many good Swedish men had not fallen in the siege of the castle of Copenhagen? Why? Because it was an unjust war! Instead of sending his soldiers against the heathen he had invaded the realm of another Christian king.(2) And that was not the worst. The kingdom was heavily burdened by the transactions undertaken by Magnus in order to consolidate it and acquire what was still lacking—the Danish provinces of Scania, Halland and Blekinge. In his perpetual need of money the Danish king, Christopher II, had been compelled to mortgage Scania to Count John of Holstein, but the Scanians were by no means satisfied with the German rule and in June 1332 surrendered the country to Magnus, and after the death of King Christopher in August of the same year Magnus assumed the title of 'King of Sweden, Norway and

Scania.' Count John did not oppose the Swedish occupation but declared that he was willing to give up the mortgage if the sum which he had lent Christopher was paid to him. On 4 November 1332, King Magnus therefore pledged himself to pay a sum of 34,000 marks in silver (over 10 million crowns or £500,000) to keep Scania, Lister, Blekinge and the island of Hvén. In this way Sweden had obtained her natural boundaries and Bridget could not but be satisfied with it. 'The bride of God,' it is said in a revelation, 'spoke to Christ and prayed for the kingdom of Sweden.' And it was revealed to her that Swedes and Danes had been together in Noah's Ark. The Swedes went towards the east, the Danes towards the west; the Swedes settled on the continent, the Danes on the islands, both were to be content with what they had and live in the land of their fathers, and within the borders of the forefathers.(3) At their meeting in Varberg in 1343 the new Danish king, Valdemar Atterdag, did, in fact, admit that he had 'sold' the whole of Scania, Halland, Blekinge, Lister and Hvén with castles and fortresses, and all royal right and authority to King Magnus. The purchase money was to be paid to the mortgagee, the Holsteinish Count, with 34,000 marks, and with 8,000 marks to King Valdemar himself. King Valdemar solemnly gives King Magnus the title deeds of the land ceded to him—in a fold of King Magnus' cloak he places a piece of turf of the newly acquired land.

In principle Bridget agreed with King Magnus, the Öresund was the natural border of Sweden. In 1333 Magnus already personally took possession of Scania. But in the past ten years he had found it difficult to pay the instalments stipulated in the contract of the sale. In vain had he tried to obtain a loan from the Hanseatic towns. In 1319, after the old Norwegian dynasty had become extinct, he had been elected King of Norway, but the income of this country could not very well be applied to the benefit of Sweden. Both the Swedish clergy and the Swedish nobility then came to his assistance and personally became sureties as hostages for the due payment of the debt. In 1331 Bridget's brother Israel paid 450 marks in silver to redeem his pledge to be surety for the redemption of Scania. Bridget herself offered her two sons Karl and Birger as hostages in order to prevent the king from levying new taxes.(4) But the burdens of taxation went on increasing. (Incidentally Bridget herself added a new tax—'Our Lady's Penny.')

Then there were the relations with Norway. Magnus Eriksson had two sons: Erik, born in 1339 and Hakon born the year after. In 1343 Haakon was already made King of Norway, with his father as guardian, at the meeting in Varberg when the sale of Scania was arranged, and in 1344 Erik was elected in Uppsala to be successor to the throne of Sweden. At that time Bridget had prayed to God for advice: 'Lord, be not wrathful if I bring yet a cause before Thee. The king has two sons and two kingdoms. One of them is a kingdom by inheritance, the other a kingdom by election. But now it happens that the younger son has been given the hereditary kingdom, the elder the kingdom by election.' The hereditary kingdom seems to her to be more stable than the elective kingdom—and the daughter of the law-man, the law-man's wife and the mother of a law-man could not approve of this slight of the elder son. In this she found agreement. 'The choice that has been made is unjust,' answered the voice in Bridget's conscience, 'and it goes against that which is for the good and benefit of the common people. It is advisable, indeed, it is necessary, that the elder son should have the hereditary kingdom and the younger be elected. If this is not done and the agreements which have been made in Varberg are not altered, the kingdom will suffer harm, the common people of the kingdom will be oppressed, discontent and disagreement will arise, the lives of the two sons will be embittered, and it will be with their kingdoms as it is written: The mighty shall be cast down from their thrones.'(5)

But to-day there is something else that Bridget has more at heart than Swedish politics. Like Saint Paul she could say: 'Who is scandalized, and I am not on fire?' *Everything* was of importance to eternity. Again like Paul she could exclaim: 'And woe be to me, if I did not speak.' The Bull of Canonization was not wrong in applying to Bridget the words of Saint Augustine: *pondus meum amor meus*—he who loves carries a burden. The path of life is easy only to those who have no love. But Bridget's heart glowed with holy love of God, and her soul burned with zeal for His honour. And this love, this zeal was now to be embodied in the church by the shores of Lake Vättern, 'of simple deed, humble and strong' and in a building of living stones, of God's friends, men and women, priests and nuns, in the two houses beside the church.

Bridget read to King Magnus the rule with which she had been inspired by Christ Himself, the rule of *Ordo Sanctissimi Salvatoris*, 'the Order of the Most Holy Saviour.' 'You know, O King,' she added, 'what I have already told you—the wrath of God is kindled against Sweden, and He will come upon it with sword and lance, and He will spare none, neither young nor old, neither rich nor poor, neither just nor unjust, but His plough will pass over the land and uproot the forests and destroy the fields, and where a thousand people once lived only a hundred shall be found, and the houses shall stand empty and the ravens shall come and feast on the dead bodies. For three sins hold sway in this kingdom: *gula, cupiditas, superbia,* "gluttony, the lust of the flesh and the pride of life." '

The terrible threats thunder over the head of Magnus Eriksson. He dare hardly look up, he dare not meet the stern eyes of a judge which he feels are gazing upon him. Bridget rolls up the parchment, but she does not leave him. Like the frightened child who has been scolded by his stern mother the king murmurs: 'God is merciful—He will not suffer all the evil you speak of to come upon us.' Now he looks up, Bridget stands before him, small and strong in her widow's attire; beneath her head-kerchief the blue eyes burn like two flames. Again he looks down.

But now Bridget's voice is suddenly gentle like a mother's. 'You are a child, Magnus,' she says quietly, 'a disobedient, naughty child. God is just, so just that He will not be unjust even to the devil in hell. But He is also merciful to those who repent and return to Him and do penance. And now Christ speaks to you in this wise: There are three things that can appease my wrath and keep back my chastisement. The first is that pride and vanity give way to humility and modesty; that moderation in food and drink and in all worldly desire is kept—and the third, King Magnus, the third and most important . . .'

Bridget pauses for a moment. Then she lifts in her right hand the roll of parchment like a marshal's staff and a sceptre. 'The third is, that because you have been slow to exercise justice and have plundered many by unjust taxes, you shall, says Christ, build a convent to the glory of Mary, and the place where you shall build it is the king's house of Vadstena!'(6)

XVI

There were still three things that Bridget had at heart, and about which she had to speak to the king. First, of course, there was the ratification of the rule of the Order by the Pope. The second was that Sweden, as a neutral country, ought to intervene and make peace between the two western powers, whose internecine strife led to nothing but mutual destruction. These two tasks might be accomplished at the same time, if a deputation from Sweden was sent to Avignon to request the Pope to ratify the rule of the Order, and to undertake the difficult charge of peacemaker between England and France. Bridget's third request of King Magnus was the easiest to realize—a crusade to Finland.

On this point Bridget's wishes agreed with the king's. Magnus had long intended to take up the Cross and set out for Finland. There were still many heathen to be converted on the other side of the Gulf of Bothnia; moreover it was said that the Russian Czar, whose name was Simeon (1340–53) would be willing to change from the Greek Orthodox confession to the Church of Rome. The war was therefore not to be carried on by force of arms, but with an auxiliary troop of Dominicans, Franciscans and Cistercians who were to accompany the army. 'For there are many heathen who desire to learn something about the Christian faith. . . . The friends of God, priests and monks, must therefore be ready to answer the heathen with divine wisdom when they come and ask them questions.' Unfortunately there were not many Swedish ecclesiastics who felt inclined to undertake this mission work— like the Jews in the wilderness they murmured against God and wished they were safely at home again among the flesh-pots of the monastery.

Bridget now warned the king against these bad missionaries. Two banners must be carried at the head of his army, the banner of mercy with a cross, that of justice with a sword. For the sword, too, has a share in mission work. It is said, it is true, that no one must be forced to enter the kingdom of heaven. No, but when the good flowers in a garden are choked by weeds is it not better to pull up the weeds so that the flowers can grow? Moreover there is another consideration, not immaterial to Bridget, that it may even be an advantage to the heathen to die young—if they were allowed to live longer they would sin more and so get a harder punishment after death.

The best mission, however, is that which Saint Sigfrid carried out when he left his own country of England to consummate the will of God in Sweden: to build churches. The bishop who goes with the king on the crusade must therefore, as soon as a little of the country has been conquered, build a cathedral to which the Christians can resort 'as to a mother.' The mission may have to begin in a small way, with one or two priests, but patience! more will surely come soon.

Concerning the ratification of the rule by the Pope, and the matter of the convent at Vadstena, Magnus reserves to himself the right to consult the Swedish ecclesiastics. Master Matthias is a learned man, Petrus Olai a pious monk, but neither of them occupies an official position which can lend weight to their words at the Papal Court. In the first instance the rule must be placed before the archbishop of the country, Hemming Nilsson, as well as three other bishops for approval and recommendation. Bridget cannot have any objection against this bureaucratic, correct method of procedure, 'and you must be assured, dear Aunt, that personally I agree with the plan and I will do everything I can to support this beautiful idea. And it would be to the glory of Sweden if a new Order, of men of a devout life and pious women, issue from this country—the various Orders have otherwise always come from the lands outside: the Cistercians from France, the Black Friars from Spain, the Grey Friars from Italy. . . . But as concerning the king's house in Vadstena, you will understand, dear Aunt, that I must talk with Blanca about it first. . . .'

Bridget remained at court. Besides, her brother Israel was there, her sons, Karl and Birger, came when their official duties in Uppland and Närike gave them an opportunity to do so. Bridget spent the winter of 1345-6 in Stockholm, no longer as mistress of the household, but as a friend and relative—and, to use a modern parallel, as a famous personality who is the guest of distinguished friends.

For Bridget was beginning to acquire fame in the land, and what gained her most fame were the signs and wonders that followed her wherever she went, and that seemed to serve as confirmation of the words that she spoke. She drove out evil spirits—and it was not only that she had the mastery over demons so that they obeyed her, but that her confessor, Petrus Olai, had been entrusted with the same gift by her—in East Gothland alone he had exorcized three demons by speaking over them the words which Bridget had taught him—and this occurred in the presence of Bishop Thomas of Vexiö and of the learned Master Matthias, Professor Theologiæ and Canon in Linköping.(2)

It was also said of Bridget that she had been given grace to look into the world which is beyond the grave. Devout persons came to her and spoke about their dear departed, asking anxiously: 'Can it be that they are condemned? Are they in the cleansing fires of purgatory? Have they reached the shores of everlasting life?' The name of the dead person was written down and given to Bridget, and then she prayed for the person whose name was written on the paper. She received the answer in prayer and could say afterwards where the soul was, what pain it had to endure, and what was to be done to alleviate its sufferings by prayer or almsgiving.(3)

People also often came to her on their own account—when a difficult decision had to be made, or when a doubt harassed them. 'Let us pray together to get light on this matter,' Bridget would answer, 'and come back in a few days.' Then only did the answer come and often in this way: 'With her hands raised to heaven the Lady Bridget prayed and said: "I am only a poor sinner, but Jesus Christ has appeared to me in prayer and said that in answer to your questions I must say thus. . . ." Sometimes the seeress wrote with her own hand in Swedish the answer which had been given her, but if she was ill she called her confessor and dictated it to him, and then she would speak the words slowly and solemnly as if she was reading them out of a book . . . and afterwards she would read through the written answer before it was sent away.'(4)

Meanwhile it was also granted to Bridget to work purely spiritual wonders. It created a great stir in Stockholm when she converted a public sinner, a girl well known to the rakes of the capital in her walking in the broad way. She was a young woman like so many others and liked an easy life, having money in hand and enjoying her youth. But in the language of the devil these three pleasures are called gluttony, covetousness and harlotry. 'And I am therefore now sitting in the midst of her body,' Bridget hears the Evil One say, 'and with five hands' (at Aspanäs Bridget had seen how many hands and claws the devil can have), 'with five hands I keep a firm hold of her. I hold the first hand before her eyes so that she may not see spiritual things. With the second I hold her hand so that she may not do good deeds. With the third I hold her feet, so that she cannot go to church. With the fourth I obscure her mind so that she cannot see how ugly sin is. I hold the fifth hand about her heart, so that it may never beat with the deep heartbeats of penitence.'

Yet this Magdalen, too, came back. In a vision Bridget is present at the dispute about her soul between the Blessed Virgin and the devil. Christ transfers His omnipotence to Mary, and the devil is compelled to answer, he is even compelled to honour the truth and to confess that this erstwhile sinner has now become different—'she repents of what she has done and weeps much over it, and she has resolved not to sin any more, but to become better as far as she can.' And now the devil is caught: 'Tell me, devil, whether harlotry, gluttony and covetousness can live together with penitence, tears and the will to live a better life?' No, the devil is forced to admit that this they cannot do. Then who is to retreat? is the next, even more pressing question. Oh, well, the Evil One admits, I suppose it will have to be the three vices! And with them the master of the vices must also depart and release the soul which he had wanted to steal from God.

Bridget saw this in spirit, and in the strength of what she had seen she made her way to the house where the harlot lived. (At Ulfåsa she had already become familiar with such places and was no more afraid of them than a Sister in the Salvation Army when visiting the slums is afraid of them at the present day. All things considered, and apart from the differences of creed, it was really a Salvation Army that Bridget wanted to found.) She finds the girl lying on the floor, unconscious like one dead—round about her the other girls are standing and telling the Lady Bridget that it is the devil who has pulled Ingrid or Margit or whatever her name was, out of bed—'we saw it ourselves with our own eyes.' Bridget orders silence, bends over the possessed woman: '*Apage Satanas*—get thee hence, devil, thou hast tormented this woman enough!' The woman does not move, she is still lying like one dead—and remains lying so for half an hour. Until she suddenly opens her eyes, points to the window and screams: 'There he flew out! I heard a voice saying to me: Woman, thou art saved! And then he flew out through the window—so terrible to look at!'(5)

As it was in the days of the Gospel, so there must also have been those in Bridget's surroundings who wondered that they could not drive the demons out of the sinner. The Catholic Church believes—also as in the days of the Gospel—in the possibility of *exorcism*, and the *Rituale Romanum* contains an exorcism of evil spirits composed by Leo XIII. 'Why could not I drive out Satan?' some priest or other may have asked. Christ answers with Bridget: 'You wonder that the evil spirit would not immediately leave the possessed woman? There you may judge of my perfect justice—I will no more be unjust to the devil in hell than to the angel in Paradise. And that which has come slowly must also leave slowly, and that was the case here.'

The fact is, there are three kinds of evil spirits, Bridget then explains. The first is like air, it comes in softly, acts like an intoxicant, and under its influence one perpetrates things of which in a sober condition one would be ashamed, but the intoxication soon goes. Bridget had seen this form of possession in a young person in Stockholm. The second spirit is worse, it torments the whole body and flesh of a human being, whose life becomes so embittered that it will rather die and in despair it commits all manner of dissipations. Then there is the third spirit, that which possessed this woman; it is like smoke that penetrates everything and only slowly curls up through the roof, covering everything with its soot; it will gradually disappear, but first many tears must be shed.(6)

The miracle of the conversion of the harlot and—almost—her raising from the dead, increased Bridget's fame, already great. In his Prologue to *Revelationes* Master Matthias indicates as one of the strongest proofs of the genuineness of Bridget's mission 'the conversion of the notorious harlot by that intervention of Christ and the Blessed Virgin through a revelation to the above-named lady' (that is, to Bridget).(7) Bridget, then, sits at her desk one day to write to the Swedish Archbishop Heming Nilsson, the man on whom it chiefly depends whether Bridget's threefold plan can be carried out, and especially also the establishment of the Order.

Now who was this man? Two years after Bridget (in May 1375) has left this world it is seen that he has gathered abundantly of those treasures which moth and rust do corrupt. In his will he leaves large estates to the churches in Uppsala and Vesterås as well as 140 silver marks and 400 Swedish pennies, corresponding altogether to about 70,000 Kroner (£3,500). Besides this, costly furs in abundance, clothes of scarlet and silk lined with ermine, twenty-two complete costumes, two sets of armour, a silver belt, a gold ring with a sapphire, seven silver jugs, twenty-one silver cups, six silver spoons, etc., etc. His kinsfolk were generously apportioned, as also his large number of servants, among whom there were two chaplains, several esquires, three pages, two cooks, a baker, a brewer, a shoemaker, two grooms, a gardener and four fishermen.(8)

It is to this man that Bridget is writing now, listening to the words that Christ speaks in her heart. As usual the revelation begins with God's testimony of Himself: 'I am He who was born of the Virgin and became Man to preach the Faith in word and deed—I am He who died that heaven might be opened, and who was buried and rose from the grave and shall come again to the judgment.'

After this Introit comes the message proper.

You wonder why I speak these words? Lift up your eyes and look about you. Open your mouth and ask. And you shall learn how I have been neglected by all men. Open your eyes and see how I am rejected by all, and there are none who rejoice in me. Prick up your ears and hear how from the rising of the sun until its setting the heart of man is hardened and he thinks of nothing but of shedding the blood of his neighbour. See how all adorn their bodies with vain ornaments, see how the desires of man are as senseless as those of the beasts. Open your mouth and ask, where are those men to be found who fight against the enemies of God, where are they who will venture their lives for their Lord? Look diligently and you will find that I have very few friends.

It is the keynote, the deepest chord in Bridget's soul, that is sounded here. With the German poet she could say: 'Break out in loud complaints thou gloomy martyr song, which I have borne so long in the silence of a flame.' Like a flame this plaint of God arises again and again in Bridget's soul and issues from her lips like that devouring fire which Prior Ragwald saw in his vision and which 'no power in the world can hinder from issuing.'

God's first complaint is directed against the Head of Christendom, the Pope in Avignon, who has set up his chair of pride against the seat of humility. And as the lord is, so are his followers, the ecclesiastics— 'the chief matter for them is to be called wise and learned in worldly things. While they can no more stomach me than they can swallow a stone, and they find me as loathsome as poison. Look how they reward my love!'

Then Golgotha rises again before the vision of the seeress.

I was tied with ropes and tortured as though in a press, my nerves were torn asunder, my veins cut apart, my muscles crushed. My brow and all my head were wounded by the crown of thorns. The blood that flowed from my head was clotted and stiffened in my beard. My mouth and tongue were filled with blood, my gums were swollen with the blows that had been struck upon my mouth.* When after this I was stretched upon the cross, my arms were stretched to such a length that they could reach to the holes in the cross-beams. My feet were pulled downwards and pierced with two nails and had no support but them. Inwardly I was entirely dried up and shrivelled. My heart was full of grief, and as it was of the soundest kind it was a long while before death came and I had to suffer longer. And as I was hanging like this in my torments I opened my eyes and saw my Mother standing there weeping, and her pain and torment afflicted me more than my own suffering. I saw, too, that my friends were in great dread, and that some of them seemed to doubt, but that others kept their faith, although it was hard for them. And with such great pain and so much woe my heart broke at last and all my limbs trembled. My eyes opened a little and my feet had to bear all the weight of my body, so that I hung like a rag. But in spirit I beheld as it were a balance, and in one scale were all the sins of the world, and in the other I laid my heart. All this have I done, and no one pays any heed. But I beg you to think of it, and I beg you to labour with me.

First and above all the archbishop must open his ears to Bridget's words and his arms to the friends of God. Next he must, doing it better than before, plough the land that has been given to him, let the plough go deeper, root up the thorns and use them as riches for the building of churches. 'Labour wisely as a wise man, doing the manly work of a man, and zealously as a friend of God.'

With his authority he must also use his influence on Magnus Eriksson. 'I bid the king,' says Christ, 'as soon as he can, to set out against the enemies. If he thinks he is doing something great for me, I have

* Bridget saw and included even this detail!

done greater things for him.' On his crusade Magnus must take with him three good comrades—two priests and a man skilled in the law. In his absence he must entrust his kingdom to the archbishop, as well as to 'a layman, who will not for gain and favour pass unjust judgments, but exercise justice without fear of men, and be wise enough to know that all is not gold that glitters, and who will therefore not be deceived into taking copper for gold.'(9)

The man whom Bridget has in mind here is her own brother Israel. Meanwhile he was not by any means inclined to assume such a position as that of regent in the absence of the king. 'He desired rather to set out against the heathen and to die fighting for the holy faith for the glory of God. . . .' Then Bridget received a revelation in which the Blessed Virgin spoke to her and said: 'If they who know the law and maintain justice, refuse to undertake the work for the glory of God and to bear this burden, how then shall the kingdom uphold its power? Truly, then, it is no kingdom' (that is, no *well-ordered state*, for that is what Bridget means by the word *kingdom*) 'but rather a den of robbers, where the wicked rule and the good are oppressed. Therefore a good and just man shall, for the love of God, take upon himself the task of ruling the common people, so that he may help many, and this my friend Israel must do, taking the words of truth in his mouth and the sword of justice in his hand, and not being swayed by consideration of kinsfolk or friends or servants, but exercising justice without respect of persons.'

Israel obeyed, and the Blessed Virgin who had called him 'my friend,' rewarded him for it. When the Finnish campaign was over and the king came back, Sir Israel resigned not only his office of regent, but also his office of law-man. And Mary 'led him by another way to his kingdom—like the three holy kings who went home to their own country by another way.' Two years later he joined the second crusade to Finland, not finding, it is true, death on the field of battle, but going with the Swedish army on the retreat to Riga, where he fell very ill. When he felt death drawing near 'he went with some of his servants to the cathedral in that city, and placed a costly ring on the finger of Our Lady's image, saying in a loud voice to it: "Thou art my Lady, and to me thou wast the very sweetest, wherefore I give up my soul to thy care and thy mercy." Whereupon he received the Sacrament of Holy Church and died. . . .' But his sister saw the Blessed Virgin lead Sir Israel by a hidden way to Paradise and present him to the mighty rulers in heaven, and she understood that it had been of greater good

I

to him to die in a foreign land than at home, where the care of the family for him could easily have distracted his thoughts from the one thing needful.(10)

Then, finally, there was still a message which the archbishop was to bring to Bishop Hemming of Åbo. Hemming was Bishop of Åbo from 1338 to 1366, and belonged to that group within the Swedish Episcopate which from the beginning was amicably disposed towards Bridget. Nevertheless, he had once doubted about her—it was when, during a visit to Stockholm, he had sat next to her at dinner at court. With some surprise he saw her help herself to an ample portion of the good things with which the table was laden (a Swedish *Smorgaas* table at the present day can still give one some idea of it), and it seemed to him that such an enjoyment of food was not seemly in a person who was famed for piety, nay, holiness. With her usual delicate perception Bridget understood what was disturbing the scandalized heart of her partner at table, and the next morning he found on his *prie-dieu* a leaf on which she had written down a revelation which she had received in the evening. The words were these: 'A voice spoke to me when I was wrapt in prayer, and the voice said: "I am he who gave to David the spirit of prophecy—was that because of his fasting? I spoke to Job as willingly when he was rich, as when he sat upon the dunghill. I am he who does with men what seems good to him without regard to their merit."' Bishop Hemming read and understood. In a repentant mood he went to Bridget, confessed that he had criticized her and recommended himself to her intercession. Then, three days later, the Blessed Virgin appeared to Bridget and gave her this message for Bishop Hemming: 'Tell him that I quite understand that his judgment of you arose from zeal for God, not from envy. Tell him, also, that because he always begins his sermons with a "Hail, Mary," I will be like a mother to him and present his soul before God.'(11)

In a vision which Bridget had later of seven bishops, symbolized by seven fabulous animals, Hemming is likened to 'that animal which fears nothing, not even death, and which has four wonderful qualities— it has always an unutterable inner consolation, it has no care for what it shall eat, it never stands but always runs and finds its rest in running.'(12) It was no wonder, then, that it was to him the difficult mission to Avignon was entrusted. Christ bids him 'bring the message to the Pope.' *The* message, in a definite form—that message which was the most important of all—the confirmation of the rule of the Order. He was enjoined to delete nothing from the rule; on the other hand, he might freely add something, provided it was 'to the glory of God and the good of souls.' In the next place he must deliver Bridget's proposal for peace between France and England, a cause which she had had very much at heart since the pilgrimage to Compostella.

With regard to the rule of the Order, Bridget had no doubts. 'Even if it were Lucifer who was sitting on the throne of Peter' (Jacopone da Todi had already had this idea—he calls Bonifacius VIII *Lucifero novello*) 'he shall carry out the will of my Son,' says Mary.

Next, she proposes that Bishop Hemming, accompanied by the faithful Petrus Olai of Alvastra, shall be admitted to the two contending kings, or rather that they shall come to him. When he arrives in France and the chieftains stand before him, he shall speak these words to them:

> God, who is the creator of all things and who deigned to descend to the Virgin's womb and to unite human nature with His divinity, yet without giving up His Godhead—God, who so loved the world that when He saw the spear and the sharp nails and all the instruments of death before Him, would rather die and rather allow His sinews to be severed and His hands and feet to be pierced than lose hold of the unalterable love He bore towards man, would that God through His suffering might deign to unite you, who have hitherto been at variance!

Hemming, Bridget adds, can also, because the spirit inspires him, speak to them about the pains of hell, about the joys of heaven, about the reward that awaits the righteous and the affliction which is the lot of the unrighteous.

Then Bishop Hemming and Prior Petrus set out on their journey to far away Avignon. As passport and written recommendation they took the letter from Master Matthias, doctor of theology and authority on Holy Writ, which now appears as a prologue to the *Revelationes*.

XVII

It was in the spring of 1346—a Swedish spring like so many other springs in Sweden. In April the ground in the woods was blue with anemones, along brooks and marshes and ponds the marsh marigolds raised their bright golden cups to the sun; the borders of ditches and dykes were strewn with the little gold coins of *tussilago farfara*; the hazel hedges shed the golden dust of their catkins; the blackthorn bush hid its pointed thorns in snow-white bridal veils.

A spring like so many other springs—for Bridget the most beautiful of all. For on the feast of Saint Walpurga, the first of May 1346, King

Magnus and Queen Blanca signed their testament in Lödöse, and with that testament they bestowed upon Bridget the king's mansion of Vadstena. 'We choose our last resting-place in that convent which we and our heirs, by the grace of God, shall build and complete in Vadstena.' Much land was furthermore added to the property of the royal estate, a costly Mass equipment was presented to the church, nay, in the following year (15 July 1347), by the so-called Norwegian testament of the king and queen, a considerable sum of money was put by for the projected conventual building.(1)

This was a victory for Bridget—a first victory. She also felt certain that her envoys would bring home a victory from Avignon in their turn; in a vision she had seen her old acquaintance of Arras, Saint Dionysius, and heard him speak with Mary. 'Have mercy on France, *thy France and mine*,' Saint Denis had said to the Blessed Virgin—'the land is mine, because I am its patron saint, the land is thine, because many in it honour thee. Thou seest how souls are in peril every hour of the day—thou seest that human beings are slaughtered like beasts—and, what is worse, thou seest their souls falling into hell like snow!'(2)

And now Bridget's eyes were opened still wider, and she sees two fearsome beasts, fighting for that fair land through which she had wandered some years agone—*la douce France*. 'One of the beasts is sorely coveting to devour everything it can get, and the more it eats the hungrier it grows. The other beast wants, in its pride, to exalt itself above all others.' Both the beasts are alike horrible—they have terrible voices—fire comes out of their mouths—one of them thinks of nothing but of devouring the heart of the other. They rend and tear at each other's flesh to get into the heart, and they will gladly sacrifice all the gold in the world and the blood of Christians, if only they can destroy each other.(3)

He who in 1940 reads these lines which Bridget's pen wrote down on a sheet of parchment six hundred years ago, sees with a shudder that nothing is altered in Europe since then. 'These two beasts signify two kings,' it continues, 'the kings of France and England,' that is Philip of Valois and Edward III. Through Queen Blanca, Bridget was informed of the course of the war—the queen's uncle, Robert, had played a part by no means honourable as a renegade from the French party to the English. And on 26 August 1346, the English gained the victory at Crécy, where the flower of the French nobility fell before the scythe. The English army consisted in part of Flemish mercenary troops. Perhaps they fought then with the same terrible weapon as at the 'battle of the spurs'—that terrible iron-mounted flail, with which they crushed both helmet and head, and which in a grim mood they called a 'good day'?

Bridget sees that the two beasts are equally strong—France and England could destroy each other, as Germany and England can at this very day—but neither of them can conquer the other. There is only one way of rescue—peace. Bridget hears three voices—one of them is that of the people, who pray daily for peace, the second is that of the friends of God, who lament over all the souls of which God is robbed by this war, the third voice is that of one of the two kings, namely that of Edward—he would really be glad to give up his plans against France, if only he could be sure that he would not lose prestige by it.

And Bridget hopes. Now, what was it that she wrote in the message that Bishop Hemming and Prior Petrus have taken to Avignon? Bridget has the draft which she wrote in Swedish, and which Prior Petrus has translated into Latin. She takes it out and reads:

> The Son of God is speaking. I am the King whom all must fear and honour. It is at the prayer of my Mother that I am sending my words to the kings of France and England. I am true peace, and where there is peace I am truly present. And if these two kings of France and England do indeed desire peace I will give everlasting peace. But true peace cannot be gained unless truth and justice are loved. . . .

For a moment Bridget had thought that the war could be ended by a marriage between the two royal houses, 'so that the kingdom can come to the right heir.' But again the voice of Christ speaks in her heart—it is not by that kind of matrimonial policy that a war, which was to last for a hundred years, can be stopped. 'I will,' the message continues, 'that the two kings shall be one heart and one soul, and that they shall increase the Christian faith where it is possible for them to do so. Furthermore, they shall do away with unjust taxes and crafty devices and love the souls of their subjects.' If they do not pay heed to this letter severe punishments await them. But there is always hope for the French people of a better future under a rightful king, 'provided they strive to attain true humility.'(4)

Naïve Saint Bridget! Neither Edward of England nor Philip of France paid heed to your words.

And yet she hoped—that if the two kings would not listen to her, her words would still find an open ear and an open heart in the Vice-gerent of Christ. But then a messenger from Avignon came to Stockholm, or to Alvastra, with a letter from Bishop Hemming. The letter did not contain good news, the kings of France and England had not appeared to be very favourably disposed to Bridget's proposals of peace, nor had he fared much better with the Pope, and now it seemed to him that he was wasting his time in Avignon, and spending his money to no purpose. Life in Avignon was considerably more expensive than at home in Finland; the bishop would like most of all to go home. There was nothing in the letter from Prior Petrus, but then it was not he who had to decide, and he was probably of the same opinion as His Lordship. Oh, these men! It is we women who have manly courage!

'Be a manly man,' Catherine of Siena was to write some decades later to one of her despondent friends. Saint Bridget did more—in spirit she undertook the long journey to Avignon. One night Bishop Hemming saw her standing by his bedside and heard her voice: 'Why are you troubled? I, Bridget, promise you that you shall come home safely and happily to your see and there gain many souls for God. But they, to whom I have sent you, and who have hardened their hearts against God, shall soon be made to feel it, and if they do not humble themselves there will be no end to their tribulations.'(5)

From her desk Bridget took out the draft of the letter she had sent to Clement VI.* Those were the words she had heard from the lips of the Son of God Himself.

Write on my behalf as follows to Pope Clement: I have exalted you and given you an office which is above all others. Arise, therefore, and make peace between the kings of France and England, who are like two fierce wild beasts. Go afterwards to Italy and proclaim there a Golden Year, and speak the words of salvation of the love of God and tread in the paths and streets of Rome which are stained with the blood of the holy martyrs, and I will give you the reward that will never end.

Bridget had understood from Bishop Hemming's letter that the Pope had turned a deaf ear to all her wishes. He had not taken any interest in making peace between France and England, he had rejected the request to leave Avignon and move the Chair of Peter back to Rome. He had not, however, objected to proclaim a year of jubilee—it was to be decreed in 1350, with plenary absolution and indulgence for temporal and perpetual punishments for all who devoutly made the pilgrimage to the tombs of Saint Peter and Saint Paul, and who in a spirit of repentance confessed their sins and received Holy Communion.

* I assume that these drafts have always been preserved; two of them, as is known, are to be found in the Royal Library in Stockholm. Copies (*minuta*) were also taken of the letters of Catherine of Siena; at the present day there are still copyists, *minutanti*, among the officials of the Vatican.

But he would not hear anything about the rule of the Order. He gave as a reason that at the Lateran Council in 1215 it had been decided that no new Orders were to be founded. 'But could not the Lady Bridget accept one of the Orders already existing, for instance that of the Augustinians? It was a rule which the founders of other Orders had also adopted, thus Saint Norbert, founder of the Order of the Premonstratensians. . . .'

Perhaps Bridget wondered that her envoys had not referred to the Franciscans, whose rule dated from 1223 (or did she know that the original rule was of 1210—she may have known it, as a Sister of the Third Order of Saint Francis). She had therefore been justified in speaking sternly to Pope Clement in her letter. She read out the words to herself, repeating them slowly and solemnly:

> Take heed to the days of your life, when you stirred me to wrath and did what you would and not what you should. But now my hour will soon be at hand when I will call you to account for all your forgetfulness. And as I have let you rise high above all, so shall I also let you descend to fearful torment of body and soul, if you do not heed my words. Your boastful tongue shall fall silent, your name, that was famed on the earth, shall be forgotten and dishonoured with me and my saints . . . I shall also question you on how slothful you were to make peace between the kings, and how much you leaned to one side.† Nor shall it be forgotten how much covetousness and worldliness increased in your time, but you did nothing against it, for you were yourself a lover of the flesh. Arise, therefore, ere the last hour comes, for it is at hand. You have but a short time left—make use of it. If you doubt of whose spirit these words are, the men and the kingdom are known to you in which strange things have come to pass. Your conscience tells you that what I advise you to do is right. If I had not in patience borne with you, you would have sunk deeper than they who have been popes before you. Look into the book of your conscience and you will see that I speak truth.(6)

XVIII

It is in the summer of 1346, King Magnus is holding his court at Örebro House. The Lady Bridget accompanies her royal kinsman, his queen and their retinue on their journey through the kingdom. They have been in Arboga, where Bridget owns a house, and in the church of the

† The Hundred Years' War began in 1339. During the seven years which had elapsed since then, Bridget thought, the Pope could have mediated for peace if he had not taken sides. Clement VI was born in 1291, the son of the nobleman, Pierre Roger de Beaufort, in 1301 he entered the Benedictine Order, became doctor of theology in 1323, abbot in the large monastery of Fécamp in 1326, Bishop of Arras in 1328, Archbishop of Rouen in 1330, finally Cardinal in 1338 and Pope in 1342. It was a rapid and brilliant career—one can understand the words addressed to him through Bridget: 'I have let you rise high above all.'

Franciscans there, if the visit has fallen on the feast of Saint Peter's Chains (2 August), she would be able to gain the Portiuncula indulgence, that indulgence for which she was later to fight so hard to gain for her own church in Vadstena. Every year on this day and on the feast of Saint Francis (4 October) the pilgrims came in their crowds to Arboga. When Bridget looked up at the paintings with which the vaults and arches of the church were adorned, she could see Saint Francis of Assisi as he stood holding up the sinking church of the Lateran—she, his daughter in the brotherhood of penance, the Third Order of Saint Francis, would do the same. She could see her Sister of the same Order, Saint Elisabeth of Hungary, standing at the convent door and dealing out bread to the poor, the sick and to cripples and pouring out something to drink from a pitcher, probably wine, for them. But she could not foresee that in this very church, dedicated to Saint Peter and Saint Paul, she was herself, at the Church Council in 1396, to be declared the patron saint of Sweden.(1)

It is not the first time King Magnus is in Örebro. In 1333, after Scania had become Swedish, that great Council meeting took place at which the clergy of the kingdom, in patriotic willingness to make a sacrifice, gave up half of the year's tithes as a help in paying the amount of the ransom. Two years later the king obtained a fresh loan from the same well-filled coffers. This was quite according to Bridget's ideas. But what would she have said if, in 1346, she could have foreseen that the Valdemar, that 'wolf in sheep's clothing' whom she hated so much, was to be received with great festivity six years later by King Magnus, as that very same Örebro house?

Bishop Hemming and Prior Petrus have but lately come home from Avignon, and it is no secret that they have returned without having achieved their object—Bridget had already spoken about it when she had received the Bishop's letter. Pope Clement has become an exalted person, and cannot remember at all that Hemming had at one time been his pupil—a professor at the Sorbonne sees so many students, who can remember them all? And *Episcopus Aboensis*—oh well, it is not a title that makes any particular impression—now if it had at least been an *Archiepiscopus*! Avignon is crowded with bishops seeking audience—the papal footmen are used to them and treat them with polite insolence. *Taisez-vous, ce n'est qu'un roi!* said the officer on duty at Napoleon's door, when the sentry saluted a king on his entering with the roll of drums reserved for the Emperor. And a Scandinavian convert, who about the beginning of the new century was sitting in the Vatican and waiting to be admitted to Leo XIII, could, while waiting, hear an exchange of talk between two of the stately door-keepers in crimson damask: *Chi é costui?* 'Who is that?'—*Mbè, uno di questi convertiti—oramai ce ne son tanti!* 'Oh well, he is one of these converts—there are so many of them at present!'

Bishop Hemming and Petrus Olai, then, had come home unsuccess-ful. The Pope had said that they might try themselves to mediate be-tween King Philip and King Edward—and neither the English nor the French ruler had taken any notice of them. For a while Bridget had sailed under a fair wind, now she felt that it was turning—it was a con-trary wind that was arising. She can no longer disarm those who criti-cize her new manner of living with a simple: 'I did not begin it for your sakes, nor am I going to stop for your sakes.'(2) There are many at court whom it does not please that the king pays so much attention to her words—why, last Saint Walburga's Day, he had even given her the royal house of Vadstena! There were opposing forces at work against her—secretly or openly, now in one way, now in another. It did not matter much, of course, what Sir Karl the king's cousin had done—in the midst of a great and brilliant gathering, where the royal-ties were present, he had given her a push in the back so that she had nearly fallen. The king was angry and gave Master Karl a severe repri-mand which he took very much to heart, so much so that he died three days after, and on his deathbed he reproached himself bitterly with having behaved so badly. Bridget willingly forgave him. With all her heart she also forgave another courtier, Sir Knut Folkesson, who one day, when she was walking through the narrow street where he lived, had opened a window and poured water over her—'and marry, it was not clean water' as Chilian says. Bridget had cried up to him: 'God bless you and may you not atone for it in the other world—I have only got what I deserve!' Bridget's brother Israel had spoken later to Sir Knut and reproved him for his behaviour, telling him also what Christ had said to Bridget the night after the incident: 'The knight who poured water over you is a man who likes to shed blood. He should take care that he die not in his blood!' Israel had spoken to deaf ears—Knut Folkesson had shrugged his shoulders and said: 'I do not believe in dreams. God is merciful and condemns no one!' But it was not long before the self-confident gentleman was found dead in his bed—he had had such a severe attack of bleeding at the nose that he had been choked in the streaming blood. 'The Lady Bridget had told him so before-hand,' the women in the quarter whispered to each other.

This was in Stockholm. And what had happened now, lately in Arboga? During dinner a man had come in and had behaved as if he was intoxicated. He had taken up a position by Bridget's chair and had begun to speak to her: 'That is right, Madam, you sit here and eat and drink like anybody else! Just you go on with that, eating well and drinking still better. You keep too much vigil and you dream too much, and after all nobody believes what you say. If God wants to speak to anybody there are priests and monks enough that He can speak to—He need not apply to fine ladies!' The King ordered the man to be taken out, but Bridget pleaded for him. 'Just let him speak,' she said, 'then I shall hear the truth for once! If people knew what I really am, they would not praise and flatter me, such as is now the case. That man knows me!' Then the man suddenly grew sober and began to weep and said: 'It was not of myself that I said all that—it was Sir Nicholas Ingvaldsson who made me drunk and made me do it.'(3)

And now Bridget was walking in the woods at Örebro (at the present day half of the district of Örebro is covered with forest, how much more, then, in the fourteenth century). Was she perhaps on the way to the convent of Riseberga where her daughter Ingeborg was a nun? That was hardly probable, the distance in a straight line is 23 kilometres, and in those days there was no motor bus. Most likely she was only walking there to collect her thoughts. During her stay at Örebro she had discovered something that grieved her—the King's tax collector for the district was not a layman but an ecclesiastic. She had spoken to the King about it—'that kind of office is not suitable for ecclesiastical persons! Priests have to think of that which belongs to the kindgom of God and not of what belongs to Cæsar!' Magnus had admitted that Bridget was right, and a suitable layman had taken over the office.

Bridget was quite assured, she knew that she had done what was right. And yet, and yet, did she not feel a little quaky about her knees when she suddenly, out here in the solitude of the forest, at a bend in the path suddenly saw the dismissed priest coming towards her? At any rate it resulted in a sharp exchange of verbal notes. 'That is a nice piece of work of yours,' the ecclesiastical gentleman exclaimed. 'I had a good office, and you have robbed me of it. Don't you think you would do better in staying at home in your own house, intead of going about and making trouble?'

It was a summer day in the woods near Örebro. Perhaps in the cathedral shade of the firs, perhaps in the light grove of the birches. The wind may have blown through the firs, or a light breeze have rustled among the birch leaves. And perhaps while the two stood opposite each other a bird may have twittered—or the wood pigeon have begun its low, somewhat ominous cooing. Bridget was silent for a moment, then she answered, gently and quietly like the soft murmur of the birches: 'What the King has done at my advice, I advised him to do for the sake of your priestly honour and for the salvation of your soul. You belong to the *clergy*, which means "God's inheritance." It is not seemly that a priest should have to do with business matters, in which he may imperil the salvation of his soul.' As might have been expected this religious argument made no impression on the ecclesiastical gentleman. 'Hoity-toity,' he snarled, 'just you leave the salvation of my soul alone—I am quite able to look after that myself.' The soft whispering in the birches fell silent and a storm of wind rushed through the branches. 'Your mouth speaks out of the evil of your heart,' Bridget exclaimed, and now her voice was strong and stern. 'If you do not take back those words and do penance for them, I tell you, *as true as my name is Bridget*, that you shall not escape God's punishment.'

But not long after this priest was also dismissed from his ecclesiastical office and died a terrible death. For he was present when a bell was being founded and the mould burst, and the molten metal flowed out and burnt him up.(4)

Before the unrepentant priest was struck down by this terrible death, however, Bridget had a vision. She sees him step up before the altar to say his Mass, as the custom is every morning of every Catholic priest. She sees him putting on the priestly vestments, first the humeral, which signifies the yoke of Christ, then the alb, signifying priestly purity, next the cincture, with which he girds his loins and which keeps the passions of the flesh in restraint, then the maniple, the chain of the commandments of Christ round his arm, after that the sign of the priestly authority, the consecrated stole, which he lays about his neck, and over it all finally the chasuble, which is red or violet or green or white, according to the Mass, whether it is for a martyr or a day of penance, or it is a Sunday, or a feast for a virgin or a confessor. And followed by his Mass server the priest comes out from the sacristy holding the chalice and paten in his hands, places the sacred vessels on the altar, takes up a position on the lowest step of the altar and begins the sacred action with a large sign of the Cross and saying: *Introibo ad altare Dei*, 'I will go in unto the altar of God. . . .'

Bridget was present at the Mass being said by the priest at Örebro. She sees him putting on the priestly vestments, but it is not an altar boy or a kind old man who is serving his Mass. It is two devils who are present invisibly to him and helping him.

And when he puts on the humeral his spirit is darkened so that he does not think or understand that my altar must be approached with fear and trembling, and how pure he must be who would stand before my face. When he puts on the alb his heart is hardened so that he thinks that his sins are not so great, and that in the worst case he will be able to endure everlasting hell, and he gives no thought to the everlasting joy of heaven. When he places the stole round his neck the devil insinuates into his mind memories of sweet sins and it becomes impossible for him to feel any remorse over them. When he puts on the maniple his hand becomes unable to do what is right for God, but he finds it easy to do what is of the world. When he binds himself with the cincture he binds himself so fast to the devil that he resolves to live on in sin, and to do all that the devil inspires him to do. When he dons the Mass vestment the devil clothes him in his falseness.

Bridget now sees the unhappy priest begin the Mass with the *Confiteor*, the confession of sins. The devils stand by his side and answer: 'You are telling a lie. You are not repenting of your sins at all! You are a Judas, saying one thing and meaning another.' But the priest does not seem to heed them, he continues the service, reads the Epistle and Gospel, intones the hymn of praise: 'Holy, holy, holy,' and reaches the moment when the priest stands bending over the bread and in trembling murmurs the words of the Holy Gospel: 'Our Lord Jesus Christ in the night He was betrayed . . .' and in his hands he takes the golden chalice: 'In like manner taking also the chalice. . . .'

At this the devils flee—for at the words of the priest, be he never so unworthy, Christ comes and is present in the consecrated Host and the holy Chalice. But they return when the priest dares to convey the Sacrament to his impure lips. 'That Communion,' says Christ to Bridget, 'is just as pleasing to me as if a harlot offered a noble gentleman a cup which she had filled with the impurities of her body. (5) And this priest shall therefore never come before my heavenly altar. I am the true pelican, who give my blood as food in this world and in the world to come. But this man shall be fed by that dreadful eagle which for a time feeds its young with the joys of the world and afterwards lets them hunger for ever.'

He was not the only ecclesiastic who was struck down by a terrible death because he would not listen to Bridget's warning voice. What was the fate of that priest who lived an immoral life and would not give it up? 'Our Lord is not so particular,' he had said in answer to Bridget's admonitions—an answer she often received and which always made her indignant—she knew well enough how particular God was. One day this priest went out into the field to bring in his horse, a thunderstorm was threatening and he was not going to let his horse stand and get drenched with the rain. Hardly had he pulled up the tethering peg than the lightning struck him and he fell dead to the ground. His servants came rushing out and brought in the body, it was uninjured, except that the limb with which he had sinned in fornication was burnt up.(6)

In a vision Bridget has heard her Bridegroom complain bitterly of 'the wicked priests who love the world and neglect Christ.' They are to be likened to the children of Israel who, when Moses was on the Mount, made a golden calf and worshipped it. The calf worshipped by these priests is named 'perfect love of the world.' It stands on four feet, which are called sloth, impatience, foolish merriment, covetousness. The calf has also a head and a throat—that is to say that these priests are so greedy that they can never have enough, and so thirsty that they would be able to drink up the whole trough of water. The calf has a rump, which is the avarice of these priests, who can never let any man have a property in peace without trying to take it from him. They think about Christ as the Israelites did about Moses—he was away a long time, and who could tell whether he would ever come back again? They attend to their official duties—offering to God as much incense and as many prayers as can be desired. And they speak and preach fair words in the hope of getting a better office. They cry to God with their lips but their thoughts wander about on errands in all other places than in the church. 'They bend their knees to me,' says Christ, 'but in reality they are not more humble than Lucifer. They have the key of my sanctuary; when they say: "Thy will be done," they open it with the key, but they close it again when they live according to their own will, and they shut me in when with their bad example they hinder others from doing my will.'

But soon there will be enough of this—'the priests have become loathsome to me,' Christ exclaims. 'To whom shall I liken them?' As in the days of His life upon earth the Saviour often speaks to Bridget in parables. 'Verily, the priests are like the fruits of that thorny bush which are called hips. Outwardly they are fair and red, but inside they are full of small prickly thorns.' It is the same with the priests—the red Mass vestment means that love of God which ought to burn in their souls, and people believe that it is so. 'But inwardly they are full of all impurities—and if one buries them others of the same kind will only come after them instead. And it is not only that they are great sinners, they pride themselves on their sin and others take courage and think: "Yes, if the priest can do such things, why should not we do so too?" And not only are they like the fruits of the hips—they are like the thorns of the bush, which no one can touch without being pricked—they will not accept teaching from anyone and think they are wiser than all others. 'But in the hearing of all angels I swear now in my Godhead and Manhood that soon I will burst open all the doors behind which they have shut me in, and my will shall be fulfilled, and their will shall be brought to nought, and they shall be confined in that torment which shall never end. For it is written that judgment shall begin from the House of God.'(7)

Of whom much has been given, much will be required. And to whom has God given more than to the priests? When a man sets out on a long journey he gives his most precious possession to a good friend who can take care of it for him while he is away. When Christ set out on the long journey from which He has not yet returned, as He has promised, He gave His Apostles five gifts. 'First I gave them my faith. Next the keys of heaven and hell. Thirdly, that of my enemies they might make angels. Fourthly, that they could consecrate bread and wine to become my body and my blood, which no angel has the power to do. In the fifth place, that they should administer this sacrament of my body.'

These five gifts were made an inheritance from the Apostles to the priests of the Catholic Church. But what have they done with these gifts? They stand in the pulpit and make long speeches like a worldly lecturer. They have lost the key of the kingdom of heaven, they have wrapped up the key to hell neatly in a white silken cloth and hidden it in a drawer. They make unjust people of the just, they turn simple people into devils, and he who comes to them with three wounds goes away with four, and he who comes with four goes away with five, for the sinner sees that the priest sins and makes bold to sin also—when the priest does it, it cannot be so bad? The priests are worse than Judas —he betrayed his Master before the Master had saved the world, the priests betray him after the redemption had been consummated. Judas was covetous—so are the priests. Out of the ten commandments of God they have made a single one—'stretch out your hand and come hither with money!' But it is not known that Judas had mistresses, and that it was for their sake that he accepted the thirty pieces of silver. The priests on the other hand—they spend their pay and the money they receive for Mass stipends on keeping concubines—'they provide for their accursed womenfolk and see that they live in comfort so that they can satisfy their lust with them and they are not ashamed of it.' And the next morning they stand before the altar as dirty as tar and touch me with the hands with which they have caressed their women. 'But the seven plagues which came upon the people of Israel shall also come upon the priests.'(8)

Bridget has no doubts about the Catholic priesthood as such—she is not a Donatist, the rightfully ordained priest administers the sacraments with the same validity, whether he be a saint or a criminal. 'Even if the worst man were a priest and said the words *Hoc est corpus meum*, he would thereby consecrate the bread to my body, and I lie before him on the altar, true God and true Man. . . . But such priests are true traitors who sell and betray me worse than Judas—and when I look upon heathens and Jews I find none who are as great sinners as they.'

Christ therefore now pronounces the great curse upon them—the curse of David of the Old Covenant upon those who do not obey God. 'He was a righteous prophet and king, and he cursed, not in wrath nor from ill will, but because it was right. But I, who am more than David, curse them who in these days are priests—not from wrath nor from ill will, but because it is right.' And now the thunder rolls, peal upon peal, from Sinai:

> Cursed be all that the priests enjoy of the benefits of the earth, for they do not praise and thank God for them. Cursed be the food and drink that enters into their mouth and nourishes the body as food for worms and the soul for hell. Cursed by their body, which shall rise from the dead to burn everlastingly in hell. Cursed be all the years of their life, which they have lived in vain. Cursed be the first moment with which hell begins for them, and which shall never be followed by the last. Cursed be their eyes, with which they beheld the light of heaven. Cursed be their ears, with which they heard my words and did not heed them. Cursed be their tongue, with which they tasted my gifts. Cursed be their hands with which they touched me in the Sacrament of the Altar. Cursed be the sense with which they smelt the pleasant things of the world and forgot me, who am more pleasant than everything else.

For a moment there is silence in the rolling thunder of the maledictions—Bridget asks: 'But how shall this curse come upon them?' She gets an answer, and the answer is this:

> Their sight shall be accursed for they shall not see the mild countenance of God, but the darkness and torment of hell. Their ears shall be accursed,

because they would not heed my words, but now they shall hear the screams and howls of hell. Cursed be their tongue, for they shall not taste my everlasting benefits, but everlasting bitterness. Cursed be their hands for they shall no longer hold me in them, but the glowing coals of hell. Cursed be their smell, for they shall never smell that which is sweetest in my kingdom, which is above all sweet smelling waters, but they shall smell the stench of hell, which is more bitter than gall and worse than the smell of sulphur. Cursed be they by heaven and earth and by all creatures having no understanding for they all praise and rejoice in God, but those others despised Him.

XIX

The Lord gave me, and still gives me, so great a faith in the priests that live according to the rules of the Holy Roman Church, that even if they persecuted me, I would yet have recourse to them because of their consecrated priesthood. And even if I had as much wisdom as Solomon, and met here and there in the parishes where they belong poor small priests, I would not preach against their will. And I would fear them and all other priests, loving and honouring them as my masters. And I would not see their faults, for in them I see the Son of God, and they are my masters. And this I do, because in this world I do not see bodily anything of that same Son of the most high God, except His most Holy Blood, which the priests receive and deal out to others.(1)

Out of reverence for the office of the priests Francis of Assisi would not see their sins. Were there, perhaps, fewer sinful priests in the thirteenth century than in the fourteenth? It may have been so. Bridget has it, that during a thousand years the wrath of God over the world has not been so great as now, in these times, which she is not the only one to think are the last.(2)

Bridget's greatest reproach against the priests, in Sweden, and later, elsewhere, is that they do not keep their vows of celibacy. In making this demand, not only (like the Greek Orthodox Church) on monks, but also on the clergy living outside monastic walls, the Catholic Church does so on the basis of Saint Paul's words about the married man, that 'he cares for that which is of the world, and how he may please his wife, and he is divided.'(3) That this commandment has always been the hard one, and that it has been difficult to make it kept, is known to everyone with any knowledge of the history of the Church, in Sweden as elsewhere. A hundred years after Bridget's time the Swedish clergy had to be forbidden at church meetings to keep concubines. There was still the same immorality of which Bridget had complained—'the priests purchase for gold a woman's body and do not consider the scandal they give in the congregation, if only they can satisfy their desire.'

The deluge, however, also penetrated within the walls of the monasteries. In her own country of Sweden Bridget never seems to have had any faults to find with her brethren in Saint Francis, but on the other hand with those in Italy. Madame de Flavigny says caustically, that it was probably because she herself belonged to the Third Order of Saint Francis.(4) Bridget tried all the more to guide the brethren in the other great mendicant Order, the Dominicans. She had at an early date come into connection with the monastery in Skara, where her good friend, Brother Algot, was the Prior. But also with other Blackfriars in Sweden —Stockholm, Skenninge, Kalmar, and quite especially Sigtuna. This old city, which had succeeded Birka as a commercial town, had since the beginning of the thirteenth century had an imposing Blackfriars monastery; the church, which was dedicated to the Blessed Virgin (and is now the parish church of the town) was built in 1240, a triple-naved church in the Cistercian style with a square chancel. The monastery was large and possessed—against the rule of the Order, but with a papal privilege of 1265—large properties. (In 1523 Gustavus Vasa received from it the not inconsiderable sum of 100 marks in pure silver). It was also against the rule of the Order that the brethren in Sigtuna strove to occupy exalted ecclesiastic positions—two of them had even become archbishops of Uppsala.

At one time or another in the period concerned Bridget must, either alone or in the royal retinue, have visited Sigtuna. She would step into the lofty, vaulted, broadly built church and think: 'Is this a church for poor mendicant friars?' for there were three other churches in the town, Saint Peter's, Saint Olof's and Saint Lars' (Laurence), so there was no lack of churches, and after the Esthonians had burnt down the city in 1187 and Stockholm had begun to assert itself as a commercial place the three shrines were more than sufficient. And now mendicant friars, yes, exactly *mendicant* friars—why should they build to the Lord such a large and costly temple with money obtained by begging?

As her custom was, Bridget took counsel of heaven. And she obtained her answer from Her to whom the church was dedicated, the Blessed Virgin.

When a church is so broad that the congregation can find room in it [said Mary], when the walls are so high that people do not knock their heads against the vaultings, and so thick that they cannot be upset by the first

I

chance wind, when finally, the roof is so water-tight that the rain cannot come in, it is enough. A humble mind in a modest church is more pleasing to God than tall buildings in which the bodies may be inside, but the thoughts are outside them. The good friars need not fill their money chests with gold and silver in order to erect large and handsome buildings—just tell them that.

It was not only in their architecture but also in other ways that it seemed to Bridget that the Dominicans in Sigtuna had transgressed against their rule. She knew very well that the Pope had allowed them to eat flesh meat because of the cold climate and to wear warmer clothes than in the South. Mary agrees with the Pope (she even says to Bridget: 'Let us excuse the Pope—he meant well!')—that more substantial diet is necessary for the friars to be able to work and preach with all their energy, and as for their habit, Saint Dominic himself had ordered that the material for it must not be too rough, but that was because the Dominicans sleep without undressing, only with the cowl over their heads, and the rough material would therefore scratch them and prevent them from sleeping. But the unusually handsome habit, the black scapular over the white robe, may of course give occasion for vanity, especially as it is most frequently women who have recourse to Dominicans. (In the 'nineties in Copenhagen the handsome Père Lange was much sought after by women for his French sermons!)

In Skenninge, too, Bridget visited the Dominicans. Nor was there here reason to be satisfied—in this monastic orchard, too, there were many trees that did not bear fruit. 'But if I pulled all of them up by the roots,' said Christ to His impatient new bride, 'what would the garden look like, with all those holes in the ground, and all that dust?' It is better to proceed like a careful and experienced nurseryman who saves what can still be saved, and grafts a new cutting on the old root (if only the root is still sound, and this it is as long as a soul can say the fourth prayer in the Our Father: 'Thy will be done'). The devil, that ugly mole, may be able to shake such a decaying tree, but he cannot uproot it, and the Prior of the monastery, Brother Ketilmund, was a tree of this kind. Like so many others he had had his doubts about Bridget— were her revelations really words spoken by God? Then it happened to him as it had happened to Brother Svenung in Compostella—he saw the Lady Bridget in a vision and saw fire from heaven descending upon her. And a voice could be heard, saying: 'No one can hinder this fire from going forth, for by my power I will send it from east to west, to north and south, and it shall set many aflame!' But from that hour Brother Ketilmund was convinced and until his death (about 1370) he was one of Bridget's most ardent spokesmen. And in a vision he saw Christ hold out His hand to him like a brother, and he heard Christ say: 'Look, Ketilmund, this is where the nail pierced through the bone!'(5)

In the Swedish Dominican monasteries, however, there were not many like Ketilmund. When lying on his death-bed Saint Dominic had besought Mary to guard and protect his brethren under her cloak, and Mary had willingly given him her promise to do so. 'But now,' she says to Bridget, 'there are fewer under my cloak than there were then under his narrow scapular.'* For what was it that Dominic required of his disciples? That they were to fight against those three evil forms of concupiscence that are displeasing to God by a life in the three great virtues: humility, continence and contempt of the world. Dominic had given his brethren a red cross as a sign by which to know them —as the sheep which are to be slaughtered are marked with red. But the devil had come and had marked the sheep with a cut in the right ear, so that they can no longer hear the voice of God, but the delicious voice of the world and the flesh. And the chastisement shall come upon them like a hunter with fierce dogs. It shall be as when a servant says to his master: 'Lord, a great number of sheep have come in here to the farm, their flesh has been poisoned and their fleeces are soiled, and their milk is not fit to drink, and they bear themselves obscenely. Would it not be best to drive them out so that they do not eat away the fodder from the good sheep and molest them with their obscenity?' Then the Lord will answer: 'Fasten all the gates with bolts except one, and place a guard by it so that no others can get in but those with which I am content. And then the hunter shall come with the dogs, and they shall tear the fleeces from the bad sheep and bite them to death.'(6)

It was also against the rule of Saint Dominic when the brethren of his Order became bishops. One of the first Dominicans, Jordanus of Saxony, wrote that it was better that a Blackfriar should die than that he should become a bishop. Here again, the Holy See had interfered— why should the church relinquish the use a pious and learned Dominican might be as a bishop? Bridget knows this, she also knows that Saint Augustine followed the rule of his Order just as well after he had become a bishop as before. If that is so all is well and she has no

* Scapular (from scapula) is the narrow piece of cloth which covers the habit before and behind—properly speaking an apron to protect it. Bridget takes the scapular as a symbol of the saint's care for the brethren both at the moment and in the time to come (*duplicem considerationem quam ad fratres habuit*).

objections to make. But how often does a saint sit in the chair of a bishop? In a vision she sees two bishops, an older and a younger, both Dominicans. She sees the former of the two in the likeness of a butterfly. The body is small, but in front there is a big mouth and two horns. The wings are broad, shining in the most beautiful colours, red, white and blue—but the colour is not fixed, if you touch them you only get a little dust on your fingers. The red colour means that he continually disputes about the Passion of Christ and the wonders worked by the saints, in the hope that he shall be looked upon as a holy man. But the truth is that nothing is further from him than the Cross and martyrdom. The blue colour means that he would like to be looked upon as dead to all earthly things and that his thoughts and longings are blue as the sky, but neither is that colour fixed, it is only dust that you get in your fingers. And the white colour—well, he wants to be accounted a man of pure living, but that is no better than the two other colours. The two horns, on the other hand, are indeed firm enough, one horn means that he wants to live in comfort and happiness here below, and have everlasting bliss after death, first the honour and glory of the world, afterwards a golden crown and a place of honour in heaven. For it is written, he says, that whosoever gives a disciple of Christ a cup of cold water shall not miss his reward—and he has done much more for Our Lord. How, for instance, would the Church have fared if he had not opened his mouth in the pulpit? So that with a good conscience he can open his wide mouth and swallow all the flies he can (Bridget did not know that butterflies suck honey and do not eat flies). But if only one single fly was left which he had not swallowed he would not be satisfied until he had swallowed that too. . . .

That was the butterfly—a prince of the Church in magnificent robes. The other bishop is likened, more modestly, to a wasp. He is not more pleasing than that. 'The wasp is of the colour of the earth and flies with great humming and stings so that the sting is felt a long time after.' It is of the colour of the earth—for in spite of the vow of poverty this bishop desired nothing better than to possess earthly goods and gold. It buzzed a great deal, for this bishop is a great preacher and makes much talk about renouncing the world, which he himself desires to enjoy. He has two wings, that is, that he likes to appear kindly and friendly to everyone, but in reality he wants everyone to obey him. The sting of the wasp is poisonous and the words of this bishop are poison to souls—he wants to appear mild and forbearing, and does not want his penitents to go to other priests, and therefore he does not cut out the boils of sin with a knife, but is content to smear them with an unction of mild words.

Bridget sees and hears these two insects—sees the butterfly flutter the gaudy wings, hears the wasp booming. But, after all, why has she to see these two creatures, she asks. To the former, the butterfly, she once in vain brought a message from the Blessed Virgin.(7) Can it be any pleasure to God to see these two perish? 'Come, and you shall hear,' Mary says to her. And now Bridget witnesses a strange talk between the two insects: the butterfly (the elder) and the wasp (the younger).

The wasp: 'Listen to me, brother, and answer me. You belonged to an Order and had vowed to live in poverty and obedience—why did you break those vows? You had renounced the world and had entered a monastery—why then, did you want to be a bishop?'

It is the wasp that stings. The wasp is no better than the butterfly, it is under the same judgment, and yet it cannot tame its poisonous tongue. Now the *butterfly* answers (with the sincerity one has when it is no longer any use to conceal anything):

'I found it irksome to obey, and God's yoke was too heavy for me, and—as the proverb says—it is better to be the driver than to be the horse.'

The *wasp* (goes on stinging): 'But why did you not make a better use of your position as a bishop? Why did you not strive after the honour and glory of this world?'

The *butterfly* (still sincere): 'If I did not appear with the show and magnificence to which my office entitled me, it was out of calculation —I hoped to be more honoured if I appeared in humility and piety. It was in order to be honoured by the world that I pretended to despise it!'

This play-acting succeeded—the episcopal coffers were filled, and the money was not wasted on almsgiving. Again the *wasp* buzzes and stings:

'Tell me, why did you give the asses a sweet drink and your brethren, the bishops, food of the mash that the swine wanted to eat? Why did you tread your bishop's mitre underfoot? Why did you spit out the wheat and begin chewing thistles? Why did you loosen the bonds of others, and bind yourself with chains? Why did you heal the wounds of others and cause yourself a mortal wound?'

To all these questions the *butterfly* has only one answer: 'Because I would not do that which I taught others to do. I laid heavy burdens upon others, but I would not touch them myself with a finger.' Then

Bridget heard a voice saying: 'This bishop shall die!' And from the depths the plaint of the dead one ascends to her: 'Woe is me, for now the bishop's mitre is gone, and the dirt that was under it can be seen. Where is that most reverend bishop, where is his reverence the priest? Where is the poor friar? Gone is the bishop who was annointed with oil and dedicated to the life of an apostle, and only the filthy thrall of dust remains. Gone is the priest who with holy words was to sanctify bread to become God, and there is left only a Judas who for worldly gain sold Him who redeemed us all with His love! Gone too, is the poor friar who by his oath renounced the world, and now I am judged because of my pride.' The play has been acted to the end, the beautiful costume is returned to the cloakroom, the silk and velvet, and the cloak of gold brocade is hung up on a peg in the sacristy. Of the public personage, the eloquent ecclesiastic, the well-known priest, of all that the world saw and that devout souls looked up to, nothing is left but a naked soul shivering with cold in the icy wind from hell. Bridget hears his last words ere he enters into the despair that will never end: '*I could have been* saved, for he who has condemned me, suffered once on the wood of the cross a bitter death for my salvation.'(8)

XX

From Örebro the journey continued westwards to Lödöse. Wherever the travellers went it was the Lady Bridget who aroused most attention, more than the king, more than the beautiful young queen. There is nothing remarkable in this, for wonderful and powerful deeds were lit like bonfires wherever Bridget appeared and her fame preceded her like beacons that are lit from the neighbour's house to the next nearest neighbour to bring a message of importance. Before the light which radiated from her the powers of darkness had to flee.

As yet there remained in corners much of the darkness of the old paganism. A short time before the arrival at Lödöse Bridget visited a peasant in whose house a devil had also established his abode. It lived in the oven and from this oven it spoke and answered any questions put to it—almost as in our days spiritualists receive an answer through a table-leg. The spirit was a spirit of divination and many people went there to consult it. Bridget discovered this and asked her heavenly Bridegroom for light that she might see what she ought to do. The answer she received was that the evil spirit visited this house because the people living in it were not Christians, but worshipped the spirits of their ancestors (the text in the testimony of Prior Petrus Olaus had *penates*). These penates were worshipped in the form of snakes, to whom were offered milk, cheese and bread as a kind of first-fruits, so that no one touched these comestibles without the snakes having first had their share. In his testimony Prior Petrus mentions that *wine* was also offered to the snakes—presumably that is why the scene of the incident has, by several authors, been laid in Italy, in the neighbourhood of Ortona. It is true that Prior Petrus does not mention the name of the village concerned, but he knows quite certainly that it is situated 'near Lödöse,' *prope Lodosiam*. There were then, in the middle of the four-teenth century, snake worshippers in Sweden, who connected this heathen worship with a no less heathen faith in *fate*. This fatalism might also be Italian—*il destino* is, unwittingly, to many a worthy peasant and peasant woman down yonder in the old Latin country, the highest divinity. After a case of a very sad death I heard this reflection: 'Yes, God is good, He does nobody any harm! but what can He do, *when fate will have it so*!' Above Jupiter is Fatum—like the Norn above the gods of Valhalla. Incidentally, however, this belief in fate does not pre-vent an Italian of the common people from going to Mass on Sunday— the people on the farm at Lödöse also went to church on Sundays, why be conspicuous? But they did not care to hear the sermon. And just because of this Bridget ordered Prior Petrus—who accompanied her also on this part of the journey—to preach to them. Like another sceptical peasant—Botolph of Gottröra in Uppland, who on Holy Thursday in 1311 was burnt because he refused to believe in the Sacra-ment of the Altar—the Lödöse peasants declared that the consecrated Host in the priest's hand was nothing but a 'little slice of bread.' Prior Petrus' sermon, however, made an impression.

'When you desire and love worldly things more than God, He permits you to thrive in temporal matters, but the devil possesses your souls. Believe in God and not in these serpents to which you pour out milk, and do not give tithes to the tomts' (the old Swedish translation of the Revelations uses this word for *penates*; the tomts are, as we know, the brownies or pixies—on whom the Lödöse folk bestowed not only Christmas porridge, but 'meat of cattle and pigs' as well as 'bread and wine and other drink'). 'And do not believe any more that it is for-tune or fate that rules everything, but that it is God who allows all things to happen, and on the altar it is not a little slice of bread but the true Body of God; believe in the Church and her sacraments: Baptism and Confirmation and Extreme Unction, and the devil will flee from you.' But when Prior Petrus had said these words they all cried, those who had come from the house and the whole village: 'We believe, and we promise to repent!' And immediately a voice was heard coming from the oven where the devil was, and the voice cried: 'Here there is no longer an abiding place for me!' And henceforth the voice of the devil was not heard there any more.(1)

A peculiar kind of demoniac phenomena consisted in women being possessed by a devil, with whom they believed they had had carnal intercourse—a so-called *incubus*. In one of these women the abdomen swelled as if she were really pregnant—but at a word from Bridget this hysterical phenomenon disappeared (modern psycho-analysis has a technical expression for it). Another woman thought that her three-year-old son was a result of her connection with such a demon—though in such a way that her husband was the father of the child's body, but that the devil had infused into it a soul. The child suffered frequently from convulsions which had to be relieved by cold spongings. Moreover, it was discovered that the boy had not yet been baptized—only, according to an old Scandinavian custom, having had water poured over him. Bridget saw to it that the child was christened.

One conversion followed another in the Lady Bridget's train. A distinguished old gentleman was lying very ill, but would not hear of making his confession. Three times did Prior Petrus try to make him listen to reason, three times he was refused. Then, in a vision Bridget saw the soul and body of the old man possessed by seven devils—one of them was actually sitting on his tongue and preventing him from uttering a confession of his sins. Bridget drove out all the seven and the old sinner came to himself again—the hard crust about his heart broke and the tears welled forth. 'Can there still be mercy for me?' he asked anxiously, keeping a tight hold of the priest's hand like a drowning man clutching the gunwale of the life-boat. 'I have done so much evil in my life, I have even seen the devil, spoken with him and hailed him as my master!' This, too, might have happened in Italy—even in modern Italy. A friend of mine, who had a property near Assisi, had a farmer who had communions with *il Demonio*—they used to meet and talk by a certain tree. There had formerly been a convent in the place and the devil had told the peasant that a treasure was buried somewhere under the ruins. Excavations were made to find the treasure, but it turned out that the Evil One—as usual—had lied. The Swedish nobleman must also have been given great promises by the devil—why, he had even denied God and sworn an oath of loyalty to God's enemy.

'Is there still mercy for me?' In one day the sick man made confession four times—it took time to clean out everything. And peace came upon him—the great peace when everything has been said. He died the next day—'I always wait until the very last moment,' said Christ to Bridget.(2)

Another great gentleman was also converted by her from his impenitence—the evil enemy even made the horse she was riding bolt, though it was usually the gentlest animal imaginable—'so that you could see all the four hoofs in the air at the same time.' The wild gallop caused her the severest pains in her back, and she felt them a long time after, but she reached her goal in time, just when the nobleman had an attack. The attack found expression in the most terrible blasphemies—'I can't help it!' he said, in answer to Bridget's reproaches. She wanted to speak to him in the name of Christ—the spirit became still more furious: 'Do not mention that man! I believe in the God that has made heaven and earth, and not in your new God, Christ!' At Bridget's bidding this madman was also cured—'he ceased speaking and fell asleep and a few days after he was well.'(3)

Mention is also made of further cures of this kind of cases of possession. In one case Bridget had to fight, not with an invisible enemy, but with flesh and blood, with a demon in the shape of a woman. The parish priest in the little town of Rinna, Master John, had been bewitched by a girl, and was so madly in love with her that he could think of nothing else either day or night. There was no longer any question of prayer, his lips mumbled the customary words, but the flesh screamed so that he did not know whether he had prayed or not prayed. For many long years he had lived as a priest ought to live—was he to give way now, at last? He knew what the Holy Scriptures say about 'the young man void of understanding' who left his house and went out into the street 'in the twilight, in the evening, in the black dark night. And behold, there met him a woman with the attire of an harlot, and subtil of heart; her feet abide not in her house. And she caught him and kissed him and said to him: Behold, I have come forth to meet thee, diligently, to seek thy face, and I have found thee. I have decked my bed with coverings of tapestry, with fine linen from Egypt. I have perfumed my bed with myrrh, aloes and cinnamon. Come, let us take our fill of love until the morning.' The parish priest in Rinna was no longer a 'young man void of understanding.' He knew that the house of such a woman inclineth unto death, and her paths unto the dead. None that go unto her return again, neither take they hold of the paths of life.' He knew it, but 'stolen waters are sweet, and bread eaten in secret is pleasant.'(4)

In this hour of need the priest John wrote to Bridget and received the answer: 'This woman is in the power of the devil. Her tongue will be her death, her own hand will kill her and the devil will write her testament!' And three days after the letter had come the woman was mad with rage, biting herself in her tongue so that the blood gushed out of her mouth, and she seized a knife and thrust it into her stomach, as she began to shout: 'Come, Satan, let us go to hell together!' And in this way she died. But the priest John left Rinna and entered a monastery.(5)

In the royal retinue there was another priest, Master Magnus of Motala. As they were nearing Lödöse he fell ill and could no longer sit on his horse—would they have to leave him behind with a peasant? Perhaps it was at that farm where the devil had taken up his abode in the oven—in any case Master Magnus was very unwilling to be left behind among strangers. 'Will you leave me here among these wild animals?' he asked Bridget. The Lady Bridget looked at Prior Petrus— they were both standing at the bedside of the sick man—'May I?' she asked with a look. He nodded yes. Then she laid her hand upon Master Magnus' brow (it was in his head that he had the pain, and he seemed to be quite confused): 'Oh, most sweet Jesus, heal him.' And immediately Master Magnus arose and went with the others, sitting his horse more erectly than before.(6)

Then they came to Lödöse where Bridget and her companions took lodgings in an inn. The rumour quickly spread round the town that she had arrived and a host of poor people soon stood outside the door, waiting for alms. It was a sight like a Saturday morning in Assisi, when the beggars go on their rounds through the town in an assembled band from door to door and receive the regulation *soldo*. Among them there are some who are privileged, they get more—*e.g.* Giuseppina, with the grey wisps of hair showing under her kerchief—she has known better days and does not beg under her own name, no, but she has a daughter who is to be married and a fair amount is needed for her trousseau. . . . The same thing happened at Lödöse and Bridget asked her treasurer (it was not yet Petrus Olai of Skenninge) to give a third of what there was in the purse. The others also received liberal gifts, so liberal that there was some difficulty in meeting the hotel bill. Rather sarcastically the treasurer remarked that it was a strange way of being charitable—first to pour out money to the poor and then to have to borrow. Bridget's answer was the evangelical one: 'Give, and it shall be given unto thee. *Deus providebit*.' Next morning when she was at Mass, she heard the voice she knew so well say to her: 'It was through love that I entered the Virgin's womb; it is love that makes God enter the souls of men.'(7)

Bridget was helped this time, as so often later, when through the giving of alms she became poor and had to beg for herself. It was probably King Magnus who with his usual generosity came to her aid. Then Bridget bade him and his Queen farewell—a message had arrived from Alvastra to tell her that Bengt was dying.

XXI

When the Lady Bridget had returned from the Swedish king to the monastery in Alvastra she found that one of her sons, who had been ill for a long time when she left him, now lay dying, and she wept a great deal over his protracted illness, as she believed that it had happened because of the sins of his parents. Then the devil appeared to her and said: 'Woman, why dost thou weaken thy sight with the water of so many tears—is it possible for the waters to rise up to heaven?' But at the same moment Christ appeared in human form to the bride and said: 'This boy's illness is not caused by the position of the stars, as foolish people say'—here as always Bridget is the sworn enemy of superstition —neither for his own sins, but because such is nature's condition, so that he may obtain a more glorious crown. If therefore he has hitherto been called Bengt Ulfsson, from henceforth he shall be called the son of tears and prayers, and I will put an end to his affliction.' And on the fifth day a sweet singing like the chirping of birds was heard between the boy's bed and the wall, and behold, the boy's soul left his body and the spirit said to Bridget: 'Now this son of tears has gone to his rest.'(1)

The same song of birds from the garden of Paradise was heard at the death-bed of Elisabeth of Thuringia. In the process of canonization one of her maids states: 'As my mistress, blessed Elisabeth, was lying on her death-bed, I heard her singing softly. She was lying with her face to the wall, and turning over she said to me: "Where are you, dear?" I answered: "I am here," and added: "Oh, my mistress, how sweetly you did sing!" "Did you hear it?" she asked, and I answered, "Yes." Then she said: "There was a little bird between me and the wall, and it sang so sweetly that I could not help singing too." This was a few days before her death.'(2)

Bengt was buried in the abbey church beside his father—his brother Gudmar already rested there. 'He went to school in Stockholm and died as a young lad' (1338).(3) Bridget now had three of her loved ones in God's keeping. Ingeborg and Cecilia were also well cared for, Karin's marriage to Eggert was the fulfilment of that dream which Bridget herself was not allowed to realize. Mereta's marriage was certainly far from that ascetic ideal, but her son Peter promised well.(4) Birger followed in the footsteps of his uncle Israel. Only Karl was her constant child of affliction. How had he behaved during his visit to the von Kyrens? At night he had crept into the bedroom of his hosts and in the morning he had made game of them because they were not lying like other married couples, 'under one sheet,' but 'like devout monks, dressed in coarse woollen garments, they lay each one apart on the floor' . . . and later, when the two couples met in Kalmar, he had raged because Karin had tried to speak a few words to his wife and had sung the song of chastity to her—'it is for the body what humility is for the soul, because as the purity of the body is to be free from the taint of persons, so humility is to be free from the taint of the devil.' 'It is quite enough to have one *béguine* in the family,' he had said, 'my wife is not also going to be the talk of the people.'(5)

Yet even with all this there was still some good in Karl. He had, moreover, in spite of his mischievous pranks, been a good boy. He showed particular devotion to the Blessed Virgin, and not only selfishly, in the hope of intercession in the hour of need and death, no, it was absolutely disinterested, because he really loved the Queen of Heaven, honoured and loved as a knight his lady. His love of Mary went so far that if it could be imagined that the exalted Lady of his heart were to lose but the smallest ray of her glory—that the least damage might touch that crown she wore in heaven—well then, Sir Karl would rather suffer the everlasting pain of damnation than that such slight harm should befall the beloved of his soul.

Karl had not inherited this love of the Queen of Heaven from strangers. 'Once when in prayer Saint Bridget meditated upon Christ's birth of the Virgin, and how God had chosen that pure maiden for His Mother, her heart began to glow with love for the Blessed Virgin, and she said to herself: "Oh, my Queen of Heaven! I am so happy that God the Most High has chosen thee for His Mother, and bestowed so much dignity upon thee, that rather would I suffer everlastingly in hell than that thou shouldst lose the least part of so great an honour and thy heavenly dignity." But after this prayer she was beside herself with emotion and filled with the sweetness of love.'(6)

When one considers what Bridget had seen in her visions of the unspeakable horrors of hell, one is tempted to doubt the genuineness of such a wish. Possibly the doubt arises because we modern Christians, and also we modern Catholics, are unable to sound the depth of that feeling, which the Germans of the Middle Ages called 'Marienminne' (love of Mary). In Bridget this feeling acquired a special character as she felt as if she were the spouse of the great Mother's Son, and as such owed her more reverence and a more devoted love than others.

Taking it altogether Bridget could think of her children without anxiety and begin her monastic life again in Alvastra. She would not return to the court any more, and no more accompany Magnus and Blanca on their travels. And she had now been to Ulfåsa for the last time. The children were there now—and the grandchildren—Ulf—and little Karl. . . .

Ulfåsa was abandoned, abandoned for ever. Yet a dream could lead her back there again. . . . It would seem to her as if she stood once more in that well-known courtyard and glanced from one house to the other. There stood Vistboden with its store of flour in sacks, and sides of bacon and hams under the roof and the big barrels of ale and one or two hogsheads with sweet wine from Spain or wine from Moselle that sparkles when you pour it into the glasses. Then there was the next building, the store of clothes, the large iron-bound chests filled with linen; cloth and linen garments, with coarse woollen material and fine clothes of the silk-worm's spinning and costly velvet and rugs of many colours woven in Baghdad and warm furs for the winter. . . . The third building was the stable—Bridget heard the stamping of the horses in their stalls and the braying of an ass, and if she peeped inside she could see in the twilight the gilding on the closed carriage. Perhaps her dream also led her through the rose garden, where the roses which Niels Hermansen had admired were in bloom, down to the edge of the lake, Lake Boren—the waves of the Vättern could splash with a sound like a tune of glass bells ringing softly, and what they rang was, 'Do you remember, do you remember? It was down here on the lake that Ulf, your husband, was in danger of his life, down here on the beach you knelt in deadly fear and prayed for him, and he was saved. Here also is the wood—one day in autumn the merry hunting party rode there, it was just after Karin's wedding to Eggert—the stalkers startled a hind, a white hind, and it sought refuge with Karin, it laid its head in her lap as she sat her horse and looked up at her with its large brown eyes—like the unicorn which only allows itself to be caught by a pure and chaste maiden. . . .'

Then the dream changed. Bridget was no longer in the flaming golden autumn wood by the shore of Lake Boren, she saw another flame—she was in the kitchen at Ulfåsa and saw a large pot hanging on its sooty iron hook over the fire. She recognized it all, but where were the cooks—and the little maid? Who was that strange man who with the bellows was so busy trying to blaze up the fire? He looked unearthly—how had he got into the house and what did he want? Bridget was frightened. 'Who are you?' she asked, 'why are you blazing up the fire so eagerly?' The strange person answered—(the answer was also strange): 'I am a merchant!' (the merchant of the Gospel, perhaps, who seeks good pearls and the pearls are souls?) 'I am blazing up the fire to make the love which you bear your children flame up so that you will decide to stay at home with them. They are young, they are rich, the world with its temptations will surround them, and if they fall into sin whose fault is it but yours, who forsook them?'(7)

Bridget awakes—*who* has spoken to her in this vision? From whom came that voice? She jumps up from her hard bed, runs to the *prie-dieu*. There lies the book she always has near her and which she carries on her breast when travelling—Bernard of Clairvaux: *Ad sororem*. She opens it and reads: 'Those servants of God who consider the well-being of their kinsfolk withdraw themselves from the love of God.' Bridget knows it—'no one can serve two masters'—'he who does not hate father and mother cannot be my disciple. . . .' Her heart shrank —must she *hate* her children, then? No, no, by no means. She reads on: 'We must not hate our nearest, but we must not allow them to hinder us from walking along the right road.'(8)

Only thus are these hard sayings to be understood.

Then Bridget receives comfort from heaven—*Mary, daughter of Joachim,** comes to *Bridget, daughter of Birger*. Bridget exclaims: 'Oh, Mary, your Son knows that you are dearer to me than all Ulf's and Bridget's children, and rather would I that Bridget, daughter of Birger, had never been born than that Mary, daughter of Joachim, should not have come into the world.' Mary then answered: 'Oh, my daughter, be assured that Mary, daughter of Joachim, will be of greater help to

* According to tradition Mary was a daughter of Saint Joachim and Saint Anne. Following the Norse custom, Bridget calls her 'daughter of Joachim.'

you than you could be of help to yourself, and Mary, daughter of Joachim, who is the Mother of God, will take a Mother's place towards the children of Ulf and Bridget.'(9)

XXII

The emotional strain of the latest years had told heavily on Bridget, but in the monastic peace of Alvastra she slowly regained her strength. Once again her vocation was present to her—the Order of Our Savour, its rule and its first convent in Vadstena. Together with Prior Petrus she reviewed, item by item, the revealed rule of the Order— here and there improving it or adding new clauses.(1) To indicate that the Blessed Virgin was the true Abbess of the convent, the office in her honour, the *officium parvum B.M.V.*—was to be sung before the usual great office. As a model of meritorious singing Christ indicated the manner in which the Carthusians sang the daily prayers—as the subject of the lecture given by the priest of the convent to the Sisters, the teaching of Saint Benedict on the twelve steps of humility.(2) From all the gardens within the boundaries of the Church Bridget gathers flowers for her altar.

Bridget is now given precise instructions as to the way in which the convent and church are to be built. Christ Himself is the master builder and spreads the plan on the table before Bridget.

The church is to lie east and west. Contrary to all the usual practices in the art of church building the high altar is to be placed at the west end and not the east, the actual reason being the simple one that the site slopes directly down to the lake, and the entrance to the church must be on the land side, which is on the east. The choir of the brethren is to be down behind the high altar, this has to be 44 feet long with only one arch over it, and this arch has to be 40 feet wide. The body of the church shall be triple-naved, roofed with five vaults, each vault has to be 40 feet wide and just as long, namely cross-vaulted. The high altar is to be 10 feet in length, 5 feet wide, and it is to stand on the top of a stair with six steps, and these steps have to be so wide that two altars can stand on each of them—one on the right and one on the left of the high altar. Between each of these two altars there must be a space of 4 feet. Round about the whole of this part of the middle aisle, where the high altar and the twelve side altars stand, there must be an iron railing, so that there will be a passage by which the Brothers can walk without getting into contact with the people, and from which a door in the chancel of the church leads into the monastery. This door must always be kept locked with a key.

In the east wall there must be two porches, one for each side aisle. Under the middle vaulting there must not be any porch, but between the two entrances the Lady altar is to stand, and it is to be 8 feet wide and 6 feet high. The choir of the Sisters is to be above this altar, it is to be supported by pillars, 22 feet from the floor of the church to the floor beams in the choir mentioned. As a precaution against fire copper plates must be laid over the beams, and over them a floor of boards, and over them again a floor of tiles, upon which the Sisters can stand during prayers. The pillars must continue up through the floor and they are to be about 8 feet high or so before they reach the vault. All the vaults over the choir and the whole church shall be of the same height and they are to be built of brick. But the actual church shall be built 'of stone from the mountains'—or 'of stone found in the meadow' [even to this very day the ploughs of the East Gothland peasants strike these huge, hard boulders]. No unnecessary decoration nor ornamentation—again the principle is stressed that the church shall be 'aff slätte gärningh, ödhmiuke oc starke.' (Of simple workmanship, humble and strong.)

In a subsequent revelation it is stated: 'there shall be three porches in the church: the first shall be called the porch of pardon for sins, through this porch the layfolk shall enter. Everyone who enters through this porch with a penitent heart and the intention of leading a better life shall find his temptations alleviated, strength to do good deeds, devotion in his prayers, the forgiveness of sins and prudence in all he undertakes.' 'This door shall be on the east,' so that it must be one of the two doors in the east wall, probably the southern one, where 'the red stone' with its promise of pardon of sins is inset in the wall. The pilgrims would enter the church here, and, after their devotions, they would go out through the northern door. For in the wall by this door there is a stone with five holes in the form of a cross, very probably an allusion to the five wounds of Christ . . . the stone polished smooth as if many hands had touched it . . . it would be the last farewell to Saint Brita from the departing pilgrims. [A later legend claims that the five holes are the marks of the five fingers of Bridget, when once the church was about to fall and she straightened it with her hand.] This porch [these porches] being placed on the east side means that the love of God shall arise in the hearts of the pilgrims and the light of faith shall become clearer.

Then there is the other door, that by which the Brethren enter the choir behind the high altar. 'This door shall be called the door of atonement and meekness, for through the faith and prayers of the brethren sinners will be drawn nearer to God, God's wrath will be lessened and the kingdom of Sweden will attain a better state. This porch shall be on the west side.'

Finally there is the third door, which leads from the church into the monastery. 'This door shall be called the door of grace and honour. For whatsoever Sister who enters by this door with penitence in her heart and with the intention of belonging only to God, shall receive grace to advance from virtue to virtue, and consolation in temptation, and honour in the life to come. This door shall face the north, for all the wickedness of the devil and the frost come from the north, and the Sisters shall therefore burn in the fire of the Holy Spirit and the warmth of the love of God.'

Petrus Olai carefully records all these resolutions (it was he, too, who added them later to the official edition of the revelations under the title of *Extravagantes*. There is a similar relation between this collection and the eight books of *Revelationes* which Alfonsus of Jaen compiled, and that between the *Speculum perfectionis* of Brother Leone and the Franciscan biography by Saint Bonaventure. We should have known less about Bridget and Saint Francis as human beings without the annotations made by these two faithful secretaries). With her clear-sighted spirit Bridget has overlooked nothing, she even thinks of 'pepper and caraway seeds, and other similar spices'; they may be of use in case of illness, but should not be put to ordinary use 'because they excite fornication.' It is better to be content with ordinary greens, such as the ground produces. Besides, she does not wish the nuns to be burdened with cooking or with any household occupations at all, all such matters should be entrusted to 'fyra stegerhus qvinnor,' four women who work in the kitchen, 'tend the fire and carry in water and fuel and throw out the refuse of the convent.' These four serving women, with the Latin name *focariae*, are not permitted to enter the choir of the nuns or their dormitory, nor may they have their meals with the nuns. They are not to live in the convent itself but in a house at the entrance, and they shall have admission to the bakery, the brewery and other places of work. They are to live on those alms or those prebends that the Abbess allots to them, and they may have their meals in the refectory 'when the Sisters are satisfied.'(4) They are to wear a special dress, a scapular without a hood. In the records in the *Diarium Vasztenense* one gets an idea of the many-sided activities of these serving-women; of one such woman it is said: 'she was the mistress of the convent bakery,' of another: 'she was, during all her time, at the head of the brewery' (which, as is known, lay within the confines of the convent of the nuns), and a third 'had managed the weaving-room for forty years,' while a fourth 'helped in the kitchen'; these *focariae* were not always—as one is easily tempted to suppose—peasants who were not suited for anything but rough physical work; one of them, Ingeborg, daughter of Nils, was an opulent widow who brought estates to the convent and was the mother of the Confessor General Ulf Birgersson (the author of a biography of Catherine which was published in Stockholm in 1483 and is believed to be the first book printed in Sweden). Another *focaria*, Catherine, daughter of Erik, belonged to the noble family of Sparre. Ingeborg, daughter of Tor, was of peasant stock. These serving Sisters were also occupied outside the walls of the convent, a certain Estrid, who died on 21 January 1432, managed property belonging to the convent in the village of Orlunda, as it happened, working together with her husband Peter, who held the same position with regard to the monks as she with the nuns.(5) For the priests also had their *focarii*, though only two in number. 'They are to be dressed like the lay brothers of the Benedictines and Cistercians, that is, without the large cowl, only with a cassock, and over the cassock a cloak with a small hood, but the cloak must be laid aside when they work,' says Bridget, with housewifely concern for the good clothes. 'And they shall wear a black leather belt'—greater precision is not possible!

Even so, however, all eventualities are not provided for. In the affairs of the convent it was often necessary to have dealings with ecclesiastical and civil authorities. For these purposes men were needed who, unlike the servants in the house of the brethren were not obliged to remain within the walls of the monastery, yet who in a certain manner belonged to the monastery. The two *focarii* are not concerned with this, they are in the monastery merely to carry out the roughest work. The Abbess is therefore permitted to choose 'four good men of mature age and good repute' and to give them accommodation on the convent farm (*i syslomanz hionagaardhin*).

Their work was to distribute alms and see that clothes were provided for the poor, and in particular they had to be 'quite competent to discuss with the civic authorities the affairs of the convent and to assist the Abbess in this task. So that these Brothers may be faithful in the affairs entrusted to them, they shall be maintained by the convent and take part in all the good works performed in it. They must live a pure life—be unmarried—and on their cassocks there must be a red cross over the heart as a sign that they love God. In worldly affairs they must obey the Abbess, in spiritual affairs the confessor of the convent . . . and they are not to place any person's commands above those of the Abbess and the confessor . . . the confessor shall decide when they shall fast and when they shall eat, when they shall observe silence, when and how they shall sleep, and how they shall go out from the confines of the monastery to the lords of the country. The confessor must also be responsible for the orderliness of their garments, and decide what they shall read and where they shall stand in the church, and when they shall go to Holy Communion. They shall have a room in which they can eat and sleep and each one must have his own bed. They must also have their own churchyard. Of these four who wear the cross, one or two may be priests . . . and one must be the leader, who shall teach and govern them according to the word of the Abbess and the advice of the confessor such as it is written in the old book in the revelation about the four *Familiares*.' (6)

The names of several of these *Familiares* or *Fratres ab extra* are known—the best known is Laurentius Romare, so called because in 1391 he accompanied Magnus Petri, Confessor General, to Rome, and was there during the time of the canonization of Saint Bridget, about which he has given a vivid and colourful description.(7)

The whole collection of *Extravagantes* is to be considered a commentary on the rule, and as giving more detail on certain points in it. Bridget knows herself down to the deepest depths, to where the poison bladder lies, and from this merciless self-knowledge she knows others. Into this new vineyard too, that she is about to plant, small foxes may creep in—those the Canticles refer to as 'those small foxes that destroy the vineyards.' (8) Bridget's Sisters were to leave the world as the children of Israel went through the Red Sea led by Miriam, the sister of Moses, singing sweetly and playing the lute to the glory of God. But in their singing they must not seek their own honour by showing what beautiful voices they have, nor must they enjoy the melodies more than the words they sing. Bridget held up the Carthusians as models to her Sisters, and warned them against the many flourishes and twists with which the Gregorian chant had gradually become embellished. (What would she say about certain modern church music? Sometimes one would think that the great reformer, Pius X, had never lived. It is true, he is dead—*et quand on est mort, c'est pour longtemps*, as a French proverb has it.)

As it may happen that one of the Sisters feels tempted to appear as an opera singer and shine with her soprano voice, the priests may also succumb to a similar temptation. What does Faust say to his familiar who thinks he can improve in his preaching by going to the theatre ? 'Yes,' answers the doctor, 'that may perhaps be useful, when the preacher is a comedian, as may very well happen at times.' To these persons, with theatrical proclivities, something even worse may happen, namely, if the preacher, instead of expounding the Word, takes pleasure in showing off his theological learning. With her clear perception Bridget has foreseen this, perhaps she is also speaking from her experience at Linköping or Uppsala, her intention, at any rate, cannot be mistaken. She says the following (the words are from the lips of Christ): 'They who preach My truth must use few and simple words, whose roots and foundations spring from the reading of the Holy Scriptures, so that those people who have come a long way can understand the preaching and not be wearied by superfluous words and long discourses and loud shouts. The priests shall not make use of flattery or cringing talk, nor shall they multiply their words, nor cut their sermons up into chapters and say, "firstly, secondly, thirdly," to show their art and their skill. The common man admires this but does not understand it, he admires the priest's learning but it is of no use to him. But those who are priests in My Order must read and explain the text for the day each Sunday. They must interpret the Bible and My words and the words of My Mother and those of My saints and the lives of the Fathers and the miracles of holy men, and they shall expound the three articles of the Faith and give beneficial advice against temptations and sins, all according to the understanding of the simple man. My dearest Mother was an exceedingly simple woman, Peter had never studied, Francis was a peasant and yet they did the souls of men more good than did the most learned of masters.'(9)

Bridget made great demands, both on her priests and on her Sisters. No wonder that now and then the thought struck her as to whether enough men and women could be found to complete the numbers in her monastery. She, personally, knew one or two, possibly there were also many women who would be glad to be admitted. But could many men be found, who would be willing to submit to a woman and obey an Abbess? Men have so many temptations of which women know nothing, the world flatters them, lures them with distinguished and well-paid positions. Many men are also puffed up with worldly wisdom. In such an hour of doubt Mary appeared to Bridget and comforted her. 'For each person thou hast in mind My Son sends thousands who will enter thy Order. Bridget shall lead these thousands to the heavenly marriage feast, which has begun here below. That day when the vows of the convent were given is the first wedding day, and from that day they will henceforth walk in the fear of God and holy joy and burning love on the right and safe road to the bridal house of the Bridegroom.'(10)

Bridget is stern, though she is anything but a doctrinaire. A mother's heart beats behind the decision stated in the rule that the Abbess has power to dispense from fasting the sick and weak, also those Sisters who have heavy work to do. She had read about David, who took the shewbread from the temple, and about the disciples of Jesus, who ate the corn they had rubbed from the ears ('heavy work,' said the Pharisees, 'on the sabbath day!'). She knew that many pious men did not drink wine, 'but did that make them nearer to God?' —and that they did not eat without first washing their hands, but what do they gain by it when their hearts are unclean? She has, however, not the slightest objection to personal cleanliness, there has to be a bath house in her convent, not only for the sick, but also for those who are well. *Sanitas servanda est*, 'one must take care of one's health.'(11)

A little recreation is also necessary: on feast days the Abbess must first give a little edifying discourse to the Sisters and then they are to be allowed to talk with each other and to 'walk in the orchard or the grass court.' To this day by the monastery church in Vadstena there are a few of the trees still standing, under the foliage of which the Sisters wandered to and fro, two and two, talking together, playing and laughing and plucking the lilies that still bloom in the 'monk's garden.' The priests and brothers in the monastery can also, if they wish it, obtain permission on special days to go out and walk.(12).

As said above, Bridget's rule, indeed, like all old ecclesiastical and mediæval rules of the religious Orders, differs on one essential point from modern Catholicism, namely on the question of Holy Communion. Bridget herself may have had a feeling about it. It is as though she would make up for a neglect, that there is a regulation which really has some connection with the growing devotion of the later Middle Ages to the Sacrament of the Altar (the feast of Corpus Christi, the hymns of Saint Thomas Aquinas). In a revelation Christ says to Bridget that just as Mary is the Mother of the new Order, He will be the Father. 'As a sign of this I give thee two proofs of grace. The first is that the Sisters must always have the Sacrament of My Body on their altar, placed in a fitting vessel of crystal or sapphire so that each day they may behold Me in that form, and thus the more ardently desire the time when they shall be filled with the truth itself.' This form of devotion anticipates the devotions to the Blessed Sacrament of later centuries. especially that Adoration of the Host exposed on the altar between candles and flowers which has become the vocation of their life for many women's Orders, such as the Sisters of the Perpetual Adoration. Bridget had already understood the intention of this form of religion which is so difficult for the uninitiated to understand. To this privilege Christ adds still one more. When a Sister has fallen ill, so that she throws up everything that is given her, and she is therefore prevented from receiving Communion, the Abbess shall be allowed to take the above-named crystal vessel, in which the Blessed Sacrament is kept —the *Holy Grail* was such a vessel—and followed by all the Sisters she must go to the sick Sister and show her the Holy of Holies. Only a priest may touch the consecrated Host—but the Abbess may carry the Holy Grail to the sick person and with it make the sign of the Cross over her and say: 'May thy faith be to thy salvation and lead thee to life everlasting!'(13)

XXIII

In the midst of these lofty visions Bridget was suddenly reminded of the fact that she too, was made of flesh and blood, and that she was still a woman of only forty-five, whose body made its demands felt. It was not a temptation of the kind that is usually called of the flesh—everything in this connection had long been to her as 'bitter as gall.' No it was much more common and therefore more humiliating—she was attacked by that demon of which the classical name is *Castrimargia*, and which appeared to her in the shape of a blackamoor (since the time of Benedict of Nurcia evil spirits had generally shown themselves as Moors). Bridget suffered quite simply from such desperate hunger that day and night she could think of nothing but eating, and now this black demon came to her, stood in front of her holding a large beautiful loaf in his hands. . . .

But Bridget was not alone with the blackamoor, a handsome young stripling also stood in her room, and he held a golden cup; he spoke sternly to the Ethiopian: 'I am this woman's guardian angel. Why do you tempt her?' The evil spirit is not cowed. 'I am tempting her,' he says, 'because now she will pretend to be an ascetic, but I know very well with how many mouthfuls she used to fill her stomach.' The angel makes excuses for her, tries to make *Castrimargia* see reason. 'You know quite well,' he says, with almost the air of a colleague, 'that you and I are incorporeal spirits, but human beings are made of earth and must constantly be repaired.' The demon does not discuss the point, he only says that 'the temptations Bridget did not have in her youth she must have now!' Then the Blessed Virgin appears: 'Silence, merchant, away with you!' (Could he be the same as the 'merchant' of Ulfåsa?). *Castrimargia* vanishes, but not without having fired the Parthian shot: 'If I can do nothing else, I will smother her with burrs that will cling to her clothes!'(1)

Everyone who has returned from a walk in the woods with trousers or skirt hem covered with burrs knows how these small, prickly things cling, and how it is almost impossible to get rid of them. Bridget was soon to know what *Castrimargia* had threatened—she was besieged by temptations which she had never known in her youth. Temptations fastened upon her, became obsessions. Christ Himself had to appear and comfort her, as does a good confessor. 'That which is not voluntary cannot be sinful, at any rate not mortal sin. For in mortal sin one must, firstly, clearly acknowledge: "This is against the will of God"—

and one must say deliberately: "but I will do it all the same!" But in your case, dear daughter, perhaps there might be a question of venial sin, if you have not immediately driven out the temptation as far as it is possible for you, or even if you have dwelt on it for a moment with pleasure. But venial sin is not punished with hell, it is blotted out in purgatory, if it has not, before this, been cleansed away by deep heart-felt sorrow at having acted against God.'(2)

Bridget was soon to fight other battles than those with the teasing devil *Castrimargia*. In Vadstena the masons had begun the alterations of the King's house, and just as at one time at Ulfåsa, Bridget carried out there too, an inspection and survey of the work. It is not far from Alvastra to Vadstena, about twenty kilometres, and the road leads through the forest-clad slopes of the Omberg and the blue Lake Tåkern of the Swans, past the old churches of Väversunda and Herrestad to the bay near Laglösaköping. Bridget usually made the journey on horse-back, escorted by a couple of armed men, perhaps also by Petrus Olai, if he could leave his work in the monastery. On fine days one has morning sunshine the whole way, the white churches of Svanshals and Strå shine in the sunlight; soon the tower of St. Peter's church shows over the trees—one has reached one's goal.(3)

Bridget had ridden along this road too often to be interested in sunshine and scenery—she preferred to take out her rosary and pray—her followers heard her faint murmurings, and now and then a louder tone recited: *fructus ventris tui Jesus Christus*.(4) But on one of these journeys something quite out of the ordinary happened—the soft prayer of the lips ceased, her hands dropped the reins, her eyes closed as if in sleep. It is that state of which she herself has said:

Oh dearest God, strange it is what Thou dost with me. For when it pleases Thee, Thou dost lull me to sleep, not bodily, but with a deep spiritual sleep. Then Thou dost awaken my spirit to see and hear and feel with the powers of the spirit. Oh, my Lord and God, how sweet are the words of Thy spirit! As often as I hear them it seems as though my soul absorbs them and they enter into the heart of my body as the very sweetest food, with great joy and unutterable solace. When I hear these Thy words I am at the same time satisfied and hungry—satisfied because I desire nothing else, hungry, because I hunger after more.(5)

Bridget's servants were not unfamiliar with this condition of their mistress. Once she had been seized with it as she was standing in a church (in Lödöse?) and was busy correcting, from divine inspiration, what she had written in a revelation. For she had misunderstood Christ—

now she heard Him say: 'Cross out what thou hast written about knighthood. Thou hast written that knighthood is dear to Me—write that it is *exceedingly* dear to Me. A knight who keeps the laws of his order is exceedingly dear to Me. For if it is hard for a monk to wear his heavy habit, it is still harder for a knight to wear his heavy armour.' Bridget was standing at the high altar correcting her manuscript, when one of the servants, who had been looking for her everywhere, came in quickly to inform her that King Magnus wished to speak to her, and was sitting waiting in the hostelry. Bridget did not answer, then the messenger laid his hand upon her shoulder, but even that had no effect. Later she gave this explanation to Petrus Olai: 'I heard the messenger quite well, but the other Voice that was speaking to me was stronger.'(6)

Again it was the same stronger Voice that spoke to Bridget as she rode on the way from Alvastra to Vadstena. Now motor cars glide along the same road—she would not have heard or seen them either. It was only when the horses stamped at last on the rough cobble stones of Vadstena that the servants dared rouse their mistress: 'We are in Vadstena, we are nearly at the King's house, Lady Bridget!' Then Bridget awoke from her vision, looked around her on that world to which she had returned, and burst into tears: 'Why did you wake me? What I saw was so wonderful!'

What Bridget saw was this:

There was a ladder reaching from earth to heaven. Heaven was open, Christ was sitting as a Judge on His throne, at His feet knelt the Blessed Virgin, and about them were all the heavenly host of angels and saints. Half-way up the ladder stood a monk who Bridget knew, a learned man, doctor of theology and well-versed in theological and other literature. On the wood-cut in the Nuremberg edition of 1500 of *Revelationes* he is shown in the Benedictine habit and a doctor's cap, with, as Bridget says, 'impatience and anger in the movements of his hands, so that he looked more like a devil than a monk.' A conceited professor, always eager for an argument, who has crept up the ladder of learning so as to begin an argument with the Almighty. In the days of the Old Covenant Job had dared to reason with God, but that was when he was sitting on the ruins of his happiness and scratching his sores as one touches memories that hurt. Not so is the professor on the ladder with which he will storm heaven—he is a man who is safely housed in the monastery, a learned gentleman who corresponds with his colleagues in different parts of Europe—Cologne, Paris, Oxford,

Bologna and other centres of learning—perhaps he is honorary doctor at one or several foreign universities. The questions which Bridget hears him put to Christ do not arise from a background of personal suffering, do not spring like a plaint from the vale of tears, but are a protest of contented worldliness against the unreasonable dogmas and unnatural claims of superworldliness. There is nothing new in his scepticism, it is as old as Celsus, and yet it has the effect of novelty each time a clever Voltaire sets up his scaling-ladder against the old fortress of Christendom.

It is the sufficiently well-known 'common sense' that speaks through the learned monk. Bridget hears him put to God all those questions that popular philosophy at all times has on its lips.

'I ask Thee, Judge, give me an answer!' he says. 'Thou hast created me, Thou hast given me a mouth. Why, then, may I not speak as I like? Thou hast given me eyes. Why may I not see what pleases me? Thou hast given me ears. Why may I not hear that which is pleasant to me? Thou hast given me hands. Why may I not do with them what I like? Thou hast given me feet. Why may I not go where it pleases me?'

Bridget hears the man's questions, hears the self-satisfied, slightly irritated voice with which he puts them. Imagine that in our times one must discuss things that are so self-evident! Of course I am my own master and my body belongs to me and to no one else. (A short time before the first world war a French novel entitled *Mon cœur est à moi* appeared, of which the thesis was that a woman has the right to kill her unborn child, just as one has the right to armed resistance against an enemy invasion. My house is my castle—my body too. The Anglo-Saxons too, are skilled in birth control.)

The professor on the ladder looks up at his adversary with a triumphant gaze. 'What dost Thou say to that?' After a little while the answer comes, then the two hands spread out like those of the Christ by Thorvaldsen,(7) and the gentle quiet Voice says, 'My friend' (Jesus said 'friend' also to Judas), 'I have given thee a mouth, so that with it thou canst speak wise and useful words, and also words that honour Me. I have given thee eyes so that thou canst see what is harmful for thee and what is to thy gain. I have given thee ears so that thou canst hear what is true and right. I have given thee hands so that thou canst work for the maintenance of thy body, so that thou canst leave the path of the world and enter into the salvation of thy soul and to rest with Me, thy Creator and Redeemer.'

This is the Christian programme of life in a nutshell. In his reply the professor seizes upon the last word of Christ's answer: the word 'Redeemer.' He does not deny the Passion of Christ—only he does not see why this voluntary suffering of God should impose upon him, the professor, the duty of any kind of following Christ. 'Thou hast of Thy own free will chosen to subject Thyself to the bitterest torment. But that is no reason why I should not live as an honourable citizen and a distinguished writer.'(8) 'Nor can there be anything wrong in acquiring this or that which one would like to possess. Now when Thou hast given me a body why may I not use my limbs as I see fit?' The monk is probably not thinking of sport and of keeping oneself 'in form' but will moderns extend the line towards the present nudity cult and other activities not exactly spiritual? On the other hand fewer people will agree with the professor in his complaint that God has promised His people peace and rest, 'but instead Thou givest us fatigue and toil.'(9) The modern person really only lives when he has much, preferably far too much, to do. The answer to this complaint is immediately obvious, that sleep and rest are good for strengthening the body, and that distress and trouble are helpful to the soul.

But all this is but fighting at the outpost of the fortress, the assault upon the ramparts of Christendom. Now the heavy artillery is suddenly directed against the centre of the citadel. It is realized that the intellectual doubts have only been used as a smoke screen in order to place the big guns in position. Behind rationalism approaches—as so often—sensualism. 'Oh Judge!' is heard from the lips of the monk: 'May I be allowed to ask Thee a few more questions? Why hast Thou given us physical senses when after all we may not live according to their impulses? Why hast thou given us food and drink, when we may not take of that which we desire? And above all—why, why didst Thou implant in man and woman the deep impulses to be united, when we may not freely follow this impulse? Why didst Thou give us a heart and desires, when we may not love that which is sweetest of all?'

From his throne the Judge answers: 'My friend, I gave man physical senses and understanding, so that he should see the way of life and follow it. I gave him food, so that in moderation he might gain strength for his work and not make himself ill with gluttony. I gave him the natural desire for union, so that mankind might increase as commanded by Holy Church. I gave man a heart, so that he might give Me a dwelling therein, and so that all his thoughts and desires might be with Me and in Me.'(10)

XXIV

The dialogue continues. It fills the whole of the fifth book of Bridget's revelations, and by the old publishers is therefore entitled *Liber quaestionum* (the Book of Questions). There are in all sixteen questions (*Interrogationes*), and each of these is divided into five smaller ones (*quaestiones*)—altogether eighty, very different subjects of doubt, to which the monk wants answers. It is clear that in foreign universities he would have studied Aristotle and Avicenna, and evidently also the *Gaya Scienza* of the Provençal Court of Love. The monk on the ladder is not Master Matthias, though he had also his doubts to contend with; but they had both been abroad, the monk had studied at the same universities as the learned canon.

After having criticized Christian morality (without being convinced by the answer) he makes an attack on a new front. Why do wild animals exist, he asks. They only go about doing harm? Why are there wolves? Perhaps so that there shall not be too many legs of mutton? Why are there worms and grubs that destroy the crops of the fields and hollow out the fruits of the garden? Why does God send us sickness and suffering, even at the actual moment of death? Why must there be pestilence and famine—why does death often come so suddenly that many people die without preparation—why are there unborn children who die without baptism and therefore cannot enter heaven—why do the wicked prosper in the world—why do unjust men exist, who worry and torment their subordinates—and, worst of all, why dost Thou allow mankind to give way to hate and envy so that it turns into revenge and war?(1)

As we all know, a fool can ask about more than ten wise men can answer. But now it is no longer a fool that talks, it is a man who has lived and is now troubled by his thoughts. It is still a doubter who leads the conversation, but the tone is altering—he has no doubt (or not much) about justifying his unbelief. His doubt is like that from which so many Christians suffer in these latest times—how is it possible that all these horrors can happen, and God Almighty watching from His heaven? Is Jesus asleep—as in the boat on the lake of Gennesaret? But on that day His disciples were able to awaken Him, and He arose and bade the waves and the storm be still. Now the prayers arise, not only of twelve fishermen, but of millions and millions of Christians, beseeching Him: 'Waken, Lord, we perish! Still the storm of war, bid the tempest of destruction cease!' The prayers ascend unceasingly, more and more fervently, more and more ardently and afraid; no answer is heard. The Vicegerent of Christ offers his life as a sacrifice—the sacrifice is not accepted. Radiantly blue the sky arches over the bleeding earth, at such Olympian remoteness in its merciless beauty. 'Did one but know in which corner of the universe Our Lord has fallen asleep!' This I heard from the lips of a French Catholic. It was no mockery of God, it was a cry from the deepest distress of a soul on the brink of perishing. . . .

But it is dangerous to think like that. 'Why were we humans not created like angels or bodiless spirits, or as animals that are not troubled with the wish to understand? Why did man become this dual being, a soul in the weak earthly vessel of the body, doomed to be born weeping, to live by work and toil, to die that difficult death?'(2) Why, why?

The monk asks about the greatest things—and about the least. That which is a matter of course, about which he does not think, to the average man, suddenly becomes a mystery to the doubter. Why life, why death? Why day, why night? The Judge answers this last question with a parable, as He did so often in the days of His earthly life. 'Under a waggon there are four wheels, so that the weight of the load can be distributed; the back wheels follow the front wheels. The world is a large and heavy load for man to pull, he is therefore given the repose of night after the toil of day, so that he may reach the place where there is neither night nor work, but everlasting day and eternal glory.'(3)

There is no question to which the monk does not receive an answer. But the heavenly Judge has no illusions that the answers will be convincing. 'Oh, my friend,' He says 'I answer thee, but not for thy sake, for I know that it is all of no use. Thou dost but persist in thy stubbornness, thou hatest the life which is the true life—therefore after death thou shalt not enter the life thou didst not love. But other souls, both those living now and in the future, shall learn about thy life and thy death, and they shall be converted and flee to Me!'(4)

But the monk continues asking, and Christ continues answering. 'Why should I strive to gain divine wisdom, when I have worldly knowledge? Why must I mourn and weep when I am satisfied with my lot? Why is it said that one should rejoice in one's sufferings—I cannot do that! Why must I live in fear and trembling when I am in the full power of my manhood? Why must I obey my superiors in the monastery—though I have a will and judgment of my own?'

Patiently the answer is given—no question remains unanswered. Somewhere in his writings Sören Kierkegaard says: 'Eternity speaks with a voice so soft that it is easy to miss it.' 'My friend,' says Christ, 'he who is wise with worldly wisdom is blind as regards Me. He who has the blessings and joys of the world is ensnared by many different cares which lead him to hell. He who is visited by suffering and illness receives a visit from Me and thus approaches everlasting life with greater ease. If anyone is strong then I am stronger, and a man's strength can be taken from him. And it is dangerous to be sole master of one's will—nothing leads so easily to hell as a will without guidance. But he who surrenders his will to Me, his God, shall inherit heaven.'(5)

'In the sight of God we are always in the wrong'—this is also a saying of Sören Kierkegaard. God is always right—no revolt like that of the Titans against Zeus is possible. For in his own breast Prometheus hears a voice which pronounces the Judge right. Even a robber must recognize and admit that he is crucified because he has deserved it. Man is of no more worth than to be buried during an earthquake or to be killed in the carnage of war. To the monk's question: 'Why dost Thou permit all this?' comes the answer: 'The sins of men demand it. Everyone who of a clear purpose injures his neighbour is akin to the devil—and is a limb of the devil's body and a tool of the devil. Just as now I use my servants to carry out what pleases Me, so must the devil be allowed to use his servants, and I should be unjust towards him if I hindered him in this. That is why I let him accomplish his malice, so that through it men may be cleansed from sin.'(6) Joseph de Maistre has explained war in the same way as Bridget explains it here. God permits mankind to punish itself, and the devil and his servants must, without wishing it, work together with God for the salvation of mankind.

A whole number of the monk's questions are theological. Why has God stooped to the indignity of assuming such a bag of worms as the human body? Why did Jesus wish to stay in the Virgin's womb for nine months and not appear immediately after the conception? Why did the Almighty not reveal Himself at once in the full beauty of His manhood? Why did he not show Himself in the glory of His divinity, then all men would have believed in Him? Why did He not let his words spread from a central position instead of travelling about and preaching? Why did He not show Himself in the power of His divinity when death approached? Why did He not descend from the cross, then all would have believed in Him!

The monk has also critical difficulties of the Bible to advance, here he anticipates modern German Bible criticism. 'If Thou wert not conceived in sin, why wouldst Thou be circumcized? If Thou wast not a sinner, why wouldst Thou be baptized by John? And if Thy Mother were really a virgin, why didst Thou not prove this by some clear sign or other, instead of exposing her to suspicion?'

There is no point in Christian theology which this sharp critic does not touch upon in his doubt. Saint Paul teaches that death is a punishment for sin. But what about the animals then? They have not sinned and no everlasting life is prepared for them, yet they must suffer and die in the same way as the sinful offspring of Adam. The monk receives an answer to everything, in the last instance this, that when Adam rebelled against his Maker, disorder appeared in all creation and the animals became partakers of the trouble and pain of mankind.(7)

The questions continue to press their way on, like a long-impeded flood. There is still much about which this extremely inquiring professor would like to have information. Why, for instance, is one unable to see the soul when it leaves the body? Or how can people who have received the spirit of God fall into sin? Why are there some souls whom the devil always troubles, others whom he leaves in peace? Then the critic of the Bible speaks again: 'Why is it written that only God knows about the day of judgment, when Thou Thyself actually art God?' The answer is: as *man* Jesus did not know it, and here He spoke as man. Half a millennium before the school of Reimarus and Tübinger Bridget's monk on the ladder has also discovered the discrepancies between the four gospels—*cur tanta est evangeliorum dissonantia?* he asks. The last, the eightieth question, runs thus: 'When the soul of man is of greater worth than the whole world, why then, dost Thou not send out Thy friends and preachers everywhere?'(8)

The answer to the question about the discrepancies in the gospel is an admission—some evangelists wrote down word for word what they had heard, some wrote the meaning of the words rather than the literal, original words, and still others wrote of what they had heard from others but had not themselves seen. The Catholic research of the Bible at the present day takes about the same point of view and warns—just as Bridget does—against placing any trust in the apocryphal gospels.(9) The answer to the last question rings in Bridget's heart—soon, soon, the friends of God here in Vadstena will go out into the whole world and preach the Word!

Then the monk is silent and Christ alone speaks. 'My friend,' He says (for ' it is hard to burn everlastingly,' Christ therefore offers His friendship 'until the last second') 'thou hast now asked Me about so many things, and I have answered everything patiently. For the sake of My bride, who stands near by'—Bridget is usually spoken of in this way, she is *sponsa quae astat*—'I will now put a question to thee. Thou art an intelligent person, wise enough to know the difference between good and evil. Why dost thou love that which perishes more than that which is everlasting?' One cannot lie when one stands face to face with Jesus—whether he will or no, his lips must speak the truth, even if this truth condemns him. His answer, which is a confession, is short: 'It is because I act against my reason and give preference to the bodily rather than to the spiritual.' Christ turns to Bridget: 'That will show thee, what it leads to when one does not resist temptation!' He then adds some words of praise about Master Matthias: '*He* did not act like this in time of doubt, when it seemed to him that all the heresies stood before him and with one voice exclaimed: 'We are the truth!' But he did not believe them, and he was therefore set free, and now he has become learned in the Holy Scriptures and knows them from Alpha to Omega.' (10)

After that Bridget no longer sees the monk on the ladder. Perhaps it is the same person who is mentioned in another vision—the reproaches of the Judge are exactly the same: 'Yet thou didst have thy understanding to know the difference between good and evil,' and likewise the answer: 'Yes, but I would rather do as I liked!' In another place a monk appears who is characterized as a chatterbox, and he is given the advice, rather to pray 'Our Father,' than to meddle with sophistical dissertations. Petrus Olai had known the monk on the ladder and mentions him in the Process of Canonization in 1379 as 'a very learned monk now living.'(11) Bridget's vision is of a time before the year 1349—the monk must therefore at that time have been a young man. Perhaps we may find a portrait of him in two of the *Revelationes* which, thirteen in number, are inserted between question and answer in the same fifth book, which must be considered as belonging to the same great revelation during the ride from Alvastra to Vadstena. Both *Revelationes* are concerned with a priest, and, almost certainly, with a monk whose prayers, in the ears of God, sound like two stones being knocked together, and whose saying of the Mass is as offensive to Him as—Bridget does not shrink from saying it and puts all her loathing of flesh and sex into the words—a soiled menstruation towel. When this priest approaches the altar and intones the Introit,* then, behind the ritual words and the harmonious recitation, God hears three voices which illustrate this man's true thoughts. The first voice says: 'I will be my own master, sleep, get up and talk about pleasant things. I will grant Nature what it demands, I will have money in my purse, soft raiment on my back, and when I have that, it is of more value to me than all spiritual gifts and blessings of the soul!' Then the monk's second voice speaks: 'Death is not so hard to bear,' it says, 'judgment is not so severe as it is written. It is because He is cautious that God threatens such a heavy punishment, but He is merciful and lets us off with less. If only I can do as I like in this world, I shall surely manage in the next one!' The third voice is just as confident. 'God would not have redeemed me if He would not give me heaven. He would not have suffered for us all if it was not His will to lead us all home to the heavenly Fatherland. If not, why has He suffered? And, by the way, who *compelled* Him to suffer? Besides, I know nothing about heaven and its blessings, except what I have heard from others, and is there any reason to believe them? If only I can get what I want I will gladly give up heaven'—like King Valdemar Atterdag, if only he could keep Gurre.

Patient as always, the Lord answers each of the three observations. To the first: 'Oh, my friend, thy way does not lead to heaven! My suffering means nothing to thee, so hell is open before thee, and because thou lovest the low and the earthly thou wilt go to the under-world.'

To the second voice the answer is: 'My son, death will be hard upon thee, judgment unbearable, and it is useless to think of flight!'

After having spoken first to 'the friend,' and then to 'the son,' Christ, in an impressive climax, addresses the sinner as brother. 'Brother,' He says, 'all My deeds were done through love, so that thou mightest become like Me—so that thou mightest repent and return to Me. But now thou dost no longer remember My deeds, My words lie heavy upon thee, My ways are not thy ways. The punishment is therefore prepared for thee, and the community of the devil. For thou turnest thy back upon Me, thou treadest My suffering under thy feet. Thou carest not that I hung upon the cross for thy sake'—and that is exactly what Bridget can never forget. Again the great lament rises from Golgotha, the lament of Good Friday with the words of the prophet Jeremiah: 'O my people, what have I done to thee?'—*Popule meus, quod feci tibi, responde mihi. . . .*

* Psalm 42 in the Vulgate.

I hung upon the cross like a man whose eye is pierced by a knife;
I hung there like a man whose heart is pierced by a sword;
I hung there like a man, all of whose limbs tremble in suffering.
What I suffered hurt more than a stab in the eye, but I endured it;
My Mother's weeping was a greater pain to me than my own pain, yet
    I came through it;
My body and everything within me trembled in agony, yet I did not give up
But thou hast forgotten everything, thou hast looked down upon everything,
    thou hast despised everything.
Therefore shalt thou be thrown away like an unclean cloth and like a fetus
    born too soon ! (12)

For alas! 'men are like children brought up in a dark room, and
who do not believe that light and stars exist, even if you tell them
so, because they have never seen them. Man has left the true light
and enjoys the dark, and has become used to it, so that what is bad
seems to him to taste sweet.' (13)

XXV

If one cared to use a modern expression, one might call the whole of
this fifth book of Bridget's revelations an *apologia* or a theodicy—a
kind of Summa in a smaller size than that of Saint Thomas Aquinas but
not of quite inconsiderable compass. The Latin text contains, roughly,
16,000 words, the Swedish about 14,000. It was of course in Swedish
that Bridget wrote down all this, which 'in about an hour' was revealed to her, and which was so clearly present to her memory, 'as if
each word had been hewn in marble.' The translation into Latin was
undertaken by Prior Petrus Olai, who by the way—which it may be
interesting to note—did not accompany Bridget on that journey from
Alvastra to Vadstena (probably he had enough to do in the monastery),
but only knew of the experience from what Bridget had told him.(1)

It is with a parable that the book of questions ends, with a parable
and a riddle. It is neither Christ nor Mary who speaks this time, it is
God the Father Himself.

There was a lord, to whom his servants said: 'Behold, thy field is ploughed,
the weeds are pulled up, when has the wheat to be sown?' The lord answered:
'The roots seemed to be pulled out but there is still old stubble to be cleared
away by the spring rains and winds; wait therefore patiently, till the time
comes for sowing.' The servant answered: 'What shall I do then, between
the spring and the time for sowing?' The lord answered: 'I know of five
cities; he who comes to them shall harvest five-fold fruit, provided he be
pure and free from pride and burning with love. In the first city there is a

I   16

vessel which is closed and yet is not closed; which is small and yet not small; a vessel which gives light and yet does not give light; a vessel which is empty yet not empty; a vessel which is clean and yet not clean. In the next city a lion was born, which was seen yet not seen; which was heard, yet not heard; which could be touched and yet not touched; which was perceived and yet not perceived; which was held fast and yet was not held fast. In the third city there was a lamb, which was shorn and yet not shorn; wounded and yet not wounded; a lamb which cried out and yet did not cry out; which was patient and yet not patient; which died and yet did not die. In the fourth city there was a serpent which lay down and yet did not lie down; which moved and yet did not move; which heard and did not hear; which saw and did not see; which felt and did not feel. In the fifth city there was an eagle, which flew and did not fly; which rested and did not rest; which grew young and did not grow young; which was happy and not happy; which was honoured and not honoured; which came and never went away.

This dark discourse is interpreted by God the Father Himself. The first of the five cities is Mary—she was closed against the devil, not closed against God; her womb is but small, yet large, as the Son of God was conceived therein; she was empty of sin, yet full of grace; her light shone before God but not before men; she was pure, because she conceived without sin, but was not pure, because she was of the race of Adam. 'Whosoever comes to the city where Mary was born and brought up, will be cleansed from his sins and become a vessel of honour.'

The first of the five cities is therefore not only Mary, 'God's city,' as the Spanish seeress has called her—it is also *Nazareth*. Of the second city it is said quite openly that it is *Bethlehem*, where the lion of the tribe of Judah was born, but is only acknowledged in the Faith. The third city, or in this case *place*, is the hill of *Golgotha*, 'where the Lamb died as a man, not as a deity, but like an eagle flew up from the *Mount of Olives* to His eternal rest which is an everlasting activity for the salvation of mankind.'

'But whosoever comes to these places, pure and with goodwill, he shall taste and see how sweet I, your God, am.' This is said to everyone, but a personal message is added to Bridget: 'When thou comest to these places I will reveal still more things to thee.'(2) This is the old promise of Arras, which is repeated and confirmed here. When from the king's house in Vadstena Bridget looks out over the water, she sees on the horizon not only the bluish coast-line of West Gothland and the distant islands beyond Olshammer. But like those mirages which, on clear summer days, can hover over the 'trollish' water, so Nazareth, Bethlehem, Jerusalem, with the hill of Golgotha and the summit of the Mount of Olives, stand out in the sky line, and through Bridget's soul rings the old pilgrim's song: 'To the land in the east I will go.' But at present she is not free to go, much work rests upon her, which she, and only she, can accomplish. 'The voice of one who stood upon the mountain was heard, and it cried: "With this drink thirst is quenched; he who is cold becomes warm; he who is mournful becomes glad; he who is sick becomes well".'(3) For this drink is the Words of God according to Bridget—*Verba Dei secundum Birgittam*. Her thoughts wander out over the whole of Christendom, even wander to the heathen lands beyond the Gulf of Bothnia to the Finns and the mission there. It seems to her that she sees something like a pair of scales hung up between heaven and earth, and upon the one scale lies a dreadful animal, on the other a no less dreadful fish. The animal represents those Christians who do not follow the words of the Gospel, but cling to earthly joys, and the fish is the heathen, who swim about in all manner of evil waves of desire. The one scale does not tip up the other—Christian or heathen—they are equally good or equally bad. Of the two the more sinister is perhaps the fish—its scales are like sharp knives, its eyes are like those of the basilisk that kills with its glance, the mouth is like that of the unicorn and spits out venom, the ears are like sharp lances. But the animal is also dangerous, from its mouth issue flames of fire, from its eyes sharp arrows, and its eyes are protected by hard steel plates, its skin is as hard as flint.

Bridget now sees three groups of people standing beside the scales —a small group, a smaller one and a very small group. To these three bands a voice from heaven cries: 'I desire the animal's heart and the blood of the fish.' And this little company must see to this! Nor are they particularly enthusiastic about the task which the voice from above imposes upon them.

The first group consists of ordinary Christians, those who, as the apostle says, live in the world without making more use of it than from necessity, leading a 'pious, sober and righteous life.' They are good people, decent folk, law-abiding citizens, good husbands and fathers, conscientious wives, loving mothers. But they are no heroes. They frankly declare that it is absolutely impossible to tackle the two beasts. The animal—to take that first which is nearest, namely the base fellow Christians—the animal has a hide as hard as flint; if we got near its mouth we should be burnt by the flames it belches forth, and its eyes would pierce us through with their arrows. And the fish is even worse! Its scales and its fins are more pointed than spears, its eyes dazzle us, its mouth pours out a poison against which there is no antidote!

Neither is the second group, consisting of the inmates of the monastery, more heroic. Only the smallest group, those who are ready to die a martyr's death, dare to undertake the task. 'Hear us, O Lord, Thou who desirest the animal's heart and dost thirst for the blood of the fish, we are ready to die for Thee. Do Thou grant us wisdom and we shall try to find a way to the heart of the animal.'

Hereupon follow detailed instructions concerning the strategy required for the fight with the two monsters. 'Oh, my friend,' says the voice from heaven, 'if thou wouldst find the way to the heart of the animal, take a sharp gimlet and *pierce thy hands*.' Only he who bears the wounds of Christ can help his Christian neighbour. 'And he who would present me with the blood of the fish let him take a net and go down to the shore.' He must go out into the waters of worldliness, yet not further than he can reach the bottom, and he must place his foot where there is a firm foundation. His net shall be the simple proclamation of the Words of God and not 'rotten philosophy' or rhetoric— 'for My church did not begin with eloquent and learned masters, but with humble fools' (as Francis of Assisi called himself). And he shall pluck out one of his eyes, namely that eye with which he sees those motives which can advise careful silence before 'the might and cruelty of the tyrants.' This eye he must pluck out. With the other eye he sees everything from the view point of eternity, and thinks only of what can be the salvation of the convert. Not only that—it can also be of earthly help. The missionary must examine the material circumstances of his convert—he should make sure 'that the unbeliever who has accepted the faith can obtain occupation by which he can live, so that he need not beg, nor be down-trodden in bondage, nor robbed of his lawful freedom.' The conversion to Christianity shall also be a charter— this was written by Birger Persson in the law of Uppland, and Bridget, daughter of Birger, heard this proclaimed by the voice from heaven. Where Christ is, there is freedom!(4)

Those Christians who go out to heathen lands must set a good example. Bridget was well aware of the sins of the Crusaders—'there are many Christians who, when in heathen lands, lead scandalous lives, kill the inhabitants and steal their property . . . this gives me as much joy,' says the Lord, 'as when the Jews worshipped the golden calf.' The Crusader must also pluck out one of his eyes, that eye which covets his neighbour's goods, and only see with the eye of the love of mankind and of compassion. It is only in this way that both home missions and foreign missions are possible—only in this way that the heart of the Christian and the life-blood of the heathen convert can be brought to God. The reward for him who does this is exceeding great—'the whole stream of sweetness shall flow into his mouth, everlasting light shall shine and enlighten his soul, and he shall enter into that joy to which there is no end.'(5)

This is the ideal, of the missionary to the heathen and the Crusader as Bridget sees them. But what was it like in reality? The crusade that both she and King Magnus desired had been set in motion—in the beginning of the summer of 1348 the Swedes advanced into Finland and after a siege of only six weeks took the strong fortress of Nöteborg which commanded the road into Russia.* Bridget had not expected that in February, 1349, Nöteborg would be retaken by the Russians, who even advanced through Finland and ravaged parts of northern Sweden. Long before this she had realized that this war was not pleasing to God. She had admonished and threatened King Magnus in vain—once again it had been proved that he was a child! Allow a child to choose between two apples—one of them is gilded like a walnut on a Christmas tree, but inside it is filled with worms and filthiness, the other apple looks quite ordinary, but fresh and good. The child snatches at the gilded fruit—and this was just what King Magnus had done. It had been so carefully explained to him how necessary it was to be spiritually prepared before setting out for this war. The soldiers were to confess—as if it were their last confession. The great ones too, ought also thoroughly to examine their conscience, and if they found that they were in possession of property unjustly acquired they had to restore it. And these Crusaders must have pure intentions, they must not wish to enrich themselves, nor covet the possessions of the heathen, 'his ox or his ass, his wife or his handmaid or anything which belonged to his neighbour.' And before the war the king himself had to travel through his kingdom and examine the state of the law and the judicial proceedings, and what sentences had been pronounced, 'for he who intends to send others to the kingdom of heaven must begin with himself, right the wrongs he has committed, and with his good example

* Nöteborg, at the mouth of the Neva where it issues from Lake Ladoga, was founded by the Swedes in the latter part of the thirteenth century as a frontier fortress against Russia. In 1323 peace was signed between Sweden and Russia, but in 1347 war broke out again. From Nöteborg the road led in a southerly direction to Novgorod (called Holmgaard by Scandinavians). In 1702 the fortress was taken by Peter the Great, who gave it the name of Schlüsselburg.

urge his subordinates along the path of virtue.' Before the actual war begins the king must offer 'Peace and faith and freedom' to the heathen. But if they do not accept the offer then the banner of mercy shall be lowered and the standard of war led forth.(6)

Warfare of this kind would have been pleasing to God, and to such a commander heaven would have granted victory. But now Bridget heard the Mother of God complain about Magnus. 'Formerly I called this king my son,' she said, 'but now he has become disobedient. When I used to come to him his heart was touched and he shed tears of remorse, and I chose him to carry the holy Catholic faith to the heathen. I called him my *new* son, for of late he had become obedient to me, and I promised him that I would be mistress of his army and protect it and his kingdom, and I would go before him in the land of the enemy. I kept my promise, for peace reigned in his kingdom while he was away at war.'(7)

Through Bridget the Blessed Virgin had admonished the king to be spiritually prepared, and the king had really tried to obey her warning. In the year 1347 he had summoned a council at Örebro, at which a law to be enforced in the whole country was to be carried through. In this new law, which replaced the old laws of the country, the king undertook to strengthen, love and maintain justice and truth, to crush all falsehood and injustice by law and by the power of the king, to be faithful and loyal to his people, so that no one, rich or poor, should suffer injury to life or limb without judicial proceedings. Neither may the king deprive anyone of his property without a trial, the kingdom of Sweden was to be ruled by men who were natives of Sweden, not by strangers, 'foreigners may not be admitted into the king's council nor give advice about stronghold and country.' . . . The king must live by the estates of the Crown and other lawful revenue, he must not impose new burdens, except if a foreign army be about to ravage his country, or some of his own people rise against the Crown. The rights of the churches, of the priests and monasteries, of the knights and esquires, which have existed from olden times, must be maintained in force, foreign laws must not be introduced, the king must not enact laws for his people without their goodwill, he must protect and save the common people and strengthen and maintain the peace of the Church, the peace of the court of law, the peace of women and the peace of the home. 'For peace increases and dissension perishes, all according as the king reigns.' Even in 1349 this new law was not quite complete, it only came into force two years later. King Magnus, however, had shown his good intentions, and in 1351 he visited Upp-sala and promised, with his hand on the relics of Saint Erik, to keep the law 'towards young and old, towards born and unborn, towards friends and foes, towards absent and present.'(8)

So far King Magnus had shown himself as the obedient son of Mary —and of Bridget. Disobedience began when he set off for Finland, for it was not as he had been told, with few and good troops, but with a large army; it was not the old-fashioned austerity that set its mark upon his warriors, but they were clothed in the newest French fashions, and the war budget was already exceeded at the very outset, without a thought as to how the money was to be obtained, and how great a famine and how much misery would be spread over the country.(9) Neither were those councillors there who had the king's ear 'the brethren of Saint Dominic and Saint Francis and of the Order of Saint Bernard,' whom Bridget had hoped to see by his side. It was therefore with good reason that the Blessed Virgin complained against the king:

'I went before him in the land of his enemies, and in one town I gathered together all the enemies that I intended to deliver into his hands.' (Nöteborg, taken by the Swedes in 1348). Many prisoners were taken, and King Magnus had at first decided to have them executed. (That was the custom then, concentration camps were unknown.) But 'certain bad counsellors' went to the king—'the tools of the devil,' says Bridget—'and their desires inclined rather to worldly gain than to the saving of souls.' The king took their advice: this was to grant freedom to the captured Russians if they promised to accept the Catholic faith and guaranteed the payment of a big ransom. The Russians took the oath and were freed, but the following year they re-turned with a mighty army, retook Nöteborg and put the garrison to the sword. 'The king took my enemies who resisted the faith, out of my hands; he allowed the wolves to run away and the lambs to be de-livered up to be torn asunder.' This was what came of Magnus having listened to his false friends and not to Bridget. 'Then he returned to his country without having gained anything, and oppressed his people and became disobedient towards God and man, and he broke his knightly vow and his oath.' Yet there is still hope for Magnus (Bridget *cannot* give him up): 'As a mother gently welcomes her son who comes to her to beg for her forgiveness, so I say again to him: "Oh, my son, be converted to me, and I will turn to thee. Rise up from thy fall and hearken to the counsel of the friends of God." ' But once again the tone becomes menacing: 'This is *the last letter* I will write to thee.'(10)

XXVI

Yet after this 'last' letter another letter came—the very last. 'Charity beareth all things, believeth all things, hopeth all things, endureth all things,' says the apostle. Even though the bridge of friendship be broken down, and the friends no longer write to one another as before, yet surely one can send a trifle to that former friend which may be of use to him—'a song that may please him or a letter with beneficial rebuke.'(1) Bridget *could* not give up King Magnus, she had, as it were, received him as a legacy from her father. It was true that he had been a disobedient son to the Blessed Virgin, the crusade had not turned out as Bridget had expected. But *another* way was open to him, he must go on a pilgrimage, he must seek out the Vicar of Christ, confess to him his many and grievous sins, and, a matter of the greatest importance, obtain the confirmation of the rule of Bridget's Order. Bridget demands great humiliations of Magnus—before the Vicegerent of Christ he must acknowledge that on account of his warfare, and his disorder in money matters he has 'robbed his subjects, broken his oath as a king and the law of the land, and wasted the possessions and wealth of the Crown.' There is no other way, but if he follows this path he will become blessed.(2)

King Magnus did *not* carry out Bridget's injunction. Instead, he made plans for a new war against Russia, that war in which Israel Birgersson met his death, and which ended in defeat for Sweden. Bridget had foreseen that the day would come when excommunication would befall him, so that spiritually he would begin to 'stink like rotten fish.'(3) *He* would convert the heathen—and he did not know what Christ had said to Bridget, that the time would come when the heathen would become so pious that the Christians, spiritually speaking, would be like their humble servants, and the Holy Scriptures would be fulfilled, in saying that there shall be one flock, one shepherd, one faith, one apprehension of God. Then many who were called shall be rejected, but the wilderness shall blossom, and the heathen shall sing: 'Glory be to the Father and to the Son and to the Holy Ghost,' with all His saints. Then that garrulous friar in Alvastra (the same who stood upon the ladder?) may say what he likes!(4)

King Magnus would not go to the Pope for Bridget. On the contrary he seemed, after about two years, to regret his great gift of 1 May 1346. Many influences had been felt at court, and from various quarters they had worked against the seeress. It was murmured in corners that she would like to see her son Karl on the throne of Sweden—the blood of the Folkungs ran in his veins as much as in those of the king. What was it that Ivar Blå had said once to Birger Jarl: 'I suppose I could shake out a king from under this cloak?'(5) From Ulfåsa too, a road led to Mora Stones. What was it that her own godson, little Erik, then only seven years old, had said to her in Båstad: 'Is it true, Aunt, that your sons are to become kings instead of me and Haakon?'(6) She had reproved the boy, but understood quite well that he had not thought of this himself. It was also very likely that Blanca had taught the child to ask her: 'Will it be fine weather to-morrow, Aunt?' Bridget could actually *hear* the queen say this, with that broken accent in Swedish which she never quite lost. Probably it was also she who was behind Magnus, when one morning he gaily asked her: 'Well, what did we dream about last night?'(7)

These were but pin-pricks. It was worse on that occasion when a learned gentleman entered the chamber where the king, the court and Bridget were assembled, and began to read aloud from the *Vitae patrum*. Bridget knew the book quite well, and had often had parts of it read aloud to her and enjoyed hearing about the pious hermits, Anthony and Paul, Theodore and Arsenius, Agathon and Macharius, far away in the desert between the Nile and the Red Sea. But the monk had not come to give an edifying lecture, it was to read about the temptations to which those holy men had been exposed, and how the devil had often betrayed them. This, he had thought, might also have been the case with Bridget and her visions. . . . Christ had afterwards appeared to her in her prayers and had comforted her; she was not to worry herself about this foolish Cistercian monk, who was nothing but a 'sackful of words.' But the learned gentleman had made an impression on the king.(8)

Otherwise how can one account for what Bridget had to see with sorrow, when one day, probably in 1348, she once again rode along the usual road from Alvastra to Vadstena? The alterations to the king's house had been begun immediately; a small group of devout women had already gathered about Bridget, like a swarm of bees about their queen. It was important to get the hive finished as soon as possible, if it took too long it was quite possible that the grasshoppers and wasps would take possession, and then it would have to be cleaned out after them!(9)

But so far from the work progressing it advanced very slowly, until at last it ceased altogether. It grew even worse, that part of the king's house which had been repaired and was now ready for use, was found one morning *pulled down*! 'This is the work of an enemy!' Bridget could say like the husbandman in the Gospel. The enemy, the old enemy, had done this. But who had been his tool?

In any case it could not have happened without the king's approval. Nor—as it was a question of a religious house, could it have been without the consent, at least tacit, of the local bishop. The bishop of Linköping at that time was Petrus Tyrgilli (Peter Tyrgilsson). This ecclesiastic was born in Skenninge, had been a canon in Uppsala, had been the chancellor of King Magnus and in 1327 his delegate to Avignon. It was indeed through the recommendation of the Pope that he became bishop of Linköping in 1342. In the old chronicles of the bishops he is praised for his righteousness and it says that 'for his virtues and great manliness' he was chosen to be archbishop of Uppsala (1351). He died in 1366.

From the first period of her conversion Bridget had already glanced towards the Swedish episcopate. Just as the apostle Saint John had written to the seven churches in Asia, so Bridget, from Alvastra, which was *her* Patmos, had sent a communication to the seven bishops in Sweden. As so often in Bridget's writings, her revelations are addressed to persons who are symbolized under the form of animals. The first of these animals 'has big horns' and is 'very eager for fight,' delights in fighting with other animals, and is probably a ram. By this animal (Prior Petrus explains) is meant Bishop Thomas of Vexiö, he travelled later to Italy to visit Bridget, accompanied her on her journey to Naples, fell ill in Benevento of gall-stones, of which Bridget cured him by applying hot compresses. He seems to have been a doubting spirit, wavering between God and the world—'he finds it hard,' says Bridget with her inspired conciseness, 'to follow the road which leads to perfect joy.' Yet another misfortune overtook him on this journey, he fell from his horse and broke a rib, just as the little pilgrim band rode up Monte Gargano. Again Bridget came to the rescue, and with prayer and the laying on of hands restored him to health. Only now does he seem to have surrendered himself entirely to God.(10)

The second animal is a unicorn. In *Lucidarius* it is said: 'There is an animal which is called a unicorn, in the front of its head it has a horn six feet long; this horn shines like a carbuncle. This animal can be caught by none but a pure virgin, and if she will sit down before it, it will fall on its knees and lay its head in her lap.' The unicorn thus becomes a symbol of Christ; in old representations the angel of the

Annunciation is seen standing before Mary, and the unicorn, which is pursued by two dogs, seeks refuge at the Virgin's knee.(11) In *Physiologus*, that mediæval encyclopedia which Bridget knew and used, the unicorn is described as a kind of horse, it is white, with a reddish purple head and blue eyes. The horn in the forehead is white and black, with a red tip.(12)

By this animal Bridget meant no other person than Petrus Tyrgilsson. Whatever may have come between them later, she never showed any of the Swedish bishops greater honour than to liken him to that animal which represents Christ. For a time he does seem to have followed Bridget's spiritual guidance: in a long letter she advises him to take Saint Thomas of Canterbury as a model. Through the lips of Bridget the Blessed Virgin promises to be the friend of the bishop, and to stand by him at the hour of his death. She herself will hold his soul in her hands and carry it up to God.(13) Even if later on a rift appears (or a less happy relation) between Bridget and Petrus Tyrgilli, yet after his death she is certain of his salvation, and in a revelation Christ says that 'the bishop for whom thou dost pray' has been saved by 'the prayers of My Mother.'(14) He suffered only 'a light purgatory.'(15)

The third bishop whom Bridget addresses is likened to an elephant. About this animal too, there were strange ideas in mediæval times. In *Lucidarius* it is called (in Asia) an animal, a *fil*,* 'it has no joints; it is the strongest animal to be found in the world, and the largest, and it can never be caught unless one is able to make it fall, because it cannot get up again once it has fallen.' It is unable to bend its knees, and so sleeps leaning against a tree; when one elephant falls all the others gather round it and with loud, plaintive cries (the elephants' trumpeting) try to raise it up.(16) It can only be caught while it sleeps, for then the hunter saws through the tree against which it is leaning, and when it has fallen, it cannot rise again. The bishop who is symbolized by this animal is reprimanded because he has married a young couple without first obtaining the papal dispensation necessary in this case. He seems to have committed this offence purely from worldly considerations— 'because all the preparations for the wedding had been made.' But to lean upon the world is like leaning against a rotten tree, and now the bishop lies upon the ground, struck by the punishment of the Church. Yet there is hope for him, provided he regulates the unlawful marriage according to the law of the Church.(17)

* *Fil*, the Arabic name for an elephant. (*Filsben* = ivory.)

A fourth bishop appears to be gentle and good and does no harm to anyone. But he has a foul breath (about which Bridget is extremely sensitive), as internally he is leprous with the leprosy of sin. A fifth bishop is likened, not to an animal, but to a well-cut block of stone, suitable for the corner stone of a church. He has his doubts, but they are pious doubts, and like Saint Thomas, the apostle, he is prepared to give them up. He is not like the Israelites, who tempted God in the wilderness, or like those who demanded signs of the prophet Jonah; he loves God as well as he is able, and is compassionate towards his neighbour.(18) The sixth bishop is not of much consequence, he is so timid that he is afraid of even his own shadow. Only of the seventh bishop do we hear once again, just as of the second, the hymn of praise full and complete; he lives in great self-denial and abstinence, is zealous for God's cause, is not frightened by threats or influenced by favours or privations, he is without fear of man and disregards loss and harm which he might be likely to suffer by speaking the truth. This knight of God without spot or blemish is Bridget's good friend, Bishop Hemming of Åbo.(19)

None of the seven bishops of Sweden could be seriously suspected by Bridget of having occasioned the abomination of desolation in Vadstena. And the king—but *can* one take the king seriously? He is nothing but a child and submits to being led by Blanca and her bad advisers. But even they would not have dared to take this step, without having had support in the highest quarter—of the Vicar of Christ. If the Pope had given Bridget's plans his blessing, if he had set his seal under the rule which Bishop Hemming and Prior Petrus had laid before him in Avignon—that rule which Christ Himself had dictated to her—why, then no one would have dared to pull down the walls of Jerusalem: Clement VI is the guilty one—he alone!

In a vision Christ appears to Bridget, and with Him Peter, the first pope. They both speak to Peter's unworthy successor. 'Thou art worse than the devil,' says Christ. 'The devil hated only Me and would kill Me to obtain My place at the right hand of the Father. But by thy bad example thou slayest those souls whom I gave into thy safe keeping, thinking that thou wast My friend, but thou hast handed them over to My enemy. Thou art more unjust than Pilate, who condemned only me to death, but thou condemnest the innocent and acquittest the criminals. Thou art more cruel than Judas—he sold only Me, but thou sellest My holy souls for shameful gain. Thou art more loathsome than the Jews—they crucified only Me, but thou crucifiest the souls of My elect, to whom thy malice and thy transgressions are more painful than if they were pierced by a sword. And because thou art the equal of Lucifer, more unjust than Pilate, more cruel than Judas, I justly lay a complaint against thee.'

Christ is the prosecutor. He leaves it to Peter to pass sentence, it is 'Guilty.' 'It is just,' says the old fisherman of Galilee, 'that he who has sat in my chair, but does the works of the devil, ought with shame to leave that chair to which he has no right, and suffer the same punishment as Lucifer.' But the punishment is the following: 'My sword shall pierce thee through from head to foot and shall be so firm that it can never be withdrawn. Thy chair shall be cast like a stone into the depths of the sea and never cease falling until it reaches bottom. Thy fingers, that are thy assessors and advisers, shall burn in unquenchable fires of sulphur. Thy arms, that are thy officers, and that should be stretched out for the benefit of souls, now only reach out after worldly honour and use; they shall be judged according to the words of David: "His sons shall be fatherless, his wife a widow, and strangers shall take his estates." For who is the widow but the soul which has missed God, and who are the sons but those virtues they did not possess, what were their possessions but the dignity which they held and which must be given to others? But they themselves shall inherit everlasting dishonour. Because they exalted themselves here above others they shall be cast into the swamp of hell, so deep that they can never hope to rise again.' The same punishment shall be meted out to the other limbs of the pope, 'namely all the priests, and all those who agree with the priests.' They shall be laid waste as a house is laid waste—as the king's house in Vadstena has been laid waste—'not one stone shall rest upon another, there shall not even be lime between the stones; and My mercy shall never come upon them, My love shall never be with them, and they shall never enter the heavenly home, but far from all that is good they shall suffer torment without end.'(20)

XXVII

But there is no longer time to write letters. The voice from Rome sounds across the world—'Come to me, and you will obtain forgiveness of your sins.' A year of jubilee was called for the year 1350 and proclaimed over the whole Catholic world. When Boniface VIII, fifty years earlier, called the bands of the faithful to Rome—Dante was among the pilgrims—it was intended that only the turn of the century was to be marked by this great indulgence. But was it just to let whole generations go to the grave without having had admission to so great a grace? Those who were born in 1300 could live to experience 1350, but in all likelihood not 1400. And it was decided that the jubilee should take place each half-century—in later years the interval between one *Anno Santo* and the next has actually been decreased to twenty-five years. The present writer has even lived to have the experience of three—1900, 1925, and the year of jubilee proclaimed by Pius XI in the nineteen hundredth year after the death of Christ. Each jubilee year begins on the last day of the preceding year—on that day when *la Porta Santa* in Saint Peter's which is usually walled up opens as the Pope strikes it with his silver hammer and chants the words of the psalm: 'Open, ye gates of righteousness!' He then steps across the threshold, which is washed with holy water and cleansed with hyssop. . . .

It had been Bridget's silent hope that King Magnus would comply with the invitation and set out on the pilgrimage. Her hope was disappointed, and she had therefore to do that which he had neglected. Yet she could not refrain from sending him a last, a very, very last letter. Perhaps it was not so very unfortunate, after all, that the king's house had been destroyed—the monastery could become more modest and more humble, without high walls and gables. Only so little was required, just the absolute necessities. But it was clear that Magnus was no longer worthy of building the monastery, he was neither a Saint Erik nor a Saint Olaf, as Bridget had so fervently hoped, had so ardently prayed for in Uppsala and Nidaros. *Another* was to come— who? God would not yet let her know this.

But in her heart she heard the strong, clear voice: 'The rule is written. The flowers are planted. Go to that city now where thou shalt see the Pope and the Emperor. Go to Rome, where the streets are paved with gold as in the heavenly Jerusalem and are purple with the blood of martyrs. There shalt thou stay, until thou seest the Holy Father and the Emperor together in Rome, and thou shalt proclaim my words to them. The rule shall be as a light in a lantern, and the heathen shall rejoice, the lukewarm be roused, the cold set afire. The corn shall be ground, and the good seed gathered into my barns.'(1)

Bridget had written to the Pope. Now she was commanded also to send a letter to the Emperor. The way had to be prepared. Her application to the two warring kings had been of no avail. But the Emperor ranked above all kings, he held the old Roman title of *Imperator*, and on 11 October 1347, Charles of Luxemburg had become Charles IV, 'Emperor of the Holy Roman Empire of the German nation.' Bridget knew that the day must come when, in Milan, he would place the iron crown of Lombardy on his head, and the day must come when he, like his great namesake, would kneel by Saint Peter's tomb and be anointed by the Vicegerent of Christ to become the law-man of God upon earth. . . .

Then Christ spoke to His bride and said: 'In My name write to the Emperor as follows:

> I am that light that came to give light to all things, when darkness covered the earth. I am that light which was invisible, but became visible. I am that light which has placed thee as a light in the world, that thou mayest lead all men along the path of righteousness and piety. I, the true light, tell thee that it is I who have permitted thee to mount the throne of the emperor, because this has been My will.
>
> I am now speaking words of righteousness and truth to a woman. Receive therefore the words which she has received from My lips and written in her books. Read them and consider them and have a care that men may fear My righteousness and desire My mercy. And thou, who art the lord of the empire, must therefore know that I, the creator of all things, have dictated a rule for nuns (*unam regulam monialium*—so that here there is no question of a dual monastery) and have given this rule to the woman who writes to thee. Read the rule therefore and speak to the Pope about this rule which I have dictated with My own lips, and which I have approved in the presence of all the host of heaven, so that it shall also be approved among men by him who is My Vicar on earth.'(2)

Is it as a postcript to this letter that Bridget 'not only on her own behalf, but also on that of many friends of God' sent to 'the Emperor's Imperial Majesty' one of those parables in which she so often clothes her thoughts? She begins as one begins a fairy tale: 'Once upon a time there was a king who had four daughters; they were so beautiful that it made one happy just to look at them.' The first of these daughters was called Madam Humility, the second Madam Abstinence, the third Madam Frugality, the fourth Madam Charity. Saint Francis of Assisi had also known four such beautiful princesses—one who was called Poverty, one who was called Humility, one who was called Charity and one who was called Obedience. They had not got on particularly well when he was alive, and after his death their fate was still sadder.(3) The four daughters of Bridget's king had also to endure a bitter life. They had been driven out of their castle and were compelled to wander about the world like beggars. Four other sisters had come and taken their place: Madam Pride, Madam Carnality, Madam Luxury and (the worst of them all, as she was dressed in clerical garments, so that no one could beware of her) Madam Simony. The emperor had now to drive these four women out of the castle, which is the Catholic Church, and lead back the four princesses who had been banished.(4)

At last all the letters were written—Bridget began to make the necessary preparations for her departure. The winter of 1348–9 proved to be her last one in Alvastra, and (but this she did not know) her last one in Sweden. Did she find the parting hard—or could it be said of her that 'pelagrims wägir är mannomen sötare än fädhirnslandet?' She foresaw—and foretold—that hard times would come upon Sweden. The merry song might still be sung: *Gaudeamus igitur* (Bridget seems to quote the same ditty that I heard the German students sing during a carnival in Cologne—*tempus nostrum breve est*). The wrath of God was to pass like a plough over Sweden, 'the birds of prey would alight upon the mountain tops,' for corpse would lie by corpse— where before thousands had lived scarcely hundreds would be living and the houses would stand empty. Alvastra would also be struck—in a vision Bridget beheld the brethren ascend to heaven like doves, and devilish blackamoors trying in vain to catch them. Some doves flew straight up to God, others had first to be tested in purgatory, others again were like one standing on a raft, with one foot in the water. When the Black Death reached Sweden the year after Bridget's departure thirty-three of the monks died in Alvastra—Bridget had foretold the names.(5) Was it perhaps a lash of that terrible deadly epidemic which had struck Prior Petrus, when, shortly before Bridget's departure, he lay sick in the monastery and thought he was going to die? Bridget prayed for him and in her prayers learned that the Prior would recover and be able to accompany her to Rome—indeed, it was actually he who was to give her Extreme Unction.(6)

A small company of pilgrims began to gather round Bridget. None of her children travelled with her—nor even her old friend Master Matthias. On the other hand the two Petrusses—Olai the Prior, who had recovered from his illness, and Master Petrus of Skenninge(7) did accompany her. Besides these two confessors Bridget also took her chaplain, Gudmar Fredriksson; a young knight, Sir Magnus Petrusson, joined them, as did also one of Bridget's friends, the Lady Ingeborg, daughter of Laurens, who was married to the knight Nicolaus Dannes (Bjelke). This lady was uneasy about leaving her husband alone at home and asked Bridget if through her prayers she would obtain that he, during her long absence, would remain true to her. In a vision it was revealed to Bridget that the Lady Ingeborg would die a pious death during the pilgrimage and her husband could then do as he pleased.(8)

Winter passed, spring drew near, soon the Baltic would be freed from ice obstructions, so that the pilgrims could set out on the voyage from Kalmar to Stralsund. There was still another pilgrimage, however, that Bridget wished to carry out in her own country: she would set off to Skara and pray by the tomb of the holy Bishop Brynjulf. Bridget was only fourteen when he died, but his office on Saint Elin of Skövde had made a deep impression on her young mind. She also wanted to say good-bye to Brother Algot in the monastery of the Black Friars in Skara—he had now become an old man, had lost his sight and also suffered from gall-stones. 'Can you not pray for me, Lady Bridget,' said the poor blind old man, when he had understood who was sitting opposite to him in the parlour. He knew, of course, how many people she had cured through her prayers. Bridget promised to do so and returned the next day with the answer: 'Brother Algot is like a shining star whose brightness must not be dimmed. If he regained his health his soul would be less bright. He has fought the good fight and completed the race, now the crown of victory awaits him. It shall be a sign to him that his sufferings shall be slightly relieved, and his soul shall become aflame with the love of God.' But not many days passed before Brother Algot breathed his last sigh. Then Bridget saw his soul ascend like a star towards heaven, and heard Jesus say: 'Now he is in Me and I am in him. As a star is not seen when surrounded by a brighter radiance, so he has now disappeared into that everlasting joy of the years that have no end.'(9)

On the feast of Candlemas Bridget went to High Mass at the cathedral of Skara. While the blessed candles were being distributed, first to the priests and then to the congregation, making the whole church look like a flower-bed filled with golden flames, the choir sang the hymn of Simeon: *Nunc dimittis*—'Lord, now lettest Thou Thy servant depart in peace.' Bridget could also sing her *Nunc dimittis*— her time in Sweden was over, her work there was ended. Like that physician she had come to the most northerly land in the world, with her message about the land of sunshine, where soft breezes blow, instead of the constant icy-cold north wind. The answer had been as icy-cold as the wind: 'We have our joys here on this earth, we enjoy sitting at a festive board and having a merry time with a good glass of

I

beer or a goblet of wine, and we have not the least desire to give up what we have here, which is something we can handle and feel, to go on a journey in uncertainty to that land of sunshine on which you waste so many words, and which perhaps does not even exist.'(10) Bridget will not go on casting pearls before swine—exactly that! What had they not done here in Skara to the body of the holy Bishop Brynjulf? By his side they buried a man like that Knut Folkesson, who had once in Stockholm poured water over her when she was walking through the street where he lived! Bridget had then in a vision seen Knut Folkesson lying on a narrow bridge over an abyss, into which he would be hurled at the least unguarded moment. On the other side of the bridge lay a ship that was ready to take up Sir Knut, if only he had the courage to make the necessary jump. But his thoughts were on quite different matters—on resting and 'drinking of the waters of carnal pleasures.' And now he has fallen down from the bridge—fallen into the depths of hell. . . .

But suddenly a sweet scent was wafted from the altar to Bridget, and the Blessed Virgin appeared to her, and by her side stood a man of great beauty, attired in the robes of a bishop. And Mary said: 'Bishop Brynjulf honoured me by word and deed while he lived, and his life was to God like that odour thou hast just perceived. His soul is now standing before the face of God, but his body lies here in dishonour —like a pearl thrown to swine.'(11)

From Skara Bridget returned to Alvastra, and on a spring day in 1349 she and her train set out from the courtyard. At Heda church they stopped a moment, Bridget wished to greet the Queen of Heaven a last time. She had prayed before this image together with Ulf, when they returned from the land of Saint James—now she prayed there alone. Perhaps Master Matthias had come down from Linköping to bid a last farewell to his penitent of many years' standing. Then they would climb up in the tower together. Down below lay Alvastra, the monastery, the church and that house to the north of the church where Bridget had lived for five years. Behind the buildings the Omberg raised its tree-clad ridges. And behind the mountain, as Bridget knew, lay Vadstena with its ruined king's house. And from Vadstena the road led to Ulfåsa. . . .

But Bridget would not think of Ulfåsa. She stood silent, and by her side, also silent, stood Master Matthias. Then from the little company down below could be heard the old pilgrim's song: 'To the land of the East I will journey' . . .

Min själ, du göre dig rede*
den langen vägen at gå
över berg och torra heder
förrn natten faller oss på.

Bridget was ready. She took a firmer hold of her pilgrim staff and gave her old teacher a handclasp in farewell. They were not to meet again on this earth.

Master Matthias remained standing up in the tower and watched the little company. Now he could scarcely distinguish them any longer —then, raising his hand, he made a large sign of the Cross: *Benedictio Dei omnipotentis, Patris et Filii et Spiritus Sancti, descendat super vos et maneat semper* . . .

Then they disappeared, down the road to Holaveden.(12)

> * My soul, do thou make ready
> on the long journey to go,
> over hills and arid moorland
> ere the night upon us falls.

NOTES

BOOK I

I

(1) *Lucidarius: A people's book of the Middle Ages,* edited by Johannes Knudsen (Copenhagen 1909), p. 133.

II

(1) *Lucidarius*: pp. 159–60.

III

(1) H. Schück. *Illustrerad svensk Litteraturhistorie,* I (Stockholm 1896), p. 55.

IV

(1) MS. Bibl. *Uppsaliensis,* No. 58, in quarto, p. 22.

(2) The confusion of the names Scythia, the region to the north of the Black Sea where the Scythians lived, and Suetia, gave rise in the Middle Ages to the legend that Christianity had been brought to Sweden by the apostle Saint Philip. 'Filippus preached for twenty years in Sithia, which is now called Sverige, from the Eastern Land to the Eastern Sound' (the Sound between Sweden and Denmark). (*Legender från Sveriges Medeltid* (Stockholm 1917), p. 79.) 'During the period of the Vikings a Swedish domination was established; by way of the Swedish colonies by the Russian rivers there was in these centuries an active communication with the Greek empire' (*Ibid.* p. 310.) A further reason for confusing the two names.

(3) *Legender från Sveriges Medeltid* . . . edited by Emilia Fogelklou, Andreas Lindblom, Elias Wessén (Stockholm 1917), pp. 285 *et seq.*—Karin Sparre: *Svenska helgon* (Stockholm 1931).

(4) The Third Book of Kings, XIX, 4. (Douay Version.)

(5) Saint Sigfrid is usually presented in bishop's vestments and carrying a vessel from which three heads protrude. Is there any influence to be seen here of the legend of Saint Nicholas about the three children who were made into salted meat by a wicked butcher, but recalled to life by Saint Nicholas? In an old French ditty the words are: *Le premier dit: J'ai bien dormi, le deuxième: Moi aussi! le troisième: j'étais au Paradis.* Bridget mentions Saint Sigfrid in *Rev.* VIII, 46: 'Sanctus Sigfridus exivit de Anglia et fecit voluntatem Dei in Regno Suetiae.'

(6) Vastovius: *Vitis Aquiloniae* (Cologne 1622), referred to in *Legender från Sveriges Medeltid,* p. 325.

(7) The Legend is incorrect in describing Magnus Henriksson as the son of a Danish king. His father was the Danish prince Henrik Skadelaar, the grandson of Sven Estridsson, his mother was the Swedish princess Ingrid, daughter of Ragnvald, son of King Ingé the Elder, and it was in his mother's name that he laid claim to the crown of Sweden. Incidentally, Ascension Day in the year 1160 fell, not on the 18th, but on the 5th of May. The 18th May was the Wednesday after Whitsunday—and therefore a day of fasting (Ember fasting)— Magnus Henriksson, however, reigned only one year—in 1161 he fell at Örebro fighting against Karl Sverkersson.

(8) *Legender från Sveriges Medeltid*, pp. 266–70. About the year 1316 the cathedral dean, Anders And, had a chapel erected on the spot where the king was killed; it enclosed the wonder-working spring; Bridget had no doubt often drunk of its hallowed waters.

Supported by C. M. Kjellberg's researches ('Erik den heliga i Historien och Legenden,' *Historisk Tidsskrift* XLV, 1898, pp. 331 *et seq.*) Westman was of the opinion that a passage in a papal letter from Alexander III (6.7.1172) would contain a prohibition against the devotion to Saint Erik. The letter in question, however, does not mention King Erik, it only complains that in Sweden a man (*hominem quendam*) is revered as a saint in spite of the fact that he was killed in a drinking bout when intoxicated (Westman, pp. 163–5). As Otto Frödin has conclusively shown, it is here not a question of King Erik, but of the Christian king Sverker, murdered at Alvastra about the year 1156, and in whose honour a chapel was erected and a holy spring arose. 'Just as unlikely as it would seem to be that King Erik on Ascension Day, at the hour before Mass, would have appeared in a state of intoxication in the church, just as probably can King Sverker be supposed on the morning of Christmas Day to have been not quite unaffected by the ingredients of the Christmas feast.' (Otto Frödin: *Alvastrabygden under Medeltiden* (Stockholm 1919), p. 74.)

(9) The consecration took place in France, in Sens, in August 1164, and the consecrating bishop was no less a person than the Danish archbishop Eskil. From the Pope (Alexander III, who was then staying in Sens) the new archbishop received costly gifts—'librum evangeliorum dictum *carla knap* et duas cruces ligneas parvas auro tectas in quibus conditum fuit lignum Domini'—namely, two gilded crosses of wood, containing fragments of the Cross of Christ. (*Chronico de episcopis et archiepiscopis ecclesiae Uppsalensis*, Script. Rev. Svec. III, II, p. 99.) On the name *carla knap*, see Knut B. Westman: *Den svenska Kyrkans Utveckling* (Stockholm 1915, p. 133, note 4.*)

---

* The following is a concise reference:

Stephen, a Cistercian monk of unknown nationality, was selected to occupy the see of Uppsala, which it was desired at the same time to raise to an archbishopric; and this desire was granted. Stephen was consecrated a bishop by Eskil of Lund in Sens, situated 10 kilometres from Paris, in 1164, perhaps on the 3rd August (on the feast 'inventio Stephani'). The Pope bestowed on the newly consecrated archbishop a book of the Gospels, the so-called *Karla knap*, and two small gilded wooden crosses, containing relics of the Cross of Christ. The name *Karla knap* is *presumably* derived from a picture on the button (*knap*) with which, according to mediæval custom, the book could be closed.

(10) Mats Åmark: *Uppsala Domkyrka genom åtta århundraden* (Uppsala 1938), pp. 16–19.

O Janse: *Uppsala ärkesätes flyttning* (Uppsala 1902).

(11) Carl Hallendorf: 'Ur Upplands historie' (in Axel Erdman and Karl Hildebrand: *Uppland* I–II (Stockholm 1905–8), p. 232).

(12) H. Schück and K. Warburg: *Illustrerad svensk Litteratur-historie* (3rd edition, Stockholm 1926), p. 285.

(13) 'sic transeamus per bono temporalia, ut non amittamus aeterna.'

(14) The name Birgitta (Bridget) came to Sweden with the daughter of the Norwegian king, Harald Gille. She was married to Birger Brosa (died 1202). Harald Gille (died 1136) was born in Ireland and had named his daughter after the Irish saint Brigid (born 451 or 452 (died 1.2.525). Her *vita* is difficult to follow, yet it seems certain that she was of princely descent. She refused several honourable offers of marriage, and with seven other young women she set off to an old Druid sanctuary, 'the holy oak' where she founded the convent of *Cill Dara*, 'the church under the oak,' the *Kildare* of our times. Kildare became a seat of study and art, such as metal work and the illuminating of manuscripts, especially of the Gospels. Round the convent, because of the pilgrimages to the grave of Saint Bridgid, a town grew up with a magnificent cathedral, under the high altar of which the saint was laid to rest. When the Vikings of Scandinavia invaded the land the relics were moved to Downpatrick, to the tombs of Saint Patrick and Saint Columba. Even to this day the name 'Brigid' is the most frequently used girl's name in Ireland and is to be found in more than a hundred place names (Killbride, Brideswell, Templebride, etc.). A modern biography was published in 1907—Knowles: *Life of Saint Brigid.* (Information contributed by Father Peter Schindler.)

V

(1) *En lustigh och trovärdig chronica om Stockholm* (1629).

(2) John Morén: *Skeningeboken* (Linköping 1929), pp. 54–9. In 1929 extensive excavations brought to light large fragments of masonry of this monastery, the dimensions of which were larger than those of Vreta. (*Svenske Dagbladet*, 20 August 1929.) Saint Ingrid, as she was called, though she was not actually canonized, died in 1282.

(3) Dahlberg's *Svecia antiqua et modierna*, quoted by Hammerich.

(4) But *not* the 'röda stugor' now so characteristic of Sweden, that Madam de Flavigny has mistakenly used to give local colour to her otherwise excellent work. It was not until 1625 that the custom began of painting the houses red. (*Uppland* II, p. 326.)

(5) O. Janse : ' Öffentliga och enskilda byggnader' (*Uppland*, description of country and people, by Axel Erdmann and Karl Hillebrandt, Stockholm 1905–8, pp. 585-8).—The chapel at Finsta in Dahlberg : *Svecia antiqva et moderna* (Holmiae 1708), plate 103.

(6) Among these cliffs the present owner of Ulfåsa, Friherre Hermelin, has had a 'grotto to Bridget' built. In the seventeenth century it was still called 'Bridget's prayer chapel.' On the estate there is an old picture of Bridget on her death-bed (illustrated by C. M. Palmgren: *Sveriges märkligsta*

kvinna, Birgitta Birgersdotter (Stockholm 1914), p. 62), of uncertain origin. On Sunday, 22 June 1930, a monument was dedicated to Bridget at Finsta. (*Stockholm Dagblad*, 23.6.1930.)

VI

(1) Arthur Nordén: *Rejsehåndbok over Östergötland* (Stockholm 1923), p. 110.

(2) Item A.D. MCCXC in Visingxö moriebatur egregius princeps rex Suecie dictus Ladulaas quem multitudo rusticorum ob ipsius excellentem et tranquillam defensionem ad sepulturam in claustro minorum versus Stokholm in propriis humeris deportarunt. (MS. Bibl. Uppsal. No. 58, in quarto, p. 23.)— Bjälbo Gaard was bequeathed by Magnus Ladulaas to the convent in Skenninge, a last proof of his good-will towards the Church.

VII

(1) The process of canonization (ed. Collijn), p. 474. Cf. *De vita beate Birgitte* in *Wadstena Klosterreglor*. (Edited by C. F. Lindström (Stockholm 1845), p. IV.)

(2) 'the chieftain of the kingdom who carried her ashore, was that duke who was starved to death . . . up in Nyköping,' Margareta daughter of Klaus relates.

(3) In the Finsta chapel in Uppsala Cathedral, on Birger's and Ingeborg's tombstone, the names of all their children, three boys and four girls, are inscribed, Bridget's name being the lowest among the daughters. This may be the reason for Margareta Klausdotter's incorrect list. But (as Hammerich has pointed out) in the division of the inheritance of 13 September 1320, Bridget is called *secundogenita*, Katharina (Karin), on the other hand, being *tertiogenita*. Israel, who takes the first place here, does so only by virtue of being a male heir. He was the youngest of all the children and cannot have been born before 1314, as on 25 March 1324, he is mentioned as not having attained his majority, and therefore not yet being fifteen years old (Hammerich: *Den hellige Birgitta og Kirken i Norden*, p. 42, note 1). On the death of their mother only Bridget, Karin and Israel were living.

(4) *De vita beate Birgitte* (*Wadstena Klosterreglor*, p. III).—Bridget made the pilgrimage to San Iago di Compostella in 1321-2. (Johanne Skovgaard: *Den hellige Birgitta* (Copenhagen 1921), p. 39, note 3.)

(5) *Processus*, p. 473.

(6) Edw. Ortved: *Cistercieordenen og dens Klostre i Norden*, Vol. II (Copenhagen 1933), p. 436.

(7) According to Schück (*Ill. Sv. Litt. Hist.* Stockholm 1926) (*Illustrated History of Swedish Literature*), this narrative, told in a popular form through the drama *The Wedding at Ulfåsa*, is entirely unhistorical. Sigrid the Fair did not belong to an unimportant family, but was, on the contrary, a woman of exalted birth, and seems to have been proud of it, and Bengt Lagman was by no means brother to Birger Jarl but grandson of Birger Jarl's brother (*op. cit.* p. 350).

(8) Svanshals, a town in East Gothland by Lake Tåkern. The church is of the twelfth century. After that is mentioned Aspanäs, also in East Gothland, by Lake Sommen.

VIII

(1) *Um Styrilsi Kununga ok Höfdinga*, edited by Dr. Robert Geete (Stockholm 1878), p. 3. According to Schück: *Ill. Sv. Litt. Hist.* (Stockholm 1926), p. 274, the author must have been King Magnus Eriksson's chancellor, Philippus Ragvaldi, of the Puke family, born before 1290, died 1332.

(2) *Um Styrilsi koninga*, pp. 15–17. Note the expression 'friends of God' among those whom a good king ought not to offend. This appears again and again with Bridget in the same connection.

(3) *The King's Mirror* (*Konungs Skuggsjá*), in a Danish translation by Finnur Jonsson (Copenhagen 1926), p. 160.

IX

(1) The three works of Honorius of Augsburg, *Elucidarium*, *Imago Mundi* and *Gemma animae*, as well as *Philosophia mundi* by Gillaume de Conches (in Normandy). The oldest Danish manuscript is of the time of Queen Margrethe (1387–1412) but presumably copied from an older one. (*Lucidarius: A people's book of the Middle Ages*, edited by Johannes Knudsen (Copenhagen 1909), pp. 32–4.)

(2) *Lucidarius*: pp. 71–8.

(3) Hammerich: *Den hellige Birgitta*, pp. 37–8. (Hail, noble martyr, soldier of Christ, hail thou honour of all kings! Oh, Erik, thou king of the Swedes, pray for us, for the forgiveness of our sins and for (everlasting) joy.)

(4) The office for the Crown of Thorns of Christ was written by Brynolf on the occasion of his having received from King Håkan in Norway (1299–1319) a precious relic, a thorn of the Crown of Thorns of Christ. As is known, this was preserved in Paris in the shrine built for it by Saint Louis, the *Sainte Chapelle* (one of the wonders of Gothic architecture), and the son of Saint Louis, Philip III, bestowed a piece of it in 1274 on King Magnus Lagaböter. (*See* Lennart Wiberg: 'En helig Västgötabiskop,' *Credo*, July 1925.)

(5) *Legender från Sveriges Medeltid*, pp. 260–1. *See also* Knut B. Westman: *Den svenska Kyrkans Utveckling* (Stockholm 1915), pp. 137–40.

(6) Westman draws attention to the fact that this canonization, supposed to have taken place in 1163, is at variance with the practice otherwise followed at the canonization of saints in the North in the twelfth century. Local saints arise and gain a cult without any other sanction than that of the bishop of the place. Papal confirmation has only been sought for two saints of the North: Saint Knud (1101) and Knud Lavard (1169). The motives for these, however, were political. Not until Gregory IX was the confirmation of Rome declared to be necessary. Westman is of the opinion that as far as Elin of Skövde is concerned, there might be a political reason for it, or that the canonization was to do honour to her house. *Cf.* Lennart Wiberg: 'Sta Helena, Västergötlands nationalhelgon' (*Credo*, July 1925).

(7) The name, Conradus Hirschaugensis, was invented by Johannes Trithemius, abbot in Spanheim (died 1516). Author of a *Chronicon Monasterii Hirsaugensis*, in which the mistake mentioned occurs.

(8) *Processus*, p. 491. (Depositio prioris [Petri Olavi] de Alvastro.)—'Samlinger utg. av svenska fornskriftsällskapet,' No. 31. The place referred to is to be found on pp. 345–51.—Bridget's ecstasy during the reading of *Spec. Virginum* also *Rev. Extrav.* 96.

(9) *Processus*, pp. 76, 305, *Wadstena Klosterreglor*, p. V.

X

(1) *De vita beate Birgitte* in *Wadstena Klosterreglor*, p. III.

(2) *Rev.* VI, 10.—Brother Algot became Prior in the Dominican monastery of Saint Olaf in Skara, on 13 December 1333. It is at my own risk that I let him preach that Lenten sermon that made so deep an impression on Bridget, and for the text of which I have made use of a Bridgettine sermon of a later time. (C. J. Brandt: *Kirkeaarets Søndags-Evangelier* (Copenhagen 1865), pp. 97–101.) We know that he was a Master of Theology and a close friend of Bridget (*familiarissimo ipsius domine Brigide*, it is said of him in the process of canonization, p. 513). In *Rev.* VI, 35, we are told that in the last part of his life—for three years—he was blind and suffered from gall-stones. He then commended himself to Bridget's intercession, but in spirit she received the following answer: 'If he regained his health his soul would be less bright. He has fought the good fight and completed the race, now the crown of victory awaits him. It shall be a sign to him that his sufferings shall be slightly relieved, and his soul shall become aflame with the love of God.'

(3) 'Ego sum quasi avis illa quae . . . nihil vult bibere nisi sanguinem purum cordis.' (*Extrav.* 50.)

XI

(1) *Processus*, p. 75. *Wadstena Klosterreglor*, p. V.

(2) Johanne Skovgaard: *Den hellige Birgitta* (Copenhagen 1921), pp. 76–7. Ingeborg Bengtsdotter died in September 1314.

(3) Andreas Lindblom: 'Birgitta och Östergötland' (*Svenska turistföreningens årsskrift*, 1938).—Sigurd Pira: 'Aspanäs. Ett Birgittaminne' (*Tranås* 1923).—The curious name, Malexander, has nothing to do with Greece. In the Middle Ages the place was called *Malgesanda*, because the little lake Malgen is here united with Sommen, and has a sandy coast. At the present day the beach at Malexander still consists of red sand. (Arthur Nordén: *Ostergötland* (Stockholm 1923), p. 310. Thor Lindell: *Ostergötland* (Uppsala 1937), p. 339.)

(4) Pira, publication referred to, p. 22. On the title page of Pira's pamphlet this seal is reproduced—showing the Blessed Virgin sitting with the Child Jesus standing on her knee; at her side a vase with a lily. Inscription: S. KATE(rin)E BAE(ndi) CS DOTER.

(5) Pira, p. 23.—The country about Lake Sommen was still, towards the close of the nineteenth century, something out of the ordinary, and well

adapted to awaken serious thoughts, especially in such an intelligent and sensitive child as Bridget. In *En bok om Sverige* (Stockholm 1893) Adolf Törneros
has given the following description: 'The peasants who drove for us warned us
about a road by which, according to their statement, no one would travel
except under extreme necessity, and never more than once in a lifetime. In the
dusk, which grew darker and darker, we travelled for two miles, the most
fantastic landscape I have ever seen. Forest and mountain wrapped us round as
though in a bewitched world. We climbed up and plunged out on steep places
coming closely one upon another, and were always consoled by the peasants
with the words: "No, it will get worse still." Deep down below us Sommen
spread out into the far distance, awe-inspiring and terrifying with its steep places
and wild shores. All this country is the very place to awaken and sustain in the
inhabitants a serious spirit and to bring their minds into close communion with
the wonderful, so that I doubt whether any place in the kingdom is richer in the
very oldest legends of a fantastic kind. The shadow-play of imagination does
not easily pale in these ever gloomy dales, and besides this the people are shut in
from the rest of the world, over whose obstructing walls the winds of the day
have not sufficient force to blow in and sweep away everything old. The people
here live isolated, and this can also be perceived in all their speech.'

(6) Thor Lindell: *Ostergöland* (Uppsala 1937), p. 339.

(7) Elias Gripp: 'Folktro' (*Uppland* II, pp. 382–94.

(8) *Rev.* VI, 28 ('enjoyed the sweetness of a mother's breast or the warmth
of her bosom').

(9) I quote from a Florentine manuscript, edited by Florio Banfi in the
Franciscan periodical *Frate Francesco* (Assisi, fourth year 1931, and later published
separately (the year not given), p. 6, notes 1 and 2. Palmgren (*op. cit.*) presumes
that the Lady Karin would consult Bishop Brynjulf of Skara (died 1317) about
Bridget's religious education.

(10) *Processus*, p. 76.

(11) *Rev.* VI, 17.—Later *Processus*, p. 305. (Katerina's testimony.)

BOOK II

I

(1) *Rev.* III, 23.

(2) 'Some years later she told her mother's sister what her conviction was
about these things, and her aunt told her to keep it in her heart and to trust in
God.' (*Klosterreglor*, p. VII.)

(3) Ulfåsa is mentioned for the first time about 1250, when the law-man
Magnus Minnesköld, of the house of the Folkungs, was the owner of the
property. 'Before the year 1252, when Ingrid Ylfwa died, she and her husband,
the knight and East Gothland law-man Måns Minnesköld, owned Ulfåsa, and
in the year 1269 the owner was the knight and law-man in East Gothland,
Bengt Magnison Minnesköld. After that the knight and law-man in Närike,
Ulf Gudmarsson (Hjorthufwud), Saint Brita's husband, was the owner thereof,

and it is believed that the property was not called Ulfåsa until after Saint Brita had moved it from the so-called Saint Brita's Ness in the big deer park, where the ruins are still to be seen on the fields of the town of Berga, where the Humle farm now is.' (Carl Fredric Broochman: *Beskrifning öfwer Oster-Götland* (Norr-köping 1760), pp. 160–1.—So that it was by his marriage with the Finsta daughter that Ulf Gudmarsson became a great landowner. 'After Santa Brita Ulfåsa passed over to her sons, the law-man of Nerike, Karl (died 1372) and Birger (died 1391), as well as belonging later to the son of the former, Karl (died 1398).' Anton Ridderstad: *Leksikon öfver Ostergötland,* II (Norrköping 1877), p. 303. The main building of the present Ulfåsa dates from the eighteenth century. The property is in the possession of the baronial family of Hermelin; a painting preserved there shows Bridget on her death-bed. (Reproduction in C. M. Palmgren: *Sveriges märkligstes Kvinna* (Stockholm 1914), p. 62.

(4) 'Sir Birger makes the marriage speech to Ulf'—the Danish word 'Giftermaal,' marriage, is here used in its original meaning: Maal, speech.

(5) C. J. Brandt: *De hellige Kvinder.* A collection of legends. (Copenhagen 1859), pp. 52–3.

(6) *Svenska medeltids dikter och rim,* edited by G. E. Klemming (Stockholm 1881–2), pp. 512–13. *Hjonalag,* the state of matrimony.

(7) *Rev.* I, 9; VI, 104. Elisabeth of Thuringia complained to her confessor, Konrad of Marburg, that she had been forced into marriage and therefore could not end her life on earth *in virginali flore* (Alb. Huyskens: *Quellenstudien zur Geschichte der hl. Elisabeth,* Marburg 1908, p. 117, note and p. 156).

II

(1) Sulpicius: *Vita B. Martini,* liber III, quoted by Durante in his commentary on *Rev.* VI, 119.

(2) *Rev.* VI, 119. This chapter is not included in the Old Swedish translation. *Cf.* Apocalypse XIV, 4, about 'those who have not defiled themselves with women, for they are virgins' (in the Vulgate *virgines*).

(3) *Processus,* pp. 77, 505, 737.

(3a) Johannes Jørgensen: *Romerske Helgenbilleder* (Copenhagen 1902), p. 100.

(4) *Romerske Helgenbilleder.* I wrote these words in 1902. They are—alas—as true of the times in 1940 as then. Bridget on the women who kill their fœtus, *Rev.* VII, 27.

(4a) Proverbs, XXI, pp. 10–30.

(5) The biography in *Wadstena Klosterreglor,* pp. VII–IX.

(6) *Processus,* p. 441.

(7) *Rev.* IV, 28; IV, 66.

(8) *Rev.* IV, 24, VIII, 48. It may be that it is brandy that is mentioned here 'burnt water which is made and made up of wines').

(9) *Rev.* I, 33.

(10) *Rev.* III, 30.

(11) *Rev.* III, 7.

(12) *Rev.* II, 4; VI, 44.

(13) *Rev.* IV, 97.

(14) *Rev.* V, 20 and VII, 28, both in the Swedish text. The remarks of Schück seem strange (in *Illustrerad Svensk Litteratur Historia*, I), p. 364. 'When one reads Bridget's writings it is as though one were standing on a height with the clouds beneath one's feet, the arch of heaven is like a vault over one's head, but not a speck of the earth can be seen.' In reality Saint Bridget would seem to be one of the most realistic writers in Swedish literature.

(15) *Vita*, p. IX. According to the testimony of Petrus Olai in the process of canonization Bridget kept still more days of fasting—he mentions, *inter alia*, the vigils of all the feasts of the Apostles, all Fridays as well as the whole of Advent and a special *Adventus Spiritus Sancti*, that is, before Whitsuntide. At these two Advent fasts Bridget ate fish only. The 'dry fast' of Margareta daughter of Klaus is here corrected to 'bread *and water*.' If to this the long fast common to all Catholics is added, one arrives at the result that Bridget fasted almost half the year.

(16) To her son Birger Bridget writes from Rome; 'When you sit at table have godly and seemly talk. Beware of the custom of swearing. Many seldom leave the table before they are like grunting pigs in the house of their fellows.' (Klemming's edition of *Heliga Birgitta's Uppenbarelser*, V., Stockholm 1883-4, p. 140.)

(17) Katerina, *Processus*, pp. 315-16. Petrus Olai, *Processus*, p. 497. Cf. *Processus*, p. 63, the testimony of Margareta of Broby.

(18) *Processus*, p. 479.

(19) *Vita*, p. IX. *Processus*, p. 79.—In spite of the intimate relations with Brother Algot, Ulf and Bridget seem to have preferred the Franciscan Third Order to the corresponding Dominican one. In a revelation it is said of Saint Francis of Assisi's rule for the brothers of the *first* Order, the Minorites or Friars Minor: 'This rule was not dictated or composed by his own reason or wisdom, but by Me' (it is Christ who speaks) 'according to My will. Every single word that is written in it was given him by My spirit.' This testimony of Christ includes also 'all the other rules which my friends keep and by which they live'—neither are they a work of human wisdom, but are written *aspiratione eiusdem Spiritus Sancti* (*Rev.* VII, 20). This almost certainly includes the rule of the Brothers of the Third Order. See further *Extrav.* 67 and 90, which clearly testify to Bridget's Franciscan disposition; moreover, she made a pilgrimage to Assisi while in Rome. It is all the more to be wondered at that Madame de Flavigny, in a work otherwise so well written as her *Vie de Sainte Brigitte*, can make the most extraordinary assertions about the Franciscan Third Order, in fact about Franciscans altogether. 'Saint Dominic, a scion of old Spanish nobility, a canon in Osma, was a doctor, a preacher, a highly intellectual genius. Following the example of the Incarnate Word he had brought the light of the truth to the people of his century. . . . He was a member of the teaching Church, he was descended from the Apostles.' Compared with him Saint Francis does not cut a really brilliant figure. He is characterized as *diacre italien*—as if there were a special race of deacons in Italy. In the next place he has issued from the citizen class in Assisi—finally 'he was a poet.' He was 'descended from the Lord's disciples, not from the Apostles,' and his rule consisted only of a few 'monastic precepts' (*des observances monastiques*). 'The brown Franciscan habit and the bare feet perhaps looked more world-forsaking than

the white habit, but in reality the elegant costume perhaps concealed greater austerity!'

As will be seen, there is a greater disagreement between Madame de Flavigny's estimate of the saint of Assisi and that of Bridget. In justice it must be admitted that in the ecclesiastical order of rank Saint Francis takes a lower place than the Spaniard—he did not consider himself worthy to become a priest (and thus escaped being one of the 'accursed priests' chastized by Bridget). But with a few 'monastic precepts' Francis of Assisi could not have created that apostolic spirit which drove him to the Orient to convert the Sultan, and in the rule of his Order—the *first* among all founders of Orders—to write a chapter 'about those brothers who go out to the infidels.'

(20) Gustaf Armfelt: *Biskop Nils Hermansson* (Norrköping 1931).

(21) H. Schück: *Ill. Sv. Litt. Hist.* (1926), pp. 247–8. (*Illustrated History of Swedish Literature.*)

(22) The monastery in Sigtuna was founded as early as in 1220, by two brothers who came direct from Bologna. It was said of the monastery church, the large, magnificent church of Saint Mary, that no church in Sweden was richer in indulgences or more beloved by the people. The school and library of the monastery are mentioned as something of great importance already in the thirteenth century. Gradually religious houses were founded in Sko, Stockholm, Uppsala, Skara, Lödöse, Vesterås, Strängnäs, Skenninge, and one in Kalmar. (E. Rosenörn-Lehn: 'Lidt om Dominikanerordenen i Norden,' *Credo* 8 Aug. 1921).

(23) Hammerich, p. 154.

(24) King Magnus' mother, Ingeborg, had fallen in love with Sir Knud Pors of Halland and lived for a long time with him before they were married. A political party gathered round the couple, and in the opinion of Master Matthias (and Bridget) it had been allowed to grow far too great. In the commentary to the description of the Feast of Tabernacles (Leviticus XXIII, 40) the words *rami ligni densarum frondium* were now translated thus: 'a ten-branched tree, that is pors (the willow)'; 'ten-branched and many-branched tree, that is pors, which grows much higher in the Holy Land than in Halland.' It is Sten Engström who calls attention to this allusion, rather unexpected in a Bible commentary, to the politics of the time, which 'has nothing to do with the flora of Halland. It is a play upon words, a spiteful allusion to the Halland duke, addressed to a circle of readers, who did not entertain any doubt that the Pors trunk grew far too high.' Sten Ensgtröm: *Bo Jonsson* I (Uppsala 1935), p. 23, note 61.

(25) Fr. Hammerich: *En Skolastiker og en Bibelteolog fra Norden* (Copenhagen 1865), pp. 151-2, 157.—According to Schück it was Abbot Svenning of Varnhem, Bridget's confessor on the pilgrimage to Compostella, who translated Master Matthias' work on the Bible (Schück, *op. cit.*, pp. 337–42).

(26) *Rev.* V, 14 (Swedish text), *Processus*, p. 83.

(27) Ellen Jørgensen: *Valdemar Atterdag* (Copenhagen, 1911), pp. 41-2, 55.—The French grey friar, Jean de la Rochetaillade, published in 1356 the treatise *Vademecum in tribulationibus* of a similar content.

(28) These fifteen signs are given in a Bridgettine sermon of the beginning of the fifteenth century. I quote from the old Danish translation of about 1450, edited by C. J. Brandt (Copenhagen 1865), p. 164.

(29) Hammerich, *En Skolastiker*, pp. 184–5.

(30) *Rev.* I, 3, 52; IV, 32; VI, 75, 89–90, V, *Interrogatio* XVI (Latin text), V, 14 (Swedish text). *Processus*, pp. 83, 530.—On Master Matthias *see* K. B. Westmann; *Birgitta Studier*, I (Uppsala 1911), pp. 10–15, 272–7.

III

(1) *Lucidarius*, p. 138.

(2) *Um Styrilsi Kununga*, pp. 59–60, 113–14. Ingvar Anderson doubts (against Hammerich, p. 55), that Bridget knew anything at all about *Um Styrilsi Kununga* ('Källstudier till Sveriges historia 1230–1436') Lund 1928, p. 126, note 2.

(3) *Rev.* I, 27.

IV

(1) Klemming IV, 132. *Vita*, p. VIII. During the years 1317–19 Ulf must often have been out on war service.

(2) *Processus*, p. 307. A sack of straw with a bear skin over it, it is said in *Rev. Extrav.* 53. But the new bed, on the other hand, was *solemnius et cariosus solito*.

(3) *Processus*, p. 480. (Testimony of Prior Petrus of Alvastra.)

(4) The biography (*Processus*, p. 98). Bridget showed the same hardihood when, on one of her journeys in Sweden, she wanted to spend the night in the open air in order not to awaken the family who would have given her shelter for the night. Her servants felt the cold, Bridget did not ! (*Rev.* VI, 84.)

(5) *Libellus quatuor ancillarum*, ed. Huyskens (Marburg 1911), pp. 21–2. Huyskens: *Quellenstudien zur Geschichte der h. Elisabeth* (Marburg 1908), p. 116.

(6) *Processus*, pp. 311, 487, 581 (the silver goblet with water).

(7) *Processus*, p. 491.

(8) *Gentiana*, *Processus*, pp. 308, 369, 439, 450, 481.—*The wax drops, Processus*, pp. 308, 364, 481.—*Vita*, p. 14. Saint Paul in the Epistle to the Galatians, VI, 17.

(9) A good prayer, which Saint Bridget used to say every day. Klemming, IV, pp. 160, 176, *Processus*, p. 78.

V

(1) Madame de Flavigny lets him come to Rome, there receive absolution from his sins by the Papal Legate, who declares that it will be more pleasing to God if Birger will return to Sweden and take up the duties of his station (*Vie de Sainte Brigitte*, p. 51). In the place indicated by her as the source in the Process there is nothing about this.

(2) Montelius: *Sveriges Hednatid samt Medeltid* (Stockholm 1877), p. 449.

(3) Schück, *op. cit.*, p. 351.

(4) Montelius, p. 485, note 2.

(5) Ortved, *op. cit.*, p. 91, note.

(6) 'The stone was not hewn in Sweden, but imported in a finished state from Flanders' (Bengt Thordeman: 'Lagman Birgers Gravsten i Uppsala Domkyrka,' in *Upplands Forminnes-Förenings Tidskrift*, 1927, pp. 19–43), Dr. C. R. of Uggla has advanced the theory that Birger himself had ordered the gravestone, when he was in Flanders in 1321 on the journey to Avignon. It is also possible that his children ordered the tombstone after their father's death in 1327. In any case it was executed after 1313, for then Israel, the youngest child of the couple, was born and of course, before the canonization of Bridget in 1391. (Thordeman, p. 37.)

(7) 'The age-old (Scandinavian) standard of value is the mark. One mark in gold was worth 8 marks in silver (M.S.). One M.S., about 210½ grammes, was divided into 8 Ører, an Øre into 3 Ørtuger (solidi). These three values were in the beginning of weight in metal, not coin, Ørtuger not being stamped until after the middle of the fourteenth century, Ører under Gustaf Vasa. Penning (denarius) was the oldest coin. Its size and weight differed in different countries, and there was therefore an unequal number of Pennings to a mark (m.p.). . . . In the second half of the twelfth century 1 m.p. was still equal to 1 mark unstamped silver. But gradually, as the metal from which the pennings were made, became commoner, it took more m.p.s to make up 1 M.S., thus . . . in the year 1340' (Edw. Ortved: *Cistercienserordenen . . . i Norden*, II, p. 28, note).

VI

(1) *Svenska Medeltids dikter och rim*, edited by G. E. Klemming (Stockholm 1881–2), pp. 485–6. The chronicle was probably composed shortly before 1523, when Bishop Hans Brask had it printed in the printing-press newly set up by him in Söderköping.

(2) Johanne Skovgaard, *op. cit.*, p. 83, Edw. Ortved: *Cistercienserordenen* II (Copenhagen 1933), pp. 507–8.

(3) Heidenstam, pp. 11–12.

(4) Information kindly contributed by the writer of local history, Pastor Karl Bäckgren of Gryt parsonage, Stojärnhov. See the same writer's paper in 'Ur fromhetslivets historia i Norra Vättersbygden' (*Till hembygden*, Stockholm 1929), pp. 157–63.

(5) The chalice from Ekebyborna is now in the National Museum in Stockholm. In the same place there is also a paten which had belonged to the church in Ekebyborna (Ekeby by Lake Boren). It has the following inscription: *Bæro de Fughilsunde et consors sua Ingrideris fecerunt me fi(eri) in honorem sancte (Ecclesiae)*.

VII

(1) *Rev.* I, 2, 7; IV, 25, 82; I, 26; IV, 83.

(2) *sponsus . . . qui abscondit se a sponsa, ut ardentius desideretur (Rev.* VII, 31). *Processus*, p. 319.

(3) *Rev.* IV, 81, 102, 111. (*See* Emilia Fogelklou: 'Birgitta och landskapslagerna' in *Årsbok för kristen humanism*, 1919, pp. 18 *et seq.*)

(4) *Rev.* VI, 23. In this *Revelatio* Bridget is designated as the bride of Christ (*peto a te misericordiam*, says Mary, *pro latrone isto, pro quo sponsa tua orando plorat*). It is therefore of a later date, but no doubt truthfully represents Bridget's feelings towards the son-in-law that was to be.

(5) '(The robber) has . . . three evil things: First much worldliness, secondly a profligate life . . . thirdly he is so haughty that he reckons no one to be his equal.' VI, 23. Next VI, 24, is quoted. 'Sigved's and Märta's son Petrus died in 1379 in Florence, on a pilgrimage to the Holy Land, perhaps as an expiation for the sins of his father.'

(6) *Vita*, p. IX. *Processus*, p. 79. *Diarium Vaztenense ad* 1399: 'fertur infantem in utero clamasse: carissima mater, noli me interficere.'

(7) The consecutive order usually supposed of Ulf's and Bridget's children is this:

Märta, b. about 1319, married (1) Sigurd Ribbing, (2) Knut Algotson, died at an advanced age.

Karl, b. about 1321, d. 12.3.1372 in Naples, married (1) Karin Gisladotter Sparre, (2) a Norwegian woman, Gyda, (3) Karin Eriksdatter Glysing, d. 1413.

Birger, b. about 1323, d. 27.8.1391, married (1) Bengta Glysingsdotter, (2) Marta Siggesdotter.

Bengt, b. about 1326, d. in Alvastra about 1345.

Gudmar, b. about 1327, d. in Stockholm about 1338.

Karin, b. about 1330, d. 24.3.1381.

Ingeborg, b. about 1332, d. after 1350, before 1373.

Cecilia, b. about 1334, d. 12.3.1390.

VIII

(1) Karl Bäckgren: 'Ur fromhetslivets historia' ('*Till hembygden*', 1929, pp. 174–89).

(2) 'Scriptura quam vos dicitis Bibliam et nos vocamus auream' (*Extravagantes* III).

(3) *Rev.* II, 15.

(4) *Rev.* IV, 41; *cf.* VI, 35.

(5) *Biaus fiz, je te prie que tute faces amer au peuple de ton royaume; car vraiment je ameroie miex que uns Escoz venist d'Escosse et gouvernast le peuple dou royaume bien et loialment que tu le gouvernasses mal apertement.* (Joinville: *Histoire de Saint Louis*, Ch. III, n. 21.)

(6) *au reaume de Noroe qui est en la fin du monde* (Ch. XCVI, n. 493).

(7) Joinville has a touching description of the stratagem practised by the two young people to meet each other in spite of the mother-in-law and not to be caught by her in being conjugally together. (Ch. CXIX, n. 606–7).

(8) *Extrav.* 59, *Processus*, p. 528.

(9) *Legenda aurea*, pp. 915 *et seq*. See Ingvar Andersson, *Källstudier*, p. 120, note 3, in which the part played by Saint Erik as a holy example is also emphasized.

(10) Joinville, IV, 29; XI, 54; XII, 59; CXXXIX, 688–9; the whole of CXLII.

(11) *In casa (here the name) non ci si mette a tavola, prima che i poveri anno avuto da mangiare!* (An ear-witness).

(12) *Histoire de Saint Louis* (Paris 1914), pp. 307–10.—'*Ce fu escrit en l'an de grâce mil CCC et IX, au moys d'octovre.*'—As Ingvar Andersson observes (*op. cit.*, p. 113), 'these admonitions of Louis IX of France to his son . . . were known in Sweden too, and translated into Swedish.' They are to be found in *Svenska fornskriftsällskapets samlinger*, 36, pp. 205 *et seq.*

IX

(1) *Rev.* VIII, 2.

(2) Thomas à Becket, whose legend Bridget had read (*Rev.* III, 13), washed even daily the feet of 13 poor people, gave them a meal and bestowed upon each of them 'forty English pennies.'

(3) *Rev.* VIII, 2; *Rev.* I, 15: 'a king should be rich, gentle, wise and open-handed.' The old Norid ideal of a chieftain can here be distinctly traced. A true king is known by his munificence. (Ingvar Andersson, *op. cit.*, p. 105.)

(4) The Book of Job, II, 1–2.

X

(1) *Rev.* VIII, 56. Cf. *Libellus de Magno Erici Rege*: 'Consuetudo regis fuit a iuventute audire missas, legere et jejunare, sed nullisfacere justitiam.' (*Scriptores Rev. Svec.* III, 1, p. 13.)

(2) *Rev.* VIII, 11: 'redire ad primam legem matrimonialis copulae.'

(3) *Rev.* VIII, 12–14. *Extravagantes* 80.

(4) This accusation against Magnus Eriksson is repeated in the polemical pamphlet of the Swedish nobility *Libellus de Magno Erici Rege*, written between 1365 and 1371. *See* Ingvar Andersson: *Källstudier* (Lund, 1928), pp. 151–73. Later *Rev.* VIII, 56, is referred to.

(5) *Rev.* VIII, 19. Richard Steffen: *Den heliga Birgittas Uppenbarelser* (Stockholm 1909), p. 290. From the words 'quem rex exaltavit in ducem contra deum et matrem ejus' Steffen deduces 'that not only Bengt himself was exalted, but even also his mother.' But 'matrem ejus' is not governed by 'exaltavit' but by 'contra' and 'matrem ejus' is therefore the *Mother of God*.

(6) *Eremus S. Francisci prope Holmiam* (Petrus Wieselgren: *De Claustris Svio-Gothicis*, Lund, 1832, p. 143).

(7) *Erikskrøniken*, written before 1332 (ref. in Schück: *Ill. Sv. Litt. Hist.*, p. 278).—*Rev.* VIII, 31: 'regnum Suetiae . . . quod quasi coeleste et quietum et justum esee deberet.'

(8) *Rev.* VIII, 57.

(9) *Aucassin et Nicolette*, VI.—Besides poetry which could not be anything but immoral worldliness to Bridget, the favour of King Magnus Eriksson's court included other interest. As Toni Schmid has pointed out, *Birgitta och hennes uppenbarelser*, Lund 1940, pp. 71–2, there lived in Stockholm at that time a German physician, Everhard von Wampen, who in a work dedicated to King Magnus, *Spiegel der Natur*, on the basis of the philosophy of Aristotle, advocated a mild Epicureanism. 'Enjoy the pleasure of love until you die, you

do not know how long you will live to do it still.' No scheme for living could be more hateful to Bridget than this. And to speak well of all people (sprek ok allen ludenwol) might do for King Magnus, but not for Bridget. 'Aristotle had not even understood the first beginning of wisdom,' it is said in *Rev.* V, *interrogatio* XIII, *resp. quaest.* 4.

(10) *Rev.* I, 27; *Rev.* VI, 80.

(11) It is the Norwegian queen, Euphemia, who is mentioned here. She was the mother-in-law of Duke Erik, and died in 1312.

(12) *Rev.* VIII, 17. Cf. *Rev.* VI, 32. According to Sten Engström (*Bo Jonsson*, I, Uppsala 1935, p. 23), Bridget, in using the word 'viper,' would have thought of the Duchess Ingeborg of Halland, married to Knud Porse, 'only by derivation possibly also . . . her daughter Euphemia of Mecklenburg.' This interpretation is also accepted by Salomon Kraft (*Ostergöta-Correspondenten*, 18.11. 1938).

(13) *Rev.* VIII, 31. Bridget had this vision in 1336 (Hammerich; *Den hellige Birgitta*, pp. 69 and 114, note 1. Sten Engström, *op. cit.*, p. 23, note 61. Steffen gives the date of the vision as 1343–48, see *Den heliga Birgittas Uppenbarelser*, p. 291, but without convincing reasons). Not till 11 years later was it explained to the seeress, 'what I revealed to thee in the dark and stormy sky.' (Klemming, IV, p. 324.) Euphemia Erik's daughter died about 1370, her husband, Albrecht of Mecklenburg, in 1379.

XI

(1) From Gustav Storm's translation of *Snorre* (Christiania, 1900).

(2) *Rev. Extrav.* 62.

(3) For the following see Gustav Ewald: 'Stenen i grönen dal,' in *Östergota-Correspondenten*, 5.1.1940, and Messenius: *Specula äller skådetorn*, 1612.

(4) Sverre Sten: *Ferd og Fest, Reiseliv i norsk Sagatid og Middelalder* (Oslo 1929).

(5) Adolf Schück: 'Sanct Olofskulten i Sverige' (*Nordisk Tidsskrift*, Stockholm 1930, pp. 409–19).—Olsmesse (Olsok) is celebrated on 29 July. The real date, however, is 31 August, as on this date that eclipse of the sun occurred during the battle of Stiklestad mentioned by Snorre (see Johannes Hohlenberg: 'Naar stod Slaget ved Stiklestad,' ('when was the battle of Stiklestad fought?'). Article in *Berlingske Tidende*, 29.7.1930.

(6) *Kongespejlet*, edited by Finnur Jonsson, Copenhagen, 1926, p. 134.

(7) Jeremiah I, 14. The verse is made use of by Aelnoth in *Passio Sancti Canuti*—Saint Knud was murdered by the rebellious Vends who had come from the north. (*Vitae Sanctorum Danorum*, ed. Gertz, pp. 82, 84.)

(8) On Pietro Quirini and his adventurous travels in Norway in 1432, see *Navigazioni e viaggiraccolti da G. B. Ramusio*, Vol. II, Venezia 1559. On 1 August Quirini is present at a feast of indulgence in Vadstena, at Stegeborg visits a fellow-countryman, Giovanni Franco, whom Erik of Pomerania had brought home with him from his journey to Jerusalem in 1424.

(9) For the following I am indebted to Jørgen Bukdahl, who in his book on the old Cistercian monastery at Bergen has devoted a whole chapter to a

study of the Draum ballad, which he dates at 1229. (Jørgen Bukdahl: *Lyseklosteret*, Copenhagen 1940, pp. 91–184.) The word *Brokksvalin* is believed to contain an Icelandic *brokk*, not known from the old literature, but possibly from the later. It means 'clouds' . . . A *sval* is a balcony. *Brokksvalin* would then mean 'the cloud path,' see Matthew XXIV, 30—'they shall see the Son of man coming in the clouds of heaven' (Professor Fredrik Paasche).

(10) *Extrav.* 51. *Rev.* IV, 130 (Swedish text).

XII

(1) 'The Saga of Saint James the Greater' (Collections published by *Svenska Fornskrift-Sällskapet*, IV, Stockholm 1847, pp. 161 *et seq.*)

(2) Emile Baumann: *Trois villes saintes* (Marseilles 1920), pp. 82–3. Emile Måle on *il Volto Santo* (*L'Art religieux du XIIme siècle*, Paris 1922), pp. 253 *et seq.*

(3) Baumann, pp. 84–5.

(4) Ciro Angelillis: 'Il pellegrinaggio al Gargano' (*L'Italia Franciscana*, January, February, 1928), and the work quoted therein of the seventeenth century by the Dominican P. Marcello Cavalieri: *Il Pellegrino al Gargano*, Vol. I, Chap. X.

(5) *Vita* in the convent rules, p. III, Johanne Skovgaard, *Den hellige Birgitta*, p. 39.

(6) Edw. Ortved: *Cistercieordenen i Norden*, II, p. 91.

(7) As Madame de Flavigny thinks (*Sainte Brigitte*, p. 67) *sous la garde de Nicolas Hermansson* (b. 1326), who, however, would not have much authority over the young men of his own age. It is more probable that the two boys stayed with their mother's sister Karin and their father's brother Magnus, especially if these two, as Palmgren thinks (*Sveriges märkligste Kvinna*, Stockholm 1914, p. 154), also had their home at Ulfåsa. In any case Karl Ulfsson became the real owner of Ulfåsa after the death of Ulf, 12 February 1344.

(8) Johanne Skovgaard, p. 86.

(9) *Processus*, pp. 494–5.

(10) Broochman, II, p. 605. Erik Lundberg: *Östergötlands romanske Landskyrkor* (Meddelanden från Östergötlands Fornminnas och Museiförening, Linköping 1927, p. 38).

XIII

(1) *Exordium Magnum*, IV, 28, quoted by Edw. Ortved, II, pp. 55–6. 'Our own archbishop too, Eskil, was given such a blessed loaf for the journey, when in 1151 he took leave of his great friend and benefactor; after the lapse of three years it was still as fresh as when it was new.' (*Vita S. Bernardi*, VII, 29, No. 62).

(2) 'Gradually Citeaux had 27 direct offshoots and 358 indirect ones (that is, founded from daughter houses of Citeaux) . . . Clairvaux 80 direct and 276 indirect. There were altogether 742 monasteries . . . 524 dating from the twelfth, 169 from the thirteenth century.' (Ortved, I, p. 3). In 1264 the total number of monasteries is believed to have been 650. Mention is made in 1369 of 1,500.

(3) From Al, the name of a little brook, which here flows into the Vättern, and Old Swedish *vaster* (ford, or *wading*-place), or perhaps from the rushes and reeds (*vass*) growing at the mouth of the brook where it flowed into the lake?

(4) Meddelanden från Östergötlands Fornminnas och Museiförening, 1917, p. 10, cited by Otto Frödin: *Alvastrabygden under Medeltiden* (Stockholm 1919), p. 5. In the following I also make use of Dr. Frödin's basic article.

(5) Joh. Sylvii translation, Stockholm 1678, p. 121.

(6) In Danish these shells (now used in Denmark for serving mince) were known by the name of Ib-shells. Vilhelm Andersen (b. 1864. Ex-professor of literature at the University of Copenhagen. Wrote special studies on classical Danish authors, such as Holberg and Oehlenschläger) has explained somewhere that the remarkable name Ib is simply an abbreviation of *Jacobus*, such as it may be read under the pictures of Saint James on the altar pictures of the Middle Ages: S C S JB (SanCtus JacoBus). Hence the well-known man's name Ib, frequent especially in Jutland.—Verner v. Heidenstam: *Heliga Birgittas Pilgrimsfärd* (Stockholm 1901), p. 78.

XIV

(1) On the journey to Rome it was *Stralsund* (*Extrav.* 67), and so probably also now.

(2) Albertus Magnus, Dominican, tutor of Saint Thomas Aquinas (1193–1280). He gave lectures in Paris and Cologne. Master Eckart, also a Dominican, worked after 1314 in Cologne and died there in 1327. Tauler (1300–61) was in Strassburg in 1347 after his years of study in Cologne, where he met Suso (1295–1366).

(3) Hammerich (pp. 134–7) also had his doubts. 'Bridget 'was a step nearer (than the friends of God), she was but very faintly affected by speculation, she knew nothing at all about their system of methods and their pantheistic trend of thought. . . . They make a display of feelings and often give themselves up to a bombastic style, while she, on the contrary, is a sober child of the North.'

(4) L. Duchesne: *Annales du Midi*, V, 1893, pp. 1–33: *La légende de Sainte Marie Madeleine.*—*Les fastes épiscopaux de l'ancienne Gaule* (Paris 1891), I, pp. 310–344; Isak Collijn: *Sur la vie de Sainte Marie Madeleine* (Uppsala 1901).

(5) *Et fornsvenskt Legendarium*, edited by George Stephens (Stockholm 1847), pp. 266 *et seq.*—The two sisters and their brother of Bethany would often be in Bridget's thoughts (*Rev.* VI, 65, in which Martha and Mary are described as types of the active and contemplative life; *Rev.* IV, 16; IV, 72; IV, 108–9).

(6) See my book *Of the Fruit of the Olive Tree*, in which there is a description of the pilgrimage as still made at the present day—or at any rate in 1925, when I was present at it. Much may have been changed since then.

(7) In the Magdalene chapel in the church of Saint Francis in Assisi there is a presentation of this miracle, in the handbooks for travellers it is incorrectly called 'the Ascension of Mary Magdalene.'

(8) *Pilon*, Provençal *pieloun*, means 'pillar,' 'column.' Originally there was on the top a column with a statue of Mary Magdalene. It disappeared when a chapel was built there, but the name remained.

(9) 'We will adore in the place where his (her) feet stood.' Ps. 131, 7.

(10) Joseph Escudier: *La Sainte Baume* (Paris 1925), pp. 22–6, 88 (the visit of Gregory XI, 20 September 1376).—'as if a child moved within her,' *Processus*, p. 81; *in corde vero senciebat quasi quoddam vividum, quod movebatur.* . . .

(11) Johannes Jørgensen: *Af Oliventræets Frugt* (Copenhagen 1925), pp. 130, 135–7.

XV

(1) *Rev.* VI, 36.

(2) *Rev.* I, 47–9; I, 56; I, 69. The *Revelationes* concerned are later than the journey to Compostella (though all of the earliest time). What was written down later, however, may have been the result of earlier experiences. No doubt Bridget on this pilgrimage had some sad experiences of French and Spanish ecclesiastics.

(3) *Rev.* IV, 104 (Swedish text VIII, 27). Here it is a question of the Hundred Years War which had just broken out between France and England (1339–1453).

(4) The testimony of Petrus Olai in the process in 1380: 'dixit idem testis quod audivit a quodam monacho nomine Svenungo qui postea fuit abbas Warnensis ordinis Cisterciensis Scarensis diocesis' (*Processus*, p. 503). Cf. *Extrav.* 63, in which Svenung is only called *hic frater.* He became abbot in Varnhem 1.3.1346.

XVI

(1) The battle at Salsada in 1340. (*Legender från Sveriges Medeltid*, pp. 96–7, 312.)

(2) *Et fornsvenskt Legendarium* I, p. 170.

(3) Emile Måle: *L'art religieux du XIIe siècle en France* (Les pélérinages, les routes de France et d'Espagne). Paris, 1922, p. 290.

(4) We do not know by what road Bridget travelled through France; it is believed that she visited Fontevrault (in Poitou), which was a double convent for men and women, and there obtained the first idea for the establishment of her order (Hammerich, p. 105). It is only known with certainty that Svenung was in Citeaux in January 1342 (Ortved, II, p. 91). In the village of Courson (Dept. of Yonne) relics are preserved of Bridget.

(5) Madame de Flavigny: *Sainte Brigitte*, p. 85, note 2.—'Birger Persson's tombstone was of Flemish workmanship, perhaps he ordered it when he was on the way to Avignon in 1321; Bridget's family was therefore known in Flanders. He left Sweden *via* Lödöse by the Göta river, the Gothenburg of the Middle Ages' (Thordeman, *op. cit.*, p. 37).

(6) 'Arras, Lens, Douai' (Clermont-Ferrand 1920), pp. 31, 56.

(7) It is Petrus Olai, the Prior at Alvastra, who testifies to this. *Peractis aliquibus annis* (Bridget) *convertit maritum suum totaliter ad Deum suis sanctis admonitionibus, orationibus et exemplis et ad castitatem vovendam eum adduxit* (*Processus*,

p. 505). Petrus Olai knows this, not only from Bridget, but also from Ulf: *etiam a dicto marito ejus.*

XVII

(1) MS. C, 240, in the university library in Uppsala, fol. 3r–3v. This manuscript had belonged to Saint Bridget, which is testified by a notice on the wrapper, now almost illegible: Hunc librum qui intitulatur doctrina Bernardi ad sororem portavit beata mater nostra sancta Birgitta continue in sinu suo, ideo inter reliquas suas asservandus est. The manuscript had been preserved in the convent library of Vadstena. On p. 3 is written in Spanish in red writing *Aqst libro ordeno sant Bernart apgarias de una su hermana ahoord Ihu Xº* ('this book was written by Saint Bernard at the prayer of his sister to the glory of Jesus Christ'). The title page is a double cross (an archiepiscopal cross), *see* the colour-print reproduction on p. 48 in Emilia Fogelklou's *Birgitta* (Stockholm 1919). The learned Horstius included the small manuscript in his edition of Saint Bernard's *Opera omnia* (Lugdani 1687), but believes it to be apocryphal (Vol. V, p. 317). To Bridget the book was genuine, which is the main thing. In the catalogue of *Birgitta Udställningen* in Stockholm, edited by Isak Collijn and Andreas Lindblom, Uppsala 1918, p. 156, there is a complete description of the manuscript. It is said in it: 'Possibly acquired by Bridget on the pilgrimage to Santiago de Compostella in the years 1341–2.' A Swedish translation of the book was made in Vadstena about 1500 (Catalogue, p. 158).

(2) *timore amittendi bonum quod non amat* (*Opera*, ed. Horstius, V, col. 1244). What delicacy of thought and expression! 'Afraid to miss a good—that is, God—which after all one does not love.'

(3) *sanctior est copula cordium quam corporum* (MS. C 240, f. 111r).

(4) *licet dixerim cum sicut cor meum* (*Processus*, p. 479, on Ulf).

(5) MS. 11v–12r.

(6) 'The saga about Saint Dionysius' (in *Et fornsvenskt Legendarium* I, pp. 343–4). 'Martyrs' Mount' is of course Montmartre, from which the white dome of the church of *Sacré Cœur* in our times sends out its light over Paris.— 'Sandinis,' Saint Denis, where Saint Dionysius (in the legend confused with the disciple of Saint Paul in the Acts of the Apostles XVII, 34), who was bishop in Paris about the middle of the third century, lies buried. He is the patron saint of France.

(7) *Predico tibi quod Deus te vult innotesci mundo.* (*Processus*, pp. 79–80, 618. *Extravagantes* 92. See also *Rev.* IV, 21, 103–4, VIII, 26). In the thirteenth century a journey to Jersualem (Jorsalafaerd) was already called 'Palmefaerd' (Palmaroferd) and the pilgrims to Jerusalem *Palmarii*. After having bathed in the Jordan, the river where Christ was baptized (and which because of the name was mixed up with Urd's well in the Edda—'Christ sits by Urda well'), the pilgrims plucked palm leaves in 'Abraham's grove of palms' (the grove of Mambre, transferred to Jericho from Hebron). It was a special sign of favour when Pope Celestine II in 1191 gave Philip Augustus and his men, who were returning from the siege of Saint Jean d'Acre, the right to wear palms on their cloaks without having been in Jericho. (Paul Riant: *Expéditions et Pélérinages des Scandinaves en Terre Sainte*, Paris 1865, pp. 46, 62, 88–9.)

BOOK III

I

(1) It was not at all uncommon for the convents to receive guests in this way, not only for the customary three days, about which the monastic witticism declares that *post tres dies vilescit et piscis et hospes*, 'after three days both fish and guest have a bad smell,' but for a longer period, even for a lifetime. There is an example of this in one of Bridget's nearest relations—Abbot Bartold in Varnhem entered upon a contract on 5 August 1352 with 'our beloved friend,' Sir Magnus Gudmarsson, Ulf's brother, married to Bridget's sister Karin. The couple were received *for life* in the guest house of the monastery and were to have the same food as the Abbot, six servants, the same board as the Abbot's servant, four horses, hay and corn. The payment for this is not mentioned, but must have been quite considerable. (Edw. Ortved: *Cistercieordenen i Norden*, II, p. 239.)

(2) *Legender från Sveriges Medeltid*, p. 256.—Rågö is an island in the belt of rocks and islands at the inlet to the Sibo Fjord in Södermanland.

(3) Saint Botvid, the apostle of Södermanland, became a Christian in England, returned home and preached the gospel, and was murdered in 1120 on Rågö in the Mälar.

(4) *quasi in mentis excessu*, Proc., p. 81, *Extrav.* 72. In both places this vision is dated at 1340 (*quarto anno obit virum sui*). But as Westman, *Birgitta Studier*, Uppsala 1911, p. 111, observes, the authority for this date is not always reliable —another revelation (*Processus*, p. 512, *Extrav.* 66) is dated by him *first* three years before Ulf's death (1341), later at three years after (1347).

II

(1) Compare the marriage ordinance of King Magnus of 1345, probably inspired by Bridget, by which the bride was forbidden to bestow her wedding dress on the *Lekare och Fidlare* (players and fiddlers) who had entertained the wedding guests—it was to be given as alms to a church or a convent.

(2) The wine mentioned here is *not* the consecrated wine, but only an ablution, so that the communicant may swallow the Host more easily. In the rule of the convent of Vadstena there is a regulation that the windows in the wall of the church, at which the nuns make their confession, and through which they receive the Sacrament of the Altar, 'shall be so shaped that the Body of God and the Chalice can be easily passed through' (*Wadstena Kloster-Reglor*, edited by C. F. Lindström, Stockholm, 1845, p. 80). There is no question of *communio sub utraque*.

(3) *Skrifter til Läsning för Klosterfolk* (Stockholm 1875), pp. 215–21. Both *Tundalus* and *Guido's Sjæls Aabenbarelse* were translated from the Latin text into Swedish in 1491 by the industrious Bridgettine monk, Jöns Budde, called Räk, in the convent of Nådendal in Finland.

(4) *Prol. in librum octavum*, cap. VI. In the fourteenth century it was already generally believed that the last times were at hand.

(5) 'The Son of God spoke to His bride: "Thou shalt be like that instrument of music called a fiddle, on which the fiddler plays sweet music".' The old Swedish has the words *fidlah* and *fidhlarin*. (*Rev.* IV, 100, Swedish). The Latin text, both here and in VII, 31, is incorrect in having *fistula* (flute): *non audiet amplius fistulam meam*.

(6) F. Böhringer: *Die deutschen Mystiker des 14 und 15 Jahrh*, referred to in Zahn: *Einführung in die christliche Mystik* (Paderborn 1908), p. 537.

Of the revelation at which the rosary was handed over to Alain de la Roche in the thirteenth century and from which is derived the devotion now diffused throughout the Catholic world, the Dominican, R. Coulon, writes: *Nous ne pensons pas, qu'il faille prendre l'assertion d'Alain de la Roche strictement. Il était ordinaire à cette époque, de présenter sous forme de révélation ce que l'on tenait à cœur de voir accepter. Ce n'était pas mensonge de la part de celui qui proposait un pareil enseignement, pas plus qu'il n'y avait méprise sur la véritable portée de ces prétendues révélations de la part . . . du lecteur.* (Article 'Alain de la Roche' in *Dictionnaire d'histoire et de géographie*, edited by Cardinal Baudrillart, VII, pp. 1309–10).

Another learned Dominican of our own times expresses himself in a similar way: *Si nous nous trouvions en face d'un livre de visions que l'Église n'eût pas reconnu comme inspiré . . . nous ne serions nullement obligés d'admettre a priori que l'auteur en ait trouvé les éléments dans ses extases personelles. Ce pourrait être . . . une forme littéraire.* (E. B. Allô, O. P. *L'Apocalypse*, Paris 1921, p. CLXIV.)

(7) 'Cujus amici videntes imaginem, quod adhuc pulchrioribus coloribus ornari posset, apposuerunt et illi colores suos depingendo super eam. Sic ego Deus præcidi silva deitatis meae verba mea quae posui in cor tuum: amici vero mei redegerunt ea in libros secundum gratiam eis datam et coloraverunt et ornaverunt illa. Nunc ergo . . . trade omnes libros revelationum eorundem verborum meorum Episcopo meo heremitae qui conscribat et elucidet et catholicum sensum spiritus mei teneat . . . Spiritus meus dimittit quandoque electos meos sibi ipsis . . . cor tuum non semper est capax et fervidum ad preferendum et scribendum illa quae sentis, sed nunc volvis et revolvis ea in animo tuo, nunc scribis et rescribis illa, donec veneris ad proprium sensum verborum meorum.' *Extrav.* cap. 49.

III

(1) Ortved: *Cistercieordenen i Norden*, II, p. 92.
(2) *Rituale Romanum. Ordo Commendationis animae.*
(3) *Processus*, p. 479: 'Quando sepelivi virum meum, sepelivi cum eo omnem amorem carnalem. . . . Quando habui annulum in manu mea, erat mihi quasi onus, quia inspiciendo eum animus meus recordabatur priorum dilectionum. Ideo ut animus meus in solius Dei descendat amorem, volo carere annulo et viro meo.' According to the same source some days passed (paucis diebus post) before Bridget parted from that ring which 'reminded her of past joys'—I have permitted myself an abbreviation. When Bridget's son Karl died in Naples, she was the only one who did not weep—'she remained sitting at a distance of eight or ten paces and did not get up, nor did she weep or complain' ('nec emisit voces ved lacrimas'). *Processus*, p. 370.—Ulf died on 12 February 1344. (*Diarium Vadst.* ad annum).

IV

(1) Ortved, *op. cit.*, II, 93. Otto Frödin has proposed the conjecture that the ruins of Bridget's house were to be found in 'the great knoll lying about fifty metres north-north-east of the convent church.' This conjecture has gained confirmation through a parchment letter found in the records of the kingdom and dated 1374, by which one Lady Ramborg Knut's daughter of Alvastra bequeathes certain properties to the monastery of Alvastra, and in return demands the right for herself and her serving-woman to live in 'the house lying in a northern direction from the monastery church, which was once occupied by the Lady Bridget of holy memory' ('hac tamen prehabita condicione, quod in parte aquilonari ab ecclesia dicti cenobii habeam curiam, in qua quondam residabat domina Byrgheta, pie recordacionis'). Otto Frödin: *Alvastrabygden under Medeltiden* (Stockholm 1919), p. 93, note 1.

(2) According to Gregory the Great (*Homilia* 34, in Matt. XVIII, 10).

(3) *Processus*, pp. 82, 619b.

(4) And David said to Achimelech the priest: 'Give me five loaves into my hand. . . . And the priest answered David and said: I have no common bread at hand, but only holy bread' (I Kings XXI, 3–4).—'Ego Deus omnium qui sum super omnes regulas, permitto tibi residere ad tempus monasterium, non ut dissolvam regulam nec ut consuetudinem novam adducam, sed magis ut opus meum mirabile in sancto loco ostendatur. Sic enim David tempore necessitas comedit panes sanctificatos.' (*Processus*, p. 82.)

(5) *Prologus Domini Alphonsi*, cap. III.—On 29 July 1348, however, Bridget signs a document in which she acts as owner. (*Flavigny, op. cit.*, p. 104, note 3). And at about the same time, when she has already taken up her residence in Alvastra, one of her peasants comes to her and tells her that there has been a big fire on a farm which she has at Tiveden, and that she has suffered a considerable loss—'much corn and many implements have been destroyed.' Far from grieving over this, Bridget praises God who has relieved her of these possessions, and to Prior Petrus Olai who is present, she says: 'It wearies me to think of all these worldly things; with all my heart I wish to be poor, nay, I would even gladly go about begging, if God so wills it.' (*Processus*, p. 494.) In Rome she had an opportunity of doing so.

(6) The text does not mention Karl; it only says: 'in illo puero deliro quem novisti nimis excessui et ineptis ejus applaudendo et congaudendo et in deliramentis ejus delectando.' (*Extrav.* 56.) It has been thought that it was a question here of a mountebank or court jester, in whose tricks and jokes Ulf was found to have taken too much pleasure. But it can hardly have been so great a fault that Ulf mentions it first. Altogether all the expressions are kept in vague terms—'a widow,' 'a man,' 'a certain nobleman.' Nor has Petrus Olai added any comments to this chapter, though he has often done so on other occasions. Even if Karl were dead, his son Karl Karlsson was living; moreover the chapter is not found in the Swedish translation, evidently out of consideration for the family.

(7) On this form of conjugal abstinence, common in the Middle Ages, *see* Peter Browe, S.J.: *Beiträge zur Sexualetik des Mittelalters*, Breslau 1932, and Dominicus Lindner: *Der Usus Matrimonii*, Munich 1929. This abstinence was

often extended—from the point of view of health no doubt commendable—
to the period in which the woman nursed the child. *See* B. M. Lavand: 'L'idée
divine du mariage' (*Études Carmelitaines*, 23 année, Paris 1938, I, p. 169).

(8) *Extravagantes* 56. The same delicate feeling concerning unjust mammon
is shown by one of Ulf's contemporaries, the knight Hakon Jonsson Lämä,
who in 1327 bestowed upon the monastery of Alvastra a farm in Näsby, with
the following clause: 'I enjoin upon my heirs, and beg them by the blood of
Jesus Christ, carefully to fulfil my obligations of debt and to pay my creditors
what I owe them. And where they can learn that any of my possessions are ill-
gained they are to return them, for they must give an account of them to
Christ, the supreme Judge.' (Ortved, *op. cit.*, II, 87.) Saint Elisabeth of Thuringia
was just as scrupulous (for she too, believed in a 'supreme judge')—one of her
serving-women testifies in the process of canonization that even when she sat
at table with many guests she abstained from partaking of those dishes about
which she did not know with certainty that they had been paid for with the
lawful income of her husband (*non utens cibis, nisi sciret de redditibus et justis
bonis mariti provenisse.* (Huyskens: *Quellenstudien*, Marburg 1908, p. 115.) In a
saint such a tender conscience is not surprising. But even the great man *Bo
Jonsson Grip*, who cannot be said to have been very scrupulous, strictly enjoins
upon the executors of his testament (of 1384, two years before his death) to see
that those against whom he has done ill are indemnified. 'And I will that everything shall be given to them in full, or their goods restored to them, so that my
soul may stand entirely without reproach before the judgment of God.' (Axel
L. Romdahl in *Östergötland*, the publication of the Home Villages Society
(Hembygdföreningens Skrift) Uppsala 1930, p. 190.)—On Bo Jonsson Grip, *see*
Sten Engström's work, *Bo Jonsson* (Uppsala 1935), of which, unfortunately,
only the first part (up to 1375) is available.

(9) *Rev.* IV, 25: 'Thou shalt be like the bride who stands by the bed curtain,
who is ready to obey at once the will of the bridegroom when he calls her.'
Rev. I, 26: 'Evil spirits fulfil and arouse in the carnal marriage the desire of
the flesh, which is nothing but a loathsome smell.'

(10) *Rev.* IV, 144. This prayer is not to be found in the Latin text. It is K. B.
Westman who has pointed out that it dates from the time before the death of
Ulf (*Birgittastudier*, p. 102, note 6), as Bridget prays for deliverance from all
carnal love of 'bonda' (husband) or of children. This agrees with the note in
MS. A, 36, that when Ulf was absent she kept vigil in prayer, and that many
prayers were then revealed to her. 'When her husband was away she watched
almost all the nights in prayer . . . and there was given her a very fairest
prayer of the passion of Christ ' (Klemming, IV, p. 132).

(11) *Extrav.* 52.

V

(1) 'One day she was uplifted in a certain exaltation of spirit, and there was
then revealed to her an exceeding beautiful prayer of the passion of Christ and
His wounds . . . which prayer she kept so well in her memory, that she
prayed it thereafter every day.' (Klemming, IV, p. 132.—The prayer which I
reproduce somewhat abbreviated, pp. 136–8.)—*Oratio secunda* (Latin text).

(2) In the biography of the two Petruses it is said that Bridget stands, and that she leaves the chapel and goes to her room ('Aufugit cameram suam et statim confessa accepit postmodum corpus Christi'). I imagine that there must have been a domestic chaplain at Ulfåsa. Or did Bridget go to the church at Ekebyborna? (See *Processus*, p. 80.)

(3) 'in corde vero sentiebat quoddam vividum secundum major es inflammationes et infusiones movebatur plus . . . et minus' (*Processus*, p. 81). 'In corde vero sentiebat aliquando quasi quoddam vividum, ac si esset ibi puer volvens et revolvens se' (*Processus*, p. 484). 'in corde suo sentiebat esse quoddam vividum, ac si infans ibi jaceret, volvens et revolvens se' (*Processus*, p. 500). Both Master Matthias and Prior Petrus made sure of these internal movements by laying their hands upon her heart when they took place ('testigerunt super vestes ipsius domine Brigide, quas habebat supra cor' (p. 600. *Cf.* p. 484 'viderunt et palpaverunt'). In *Revelationes* VI, 88, it is related that on a Christmas night in Santa Maria Maggiore in Rome, Bridget felt this mystic state with unusual strength. It was verified not only by the confessor but by others who were present, 'visu et tactu.' And at the High Mass on Christmas Day Mary appeared to Bridget and set her mind at rest. This feeling 'as of a child that moves and turns,' is not any allusion, but a kind of repetition of what Mary herself would feel when she became a mother and the child 'came out of her virginal womb' ('clauso meo virginali utero prodiebat'). The same joy that Mary felt then, Bridget feels now, for Jesus is born in her heart.

VI

(1) *Rev.* I, 3, Declaratio: 'iste fuit tentatus a diabolo subtilissime de multis hæresibus contra Fidem Catholicam'; IV, 32 (he is tempted against belief in the Trinity); V, Interrogatio XVI, Quaestio I, Responsio: 'magister tibi notus, cum ipso quippe descendit spiritus tentans eum, in tantum, quod quasi omnes haereses essent ante eum stantes et quasi loquerentur uno ore: nos sumus veritas.' Cf. *Rev.* VI, 75, 89–90; *Rev.* I, 3, Declaratio. *Processus*, p. 83.

(2) The text has 'canale meus' (*Processus*, p. 81).

(3) Master Matthias has himself inserted this revelation in the preface which he wrote for the first collection of the *Revelationes*. The Prologue is to be found in all editions.

(4) 'Ego sum quasi cursor litteras domini deferens' (*Processus*, p. 195). 'Ego sum ad modum vilis cursoris, qui cum portet litteras magni domini ubi sunt magna negocia scripta' (*Processus*, p. 233).

(5) Master Matthias makes no secret of the doubts he has had from the beginning with regard to Bridget ('Ignisque zeli exardescit injusto, nondum virtute patientiae et mansuetudinis perfecto, contra peccatores, ut patet in pharisæo, qui . . . indignationis igne contra publicanum sicut et Symon contra Magdalenam fervebat. Sed non est in tali fervore dominus.' *Prologus*).

(6) *Processus*, p. 632: 'quia magni domini et magistri nolunt venire ad me, ego colligo pauperes et idiotas in regnum coelorum.'

(7) *Processus*, p. 191: 'oculos ad coelum non elevabat, nisi petita et obtenta licencia a suo patre spirituali.' *Cf.* pp. 40–1.—*Prologus* in fine: 'Cum autem persona, qui haec fiebat revelatio, ingemisceret et judicium nimis durum conqueretur . . .'

(8) *Processus* 82 and 619: 'in principio revelationum statim tibi preceptum fuit obedire eidem magistro Mathie in theologia et stare in monasterio mona-chorum Cisterciensis ordinis sancte Marie de Alvastro.' Third Book of Kings, XIX, 9–12. (Douay Version). Master Matthias quotes the place in the beginning of the Prologue.—All sources are agreed that this very revelation with its judgments of punishment over Sweden is the *first* (*see e.g.* the biography of the confessors, *Processus*, p. 81, in which the introductory words are given, so that there cannot be any doubt, after which it says: 'Et haec est prima revelatio' with the date 'anno Domini millesimo III° XLV^to,' *i.e.*, 1345.) On psychological grounds one might be tempted to place it at a later point of time, *after* the bitter experiences which Bridget had during her second stay at the court. But psychology must yield to the chronology attested by the sources.

VII

(1) The tombstone now preserved in the State Historical Museum, in Stockholm, is not the original one, Ulf being mentioned as 'erstwhile married to Saint (beatae) Bridget.'

(2) *Processus*, p. 535 ('quodam fratre Nicholas monacho ipsius monasterii qui scriptor revelationum domine Birgitte ante fuit,' *ante, i.e.*, before Petrus Olai); it was he who in the year 1380 gave testimony.

(3) *Processus*, p. 510. Thereupon there is a quotation from *Rev.* I, 13. *Extrav.* 48.

(4) *Rev.* I, 13. Steffen is of opinion that this revelation was directed against Ragnvald (*Den heliga Birgitta's Uppenbarelser*, Stockholm 1903, pp. 3 *et seq.*). But Ragnvald was Abbot, not Prior, and did not die until 22 May 1350, *after* Bridget's stay in Alvastra. It is most probably not correct that this Prior can be identical with the one mentioned in *Rev.* VI, 30 (*see Proc.*, p. 532).

(5) *Processus*, pp. 510–11.—The relation between Bridget and Petrus Olai is plastically presented in a wooden statue (27 inches high) in the church of Njutånger (Helsingland) of about 1520. Petrus is here kneeling, a quite small figure, at the feet of the enthroned Bridget, and supporting with one hand the book in which she is writing.

VIII

(1) *Rev.* VI, 88. The Swedish text here is more detailed and more per-spicuous. 'And even as the father and mother entrust the housekeeping to the son's wife, and leave the work of it to her, and tell her what has to be done in the house and on the farm, so will God and I, who now are old in the hearts of men. . . .'

(2) 'in XXVIII annis . . nunquam ibat nec faciebat aliquam mutacionem ad alias civitates . . . nisi secundum infusionem et preceptum Spiritus Sancti' (*Processus*, p. 97).

(3) *Processus*, pp. 369, 488.

(4) *Processus*, p. 630a, from the Panisperna manuscript. The Stockholm manuscript has only: 'incitat hominem ad luxuriam.' The first reading agrees with what we know otherwise (Bridget's reproach against King Magnus).

(5) *Rev.* I, 13.

(6) *Processus*, p. 532. 'in requie Lazari evigilabit'—an echo of 'et cum Lazaro quondam pauperia eternam habebis requiem' of the Office for the Dead: *Rev.* VI, 30.

(7) *Processus*, p. 92 ('frater quidem conversus . . . sancta vitae'), p. 522.

(8) *Processus*, pp. 539–40.

(9) *Processus*, p. 545. When the Black Death reached Sweden in 1350, no fewer than 33 of the monks in Alvastra died. (*Rev.* VI, 113.) Gerekinus was canonized in the catalogue of saints of the Cistercian Order on 25 July.

(10) *Extrav.* 55. After that *Rev.* IV, 121.

IX

(1) *Rev.* VI, 30. (Declaratio). *Processus*, p. 628. As mentioned earlier, Steffen believes this doubting Thomas to be Abbot Ragnvald and regards the *Declaratio* written by Petrus Olai as an 'amende honorable.' I believe that here it is a question of an entirely different person. There were no doubt many in the monastery who doubted, *e.g.*, that Brother Paul who later became Prior in Alvastra (from 1359 to 1363), and who declared openly that Bridget was not quite right in her head. This was told to Bridget, who declared shrewdly that Brother Paul was right—'I was not quite wise when I loved the world more than God'—and with pious courtesy she commended herself to his intercession. (*Processus*, p. 488.) Perhaps it is he with whom the above-named passage is concerned.

(2) Karl Bäckgren, *op. cit.*, pp. 152–6.

(3) Cf. *Rev.* IV, 7: 'Thou art to know also, that the fire which burns in the furnace (hell), burns in everlasting darkness. But the souls that burn have not all the same great torment. And the darkness thou seest about the furnace of fire is called *Limbus*'—the place where the souls of the just awaited the coming of Christ (Grundtvig's hymn 'This night there was a knock at the door of hell,' and Joachim Skovgaard 'Christ in the kingdom of the dead' of 1894).*

(4) *Rev.* II, 15.—Next I John, II, 15–17.

(5) *Rev.* VI, 52. The revelation dates from Bridget's first period.

(6) *Rev.* VI, 26.

---

* Grundtvig, N. F. S., b. 1783, d. 1872, was a religious personality with the gifts of a genius. Believed that faith should be founded on the symbols, as being older than the gospels. Showed an active interest in education, and the People's High Schools, for which he gave the model, are due to his efforts. In these schools adults of both sexes can complete their education, and they are a characteristic feature among Scandinavian institutions.

Skovgaard, Joakim, b. 1856, d. 1933. A son of the Danish painter, P. C. T. Skovgaard, exhibited his first pictures in 1878. Studied the art of ancient Greece and Italy, also early Italian art, from which he learnt simplicity and emphasis. At first a landscape painter, but turned afterwards to figure painting, and then to Biblical subjects. Was chosen to carry out the work of the decoration of Viborg Cathedral in Jutland. In this he may be said to have reached the climax of his art. It is his greatest work and will carry his name far beyond the shores of his own country.

(7) *Rev.* I, 27. In the book which Saint Bernard wrote 'for greater knowledge and much use for all those who are given to a life of purity in the monastery,' one of the chapters has the heading 'To avoid vain pleasures and weep over one's sins' . . . 'It shall be seen here that it is foolishness and vanity to have some sensual or only worldly pleasures in this world.' 'Every one must be ashamed who does not weep, when even the newborn child, who is not a night old, tells us with its weeping that "we are in the dark kingdom of death," and that "true lovers of Jesus Christ" have therefore no choice but to deny their own will, take up their cross and "forsake a worldly life, remembering the mockery suffered by Jesus Christ and bearing in their bodies the likeness of His death, that the life of Jesus Christ may be revealed in their mortal bodies." (MS. A 27 in the Royal Library in Stockholm, f. 32r, f. 34r, f. 87r). Krogh Tonning justly says: 'Die tiefe, mächtige, oft gar bewunderungswerte mitteläterliche Aszese beruht auf der Ansicht, dass die Sünde in ihrem tiefsten Wesen *Weltlichkeit* ist.' (*Die heilige Birgitta*, München 1907, p. 67.)

X

(1) *Rev.* I, 15. I quote from the Swedish text, which is more worked out in details.

(2) It is under this name that Christ speaks most frequently to Bridget. Theology generally refers creation to the first person in the Trinity, the Father, while the Son is He by whom creation has been effected (*per quem omnia facta sunt*, as it is said in the Credo of the Church). With Bridget Christ is the Creator; 'Ego sum Creator Coeli et terrae qui in utero virginis verus Deus et verus homo fui' (*Rev.* I, 34; *cf.* I, 1, 2, 4, 11: 'Ego sum creator coeli et terrae et corpus meum verum est quod in altari consecratur,' the body of God is consecrated on the altar: I, 19 'Ego sum creator coeli,' Christ is the Creator of heaven, I, 25, 40, 44, etc.)—In a village school in Italy the priest asked a little girl: 'Who has created you?' She answered without hesitation: 'Christ!'

(3) *Rev.* I, 15,

(4) *Rev.* I, 1, 46 (less than a dog).

(5) *Rev.* I, 2. The two 'Ve' only in the Swedish text.

(6) *Rev.* I, 1, 2: IV, 137 Swedish text = *Rev.* V, 11 in the Latin text.— The prophet, *i.e.*, Elias, in III Kings, XVII, 14: 'For thus saith the Lord, the God of Israel: the pot of meal shall not waste, nor the cruse of oil be diminished, until the day wherein the Lord will give rain upon the earth.'

XI

(1) *Rev.* I, 44; II, 19, 20.

(2) *Rev.* II, 12 in the Swedish text: 'His voice shall be like the voice that is heard in the woods.'

XII

(1) Petrarch, *Sonetti* CV–CVI (*L'avara Babilonia* and *Fontana di dolore*. See also *Ep. sine tit*, 5, 8, 17–19; *Rerum Senilium*, Lib. VII and IX. P. M. Baumgarten: *Die Papstveste von Avignon* (Festschrift an G. v. Hertling, Kempten

1913), pp. 272 *et seq.* G. Mollat: *Les Papes d'Avignon* (Paris 1912), p. 302.—Pope John XXII, so severely attacked by the Spirituals, seems to have cherished a deep contempt of so-called 'public opinion.' *Qvicqvid laudat vituperio dignum est*, he is supposed to have said, *quicquid cogitat, vanum; quicquid loquitur, falsum; quicquid improbat, bonum; quiquid extollat, infame est.* (Bzovius, ad annum 1344.)

(2) A florin = about 6 gold francs. (G. Mollat: *Les Papes d'Avignon*, Paris 1912, p. 361.)

(3) Petrarch: *Rerum senilium*, Lib. XV.

(4) Casanova: 'Visita di un papa avignonese' (*Archivio della Società Romana per Storia Patria*. T. XXII 1889) pp. 371–81.—The palace which Annibale Ceccano had built in Avignon served Catherine of Siena in 1376 as a residence during her stay at the papal court.

(5) G. Mollat, *l.c.*, pp. 358–61.

XIII

(1) *Vita*, p. 12 in the Old-Swedish translation.

(2) *Processus*, p. 518.

(3) *Rev.* III, 31.

(4) *Extrav.* 73 and 74.

(5) Carl M. Kjellberg: *Vadstena i Fortid och Nutid* (Linköping 1907), pp. 200–202. A part of the town, about where Marten Skinnares house now stands, is mentioned early under the name of Laglöseköping. Mention is also made of a kind of harbour. *Susenborg*, built on piles in the lake to the north of the king's house. Perhaps Laglösa is the oldest name of the town. Names ending in -lösa are also to be found elsewhere in the district. *See* Charles Bengtsson: *En bok om gamla Vadstena* (Vadstena 1921), pp. 249–50. Andreas Lindblom: *Vadstena* (Stockholm 1925), Axel Ripa (1883), Sven Wallin (1940) as also Arthur Nordén in *Östergötland* (Norrköping 1923), pp. 54–110. *Diarium* for 19.3.1514 mentions a lay brother who had been the steward of the monastery in Susenborg.

(6) *Extrav.* 21 (Swedish 19).

(7) Steffen, p. 305: 'perhaps also a place of sacrifice, as it is pointed out separately, such as "the home of the devils"—*in isto vero loco fuerunt habitationes dæmonum.*'

(8) *Extrav.* 25 (Swedish 30) and 26 (31).

(9) *Extrav.* 32 (Swedish 38). *Processus*, pp. 374, 497.—Torvald Höjer: *Studier i Vadstena Klosters och Birgittinerordenens Historia* (Uppsala 1905) Excursus A: 'De äldsta förordningarna om Vårfrupenningen.' (Denarius beatæ Virginis), (The oldest ordinances about Our Lady's Penny).—Sten Engström, *op. cit.*, pp. 265 *et seq.*—Ulf's testamentary bequest 'to Wadstena Convent, which is now being built there,' Höjer, p. 33, note 1.

XIV

(1) *Regula*, cap. 1.

(2) *Oratio quarta* (Swedish text), Klemming IV, pp. 143 *seq.*

(3) 'My Lord Jesus Christ, may Thy teeth be honoured for every time they were opened and closed in biting, when Thou didst chew with them' (*Oratio tertia*, Klemming IV, p. 137).

(4) *Regula*, capp. II–III. As a heading of the third chapter the Swedish text has 'she (Bridget) shall be the finest vine in His vineyard—from which shall grow fruitful branches.' Bridget is not only to plant a vineyard, she is herself the vine.

(5) Höjer, pp. 35–43. In the letter to the Emperor Charles IV, Bridget says emphatically that Christ has dictated her 'unam regulam monialum.' *Rev.* VIII, 51.

(6) *Rev.* VI, 23–4. It was for Bridget's son-in-law, the robber, that the Blessed Virgin here prayed for mercy.

(7) *Rev.* I, 18. The Old Swedish translation is also of the opinion 'that this chapter is generally believed to allude to the convent of the Blessed Virgin Mary in Vadstena,' Klemming, Vol. IV, p. 88.

(8) *Regula*, cap. 12.

(9) *Regula*, cap. 4.

(10) *Extrav.* 13.

(11) *Regula*, cap. 25. Madame de Flavigny is mistaken when she declares (p. 180, note 1): 'tous les historiens indiquent Alvastra comme le lieu où le Christ dicta les constitutions de son ordre.' It is distinctly stated (*Regula*, cap. 30) that a convent was to be built 'in loco qui tibi, *regulam audienti*, demonstratus est'—and the convent was not built in Alvastra, but in Vadstena. Madame de Flavigny is perhaps thinking of the rule being translated into Latin by Patrus Olai—this was done in Alvastra. Cf. *Rev.* IV, 137.

(12) 'habere necessaria cum moderantia, utilia, non superflua, honesta et expedientia, omnia humilia, nullaque superba' (*Rev.* IV, 127). Among the rules of earlier founders of Orders, which can be used in completing the Bridgettine rule, is *Regula*, cap. 26: 'Deinde ista regula per Papam confirmata, inquirantur aliqui devoti fratres, de regula Benedicti vel Barbardi, qui huic regulæ inscribant quomodo excessus emendandi sunt in monasterio inscribant quomodo mortui sepeliendi sunt' etc.—'The body an ass,' *Rev.* IV, 126. Cf. *Regula*, cap. 24: 'Necessitati cum discretione satisfaciat et prout natura infirma petit.'

(13) 'Haec per proprietatem, fallente Diabolo, graviter contra Deum et ordinem peccavit.' *Regula*, cap. 118.

(14) *Regula*, cap. 19.

(15) *Regula*, cap. 20.

(16) *Regula*, cap. 27.

(17) *Regula*, cap. 11.

(18) *Rev.* III, 18. *Extrav.* 31 and 28.

(19) Ortved I, *op. cit.*, pp. 74–5.

(20) *Regula*, cap. 17.

(21) *Regula*, cap. 14.

(22) *Regula*, cap. 27.—('and the windows shall be so shaped that the Body of God and the Chalice can be passed through easily' (*Wadstena Kloster-Reglor*, cap. 22). *Regula*, cap. 25, does not contain the rule about the chalice.

(23) Ortved, *op. cit.*, I, p. 76.

(24) *Regula*, cap. 25.

(25) *Regula*, cap. 27.

I

(26) *Regula*, cap. 13.

(27) *Regula*, cap. 23.

(28) *Jungfru Mariä örtagård*, ed. Geete, Stockholm 1895, pp. 6–7. The office 'is written and composed by the Reverend Father, the holy master Peter, the confessor of Saint Bridget.' Master Peter wrote 29 of the hymns of the office.

(29) *Regula*, cap. 29, 'the pious friend of God' *i.e.* Prior Petrus Olai.

XV

(1) 'reduco Regi ad memoriam qualis gratia facta est in Regno ejus. Nam filius meus qui sedet in summo throno majestatis exelsae, loquiter frequenter tibi, quae es nata de Regno ejus' (*Rev.* VIII, 47).

(2) *Rev.* VIII, 2. The fight for the castle of Copenhagen took place on 26 June 1342.

(3) *Rev.* IV, 3 (Latin); VIII, 41 (Swedish.)

(4) 'cum quodam tempore rex Suecie gravare vellet subditos in toto regno magnis exaccionibus ut soluerunt quamdam pecunie quantitatum, in qua ipse tenebatur, creditoribus, ipsa domina Brigida ad dictum regem accessit, et dixit eidem: Domine mi rex, noli hoc facere, sed recipe duos filius meos et pone eos obsides pro ipso debito, donec soluere poteris, et non offendas Deum et subditos tuos.' (*Processus*, pp. 374–5.)

(5) *Rev.* VIII, 41 (Swedish); IV, 3 (Latin).

(6) *Extrav.* 74, *Extrav.* 43 (King Magnus a child), *Rev.* VI, 41.

XVI

(1) *Rev.* VIII, 40–43–46.

(2) *Processus*, pp. 90, 539, 'unus demoniacus in Osgocia . . . liberatus est ad verba ipsius testis, quorum formam ipsa domina Birgitta a Christo audivit et ipse testis . . . ad demonem dixit.' The text of this exorcism is to be found in *Rev.* VI, 34 'Deus Pater qui es cum Filio et Spiritu Sancto Creator omnium rerum et judex eorum quae facta sunt, qui misit benedictum Filium suum in viscera Virginis Mariae propter nostram salutem, præcipio tibi, immunde spiritus, ut ad gloriam ejus et propter Virginis Mariae, exeas de ista creatura Dei, in nomine ejus qui natus est de Virgine, Jesus Christus, unus Deus qui est Pater et Filius et Spiritus Sanctus.'

(3) *Processus* (*Vita*), p. 85.

(4) *Processus* (*Vita*), p. 84 'referebat ei verba illa in vulgari sua cum quadam attenta elevacione mentali quasi si legeret in libro.'

(5) *Rev.* I, 16. *Extrav.* 51.

(6) *Extrav.* 51. *Rev.* III, 31. *Cf.* Steffen, pp. 285–7. Bridget's answer is not quite clear, for the converted harlot did emphatically *not* belong to the third category of possessed persons.

(7) 'conversio unius publicae meretricis, per Beatae Virginis cum Christo dictae dominae apparentis subventionem' (Master Matthias in the *Prologue*).

(8) Montelius, II, p. 17.

(9) *Extrav.* 51; *Rev.* IV, 130 (Swedish).

(10) *Rev.* VI, 95 (Swedish VIII, 29).

(11) *Extrav.* 104. The text has 'qui implevi pastorem spiritu prophetiae.' I have thought it possible to identify this shepherd boy with David, who was accounted a prophet ('teste *David cum Sibylla*,' it is said in Thomas a Celano's *Dies irae*).

(12) *Rev.* IV, 125. Petris Olai says in his *Declaratio*: 'hic cum se posuisset ad orationem, reddidit spiritum . . . fuit Dominus Hemingus Episcopus Aboensis et amicus Beatae Virginis Mariae.'

(13) *Rev.* VI, 34. Cf. *Rev.* I, 52: 'dic amico meo et patri tuo quod haec verba conscripta exponat diligenter et ipso Archiepiscopo et postea alij episcopo.'

XVII

(1) Höjer, *op. cit.*, p. 55.

(2) *Rev.* IV, 103 (VIII, 26, Swedish).

(3) *Rev.* IV, 104 (VIII, 27, Swedish).

(4) *Rev.* IV, 105 (VIII, 28, Swedish).

(5) *Processus*, p. 525. It is Prior Petrus who reports this, 'quod audivit in confessione ab episcopo Aboensi cujus socius tunc erat.'

(6) *Rev.* VI, 63 (Latin) IV, 132 and IV, 63 (Swedish).—With the words 'ecce regnum et persona nota sunt in quibus stupor et mirabilia facta sunt' Bridget of course alludes to the *Prologue* of Master Matthias: 'Stupor et mirabilia audita sunt in terra nostra.'—One of the reasons why Bishop Hemming, above all others, was chosen for this mission was that while he was studying in France the future Clement VI had been his professor ('quidem doctus episcopus qui in scolis discipulus pape Clementis fuerat.' *Processus,* p. 105).

XVIII

(1) G. Bergström: '*Medeltidsmålingerna i Arboga stadskyrka.* Örebro 1898, pp. 3, 10–13. Birgitta's house in Örebro. G. Bergström: *Arboga Krönike,* Örebro 1898, p. 20.

(2) *Rev.* IV, 3. (Swedish VIII, 41), VIII, 16.

(3) *Processus*, pp. 492–3. *Rev.* IV, 113—with the following Declaratio by Petrus Olai: 'Dominus ille compunctus est et reconciliatus est Dominae (Birgittae) venit ad Romam et ibi laudibili fine quievit.'—The same doubt about Birgitta's revelations were entertained by an ecclesiastic not more clearly specified (religiosus authoritatis, *Rev.* VI, 90), who was punished by being struck with paralysis, and dying in that state.

(4) *Processus*, pp. 518–19, *Rev.* VI, 9.

(5) 'ac si meretrix menstruum in vase positum offerret alicui nobili ad bibendum,' *Rev.* VI, 9.

(6) *Rev.* II, 2, Petrus Olai's Declaratio.

(7) *Rev.* I, 48. Ezechiel IX, 6. I Peter, IV, 17.

(8) *Rev.* I, 49 (Swedish), IV, 132 (Latin).

(9) *Rev.* I, 47. Cf. II Samuel, XXIII, 6. (II Kings). The Swedish text adds: 'And not only the priests, but all they who mock at the commandments of God and His holy will.'—Of the bad priests ('these accursed priests') *see further* I, 48, 49 = IV, 132, 133, 134 and 135 in the Latin text. The MS. A 5a

(Stockholm) has *Rev.* I, 47–9 and the chapters identical with them, IV, 132, 135, omitted in the translation, not to cause scandal and harm the clergy. Yet the first three chapters are included in Latin with the following excuse: 'After this something is said about priests, and since it is not of much use to laymen to have knowledge of it, and the monks prefer to know and read Latin, this next chapter is therefore for their sakes written in Latin.' Then follows the Latin chapter heading with this addition: *et ponitur hic in latino ne Clerus skandalizetur a laicis et dampnetur.* The manuscript is of the beginning of the fifteenth century and belonged to Mr. Sten Christiernsen of Salstad (d. 1516), of the family which later took the name of Oxenstierna (Klemming, V, pp. 146–8).

XIX

(1) Johannes Jørgensen: *St. Francis of Assisi* (Longmans, 1912), p. 325, and also *Den hellige Frans af Assisi* (3rd edition), Copenhagen 1926), p. 282.

(2) 'For a thousand years the wrath of God over the world was never so great as now' (*Rev.* I, 49 (Swedish), IV, 134 (Latin).)

(3) I Cor. VII, 32–3.

(4) Flavigny, *Sainte Brigitte*, p. 152.

(5) 'excusamus Papam,' *Rev.* III, 18.—*Rev.* VI, 30. *Processus*, pp. 503, 628. 'Per istud . . . solidum os intraverunt clavi.' On the shroud of Christ preserved in Turin—*il Sacro Sindone*—the wound in the hand is not seen, as generally shown, in the middle of the palm, *but in the wrist. See* Pierre Barbet: *Les cinq plaies du Christ* (Paris 1935), pp. 14–19.

(6) *Rev.* III, 17–18.

(7) *Rev.* III, 14: 'Numquid recolis, quod misi te ad quendam episcopum quem vocavi servum meum? Ideo nunc similamus cum papilioni.' *Cf.* VI, 73, where it is a confessor who is likened to 'a butterfly that has broad wings and a small body.' Here it is a question of a Roman prelate who became an archbishop 'and died the same day.'

(8) *Rev.* III, 18, 19, Additio. One of these two bishops had a beautiful death, the other perished by a wall falling upon him.—The bishop of Vesterås was a Dominican, but survived Bridget.

XX

(1) *Processus,* pp. 540–41, 629b–630a. *Rev.* VI, 38.—Emilia Fogelklou: *Ur fromhetslivets svensk-historie*, II, 1 (Stockholm 1917), p. 115.

(2) *Processus*, pp. 541–3, 630a–631a.—The sixty-year-old sinner was a captain at Falkenberg Castle.—In Karlfeldt's poetry there are allusions to the widespread belief in Dalarne in the time of the witch trials, in a devil with whom women had sexual intercourse (Torsten Fogelqvist: *Karlfeldt*, Stockholm 1940, pp. 212–13).

(3) *Processus*, pp. 89–90.

(4) Proverbs of Solomon, VII, 7–18; II, 18–19; IX, 17–18.

(5) *Processus*, pp. 513, 627; *Rev.* VI, Declaratio.

(6) *Processus*, pp. 534, 628.

(7) *Processus*, pp. 499–500.

XXI

(1) *Vita* in the convent rules, p. XIII; Johanne Skovgaard: *Den hellige Birgitta*, pp. 50–51; *Processus*, pp. 92, 625.—I deviate here from the general chronology, which places Bengt's death at 1345 (21 March). According to this he would have died only one year after his father (12.2.1344). It was *after* the sojourn at court that Bridget returned to Alvastra and found her son ill ('Reversa igitur domina Brigida a rege Swecie ad monasterium Alwastri invenit filium suum, quem infirmum diu reliquerat iam in extremis agentem') (*Processus, l.c.*). Provided the old Cistercian list of saints is right in giving the date of death as 21 March (*see* Edward Ortved, *op. cit.*, II, p. 95), the whole of Bridget's journey would have taken place in the winter, and then one does not walk in the woods, either at Örebro or elsewhere. The 21st March 1347, on the other hand, might be the correct date. And provided the chronology of the Order reckoned the year from 25 March (which, as is known, was often the case in the Middle Ages) the day mentioned would in any case fall in the year 1346. Margareta Claus' daughter only knows of Bengt that he 'died young and was buried in Alvastrum.'

(2) 'Elizabet, ancilla domine lantgravie, dixit: "Cum domine mea beata Elizabet ultimo decubuit lecto, audivi vocem quasi intra collum ejus dulcissimam et jacuit ad parietem versa." Post horam vertens se ad me dixit: "Ubi es dilecta?" Respondi: "Ego sum hic" et adjeci: "O domina mea, quam dulciter cantastis," et quesivit, si ego audivissem. Et ego dixi quod sic. Ait illa: Dico tibi quod inter me et parietem avicula quedam michi jocundissime cantabat. Cujus voce excitata oportebat et me cantare? Hoc fuit aliquot diebus ante mortem ejus.' (Huyskens: *Quellenstudien zur Geschichte der hl. Elisabeth*, Marburg 1908, p. 138).

(3) *Margareta Klausdotter* (Johanne Skovgaard, p. 85).

(4) 'The Lady Mærete had a son by her lord, Sigvid Ribbing, and he was called Sir Peter Ribbing. . . . He fared to the Holy Tomb and died on the way' (*Margareta Klausdotter, op. cit.*, p. 78). The Finsta blood was the strongest in the 'robber's' son—like his forefathers on his mother's side he, too, wanted to go on a pilgrimage. On 13 April 1379, he was in Rome and there, in the presence of his mother's sister Karin, bequeathed some farms to the convent of Vadstena. He died the same year in Florence, on the way home.

(5) *Vita Catharinae*, cap. 2, 'Cohibentes se ab illicitis, immo etiam a licitis et concessis.'—During a stay in Kalmar the two sisters-in-law pray in a chapel dedicated to Our Lady, and Karl's wife then sees that the image of the Madonna looks with favour upon Karin, the daughter of Ulf, but looks at herself 'torvis oculis et irato vultu' (*ibid.* cap. 3). 'Sicat munditia carnis est immunitas a pollutione hominum, sic humilitas est immunitas a pollutione dæmonum.' (*Vita*, cap. 1).

(6) *Rev.* VII. 13 : 'si possibile esset, quod ipsa (Maria) in uno puncto minimo, a dignitate in qua est, a Deo remotior fieri posset, ego magis mihi in permutationem eligerem in profundo inferiori æternaliter cruciari.' It is Karl who says this on his death-bed.—The text of Bridget's prayer is: 'O domina mea, Regina Coeli, in tantum gaudet cor meum ex eo, quod altissimus Deus te praeelegit matrem et tantam dignitatem tibi conferre dignatus est, quod ego

magis mihi eligerem in inferno æternaliter cruciari, quam quod tu uno minimo puncto de tanta excellenti gloria et tua coelesti dignitate careres.' (*Rev.* VII, 1.) The prayer dates from Bridget's Roman period, but this heroic love of Mary can hardly have arisen then. Cf. *Extrav.* 63 and *Regula*, cap. 30 ('æterna supplicia sustinerem').

(7) *Rev.* II, 24. *Extrav.* 95. Cf. *Extrav.* 54.

(8) 'Servi Dei qui parentium suorum utilitatem procurant, a Dei amore se separant. . . . Non debemus odio habere parentes nostros, sed impedimenta eorum qui nos a recto itinere deviant' (*Ad sororem*, cap. VII).

(9) *Extrav.* 63.

XXII

(1) *Regula*, cap. 30. *Extrav.* 2. 'Carthusia nunquam reformata quia nunquam deformata.' In Bridget's time there were no Carthusians in Sweden. Not until Sten Sture the Elder (about 1440–1503) called them to the country and founded the monastery of Mariefred (Peace of Mary), which was and remained the only one.

(2) *Extrav.* I. *Regula* Sancti Benedicti, cap. 5.

(3) *Extrav.* 31 (Latin), 37 (Swedish).—Here again the North is looked upon as the seat of the devil.—On the 13 altars, *see Extrav.* 34 (Latin), 40 (Swedish).

(4) *Extrav.* 35 (Latin), 41 (Swedish).

(5) Carl Silfverstolpe: *Klosterfolket i Vadstena* (Stockholm 1898), pp. 73–5. On Lars Romare, *see Diarium* ad 1394 and 1398.

(6) *Wadstena Kloster-Reglor*, p. 5. 'Den gamle Bog,' *Extrav.* 33 (Latin), 29 (Swedish).

(7) *Wadstena Kloster-Reglor*, pp. XXXIV–XXXIX. Johanne Skovgaard, pp. 185–203.

(8) Canticle of Canticles II, 15.

(9) *Extrav.* 4 (Latin), 9 (Swedish); 23 (Latin), 28 (Swedish).

(10) *Extrav.* 19 (Latin), 24 (Swedish), 17 (22) *Rev.* IV, 139 (Swedish).

(11) *Extrav.* 13–14.

(12) *Extrav.* 12 (Latin), 17 (Swedish).

(13) *Extrav.* 37 (Latin), 43 (Swedish).

XXIII

(1) *Processus (Vita)*, pp. 93, 626. The second part in the name of the demon in question probably comes from the Greek *margos* (mad).

(2) *Rev.* III, 19. 'Tu enim miraris cur tentationes accrescant tibi in senectute quae nec in juventute, nec in conjugio experta es.' (*Rev.* VI, 94.)

(3) The church of Saint Per, of which only the tower is still standing (röda tårnet), is older than the convent church. In his testament of 1.5.1346 King Magnus ordains that he is to be buried provisionally in the 'parish church in Vatzstenom,' until the convent church is finished (Kjellberg: *Vadstena*, p. 57).

(4) The Catholic *Ave* consists, as is known, of three parts: St. Luke I, 28, St. Luke I, 42, as well as the invocation: 'Sancta Maria, Mater Dei, ora pro nobis peccatoribus, nunc et in hora mortis nostræ.' Originally the prayer had only the two first pieces, that is, the two Gospel texts; in 1184 it was used by

the Cistercians, in the thirteenth century it had become general to recite it, though without the addition *Jesus* at the end of St. Luke I, 42 *ventris tui.* In the Bridgettine Office (Cantus sororum) the prayer was said as follows: 'Ave maria gracia plena, dominus tecum, benedicta tu in mulieribus et benedictus fructus ventris tui ihesus christus' (*Jung fru Marie Örtagård*, edited by Robert Geete, Stockholm 1895, p. 209). This is no doubt the form used by Bridget. In the *Myroure of our Lady* originating from Lyon Abbey it is said: 'Some saye at the begynning of this salutation *Ave benigne Jesu* and some say after *Maria, mater Dei,* with other addycions at the ende also.' (Herbert Thurston, S.J., in the *Catholic Encyclopedia*, Vol. VII, column 110 *seq.*). In 1447 the Bridgettine nuns in Vadstena resolved to add the words *in æternum* after *Jesus Christus,* and in this form the prayer is still said every morning, except Saturday, after Terce. (*Diarium,* ad annum). Not until the Council of Trent (1568) did the 'Hail, Mary' receive its present form.

(5) *Rev.* IV, 77.

(6) *Processus,* p. 627b.

(7) 'Christus judex ad illas questiones cum gestu mansuetissimo et honesto, sigillatim et compendiose, sapientissime respondebat.' *Rev.* V, *Prologus,* 'Resondit judex sedens in throno cujus gestus erant mansueti et honestissimi.' (*Rev.* V, Interrogatio I, Quaestio I, Responsio.)

(8) 'O christe judex, tu voluntarie amarissimam sustinuisti poenam. Cur propter hoc ego non debeo honorabiliter me habere et in mundo superbiæ?' (*Rev.* V, Interrogatio II, Quaestio 1).

(9) 'Why hast Thou let us know toil and weariness while Thou didst promise us rest and quiet?' (Swedish text, V, 1).

(10) *Rev.* V, Interrogatio III, Quaestio 1, Swedish text V, 1. *Processus,* pp. 86, 622a: 'liber questionum qui ea equitant et itinerante ad villam Wastenum divinitus sibi datus infusive a spiritu sancto miro modo quasi in una hora.'

XXIV

(1) *Rev.* V, Interrogatio IV, quaestio 1; V, quaestio 1; VI, 1; IX, 1.

(2) Interrogatio IX: 'homini vero dedisti vas terrenum et spiritum, et nasci cum ploratu, vivere cum labore et mori cum dolore.' Swedish V, 7: 'born with tears, living in toil and hardship and dying in pain.'

(3) Interrogatio IX, Responsio questionis quintae. Swedish text V, 7.

(4) 'Respondeo tibi et non tibi' (Interrogatio XI, Responsio quaestionis primae).

(5) Interrogatio IV.

(6) Interrogatio VI, Responsio quaestionis quintae.

(7) Interrogatio X–XI–XII–XIV.

(8) Interrogatio XV–XVI.

(9) Interrogatio XVI, responsio: 'illi Evangelistae solum—recipiendi sunt, quos Ecclesia mea recipit.'

(10) Lib. V, *Rev.* XII. Interrogatio XVI, responsio: with Declaratio. *Cf.* about Master Matthias, *Rev.* I, 3, 52; IV, 32; VI, 75, 89 and 90, where he disputes with 'quodam religioso magnae authoritatis' (the monk on the ladder?).

(11) *Rev.* I, 77: 'quid dixit tibi ille frater loquax?' But here it seems to concern an Augustinian monk. *Rev.* IV, 102: 'nomen erat monachus.' *Processus*, p. 522: 'quidam religiosus adhuc vivens magnus litteratus,' cf. *Rev.* VI, 90. In Interrogatio VII the monk describes himself as 'pulcher et de nobili progenie' and 'dives.'

(12) Lib. V, *Revelatio* septima et octava. Cf. *Rev.* VI, 19, where the three forms of address also occur: 'Friend—Son—Brother.' But here it concerns a monk in San Lorenzo in Rome.

(13) Interrogatio XV. Swedish 13: 'men are like children brought up in a dark room.'

XXV

(1) Prologus Libri quaestionum: 'ac si in tabula marmorea totus sculptus fuisset.' *Processus*, p. 522 (Petrus Olai) 'audivit a domina Brigida.' Cf. *Processus*, pp. 86, 622.

(2) *Rev.* XIII (Swedish 21). 'Itaque cum veneris ad ista loca, ostendam tibi plura' (not in the Swedish text).

(3) *Rev.* XI.

(4) *Rev.* IV, 2 and IV, 129. 'Likewise shall the just man bear in mind . . . how the unbeliever, who has been converted and come to the faith, can get what he needs for living, so that he need not beg or be oppressed as a thrall, or be robbed of his lawful freedom.'

(5) 'the streams of all sweetness shall flow into his mouth, everlasting light shall enlighten his soul, and his joy shall be for ever renewed' . . . 'sweetness in abundance and everlasting joy.' (IV, 129 Swedish).

(6) *Rev.* VI, 41, additio. VIII, 39–40. VIII, 43.

(7) *Rev.* VIII, 47. *Cf.* VIII, 43 and VIII, 44 (= VI, 41).

(8) Montelius, II, pp. 4–8.

(9) VI, 41 with additio.

(10) VIII, 47.

XXVI

(1) VIII, 43 'sive . . . cantilena lætitiae . . . sive littera reprehensionis salutaris.'

(2) *Extrav.* 43. This revelation is derived from Bridget's Italian period, as it mentions the excommunication which Magnus incurred because he did not in due course pay back the 22,000 marks (about £37,500) which had been lent him by the papal legate for Sweden, Jean de Guibert, from the Peter's pence collected there. After waiting a long time the Pope (Innocent VI) decided to excommunicate Magnus, but this excommunication did not take place until May, 1358 (Montelius, II, pp. 18–19). I am of the opinion, however, that the thought of this 'other way' to salvation for King Magnus had been vivid in Bridget's mind, towards the end of her time at home in Sweden too.

(3) *Rev.* VI, 87.

(4) *Rev.* VI, 77 and 83. I translate 'populus non intelligens' by 'the heathen,' as it seems to me to appear that this is what is meant.

(5) Carl Grimberg: *Svenska folkets underbara öden* (Stockholm, 1938), p. 339.

(6) *Processus*, p. 514. Here I follow Madame de Flavigny (p. 238, note 1), who supposes that the 'Haquinus' is an error in writing for 'Ericus.'

(7) *Processus*, p. 313.

(8) *Rev.* VI, 92 'saccus verborum.'—*Vitae patrum*, in the old Swedish translation 'Helga manna lefvarne' edited from a Vadstena manuscript by G. E. Klemming in *Klosterläsning*, Stockholm, 1877–8, pp. 179–304.

(9) *Extrav.* 43.

(10) *Rev.* IV, 125. Declaratio.—*Rev.* III, 12 with two Declarationes belonging to it. At Bridget's advice the Bishop stayed for a while yet in Rome, and thus avoided coming home during the disturbed scenes in 1365—on his return he found 'Regem captum et totum regnum turbatum.'

(11) *Lucidarius*, edited by Johannes Knudsen (Copenhagen, 1909), pp. 144–145. It is said there that the unicorn lies down and sleeps so soundly in the lap of the virgin 'that she must kill that animal' (must = can). Likewise with Bridget 'Hoc animal non capitur nisi per virginem, qua visa curris in sinum ejus et sic ab ipsa interficitur.'

(12) Remy de Gourmont: *Le Latin mystique* (Paris, 1922), p. 183.

(13) *Rev.* III, 13. Here it is said emphatically: 'Haec revelatio facta est de Episcopo Lincopen, qui postea factus fuit Archiepiscopus.'

(14) *Rev.* VI, 22.

(15) *Rev.* III, 13, Additio.—Steffens' supposition that the Bishop mentioned in *Rev.* III, 4, would be Peter Tyrgilsson, and that the 'rather book-learned canon' who, unfortunately in vain, tried to convert him, would be Master Matthias, seems to me to be untenable. For it is said elsewhere about the said canon that he was an aspirant to a bishopric, but because of intrigues had been hindered in attaining to that dignity, for which he was so well qualified. (*Extrav.* 79). Nor does what is said of him (*Rev.* III. 4) fit very well into the picture of him that one gets otherwise of the quiet scholar—as it is said of him that he 'had what was needful of money,' that he kept a horse, but 'did not groom it himself, nor did he light the fire himself in the kitchen, when he was going to have a meal'—in other words lived in a manner of which Bridget seemed to disapprove. Meanwhile, that which makes it quite impossible that the two men in question can be Bishop Petrus and Master Matthias is the revelation in which Bridget sees that anonymous bishop before the judgment seat of God, where to his everlasting shame and disgrace, he is clothed, instead of in the bishop's robes, in 'a sheet from the bed of a harlot') (*pannus meretricolis*), has an excrement put on his head instead of the mitre and is led away to hell by devils. Toni Schmid, too, has seen that there cannot possibly be any question here of Peter Tyrgilsson (*Birgitta och hennes uppenbarelser*, Lund 1940, pp. 50–54). She tries to find a bishop, contemporary with Petrus Tyrgilli, who might be a possibility. Perhaps the solution of the riddle is to be found in the word which caused Steffen (p. 284) so much trouble: 'Tu, filia, cogitas quae fuisset remuneratio Canonici illi Aurelianen, si Episcopus suus fuisset conversus?' (*Rev.* III, 12). There is, says Steffen, no trace elsewhere in Bridget that she 'had known priests from Orleans or visited this city herself.' That is correct. *But Nicolaus Hermanni knew Orleans*—he had even studied there. And it can be imagined that this ecclesiastic, with whom Bridget was so intimate, may have told her about the times he spent there on his studies, and about the good canon and the bad bishop in Orleans. Bridget was interested in France, and the *Revelation* III, 4, might be a transposition of Nils Hermansson's account. (An investigation in

Orleans would perhaps confirm this interpretation of mine. But in February 1941 it was not easy to go to France.)

(16) *Lucidarius*, p. 145. Cf. *Physiologus*, in Migne's *Patrologiae Cursus completus*, Series Secunda, Tomus CLXXI, Paris 1854, pp. 1217–18.

(17) On this bishop, *see also* IV, 130. The newly-married were personally known to Bridget ('Tu vero, filia, scribi conjugi tibi noto').—On this fourth bishop, *see* VI, 97, on the fifth, III, 33.

(18) *Rev.* III, 33. Declaratio.

(19) *Extrav.* 104. *Rev.* IV, 130, in which there is a milder judgment on the bishop who is so timid—he is ready to die, if God wills it, or to live on, if God wishes it of him. But the leper 'shall die with those whose God is their belly, he shall be buried in the churchyard of the lepers and not have a seat with those who are to judge the world' (that is, the twelve apostles on the Last Day).

(20) *Rev.* I, 41. The Swedish text: their members (all who are of the same body), all the priests, their followers and adherents.'

XXVII

(1) *Extrav.* 26 and 27.

(2) *Processus*, pp. 94, 477. *Extrav.* 8 and 40–41.

(3) *Rev.* VIII, 51.

(4) 'Regina Sapientia, Dominus te salvet, cum tua sorore sancta pura Simplicitate. Domina sancta Paupertas, Dominus te salvet, cum tua sorore Humilitate, Domina sancta Caritas, Dominus te salvet cum tua sorore sancta Obedientia.' (*Opera Sancti Francisci*).

(5) *Rev.* IV, 45.

(6) *Extrav.* 74, *Diarium ad* 1365.

(7) *Rev.* VI, 113.

(8) *Processus*, p. 641.

(9) 'ad Romam peregrinando devenit . . . habens semper secum . . . duos seniores antiquos et maturos et expertos patres spirituales qui usque ad mortem ei secuti sunt.' (Prologus Alphonsi in lib. octavum, cap. 3.) One of these two is 'monachus et prior Cisterciensis,' the other 'quidam presbyter de Suetia,' who in Rome ruled over Bridget's house and gave her and her daughter lessons in Latin and singing.

(10) Gudmar Frederiksson, *Diarium ad* 1389; Magnus Petri, *Diarium ad* 1396; Silfverstolpe, p. 79. Magnus Petri (Three Lilies), died in 1391 in the monastery of Paradiso near Florence.—Ingeborg Dannes, *Rev.* VI, 102, *Processus*, p. 631. *Diarium ad* 1401. The process of canonization places her death in Milan; *Rev.* VI, 102, says that she lay ill in Rome, the Vadstena diary that 'she was with Saint Bridget in Rome and died there.'

(11) *Processus*, pp. 83, 620.

(12) Holaveden—the big forest between Östergötland and Småland.

SOURCES

A. BIOGRAPHIES

(1) The *Vita* written by the two confessors, Petrus Olai of Skenninge and Prior Petrus Olai of Alvastra for use at the process of canonization in 1373. Printed from MS. A. 14, Royal Library, Stockholm, in Collijn's edition of the process (Uppsala 1924–31), pp. 73–101, and from the Panisperna manuscript found by Collijn in 1929, in the same place, pp. 614–64.

(2) *De vita beate Birgitte*, Swedish, of the close of the fourteenth century, printed in *Wadstena Klosterreglor*, Stockholm 1845, pp. II–XXI, also *Script. Rev. Svec.* III, 2, pp. 185–206.

(3) *Vita abbreviata*, in the various editions of *Revelationes*. I have been able to make use of Olaus Magnus' edition (Rome 1553).

(4) *Vita sanctae Birgittae, auctore Birgero, archiepiscopo Uppsaliensis*. Printed in *Acta Sanctorum*, Oct. IV, pp. 485–93 and *Script. Rev. Svec.* II, 1, pp. 383–8. Birger Gregersson was elected archbishop in 1366, died 1383. (Chevalier, *Rép. bio. bibliogr.*, I, 605.)

(5) *Vita*, written by the Bridgettine monk, Berthold, in the first half of the fifteenth century. Berthold—Bartholdus de Roma—became Confessor General in 1429 in the convent *Paradiso* at Florence. His work is an extract from the process of canonization. Printed *Script. Rev. Svec.* III, 2, p. 187 *seq.* and *Acta Sanctorum*, Oct. IV, pp. 495–533.

(6) 'Margareta Klausdotters Krönike' in Swedish, edited in *Script. Rev. Svec.* (1871), pp. 207–16. Margareta Klausdotter was abbess in the convent of Vadstena from 1472–86 and would undoubtedly have at her disposal documents now vanished.

(7) Master Matthias' *Prologue* to the Revelations.

(8) Alfonsus of Jaen's Preface to the eighth book of the Revelations.

(9) The Bull of Canonization, like (7) and (8) printed in the various editions of the Revelations.

(10) Nicolaus Hermanni's Office of Saint Birgitta *Rosa rorans*, of 1373, is chiefly founded on No. 5. (*See* H. Schück: '*Rosa rorans*. Ett Birgitta Officium,' in *Meddelanden fr. det litteraturhistoriske Seminariet i Lund*, II, Lund 1893.)

B. LETTERS FROM BRIDGET

(1) 'Sancta Birgitta skreff sin soon tiil aff room her byrier wlffson lagman i närike.' Printed from a list in Arvid Trolle's law book, Klemming's edition of the Revelations, Vol. V, pp. 140–41.

(2) Two letters to the Spanish Condottiere Gomez d'Albornoz, printed in K. G. Westman's *Birgittastudier*, I, Uppsala 1911, pp. 297–301, translated into Swedish by Isak Collijn, *Birgittinske Gestalter*, Stockholm 1929, pp. 58–62, and

into Danish by Johanne Skovgaard, *Den hellige Birgitta*, Copenhagen, 1921, pp. 152–8, Lolland Falsters historiske Aarbog for 1914.

(3) A letter to a lady of the Italian nobility, Lapa Buondelmonte, printed in Isak Collijn's *Birgittinske Gestalter*, p. 19, translated in Swedish, *ibid.*, pp. 16–17. The letter is signed *Brigida de Rachman* (?) *de Norvegia*.

C. OTHER SOURCES

(1) *Vita sive legenda . . . domine Katherine sancte memorie filie Birgitte de regno Svecie*, written by the Vadstena monk, Ulf Birgersson, in 1426 and 1427. Printed in all editions of the Revelations, as also in *A.S.*, March III, pp. 503–30 and *Script. Rev. Svec.* III, 2, pp. 244–75.—To this is joined the letter published by G. E. Klemming from Katerina to Archbishop Birger (*see* Andreas Lindblom: *Den heliga Birgitta*, Stockholm 1918, p. 9).

(2) *Vita Magistri Petri Olavi, confessoris Sanctae Birgittae, et miracula* (Fragment, edited by K. G. Grandison, Karlstad 1888).

(3) *Diarium Vazstenense* ('Klostersens tänkiebok'), from 1344 to 1545, edited by Benzelius, Uppsala 1721, Swedish translation by A. W. Lundberg and Andreas Lindblom, Stockholm 1918.

(4) 'Diarium Minorum Holmiensium,' *Script. Rev. Svec.* I, 1, No. XVIII.

(5) *Commentarii historici super nonnullis revelationibus sanctae Birgittae de rege Magno Erici et successoribus ejus* (written by a priest in Linköping after the election of Erik of Pomerania in 1397), *Script. Rev. Svec.* III, 1, pp. 16–20.

D. BRIDGET'S REVELATIONS

(1) Original Manuscripts (in the Royal Library in Stockholm).

(a) Fourth Book, Chapter 49 (Revelation on the state of the Church, 1367?) in Swedish.

(b) Eighth Book, Chapter 56 at the end, also fourth book, Chapter 141 in the old Swedish translation or *Extravagantes* 80 in the Latin text), in Swedish. (*circa* 1360.)

(c) Third Book, Chapter 8 (the letter to the unknown Master in Milan, in Latin, probably written from Bridget's Swedish original by Prior Petrus of Alvastra.

All three manuscripts are printed in Klemming's book, IV, pp. 177–85 and pp. 192–6.

On the back of (a) this addition has been made in a later handwriting: 'Sancta birgitta scref thässa ordh mz sinne eghne hand som röre pawan oc cardenales.'

(2) Editions of the Revelations

(a) *Manuscripts*

Long before her death Saint Bridget had thought of settling up her literary estate, consisting of the revelations dating from different periods of her life. The first, second and fifth of the eight books into which they are divided date, roughly speaking, from the time after the death of Ulf until the departure of Bridget from Sweden, that is, from 1344 to 1349. The third book contains the revelations dealing with the ecclesiastics. Such as these, however, are also to be found elsewhere. The greater part of the fourth book was written in Italy. The sixth book is a kind of aftermath, containing revelations from all periods of Bridget's life. The seventh book, one might be tempted to say, is a travel diary of the great pilgrimage to the Holy Land. The eighth book—*Liber coelestis Imperatores ad Reges*—is Bridget's political testament. In both of these books traces are to be found of the arranging hand of her secretary and last confessor, Alphonsus of Jaen.

But those among whom Bridget lived had begun still earlier to collect her Revelations. For this first collection Master Matthias wrote a preface—it is this collection which was authenticated by Archbishop Hemming Nilsson, and which Bishop Hemming of Åbo and Master Matthias brought to Avignon in 1347. Westman is probably right in supposing that originally it consisted only of the present first book; for the rest I must refer to this author's thorough and ingenious examination of this difficult and complicated question (*Birgitta Studier*, pp. 10–28).

During the sojourn in Italy the *Liber coelestis revelationum*, divided into seven books, gradually came into being, and new revelations were continually being inserted into it (*see* the remark on the original manuscript (c) *scriptum in libro magno*). After Bridget's death Alphonsus of Jaen extracted from this book the *liber magnus*, the revelations addresses to kings and princes, and collected them in an eighth book, to which he added a series of similar pieces from writings left by Bridget. Later came the rule of the Order, *Sermo angelicus* or the Bridgettine Office, and four prayers revealed to Bridget. Finally Prior Petrus had among his possessions a great number of papers which served as a more detailed explanation or elaboration of certain difficult places; they were inserted under the title of *Declaratio* or *Additio* or actually formed a supplement, to which was given the title *Extravagantes*, standing in the same relation to Alphonsus of Jaen's edition of the Revelations as Brother Leone's *Speculum perfectionis* to Thomas of Celano's official biography.

The process of canonization began in 1377, when probably only the seven first books were available in a complete state, and in this form the *Revelationes* were copied for the first time. In a letter of 15 January 1378, Alphonsus could write from Rome to Archbishop Birger of Uppsala that 'the books of the saintly Bridget (*libri celestes*) are read in Spain, in both Sicilies and Italy,' and that new supplies are continually being issued. (Westman, *loc. cit.*, p. 21, note 5). An anthology compiled by him (*Celeste viridarium*) of all the revelations dealing with the lives of Jesus and Mary, was a publication independent of the large edition; the book was translated into Swedish by the diligent Bridgettine monk, Jöns Budde of Åbo, but did not obtain a very wide distribution.

(b) *Printed Editions*

It was the text arranged by Alphonsus and provided by Petrus Olai with annotations and additions that was issued in 1492 by B. Gothan in Lübeck. The *Diarium Vazstenense* contains the following notice of this great event: 'In the year of Our Lord 1491 on the feast of Saint Cosmas and Saint Damian (27 September) the brothers Petrus Ingemarsson, priest, and Gerardus, lay brother, set forth for Lübeck to cause to be printed the heavenly books of Saint Bridget's revelations. And after the lapse of a year, after eight hundred copies had been printed on paper, but only sixteen on parchment, they came back to their monastery in the year of the Lord 1492, about the feast of Saint Catherine, Virgin and Martyr (25 November). Glory be to God Almighty. Amen.'

The edition is very sumptuous, 864 pages in folio, with fifteen woodcuts, among them the well-known one of the monk on the ladder, and the equally well-known one of Bridget sitting on a throne and distributing her book to kneeling kings and emperors. As Klemming has surmised, these woodcuts have perhaps been executed by the same lay brother, Gerard, also mentioned in the *Diarium* of 1487—'by birth he was German, he could carve and paint,' or, as it was said of him at his death in 1515, 'he was a good painter.' So he was, the best of these woodcuts are not inferior to Dürer's. A copy of the book cost 5 Lübeck marks.

It is not intended, however, here to give a list of the later editions of the Revelations—this can be found in Klemming's fifth volume of his edition of the Old-Swedish translation of the Revelations (Stockholm, 1883–4, pp. 182–243). I will only mention that for my work I have made use of the following editions:

Revelationes Sancte Birgitte, Nuremberg, A. Koberger, 1500 (Klemming's Bibliography No. 2);

Olaus Magnus' edition of 21 August 1557, printed in *aedibus divae Birgittae viduae* (No. 4 in Klemming);

The Antwerp edition in one volume of 1611, and the edition in two volumes, Rome 1628.

Further, among Bridgettine literature may be reckoned the well-known indictment, *Onus mundi*, against the clergy, an extract from the Revelations, undertaken about the year 1433 by Master Johannes Tortsch in Leipzig. The author sent his work to Vadstena, but did not thereby give any pleasure to the Brethren—'Our hearts became as though dead within us, when we understood that this writing had been sent to cities, countries and princes,' for it contained the severest of Bridget's pronouncements against the clergy, and just then the meeting of the Church was convened in Basle, and feelings for Bridget were anything but favourable.

In the same spirit as *Onus mundi* is the scathingly ironical 'Mass in honour of the Lady Simony,' a parody in honour of Maria Assumpta. (The Assumption of Our Lady.) It is to be found in a complete reprint in Toni Schmid: *Birgitta och hennes uppenbarelser* (Lund 1940), pp. 40–43. Toni Schmid is of opinion that 'we are indebted to Alphonsus of Jaen for its formal completion.'

E. THE PROCESS OF CANONIZATION

Next to the Revelations comes, no doubt, the process of canonization, namely, the collected testimonies about Bridget and her cause, the most important source of knowledge about the great seeress.

The first examination of the cause was entrusted by Pope Gregory XI to Bishop Galhardus of Spoleto, who had perhaps made the personal acquaintance of Bridget when she made her pilgrimage to Assisi in 1355. Bridget died on

23 July 1373—on 14 December of the same year the biography written by the two confessors (*see above* under A(1)) was already in Bishop Galhardus' hands. The first meeting on the cause was held in the Franciscan church in Montefalco (confused by several authors with Montefiascone), not yet adorned with those frescoes by Benozzo Gozzoli which have since drawn so many friends of art thither. The wonderful view would be there, though, which has obtained for the city the title of *La ringhiera dell' Umbria*; it is as though, from a balcony high up, you look out over the country of Umbria blessed by God and man. For the present writer Montefalco became at an early date the scene of a great experience, and during many long years I have from my windows in Assisi seen its towers in the distance. Often have I been there with friends and acquaintances, and the old church of San Francesco became still more homelike to me when I read in the process of canonization that Bishop Galhardus had summoned as witnesses 'Venerabiles viros dominum Petrum Olai de civitate Skenengensi . . . et fratrem Petrum Olai, priorem monasterii sancte Maria de Alwastro diocesis Lincopensis ordinis Cisterciensis de regno Sweci' and likewise 'the son of the above-named lady, Sir Birger from Sweden.' Under these vaults, between these walls had they stood, Master Petrus and Prior Petrus and Sir Birger Ulfsson—here they had entrusted to the care of the Bishop 'a manuscript paper (*quemdam quadernum papireum*) in which were written the life of the above-named Lady Bridget, and the record of some miracles, and on oath they confirmed that what was written in this manuscript was the sheer truth, and what they had heard and seen themselves and been present at.' (*Acta et Processus Canonizationis Beate Birgitte*, edited by Isak Collijn, Uppsala, 1924–31, pp. 72–3).

After this preliminary examination comes the official process of canonization, which takes place in Rome before a commission of four cardinals, and lasts from December 1378 until August 1380. The cause was not yet definitely decided with this, however, as a new examination followed in 1391, and not until 7 October of the same year did the canonization take place. On this occasion the Confessor General of the convent of Vadstena, Magnus Petri, presented the Pope with a copy of the whole process from beginning to end, and 'as the Cardinals also wished to have a copy' (says the eyewitness, Lars Romare), the Pope requested Magnus Petri to grant them their wish. Magnus then orders no fewer than thirty writers to make the necessary copies 'och lätt så hwar Cardenal bekomma Enn Book well och stådthellig inbundena, sa att hwar Book kostade honum Tiwggu Ducater,'* says Lars Romare. This entailed an extra expense of 600 ducats, which the worthy *frater ab extra* notes without much enthusiasm.

Perhaps it is one of these thirty copies which has found its way to the royal library in Stockholm under the signature A. 14, and from which Isak Collijn made the critical edition mentioned above. In this invaluable original writing are to be found—besides the biography of the confessors—such important testimonies as those given by Bridget's daughter Katherine and Petrus Olai, Prior of Alvastra. Thanks to Collijn the Bridgettine student is no longer under the necessity of going to the Royal Library in Stockholm in order to study the

* 'and let each cardinal then receive one book, well bound in so stately a manner that each book will cost him twenty ducats.' (Tr.)

manuscript for himself, but can have it lying in a printed edition on his writing-table. One cannot be grateful enough to Dr. Collijn.

Naturally I have had to have recourse to many sources of help in the present work. It would be an easy matter for me to fill several pages with a list of the works consulted. Meanwhile all the sources used will be found in the Notes. I will therefore only mention briefly the most important biographies (Hammerich, de Flavigny, Krogh-Tonning, Emilie Fogelklou, both the Swedish and German edition). Next G. E. Klemming's edition of the old Swedish translation of the Revelations, Stockholm 1857–84, Richard Steffen's *Den heliga Birgitta's uppenbarelser i urval och öfversätning* (Stockholm 1909) as well as the following works on special subjects:

Torvald Höjer: *Studier i Vadstena's Klosters och Birgittinordens Historia* (Uppsala 1905);

Knut B. Westman: *Birgitta-Studier* I (Uppsala 1911);

Andreas Lindblom: *Den heliga Birgitta . . . i Skulptur och Måleri* (Stockholm 1918);

Ingvar Andersson: *Källstudier til Sveriges Historia* (1230–1436) (Lund 1928);

Isak Collijn: *Birgittinska Gestalter* (Stockholm 1929);

Salomon Kraft: *Textstudier til Birgitta's Revelationer* (Uppsala 1929);

Sten Engström: *Bo Jonsson*, I (Uppsala 1935).

At the last moment I also had the opportunity of reading and in part making use of Toni Schmid: *Birgitta och hennes uppenbarelser* (Lund 1940).

INDEX

SAINT BRIDGET OF SWEDEN

SAINT BRIDGET
OF SWEDEN

by
JOHANNES JØRGENSEN

Translated from the Danish by
INGEBORG LUND

VOLUME II
(1349–1373)

1724

LONGMANS GREEN AND CO
LONDON · NEW YORK · TORONTO

LONGMANS, GREEN AND CO LTD
6 & 7 CLIFFORD STREET LONDON W I

ALSO AT MELBOURNE AND CAPE TOWN

LONGMANS, GREEN AND CO INC
55 FIFTH AVENUE NEW YORK 3

LONGMANS, GREEN AND CO
215 VICTORIA STREET TORONTO I

ORIENT LONGMANS LTD
BOMBAY CALCUTTA MADRAS

First published 1954

NIHIL OBSTAT: DANIEL DUIVESTEIJN, S.T.D.
Censor deputatus
IMPRIMATUR: E. MORROGH BERNARD, *Vic. Gen.*
WESTMONASTERII, *die 24a Martii 1954*

PRINTED IN GREAT BRITAIN BY
SPOTTISWOODE, BALLANTYNE AND CO. LTD.
LONDON AND COLCHESTER

TRANSLATOR'S NOTE

In Swedish the letter a with a circle above it—å—is pronounced like the English a in au or aw, but a little more closed.

The a with a diæresis above it—ä—is pronounced like the English e in best.

The letter o with a diæresis—ö—is pronounced approximately like eu in French, *e.g.* heure; the final e in all words is always pronounced, forming a separate syllable. Example: Dovre, in Dovre Fell. It is approximately like the French e in le, ce, but more open.

The word 'ur,' primeval, is pronounced like 'oor' in 'moor.'

The letter i is pronounced like ee in English, *e.g.* keep, and the final e as above, forming a separate syllable.

PREFACE

Aliquando contigit quod de nigro camino exit pulchra flamma.

Revelationes VII, 12

'It happens at times that from a black furnace comes forth a bright flame.'

THIS, the second—and last—volume of my book about Saint Bridget has not been written under circumstances as favourable as the first. Occurrences over which I had no control compelled me to break away from Vadstena and to continue my work at first in a home of recreation in Sealand in Denmark, and after that in a convent on the island of Funen. My original plan of writing this volume in Italy, near the old Bridgettine convent of *Paradiso* near Florence, could not, for reasons which I need not explain, be realized.

I must be allowed to say a few words to the critics, on the whole favourably disposed, who reviewed the first part of my book. I have been reproached, for instance, with placing too much confidence in the testimony of the process of canonization, which is believed to be more or less falsified with the intention of attaining the desired object—the canonization of Bridget as a saint. He who wrote this has evidently not made himself familiar with the process in question, such as it is presented in the exemplary edition by Isak Collijn, for it clearly shows how the ecclesiastical authorities take every precaution to prevent the testimony from being influenced by other considerations than that of truth. Each one of the witnesses has to take an oath 'to speak the pure, full and entire truth' (*puram, meram et plenam veritatem*) without allowing himself or herself to be influenced 'by prayer, bribery, affection, fear, hate or feelings of kinship' (*prece, precio, amore, timore, odio, gracia et affectione remotis*. The *Process*, pp. 38–9). This oath is taken by every witness, 'with his/her hands upon the Holy Gospel.' Here one is in the presence of honest people—among them Bridget's own daughter Karin, the confessors, the Roman noblemen who, after having taken an oath which binds them and places them under a responsibility, bear witness to what they have seen and heard or learnt in other ways. There can be no doubt about the subjective truth of these testimonies—but there is

also reason to rely upon their objective truth. For, as it happens, th
process of canonization when compared with the *Revelationes*, is see
to be the primary source, whose testimony is to be preferred. I will giv
only *one* example of this. In Book 6, Chapter 78, of the Revelation
there is a remarkable story of how Bridget and her confessor, the Prio
of Alvastra, Petrus Olai, stay overnight with some peasants who ar
found to be *snake worshippers*. They sacrifice the firstfruits of their pro
duce, both milk, meat, pork, bread and wine to the snakes. At Bridget'
request Petrus Olai now preaches to them and reproves them with thi
idolatry, upon which they are converted. On account of *wine* being
found among the gifts offered up to the snakes, earlier writers have
laid the scene of the incident in Italy. Petrus Olai's own testimony, however, is to be found in the process of canonization. The text is the same
word for word—with only a single, but decisive addition. The inciden
took place, he says, in a peasant farm, the name of which he does no
remember, *but which lay near Lödöse* (in quadam villa que est prop
Lodosiam. The *Process*, p. 540). Alphonsus of Jaen would have this tex
beside him when making the final edition of the revelations, but he lef
out the mention of Lodosia, a name which did not mean anything to
him, as he was a Spaniard.

Furthermore, those who are well acquainted with the subject wil
find that in this volume—as in the preceding one—I have mixed too
much of my own flour in Bridget's sack. It is true, and I must apologize
for it. But as it happens, I am used to having my *franches coudées* when
I write, that is, a little elbow room for my personal whims, and I do
not think I shall get better in the time remaining to me.

I pass on then, to expressing my gratitude to the Carlsberg Fund
and its president, Professor Johannes Pedersen, who has been willing to
support me in the completion of my work. Next I present my cordial
thanks to the Bridgettine Foundation and its President, Prince Eugene,
Duke of Närke (the province of which Ulf Gudmarsson was law-man)
for the support and recognition granted to me.

And then comes the final leave-taking of a work which has for so
long formed the central point of my existence. I was not permitted to
finish it by the shores of Lake Vättern, but my thoughts have often
wandered thither. In far away Rome Bridget would no doubt often
turn towards the north and across the miles of lands beyond the mountains, and listening she would hear the rippling of the waves against the
shore at home in Vadstena. But she never saw the church that is now

anding over her grave like a shrine over the tomb of a saint. On how
any evenings when it was moonlight, have I not stood in the garden
f the monks before that mighty façade rising like a mountain (a
ountain moved thither by faith), or like a face in ecstasy looking
wards the sunrise. And then it has been as though from within the
urch I heard a voice, quiet and strong, stern and gentle, saying: 'Oh,
ou sinful being, turn back for thou art walking in peril, and because
y heart is dark thou seest not the dangers on the road.' (*Rev.* II, 11.)

JOHANNES JØRGENSEN

alum. The Feast of St. Catherine of Sweden, 1943.

CONTENTS

BOOK IV

ROME

The scribes and the Pharisees have sitten on the chair of Moses. All things therefore whatsoever they shall say to you, observe and do: but according to their works do ye not. For they say, and do not.

St. Matthew xxiii, 2–3

I

THEN again it was Stralsund as it was eight years ago, when Ulf and Bridget set forth together to go to Compostella. But now she was sitting alone in her room in the German hostelry. The widow of Sir Ulf Gudmarsson, erstwhile mistress of Ulfåsa, now a poor pilgrim among other poor pilgrims on the way to the tombs of the Apostles, down yonder in 'Rome the Great' (as Babylon in the Revelation of Saint John is called 'Babylon the Great'). And none of her own people was with her on this pilgrimage. Her thoughts went out to them, most likely to Birger and Karl in their doings by the shores of Lake Boren or in the castle of Stockholm.

It was in Kalmar that Bridget embarked on the vessel that for ever was to take her away from her own country. Kalmar, 'the eye of Sweden, its bulwark and key,' as the city was called because of its strong castle, and its harbour protected by the long mole of Öland, was not an unknown city to Bridget, and she could not be indifferent to it. Here King Magnus Ladulås had celebrated his marriage with Princess Hedwig of Holstein—and though Bridget had never had any personal acquaintance with this great king (he died thirteen years before she was born), she had heard enough about him at home in Finsta, and when the goblets were emptied at feasts at Ulfåsa. There were many things that these noble gentlemen could not forgive the pious and just king, and among them this, that he had 'put a lock on the door of the peasant's barn,' *i.e.*, that he had forbidden the custom hitherto prevailing, of the great lords, on their journeys about the country, 'though they were never so rich, of not being ashamed of going into the houses of poor men, and there demanding food without paying for it, and thus in a short space consuming what the poor had laboured a long while to obtain.' When many years later Bridget had her great vision of the three kings before the Judge, the second of these kings—and that was this very Magnus Ladulås—had to confess, among many other misdeeds, that he had 'thought out new and unlawful imposts and taxes . . . to the harm of many men in the kingdom, as also of many wayfarers and merchants.' The 'fault' of which Bridget here makes him accuse himself, is none other than that by which he

2

ordered travellers, both the nobles and merchants, to pay for what they consumed.(1).

Bridget, however, had also a more personal connection with Kalmar. In June 1332 both her husband Ulf and her brother Israel had been present there among other lords and good men of the kingdom and had been sureties for the ransom of Scania and Blekinge. The ransom, which was to be paid to Count John of Holstein, to whom both provinces had been mortgaged by the Danish King Christopher II, amounted to no less than 34,000 marks in silver. In the year 1334 Israel Birgersson paid, as his share, 450 marks in silver—Bridget might also be thinking of this as she walked about the streets of Kalmar and bought provisions for the journey from the German traders, dominating here as everywhere else in Sweden.

But there was one thing that she could not imagine (and if she could have done so what would she have felt?) that here, in this same city of Kalmar, on Trinity Sunday, 1397, a daughter of her bitterest enemy, Valdemar Atterdag, brought up by her own daughter Märta, was to crown the fifteen-year-old son of a Pomeranian duke with the three crowns of the northern kingdoms. . . .

Like so many other things this, too, was hidden from the eyes of the seeress. But from the ship that took her away from Sweden (she did not know that it was to be for ever), she would send a greeting to the Cross on Kläppinge Ness, for it was there that it had been raised in memory of Duke Erik's rescue of her mother and herself while yet unborn from the shipwreck. It may also have turned her thoughts to Duke Erik's son—to Magnus the Young, the *degenerate* son of Duke Erik—Magnus with the heart of a hare, who wanted to get through life with caresses—Magnus who sat on his throne like an ass with a crown on the long ears (did Blanca sometimes pull them?)—Magnus, that stupid Magnus whom she could not help being fond of. . . . But why, then, had he submitted to the guidance of bad advisers, destroyed the convent building in Vadstena, undone all that he had promised on that beautiful day of Saint Walburga's feast only three years ago? And what was to be done now about Bridget's dream of the convent on the shores of Lake Vättern ?(2)

Bridget gave herself up to prayer, and in prayer she received an answer. In her inmost soul she heard the voice she knew so well—Mary's gentle, motherly voice: 'Fear not, my daughter,' said the voice from heaven. 'Even though thou shouldst die ere thou hadst fulfilled the work entrusted to thee, thou shalt, for the sake of thy good will, be accounted a nun in Vadstena and shalt have a part in all the good that is to come to pass there.'(3)

There was a knock at the door—Bridget struggled out of the ecstasy, back to reality. Again a knock and the door was opened carefully—it was Master Petrus of Skenninge. 'Dinner is ready, Lady Bridget, we are all waiting.'

She followed Master Peter. There they all stood ready about the table—Prior Petrus in his white habit—Sir Magnus Petri of Eka, the knight without fear and reproach, who lived that genuine life of chivalry, which was stricter than that of the monk in the cloister, 'as true as a breastplate is harder than a monk's habit'(4)—beside him stood the young priest, Gudmar Fredriksson, the Lady Ingeborg, daughter of Laurens, who had been permitted by her husband, Sir Niels Bielke, to accompany the Lady Bridget on the pilgrimage—and some menservants and handmaids.(5)

The Lady Bridget went and stood behind her chair at the upper end of the table and nodded to Master Peter.

In nomine Patris . . . Master Peter began saying grace.

II

It was the plague, 'the Black Death,' that Bridget was to meet on her journey. And it was not long before it also reached Sweden. In the spring of 1350 King Magnus Eriksson sends out a circular letter, in which he mentions:

> a terrible news, that every Christian man and woman must sorely fear, for God, because of the sins of men, has sent a great plague upon the whole world, so that the greater part of the people who live in the lands lying to the west of our land, have died a swift death, and now this flying sickness is all over Norway and Halland and will soon be here, and it takes such a hold that before they are sick people fall down and die without the sacraments, and wherever it comes there are not so many people left that they can bury the dead.

As King Magnus says, this terrible sickness had come first to Norway. In the summer of 1349 an English ship, laden with woollen goods, ran into the harbour of Bergen and brought the infection with it. The sickness appeared at first like a violent fever with attacks of alarm and fear, then boils broke out all over the body, the breath grew fetid, the tongue black, as if burnt, violent vomiting of blood rushed from the mouth and nose. The time granted by the plague was but short—at the most two or three days, most often only a couple of hours. No one dared come near a sick person—'in vain did a wife call for her husband, the husband for his wife, the child for its parents,' says an old chronicle. In deadly fear the priest hurried with the Sacrament from one deathbed to another, until he fell down himself and expired, struck by the infection.

Medical skill of the time was helpless with its well-meant and ineffective advice to use the smoke of cinnamon bark, of mace and juniper, or to place a vessel with a solution of vitriol in the sick-room —'that water draws the poison to itself.' With the knowledge how useless these and many other measures were, many physicians advised their patients to enjoy life and take their fill of wine, 'for to-morrow we die.' It is said in an old medical book: 'one must drink old ale, not too strong, be reckless and enjoy oneself with one's friends, sing, play the harp, beat the drum and join in other games and merriment.' Even in the sixteenth century Benedict Olai, the physician of Erik XIV, in 'his useful physician's book' gives the following recipe: 'In times of pestilence man must be of good courage and be glad, and delight in many kinds of merry games and music, in the lute, harp and fiddle, love clean and comely raiment and not think of death.'(1) That was just what Florentine youth did in Boccaccio's *Decameron*. And yet one day Death stood among the rose-wreathed guests at the festive board— as in the old play about Everyman.

In Norway two-thirds of the inhabitants of the country died, in Sweden only half as many, but that was enough. In Uppland only a sixth of the population was left—both there and elsewhere people had to think of Bridget's prophecy. Nor could the king help remembering that dreadful day when she had stood before him and spoken to him in the name of Christ:

> Thus saith the Son of God: I will visit this kingdom with the sword and lance and with wrath. In vain do they say: 'Let us do as it pleaseth us, life is short, God is merciful, He will do us no evil!' Hearken to what I now say to thee. I will rise up in all my power and will not spare either young or old, rich or poor, just or unjust. I will come with my plough and pull up the trees by the roots, so that where there before were a thousand people only a hundred will be left, and their houses shall stand empty.(2)

King Magnus summoned the lords and good men of the kingdom to Lödöse, to take counsel with them on what had to be done in this distress. Among those who had been bidden were Bridget's brother Israel—he would surely know about his sister's threats,—the bishop of the diocese of Linköping, the bishop of Skara, the canons of the dioceses whose bishops could not come. All were agreed that now they would have to find out 'by what service and humility it would be possible to appease the wrath of God.' All over the kingdom the following royal decree was issued:

> All the people in the kingdom of Sweden, priests and laymen, old and young, men and women, shall come every Friday to their parish church, clothed in woollen garments and barefoot, and they shall humbly before God admit His justice and great power. They shall walk round the church with the holy things [the relics that were preserved in the church] and with pious devotion they shall on those days hear Mass and offer up on the altar such money as they are able. 'These gifts shall be given to the poor. They shall by no means be given for the use of the priest.'

But it was not enough to go to church and to give alms—the spiritual preparedness of 1349 demanded more. Everyone was advised to purify his soul and to go to confession, and to set right what was wrong, so that, if called away by God, he might be found ready to yield up his soul into God's hands.(3)

But the Black Death could not be turned away. In the *Diarium Vazstenense* of the year 1350 it is said: 'At that time a great mortality prevailed in Sweden, greater than any could remember to have been before or since, which mortality Blessed Bridget had foretold long before would come. For Christ foretold it in a revelation, saying: "I will pass over the world with my plough. . . ."'

On their way down through Germany Bridget and her escort everywhere met crowds of penitents. With Cross and banners, singing *Miserere* and *De profundis*, and saying the rosary, they walked from one shrine to another, in order to meet at last on the way to Rome. The pilgrims' singing could be heard—the beautiful spiritual songs of Catholic Germany—and Bridget, who was used to hearing and speaking German, not only with her son-in-law Eggert von Kyren, but also with the German tradespeople in Skänninge, would no doubt be able to join in the singing, when they sang the hymn about the loveliest rose:

> Es ist ein Reis entsprungen
> aus einer Wurzel zart,
> davon die Alten sungen
> vor Jesse kam die Art
> und hat ein Blümlein bracht
> mitten im kalten Winter,
> wohl zu der halben Nacht.

And the other beautiful song, which is said to have been written by Tauler:

> Es Kommt ein Schiff, geladen
> bis an sein'n höchsten Bord,
> er trägt Gott's Sohn voll Gnaden,
> des Vaters ewiges Wort.
> Zu Bethlehem geboren
> im Stall ein Kindlein,
> giebt sich für uns verloren,
> gelobet muss es sein!

Could Bridget have any greater desire than to kneel by the Crib in the stable at Bethlehem? Had she not been given the promise again and again, that one day she would come there? Rome was only to be a halting-place on the way to *Hierusalem*, as she had seen it written on a guide-post down yonder in the Pyrenees, when she was there with Ulf. Now she had to wander on the road alone!

> My soul, do thou make ready
> to walk the long way
> over hills and dry moorland
> before the night overtakes us.

Over the arid moors of North Germany, among the green mountains of South Germany the road led the pilgrims. One evening the Swedish pilgrims made a halt in the little town of Maihingen in Swabia, letting their horses graze on a meadow outside the gate. When the peasant who owned the meadow asked for payment, Bridget with a magnificent Swedish gesture bought the whole meadow—and with another magnificent gesture gave it to the town. Her gift came back to her, in the year 1472 a Bridgettine convent was founded there, and about ten years later the famous, still existing convent of Altomünster was founded from it.(4)

From Maihingen the Swedish pilgrims would probably set their course towards Basle, then as now the great gate from Germania, especially from Western Germany, to Switzerland. From Basle the Roman road led across Great Saint Bernard; *Bjarnardsspitali* is mentioned already in the book of travels of Abbot Nikolas of Thingerar (in the middle of the twelfth century). The first station on the other side of the Alps was Aosta in Savoy; the Icelandic abbot speaks well of the town. Then the road led on to Ivrea, Vercelli, Pavia, Piacenza.(5) Bridget seems to have chosen another route, perhaps one leading to the place of pilgrimage at Oropa,(6) for Milan is her first station in Italy. That marble cathedral among whose vegetation of spires and finials the modern tourist wanders about, did not yet at that time rise in luminous beauty above the capital of the Lombards, the golden *Madonnina* on the highest pinnacle did not yet bless the fertile land. Bramante had not yet built Santa Maria delle Grazie, and a century and a half were to pass before Leonardo was to paint his 'Last Supper' on the wall of the refectory in the convent. Even if it had existed Bridget would perhaps not have walked two steps to see it. In any case her first walk was to Sant' Ambrogio, the old Romano-Lombardic Cathedral of Milan; Saint Ambrose lies buried in the crypt, and he was a bishop after Bridget's own heart, who had bravely withstood the great Theodoric. She knelt by the tomb, in the stone of the sarcophagus a single word was engraved: *HUMILITAS*.

Bridget knew who Ambrose was. 'His heart,' she says of him, 'was full of godly joy, he brought his body into subjection and denied himself an excess of sleep, he made good and seemly use of his time. He healed the wounds of sinners with the words of truth; by his example he kindled those whose hearts were cold to godly love; with the purity of his life he brought coolness to those who burned with the desire to sin. In this manner he helped many souls that they should not go to everlasting death and hell.'(7)

Ambrose had been a bishop after God's heart. But what manner of man was he who was now sitting in his chair? At that time the Lombardic archiepiscopal see was occupied by the Italian nobleman Giovanni Visconti, a Renaissance priest of the type which culminated in Alexander VI. By his contemporaries he was called 'the great serpent,' one of the most unscrupulous and crafty personalities of the time, a man with unlimited ambition, not so much on his own account as on that of his country—by all means, permissible or not permissible, he tried to extend the domain of Milan. He had acquired dominion of one of the best territories of the State belonging to the Church: Romagna with its capital, Bologna, the 'learned' and 'fat' Bologna. The Pope, Clement VI, therefore took the opportunity of excommunicating him, which did not distress him particularly. On the other hand, he made his armies advance further towards the south and threaten Guelphic-minded Firenze, which tried in vain to gather the other Tuscan republics to a common resistance against the warlike archbishop.(8) Bridget, not unjustly, called him 'a ravening wolf in sheep's clothing.' Or was he not rather like a snail, that creeps about in the dirt of the earth, or a bellows, blowing up the fire of war, so that souls drip down into hell like melted ore ?

In the crypt of Sant' Ambrogio she prays long and ardently. Like once the Hebrew prophet she cries to God: 'Descend, Oh Lord, and save Thy people Israel. For we are as on a ship in a storm and the masters of the ship steer whither the storm rages most fiercely, and few are they who reach the harbour of salvation.' And who are these bad steersmen? Bridget knows it—they are simply *all* those who have power here upon the earth, be it worldly or spiritual.

For most of them love their own will so much that they pay no heed to what is good for the souls of their subjects, but they sink down in the world's most evil wave, which is pride and covetousness and the unclean lust of the body, and the poor common people believe that it must be so, and thus everyone slays his own soul, and all follow the will and desire of their body.

Bridget prays a long time at the tomb of the saint, and at length she receives an answer. 'The truth has grown dark to many,' she hears Ambrose complain. 'When anyone would point out the road to the heavenly fatherland, he is told: "Thou liest!" The people would rather follow those who sink down in all manner of sins than they will believe and obey those who preach the truths of the Bible.'

Therefore must a *new beacon* be lit, which can guide the souls of the human beings who are tossed about in danger of death on the waves of worldliness back to the harbour of salvation. And *Bridget* is to be this new beacon—here in a strange land as she was at home in Sweden. Saint Ambrose himself sends her out in the name of God to speak the words of repentance: 'At the prayers of thy friends God has called thee so that thou mayest in spirit see and hear and understand, and what thou hast thus heard in spirit thou shalt reveal to others.'(9)

Italy has become Bridget's new domain of work and her mission field.

III

When a Scandinavian at the present day enters Italy for the first time, and glides from a tunnel out to the light, he is dazzled by the bright sunshine. The pilgrims of the Middle Ages would not feel the transition so abruptly, either when they crossed the Alps, walking with a pilgrim staff in their hands or—as Milles has presented Bridget on the well of the Folkungs in Linköping—riding on a humble ambler. Bridget, however, had seen the sun of the south in Spain.

But she was dazzled spiritually by a light that was strange to her. She came out into the springtime of the Italian Renaissance—the great

Trecento. She came from the cloister and was faced with that worldliness that she hated most of all, clad, it is true, in the Stoic toga of philosophy, but wearing a wreath for the symposium with flowers from Helicon. At home she had only had to fight with trolls and devils, and they were so hideous that everyone who saw them would be filled with horror. But in the Latin light the statues of idols stood nude and beautiful, and instead of the Gospel the works of heathen philosophers lay on the ecclesiastic's table. What was this kind of study but chewing straw and throwing away the ear of corn with the full nourishing grain? How like that Master of Arts, with whom the Swedish pilgrims had made acquaintance here in Milan, and who was more at home in Cicero and Seneca than in the Holy Scriptures! Bridget found that he behaved more like an ass than like a learned scholar—besides, an ass feeds on straw, not on grass.(1)

We do not know who this Master of Arts was, of whom Bridget speaks. She may have sought communication with him, in order to obtain through him an introduction to the archbishop. The letter which Prior Petrus Olai wrote to the Master in his best Latin is still preserved. The Master paid a visit to the Swedish travellers, and there, in the presence of Prior Petrus Olai, he had a talk with Bridget. When he had gone Bridget had that revelation which Prior Petrus now sends to the foreign ecclesiastic, and which is sharpened into three questions of conscience put to the learned gentleman.

(1) Will the Master risk falling into disgrace with the archbishop in order to save the soul of the latter? (2) Will he risk a pecuniary loss by such a step? (3) Finally, will he stake his esteem as a scholar, and exchange his seat among the other supporters of culture for the humble place of a poor Franciscan among the simple-minded and the foolish? For only when he is inspired by such selflessness can he really be of use to the archbishop, only then can he stand fearlessly before him and tell him the truth, instead of, as hitherto, talking only to please him and letting him be right in everything. If the Master is not able to do this, why then he must go on chewing the bed-straw of worldly wisdom, feeding on it like the ass he is. 'But he must know this, that the sun shines even if the blind man cannot see it, and the waterfall roars even if the deaf cannot hear it, but plunge straight into it, and even if the dead, lying rotting among the worms, can no longer lift a cup, the wine is there just the same, and he who is living drinks it and enjoys it, and is encouraged by it to manly deeds.'

The Master did not find it necessary to answer this letter at any length. He only, as a competent official, supplied it with three short marginal notes:

(ad 1) I prefer to benefit the bishop in a spiritual manner; (ad 2) I have no personal property and rejoice more in the poverty I have made a vow to keep [the Master would therefore be either a Franciscan or a Dominican] than in all the riches of the world; (ad 3) It is more precious to me to be called a simple-minded friar than to be honoured as a learned Master of Arts.(2)

Correct answers—what else could a distinguished ecclesiastic answer a pious lady? For he could not very well confess that he preferred by far his pleasant and well-paid position with the archbishop to telling his lord and master unpleasant truths because of something so much of a problem as that of saving his soul. Nor could he say that it tickled his vanity pleasantly when, walking through the streets of Milan, people swept their hats deeply to him, and he heard the women whisper: 'That is the archbishop's confessor! *Un uomo tanto istruito*—such a learned gentleman!' '*E anche pio!* And very pious too! He says his Mass so devoutly!' Besides, what right had this seeress from the barbarous North to come here and trouble his conscience? He had to read a chapter of *De officiis* in order to regain his composure. . . .

Bridget was not deceived by the Master's answer. She showed the Blessed Virgin the letter, and it was at once clear to Mary that the learned gentleman's pious words were not to be trusted.

I have brought the Truth into the world [she said to Bridget] and I fully understand whether people are speaking the truth or not. The Master's answer would have been excellent if he had meant it. But there was not a vestige of truth in what he said, and I now predict three things for him: There is something that he desires with all his might at this moment; he will never get it. Next: what he possesses now with so much worldly joy, he will lose ere very long. The third is that the little ones and the humble shall enter into the kingdom of heaven, and the great and mighty shall stand outside, for the gate is narrow.(3)

Bridget was not deceived, nor would she be put off. If the Master, that ruminant ass, would not speak to the archbishop, she would do it herself. It was not as a jest that Saint Ambrose had sent her. Prior Petrus had again to exercise his most classical Latin—(of course it was not proper Ciceronian like that of the Italian humanists)—in order to convey in the language of Rome what Bridget had said to him in 'the Swedish tongue.'

It was a parable that 'Ambrose the Bishop had told her,' because 'thy heart is not able to understand spiritual things without a bodily likeness.' And the likeness said:

There was once a man who had a fair and good wife. But he cared more for the handmaid than for his wife. And this led to three things. Firstly, that the words and smiles of the handmaid pleased him more than those of the wife. Next, that he clothed the handmaid in the finest raiment and paid no heed to his wife being poorly clad, in common stuff, in rags and patches. Thirdly, that he spent nine hours with the handmaid, while he spent one with his wife. Of the nine hours he spent the first in looking at the handmaid and rejoicing at her beauty. In the second hour he slept in her arms. In the third hour he worked gladly for the use and benefit of the handmaid. In the fourth he took his midday sleep with her. In the fifth hour he was troubled in his mind to provide well for her. In the sixth hour he was glad because she was grateful to him for having provided for her. In the seventh hour he grew hot with carnal desire, and in the eighth hour he consummated his desire with her. In the ninth hour he omitted to do some things which he would otherwise have done, and in the tenth hour he did something he did not like to do, and that was the hour that he spent with his wife. But now one of the wife's kinsfolk came to this adulterer and rebuked him severely and said to him: 'Incline thy heart again to thy lawful wife, love her and clothe her becomingly, and be with her nine hours and only one with the handmaid. If not, then know that thou shalt have a dreadful death.'(4)

Now what did this story about an unfaithful husband mean? Bridget may have known of it as actually happening, and Giovanni Visconti may have read it with a slight smile—perhaps as he read Boccaccio later on? For that matter it could well have fitted into the *Decameron*. But it was a parable, not a novel—and now came the interpretation. Bridget had 'no hair on her tongue' as the Italians say (*non aveva peli sulla lingua*)—she called a spade a spade and Rolet a scoundrel. 'By this adulterer I mean and understand,' she wrote, 'a man of the Church, who has the office of a bishop and who lives like an adulterer.' It is not an accusation against bishops as such in general, which one can take to heart or not take to heart. It is Giovanni Visconti to whom she is speaking—'this head man and ruler of the Church.' *He* is the man—as David was the man when the prophet spoke to him.

Why, then, is he an adulterer?—Yes, as a bishop he is wedded to the Holy Catholic Church as a husband to his wedded wife. But now he has left his lawful spouse to seek adulterous joys with the world. In the first hour of the parable he looks with pleasure upon the beauty of the world. In the second hour he sleeps in the arms of that world, that is to say, he believes himself to be safely hidden behind the high walls of his castle, with armed men on guard at the door. In the third hour he works for worldly gain, in the fourth he rests with the consciousness of having done good business. In the fifth hour he is troubled about his position and esteem, but in the sixth he is again of good courage, as he sees that all men treat him with courtesy and respect. In the seventh hour he is heated with desire for worldly things and in the eighth he succeeds in getting possession of them. In the ninth hour he imposes a certain abstinence upon himself, but only out of consideration of what people will say. At last, in the tenth hour he does something good—and he offers up that hour to his bride, the Church—but he does it only because of fear of the everlasting punishments in the life hereafter. For, like King Valdemar in the legend—he cares not a whit for the blessedness of heaven,—'if only he may live always on the earth, be always in good health and have the riches of the world in abundance.'

And now Bridget admonishes the adulterer to return to his deserted spouse. If not his soul will be struck by a punishment just as severe spiritually, as if someone had such a blow on the head that the whole body was crushed by it, veins and nerves burst, and the bones crushed so that the marrow flowed out of them. (That was what happened to certain criminals—the bones were crushed, before the transgressor was yet dead. Bridget often applies this image to give an idea of the punishments in hell.)

Her threat, however, had no effect. She had to admit that 'this bishop is like a tortoise, on whose hard shell all blows glance off, and who is content to crawl about with his head on the ground and not desiring anything better than the filth he is used to.'(5)

Bridget's hand—as it is written on the back of one of her own drafts for letters—'was to touch the hand of the Pope and of Cardinals.' It was to be harder for her to touch their hearts.(6)

IV

The Lady Ingeborg, daughter of Laurens, the wife of Sir Nicolaus Dannes, who was a member of Bridget's escort, was ill when they arrived at Milan. Her husband had not been very willing to let her venture on this journey—it is true that he had permitted it, but he had regretted it and had asked some of his friends to dissuade her from the long and dangerous journey. She had also herself been anxious—her husband was not old yet—would he remain faithful to her during such a long absence—would she not imperil his soul by leaving him behind alone? In the end she had put aside all mere human considerations and had set out on the great journey to win the forgiveness of her sins, as the Argonauts set out to find the Golden Fleece.

But the Lady Ingeborg was not strong enough to bear so great a responsibility. Day and night she was harassed by the thought of what might be going on at home. Was Sir Niels perhaps making merry with one of the pretty girls at the farm? Or was he making love, perhaps to a frivolous lady at the court? In her distress the Lady Ingeborg turned to Bridget—she who could obtain so much from God was to achieve that Sir Nicolaus stood firm in all temptations. But when the little company of pilgrims reached Milan the Lady Ingeborg was so ill that they could not continue their journey. Bridget asked God for advice —had they to wait in Milan until the Lady Ingeborg grew well or to continue their journey? The answer came and it was that the pilgrimage was not to be broken off, and that the matter would be settled by the death of Lady Ingeborg. And thus indeed it happened. But after the funeral Bridget heard a voice from above say to the devil: 'Thou hast tormented her body but chastened her soul, so that now it belongs to Me.' In Milan the Lady Ingeborg, Laurens' daughter, rests *in pace*.(1)

The little company of pilgrims, lessened by one in number, journeyed on—towards Genoa. In Pavia Bridget had knelt by the tomb of the great Father of the Church, Saint Augustine—the pious king of the Lombards, Luitprand, at some time in the eighth century brought the body of the saint thither from Cagliari in Sardinia (whither it had been brought from Hippo from fear of the Vandals. In the world there are always barbarians of some kind or other to flee from!). In the old cathedral of Pavia with the beautiful name of *San Pietro in Ciel d'Oro* the great Father of the Church rests under the golden sky of mosaics in the chancel. Another of the great Christians of antiquity has found his grave here, the philosopher Boëthius, Theodoric's minister, murdered by the Aryans in the year 524, a martyr of orthodoxy. Bridget would hardly have read his famous book *De consolatione* —but with Dante she knew that he had come from martyrdom to peace with God—*e di martiro venni in questa pace*.(2)

From Pavia the road to Rome then went on to Piacenza, where all the pilgrims 'of the Danish tongue' (practically speaking all Scandinavians) were entitled to spend the night in the hospice founded by Erik Aye-good, and there 'to drink as much wine free as they pleased'(3)—a privilege which the much-drinking Northerners would doubtless appreciate. The road now led them across the Apennines; in Lucca Erik Aye-good had provided for his fellow-countrymen by a similar foundation—moreover they could in the cathedral venerate the wonderful *Volto Santo*, a 'clothed crucifix' (*Cristo velato*), according to the legend the work of none less than Nicodemus. This personality, known to us from the Gospel, was said to have been a wood carver; on his return from the tomb of Christ he had tried to reproduce the features of his dead Master, in a block of wood, but the work did not succeed until an angel finished the image while Nicodemus slept—'a legend,' says Emile Mâle, 'containing the deep meaning that all great art has a heavenly origin.'(4) When the Holy Land was conquered by the Turks the sacred image fled, on a ship without a crew, without sails and oars. It reached the Tuscan coast where the Bishop of Lucca went on board the ship and found the crucifix. The inhabitants of the seaport of Luna made a claim for the image—it was then laid upon a cart drawn by two oxen which had never been yoked to a plough—and with this team the crucifix came to Lucca and found its place under the Romanic arches of the cathedral of San Martino. As only the face of Christ was visible, the cross was named *Volto Santo*, 'the Holy Face' (in French *le Saint Vou*), and it is said that among many other pilgrims Ogier the Dane also visited it and prayed before it.(5) *Il Volto Santo* was known also in the North—in Kliplev near Aabenraa it was venerated under the name of 'Saint Helper.'*

From Lucca the road continued via Altopascio (the church of *Saint Jacques du Haut Pas* in Paris is named after this mountain pass, because it was here the pilgrims received the mark which gave them admission to the travellers' hostel in Altopascio, founded by none less than the Markgravine Mathilde, the pious friend of Gregory VII). By way of Poggibonsi and through the Val d'Elsa (both names are well known to the modern visitor to Italy) the pilgrims reached Siena. In the guide book of the Iceland abbot there is a small note on Siena, which later wanderers in Italy have had no cause to contradict— 'there the women are fairest.'(6) 'Oh, ye fair women of Siena, never shall I forget you,' wrote the French condottiere, Montluc, a century or two later in his memoirs (as female warriors the young Sienese women had fought at his side on the city walls against their common enemy).

From Siena the road to Rome led by way of Radiofani (called by the Icelandic abbot 'the castle of the wicked woman'—whoever this wicked woman may have been) to Bolsena (here that miracle occurred, which Raphael immortalized) and to Montefiascone. The grave of the Augsburg bishop John Fuggers bears the warning inscription: *Propter*

---

* Vol. I, Book II, Ch. XII, *il Volto Santo*.

nimium Est-Est Dominus meus mortuus est—the good bishop here drank himself to death in the sweet wine of the place, Est-Est (but this would probably not deter the pilgrims from having a good taste of the wine—a traveller still likes drinking a fiasco Est-Est). Then at last they came to 'the mount of joy,' *Montjoie,* now Monte Mario, from which there was a view over Rome, and where the pilgrims on their knees prayed to the holy princes of the Apostles, by whose graves they were soon to kneel: *Sancte Petre, Sancte Paule, misericordia!*

Bridget, however, chose another route. From Pavia she took the road to Genoa—she intended to make the rest of the journey by sea. A local tradition maintains that she had stayed in *Quarto*—now *Quarto dei Mille,* because it was from the harbour of this little town that Garibaldi and his thousand men set out to deliver Sicily from the dominion of the Bourbons. That was in 1860—Bridget did not look so far ahead as that! Nor had she any idea that here that man who was later to become her best friend, Alphonsus of Jaen, was to found the Olivetan convent of San Girolamo di Quarto, and in it to close his eyes on 19 September 1388, after many years of faithful work in Bridget's service.

Bridget and her escort were not alone in landing in Ostia. The concourse of pilgrims for the opening of the year of jubilee on Christmas Eve was enormous. Between Christmas and Easter there were at times a million strangers in Rome. From Easter to Whitsuntide the lowest number was 800,000. During the hot summer the stream lessened somewhat, but towards the close of the jubilee year it rose to its original height. These pilgrims were mostly Italians and Germans. France and England were at war, and although Clement VI —perhaps remembering Bridget's admonitions six years earlier— succeeded in getting a truce arranged just for Christmas, it was still some time before the English and French pilgrims could come so far. Besides, the roads were unsafe—the mercenary troops, which had suddenly become unemployed, went in crowds through the countries, attacking and plundering wayfarers.

From Ostia the pilgrims followed the old *Via Ostiense;* on the way they prayed and sang, each in their own tongue, but now and then all voices joined in the common language of the Church. The road led along the Tiber, the yellow Tiber then as now, and the Campagna was the same as that of five hundred years later, with the broken arches of the old aqueducts, with grazing herds of buffaloes and picturesque herdsmen on horseback. (The land reforms of Fascism have done away with most of this decoration, and a good thing too!) At the Cistercian monastery of *Tre Fontane*, where no malarial febrifuge eucalyptus woods had yet been planted, the pilgrims drank of the three springs which had gushed forth where Saint Paul's head when struck off by the executioner's axe had three times touched the ground. And now they were near Rome—at a turn of the Tiber they had the view of the first of the seven pilgrim churches, San Paolo. It had been partially destroyed the year before by the great earthquake, but the *baldachino* rose undamaged above the grave of the apostle, who had never seen the Lord in the days of His flesh, but who had become his most zealous envoy—*Sancte Paule, ora pro nobis!* Where Bridget now prayed, her spiritual leader, Catherine of Siena, was to invoke a few years later *quel dolce Pavolo*. . . .

Then they came to the walls of Rome and Porta San Paolo; to the right of the gate rose, then as now, the pointed tent of the Cestius pyramid, which was later to stand as a protection over many a traveller from Bridget's country (but not of Bridget's faith). And now they were in Rome—walking through the dingy and dirty alleys of the Ghetto, finding their way out to the Tiber, coming to Castel Sant' Angelo—and then they came to the narrow Borgo, full of shops and taverns—until the Piazza San Pietro lay spread bright and open before the company of pilgrims—*Sancte Petre, ora pro nobis!*

It was the mediæval church of Saint Peter that Bridget saw— Raphael painted it in the background of the *Fire in the Borgo*. The pilgrims mounted by a high stairway up to the three portals and so came into the forecourt surrounded by arcades, in the midst of which stood *la Pigna*, the gigantic pine cone of metal which spurted water from all its scales; it had stood once in a heathen temple; here, instead of the *Kantharus* of the ancient basilicas, it served for washing the hands of the faithful. From the forecourt one entered, then as now, into an entrance hall with five doors leading into the church—*Porta del Giudizio* ('the gate of judgment,' through which funeral processions passed), *Porta Trasteverina*, *Porta Regia* (of silver), *Porta Romana*, finally *Porta Guidonia* (for the pilgrims the *Porta Santa* of those days). High up on the façade of the entrance hall could be seen Giotto's mosaic, *la Navicella*, the Ship of the Church in the storm of the world, that Ship under whose burden Catherine of Siena was to sink exhausted to the ground. . . .

The purple curtain before *Porta Giudizia* fell back heavily behind the pilgrims, they stepped into the vast, five-naved basilica with its four times

II 2

five and twenty columns of marble, red granite, green granite. In the middle nave the main walls over the columns were still adorned with mosaics of the time of Constantine; in the distance the azure ground shone in the mosaics of the triumphal arch, and up above, under it, borne by six alabaster columns, rose the gilded silver *baldachino* over Saint Peter's tomb.

The church was thronged with pilgrims—carried by the crowds rather than walking by herself, Bridget advanced over the mosaic floor of Saint Peter's church, against her feet she felt the cold of the stones and the small roughnesses in the mosaic floor. Further and further on she was borne with her Swedish friends—now Master Petrus and the Prior, who were both taller than she, began to speak of the Apostle's grave, which they could glimpse in the distance. Now they read aloud the inscription on the triumphal arch, and translated it for her: 'Because the world, Oh Peter, has under thy guidance ascended victorious to the stars, Constantine has after thy victory dedicated this temple to thee.' Now she saw the inscription herself and read it—now she approached the golden radiant *Confessio*—now she trod on the steps leading down to the crypt—Bridget, Birger's daughter, from Finsta in Uppland, Ulf Gudmarsson's widow from Ulfåsa in East Gothland, knelt at the grave of the Prince of the Apostles. . . .

In the midst of the crowd she prayed a long time, without stirring, until Master Petrus touched her shoulder: 'Lady Bridget, it is time to go and eat.' Bridget obediently went with the others—perhaps to that *Albergo dell' Orso* on the left bank of the Tiber, just opposite Castel Sant' Angelo, where Dante had lodged fifty years earlier. But if she had been allowed by the strict Master to look about her it would not be any joyful sight that would meet her eyes. Cattle were grazing on the open squares, the churches which the Swedish pilgrims passed were lying roofless, the floor overgrown with grass and wild herbs. At one corner they had to retreat before two men who were fighting with knives, and when they came into a narrow street shameless women showed themselves with uncovered breasts at the windows and beckoned to her ecclesiastical escort, although they were wearing priestly clothes. Bridget sighed deeply and exclaimed: 'Alas, Master Petrus—is this Rome?'

And through her soul there was an echo of Jeremiah's Lamentation over Jerusalem:

In times past justice had her seat in this city, and her princes were princes of peace. Now she has become despised, and her princes have become slayers of men. In times past the city was dyed purple with the blood of martyrs and built up on the bones of saints. Now her gates have been thrown down and are lying on the ground, her altars are desolate, her walls without watchmen. Oh, Rome, if thou knewest the day of thy visitation thou wouldst weep and not rejoice. Oh Rome, Rome, be converted and turn to the Lord thy God.(7)

V

'God, who drew thee out of the nest, will care for thee until death.'(1) At this word Bridget had left her fatherland, at this word she had journeyed to Italy and had come to Rome. And whether it was at the *Albergo dell' Orso* or another inn where she and her escort, poor pilgrims that they were, had first sought a lodging, their stay there was not for long. One day a messenger came and said that he was to bring greetings from his master, Cardinal Hugo de Beaufort, and to say that the palace, which he did not use during his sojourn in Avignon, he would be glad to place at the disposal of the Swedish *principessa*. Cardinal de Beaufort was a brother of Clement VI—it must have been imperative to the latter to show Bridget a kindness. He had not forgotten her suggestions for peace between France and England; probably he also knew through Bishop Hemming of Åbo what a person of consequence she was.

Bridget accepted the offer. The Cardinal's palace was situated next to the church of San Lorenzo in Damaso—on that site where now stands the papal *Palazzo della Cancelleria* with its noble Renaissance façade. . . . The church and the palace, as we see them now, are the work of Bramante; in Bridget's time the old basilica was still standing, as when Pope Damasus (hence the name *in Damaso*) had caused it to be built about 370, in honour of his fellow-countryman Saint Laurence. Later the church had been restored by Leo II (795–815) and one may venture to imagine it as a basilica in the style of Santa Maria in Cosmedin or San Marco (by the Palazzo Venezia), richly adorned with mosaics like San Clemente or San Prassede. The palace itself probably appeared like a high and lofty building with substantial doors, as few windows as possible, and a powerful tower in the style of *Torre delle milizie* or *Torre de' Conti*, which are both of the thirteenth century, Rome in the later Middle Ages being a city of towers—as still in our times San Gimignano (*la città delle belle torri*) or the old papal city of Viterbo, where the picturesque San Pellegrino quarter perhaps gives the best idea of mediæval Rome.

Of the nine hundred towers in the papal city about two hundred were church towers which were also towers of defence; three hundred served as watch-towers on the city wall; many were built into the ruins of ancient Rome—in the mausoleums of Hadrian and Augustus, the theatre of Marcellus, Circus Maximus, the monument of Cecilia Metella on the Via Appia.(2) The Rome into which Bridget entered with her escort was like a hedgehog, with all its spines sticking up towards the sky.

And just as irascible as a hedgehog, that hisses and bristles at the least touch. Or rather, like *two* hedgehogs fighting. The two hedgehogs were the two Roman families, the *Orsini* and *Colonna*, who had simply divided Rome between them. The Orsini ruled from Campo de' Fiori to Saint Peter's—the rest belonged to the Colonnas, the Colosseum, the triumphal arches, both Constantine's and that of Titus, everything was changed into fortresses. Between these lay the hills of Rome, full of ruins, copse woods and grazing cattle. Only the hollow from the Capitol to the Vatican was built upon, no one could live on the hills, because the old aqueducts which formerly led water up to them were broken down. The great earthquake in 1348, the year before Bridget came, had further increased the number of ruins, the churches Fuori le mura, the Lateran and Santi Apostoli had partly collapsed, part of the Colosseum also fell. Wherever Bridget came she saw only ruins—the ruins of antiquity, early Christian ruins, ruins of her own time. All this became to her a picture of the ruin that she mourned more than the ruins of ancient Rome, the great ruin called the Holy Catholic Church.

The Swedish pilgrims presumably occupied only part of the big palace of the Cardinal. Master Petrus was the rector of the house, whom Bridget and the other members of the little family—Prior Petrus, however, probably excepted—obeyed in everything. It was he, too, who attended to the material needs, went out marketing and spoke with the workmen when any repairs had to be done in the house. In his eagerness he once fell down from a flat roof and sustained an injury to his leg so that afterwards he was lame. It was Christ Himself who by the lips of Bridget dictated the rule that was to regulate the daily life in the house. This rule of the house, however, did not consist of strict commandments, which had to be kept without murmuring— it was mild in form, the words forbearing with human frailty. 'I advise you to'—*consulo vobis*—was how it began; it was a kind adviser, not a stern and strict lawgiver who spoke. 'I advise you to sleep four hours before midnight and four hours after midnight'—eight hours' sleep. If anyone *can* sleep less then it is his or her spiritual merit, but— health must *not* suffer because of piety! So to bed at eight or nine o'clock, at four or five the person on duty will come and knock at the door: *Venite adoremus*, 'Come, let us adore.'

Then they all assembled in the chapel, each of them in their places, and in his beautiful voice Master Petrus intoned the office of the day: *Deus, in adjutorium meum intende*. 'O God, come to my help.' *Domine, ad adjuvandum me festina*, 'O Lord, make haste to help me,' the response is given by the sweet voices of the Sisters. During four hours in succession this service of hymns of praise, of prayer and intercession continues—*opus divinum* as it is called in the rule of Saint Benedict. In this Bridgettine domestic rule there is no mention of that which in a modern Bridgettine convent (and in convents of the present day altogether) is an absolute matter of course: *the daily Mass and daily Communion*. It only says that four hours are to be spent in saying the Office, 'and to be engaged in other godly deeds and customs and useful occupation, so that no hour may be without fruit.'(3) It seems then, that Communion is left entirely to private initiative; at a later date, in the convent rule, Communion is only prescribed at the great feasts, 'yet those Sisters who feel a particular need thereof may ask the confessor for permission to go to Communion every Sunday.'(4) Nor was there in the Middle Ages always an opportunity to receive Holy Communion daily, as not all priests said Mass every day; Saint Catherine of Siena had actually to importune her confessor to permit it, and that was even one of the most devout priests of the time, Raymond of Capua. No one dared without previous confession to kneel at the Communion rail—they well knew the words about eating and drinking oneself to judgment. At this very day an Italian of the people prefers— in spite of the exhortation of Pius X that if we are not conscious of mortal sin, confession is not required but sorrow and sincere contrition are sufficient preparation for communion—to let the confessor decide whether the soul is in a state of grace or not. . . .

From the chapel the next step in the day leads to the refectory and there is permission to sit at the table for a whole hour (but of course there is merit in not sitting so long. 'Sitting a long while at table' was one of the sins Ulf Gudmarsson had to atone for in Purgatory). The bill of fare was not particularly ascetic—it included soup or cabbage, two kinds of meat dishes or fish dishes ('if more is offered, refrain from it for love of Me,' says Christ). Bread *à discrétion*, likewise drink (at home it was ale, in Rome probably wine, according to Italian custom mixed with water). If any member of the household is not well, or needs a specially nourishing diet, he can have extra food. Three meals a day—in the morning a slight collation, then the midday meal and in the evening supper, which is evidently the chief meal, as with the recreation after it it may last two hours—'then you may have seemly talk with each other and be refreshed thereby, before you go to bed.'(5)

The room in the large cardinal-palace which Bridget came to love most was the chapel on the first floor, with a window looking into the church. From it she could see the high altar, from it she could be present at the Sunday Mass. This room became Bridget's oratory— soon it was to become that cell of work in which, at the dictation of an angel, she wrote down *Sermo Angelicus*. Daily Bridget spent hour after hour there in prayer, her eyes directed at the high altar under the many-coloured mosaic vault of the choir. And in the accustomed way a voice came to her one day from the world beyond—it was none less than the Prince of the Apostles, Peter, by whose tomb she had knelt on her first day in Rome. Peter spoke to Bridget and said:

Oh, my daughter, this city of Rome was in times past a city in which dwelt the warriors of Christ, its streets were strewn as if with gold and silver. But now all its precious sapphires are lying in the mire, and there are but few of its inhabitants who have plucked out the right eye and cut off the right hand.* Toads and vipers build here, and the fishes from my draught are afraid of their poison and dare not lift their heads. Yet shall the fishes still be gathered here, though not so many as in times past, but tasting just as good. And they shall have courage to fight against the toads, and the vipers shall be changed into lions, and the lions shall again be changed and turn into doves sitting on the roof of the house and by the windows. And moreover I tell thee that thou shalt live long enough to see with your eyes my vice-gerent come back to Rome, and thou shalt hear the people cry: Evviva il Papa!(6)

VI

Few other things so outraged Bridget's mighty soul as did scandal— provoking holy anger, relentless like that movement of the hand with which in Michelangelo's fresco in the Sixtine Chapel, Christ plunges the damned into hell—'Depart from Me! I do not know you!'

Bridget was not alone in being scandalized.

He who is ashamed to go begging, does he not deny Christ in the crib of poverty? He who will not ride on a humble ass, but demands that a mettle-

---

* An allusion to the words of Jesus, St. Matth. v, 29-30.

some steed shall be led forth to him, does he not despise his Lord and Master, who made his entry into Jerusalem riding on the foal of an ass? It is time now to return to the apostolic life, when Christians did not strive after obtaining earthly goods, but sold what they possessed and gave the money to the poor. He who would really be the disciple of Christ must not have any other possessions than his lyre.

This might have been said by Bridget—and *she* had a fiddle too, with which she went, playing, through the world.(1) But they are much earlier—they are by the Cistercian, Joachim de Fiore (not of Santa Fiora, as I wrote erroneously in my book about Saint Catherine of Siena—Santa Fiora is a town on Mont' Amiata, Fiore is in Calabria).

And now the question arises—would Bridget know anything about the spiritual movement that had issued from Joachim? On one main point they are agreed that the primary cause of the corruption of the world is a sin of pride—the revolt of Lucifer against God. But are there other similar points?

It was on a morning of Pentecost, one day between the years 1190 and 1195, that a spiritual wind fell upon Abbot Joachim in the monastery in Fiore, high up in the Calabrian Apennines, in the forest-covered mountain country of *la Sila*. 'In the hour when Christ arose from the dead'—that is, at daybreak—he took his Bible in his hand, as his custom was, and opened it at the Apocalypse. The whole of the Middle Ages pondered this mysterious writing, at home in Sweden Bridget had studied it together with Master Matthias. But in the twelfth chapter of the Apocalypse it is said:

> And a great sign appeared in heaven: A woman clothed with the sun, and the moon under her feet, and on her head a crown of twelve stars. And being with child, she cried travailing in birth: and was in pain to be delivered. And there was seen another sign in heaven. And behold a great red dragon, . . . And the dragon stood before the woman who was ready to be delivered: that, when she should be delivered, he might devour her son. And she brought forth a man child, who shall rule nations with an iron rod. And her son was taken up to God and to his throne. And the woman fled into the wilderness, where she had a place prepared by God, that there they should feed her a thousand two hundred and sixty days.*

Now who was this woman in the wilderness, and what is meant by these 1,260 days? To the exegetists of the Middle Ages 'days' in the Bible texts were the same as years—but what, then, do these 1,260 years mean? It was exactly on a Whitsunday morning that Abbot Joachim sat pondering this, and with all his soul he prayed to

* The Revelation of St. John, xii, 1–6.

the Holy Ghost for light. And light was sent to him, in a vision he saw how the work of God for the salvation of mankind is like a drama in three acts, a trilogy, composed by the three Persons in the Holy Trinity. The first act is the *Father's* and comprises the period of the Old Covenant. The second is the *Son's* and it is still going on. The third is the period of the *Holy Ghost*—it is that which is drawing near. The first of these three periods is that of the Jewish Temple, the second is that of the Catholic Church—and in the third the Holy Spirit shall build up a house of God with living stones. There are three steps in the order of salvation—in the first we were under the Law, then under Grace, and now we are to receive Grace above Grace. The first age was that of Science, the second of Wisdom, in the third we shall receive the fullness of knowledge. The first age was the age of bondage, the second of filial obedience, in the third we come to the freedom of the Spirit. The first was the age of Fear, the second is that of Faith, the third of Love. The first is the age of slaves, the second of the free, the third of friends. The first is the age of boys, the second of men, the third of the old. The stars shine upon the first, the rosy dawn upon the second, in the third it is full daylight. The first age belongs to the winter, the second to the spring, the third to the summer. The first brings *Primula veris*, the second roses, the third lilies. The first brings grass, the second corn, the third the ears of corn. The first brings water, the second wine, the third oil. In the ecclesiastical year the first age corresponds to Advent, the second to Lent, the third to Pentecost—to that radiant morning in June when Abbot Joachim had his revelation. . . .

But when is this age of the Holy Spirit to dawn? Joachim finds the answer in the very text he has before him—the woman in the wilderness, who is she, if not the revealed Church? It is not that Abbot Joachim—like other reformers—wishes to break with the Roman Catholic Church; he does not doubt the right of this Church to call itself by that name. For those who live in another age, that is, between the birth of Christ and the coming of the Holy Ghost, the Catholic Church with her hierarchy and her sacraments is an indispensable condition of salvation. Without the slightest hesitation, exactly like Bridget, Joachim accepts the lawfully elected Pope as the Vicegerent of Christ. But he also knows that papacy, hierarchy and sacraments are only valid for the age that is now drawing to its close. For the 1,260 days are to be understood as 1,260 years. Other Bible texts confirm him in this conviction : Judith's widowhood lasted three and a half years of 360 days, that is, 1,260 days. The prophet Elija lived for three and a half years in the wilderness, again the same number. So that from the birth of Christ 1,260 years were to pass before the beginning of the new age—'*jam est in januis*, it is already at the door.' . . .

And if anyone were to ask Joachim whether the Roman hierarchy (like that red dragon in the Apocalypse) would not devour the Church of the newborn spirit, he is full of confidence. 'As the aged Simeon took the child Jesus into his arms,' he says, 'so shall Peter's successor, to whom it is given to distinguish between clean and unclean beasts' (allusion to the Acts of the Apostles, x, 9–14) 'with his authority protect the church of the spirit and establish its rule of life with his word and seal.'(2)

Joachim fell asleep without having seen the dawn of the new age. In the lonely convent of Pietralata, high up in the wildest and most lonely Abruzzi, where the religiosity of Italy has always flowered most richly, he closed his eyes for ever in 1202. In the same year a young dreamer and enthusiast sat in a prison in Perugia, who was later to say of himself that he was the herald of a great king. When a few years later he put off his worldly clothes it was a corner of the Calabrian prophet's mantle that he cast about his shoulders. And if something jingled under the mantle, it was not a purse with gold and silver (the robbers on Monte Subasio found nothing they could take from him), but it was Joachim di Fiore's zither, with which God's fiddler was to go out into the world. . . .

'The true men of the spirit'—Joachim had said—'are not to have a pleasant nest like the sparrows under the peasant's roof, but they are to live in the clefts of the mountains, in rock caves, where there is a cold draught and the water drips from the wet stone walls.' It was just like this that the disciples of Francis of Assisi lived, who remained faithful to the Master—such was the manner of life of the strict Franciscans, the *Spirituals*, in Carceri, in Greccio, Fonte Colombo, Poggio Bustone. And in these small mountain convents and hermitages the writings of Joachim di Fiore were read—read aloud by the fire in the evening, in the light shed by a single oil lamp, while the wind roared outside, and Brother Wolf slunk howling about the convent, or Brother Robber knocked at the gate and was admitted. . . .

Saint Francis had himself told the great Innocent about the poor but beautiful women in the wilderness, who bore children to the king, and the children came and presented themselves to their father, and he opened his arms and received them well: 'Strangers eat here at my

table, how much more, then, you who are my own legitimate sons.'
And the king sent a message to the woman in the wilderness that she
was to send all her sons to him.(3)

Then at last that year came which Abbot Joachim had foretold.
The year 1260 came as all other years had come. But no millennium
was revealed, Simeon did not take the Child into his arms, the king did
not bid the woman in the wilderness and her sons to his table. That
struggle between the Spirituals and the papal chair began which
found its extreme expression in the writings of the Franciscan, Pierre
Jean Olivi, in which the Catholic Church, such as it had developed in
this, the latest years of the *second* period, was simply declared to be the
'great harlot' of the Apocalypse, 'Satan's church,' 'the temple of
Antichrist.' John XXII, who was the Pope, answered by a bull of
12 November 1323, in which a number of passages in Olivi were
condemned as heretical. When the General of the Franciscan Order
took Olivi's part he was called to Avignon and was there thrown into
prison; he succeeded in escaping and took refuge with King Ludwig
of Bavaria.

Henceforth the religious strife becomes a political fight. Ludwig
is excommunicated, defies the bull of excommunication, goes with a
great army across the Alps to be crowned as a Roman emperor.
Wherever he advances, the Franciscans of Olivi's school go with him,
the churches, which were kept closed by the local clergy faithful to the
Pope, were opened by force, and from all pulpits thunderbolts were
hurled against Antichrist in Avignon. On 17 January 1328 the excommunicated king was crowned Roman emperor in Saint Peter's church;
Sciarra Colonna, the same who twenty-five years earlier had laid
hands on the person of Bonifacius VIII, in the name of the Roman
people places the crown on the scion of the house of Wittelsbach.
Then one day in April of the same year the great bell of the Capitol
called the Roman people to parliament. The emperor sat on his throne,
at his side *gli Anziani*, the oldest citizens, a kind of Senate. And now
a solemn complaint was laid against Pope John. He had proved to be
Antichrist by contending with the Spirituals and their doctrine of
evangelic poverty. He had neglected the duties of his office by not
coming to Rome and taking his seat on the Chair of Peter. 'The priest
Jacques from Cahors, who had taken the name of John XXII' was
therefore unanimously declared to be deposed.(4)

John XXII continued being Pope, also after the year 1328; he did
not die until 1334. True, the anti-pope who had been elected at the

Capitol, a pious hermit, who took the name of Nicholas V, crowned Ludwig emperor (once more!). But the German army soon had to retreat, and the simple-hearted Pope Nicholas had to walk as a penitent pilgrim to Avignon to beg for forgiveness. The dream of Joachim and the Franciscan Spirituals of a Church of the Spirit seems finally to have failed. But in the crowd of people on that day in April 1328 thronging about the statue of Marcus Aurelius (of the Emperor Constantine, it was believed) there was a boy of fourteen called Niccolà di Lorenzo —the later *Cola di Rienzo*. It was to fall to his lot to make a last attempt to create a kingdom of the Holy Spirit. And Bridget was to see how it perished.

VII

Cola di Rienzo—abbreviation of Niccolà di Lorenzo (Niels Laurenson) —was born in 1313, in the same year as Boccaccio and ten years later than Bridget. His father had a small sailors' tavern by the Tiber, but the profits were not big, so that his mother had to go out doing washing for people. She died early and Lorenzo then sent the boy to relations of his in Anagni (the summer residence of Bonifacius). In this little mountain town—about 1,400 feet above the sea—Niccolà grew up. The inhabitants of Anagni had not forgotten (and if they were to forget it, Dante's verse in the Divine Comedy was there to remind them of it), how 'the envoy of the French lily, Nogaret, on the eve of Our Lady's feast in September, in conspiracy with Sciarra Colonna, had laid hands on the old Pope and struck the Vicegerent of Christ in the face.' From that day a curse seemed to rest upon Anagni. The successor of Boniface VIII to the Chair of Peter had cried woe upon that town, whose inhabitants had been capable of allowing so great a crime to happen—'Woe upon thee, Anagni! Neither dew nor rain shall from henceforth fall upon thee, the clouds shall pass thee by, and from now on the rain shall fall upon other hills!' And when Bonifacius died, only a month after the outrage, the papal court left, and the tradespeople of the town, hitherto purveyors to the papal court, lost their main source of income.

But with its numerous religious houses Anagni was still a centre of culture, and Cola di Rienzo, who quickly gave evidence of being highly gifted, received, during the ten years or so that he lived in the town, the best education of the time. And in the fourteenth century that meant, above all, one thing—he became a perfect Latin scholar, a humanist who could be classed with Petrarch.

This is not the place to recount the fantastic story of Cola di
Rienzo. But Bridget must have heard her friends in Rome speaking
about him. By force of his great oratorical gifts alone this son of an
innkeeper acquired political influence; he called himself 'the advocate
of the widows, the fatherless and the poor'—this indicates sufficiently on which side he stood. The Colonnas, the Orsini and the rest
of the noble gentlemen had no more dangerous enemy than this young
tribune of the people. Bridget nowhere mentions Cola—either for
good or ill. But the mistress of Ulfåsa, in whose veins flowed the bluest
blood of Sweden, cannot have taken much interest in this son of a
tavern keeper.

And yet he was to become her collaborator, indeed prepare the
way for her. In the year 1341 Petrarch had come to Rome to be crowned
poet laureate on the Capitol; Cola, who was as yet only one of those
upon whom the upper classes looked with disfavour, who gave legal
help free, had therefore no means of approaching the great poet. But
in 1342 a democratic revolution broke out in the city on the Tiber,
the nobles were deposed from power and Cola was sent to Avignon to
plead the cause of the new government with the Pope. John XXII had
died in 1334—his successor, Benedict XII, followed him to the grave
a few years after—and since then the Chair of Peter had been occupied
by Roger de Beaufort, who had taken the name of Clement VI. By
this nobleman of an old family, and scholarly humanist, Cola was now
received as the envoy of Rome, and by his classical Latin and his poet's
eloquence he awoke the Pope's interest and goodwill. The young
Italian described, as Bridget was to do later, the abomination of desolation in the Eternal City, concluding with a pathetic appeal to the
Vicegerent of Peter: 'Rome sits like a sorrowing widow longing for
her bridegroom.' Finally Cola begged the Pope that a year of jubilee
might be proclaimed in the year 1350, and this was readily granted by
Clement. As to a return to Rome, the Pope was more careful—true,
he could think of it, but for the present there was this war between
France and England—at the moment he could not very well leave
Avignon.

Clement was pleased with the frank and eloquent young man, and
so was Petrarch, whom he now approached, and when Cola at length
left the city on the Rhone, it was with an appointment in his pocket as
papal notary in Rome (monthly salary five gold florins). He now had a
position and could work for his cause—and his cause was neither more
nor less than the creation of that *kingdom of the Holy Spirit*, which had

formerly been purely religious, but which Cola carried over into the sphere of politics. He quietly prepared a *coup d'état* which was not to be carried out 'by force or strength, but solely by the spirit of God.' Again came the dawn of Pentecost, 29 May 1347; Cola and his adherents spent the night before it in the little church of Sant' Angelo in Peschiera (perhaps chosen in defiance, as it belonged to the Colonnas). Cola had ordered thirty Masses in honour of the Holy Ghost—at all the altars in the little church could be heard incessantly the little Mass bells, and the priest read the sequence of the feast, the *Veni sancte Spiritus* of Innocent III. Not one of the Latin words escaped Cola, they re-echoed in his heart and could be heard from his lips: *Veni, pater pauperum*, 'oh come, thou Father of the poor'—*lava quod est sordidum*, 'wash the sinful stains away from the majestic countenance of Rome'—*flecte quod est rigidum*, 'humble the stiff and proud neck of the nobility'—*rege quod est devium*, 'lead us from our own wild path by the royal road to heaven'—*da perenne gaudium*, 'grant us everlasting joy!' With this prayer in his soul Cola di Rienzo went to Holy Communion—and after Communion a procession was formed outside the church. By Cola's side rode the papal Vicegerent, Bishop Raimundo of Orvieto, over his head waved the banner of Saint Peter with the two crossed keys. Twenty-five armed men formed Cola's bodyguard, one hundred young horsemen in armour completed the train. Without meeting any hindrance the procession reached the Capitol, and there Cola stood forth and spoke to the assembled Romans. The young tribune of the people stood there, in the sunshine of Pentecost, bareheaded and unarmed, and proclaimed in enthusiastic language the great tidings that now the kingdom of justice had come. The people acclaimed him with joy, and when one of the doves of the Capitol, frightened by the noise, hovered for a moment above the head of the speaker, everyone was seized with a trembling—*Ecco lo Spirito Santo!* 'It is the Holy Spirit!'

Cola had at one stroke become absolute master of Rome—and had done this without shedding one drop of blood. During the short time his dictatorship lasted he introduced great reforms. An account only ten years later says:

> The forests rejoiced, for they had been cleared of robbers, the peasant could plough his field in peace, pilgrims went to the shrines of pilgrimage without being molested and plundered, merchants could leave their wares in the street overnight and find them again next morning. All good people rejoiced, but the tyrants were seized with fear and trembling [*i.e.*, the nobles].

A great spiritual rebirth passed over Rome. Like Mussolini six hundred years later, Cola issued draconian prohibitions against swearing and indecent talk (*turpiloquio*). Adultery and concubinage were severely punished. The greatest scourge of the time, the everlasting family quarrels, were dealt with by the tribune of the people by the establishment of a court of a kind hitherto unknown, a court of the people in which no jurists or great gentlemen had a seat, but only worthy citizens. The task of this court was not to accuse or judge, but solely to *make peace* between contending parties—a court of arbitration. So great was the faith that the kingdom of the Holy Spirit, of the spirit of love, was now to prevail, that during the short period of Cola's government no fewer than eighteen hundred mortal enemies became reconciled.(1)

When Bridget came to Rome Cola's kingdom of justice had long since perished—he had himself transgressed its laws. From the Capitol there are but few steps to the Tarpeian Rock. Instead of the white dove of Pentecost an owl sat hooting in the November evening outside the window of the tribune of the people. He ordered his servant to drive it away, but it persisted in coming back. The modern Italian also looks upon the night-owl, *la Civetta*, as a bird of ill omen, that gives warning of disaster with its shriek. Only a few months after the triumphal procession on a morning in May, the nobility were again masters of Rome. The Pope dropped Cola, Petrarch broke off his friendship with him, and one black day in December 1347, the cry went through the streets of Rome: 'Death to the Tribune!'(2)

Like most of those who possess great gifts of oratory, Cola di Rienzo was not a hero. Deserted by everyone, he knew of no other means than flight—first to Castel Sant' Angelo, afterwards to Civita Vecchia, finally to Naples, where he intended to seek the protection of Queen Giovanna. Here he was met by the plague, and again he fled, this time to those mountains to which so many a homeless wanderer (above all of them Dante), like the Psalmist, had lifted up his eyes—'for thence cometh my help' (Ps. CXX, 1). One day the poet who had written *La Divina Commedia* stood outside the gate of the monastery of Fonte Avellana, and when the Brother at the gate asked him: 'What are you seeking?' he answered in a single word *Pace*, 'Peace!' Cola turned his steps to the hermits on Monte Majella in the Abruzzi, to that monastery from whose solitude the pope of the Spirituals, Celestino V, had come forth, and to which he had returned after having resigned the tiara. (Dante could not forgive him this *gran rifuto*

—why had he not stayed at his post at the helm of the Church, why had he not, the disciple of Joachim di Fiore, staked his life to prepare the way for the coming of the Holy Ghost?) The strict Franciscans lived up there in the wild and desolate mountains; in the monastery, which consisted mostly of rock caves, they tried to realize Francis of Assisi's programme in all its original austerity. Even at midsummer you can still see, from Sulmona, the snow lighten the summit of Monte Majella. Life up there in the monastery was hard, food was scarce, nothing but the herbs growing in the garden, and the fruit that might be found growing wild in the woods; money was never touched by *i fraticelli*, as people called them, they could therefore not go down to the villages in the valley to buy bread. It was not the temperate asceticism of a Benedictine monastery that was the rule up here on Monte Majella—it was a continual fast, cutting through bone and marrow like the north wind. True, Cola di Rienzo did not come to seek admission to the Order, but even as a guest, and an esteemed guest, he lived the same austere life as the Brothers. He persevered in it for nearly two years, those years when the Black Death passed like the punishment of God over the worldliness of the world. Among the hermits Cola had in particular become intimate with a certain Brother Angelo, who had come thither from Etna, and who was therefore called *di Monte Volcano*. This Sicilian hermit led Cola still deeper into the thoughts of Joachim and the Franciscan Spirituals, and inspired him to write that series of 'spiritual letters' which he issued later during his sojourn in Prague. In these writings Cola openly proclaims the downfall of Avignon and the Church of the Popes: 'the times have grown old and grey in sin—love is dead—the Church that was once the house of the Holy Spirit has become a Babel—never has the Church gone more astray than now, never has the path of love been so deserted, never before has vice prevailed as now.' In this conviction Cola was confirmed by reading a book which Brother Angelo put into his hands, a book containing 'a prophecy written in heaven,' called *Cyril's Oracle*. According to this the third General of the Carmelite Order, Cyril of Constantinople (*d.* 1224), had received from an angel two tables of silver, on which were written in Greek a prophecy of the things that were to come. This prophecy was believed to have been translated into Latin by Joachim di Fiore, and to have been provided with a commentary. In reality neither Cyril nor Joachim had had anything to do with the book. The 'Oracle' was one of those numerous mystical-prophetic writings of which there were so many in those centuries. Cola, however, sucked up the book as a calf drinks milk—in a letter he writes: 'I would not have believed so easily that Cyril's prophecies had come down from heaven, and that God Himself had been their author, if I had not in Avignon seen with my own eyes the Pope and his whole court and been witness to their corruption.' (3)

Here the worthy Cola seems quite to have forgotten how well he had been received in Avignon a few years earlier, and that it was really the nomination to papal notary to which he owed everything. An infinitely higher title now stood shining before him—Cyril's *Oracle* speaks of a Saviour who is soon to come, and who is designated as the *Sun*. Like the real sun he was to pass through a zodiac of enemies —lion, bull, crab, scorpion. Cola now began to apply all this astrology to himself, and Brother Angelo confirmed him in it (Cola was later to accuse him of it). Had he not had many enemies to fight against, the Colonnas, the Orsinis and other beasts of prey of the nobility? Was he not living as though in a nocturnal darkness? But the sun would conquer in the end—Cola would come out radiantly from his hiding-place when the hour had come. . . .

In June 1350 he left Monte Majella to go to Rome and to gain the jubilee indulgence which he had himself effected with Clement VI.

VIII

The first church in Rome is that which was originally called the basilica of the Saviour and is now generally called San Giovanni in Laterano; it was built by the Emperor Constantine in a wing of his palace. It was consecrated by Pope Silvester and dedicated to Our Saviour Jesus Christ and to John the Baptist and Saint John the Evangelist, and it is said that Pope Silvester and after him Pope Gregory granted so many indulgences to those who devoutly visit this church, and no one but God alone knows how many they are. But in the church there is a very old inscription, on which it is written that at the high altar there is an indulgence of forty-eight years and forgiveness for a third of all one's sins. For when the Emperor Constantine had been baptized, and in baptism had been cleansed from his leprosy, he said to Pope Silvester: 'Father, behold I will build a church in my house— do thou bless it and with it all who come into it.' And Saint Silvester said to him: 'Our Lord Jesus Christ, who has healed you of your leprosy and cleansed you in holy baptism, heal and cleanse all those who come hither from all their sins—at whatever season of the year they may come.' And Pope Gregory dedicated this church anew, after the heretics had destroyed it, and he confirmed all that Pope Silvester had resolved. And when Pope Silvester dedicated this church the first time, a picture of the Saviour appeared on the wall, and all the people saw it, and the church was twice burnt down, but the picture remained on the wall and was not burnt. Here there is forgiveness for all sins, and the same is true of the baptistry, and in the chapel called Sancta Sanctorum, but into that women may not enter. If people knew how much indulgence there is in the Lateran church, no one would need to travel beyond the sea to the Holy Sepulchre.(1)

It is an old pilgrim guide that contains this information—very different from what is to be found in a modern Baedeker. After the Lateran comes Saint Peter's—here the praying pilgrim can again obtain an indulgence of forty-eight years and forgiveness of a third of his sins. He is absolved from the last third in San Paolo fuori le mura —and then, if he likes, he can continue his wandering to all the other old churches in Rome—for spiritual benefits are to be found in all of them. This applies in particular to the seven pilgrimage churches: Saint Peter's, Saint Paul's, Saint Mary Major, the Lateran church, Santa Croce, San Lorenzo outside the gates and Saint Sebastian on the Appian Way. The pilgrims walk from one of these seven churches to the other by a road called *Via delle sette chiese*; in the twentieth century it is still those to which the jubilee indulgence is attached.

In order to avoid certain associations of ideas I ought perhaps to have omitted the use of the Danish word 'Aflad,' or leaving off, which is almost an improper word in Northern Europe. The Latin term *Indulgentia* is perhaps rather better—it means forbearance. God bears with His children, when they try, as well as they can, to make reparation for what they have done wrong. The book spoken of in *Dies irae* —*liber scriptus proferetur*—is a pass-book between God and man—so much on the debit side, so much on the credit side. A child who has grieved his mother tries to make up for it by being willing to serve and help her—'you must not carry all that wood into the shed—I will fetch it.' A harsh word, a moment's disobedience, is counterbalanced by a willingness to serve, and the reward is a caress and a kiss. 'Of course I knew that you are my own good boy.' The transgression is not only forgiven, it is also blotted out—the mother does not think any more of what the child has done to displease her—'let us forget it!' In this way God also forgives—and forgets the bad for the good. 'There, we will not think about it any more—I can see that you want to please me.' This is God's forbearance, and our so-called 'good works' are in fact nothing but the works of children. When God is satisfied with them and is not angry any more and not using the rod—well then, the indulgence has been gained.

It is of course a foregone conclusion that he who wants to gain the indulgence *is* a child of God—even though a disobedient one, that is, that he is in the grace of baptism, or, if he has lost it, that he has regained it by a contrite confession. The strict calculations of the old pilgrim guide must be understood from the penitential rules of the early Christian Church—an indulgence of forty-eight years means a penitence carried on throughout forty-eight years, to which the pilgrimage is an equivalent. It would seem to be doubtful whether the forgiveness of sins is distributed in portions of thirds, and yet the thought underlying it is right—one must make oneself worthy of the friendship of God, and be thankful too if one can gain it little by little. How much more then, must one not rejoice when one reads, as in the chapel *Sancta Sanctorum*—'Here is pardon for all sins and forgiveness for all punishments'—*Indulgentia plenaria a peccato et poena*. A plenary indulgence like this had been gained by Saint Francis of Assisi for the Portiuncula chapel—and it was Bridget's desire to obtain such a plenary indulgence for the convent church in Vadstena. . . .

For the present, however, she had to be content with obtaining an indulgence for herself in the seven Roman pilgrimage churches. She had a special predilection for San Lorenzo fuori le mura—for Saint Laurence was no stranger to her, the cathedral in Lund was dedicated to him, as also the parish church at home in Linköping, Saint Lars. She had read about him in the book of legends, she knew that he had not been a priest but a deacon, archdeacon under the martyr pope, Saint Sixtus, who before his death had bidden him distribute the gold and silver to the poor, which the pious Emperor Philip had given to the Church.* After Pope Sixtus had been killed Laurence was seized and imprisoned. He was ordered either to deliver up the gold and silver or to sacrifice to the gods. As he would not do either one or the other he was subjected to various tortures, but he did not give way.

Then Decius commanded an iron bed to be brought up, and Laurence was told to lie down and rest. Laurence was undressed at once and laid upon this gridiron, and a fire was kindled under it, and above him the executioners tortured him with iron forks. Then Laurence said to the chief of the executioners: 'Know this, that this fire will bring me coolness, but to you it will bring an everlasting fire. For I confess Jesus Christ and do not deny Him, and while I am being roasted I give thanks to God and praise Him.' He spoke also to Decius, gently and smilingly: 'You poor man, now you have roasted one side of me. Now turn the meat and eat that which is roasted enough! But I give thanks to Thee, oh God, for making me worthy to enter

---

* The Emperor Philip, called the Arab, was a Christian. He reigned from 244 to 249 and was succeeded by the Emperor Decius, notorious for his persecution of the Christians.

through Thy gates!' And while thus speaking he gave up his spirit to God.(2)

Another legend has it that when the heathen judge pressed Laurence hard to tell him where he preserved the gold and silver of the Church, he brought a crowd of poor people before him, stretched out his hand over them and said: 'Behold here the treasures of the Church. Christ has no better wealth than these, in whom He is Himself present. For it is written: *I* was hungry, and you gave Me to eat; *I* was thirsty, and you gave Me to drink.' After that Laurence was taken to the place of martyrdom.

In the church of San Lorenzo, which Bridget was soon to frequent, she was shown the place where the gridiron had stood, and where the fire was kindled. A piece of the gridiron has been preserved in the church of San Lorenzo in Lucina. The martyr was buried by a Christian lady named Cyriaca at her country residence *in agro verano* outside the Tiburtine Gate, on the road to Tivoli. Soon a subterranean cemetery was formed round the martyr's grave and Constantine built a basilica over the catacomb which had thus been formed. Close up to the rear of this basilica, apse against apse, another church was built in the fifth century, dedicated to the Blessed Virgin, and in the year 1220 Pope Honorius joined these two churches into one, so that the basilica of Constantine became the chancel of the church, and the martyr's grave came to lie before it. In this form the church stood in Bridget's time, and stands so still; *San Lorenzo fuori le mura*, as it is called, with its mosaics of the sixth century, its ambonas and its inlaid marble floor of the thirteenth century, is one of the most beautiful churches in Rome. It gained a further value for pilgrims when Pope Pelagius II in the year 578 entombed the body of the protomartyr Saint Stephen in the same sarcophagus as Saint Laurence. They were both deacons; according to the legend they were believed to be cousins and both came from Spain—Pope Sixtus had brought them with him to Rome.

Saint Laurence and his colleague Saint Stephen kept watch by the road to Tibur. Other roads of pagan Rome were also occupied by Christian guard-posts. At the Via Ostiense the great apostle of the Gentiles stood at his post, leaning upon the sword with which he had been beheaded (as a Roman citizen he had a right to this form of execution). At the Via Appia it was the Christian soldier, Saint Sebastian. At Via Nomentana stood the church which the Emperor Constantine's daughter Constantia had built over the grave of Saint Agnes.

At home in Sweden this saint was well known to Bridget. She knew that Agnes, in the first loveliness of youth, only thirteen years old, had been asked in marriage by a Roman youth, the son of the Proconsul Simphorinus. It was during the persecution of the Emperor Valerian, in the middle of the third century. Agnes refused to accept the offer, although the suitor 'gathered all the precious jewels to be found in Rome, and sent them to her, and he offered her riches, house and land and all the good things of the world, to make her take him for her husband.' The young man was deeply grieved by her refusal, 'he was so filled with sorrow that he took to his bed. But when his father heard that his son was ill because of her, he sent a messenger to her and repeated his son's request.' Agnes now lets him know that she has given her troth to another and will not fail her betrothed, who is Christ. Then Simphorinus said: 'Choose one of two things—either to sacrifice to my gods, or to be led to a house of harlots and there in uncleanness to lose thy maidenhood, so that Christian men will despise thee.' But Agnes refused to sacrifice. Then they took her and unclothed her and led her to the unclean house, and made their servants scream and shout these words: 'the maid Agnes, who has denied the gods, shall be led to the house of unclean women.' But when she was unclothed her hair grew so much that it clothed her in far greater beauty than the fairest raiment. When she came into the unclean house the angel of God stood there waiting for her, and shone about her with so bright a light that no man could see her for the shining light. And the more a man desired her, the weaker grew his eyes, because she was so bright. And when she knelt down and said her prayers a white garment appeared before her, and in this she clothed herself and said: 'Lord Jesus Christ, I give Thee great thanks, that Thou hast counted me among Thy handmaids and hast clothed me.' The same garment was so white and fair that no one knew but that it had been made by the hands of angels.

But the son of Simphorinus came with his companions to the house where she was, and thought he could have his will with her. But before he could lay his hand upon her he fell down, as dead as a stone. When his companions saw that he tarried there so long, one of them went in and found him dead, and began to shout: 'Noble Romans, this witch with her evil wiles has killed the Proconsul's son.'

Agnes is now sentenced to be burnt at the stake, but 'the fire divided into two flames, and the fire burnt on both sides the people standing about it, and hurt her neither little nor much. Then the pagan judge took a sword and severed her throat, and thus Our Lord dedicated to Himself a martyr and a bride. Her parents did not mourn, but with great joy they took her body and buried it by a road called Nomentana. And when Saint Agnes' parents prayed by her grave at night they saw at midnight a great company of virgins, all clothed in raiment of gold tissue, and walking in a great light. Among them was Saint Agnes, and upon her right hand was a lamb as white as snow. When they had seen this they were seized with great dread, but Saint Agnes bade the maidens wait while she spoke with her parents. Then she said to them: "Rejoice and be glad with me, because I have received my reward in heaven with those whom ye see, of Him whom I loved with all my soul when I was here upon the earth." And when she had said this she was gone from their sight. And this vision was revealed by them who saw it. But I, Ambrose, the servant of God, could not suffer that this should not be put into writing, and in her honour who was so dear a martyr, I have written of her deeds.'(3)

The punishment to which the heathen proconsul sentenced Agnes is not an invention of the author of the legend (whether this was Saint Ambrose or another). Tertullian had already said, with a play upon words: *ad lenonem demnando christianam potius quam ad leonem*, 'the Christian virgin is oftener thrown to the pander than to the lion.'

Not far from where Bridget lived, on the present Piazza Navona, there is a church dedicated to Saint Agnes—it is said to have been built where the ill-famed house stood. In the *Acta Sanctorum* it is said that the house stood *juxta theatrum*, 'beside the theatre,' which may have meant the circus of Domitian, the site of which is exactly occupied by the Piazza Navona, and whose oblong shape is still reproduced by the modern piazza. Houses of ill-fame and wine-shops formed natural surroundings for the race-courses and theatres.

As the legend says, the body of Saint Agnes was buried 'beside the road called Nomentana.' It was either because her parents had a property there, somewhat further than the present Porta Pia, or there was already a Christian catacomb in the place. This cemetery, however, did not become of importance until Agnes was buried there, especially after her foster-sister Emerentiana suffered martyrdom there, being killed while praying at her grave. The pagans took Emerentiana's life by stoning her from above through the holes admitting light in the crypt. The two young girl saints now rest together in the basilica built by Constantine's daughter, Constantia, and next to which she had a church built as a mortuary chapel (Saint Costanza, famous for the mosaics in the vault; the connoisseur Schück says of them that there is 'a freshness about them hardly to be equalled by the pagan paintings of the same period, those of the third century').

It is not only art historians and archæologists who in our own times visit the two old churches outside Porta Pia. Every year on 21 January, on the feast of Saint Agnes, her semi-subterranean basilica is filled to overflowing. For on that day two lambs are blessed during Mass, two tiny lambs, from whose wool are to be woven the palliums (shoulder bands) which the Pope sends to the archbishops as a sign of their dignity. The lambs are dedicated here in Saint Agnes' church, because the saint's name recalls the Latin word *agnus* (lamb) and because her purity and piety was like that of a lamb without blemish. The two lambs are then entrusted to the nuns in a convent in Trastevere; they have the task of tending them until they are ready for shearing. Then the palliums are woven, again by virgins dedicated to the cloister, and when they are finished they are taken to Saint Peter's, where, on the eve of the feast of Saints Peter and Paul (29 June) they are laid on Saint Peter's tomb and left there overnight. They are then sent to all the Catholic archbishops all over the world as a symbol of the spiritual bonds by which they are connected with Rome, with Saint Peter's tomb and the Chair of Peter. . . .

All the year round Saint Agnes' basilica lies rather deserted. But on the feast day it is filled with dense crowds. Its marble floor is strewn with twigs of boxwood, green garlands are hung about the marble balusters of the high altar, and the Mass is sung by a bishop. In the closely packed crowd about the high altar can be heard all the tongues in the world, even Danish and Swedish. And there is an immense crowding up and stretching of necks when the two lambs, snowy white and newly washed, with pretty little pink muzzles, and all four legs tied with rose-coloured silk ribbons, are carried up to the altar in two flat baskets towards the end of Mass. They are placed before the bishop, one on either side of him, they lie quite still in their baskets, perhaps they lift their heads a little to snatch at the flowers on the altar. But they do not utter a sound, not even when they are sprinkled with holy water and the cloud of sweet-smelling incense waves about them—though yes, perhaps one of them sneezes, a dainty little sneeze, which makes the English Misses exclaim: 'Oh, how lovely, aren't they dears?'

Then the lambs are carried away, the Mass is finished, the candles are put out, little by little the church is emptied. Only a single pilgrim remains, sits and falls into meditation, as he looks up at the mosaics in the arches of the chancel. Down from the cloud the hand of God is stretched to bestow the crown of martyrdom upon Saint Agnes; on her left stands Pope Symmachus, on her right Pope Honorius, who on his hand holds the basilica rebuilt by him, and offers it to the saint (as in Denmark it is offered up in Fienneslev church by Asger Rig and the Lady Inge).*

And if the pilgrim has come from the North, it makes him think of Saint Bridget, for this church is one of those to which she made the most frequent pilgrim visits.

IX

Easter came early that year, on 28 March. Lent began in February, Ash Wednesday fell on the 11th.

With the season of Lent the pilgrimages to the *stations* of the Roman churches began. In the Middle Ages a certain church was appointed for each day in Lent, and to this the whole of the Roman clergy proceeded in solemn procession to celebrate the liturgy together. The names of the churches are to be found in the Roman Missal. In our own times this custom is still observed. On the day of the station the church in question is adorned as though for a feast, the pillars are draped in crimson, the mosaic is strewn with boxwood, and the bitter scent of the crushed leaves blends with the sweet fragrance of the incense from the altar, where the candles burn in bright golden flames during the singing of Mass.

Bridget and her household would make these pilgrimages. They begin on Ash Wednesday, when the pilgrims go to Santa Maria in Cosmedin down by the temple of Vesta, and then up the Aventine to Santa Sabina. In Rome Santa Sabina is the mother church of the Dominicans. In the adjoining convent is shown the cell in which, as an inscription says, 'the holy men, Dominic, Francis and Angelus the Carmelite, spent the nights in talk about the things that belong to the kingdom of God.' Francis was Bridget's spiritual father, she wore about her body, tightly drawn, the cord of the Third Order with the three knots.(1) At home in Skara Brother Algot would tell her about Saint Dominic, she would also have heard about him when she was in Spain. Later she

* Symmachus was pope from 498 to 514, Honorius I from 625 to 640. Saint Agnes suffered martyrdom in 304, therefore not, as the legend would have it, under Valerian, but under Diocletian.

was to get many Spanish friends, and a Spaniard, Alphonsus of Jaen, became her last spiritual director. Out in the convent garden she had stood before the orange tree which Dominic himself had planted—a good tree bears good fruit. . . .

Every day in the long fast took the pilgrims from the North to new holy places. They would go to San Giorgio *in Velabro*, 'in the swamp, down by *Forum boarium*—and Bridget would pray to Saint George, the patron saint and ideal of all Christian knights.(2) On another day the goal of the pious wandering would be San Gregorio Magno, where the ancestral home of the great pope once stood, and you see the dining-hall where Gregory daily fed twelve poor people. Twelve crosses, hewn in the marble of the table top, denote the twelve places. One day a thirteenth came, and this unbidden guest was also given food. But when the stranger had received his food from the hand of the gentle pope, he got wings and became an angel. . . . Bridget knew this; she also knew that the great pope had prayed for the pagan emperor Trajan and had saved him from hell; there was a soul whose eternal salvation caused Bridget great anxiety—she prayed for him here as Gregory had prayed for Trajan.(3) . . . On another day Bridget and her companion, who on that occasion was her chaplain Petrus Olai, found a poor woman lying outside the church of Santa Prassede, where that pillar is preserved to which Christ was bound during the scourging. The pillar is low, for the technique of the scourging required the delinquent to stand with a bent back. Most artistic representations are incorrect in letting Christ stand erect, with His back to the pillar. Blows struck better and smarted more when they swept down over the back and across the chest, out of whose muscles the fine iron hooks of the scourge tore small pieces. The woman lying in front of Santa Prassede turned out to be from Norway—in the process of canonization she is given the not very Norwegian name of *Junon* or *Juron*, whatever it may actually have been. With her usual energy Bridget took hold of the Norwegian woman and wanted to carry her to the hospital of Saint Anthony near by, and Magnus Petri had to help her. At the hospital it turned out that 'Junon' or 'Juron' suffered from the falling sickness; Bridget paid for her to stay there, and when she was better took her into her house.(4). Something always happened to Bridget on these pious morning walks. On another day there was as usual a crowd of beggars standing before the Lateran, and Bridget distributed, also as usual, her soldi to the whining multitude. One of the beggars was holding a little boy by the hand and complaining more than the others: *Un soldino, Signora, per queste povero figliuolo!* Bridget looked keenly at the two—the boy was Jewish! 'That is not your son,' she said to the pretended father, 'You have stolen him to arouse people's compassion when you beg!' In this way the Jewish boy was taken from the enterprising beggar, and Bridget saw to it that he was baptized.(5)

It is no wonder that in Rome there were those who already saw the saint's halo shining about Bridget's head. A pious hermit, John of Pornacio, from Lombardy, then living in Todi, often met her on her pilgrim walks, and one evening—he was on his way from the church of San Giuliano to Santa Croce—he saw her coming, and her face shone so brightly that the light dazzled him, and he had to turn his eyes away. Another time he met Bridget and her little flock near the Colosseum—the others walked with their feet firmly on the ground, but Bridget—she floated—'like a ship borne up by the waves.' . . .(6)

In the same way John of Pornacio saw her another time moving through the air—it was in the church of the Lateran; High Mass was being sung at the altar of the canons, and after the Epistle had been sung he saw her rising up above the floor as much as half the height of a man and moving, again 'like a ship over the water,' to the chapel of the *Sancta Sanctorum*. No doubt was possible, the worthy hermit averred when he gave his testimony in the process of canonization— 'I stood up and followed after her right up to the chapel.' *(7)

The pious hermit from Todi recounted from time to time in Rome his strange experiences with the foreign woman saint. They are told in many places in the process of canonization by different witnesses, but always with John of Pornacio as their source.(8) Not even Bridget's daughter Karin knew anything about them, except from the tales of the Todi hermit. Nor did Petrus Olai of Alvastra know any more. But all over the city of Rome these rumours passed from mouth to mouth and Bridget's fame spread all over the city.(9)

And then she, of whom such great legends were told, was sitting alone out in the basilica of Saint Agnes on the Via Nomentana. There was no feast to-day and no crowd—Bridget was alone in the stern

* The chapel Sancta Sanctorum, above the Scala Santa, was in the Middle Ages part of the Lateran Palace, of which there was a wing, where the Piazza San Giovanni now stands. In the Triclinium Leonianum Bridget would be able to see the old Mosaics—Christ giving the keys to Saint Peter and the Labarum to the Emperor Constantine—and Peter giving the stole to Leo III, and the banner of the empire to Charlemagne. Pope and emperor—when was Bridget to see them together in Rome?

silence of the church and the white figures of the mosaics on a golden ground up yonder in the vaults of the chancel. On her knees and leaning her forehead against the marble baluster around the saint's tomb she prayed a long while. 'Before the face of kings I have testified to thee, oh Lord, I shall not be confounded,' it was said in the Mass of Saint Agnes. Agnes paid for her testimony with the death of a martyr—no martyrdom no crown! Bridget too had testified before the face of kings—but what is her martyrdom? She lives in comfort in the cardinal's palace—Petrus Olai has seen to it nothing is lacking—she and her household live a regular, well-ordered life—Mass, breakfast, visits to churches, dinner, prayer in the chapel, needlework, supper, recreation, early to bed, good and sound sleep—what martyrdom is there really here? Can this be called following Christ? She does not need to work for her daily bread—money comes fairly regularly from Sweden—now during the year of jubilee many Swedes come to Rome and they can bring messages. Some bad news they bring too, of course, the worst was what the cook came and told her to her great grief. 'Very sad tidings, Lady Bridget. I have just heard it from a Swedish pilgrim whom I met in Saint Peter's—your son Karl is dead, he was hanged!' Bridget had not wept when she sat by Ulf's deathbed—nor did she weep when, shortly after her arrival in Rome, she had received confirmation that Petrus Olai's dream had been true when he dreamed that her old teacher, Master Matthias had died. But Karl, her child of affliction, the son of her tears, was not ready to stand before the seat of judgment—he was still a child of the world, entangled in the snares of the Devil—he must not depart yet. It was with weeping that she stammered her: 'Thy will, not mine, oh Lord, be done!'

Later on a letter had come from home to tell her that Karl was living and perfectly well, and it was discovered that the cook, out of pure spite, had made up the whole story just to grieve his strict mistress! Nor was it to be wondered at that this spiteful fellow had died soon after the truth had been found out. He begged Bridget's forgiveness on his deathbed, and she forgave him. But seven days after the funeral she had a vision—she saw him sitting on a beam that was laid across the abyss over hell. (She had also seen another of her enemies, Sir Knut Folkesson, sitting like this.) And the Blessed Virgin had appeared to Bridget and had said to her: 'No one can imagine the dread in which this soul is sitting here. It is his punishment because while living he grieved the friends of God. But this thou shalt know, that he is yet numbered among those who shall be saved.'(10)

To-day Bridget had another vision. Saint Agnes appeared to her and what did she hold in her hand? A golden crown in which were set seven precious stones. Each of them was a reward for Bridget's patience in suffering. The first stone was a *jasper*. 'This stone was given to you by him who said that you would do better to stay at home and spin like other women than to dispute about the Holy Scriptures.' The second stone was a *sapphire*. 'This was given to you by him who spoke kindly to you when you were present, but spoke ill of you behind your back.' The third stone was an *emerald*. 'This was given to you by him who lied about you and asserted that you had said things which you had neither thought nor spoken.' The fourth jewel was a *pearl*. 'There was a man who in your presence spoke ill of one of your friends'—by whom was meant Master Matthias—'and it pained you more than if he had spoken ill of yourself.'(11) The fifth stone was a *topaz*. 'There was one who spoke bitterly and harshly to you and you blessed him.' The sixth was a *diamond*. It was set in Bridget's crown when Knut Folkesson had poured water upon her head, and she would not have Birger and Karl to take revenge upon him for it.(12) But the seventh stone was the most precious of all, it was a *carbuncle*. And this stone she had gained here in Rome—'it was given to you by him who falsely told you that your son was dead, and you bore your grief with resignation to the will of God.'(13)

The sources do not indicate when Bridget had this vision. In placing it in the first year of the sojourn in Rome, I have done so because the memories of the injuries suffered in her own country were still so vivid in Bridget's memory—later, however, the numerous impressions of the foreign surroundings must have covered them. But at present the thorns were still fixed and smarting.*

Altogether Saint Agnes was, among the Roman saints, that one to whom Bridget was drawn from the beginning. When she sat writing her Latin exercises for Master Petrus and had difficulties with the grammar, it was as though the gentle Roman maiden came and sat down beside her and helped her with the work. Bridget's old brain did not always grasp things so quickly, she had even to give up some of her long and numerous prayers in order to practise the inflection of adjectives: positive, comparative, superlative. Sometimes it was

* The seven precious stones are perhaps a memory of the Apocalypse of St. John, xxi, 19–21, in which the foundation stones of the heavenly Jerusalem are enumerated: 'the first foundation was jasper, the second sapphire . . . the fourth an emerald, the tenth a topaz . . . and the twelve gates were twelve pearls.'

difficult to connect substantive and adjective so that both had the right ending. There was also the matter of active and passive—the difference is so slight, only an *i* at the end instead of an *e, e.g., praevenire* and *praeveniri,* and yet it makes the meaning quite different.(14) But with a teacher like Agnes Bridget could not but make great progress—'in a short time she got so far in the grammar that she had a sufficient knowledge of Latin and could speak the language herself.' It is Petrus Olai who bears witness to this; it might be thought, perhaps, that he was not a quite impartial judge.(15) But a lady of the Roman nobility, Golizia Orsini, testifies in 1379 in the process of canonization, that Saint Agnes 'taught the said Lady Bridget (Latin) grammar and helped her so much that the Lady Bridget spoke the language almost perfectly and made long speeches in Latin.'(16) Golizia Orsini was forty years old when Bridget died, and she would often have heard her make her 'long speeches'; she and her husband, Latino Orsini, were close friends of the Scandinavian saint, who by her intercession had healed their son, Gentile, of a serious illness.

Both heaven and earth, both Bridget's own tremendous energy and the consoling and helping presence of the gentle saint, had to be strained to the utmost. For unless she could speak the international language of the time Bridget could do nothing. When later on Catherine of Siena took up the work of the Swedish saint she had not passed through any course in Latin—Raymond of Capua had to serve her as interpreter before Gregory XI. But then it was easier to translate from Tuscan to Latin than to reproduce Bridget's Uppland Swedish in the language of Rome. Finally it might also be supposed that Petrus Olai would have his misgivings about reproducing the unsweetened speech of the seeress in a suitable official style. In any case Bridget did not intend to stand before the Pope as a dumb person, she would choose her expressions herself. She would therefore have to study, and the rosary would have to take care of itself!

And one fine day Bridget could really sit down at her desk and write a Latin letter to the Cardinal of Albano, Annibaldo Ceccano, whom Clement VI had sent to Rome as his legate during the year of jubilee.

X

Most Reverend Father. It is a widow who writes to you to tell you the following: A woman had, during the time when she lived in her own country, many visions of wondrous things, and these visions were examined by bishops, cloistered folk and priests and have been found to have their origin in the Holy Ghost, of which also the king and queen of that country have been convinced.* This same woman left her country and journeyed to Rome, and one day, when she was praying in the big church of the Blessed Virgin,† she was caught up in a spiritual vision, in which her soul was, as it were, asleep, but she did not sleep. Then the Blessed Virgin appeared to her. The woman was troubled and feared a deceit of the devil, but the Virgin who appeared to her said: 'Fear not that what you now see and hear has come from an evil spirit. For as the sun brings light and warmth, which the dark shadow does not bring, so the Holy Ghost, when it enters into the heart of a man, brings two things: the warmth of love and the light of faith. You feel these two now, and they do not go with the devil, who is like the cold shadow.'

Send therefore this message to him whom I have mentioned to you. And albeit I know his heart and foresee his answer, you are nevertheless to send him my words.

In Rome Bridget had seen the churches that were falling into ruin and ravaged by fire—there were cracks and rifts in the arches, so that bricks and large pieces of lime fell down on the heads of people. Many of the pillars of the old basilicas stand crooked and are on the point of falling down. The mosaic floor, which was once new and beautiful, is now full of holes, so that one stumbles at every step and risks a twisted ankle. The whole Church is on the point of falling, and the fall will be so great that it will be heard all over Christendom.

What you have thus seen [says the Blessed Virgin] is a sign of what will soon come to pass. I am like the rainbow, standing in the cloud, but touching the earth at both ends—thus do I also stoop over the world with my prayer. I stoop to the good, that they may remain steadfast, I stoop to the evil, that they may not continue in their wickedness and become still worse. But do you now make known to him, to whom I send these words, that from a certain quarter a dark and terrible cloud is rising with the brightness of the rainbow. By this cloud I mean those ecclesiastics who live with harlots, and whose greed of money is bottomless like the sea, and they scatter gifts and favours about, so that men may see what great persons they are. Most of the men who govern the Church are now living in these vices, and their sins rise up before the face of God like a dark cloud against the brightness of the rainbow. And such persons shall not be exalted in the Kingdom of God, but shall be cast down.

But if any will begin to shore up the Church and make the floor smooth and straight, I will help him. And if any will go into the vineyard which my Son planted and watered with His blood, I, the Queen of Heaven, will come to his aid with all the hosts of heaven and root up moss-covered stumps and barren tree trunks and cast them into the fire to be burned, and plant fruitful trees in their place.

* Otherwise Bridget has no great opinion of Magnus and Blanca!
† Saint Mary Major.

All this, most reverend Father, the Blessed Virgin and Mother of God bids me send to you in writing. And this you must know, that I who send you this letter, swear by Jesus Christ the True and Almighty, and by His holy Mother, as true it is that I will that they shall help me in my last hour, that I do not send you this letter to gain favour with men or honour in the world, but because I have been bidden to do so.(1)

'Who was Annibale di Ceccano? He was one of the most influential cardinals in Avignon, after the Archbishop of Rouen, Roger de Beaufort had been elected Pope (Clement VI) in May, 1342. It was Ceccano and another cardinal who wrote to the English king, Edward III, that the election had taken place ('exclusively by divine inspiration').(2)

He it was too, who in honour of the newly-elected Pope gave that fantastic banquet which is mentioned in the first volume of this work (pp. 163–4). This is the man to whom Mary speaks by Bridget's pen —and Christ Himself adds a postscript to the letter:

Blessed is he who tries to drive out the vices of the world, for they have more than ever gained dominion. Many who are now living will see the sun lose its brightness, the stars be darkened, wisdom despised, the humble crushed to the earth, the proud triumphing. May he who has the power to reason heed these words and be prepared in time.(3)

The Cardinal did not heed the warning and did not prepare himself. 'With all his heart he clings to earthly things, his eyes are not turned to heaven but to the earth.' He may have the face of a man, but otherwise he is hairy like an animal—most of all he is like an ape.

To the Pope's vicar, in the capacity of Bishop of Rome, Ponzio Perotti, Bishop of Orvieto, Bridget also sent a letter. Neither did he pay much heed to the admonitions and wishes of the seeress. Christ then proclaimed to His bride the punishment that would befall the man.

It will be with him as with a dog whom a man has deceived. He takes an iron and smears it with fat meat, and when the dog thinks it is a bone and wants to eat it, it gets the iron into its throat, and is choked. Thus will the Devil show this bishop all the pleasures of the world, and make him believe they are a sweetness to the soul, and that all his riches are only what is right for his station. He has therefore not thought of giving up any of the treasures that are his toys, for the good of his soul, and when death comes he must leave it all, and has no fruit for eternity. Only wait and you will see it!(4)*

It is Bridget's constant theme—the theme of the old play of 'Everyman,' and of the Gospel: 'This night thy soul shall be required of thee.'

---

* A rebellion drove Perotti from Rome, but he succeeded in getting back to Avignon and died there.

The Gospel is on Bridget's side, God Himself speaks through her—why then, do her words glance off so ineffectively against the purple of the cardinal of Albano and the bishop's cope of Ponzio Perotti? She remembers her doubts after the first great revelation—at that time she hurried to Linköping, to Master Matthias, and he helped her. But Linköping is far away, and Master Matthias is dead. True, she might ask Master Peter of Skenninge—but his time is so much taken up with the management of the house and with his new position as confessor for all the pilgrims 'of the Danish tongue.'* And it is more likely that he will seek advice of Bridget—like that time with the pilgrim from Åbo, who knew nothing but Finnish, spoke neither Swedish nor any other Christian language. Master Peter could not absolve him, he did not understand a word of what the man was saying! So he sends his Finn to Bridget—and Christ speaks to her and says that the good Åbo man can be quite easy in his mind, if only he has a good will to be sorry for his sins and to do better. 'For what is it that opens the gate of heaven? It is the will to do what is good and to hate what is evil. And what is it that produces hell?' (*facit infernum*, it says in the text. As a good psychologist Bridget knows that heaven and hell are created by man himself). 'It is the will to what is evil and to inordinate love.' The good Finn need therefore not be troubled about confession and absolution—when he gets home to Åbo he can make his confession (perhaps to Bridget's good friend, Bishop Hemming). 'And if he should die on the way, he will, like the Good Thief, hear the blissful words: To-day thou shalt be with me in Paradise!'(5)

Again at another time Bridget had to help Master Peter in his work as confessor. It was not always an innocent confession like Queen Dagmar's† that was confided to him through the grille—the year of jubilee with its great indulgences was sought rather by old sinners whose lives were declining, and who had been driven out of the Paradise of their guiltlessness by the angels of death of the plague. In this way a distinguished gentleman from Sweden came one day and confessed a number of serious transgressions of the sixth commandment. Altogether he had seduced or ravished almost two hundred

---

* It was Pope John XXII who instituted this office.

† Queen Dagmar: A Bohemian princess who was married to King Valdemar, called the Victor, because of his victory over the heathen Wends on the coast of the Baltic. Queen Dagmar won the affection of the Danish people because of her gentleness and her care for the poor. It was said of her when she was dying that she could not remember any sin, save that she 'had laced her silken sleeves on a Sunday,' and this became a proverb about innocent confessions.—Tr.

women and among these there were four pairs of sisters—he had had first one, then the other of each pair . . . Perhaps in the Swedish knight's confession of sins there was a note of self-complacency—'One has not always been a child of God, Father!' Nor does one object to boasting of one's *bonnes fortunes*. Anyhow, Master Peter did not want to hear any more of this mediæval Casanova's memoirs—he closed the hatch behind the grille with a bang. But the Swedish gentleman placed the matter before Bridget—and she did not agree with Master Peter. In prayer she received a distinct answer: 'Master Peter must deal with *all* who want to confess to him, in so far as they are of his people and speak his tongue.'(6)

Bridget is able to help others, but now she is in distress herself. More than ever before she is in doubt about her vocation. In vain does John the Baptist reveal himself to her: 'He who speaks to you is really the same Son of God whom I baptized in the Jordan—I ought to be able to recognize Him!'(7) The words of the Baptist are not enough for Bridget—she turns to Mary. 'It seems to me,' she says to the Blessed Virgin, 'that I am standing between two houses. One of them is very light, the other very dark. And if I turn my eyes to the dark house it seems as if everything I have seen in the light house is like a dream in the night.'

Mary answers with a question: 'Tell me what you saw when you looked at the dark house.' Bridget gives the following answer:

I saw an entrance to this house, and the passage went straight through the house to a gate, and beyond this gate there was a light, wherein was all brightness. But from the entrance door leading to the gate to go out five men were standing, and they were deadly enemies of those who wanted to go through the house. The first spoke sweet words of flattery, but if one listened to him it was as though a thin flame darted through one's brain. The second held in his hand flowers and fruits fair to behold, but if one looked at them with desire to own them, a sharp lance was stuck through one's eyes. The third had a cup full of poison, but the rim of the cup was smeared with honey. The fourth was a pedlar, who offered for sale cunningly made ornaments of gold and silver and precious stones, but they who held out their hands to take them were stung by a poisonous worm. The fifth was a servant who placed a soft cushion before one, but if any wanted to rest upon it, it was pulled away and one fell down on the hard rock.(8)

It is better then, to go through the dark house and not to be enticed by any of the pleasures of the world. There was nothing for Bridget to seek on the earth, not even if all that she had seen a glimpse of in the home of light were only to be like a dream in the night. . . .

XI

On Saint Valentine's day, 14 February, winter is over in Rome, that is, for the most part. On the Piazza di Spagna the lowest steps of the stairs up to the Trinità de' Monti are turned into a florist's shop, daffodils, narcissi (regardless of the calendar), white-blossomed branches of almond trees, pink-blossomed twigs of peach trees. Up and down the steps little girls from the Albanian mountains run about with big bunches of scented violets—*le vere mammole di Nemi, Signorina!* And the Signorina, who as a rule is an English 'Miss,' buys for a few soldi a bunch of the big dark-blue flowers and puts them in water at home in her room in the Hotel Eden, and the whole room is filled with their sweet fragrance. And if the English Miss knows Italian, and most of the Misses do—she will perhaps take up Pascoli's *Limpido rivo* (it stands in a beautiful Florentine binding next to the *Fioretti* and Petrarch's *Canzoniere*), and read the sad poem about the violets that bloom every year in the wood round the Capuchin monastery—violets, blue and big like those standing before her in the glass—*ma quello ch'era non sarà mai piu*—'but that which was, will never return.' . . .

Up to twenty years ago a Roman spring might still have been like this—and for others as well as English Misses. In 1942 there is no longer anyone who has time to sit and be sad about a bunch of violets. Nor was there time for it in 1350—and besides, Bridget probably never knew anything about the wistful longing of later generations for what was past. Her eyes were bent on the future—her castle did not lie in the valley of regret for the past. Finally the Rome that she saw about her was different from what the æsthetes of the nineteenth century wandered about in—there were neither picturesque models on the Piazza Montanara or Babington's tea room on the Piazza di Spagna—on the other hand there was a lower class in wild revolt against the Papal Legate, who because of the difficult conditions of billeting had commanded the pilgrims to be content with a sojourn in Rome of barely a week instead of the fortnight originally fixed.

The state of affairs in the Rome of the year of jubilee was therefore not one that invited anyone to make a longer stay. The crowds in the narrow streets were so great that several times people were pressed and trampled to death. It was difficult to find houseroom, many pilgrims camped in tents outside the town. There was a rise in prices on all comestibles—it was said that the shopkeepers in Rome prevented all supplies of flour, oil and wine from coming in in order that they might charge as high prices as they liked. There was great insecurity in the town, it happened constantly that pilgrims were attacked in the streets, and plundered and killed. Even in Saint Peter's the canons fell to quarrelling about the indulgence money that had been collected. It was striking the Romans on their purses when Annibale di Ceccano shortened the stay of the pilgrims in Rome to half its length. The wit of the Roman populace, which was later to find expression in the Pasquinades of the baroque period, sent its arrows against *la scimmia francese* (the Cardinal Legate seems to have resembled an ape—as Bridget uses this pet name for him). But real arrows, too, were shot against Annibale di Ceccano—one day, when he was on his way in a great procession from San Pietro to San Paolo, an arrow was shot at him with a crossbow from a house near San Michele in Borgo, and one of the arrows pierced his red hat. It was said that Cola di Rienzo was behind this attempt—there were some who had seen him among the pilgrims. (He did not come, however, until the beginning of June, after the attempt, and left the town at once.) The Cardinal Legate retorted by issuing an interdict on Rome for a week—'I would rather be a little parish priest in Avignon,' he said, 'than papal legate in Rome!' He was glad when in July he was sent on a mission to Naples to arrange the political affairs there. He did not get so far, still less did he come back to the little presbytery among the olive groves of Provence of his dreams. He died (1351) on the journey to Naples—it was said of poisoned wine. (This poisoning may have been mentioned to Catherine of Siena, when she was staying a few years later in Anniable di Ceccano's palace: 'That is just like Italians!' 'Oh well,' she answered unabashed, 'poisoned wine may be found in Avignon too!') And now Bridget is present when the proud prince of the Church is standing before judgment—'trembling and naked.' As so often in her visions it is a policeman who leads the poor soul up before the Judge; the Devil, black though he is, has admission to heaven as God's policeman. 'Why did you not follow your own teaching?' was the Judge's first question to the Cardinal. 'Because stench was more pleasing to me than fragrance,' answers the accused. Again comes the Judge's question: 'You were to be like a candle in a candlestick to give light to your people, both by your words and your example—why were you not this?' In all sincerity the disheartened answer is: 'Because love of Thee, Lord, was scraped from my heart. I wandered like a man who does not think of what he is doing—like a vagabond who lets the fiddle mourn, and does not think of what the end will be!' The policeman now thinks he has won the game 'This soul belongs to me,' he cries. 'What shall I do with it?' Without waiting for permission he pours a drink of liquid sulphur into the mouth of the miserable soul and tears out his eyes. Judgment has not yet been given—'Put him in the press for a time,' it is said (one of the most terrible forms of torture in the Middle Ages was to lay a human being between two planks and to lay a weight of heavy stones on the upper plank, continually more and more, so that the unhappy victim was literally pressed to death. The method was still applied in England under Henry VIII against Catholics, especially against women; for the sake of decency they were crushed fully clothed). After the Cardinal's soul has been pressed and squeezed the matter is to be taken up again—'We will take counsel later and hear what the man's friends and enemies have to say.' No one is to be judged without his possible defender having been able to speak for him.(1)

Bridget sees the final judgment. This soul too must sit, 'in human form'—on that sinister beam which is laid across the flaming abyss of hell; only those whose conscience is clear will not be giddy. Then the four 'policemen' draw near, take hold of the Cardinal and lead him away. But not to save him, much more to force from the soul the only valid judgment—man's judgment of himself. In order to obtain this they bring back the dead man to the palace in which he once gave such stately entertainments.

But he feels no joy in revisiting as a ghost what had been his home. The four policemen take him through four rooms. In the first there are fine clothes, in the second gold and silver and jewels, in the third food and sweet-smelling things, in the fourth his Eminence's well-groomed saddle horses stamp their feet. But the soul finds no joy in seeing these sights again. In the first of the four rooms he feels miserably cold and reproaches himself bitterly with having been so fond of showing himself in beautiful and costly raiment. In the second room there is burning tar round about him and he exclaims: 'Woe is me! I drank and drank and loved a brimful cup—now I must drink the devil's wine!' In the third room there is a horrible smell, fiery snakes twine about him, and he cries: 'Woe is me, I loved all sweet things, and now I must taste this bitterness!' Like the Cardinal of Milan he had 'loved the bondwoman and neglected his lawful wife and queen, Holy Church.' In the fourth room, which is the stable, it is not his favourite mare that greets him with a whinnying, as in old times when he was going out for a ride, and he laid a piece of sugar in his hand, felt the animal carefully take the sugar with its soft muzzle, and then look up at him with big, bright eyes to thank him. But a terrific peal of thunder shakes the room, everlasting justice booms towards him, and in hopeless horror he screams: 'I have deserved to be damned.'

And as at Sinai a voice is heard through the thunder:

> What do those people think who go about believing that the Son of God lies when He says that an account shall be given of everything until the smallest farthing? Verily I say unto you, even more than that, an account shall be given of every hour and every penny, and of food and drink, and of all thoughts and words—except they have been scraped off in repentance and confession. What do the clerics and cardinals and bishops imagine? As if I should not require of them to give an account of the alms which Christian men have given them, and which they do not consume frugally and in the fear of God, but swallow them up uselessly.

At home in Sweden Bridget herself had added much property to the Church, she had founded masses for the soul of her dear Ulf. Now she heard the Voice from above complain that the gifts intended for the good of souls were wasted in keeping a large household and living in worldliness. And from purgatory the souls that have thus been cheated cry to heaven for revenge. 'Verily,' says the Lord, 'I shall make careful search, by what right such priests consume the victim on my altar, and they shall be judged by men and angels. For I and my friends bestowed gifts upon my Church, so that the priests might serve me without wordly cares. But now the priests are no longer my friends, and their prayers will no longer be heard in heaven.'(2)

After the departure of the Cardinal Legate and the flight from Rome of the Vicar of the Pope, Rome was left a spiritual wilderness. The pilgrims continued to come but did not find what they sought. Then Bridget again took up her staff, and accompanied by Prior Petrus, she left Rome by the Porta Salaria.

XII

The name of the last French station, on the railway line Paris–Turin, thirty kilometres before Modane, is Saint Jean de Maurienne. Nowadays there is nothing remarkable about it, except just this, that it is the last station on this side of the Alps, and that you begin to prepare for the coming control of passports, customs and currency at the border. But about thirteen hundred years ago a devout priest named Thomas lived here. Like so many others he also went on pilgrimage to the Holy

Land, and one day he prayed by the tomb of Christ in Jerusalem. The times were evil, as they are for the most part, the world was torn asunder by war—it usually is—the children of Cain continued their father's work and slew the race of Abel—and that is what is called the history of the world. It was about the year 600, the Lombards were engaged in extending their sphere of living space. Rotari conquered Liguria, Padua and Mantua were under the rule of Agilulf, who in the year 605 also brought Perugia under his dominion, as well as Gubbio and other cities in Central Italy. Grimwald was Duke of Benevento, soon Luitprand was to advance plundering through Italy and not to stop until he stood before the gates of Rome, whither Gregory went to meet him and saved the city—a new Leo before a new Attila. . . .

The times were evil, the world was evil—whither could one flee to find peace? *La pace non si trova che nei boschi*, the great Michelangelo was to say nine hundred years later—'Peace is to be found only in the woods!' And the Blessed Virgin appeared to Thomas of Maurienne, as he was praying by the tomb of Christ, and showed him in a vision a wooded hilly country, and in the midst of the hilly wood, in the heart of an inaccessible wilderness, a monastery half in ruins—thither Thomas was to go! The road was long, the monastery was in Italy, in the Sabine mountains, on the bank of a little river called Farfa. A temple had once stood there to Vacuna, the goddess of the Sabines, but in the fifth century the pious Bishop Lorenzo built a church there to the Blessed Virgin, and next to the church a monastery, where he ended his days himself. The church had now long since fallen into decay and was deserted—Mary therefore wished it to be built up again. It was a long way, Thomas was to have provisions with him for the journey—the Blessed Virgin gave him a big, exceeding fair and white loaf which she had baked herself, and promised him that he and those who would go with him were never to lack bread.

Thomas obeyed, came to Italy, came to Rome, set out on a journey of exploration in the Sabine mountains. Thomas left Rome by Via Salaria, and that road was good for walking. But soon he had to leave the old Roman road, by steep mountain paths to get up to Passo dei quattro venti, where the wind blows from all the four corners of the world, and then down to the valley through which the Farfa, Ovid's and Vergil's Pharpharus, flows towards the Tiber. Round about on the hills there are shining white little towns—Castelnuovo, San Valentino, Castel San Pietro—in the distance can be seen the snow-covered summit of Monte Terminillo and the 'nive candidum' of Horace's Soracte. But no one knew anything about Bishop Lorenzo's monastery, it is also possible that the peasants of the countryside did not understand the stranger's dialect—he was from Savoy! And Thomas, the Savoyard, was suddenly homesick for his presbytery in Saint Jean de Maurienne—what was he doing here among Italians?

But then he heard, speaking to him, the same gentle voice that he had heard in the Holy Land: 'Brother Thomas, you are on the spot! Look at the three cypresses over there on the hill—there are the church and the monastery.' Together with his companions he made his way to the three cypresses, and sure enough, they found there the ruins of Bishop Lorenzo's buildings. By prayer and work, according to Benedictine custom, the monastery arose anew. The Duke of Spoleto, the Lombard Faroald, took it under his protection, many monks came and placed themselves under the abbot's crozier of Thomas of Maurienne. Pilgrims journeyed to the old shrine of Our Lady, now risen again, pious benefactors added land to the monastery. The Saracens destroyed it but popes, emperors, and kings bestowed new riches; beside the basilica arose a splendid palace in which the Abbot lived, and where distinguished guests found hospitality. Round about it lay the dwellings of the monastery servants, a strong wall with towers of defence protected everything. In the ninth century Farfa was one of the richest monasteries in Italy—it even owned a ship, which had the right to sail into all Italian harbours and not pay duty on imported goods. In the eleventh century the abbey came into possession of the whole of the Piazza Navona in Rome.*

Then the decline began. A monk named Campone poisoned Abbot Roffredo, made himself master of the monastery and began to plunder the treasury. The other monks helped him. Most of them lived in the various farms belonging to the monastery, each with his concubine, and only came to Farfa on Sundays to enjoy themselves. All of them were guilty of pilfering. The monks' mistresses made beautiful costumes for themselves out of the gold-embroidered church vestments, and the precious stones in the chalice and other sacred vessels were taken out and set in rings and bracelets. The rumour of the vices of the Farfa monks reached Cluny and a group of French monks was

---

* *Vita Catharinae*, Cap. V, erroneously places Farfa in the country about Bologna. In the church of San Petronio, however, in this town there is a fresco representing Bridget. On her journey down through Italy did she perhaps visit the city, and does the fresco commemorate it?

sent thither to effect a reform; they were simply stabbed to death
with good Italian daggers. The disorder did not come to an end until
Pope Boniface IX (1389–1404) interfered; after the death of Abbot
Nicholas II he gave Farfa to his nephew Cardinal Tomacelli.

It was to this corrupt monastery that Bridget now directed her
steps in the summer of 1350. She would probably follow the same road
as the pious Thomas de Maurienne—first by Via Salaria and then up
to Passo dei quattro venti. But she would not need to ask her way—
from afar off she could already see the mighty tower of the abbey. In
Rome Bridget had heard the voice of Christ saying: 'Go to Farfa, a
room is ready for you there.' She now came together with Master
Petrus and others of those who usually accompanied her, and gave her
name at the gate. She may have thought that in the large and excellent
guest-house there would surely be room for her and her escort. But
she was turned away—'It is not our custom to have women living in
the monastery,' was the message which the porter had to give from
Abbot Arnaldo. 'But you can be allowed to spend the night in the shed
over there.' A shed, an outhouse, in which the monastery porter kept
his tools—that was the room that was prepared for her! 'Just that,'
said Christ to her in prayer—'in former times you have lived in fine
houses and lofty rooms, now you can learn what my saints had to
endure in the caves in rocks!'(1)

Bridget did not get any sleep that night. Vision followed vision—
Master Petrus had to keep watch and write. Christ spoke by Bridget to
Abbot Arnold.

> You ought to be a mirror to your monks [said the judging and warning
> Voice] but you are a woman hunter, which is amply proved by all the
> children you have. You ought to be the father of the poor and the providence
> of the needy, but you use the goods of the monastery to play the fine gentle-
> man, and you would rather live in castles than in a monastery. You ought
> to be a teacher and a mother to your brethren, but you have become a
> stepfather and a stepmother to them. And if you do not mend your ways
> I will drive you out from your castles, and you shall not, as you believe,
> return to your own country [Abbot Arnold was a Frenchman] and to *my*
> country you shall not come either!

For a moment it is as though Bridget hesitates—'What faults do
you really see in this abbot?' the Blessed Virgin asks her. Bridget
answers that he only says Mass very rarely, and that he does not wear
the habit of his Order, the black habit of the Benedictines, but is
clothed like a great man of the world. As to the first, he is not alone
in it—in the Middle Ages there were many priests who only said Mass

on Sundays and holy days. The second may be a custom which in itself is not punishable. But he has faults that are worse. 'His heart, in which God ought to rest, is in the breast of light women. He promised to deny himself, yet in all things he follows his own will. He is not open-handed, but he will gladly take what belongs to others. God created his soul as fair as an angel that he might live like the angels— now he is like the angel who out of pride left God. He is esteemed by men but what he really is, God alone knows. God keeps it hidden for a while, as when children play and ask: "Can you guess what I have in my clenched hand?" But one day God will open His hand.' 'This man,' it says in Petrus Olai's commentary to this revelation, 'was a very worldly abbot, who thought but little of his soul. He died suddenly without confession and the consolation of the Church, and the Holy Spirit said to him: 'Oh soul, thou hast loved the earth, and now the earth is taking thee. Thy life is dead, and thou shalt not have a part in my life, because thou didst seek communion with him who left me in pride.'(2)

Nor were the monks in the monastery of Farfa any better than their abbot.

The fire which issued from Saint Benedict kindled three kinds of men, who were like three kinds of fuel. First there were those who burned like incense —those who left the world for love of God. There were those who burned like withered grass—they who forsook the world out of loathing of the vanity of all things. And there were those who burned like twigs of olive with a bright and pure flame—those who were ready to die for Christ. Such as these were the first Benedictines—monks, ascetics, missionaries. But now the spirit has retreated from the sons of Saint Benedict, the torches are lying on the ground, giving no more light but only smoking—the smoke of impurity and avarice.(3)

There was a time when good monks lived in Farfa, 'but they who live there now are like goats that have come into a sheepfold.' Is it of any use at all to speak or write to them? Bridget often feels discouraged —all her sermons are of so little effect. But at once she takes comfort— there will always be some who pay heed to her words—even the Apostles did not convert everyone.

Bridget, then, sends a last message to the Abbot and monks in the monastery before she shakes the dust from off her feet. It is Christ who speaks:

Tell them that if they do not repent I will come upon them hastily like the most terrible enemy, and I will judge them as thieves and swindlers. I will come upon them with a sword, I will fill their throats with boiling fire, for

I have warned them as a father admonishes his children and they have not hearkened to me. Heathens would have heard me! Therefore I will not spare them—it is of no use for my Mother and my saints to pray for them, for so long as I am in my glory, so long shall they be in their torment.(4)

Like a thunderstorm among mountains is the booming of Bridget's words. But the storm passes away and the rain falls. 'While the soul is in the body there is always hope,' she adds.

XIII

Bridget did not return to Rome immediately. Perhaps she expected that her stern words would make an impression on Dom Arnold— if not immediately, then after he had had time to think over them a little. 'We will stay here,' she said to Master Petrus. But to her great surprise he did not agree with her at all. 'I do not know what is the matter with me, but I seem to have an impulse that I must return to Rome.' Bridget reluctantly let him leave, and when Petrus had come back to the Eternal City and wandered about alone to the churches which he had formerly visited with Bridget, he was really in doubt why he had left Farfa. Among the companies of pilgrims who, after the interdict had been raised, were again crowding into Rome, he walked about with a feeling of loneliness from church to church—and in this way also came to Saint Peter's. And there something happened to him —just as he was kneeling by the Apostle's tomb, a hand was gently laid upon his shoulder, and a woman's voice spoke his name. He looked up, a young girl with fair golden hair and blue eyes was standing behind him: 'Master Petrus, do you not know me?' The good Petrus was quite bewildered—was it a vision? was it a dream? was it reality?—for the young girl, the young woman, why, it was *Karin*, Karin Ulf's daughter, the wife of Eggert von Kyren! 'Where is Mother?' she asked, and there was a note of fear in her voice, 'we have looked for her everywhere in Rome!' Only now did Master Petrus see that the Lady Karin was not alone—a beautiful, youngish lady was standing near her, Karin's cousin, the Lady Ingeborg, daughter of Magnus, with her husband, Sir Gustaf Turesson Bielke, and some others, quite a little Swedish company.

'I could not bear it any longer at home,' said Karin, when she was alone with Master Petrus.

I longed so much for Mother that I could neither eat nor drink nor sleep, and I could no longer find a joy in anything. Eggert saw how I was wasting away and at last he said that I had better go. Eggert is not well, he could not come with me, but Brother Karl wrote to Eggert that it would be sheer madness to let me go, he thought I was too young, and in fact I am only eighteen; he also thought I was too good-looking, I don't know anything about that! But now it happened by good luck that Eggert was not at home when Karl's letter came—I opened it, read it, closed it again and sent it to Uncle Israel. And he arranged for me that I could travel with the Bielkes. And a good thing too, for it *has* been a severe journey —first the sea, I was ill all the time until we ran into harbour in Stralsund, then Germany—and the Alps—and Italy. But now I am here at last—and so *where* is Mother?(1)

Well, Mother was in Farfa, and Petrus Olai took Karin there. It may have been that Dom Arnold had meanwhile taken Bridget's admonitions to heart, or perhaps it was because Karin was young and beautiful, *una bella bionda*—anyhow it is said in her biography that when Petrus Olai again knocked at the gate of the monastery in Farfa, with the Swedish young woman by his side 'they were received with reverence' (because of the Abbot's admiration of the Lady Bridget, the author, the Vadstena monk Ulf Birgersson, has thought it correct to add).

Together mother and daughter returned to Rome, together they went on pilgrimage to all the holy places with which Bridget was already well acquainted, and which she was now glad to show her daughter. Those who have lived abroad know the joy it is to show their fellow-countrymen round—it seems to make everything new again, in the quality of one who is acquainted with the places one sees that one's guests are impressed at finding that one is on an intimate footing with the people one meets—it may be that one even makes the intimacy look greater than it is to show one's good standing with people in the town . . . vanity? Ah well, vanity—of course Bridget would not feel that! But now, as she walked beside her young and beautiful daughter, and when they had intimate talks with each other at the fireside in the evening, and talked about those at home, and when she thought that it would all soon be over, that soon she would be walking alone on all those pilgrim roads, along which she had walked with Karin (what is more desolate than a road where you have walked with one who was loved, and now have to walk on alone?) why then Bridget could not believe that this was what God intended! Nor *was* it that, indeed.

Tell your daughter, who has lived with you for a time [said His voice], that it is more useful for her to stay in Rome than to go home. It is with her as with a maiden who has two suitors. The one is poor, the other rich. Her father, who is a sensible man, sees that the girl loves the poor one, but betrothes her to the rich one. He makes it up to the poor one with fine raiment and other gifts. Your daughter loves her husband, but she also loves Me. And I am the rich suitor, for I am the Lord of all things. I will therefore have a care for her husband and bestow upon him the gifts that are best for his soul, for soon I will call him to Me, for the sickness that he is suffering from now will be a sickness unto death. With his account in his hand he shall take his stand before the Almighty and be set free from the prison of the flesh. But I will lead and guide her until she has become fit for the work for which I have destined her from eternity.(2)

Bridget was in no doubt what this work was. And one day she came to her daughter with the great demand: *Leave all things!* house and home, friends and kinsfolk, fatherland and mother tongue, all, all! 'Eggert too, my poor darling Eggert, who is lying ill at home, and whom I love more than my own body?' 'Eggert too! He that loveth father or mother more than Me is not worthy of Me. And everyone that hath left house, or brethren, or sisters, or father or mother, for My sake, shall receive an hundred-fold and shall possess life everlasting.' *

Bridget stands before her daughter, as she stood before Ulf on her wedding night, and as she had stood before King Magnus. Her blue eyes gleam in her pale face. Her mouth is closed, her lips firm and stern, like the words that have passed over them. And like the others Karin cannot say no, either. 'Dearest little Mother, I love you so much, I will not leave you, you shall not go about here alone, without anyone of your own near you. Mother, my own darling Mother, I will stay with you. Your will is God's will, goodbye, dear Eggert at home!'

Sobbing she throws herself into Bridget's arms, crying helplessly against her shoulder. Bridget lets her have her crying out, then she quietly strokes her daughter's golden hair, pats her cheek and, when the weeping at last grows calmer, she whispers into the young woman's ear: 'There is something I must tell you, Karin, something that no one knows but me, because God has told me. Karin, Eggert is dead!'(3)

Yes, Eggert was dead, dead, moreover, on Good Friday; soon the pilgrims from home brought the sad news. On that same Good Friday Karin had been with her mother and the other pilgrims to Saint Peter's to see the kerchief of Saint Veronica, which on that day is shown to the people. On that day she did not think that at home in Sweden there

* St. Matth. x, 37; xix, 29.

was one whom she loved more than herself, who lay dying, and she was not sitting by his bed, she was not there to wipe away the cold sweat from his brow, to hold his hand in hers, until it grew stiff and no longer responded to her handclasp, to close the dear eyes to the last sleep, to press the last kiss on the cold lips. . . . *O caput cruentatum* rang the hymn on that day in honour of the Holy Face—'O Head so highly despised.' She had not then been thinking of her husband's face, which at that same hour was perhaps growing pale in death. . . . She had said goodbye to someone living—one day, perhaps, they might meet again—she and Eggert. . . . They could not meet again now, nothing was left but memories. And it is hard to fight against memories. . . .

Later in the summer the other Swedish pilgrims went home, and among them Gustaf Turesson, who had accompanied Karin to Rome. About this man Bridget had a very strange revelation. It seemed to her that she was at home in Sweden, out in the country. It was not at Ulfåsa, exactly, but some place like it. There were many people at work—there were rope-makers, twining ropes; there were smiths beating iron rods; there were carpenters erecting a gallows; and there were stable-boys laying harness on mettlesome steeds. Bridget stood looking at all this activity but without understanding any of it. There was someone else also looking at it—a young woman who looked very sad. From her Bridget gets the explanation—Gustaf Turesson's soul is to be bound with the ropes; the horses are to drag his body through the streets, as it is done with the lifeless body of a great criminal; the tongs in the hands of the executioner are to tear asunder his nose and eyes, and ears and lips; he is to be hanged on the gallows. Yet there is still time for mercy, and if he repents 'the ropes shall become golden girdles, angels shall carry him through the gates of the heavenly Jerusalem, his nostrils shall be filled with a fragrant odour, his mouth with a sweet taste, his eyes shall behold the fairest sight and his ears shall hear the most pleasing songs.'(4)

Gustaf Turesson was a great sinner, but he repented. In his commentary on the place in question Petrus Olai says:

> This man was the richest high constable in Sweden. He came to Rome in such great humility and penitence that he went bareheaded to many churches and prayed to God not to let him return to his own country and to fall back there in the old sins. His prayer was heard, for he died in Montefiascone on the journey homeward from Rome.(5)

'The old sins'—Bridget knew them well at home—'the custom

of Sweden,' against which she later warned her son Birger. If only
they would bear in mind at home that

> superfluity in food and drink and great feastings hinder the visitations of
> the Holy Spirit. But never do they tire of enjoying the world and of
> having an abundance of gold and silver, of household goods and clothes, of
> servants and horses and cattle. They drive away the angels of God who
> come to serve them, but they entice the devils, the accursed rabble!(6)

Gustaf Turesson was to die in Montefiascone, his wife, the Lady
Ingeborg, daughter of Magnus, had to travel home alone, but her
heart remained in Rome. Later she fled back to Bridget, lived for five
years in her house, and in the process of canonization she could testify
to the self-denying life Bridget had led there. 'She prayed constantly
in churches and chapels, earnestly and in tears, and she sang daily the
prayers of the canonical hours with the priests, before she went out to
gain indulgence.' Petrarch, and after him Cola di Rienzo, had been
enthusiastic about ancient heathen Rome and its ruins—Cola had
studied them with the eager interest of an archæologist, but Bridget
had neither ear nor eye to spend on such vanity—to her Christian
Rome was everything, she did not want to hear anything about that
vana pompe mundi quae Romae antiquitus fuerat, the pomp and splendour
that had reigned in ancient Rome.(7)

The Swedish pilgrims went home. In later, happier times, in
Thorvaldsen's century, it was customary for the Scandinavians in the
Eternal City to go with their fellow-countrymen part of the way—
out to that Pons Milvius, where Constantine had once gained a victory,
but which was now in the Roman language called Ponte Molle. Here
the last bottle of golden Frascati wine was drunk—'*non troppo dolce,
sulla vena*,' said a connoisseur of wine in the company, to get the right
taste, neither too sweet nor too dry—and the homeward bound
northerners went away, with the longing for Rome fixed like an
arrow in their hearts. There can be no doubt that already in the
fourteenth century there was an osteria by the old bridge, where two
of the great highways parted—Via Flaminia and Via Cassia. Bridget
would not be afraid to drink a farewell cup with the departing kinsfolk
—'Wine is wholesome, gives health to the sick, joy to the sorrowful,
courage and bravery to those who are well.'(8) Perhaps she would
gladly have gone with them as far as Bolsena, where a great miracle
had occurred with the blood of Christ: a priest who doubted (as so
many did, whom Bridget knew) the Real Presence in the Sacrament
of the Altar, happened accidentally during Mass to upset the chalice

with the consecrated wine—and behold, the stains of wine on the altar cloth were stains of blood! This miracle occurred in the year 1263, when Urban IV was Pope, and Urban ordered this wonderful altar cloth to be transferred to the new cathedral which he caused to be built in Orvieto—one of the most beautiful temples in Italy. It is preserved there to this day and is shown to pious pilgrims, and in the murals of Raphael the tourist sees, recreated by the master's brush, *il miracolo di Bolsena*. . . .

Karin may also have wished to go with them—for the sake of the miracle in Bolsena or to taste the sweet wine of Montefiascone? It may rather have been to walk the long way back over the mountains of Italy and the arid heaths of Germany, to Stralsund, where the ship was waiting to take her to Kalmar, and then to wander up through the forests of Småland, where she would at length reach the grave where he rested, who had been dearer to her than her own body. . . .

Bridget touched her arm—'we must be at home before sunset, Karin!' Petrus Olai took out his rosary, Bridget did the same—Karin saw that she had tied some knots on it, she knew what that meant, they were knots that Bridget tied to remind herself, when some incorrect or unkind word had escaped her. Praying as they walked they wandered towards Rome.

XIV

There was not time to miss those who had gone, others soon took their places and filled the rooms which they had vacated. The year of jubilee continued to draw pilgrims to the Eternal City—even the great Petrarch left his peaceful home in Provence and again set his course towards Rome. Not as when eight years earlier he was crowned with worldly laurels, but like another poor sinner to seek peace with God. On the way the famous poet had a somewhat unpleasant experience. As travelling companion he had an old abbot; both of them were on horseback. In the neighbourhood of Viterbo, the otherwise peaceful steed of the old gentleman seemed to have become possessed of an evil spirit, it began kicking with its hind legs, and one of these kicks struck the poet, who was riding alongside, on one knee. Petrarch had to break his journey at Viterbo, have the wounded knee bandaged and go to bed. Next morning, however, he was well enough to continue the journey.(1)

Bridget did not make Petrarch's acquaintance; if she had read his sonnets to Laura she would not, perhaps, have approved of them. Nor did she share his enthusiasm for the antiquities of Rome. Besides, she was occupied with the great number of guests that came to her from Sweden. It is only natural that the traveller, visiting the country for the first time, seeks out the fellow-countryman living in it, to get his advice and guidance. 'Good day to you, I am a Scandinavian!' At these words the door is willingly opened, and the table is laid with the best the house can provide. And it is but seldom that hospitality is not rewarded with thanks.

Yet this did happen once to Bridget. Usually she was able to see clearly enough. This was the case, for instance, with the three Swedish knights who presented themselves to her one day. Bridget's keen blue eyes saw right through them; in a chapter of the *Revelationes* she drew the spiritual portrait of the three men.(2) Of the first it is said briefly that he is of the kind that perhaps out of the fear of God will avoid one sin, but is ready to commit ten others, if only it can be profitable to him. The second is a piece of rotten meat, on which God will not waste any more spices—for 'spices are the temporal tribulations that are useful to the spirit'—all he hankers after and desires is to gain worldly honour, wealth is more precious to him than poverty, and 'the pleasures of the flesh are sweeter to him.' About the third one might be mistaken—he likes talking about spiritual things, is easily moved to tears. But Bridget is not deceived. Why is this old gentleman so easily given to weeping? He is like a cloud that gives rain, snow and hail. The rain is the tears this man weeps when he considers that he must soon die and leave all that is dear to him on the earth. The snow is like the tears he sheds when he reflects that death is bitter and hell a misery. These tears melt like the snow. And the tears that are cold and hard like hail are those he sheds at the thought that he shall no longer enjoy the pleasures of the flesh. He does not weep—those would be the true tears—because in him God has lost a soul which He has redeemed with His blood, he only weeps out of pity for himself. And to come to the vision of God and everlasting bliss is a matter of complete indifference to him, if only he might here, or hereafter, have a little room in which to enjoy peace and comfort. Valdemar Atterdag was not alone in not caring about heaven, if only he might keep his castle of Gurre.*

Petrus Olai gives more detailed information as to who these three knights were. The first was from Scania—his fate was better than

* See note on p. 157 of Book III, Ch. XI of Vol. I.

might have been expected. After his death he appeared to Bridget clad in red—like Dante's Beatrice in *color di fiamma viva*—but with a few black spots. The red meant that his soul was saved—in Rome he had gained pardon for his sins. The black spots signified his faults—the worst were his far too great love of his family and his consequent longing to get home. It would have been more perfect to stay for a while yet at the tombs of the apostles.(3) The second Swedish gentleman was from Halland—the country of Knud Porse and the Duchess Ingeborg, for whom Bridget did not feel particular sympathy—besides, the Hallander was a chatter-box and a boastful windbag (*magni loquax et flabellum ventorum*). Bridget took him with her on Good Friday when Saint Veronica's kerchief was shown to the people—he spoke in doubt about the genuineness of the relic and made jokes about the loud-voiced prayers of the pilgrims—but 'they who do not feel compassion with the supplicants shall themselves supplicate and not be heard.' The third knight was from Sweden proper—he was saved, because his wife rescued him 'with both hands' from the claws of the devil, 'above all by prayers and tears and good works', next by her admonitions and her example, 'so that he is now on the way to salvation.'

Bridget had a hard spiritual struggle with a certain Sir Birger, who was collector of taxes in East Gothland. Perhaps she had a liking for him because he was an East Gothlander, in any case her usual clear and keen sight seems to have failed her in respect of this man. In a vision the Blessed Virgin reproaches her with having received this man in her house—'he is a braggart and lives a worldly life.' Bridget defends herself—'I did not know anything discreditable about him,' she says, 'but if I had known it I would rather have opened my house to a serpent than to him.' Mary gives her further warning: 'He is a wolf in sheep's clothing; the devil has sent him to you so that he can find something to criticize and to carry tales about.' Bridget still defends her guest—'We thought he was devout and penitent; he went on pilgrim walks with the rest of us and said that henceforth he would not sin any more.' 'May I ask you a question?' the Blessed Virgin then said. 'What is the best to eat on a goose, the meat or the feathers?' Naturally Bridget does not know what to answer, or rather: only one answer is possible. The Blessed Virgin must mean something else. And so she does, she has spoken in a parable and now she explains it:

'The Church,' she says, 'is like a goose.' The body of Christ in the Sacrament of the Altar is 'like the freshest meat.' The other sacraments of the Church are like the heart of the goose, its liver, kidneys and other internal parts. The wings are the works of holy men. The feathers are the indulgences and grace they have gained with God. The fine, soft down is the love and patience of the saints.

The parable is grotesque, and it is not yet quite clear to Bridget what it can have to do with her East Gothlander. At last she gets the solution—'he who is willing enough to confess, but does not change his life after confession, is like one who thinks he can live on goose quills.' If one has eaten too much, and feels unwell, one tickles the throat with a goose quill (Bridget had seen it so often), that makes one vomit and it gives relief. Such a goose quill is confession, but after that one must take nourishment—receive the other means of grace of the Church and live as a Christian ought. And Bridget knows better than most what this means—it means the will to flee from sin, to restore goods unjustly acquired (in the Middle Ages it was not enough to say 'Lord, Lord!' one had to show one's faith in one's works!), not to earn anything by dishonest means, not to live even a single day except according to the will of God. In good fortune and ill to submit to God's dispensations, to flee from worldly honour and friendship—'He who does this will get forgiveness of his sins.'

Bridget may have had her doubts, whether so much could be required of a royal official and a collector of taxes—she puts in a word more of pleading with Mary. 'There is a stone lying at the door of that man's heart,' is the answer, 'that stone hinders my Son from getting in.'(4)

But the stone was overturned. Bridget spoke to her guest, as earnestly as only she could do it. At first he seemed entirely to resist her persuasion. 'What is all this talk with that "spirit" which you say that you have and that I have not? I think it is perhaps nothing but your imagination—or perhaps it is an evil spirit?' Bridget was standing so close to her guest that she could smell his breath—it smelt of sulphur! She recoiled a step—'Now I know who it is that speaks through you!' she exclaimed. 'Take care!' Sir Birger left in anger. But in the night while he was sleeping he heard countless voices crying: 'Come, let us drag this pig along to the pig sty!' (One of Saint Francis of Assisi's first disciples had heard the same cry—he was an advocate and in a dream he heard the devils shriek: 'To the pig sty with the pigs and to hell with the advocates!' And he repented.) Sir Birger also understood—he went to Bridget and gave himself up. 'And afterwards, when she was sitting with him she no longer felt the stench of sulphur, for his breath had now become sweet!'(5)

Bridget had yet another great joy—Sir Niels Ingvaldsson, who in Arboga had made a man drunk, and made him go into the dining-hall where Bridget was sitting at table with the king and queen, and insult her(6)—Sir Nicholas Ingvaldsson *came to Rome*. In spirit Bridget had already heard the judgment proclaimed upon the proud keeper of the castle at Stockholm—it is, as often with Bridget, a *conditional* judgment. Conditional, but severe.

> May grief and affliction in the company of the devil be your lot, and just as much as you have had of pleasure on the earth, you shall now have of suffering in the flames, just as great as your name has been among men you shall now be accursed, and from your place of honour you shall be cast down to the lowest disgrace. You have been a famous man on the earth, you shall also become famous in hell,

the mocking voice concluded. According to her custom Bridget did not keep silence about what she knew. Sir Niels Ingvaldsson came to Rome in the year of jubilee, sought out Bridget, begged her pardon, and received forgiveness, and also the forgiveness of God. He did not return to Sweden but stayed in Rome, where he died a good death in the following year.(7)

Bridget gained a still greater victory—(in spite of the saying that 'a man's household shall be his enemies')—over one of her nearest kinsfolk, the husband of her sister Karin, Ulf's brother Magnus Gudmarsson. Magnus seems to have been of a less pious disposition than his elder brother, or Karin may not have had the same good influence on him as her sister on Ulf. But Bridget had not forgotten her brother-in-law—all the four of them sat together at the wedding table at Ulfåsa, together they were all to sit at the heavenly banquet! Bridget prays to Mary for help, but she receives but a chilly answer. 'The man you pray for has no love of my Son, and he has but little to spare for me. If he had died in his evil deeds he would have suffered endless torment, but I did not forget him, and there is hope for him if he will do something himself to help. For now he repents of his sins and has the will to do better, but his heart is cold and without piety.' He must therefore daily meditate upon the Passion of Christ—'how the Son of God and the Virgin, who is one God with the Father and the Holy Spirit, was tormented'—and thus, little by little, he will grow warm in the faith, and Mary will 'lay him like a child to her two breasts,' which is interpreted as her two virtues: the fear of God and obedience. 'And I will give nourishment to his will, so that he will obey God in all His commandments.'(8)

Did Magnus Gudmarsson come to Rome—or was it only by a letter from Bridget, perhaps brought to him by his daughter Ingeborg, that the message of the Blessed Virgin reached him? However that may have been his conversion was as complete as she could desire—not much more than two years were to pass, ere he and his wife followed the example of Ulf and Bridget. They did not turn to Alvastra, but to its daughter convent of Varnhem in the diocese of Skara. If Alvastra could show the grave of King Sverker, the convent church of Varnhem was the last resting-place of Birger Jarl himself, and the Swede who had gone with Ulf and Bridget on the journey to the land of Saint James was Abbot there. It was not he, however, but his successor, Bartold, who on 5 August 1352 entered upon a contract with 'our beloved friend, the knight Magnusson, brother of the husband of the Lady Bridget, and married to her sister Karin.' The couple were received for life in the convent and were to be provided with the same food as the Abbot, six menservants the same food as the Abbot's servants and 'four horses were to be kept with hay and straw.' The remuneration is not mentioned, but no doubt it was considerable.(9)

It must have been a great day for Bridget when these good tidings were brought to her in Rome.

XV

Actually it was not a religious motive that had made Karin stay in Rome when her mother asked her to do so. She had simply been sorry for the older woman (Bridget would soon be fifty), who was to live there in a foreign country, without any of her own people about her. To be sure, there was Master Petrus, but it was mostly household matters they had to discuss—there was also Dom Petrus Olai, but he was Bridget's confessor and secretary, and translator of the Revelations, moreover they were both priests, whom one treated with a certain diffidence and with whom one could not have exactly intimate talks.

But now it appeared that Bridget did not seem to be in any need of such times for talks, such as Karin had imagined. She had simply no time for them. One of the witnesses in the process of canonization, the Spaniard Ludovicus Alphonsi, who had known Bridget well, relates the following: In the night she got up several times to pray (this was also known to a daughter of that Lady Ingeborg Dannes who died in Milan; the daughter came to Rome and lived with Bridget). The first thing she did after she had had her night's sleep was to go to confession to one of the priests in the house. At daybreak or a little later she would leave the house to begin her visits to the churches, and she seldom returned before noon. Then she went to table at once, but standing in front of her on the table she had a sheet of parchment, on which she had written down how she was to comport herself at the table, both as regards eating and drinking and everything else. Three times during the meal she would remember the Passion of Christ, at the beginning, half way during the meal and at the end. Talking was not allowed during the meal, but reading aloud from a book about the Passion of Christ, and often Bridget was transported in spirit, so that she knew nothing of what was going on around her—the others would then see her with folded hands and her eyes uplifted. After the meal she went to her room and prayed or busied herself with needle-work, such as altar cloths or embroidering vestments, 'for she would not occupy herself with other work,' says the Lady Dannes' daughter. The work continued until Vespers (three o'clock), whereupon Bridget went to Saint Peter's or another church. She did not return until it was time for supper, and before supper she said Compline (the last office of the day, see Vol. I of this work, p. 101, footnote) and other prayers. If it was a day of fasting she partook of the meal first, after which she went with her daughter and the confessors and the whole household to the chapel, where they sang certain prayers and pious songs and then retired to their own rooms. Bridget then stayed in her room with her daughter, but no one dared speak to her until the next day after Prime, that is, after six o'clock.(1)

Everything Bridget did throughout the day was accompanied by prayer. Like the priest when putting on the vestments for Mass, she too, had special words for each garment—Christ Himself had dictated them to her. When she put the kerchief on her head she was to say: 'Oh Lord, I thank Thee for bearing with my sins, but I cover my head for I am not worthy to see Thee.' When she put on the veil: 'Have mercy upon me, Lord, that I did not preserve the beauty of my face for Thee alone, I therefore veil my forehead.' When she put on her shoes she was to say: 'Blessed be Thou, my God, who hast permitted me not to walk barefoot' (like the Franciscans)—'do Thou give me strength to walk in the ways of Thy commandments!' And so on with all the other garments. She had also been inspired with a special grace before meals—it was: 'Oh my Lord and my God, if it were Thy will (as it might be), that I should live without food, I would rather that. But as Thou dost bid us to take food, I beseech Thee that by Thy

grace I may eat according to what nature demands and not according
to the pleasures of the body.' Then, when all the prayers of the day had
been said and Bridget entered into silence (the *silentium magnum* of
the Cistercians), came the last prayer: 'Blessed be Thou, Oh God, who
makest the times change for the consolation and comfort of the soul,
I beseech Thee, give my body rest in this night and preserve me from
the force and guile of the enemy'—from 'the force and crushing of
the enemy,' are the words used in the old Danish song of the night
watchman. . . .(2)

But it was as though, because of all these prayers that permeated
her day, Bridget forgot her daughter. The Blessed Virgin herself had
to remind her of Karin's existence. One day Bridget addressed the
following prayer to Mary: 'Help me, dearest Mother, entirely to love
thy Son. I feel so weak and unable to love Him as I ought. I beseech
thee, therefore, that thou wilt now bind love of Him about my heart
and draw me to Him, taking it away from all carnal love. And draw
it the stronger, because it was the heavier.' The Blessed Virgin's answer
is rather chilly—it is, of course, a beautiful prayer that Bridget has
addressed to her, and there is sweetness to be found in such ardent love
of Christ—'but now it will be better for thee to go and do some
mending of your daughter's clothes. It is not a silk gown but a common
woollen one, which is both old and patched.'(3)

Anyhow Karin could be with her mother on the daily walks to the
Roman churches. They also made pilgrimages together to San Sebastiano on the Via Appia and to San Lorenzo fuori le mura. For a while
this did very well. But soon people began to notice the pair—Bridget,
small, insignificant, dressed in her widow's garb, and by her side the
tall, beautiful Karin, 'stately and well grown in all her limbs.' *Una
bella bionda* has always made an impression on the hearts of Italian men,
and soon Karin and her mother could not walk even that short way
from home to Castel Sant' Angelo and from Castel Sant' Angelo to
Saint Peter's without being surrounded by young gentlemen who
sent the beautiful blonde dangerous looks and whispered fond words
in her ears, as they glided past: *'Come siete bella! Vi voglio bene!'*
Karin was in despair—'What can we do? The men are running after
me everywhere!' Bridget comforted her, yet she was not assured—
'nothing bad shall happen to you.' It had just happened that a young
girl of the Swedish nobility had been violated and had had to return
home, shamed and dishonoured. Bridget had taken the matter very
much to heart, and had spoken to the patron saint of virgins, Saint

Agnes, about it. 'If this has happened against her will, it cannot be accounted as a sin to her. The young girl must shake it off, as a swan shakes the water off its wings,' Saint Agnes had answered.(4) Nevertheless Bridget would rather preserve her daughter from such a fate—Karin would have to stay at home, while Bridget, Master Petrus and the others went on their visits to the churches.

The young woman, then twenty years old, sat in her room alone. And gloomy thoughts hovered about her like birds of ill omen. Here she must live like a prisoner within four walls, while the others visit churches, hear services, gain spiritual merit. 'At home in Sweden my brothers and sisters live in peace, why must *I* alone fall into this misery? It would be better not to exist at all, than to live such a life as this, which is useless both to body and soul.'

Was there a mirror in Karin's cell? It is hardly likely. But she could not help knowing that she was fair to behold. For every day she received messages and letters from those who were overcome with love of her beauty. Large gifts were sent, and larger ones still were promised by a still larger number of distinguished gentlemen if she would consent to a union with them. She gave refusal after refusal—notwithstanding that Bridget had allowed her to decide freely(5) and in her distress she thought of simply destroying the beauty which was the cause of her never being able to go out of the house.

> She had a horrible and loathsome ointment prepared and said to her confessor, Master Petrus, and to her mother, that she would smear and spoil her face with it. Both her mother and her confessor, however, forbade her to do so, and said that she should put her trust in God in heaven, who would guard and protect her against all shame and dishonour. Nevertheless she would carry out her intention secretly and sat down below a big stone so that she could smear her face unseen. But God, who had made her so beautiful, did not permit it. From the rock or the mountain below which she was sitting, a big stone immediately fell down on her head and caused a wound so big that the scar can still be seen in her skull.(6)

Heidenstam is probably right in letting this scene take place after Bridget and her family had moved to the Casa Papazuri, the present Casa di Santa Brigida on the Piazza Farnese; in the garden of the house there was perhaps, not a rock but an antique column or a piece of old masonry, from which a brick or stone may have become loose. One of the two skulls preserved in the saints' shrine in Vadstena has a scar.

There was nothing else to be done—Karin would have to stay at home. Little by little she was seized with utter listlessness. Convents and monasteries are well acquainted with this spiritual disease, this *accedia*, which is one of the seven chief sins (not to be confused with mortal sins) and which arises from the everlasting sameness within the perpetually same walls and in company with always the same people. And one evening when Bridget, Master Petrus and the others, come home happy and pleased after their walk and after the beautiful religious impressions they have received, they find Karin sitting motionless in her room. She does not get up, she does not rise to meet them—she sits there in a corner, silent and sad. Bridget asks her: 'Whatever is the matter?'—Karin is so weary that she cannot utter a word. Bridget gets serious: 'In the name of holy obedience, *answer me*!' 'I cannot!' She is as pale as one dead, her glance is strangely wild. Bridget and the Master quietly retire.

But in the night Karin has a gruesome dream. She sees the whole world on fire, and she herself is standing quite alone on a small island in the midst of the flaming ocean which will soon devour her. 'Holy Mother of God, help me,' she cries. Mary does indeed appear, but will not help her. 'You are thinking only of getting home to your own country, to your friends and your kinsfolk. You have forgotten the promise you gave your mother—you have grown faithless to her, to your spiritual father, Master Peter, to me and to God Himself!' Next morning Karin hurries to Bridget, tells her about this dream, confesses her faithlessness, begs forgiveness and promises always to stay with her mother in her exile. 'This is the work of the Highest,' Bridget exclaims.

She now hands Karin over to Master Petrus, so that she may be entirely under his guidance. Above all she begs him to chastise her corporally—that was how she was brought up herself at Aspanäs. And every day Bridget and Master Petrus go to Karin's room. Besides the Latin grammar which the young woman has begun to study they bring a rod of supple twigs of olive. And the beautiful white shoulders, which Eggert would hardly have dared to touch with a kiss of love, are now zealously uncovered by Bridget for the chastener. Karin bends submissively under the punishment—'strike harder, Master, you have not yet struck my hard heart!' Until one day, 'with a merry countenance,' she says: 'That is enough! I feel that my heart is changed, and every trace of the temptation has vanished.'(7)

With the temptation fear has also vanished. As Bridget found her heavenly friend in Saint Agnes, Karin found hers in Saint Sebastian, the soldier martyr, whose grave she had visited on the Via Appia. 'He shall guard my virginity, as Eggert did it aforetime.'(8)

From that moment Karin was another person. She had become that *Sancta Catharina* of whom Urban VI was one day to say: 'Of a truth you have drunk of your mother's milk.'(9)

XVI

'You shall stay in Rome until you see the Pope and the Emperor together, and then you shall proclaim my words to them.' This had been the order spoken from heaven at home in Alvastra. The year of jubilee was now nearing its close and the Pope had not come to Rome. And the Emperor, what was there to say about him?(1)

The Emperor was King Charles IV of Bohemia, elected emperor in 1346, but not yet crowned. In the long row of 'römische Kaiser deutscher Nation' he is not one of the most prominent. Although he was only thirty years old when the choice fell upon him, there was nothing youthful in his manner. To strangers who visited him, he chiefly gave the impression of being a quiet scholar. He liked to gather men of science about him, and in 1348 he founded the first German university in Prague. Petrarch visited him in 1356 and was surprised at the atmosphere of culture that he found at the court; to a friend he wrote: 'I must confess that I have not seen anything less barbaric, more humane than the Emperor and his highest officials. They might have been born in Athens.'(2)

Charles IV was a humanist, he was also a devout Catholic. At his castle of Karlstein he had established a considerable collection of relics; everywhere he founded convents and churches, he had himself, like Francis of Assisi, received the orders of a deacon, and on solemn occasions he read the Gospel at Mass. He was active, too, as a religious author, among other things he wrote a biography of the patron saint of Bohemia, Saint Wenceslaus. From the Pope he had received permission to take a portable altar with him everywhere, so that his chaplain could everywhere say Mass, including those places where there was an interdict.

He declined, however, to take any sympathetic interest in the various mystic currents of the time. In Strasburg he had heard Tauler preach, but the words of the great Dominican had not found a way to his heart. He was obdurate against Bégards, Béguines and other schools of free religious thought, and he persecuted them as heretics. The flagellants of the year of plague were not allowed to come within his dominions. In Bohemia and Silesia the Jews were allowed to live in peace, Charles IV did not believe the stories that they had poisoned the wells and caused the plague. Prague became a real centre of culture, where not only men of science but also artists felt at home.

To this very day [a connoisseur has said] numerous buildings in old Prague and on Hradschin give evidence of the art of master builders and sculptors. Manifold European influences met here and created a peculiar style, full of moderate gaiety and elegance, of aristocratic joy in living and the cult of beauty. The Prague of Charles IV is at the same time Weimar and Sanssouci. In spite of his Slavic origin (or perhaps just because of it?) this emperor was a perfect European, who could not put up with narrowness or provincialism, but, on the other hand, he could not bear any exaggeration or extravagance.(3)

This was the man in whom Bridget now placed her hopes. And—as in Avignon—she had in Prague an unknown collaborator: Cola di Rienzo. In Rome dressed as a pilgrim, that he might not be recognised by anyone, he had gained the indulgence of the year of jubilee, and from Rome he had in 1350 arrived at the capital of Bohemia. He had no difficulty in obtaining an audience of Charles IV—it was known at court who he was, and the king took a particular interest in famous men. One fine day, then, the young Roman stood before the king and his council, and with Italian eloquence he made one of his great speeches in a Latin which Petrarch could not have excelled.

But in his ignorance of the king's character the Roman tribune of the people was not fortunate in the means he had chosen to gain an effect. He struck exactly that mystic and prophetic-apocalyptic note that Charles IV disliked. The man on whom Tauler had not made an impression was not moved by a message from Brother Angelo at Monte Majella. Of course he knew all about it—'the kingdom of the Holy Spirit was at hand, a new Pope was to come, and with the stones of the Roman Church, now grown so worldly, he was to build a temple of the spirit, to which the heathen too, would make pilgrimages.' And he understood exceeding well what Cola di Rienzo really meant, when Brother Angelo's prophecy ended with the prediction that the pope and emperor were to meet soon in Rome, and that he, Cola, was to prepare the way for the emperor.

This was the core of the lecture, and in *this* matter King Charles agreed with Cola, that he would have to go to Rome to be crowned emperor. Cola had been a mighty man in the Eternal City, he might become that again. Meanwhile he was asked to send in his lecture in writing and for the present to be the king's guest.

Bridget could not go to Prague, and Charles IV did not come to

Rome until 1354. A letter from her, however, reached him. The heading was: 'The Emperor Christ writes to the Emperor of Germany,' and the content was a command to Charles IV to make himself acquainted with 'the rule, which I have dictated to the woman who is now writing to you. Read through the rule, and see to it that what I have approved before the face of my heavenly host is also approved by my Vicar on earth.'(4) A subsequent letter repeats the parable of the four good sisters Humility, Abstinence, Frugality and Charity who have now been ousted by the four wicked maidens, Pride, Carnality, Luxury and—the worst of them all—'Madam Simony, from whom hardly any ecclesiastic can escape. Do thou Lord, therefore help the four good sisters, who are now suffering tribulation and oppression in that God's inheritance, which is the Holy Catholic Church.'(5)

Neither Cola di Rienzo's speeches nor Bridget's letter moved Charles IV to leave Prague (where, by the way, he was lying ill of rheumatoid arthritis, and was suffering so much from the disease that in Germany the question of who was to succeed him was already being discussed). Not even a communication from Petrarch himself had any effect: it was in vain that the famous poet called the king 'the saviour and liberator sent by God,' and reminded him of his grandfather Henry VII, Dante's emperor. Charles IV answered courteously but with a rejection; as the humanist he was he quoted the words of Tiberius in Suetonius: 'You do not know what a monster the empire is,' and was ironical enough to make Cola di Rienzo, none other, convey this refusal in writing. The Roman tribune had to send his friend and fellow-partisan that No which was the death-blow to their dearest dreams. Neither of them knew that Charles IV had by no means given up the thought of the coronation as emperor, but that he was only waiting for a favourable wind. He therefore kept Cola at his court for two whole years until the moment had come when he could make use of him.

Expectans expectavi—the great French writer Léon Bloy had taken those words of the Psalms for his motto—'I waited and waited.' One of the pithy sayings of Saint Theresa of Avila was *la paciencia todo lo alcanza*, 'patience achieves everything.' The only thing Bridget could do was to wait. From Sweden came one message of death after another—Eggert von Kyren, Master Matthias, Bridget's daughter Ingeborg in the convent of Riseberg, Bridget's brother Israel, Archbishop Hemming of Uppsala. Although Bridget had barely reached the half century she was already beginning to learn how death can clear the space around one. One by one they go away, those with whom one has been young together. Trees are cut down—where the old trunks stood a new young wood is growing up. And articles are written about one that already sound like obituary notices.

Many messages came from home, one of them pierced Bridget to the heart—Cecilia, her fourth daughter, had fled from the nunnery in Skänninge, and it was of course her brother Karl who had helped her to escape! After she had got over the first anger, Bridget, however, gave her consent to the marriage into which Cecilia intended to enter.

> The Son of God said to His bride: thy daughter whom thou gavest Me is like a vine. And as I know now of a better place for her to grow, I will replant her elsewhere. Thou shalt not mourn over having now consented to this, thou gavest Me thy daughter, but I did not show thee which was the more pleasing to Me, the state of virginity or marriage, nor whether thy sacrifice was pleasing to Me or not. And what has been done in ignorance should be changed and corrected, now that thou knowest the truth.

In her Bible Bridget finds two devout women, namely Susanna and Judith, and in the Roman martyrology Saint Tecla. The first was married, the second was a widow, the third a virgin, 'and yet they were all equal in merit before God.' It is equally pleasing to Christ whether Cecilia lives as a virgin or in matrimony, if only she lives in all things according to His will. 'For what could it avail her that her body sits in the convent when all her desire is outside?'—as with those nuns who sang: 'God grant that such an angel might come and take both thee and me!' (and the angel was a handsome young knight). It is therefore better for Cecilia to be married—'but he who is to take her to wife must have three things: house and clothes and food.'(6)

Cecilia was married twice, perhaps three times. A daughter of hers named Bridget became a nun in Vadstena, where she herself also lived as a widow during her last years. She was buried beside her brother Birger in the convent church. An adopted daughter of hers, a certain Kristina Esbjörn's daughter, also entered the convent.(7)

Bridget did not receive any answer to her letter to Charles IV. A message now came from Avignon that the Pope was very ill—it was said by some that it was the kidneys that caused the trouble, others that it was the disease that was called the French one.(8) One day, when Bridget was praying in church for the sick Pope, Saint Laurence (to whom the church was dedicated) appeared to her. 'When I was living in the world,' he said (and thought of the time when he, as a deacon, had had the care of the poor), 'I preached the word of God with zeal, distributed the treasures of the Church wisely and with joy bore scourging, fire and death. But this bishop' (Saint Laurence evades calling him pope, is content to use the title to which at any rate he is lawfully entitled)

—this bishop permits and endures the fornication of the priests and makes as though he knows nought about it. He gives that which the Church owns to the rich and thinks only of himself and his friends. The prayer of the Mother of God for Holy Church is still hovering like a light cloud over the earth, but it is hidden by the dark smoke from that fire of unrighteousness and ungodliness that is now devastating the world. I therefore counsel this bishop to repent, to govern himself and those under him well, and to admonish them to what is good with his own words and example. For if he does not he will soon feel the hand of the judge.(9)

Saint Laurence vanishes, and another vision appears. Bridget sees a knight, tall and stately, clad in a shining armour. But she is not impressed—with a quick movement she goes up to him and takes the helmet off his head, as she did so often when Ulf came home. And what she sees is not a head with fair or brown curls, that she can stroke with a gentle and motherly hand—what she *sees* was perhaps once a human face, but now, what a horror!

'His brain is uncovered, his ears are on his forehead, his eyes are in the back of his head. His nose is cut off, his cheeks are shrivelled as on a dead person. On the right side half of the jaws and of the lips are gone, so that you see the naked throat. His chest is full of crawling maggots, his arms are like two serpents, in his heart lies the worst venomous worm, whose name is *scorpione*. His back is charred like coal, his entrails stink like rotten meat, his knees lie bent like a dead man's knees, his feet are dead and are of no use for walking.'(10)

It is the sick Pope whom Bridget already sees consigned to corruption. And this external horror is a sign of inner putrefaction. To men it may seem that Clement VI looks like a man who does a great deal for the benefit of his neighbour. When the Black Death reached Avignon, he did not flee from it, but stayed and organized the health service. He paid physicians who were to have the care of the sick, and hired carters and grave-diggers to carry away and bury the dead bodies. When the persecution of the Jews broke out Clement took them under his protection. By two bulls he excommunicated every one who molested them, and opened his country (the county of Venaissin) to the persecuted. Nor did he neglect to invoke help from above—he instituted a special Mass to obtain from God the cessation of the plague.(11)

Bridget probably knew nothing about all this. And even if she had known, her point of view was different. Clement is not what he seems to be—'if the helmet were to be taken off his head, that is to say, if men were to see what his soul was like, he would be the most hideous of all men.'

Bridget now examines in detail all the signs of the Pope's spiritual corruption. His brain is uncovered, for he lives imprudently, recklessly. He has ears in his forehead that he may the better hear all the flattery that is said openly to his face. He has eyes at the back of his head—he attends only to the demands of the flesh and the welfare of the world, and does not think of saving souls. His nose is cut off—he can no longer smell the difference between the fragrance of virtue and the stench of sin. His cheeks are withered, they are no longer coloured by the blushes of modesty. Half of his mouth is gone, he cannot preach the word of God, but the throat is open and can never have enough of food and drink. Worms are crawling in his breast for all manner of worldly griefs and cares gnaw at his mind, so that he never gets time to think of what belongs to the spirit. And in his heart, where God Himself would dwell, lies the worst vermin, 'which stings with its tail, but licks with its tongue.' For from the Pope's mouth come forth 'mild and fair and wise words'—it was he, for instance, who made a league with Venice, the king of Cyprus and the knights of Saint John to cleanse the Mediterranean of the Turkish pirates, in which they also succeeded after Smyrna (1344) and the victory at Imbros in 1347. But because of these undertakings in war he neglects his office as the ruler of the Church. His arms are like two snakes, he turns and twists everything as it suits and serves him best. He is so wise and crafty that there is hardly anyone who can understand, and perhaps he also thinks that he can deceive God, and that God is a nice man who will not punish him for his cunning. He is like the most loathsome snake, and just as the serpent is the animal that is most hated of men, so he is more abominable in the sight of God than any other. His back, which ought to be like white ivory as a sign of his pure and white deeds, is black as coal, for he does everything out of black self-interest. All his thoughts and wishes stink like rotten meat, but that his feet are dead means that he will neither walk in the narrow way of repentance, nor in the path of good deeds. And in his bones there is no longer any marrow of virtue, all that is left are only the hard joints of obduracy. 'And no holy person can endure the stench of him any longer, but all turn away their faces from him and pray that judgment may be passed upon him.' In this form he stands before God. But—Bridget never forgets the postscript—'so long as the soul is in the body mercy is to be found.'

Bridget received no answer from the Pope, no more than from the Emperor. A year passed, and two years. But one day in the beginning of December (2.12.1352) something quite unusual for the time of year occurred. Perhaps there had been a scirocco, a heavy and stifling wind from Africa. And suddenly a thunderstorm burst over Rome. Flash came after flash of lightning, peal after peal of thunder. Bridget had a blessed taper lit, and after every flash that lit up the window, she crossed herself—*a fulgare et tempestate, libera nos, Domine!* 'from lightning and tempest deliver us, oh Lord!' Then came a terrific peal, followed by that sharp crackling which is not to be mistaken—'that struck, Mother,' said Karin. 'And not far from here,' added Master Petrus. They were both right—the lightning had struck Saint Peter's itself and had melted the bells!

When Master Petrus went down next morning to do the shopping (in Rome it is generally the master of the house who goes to the market—the women are at Mass meanwhile!) he met serious faces everywhere in the dingy shops, where the oil lamp burns before the picture of the Madonna between the hams hanging from the rafters and the horse-milk cheeses. *E che cosa ne dite Voi, Maestro Pietro?* 'And what do you say, Master Peter?' Well, what was Master Pietro to say —except what everybody said: 'The Pope is dead! He is dead and buried in hell, as it is written of the rich man in the Gospel—*et sepultus est in inferno.* Blessed be this day—and cursed this Pope!

Bridget agreed with the worthy folk here and there in the shops. 'For he who was to cry: "Come hither to me and find rest for your souls," he cried: "Come hither to me and see me in my splendour, which is greater than Solomon's. Come hither to me in my court and empty your purse, and you shall find the perdition of your souls." Therefore shall I condemn him, because he has neglected the flock which I gave into Peter's care, says the Lord.'(12)

XVII

Antichrist on the Chair of Peter was dead—perhaps the age of the Holy Spirit was now to come and a new, chastened Church arise? Bridget heard Christ proclaim it—'now will My friends bring to Me a new

bride, fair to look upon, joyful to embrace, honourable in her conduct.'
These *friends of God*, who are also known to German mysticism, must
be 'quick as flying birds, so strong that they can overturn walls, great-
minded and bold, not fearing death, ready to risk their lives.'(1) Are
there many of them in the world? asks Bridget. Mary answers her:
'My Son is like a king, in whose kingdom there are seventy principalities, and in each of these principalities there is only one man who is
faithful to the king.'(2) A small army but a chosen one! Bridget must
not be troubled—'I, who speak to you, am the same who once made
His voice heard over the earth and the mountains and said: This is My
Son, the well-beloved! Very soon my words will be fulfilled!'

Meanwhile the Cardinals, twenty-five in number, met together in
conclave in Avignon. Then as now each of those princes of the Church
who were entitled to vote—and eligible—was allotted a cell, which
they might not leave until the election had taken place. In earlier, more
austere times, it was really an ascetic monastic cell to which the
exalted gentlemen were shown, but Clement VI had introduced
certain improvements—a handsome canopied bed in which to sleep,
two servants to attend upon them, the midday meal and supper a
generous one : soup, a fish or egg course, meat, cheese, fruit, bread and
wine. The conclave, however, was only of short duration—Clement VI
died on 6 December, the Cardinals assembled on the 16th, on the 18th
the erstwhile Professor of Jurisprudence at the University of Toulouse,
Etienne Aubert, now Bishop of Ostia and Grand Penitentiary, already
came forth from the urn of election. As Pope he took the name of
Innocent VI. Bridget hailed the election with satisfaction. 'This Pope
is of better metal than he who went before him,' said the voice in her
soul. 'He ought to be painted in the best colours.' If he will listen to
the words to be found in Bridget's *Revelationes* he will become still
better (this is probably what is meant by saying that he must be
painted), and those who will convey Bridget's words to him will
receive a great reward for it from God.(3)

None of those friends of God upon whom Bridget had counted
seems to have been willing to undertake such a mission, and justly so.
The fact was that the erstwhile professor of law was not in the least
interested in prophecies and revelations—on the other hand he took
a great interest in the university in Toulouse, where he founded
a college, and in that of Bologna, where he established a chair of
theology. He was an upright, straightforward, honourable man, who
immediately set to work on cleaning out Avignon. The ecclesiastical

office-hunters, who under Clement VI had crowded about the Pope's richly-decked table and hoped that a bite would fall to them, were sent home and threatened with excommunication if they left their posts again. Acquaintances and testimonials were no longer of any use, only real ability. Indeed, a chronicler of the time complains that this Pope was 'hard upon the clerics.'(4)

So far as this Bridget could agree with him. Was there anyone so 'hard upon the clerics' as she was? But it was soon evident that Innocent VI was as firm as his predecessors in his attitude towards extreme Franciscanism. The Inquisition took action. Two Franciscans, followers of Joachim of Fiore, had to die at the stake, a third, Jean de Roquetaillade, escaped death in the flames, but was kept in prison for life. The wind was against the prophets.

There was one who had had an inkling of it, and who with a sudden movement turned quite round and wholly renounced his past —this was Cola di Rienzo. His mystic lectures had not had the effect upon Charles IV that he had expected. Nor had that neat little romance which he had invented, about his real father not having been the inn-keeper on the banks of the Tiber, but the grandfather of King Charles himself, Henry VII; during his sojourn in Rome in 1312 the latter was believed to have had a delightful adventure with the handsome washer-woman, Cola's mother! Charles IV did not believe in the romance. And when Clement VI, in a letter to King Charles (and another to the archbishop of Prague), demanded that Cola should be delivered up on an accusation of heresy, the king complied with this wish. Cola's sojourn in Prague had mainly been of a kind that has later been called 'Schutzhaft,' that is, that he was 'in protective custody'; in Avignon he was put in the prison-tower like any other criminal. He hears there all the bells of Avignon tolling for Clement VI— and here a light suddenly dawns upon him—he sees that Brother Angelo on Monte Majella, who initiated him in the teaching of Joachim of Fiore, has been an angel of Satan (did he not also come from the volcano of Etna, in which is the descent to hell?) In a letter to the Archbishop of Prague Cola writes: 'The woman Jezebel, who interpreted is that synagogue of Satan, who everywhere aims at sowing disunion and quarrelling in the Church of God, shall no longer have any cause to rejoice over me. That angel of Satan in human form, who deceived me with his apples' (as the serpent deceived Eve) 'and up there in the woods brought me away from the Church, has again turned to me with his interpretation tricks'—but this time Cola was determined. It was a vital matter for him—and it was above all necessary for him to go to Rome. He therefore turns everything upside down—the wicked queen Jezebel, who once signified the Catholic Church, is now the symbol of the Franciscan fraternity up yonder in the Abruzzi, the friend, Brother Angelo, has become a Satan in disguise, but the worthy Cola has happily escaped his claws and is returning in penitence to Peter's successor.(5)

It could not be otherwise but that this news of Cola's conversion to the Church which he had, only two years ago, called the synagogue of Satan, would reach Rome and make an impression there. Perhaps it is in connection with this change of direction that Master Petrus, in his memoirs, gives an account of a great demonstration against Bridget.

> During the first fifteen years when the bride of Christ was in Rome and awaited the coming of the Pope and Emperor, she received many revelations of the conditions in Rome, in which revelations Christ reproved the inhabitants of Rome for their sins and threatened them with severe punishments. And when these revelations were made known and read to the inhabitants of Rome they were inflamed with a deadly enmity against the Lady Bridget, and some said that she was a sorceress and wanted her to be burnt as a witch.(6)

The anger of the Romans—from their point of view—was not unjustified. For from the cardinal's palace by San Lorenzo in Damaso a doomsday trumpet continually thundered over Rome.

> And now I must speak to Rome like the prophets to Jerusalem. In former times justice dwelt in the city, its chiefs were princes of peace, but now they have become slayers of men. Oh Rome, if thou hadst known this thy day, thou wouldst weep instead of rejoicing. In times gone by Rome was like a linen cloth, woven with the finest thread, painted with the fairest colours. The earth was dyed with a red colour, which is interpreted: with the blood of martyrs and blended with the bones of saints. But now its gates are destroyed, the walls are thrown down and left without defence, for the priests and the common people, who are God's gates and walls, have no care for aught but what is the will and use of the flesh. The sacred vessels of God are sold, God's sacraments are served out and exchanged for money and the favour of men. The altars are laid waste, for he who handles the sacred vessels does it with loveless hands. He holds God in his hand, but God is not in his heart, for it is full of the vanity of the world. High Mass is no longer celebrated in the sanctuary, but in the porch, which is the world, for all divine love has been turned into worldly vanity. The altars are destroyed, and the sacrifice is laid in the taverns!(7)

Christ has made His plaint to Bridget—He would gladly come to Rome. He would come by three ways: by the way of the fear of God, by the preaching of the Word of God, by the inspiration of the Holy Spirit. But Rome has barred these three ways—the first with the rock of obduracy, the second with the lance of self-will, the third with the pit of worldliness. And above all the Romans offend Christ by their terrible blasphemies (Mussolini had great trouble in driving out *bestemmia* and *turpiloquio* from Italian speech). 'In jest or in earnest, in joy or in anger,' the Romans always use oaths and curses—*che ti possa pigliar un accidente*, 'may you die a sudden death,' *ti auguro di morir ammazzato*, 'I wish you may be murdered'—in both cases without a priest and confession, with the prospect of landing in hell. . . .

> They will not go to holy communion—they loathe the Eucharist as if it was poison. But now I will come to them in a way they do not expect—*My* stone on the way is called sudden death, *My* lance is My justice, which removes them from Me, so that they shall never behold My beauty, *My* pitfall is the dark deep of hell. All My angels in heaven shall condemn them, and all devils and all condemned souls shall curse them! For I am the same as when I hung upon the cross and opened heaven to the good thief, and to the bad thief I opened the gates of hell.(8)

In the second revelation Rome is likened to a field which is over-grown with tares. The fire must pass over it, next the plough, next to that a yoke of oxen drawing the harrow, before corn can grow there again.(9)

These prophecies, these omens, these threats passed from mouth to mouth. When the workmen sat over their wine in the evening, when the peasants from the Campagna came into the city to hear news, when the priest sat down to table with his illegitimate companion, the talk was of *quella principessa norvege* in the cardinal's palace. 'A witch, that is what she is—and a *jettatrice*! It is she who has cast her evil eye upon the city so that everything goes wrong. Has ever the state of affairs in Rome been so crazy as now? We hardly know any more who is master in the city! Is it the Pope's vicar, the Bishop of Orvieto? Is it he, Giovanni Cerroni, poor fellow—he was only a man of no account, he could not hold his own against the grand people, these Savelli, Orsini, Colonna gentlemen, and whatever all that grand rabble is called—*che possano morir ammazati tutti quanti*! May they all be murdered! Though Cerroni, by the way, was wise enough, he saved himself in time, took what money there was in the Treasury, and purchased a property for himself devil knows where, up yonder in the Abruzzi—*beato lui*! Here in Rome we have hardly more than enough for a plateful of *pasta sciutta* and a *fiasco Frascati*! Now how was

it last Saturday? We stood ready with the money in our hands—but
corn was not to be had. Nothing had been brought to the market, it
was said. It is the landowners—they would rather sell to these captain
fellows who drag about the country with their bands and carry on
war, now here, now there—to him, Giovanni di Vico, and him, Fra
Moriale, and him, that German, Guarnieri—he is the worst of the lot—
he has had it embroidered on his jerkin that he is "the enemy of God,
religion and mercy," he is a real *tedescaccio*—like those who once
burned Milan, Barbarossa and his bandits . . . and they eat up everything we have—Messer Giovanni alone has an army of 12,000 men and
700 horsemen—it takes a deal both of corn for bread and fodder for
horses to feed so many . . . and they pay well, they have plenty of
money, they take it out of other people's pockets—and then *we* can
starve! However—the old Count Bertoldo Orsini, we did get at him—
we caught him, as he ran up the steps to the Capitol—he could not
jump as quickly as that other one, Stefano Colonna—there was a pile
of stones two feet high over his corpse. . . . And we shall get our
fingers, sure enough, on her who lives near San Lorenzo in Damaso.
They say she is a *contessa* or *principessa*—no better than the other
riffraff of the nobility. . . . And our new Holy Father, he does not
believe in all these soothsayers and witches—he has already had two of
them burnt in Avignon—now it is the turn of the witch over there.
Come to think of it, what business has she to be here among us? She
has come down here to bask in the sun and drink our good wine
and to speak ill of us as thanks! Out with her—she shall go to the
stake!'

One evening, then, a menacing crowd gathered in the square in
front of the cardinal's palace. Flaming torches sent up their crimson
smoke towards the windows, wild shouts arose from coarse throats,
shrill screams of women: *Abbasso la straniera! Fuori la strega! Fuoco
alla casa!* 'Down with the stranger! Out with the witch! Set fire to the
house!' Within alarm prevailed, Master Petrus barred the massive
door with yet another iron rod, the cook shook in his shoes, the women
servants wept, Karin sat pale with terror in a corner—what might she
not expect, if the furious mob forced its way in—a disaster worse than
death? And where was Bridget? They found her in the little oratory,
from which she could look down into the church. She had asked her
Bridegroom whether it would perhaps be right and wise of her to
leave Rome for a time—she endangered, not only her own life, but
the lives of others by staying? The answer was an absolute No. 'Your

enemies cannot do you any harm, but what I permit them. And they
will *not* get My permission!'

Bridget trusted confidently in her heavenly Bridegroom's word,
and disregarding the tumult outside she gathered her household about
her in the chapel. 'Is it not time to sing Vespers, Master Petrus?' Yes,
it is time for Vespers—perhaps even a little past it. And while stones
shatter the windows, and the blow of clubs thunder against the great
door, the singing can be heard of the hymn to Mary, 'Hail, thou Star
of ocean'—*Ave, Maris Stella* . . . arises within.(10)

XVIII

They were right, who murmured about it in the taverns of Rome—
the Swedish Principessa was on friendly terms with the Roman
nobility and especially with the Orsini family. The acquaintance had
been begun in a somewhat remarkable way. Among the suitors who
had been refused by Karin there was also an Orsini, and he would not
submit to a refusal, but resolved to take by force what he could not
obtain by fair words and handsome presents. Like his Roman forbears
he too, would seize a Sabine bride.

The only possibility of capturing 'so fair, so noble, so modest a
maiden' (as the old Swedish legend has it) was when she and her
mother went out on their pious walks. The young man had therefore
once lain in ambush on the Appian Road—Karin was in the habit of
making pilgrimages to the shrine of her favourite saint, San Sebastian.
But before she came Orsini had caught sight of a stag, that came
skipping out from the Campagna, the hunter in him gained the victory
over the lover, and Karin could escape, herself a hunted hind. Then
came August 10, the feast of Saint Laurence (on the eve of it heaven
weeps stars—they are the tears of Saint Laurence!). In Rome the feast
is celebrated at the saint's grave at Via Tiburtina, San Lorenzo fuori le
mura. Early in the morning pious crowds are on their way thither, but
ahead of all of them young Orsini had set out with a small company
of his men and had taken his stand in a vineyard on the way. Bridget
and her daughter also intended to go to San Lorenzo; Karin was
anxious, but Bridget gave her courage, and 'armed with a quintuple
sign of the Cross in honour of the five wounds of Christ' they set out.
And now the following happened: the young nobleman and his
troop lie in wait from the early morning in their ambush in the vineyard. A Roman vineyard is not an unpleasant place in which to spend

a summer morning—the branches build a roof over one's head, shelter one from the dew of night, provide a shade from the sun— it may be that so early as on Saint Laurence's day a bunch or two of ripe grapes can be found among the leaves? But hour after hour passes, the morning is not cool any longer, there is dust from the road where the ox-carts roll by, one company of pilgrims follows after another— 'how long are we supposed to stay here?' Not till now does the young count say for *whom* they are waiting. 'The Swedish countesses?' is the astonished answer—'It is a long time since they passed by!' The enamoured youth had seen nothing—does not see anything now—as a punishment of his presumption *he has become blind!* He now submits to being led to the church, finds Bridget and Karin in it, in tears he confesses his guilt, and by the prayers of the two women he regains his sight! Henceforth he is no longer lover and suitor but a friend and protector, Ulf Birgersson says in his biography of Katherine, though without mentioning the man's name.(1)

Bridget found several friends among the Orsinis. One of them, Count Nicholas of Nola in the Campagna, took a particular interest in her, and perhaps it may have been said of him, what Ulf Birgersson says of that hunter of women, that later he recounted the miracle himself 'before Pope Urban V and the Cardinals.' In the process of canoniza- tion preserved to us there is no mention of it. Count Nicholas only relates that in the year of jubilee he came from Nola to Rome, and there his aunt, Selena Orsini, drew his attention to the two devout women from Scandinavia. He would often see them on their pilgrim walks to the churches in Rome, later on he had an opportunity of rendering them several services. When the Bridgettine rule had to be approved by Urban V it was seen that it was written in a rather barbaric Latin, deviating a great deal from the humanistic style of the Curia, and Count Nicholas, who in Naples had known Petrarch and other stylists of the time, then improved Petrus Olai's text. It was he, too, to whom the Bull confirming the rule of the Order was delivered—'I held it in my hands,' he says, glad to have been of use. He continued to be a faithful friend of Bridget and Karin. But it is a long way to conclude from this that he is identical with that woman-hunter who was struck blind. And if he really did confess the error of his youth to Urban, it was at any rate not mentioned in the records.(2) He died in the year 1399.

Nor do we know who was another Orsini, whose weal and woe Bridget had at heart. He seems to have been the black sheep of the family, and in the more intimate intercourse with the Orsinis, Bridget would hear about him, indeed; a troubled mother confided her anxiety about her son to her and his straying on the paths of sin. Like the Jewish King Ahab he had seized his neighbour's vineyard and would not restore the goods unrighteously acquired. To the social Christianity of the Middle Ages, and especially to Bridget, this was one of the sins that cried to heaven. In her Bible she had read about the unjust King Ahab and his wicked queen Jezebel, who had Naboth murdered in order to be able to take his vineyard.

> And the word of the Lord came to Elias, saying: Arise, and go down to meet Achab, king of Israel, who is in Samaria: behold he is going down to the vineyard of Naboth, to take possession of it. And thou shalt speak to him saying: Thus saith the Lord: Thou hast slain. Moreover also thou hast taken possession. Thus saith the Lord: In this place wherein the dogs have licked the blood of Naboth, they shall lick thy blood also. And of Jezebel also the Lord spoke, saying: The dogs shall eat Jezebel in the field of Jezrahel.*

Bridget had read this, and in the spirit and power of Elias she now writes to the Italian Achab, God is the same now as in the time of the Old Covenant, now as then there is no blessing on unrighteously acquired goods. '*Urse, Urse*,' she exclaims, with a play upon the word *Ursus*, bear, and the family name Orsini—'God is my witness that I do not write this of myself, I do not even know you, but in my prayer I have heard an angel cry that you have dared to set yourself up against God and justice (the two are one in Bridget's view). Your self-will has gained the victory over your conscience; conscience is silent now and only self-will speaks. But soon you will come before judgment at the judgment seat of God, there your self-will will be silent, and your conscience will speak and condemn you.'(3) Neither was this member of the family mentioned by name. On the other hand another Orsini, Latino, relates that once, after she had come back from the Holy Land, Bridget behaved very strangely to him. He came to pay her a visit, and found her in the company of Master Petrus. Instead of responding to Messer Latino's greeting she covered her nose with her hand—and when the Italian asked Master Petrus for an explanation the latter said: 'She does this when she can smell sin in people!' The nobleman thought this over—what could he have done? Yes, he had had a great dispute with some of his vassals, and the court had not taken his part!(4)

* III Kings xxi, 17–19.

For Karin the acquaintance with the Orsini family became a great consolation. Here she found at last those to whom she could attach herself. First, and above all, there was the Lady Golicia herself (as the mother of her firstborn child of seven she would, at the time when Karin became acquainted with her, have been in the middle or at the end of the twenties). It was Monna Golicia's sister Perna who later (in 1361) became a nun under the name of Constancia with the Poor Clares in San Lorenzo in Panisperna. There was Angela, married to an Orsini named Matteuccio; there was Francesca, who also ended her days with the Poor Clares. In the Palazzo Orsini there would be a chirping nestful of sweet-voiced young Roman girls, and Karin, who at home with Mother Brita never heard anything but Swedish, would listen to the delightful Italian tongue and learn to speak it herself. It happened at times that some of the Orsini came to visit their Swedish friends, but then the Lady Bridget—despite her Franciscan convictions—was shy of letting them see the poverty in which she and her daughter lived. Once Karin was lying ill, and the Baron himself (Ludovicus, the Catherine legend calls him, but it must have been an error for Latinus) announced his visit. Bridget was miserable—for like herself Karin slept on a sack of straw with a rough pillow under her head, and for a blanket an old, patched travelling cloak. But when the distinguished gentleman and his whole train arrived his sight became confused, and it seemed to him that Karin was lying in a magnificent bed with a rug of gold-embroidered purple over her. The miracle—for such it was—produced, however, in the realistically-minded Italian the rather natural reflection that it was strange that these ladies did not prefer to sell their costly furniture rather than to go about and borrow money of others (first and foremost, perhaps, of himself)—which Bridget in a matter of necessity actually did.(5)

Another miracle of vanity (one may perhaps venture to call it) is recounted in this manner: It was at the time of the vintage, and the young ladies of the Palazzo Orsini came and invited Karin to go with them to a *Scampagnata*, a trip out to the country to eat grapes in one of the vineyards belonging to the family. In such good company Bridget could safely let Karin go, yet nevertheless she was anxious—the cloak that her daughter was wearing was fairly neat, but when she was to gather grapes out there in the vineyard the sleeves of her dress would be seen by the others—and they were darned and patched. . . . Again Mother Bridget's vanity on her daughter's account was satisfied by a miracle. For when the young women came out to the vineyard they saw some unusually big and fine clusters of grapes hanging down over the wall. The small Italian girls stood on their toes, strained and stretched themselves, but they were too short. *Ma te, Caterina, che sei cosa alta!* 'You are so tall, can you not reach them?' Yes, Karin could,

> for she was the tallest of them all, and slender as a lily. And now, when she had to stretch her hands and arms, she was ashamed of having to let all these richly dressed ladies see her bare arms and patched sleeves. But Almighty God, who loves voluntary poverty and who was poor for our sakes in this world, honoured her in her poverty in such a way that when she lifted up her arms it seemed to all the ladies as if she had sleeves shining with gold, cunningly adorned with precious stones. And as they were wondering at this they went up to her, one by one and looked closely at the sleeves and felt them, and in their Italian tongue they said to her: 'Oh, Monna Catherina, who would have thought that you, who honour poverty so highly, would wear such fine and costly sleeves?' But she herself saw nothing of all this splendour.(6)

XIX

Gradually Bridget found courage also to go with Karin on bigger pilgrimages. First and above all she intended to go to Assisi—she was a Sister in the Third Order of Saint Francis. Saint Francis himself invited her—on his feast day, 4 October 1351, she was praying in the church dedicated to him in Trastevere (*San Francisco a Ripa*). And *il Poverello* appeared to her and said: 'Come to my room to eat and drink with me.' Bridget accepted the invitation the next summer. On the first and second August may be gained in the Portiuncula chapel the great indulgence which Pope Honorius granted to Francis—the same indulgence which Bridget hoped to be granted to Vadstena. Bridget was accompanied, besides Karin and the priests, by a young Roman lady of the nobility, Francesca Papazuri, who was later to become a so faithful friend of her and Karin.(1)

It was at the height of the Italian summer when the Swedish pilgrims to Assisi set out, The *solleone*, when the sun is in the sign of the Lion—the glowing July, of which Carducci has sung: 'Behold, it is summer, a song rises of love over the plain, where the harvest is being gathered in'—the languishing singing of the harvesters, which is always a song about love, a *stornello d'amore*. Labour and love, *lavoro* and *amore*, the Italian summer burns in both these words. July is a month of glowing heat, a month of fire—he who sits indoors behind closed shutters and sees the sunlight like a white flame behind the green

slats of the blinds can be afraid of it. And then he will perhaps write
lines like these:

> Italy's sun, Assisi's chiming bells,
> The noonday heat of a Sunday in July,
> With the gay twittering of swallows,
> Darting to and fro as on the first day of spring;
> And in the crackling leaves of the olive,
> The cicadas shake their silver sistra.
>
> The white fire, high summer's melting flames
> Scorch the fields to yellow and dry up the meadows.
> Soon every elm is robbed of its leaves
> That should be fodder for beasts in stable and fold.
> And soon the streams, where still a little water flows,
> Will turn into white and dusty roads.

Yes, so it is! But have no fear, Northerner, throw yourself out into
the white fire, as you throw yourself into the water. An Italian proverb
says: 'Better a piece of bread under a tree at noon than a richly decked
table within four walls.' Jump out in the light of noon, Northerner,
and you will find the old Italy, the Italy of antiquity, the Italy that
Vergil saw, and of which he sang—and Carducci saw it two thousand
years later. There is more than one Italy. There is that in which English
'Misses' delight—'Mornings in Florence' and 'a nice cup of tea' at
Babington's in the Piazza di Spagna. There is the Italy of the Danish
painter Marstrand, with scenes in *osterias* and *abbates*. But the deepest
Italy, that which supports everything, is the Italy of Vergil's *Georgic*,
everlasting Italy. . . .

Through this Italy, then, Bridget set out with her escort for Assisi.
At Ponte Molle, where they had bid farewell to the homeward
bound kinsfolk, they turned into the Via Flaminia—Bridget knew the
road from the time when she made her journey to the Benedictines
in Farfa. But this time she passed by the inhospitable convent on the
left and walked on. Under the feet of the pilgrims the dust rose in
clouds, above them the sky was relentlessly blue, in the noonday heat
the stringed music of the cicadas came deafening and monotonous
from the olive fields. Could it be to seek a little coolness and a little
shade that the Swedish pilgrims, when they came near to the town of
Narni, took refuge up in the mountains? Even at midsummer it can
be cool up there in the deep ravines, at the bottom of which a mountain
stream runs purling between big stones. Oak woods and groves of
chestnut afford a shade, on a glade in the woods a half-naked shepherd

boy tends his herd of black pigs. Then the road leads over the bare, grey and flat stones of the heights where junipers grow (Saint Francis of Assisi had a 'Brother Juniper' among his first followers and wanted a whole wood of them), but the gorse has long since finished flowering (in June it is golden and sweet-smelling), now only the stalks are left— the peasants gather them and make brooms of them. At one place the road leads past a *maestà*, a wayside chapel—behind the grating a Madonna looks out at you with great black eyes—flowers have been stuck into the rusty grating or stand in a chipped vase—and inside, round the picture of the Madonna (a fresco by a village artist, who may have watched Giotto painting, when, half a century earlier, he worked in Assisi)—inside, round the picture, the space is filled with votive gifts—some of them rather odd—small scraps of cloth from the garments of sick people who have been healed, a small painting representing an eye, an infant in swaddling clothes of wax. . . .

And so the day wears on. There is no longer any road to be seen, no traces to be followed. You do not meet anyone, far and wide no human dwelling can be seen. Dusk is falling—the fire-flies begin their glinting dance among the gorse bushes. It becomes evident to the Swedish pilgrims that they have lost their way. At long last they reach a *taberna*, a hostelry—but, as in Farfa, they are rather unkindly received, the innkeeper takes them to a place in a shed, where the sky can be seen through gaps in the roof. And then, if they had been allowed to be alone there! They were on the way to Saint Francis, the saint vowed to poverty—perhaps, Bridget thought, this shed was the *camera* to which he had invited her. . . . But there are other way-farers seeking lodgings for the night here, a sinister-looking company of men, neither more nor less than a band of robbers, come storming in. They make a fire on the hearth, and by the light of the flames they discover the frightened crowd of pilgrims, huddled together in a corner. They discover the pilgrims—and they become aware of Karin, sitting behind her mother and the priests, in fair and radiant beauty. Black and sooty hands are already reaching with lustful desire for Eggert's virgin bride—then suddenly, a screaming as of many voices and clash of arms is heard outside the house. The robbers are seized with horror, they believe they are discovered, pursued, surrounded— and flee. . . . But when the pilgrims came out to thank their rescuers, they saw no one, it was God who had sent his guard of angels! And the next morning they continued their journey and without hindrance they reached Spoleto, where the Umbrian plain begins.(2)

From Spoleto the road goes on to Foligno, Saint Angela's town. Bridget does not seem to have known anything about this sister of hers in Saint Francis, or she would surely have prayed at her grave. On the other hand she may have paused a while at the ancient church of Santa Maria fuori portas, in the chapel where the Apostle Peter is said to have said Mass on one of his mission journeys in Italy. Nor did Bridget probably know anything about Angela's contemporary, Saint Clare of Montefalco—the nun on whose heart the instruments of Christ's Passion were found imprinted: the Cross, the Scourge, the Crown of Thorns, the Nails, the Tongs. Bridget would have been able to greet her, too, as a kindred spirit—did she wish anything higher herself than always to bear the Passion of Christ in her heart? From Foligno you can look across the Umbrian plain to the towers of Montefalco—Karin and Master Petrus could not dream that twenty years later they would stand there before the Archbishop of Spoleto as witnesses to Bridget's life and death and miracles. . . .

At Foligno the wayfarer leaves the Via Flaminia which now bores into the Apennines, in order to come out at the Adriatic by way of the mountain pass of il Furlo. The road to Assisi goes across the little river Tupino, whose wild waters carry messages from Gubbio and from Sant' Ubaldo, the bishop saint of that town—'the water flowing down from the hill, where Ubaldo chose to live,' says Dante. You come through the old Roman town of Spello (the town gate with the antique statues still bears witness to the antique Hispellum), and then comes the great moment when you can see ahead 'the city that stands on a hill and cannot be hid,' the city of San Francisco! There it stands in the light of the evening sun, with its stepwise ascending rows of houses, with walls and gates, with churches and towers, with the convent of Santa Chiara in the west, and the mighty Sagro Convento in the east, setting its buttresses deep down in the valley and soaring high up towards heaven with its double church and the square campanile.

At the little rustic chapel of Santissima Trinità the road begins to climb up the mountain side, away between the olive fields, to reach up to Porta Sementone, the town gate through which the dying Francis was carried out, lying on a stretcher—on the last journey down to the Portiuncula chapel, where he wished to die. But now, when I had reached the spot where the path goes up to Assisi, a voice within me said:

' "My dear daughter, my dear bride! There are so few good people in the world and so little faith. So great is my love for the soul that loves me without any guile, that if such a soul could be found, it would be able to obtain still greater grace than all the saints that have ever lived. And no one can excuse himself because he has not that love, for all can love God, and God asks nothing but that the soul should seek Him and love Him, and He is Himself that love that the soul feels." And God reminded me of all that He had suffered for us, of His coming to the earth, of His Passion and His Cross.'

These words might well be in Bridget's *Revelationes*—actually they are by Angela of Foligno.(3) Though separated by a hundred years the same complaint can be heard from both of them—'there is so little faith in the world.' And therefore there are so few who will really follow Christ. Even among the disciples of Francis there are more 'children born out of wedlock,' says Angela, than those who are lawfully born. 'The children born out of wedlock are all those who throw away the yoke of the rule and wander about in the lusts of the flesh. But the children born lawfully are all those who would strive to become like their God in poverty, suffering and contempt.' Bridget did not think differently.

Like Angela Bridget would kneel at the high altar in the church of Saint Francis. The crypt, which now makes it possible to go down to the grave, did not exist at that time—it was built in 1818. But above the altar she could contemplate Giotto's frescoes in their pristine beauty—the three Franciscan virtues and the wedding of the Lady Poverty to *il Poverello*. Giunto Pisano's crucifix, now vanished, hung in the choir of the upper church (painted in 1236)—but why is it not Francis who, kneeling, embraces the feet of the Crucified, why is it another, why is it *Brother Elias*? Bridget reads the little rhyme at the pediment of the crucifix: *Domine Jesu pie, miserere precantis Elie,* 'good Lord Jesus, have mercy upon praying Elias'—yes, indeed, Brother Elias might have good cause for praying! For was he not that *frater Adversarius,* that 'Brother adversary,' who had entered the Order with the praiseworthy resolve, that

when the others fast and observe the holy silence I will, with my friends, do the opposite, that is, eat and drink and talk...? And I will study and become learned to become a man of repute and obtain a good position— perhaps a bishopric. And then I will keep horses and have fine clothes and buy myself costly jewels and a table service of silver, and if anyone reproves me for it, I will say that my rank and dignity require it of me.(4)

Did Bridget know that it was this very Brother Adversarius who had built the church over the grave of Francis? In any case it is hardly probable that she would like it. Ought not the sunshine to fall pure and clear through the windows, and ought they not therefore to be of

white or at most of yellow glass? While here the coloured panes glowed
and shone like rubies and emeralds and amethysts—a worldly splendour
that was not seemly at the last resting-place of *il Poverello*. And nowhere
was there, among all the many-coloured frescoes covering the walls
like costly tapestries, a single presentation of the Day of Judgment.
Nowhere could be seen here—as in the paintings of Luca Signorelli
in the cathedral of Orvieto—devils bearing on their backs shrieking
naked women down to hell and throwing them into the fire, while
angels in armour looked on immovably from their cloud.(5)

Above in the upper church Bridget and her escort—like the modern
tourist at the present day—would go from fresco to fresco in the long
row of pictures describing the life of the saint. Before one of them, the
twelfth, she would surely pause. It is that which describes the event in
the hermitage of Fonte Colombo, where Francis was writing the final
rule of the Order.

It happened that there was a great commotion among all the Brothers in
Italy, because Francis was writing a new Rule, and the one minister excited
the next. And all who were in Italy went to Brother Elias who was then
Vicar, and said to him: We have heard that Brother Francis is writing a new
Rule, and we are afraid that it is too hard to keep . . . Say this to him,
therefore, before it is ratified by the Pope.

Then Elias answered that he would not go alone to Francis, and they went
together. And they came near to the place, and Brother Elias called out,
'The Lord be praised!' Then Francis came out and saw them and asked
Brother Elias, 'What do these Brothers want? Have I not said that no one
was to come here?' Brother Elias answered, 'It is all the ministers in
Italy, who have heard that thou writest a new Rule, and now they say that
thou shalt write it so that they can obey it, for if thou dost not do this,
they will not bind themselves by it, and so thou canst write it for thyself
and not for them!'

Then St. Francis lifted up his voice and cried out, 'O Lord, answer
thou for me!' And then all heard the voice of Christ in the air, which
said: 'Francis, there is nothing in the Rule of thine but it is all mine,
whatever it is, and I wish that the Rule shall be literally obeyed, literally,
without interpretation, without interpretation, without interpretation! And
whosoever will not obey it may leave the Order!' Then St. Francis turned
to the Brothers and said to them, 'Have you heard that? Have you heard
that? Or shall it be said once more to you?' But the ministers went away
terrified.(6)

Bridget was also to cry such a *sine glossa* to those whom her spiritual
kinswoman, Angela, had called the 'children of the concubine.' In the
chapel dedicated to Saint Mary Magdalene she may have lingered a

moment before the fresco depicting the miracle of the angels bearing
the penitent sinner up to *le Pilon*—she had been there with Ulf.(7)
Or was that perhaps a reason for *not* looking at the picture? She does
not seem to have come to San Damiano during the five days of her
stay in Assisi. Her chief interest would be in Portiuncula and the
indulgence. With Karin, Francesca Papazuri and the priests she would
then mingle in the crowd of pilgrims before the chapel and the convent. Here carriages were ranged up closely, row behind row; dusty,
sunburned pilgrims, easily recognizable by their cross staves, filled all
the booths where food was to be had, and crowded about the tables
where gigantic water melons were cut out in rose pink slices, full of
big, black seeds. In front of the chapel and the little convent next to
it enterprising inhabitants of Assisi had set up tent by tent, where one
could buy wine, the light, yellow Umbrian wine, and merchants had
come from Naples, offering for sale rosaries, crosses of mother-of-pearl
and medals with the heads of Saint Francis and Santa Chiara. On the
second day of the Indulgence there were already many who were
thinking of departure, they were those who had the longest way home,
those from Apulia and Calabria. One carriage after another was filled
with old, straight-backed women, whose brown faces were framed in
the white *pannicella*, and to the cry of *Evviva Maria* the carriages were
started, rolling away in thick, steaming clouds of dust. Then from the
chapel came a small company that was to go home on foot. Backwards,
their faces turned towards Portiuncula, they set out on their journey.
A large crucifix was carried by a young man, all had cross staves, on
which they had hung their bundles. Slowly they wandered away, still
going backwards, their eyes steadily fixed, as if in ecstasy, on Portiuncula. And as if they did it unaware they sang continually one and the
same, half plaintive, half wild melody: *Evviva Maria e chi la creò—
evviva Maria—Maria evviva* 'live Mary, live He who created her. . . .'
A long while did the singing go on, till at length it died away on the
plain in a last cry, which was like a scream: *Evviva Maria!*

It was the pilgrims. But Bridget stood there in the crowd and
dared not go with them into the chapel. What had not the learned
Fathers said up there in the *Sagro Convento*, who had studied at the
university in Bologna—what had they not said to her? With what
contempt had they not spoken about the brown brethren down there
at Portiuncula—*i zoccolanti*, the brothers with the wooden shoes, who
did not wear boots like respectable people, but sandals! And then this
indulgence—it was said that Honorius had granted it. . . . But was

it not there to be read in Brother Francesco Bartholi's book, that Saint Francis departed from the Pope without having got anything in writing? We, on the other hand, up here in Sagro Convento, we have the Bull with the confirmation of Honorius III, not on any indulgence, but on the rule of the Order: *Honorius Episcopus, Servus Servorum Dei, fratri Francisco* etc. And it is therefore *our* church which is *Caput et Mater*, the Head and Mother of the Franciscan Order. . . .

Bridget listened in sorrow and disquiet to these critical and mocking voices which found an echo within her. Was all this affair of an indulgence something that Francis had invented? Slowly and reluctantly she went with the stream of pilgrims—Karin walked by her side, Francisca Papazuri and the priests followed behind them—Bridget envied them, *they* had no doubts, if only one could believe like them! Now they were at the chapel door, narrow like the gate into the Kingdom of Heaven—and indeed, there was the inscription above it: *Haec est porta vitae aeternae*, 'this is the door to life everlasting.' . . . And now they stepped in—after the bright sunshine outside they did not see anything at first, but Bridget heard something, heard that Voice speaking to her that she knew so well. 'Tell Me,' said Christ to her, 'what it is that troubles your heart.' And Bridget confesses her doubt. The answer comes clearly and with dignity—as it is fitting for Him who speaks with authority and not like the scribes. 'My friend Francis was truth itself and what he said was truth. He prayed that everyone who came hither with an empty soul should have it filled with blessing and be absolved from his sins. And as he prayed from love of men, and as I am love, I gave him what he prayed for.'(8)

Then the darkness passed away from Bridget's soul and from her eyes. She saw the little chapel where the pilgrims thronged to get to the front, go up to the altar, kneel down in prayer, rise again and go out through the side door by Pietro de' Cattani's grave. (It was he who after his death worked so many miracles that Francis was at last, in the name of obedience, compelled to bid him desist, because the concourse of people became too great.) Ilario da Viterbo's beautiful fresco of the Annunciation was not there in Bridget's time—it dates from 1393. Nor would Bridget have seen it. For on the altar there was no picture, but Saint Francis stood there himself. From the wounds in his hands and feet, and from the print of the nails in his side there were golden rays, and the rays pierced Bridget's heart. And the saint spoke:

Welcome to my room, Bridget. Well met here in my room, to which I bade you come. But there is a room which is still more mine—it is *obedience*.

Obedience was the virtue which I practised above all others; always I had a priest with me, whom I obeyed in all things ['as I obey Master Petrus,' Bridget may have thought]. Obedience was my room; the food that refreshed me was to draw my neighbour away from the vanity of the world, and the drink that quenched my thirst was the joy I felt when I saw my converts live in prayer and contemplation and poverty and guide others to a good life. Behold, my daughter, this was the drink that made my heart rejoice so exceedingly, that everything in the world lost its taste for me. Go therefore into my room, eat that food with me, and drink with me that drink, and you shall for ever be refreshed with God.

BOOK V

THE TIME OF WAITING

Expectans expectavi Dominum.
Psalm xxxix, 1

'I have waited patiently for the Lord.'
Psalm xl, 2

La paciencia todo lo alcanza.
Saint Theresa of Avila

'Patience obtains everything.'

I

BRIDGET and her 'family' were back again in Rome. But now the events of the world began to intervene in her life and to knock at her door. For about four years she had lived as a guest in the Cardinal's palace at San Lorenzo in Damaso. But one day a message came from Avignon that the Cardinal might soon be needing his house, and Bridget was politely requested to seek another lodging.

Bridget ought to have been glad to receive this notice to quit, as it could only be understood to mean that the papal court would return to Rome. For the present, however, Innocent VI was thinking of what was most urgent—regaining the papal State. In reality this was no longer in his possession, but had passed over to a number of great lords who ruled nominally in the Pope's name, bearing the title of Papal Vicar, paying the papal see a yearly tax, but ruling with entirely sovereign power. The Polenta family reigned in Ravenna, the notorious Malatesta in Rimini, the Counts of Montefeltro in Urbino, the Verani in Camerino. Rome and the Roman Campagna was divided between the Orsini, to the east of the Teverone, the tributary of the Tiber, the Colonnas about the strong fortress of Palestrina, the Savelli in the Alban mountains, the Frangipani north of the Pontine marshes, the Farnese family to the west of Lake Bolsena. Towards the middle of the fourteenth century only the little mountain city of Montefiascone was in the Pope's undisputed possession. For the great work of driving out all these petty tyrants Innocent had the good fortune to find the right man—the Spaniard Alvarez d'Albornoz from Cuenca in Castile. Albornoz had studied canon law at the University of Salamanca, had become archbishop of Toledo in 1337, came to Avignon as Spanish ambassador, and was made a cardinal by Innocent VI, who had a good judgment of men, and who then sent him to Italy as papal envoy. He was not only one of the usual warlike bishops of the Middle Ages, he was also a diplomat. Nor was it with any great army that in the summer of 1353 he went across the Alps. Italy was like one great battlefield where all fought against all. Archbishop Visconti of Milan had seized Genoa and the whole of the Riviera. This did not suit the other great mercantile republic of Venice, which therefore tried to create an alliance between the minor Lombardic tyrants and the Tuscan cities. The Emperor Charles, too, was gained for the fight with 'the great

98

serpent' of Milan. But then dissension broke out within the league—Verona and Mantua came to loggerheads. And to complete the confusion there were great bands of mercenary troops that marched about in Italy, fighting now on one front and now on another, according to the payment they received. North of Rome Giovanni di Vico had cut out a considerable portion of the church State for himself. In Rome itself revolution followed revolution—after Cerroni's short-lived government came the dictatorship of Francesco Baroncelli, a still more short-lived imitation of that of Cola di Rienzo. To engage in Italian politics was like putting one's hand in a nest of scorpions.

But here it was that Albornoz showed his talent as a diplomat, in playing one of the contending parties against the other. In order to prevent the papal envoy from joining the Venetian league Visconti placed auxiliary troops at his disposal. This did not prevent Albornoz from also accepting an offer of help from Florence. Rebellion was smouldering in those parts of the papal State which Giovanni di Vico had conquered. Perugia placed troops at the disposal of the Pope, Siena followed its example. Gradually Albornoz had collected a rather considerable army and set up his headquarters in Montefiascone.

The main object was to conquer Rome—first and above all spiritually. And there was only one man who could do this: *Cola di Rienzo*. The erstwhile Joachimite had long since forsworn the errors of his youth, and seemed to Innocent VI to be a fitting tool. In September 1353 Cola was released from his prison and sent to the papal headquarters in Montefiascone. When in Rome he was to get Baroncelli, whom the Pope did not believe to be reliable, out of the way, and to take over the rule himself, not in his own name but in that of the Pope.

Meanwhile, in December of the same year, the Romans themselves murdered Baroncelli, and furthermore sent an embassy to Albornoz to give assurance of their fealty to the Pope as their true lord and master. Cola had now become superfluous—nay, much more: he had become dangerous. Did not the Spaniard see how the Roman envoys gathered round the former tribune, clasped his hands and assured him, with tears in their eyes, that they had never forgotten him? Albornoz resolved to remove the Roman and sent him to Perugia with strict injunctions to keep quiet; the Cardinal himself began a campaign against Giovanni di Vico.

Cola di Rienzo was a man of about forty. Many dreams had failed —yet he went on dreaming. He was not yet by any means an old man

—and like a giant he felt his strength returning at touching the soil of his ancestors. Roman eyes had again looked into his, and after the barbaric language of Bohemia and the musical tongue of Provence he again heard Italian as it is spoken in Trastevere and on the banks of the Tiber, where his father had his *osteria*. Like Garibaldi's soul five hundred years later, the same words sounded in his: *Roma o morte*, 'Rome or death.' . . .

It was in Perugia that he found the man who could help him to realize the dream of Rome—the greatest condottiere of the time (formerly Prior in the Order of Saint John, therefore called Fra Monreale, 'Brother' Monreale). The sojourn in Avignon now stood him in good stead—in Perugia, where he went about freely, he made acquaintance with two young gentlemen from Provence, two brothers, Brettone and Arimbaldo, one of them doctor of laws, the other a knight. Both of them were glad to find a man who spoke their language, and Cola cultivated the acquaintance, especially when he discovered that the two young men were own brothers of the terrible Fra Monreale. If Albornoz was a diplomat, Cola was so too, and now that game began which was to lead him back to Rome.

In the first place it was evident to him that Monreale was the most powerful man in Italy. No one could cope with his army, made up of Italian, German, French and Hungarian mercenary troops. He was not troubled with any kind of religious or political convictions—he had only one aim: to rule and to rule in order to plunder. The 'great company' (as his band was called) was strictly organized with the above-mentioned aim in view. The booty was shared among the various divisions of the troops according to special rules—the individual soldier received his share of the booty just as surely as a shareholder his dividend in an industrial enterprise. The incomes were considerable. Towns like Florence and Rimini paid enormous sums only to be spared the marching in of the band. Others hired the company and paid huge fees for it—thus Monreale received from Venice one hundred and fifty thousand gulden for helping the republic on the lagoons against Milan. It is no wonder that he had large deposits in the banks in Rome, Padua and Perugia. And no one in the last-named town could be ignorant about it, nor could Cola di Rienzo.

There is a saying by Charles Péguy which runs into my pen again and again when I write about men—it is this: *Quarante ans, c'est un age terrible*—c'est l'age ou l'on devient *ce qu'on est*. It is at the age of about forty that one becomes *what one is*. Cola di Rienzo completed his fortieth year in 1353. That day was already far away when he was crowned in Santa Maria Maggiore with the silver crown and was given a sceptre in his hand, and the Prior of the convent of Santo Spirito said to him: 'Receive with this crown and this sceptre the gifts of the Holy Spirit.' It was no longer the Holy Spirit that Cola was invoking—as on that eve of Pentecost before the *coup d'état*. It was in Fra Monreale's full money-boxes in the bank in Perugia that he put his trust. The two young gentlemen from Provence introduced him to their brother—and once again Cola's eloquence gained a victory. Monreale advanced him a loan—when the erstwhile tribune again became the lord of Rome the loan was to be paid back. And while Albornoz carried on a war against Giovanni di Vico and reconquered town after town for his master, the Pope, so that di Vico at last had to surrender, Cola equipped, with Monreale's money, a small armed company of about a couple of hundred men. At the head of this he marched to Montefiascone and presented himself, arrayed in a purple cloak as in former times, to the Spaniard. From his pocket he took a letter from none less than Innocent VI—a letter addressed to the government in Perugia, in which the Pope approved the respectful request of that government that Cola might be sent to Rome with the title of 'Senator of the Eternal City.' No doubt Cola was indebted to Monreale for this letter also. Albornoz could not keep back his former prisoner, but he gave him no support with either troops or money. Nor was it necessary; in the morning of 1 August 1354 Cola had reached Orte, where he was met by a company of horsemen who bade him welcome with olive branches in their hands.

Cola's march to Rome proved to be a triumphal march. It was just at harvest time, the peasants left their work in the fields, standing along the roadsides and greeting the returning tribune with shouts of rejoicing. A steadily increasing crowd followed him into the city. Rome received him with triumphal arches and banners, the streets were crowded with people, from windows and roofs flowers rained down upon Cola, who rode at a foot pace through the crowds. Everywhere hands waved with palms and olive branches, and like a surf the shout roared along the road: '*Evviva il Tribuno! Evviva Cola di Rienzo!*' The train reached the Capitol, reached the palace of the Senate. Cola rode in, the gate was shut after him. But the people did not go away, everyone wanted to see him, hear him—*fuori il Tribuno! Fuori!*

The door of the balcony was opened—Cola di Rienzo stepped out. Dead silence fell upon the whole of the great square. Everyone's eyes

were fixed upon the figure of this man in the purple cloak—stocky
but powerful—and with such a beautiful head! And then the mighty
voice of bronze rang out over the multitude—yonder on the statue of
Marcus Aurelius the doves flew up—(but this time none hovered over
his head). 'Romans,' rang the voice, 'I bring you peace, freedom and
justice.'(1)

II

It is not probable that Bridget would be among those who stood on
the Capitol and acclaimed the tribune of the people—she had had other
things to think about. From the cardinal who owned the palace in
which she lived she had received a respite of a month in which to seek
a new home. Most likely it was the Jack of all trades of the little family,
Master Petrus (father of the household, confessor of all visiting Scandinavians, later also hymn-writer and composer), who was sent out to
find something and who came limping back with nothing achieved.
There was a housing shortage in Rome—and Bridget was not popular.
Moreover it seemed that her financial affairs were not in a good state—
she borrowed money both here and there, first from her friends in the
nobility, and when they would not continue then from persons who
lent money at interest. There was, for instance, the German who
came again and again to assert his claim—and who was always put off
with the assurance that he would get his money at Whitsuntide. 'Did
he get it then?' Well, that depends on how you look at it—on Whitsunday he called on Bridget, but she was not at home—the whole
family were at High Mass in Saint Peter's. It was a matter of a fairly
large sum, and the German therefore went on to Saint Peter's to
demand his money. He met her in the forecourt by the big pine cone—
she was with the Lady Francesca and several others, among them two
gentlemen who appeared to have just come from a journey. The
German went straight to Bridget, and in no gentle terms asserted his
claim—'It was the great feast of Pentecost—and where was his money?'
With an air as if she might have been the queen of Naples herself
Bridget turned to the two gentlemen—'Open your money bag,' she
ordered. And now one of the gentlemen took out from under his cloak
a big purse and opened it—full to the top of gold and silver, florins and
ducats and sequins . . . 'Take what is yours,' was uttered by Bridget's
lips; she had prayed to God to let her have this money at the stated
term—and she had it.

Another time also Bridget and her little family were helped in their need in a strange way. Like her mother, Karin liked to go to Saint Peter's, besides, it was very near the Cardinal's palace. One day she was praying before the altar dedicated to Saint John the Evangelist, when a woman approached her and spoke to her in Swedish. The woman looked like a pilgrim, she was dressed in a white robe, black cloak, a girdle round her waist, a white kerchief—so many were dressed like that and many such had been the Lady Bridget's guests. The strange woman knelt down beside Karin and quietly said to her: 'Dear Lady Karin, pray for the soul of the Lady Gisla.' Gisla was the name of Karin's sister-in-law, Karl's second wife. Hearing this name Karin stood up and asked the stranger to go home with her. But the woman said that she had not time, only saying again: 'Pray for the soul of the Lady Gisla,' and then added:

> Here below you have hard times and suffer great poverty, but God has help in readiness for you. In a few days a messenger will come to you from Sweden with the money you have prayed for, and besides that a crown of gold which the Lady Gisla has bestowed upon you as her last token of friendship, and that you may faithfully pray for her soul.(1)

After these words the woman vanished, and when Karin asked those who were with her, if they had seen whither the stranger went, they answered that they had not seen anyone—'We did hear you speaking with someone, but we saw no one.' (Swedenborg spoke in the same way with Vergil; those who were waiting in his anteroom heard him speak, but did not hear any answer. Then the door was opened and the Swedish scholar saw his invisible guest out.) But not many days after Sir Ingvald Ammundsen came from Sweden and brought with him the Lady Gisla's bridal crown, which was of gold and set with precious stones, and was so valuable that with the money Bridget obtained from the sale of it, the little family could live a whole year.(2)

But the day came when the Lady Gisla's bridal crown was eaten up too. Master Petrus came to Bridget and declared that he had come to the end of his resources. 'We can just manage for to-day, but to-morrow I have not a soldo left. And no one will give us credit here in the quarter.' Petrus left; in her distress Bridget turned to her Mother in heaven. At first she was only answered with texts from the Scriptures: 'If you would be perfect, go and sell everything and give the money to the poor.' 'Be not anxious for the morrow.' 'Behold the birds of the air, the heavenly Father feedeth them. Are you not of much more value than they?' 'Seek first the kingdom of God and his justice and all these things shall be added unto you.' Bridget listens reverently to the heavenly voice, but then she says:

> Oh dearest Lady, you are always rich because you are the friend of God, who have never sinned, and you are a pattern of all virtues. But I am only a poor sinner, without much virtue, and with me it is a different matter. To-day we have only what is enough for our barest needs, but to-morrow we have no money at all, how can we not be anxious when we have nothing? It is true that the soul can rejoice in the Lord, but Brother Ass [Bridget had been in Assisi, and Francis had taught her that the body is our Brother Ass], Brother Ass must have his food!

Bridget talks sense, and the Blessed Virgin puts aside the strict ideal demand and discusses the matter in an earthly way. 'Have you anything you can sell or pawn?' she asks. No, Bridget has not—the bridal crown from home has long since been eaten up. 'We have nothing but our clothes,' is her answer, 'and a few things for the table; the priest has his books, and we have a chalice and the vestments and other things required for the Mass.' The Blessed Virgin answers: 'The priest cannot be without books, and you must have your Mass. And you cannot go about naked!' 'Ought I perhaps to raise a new loan?' the anxious Bridget now asks. 'If you are quite sure that you will be able to pay it back—yes. If not—no. It is better to starve than to make promises that one cannot keep.' Bridget thinks this over: 'Shall I try to find work?' The answer is: 'What are you doing at present?' 'I am learning Latin, and then I pray, and I also write.' Bridget, however, ought not to give up her studies, her prayers, nor her work of writing. But what then? The answer comes, short and clear: 'Beg for alms in the name of Jesus Christ!'(3)

Next morning the former mistress of Ulfåsa sat down among the church beggars outside the convent of San Lorenzo in Panisperna.

III

'I study Latin grammar, I say my prayers, and I write.' The Blessed Virgin had declared that Bridget ought not to give up any of these three occupations—so much the less because she was just then engaged on some work to the glory of the Blessed Virgin. And there was no time to be lost—Bridget wanted to finish it before moving. Here in the Cardinal's palace she had a good room for her work, the little oratory on the first floor, from which she could look down into the church. Would she be able to find such a suitable study anywhere else? Besides, it was a very important matter, that of arranging the daily service as it was to be held one day under the arches of the convent church of Vadstena. No resounding organ was to be heard there —Christ had said it Himself to Bridget.

> The children of Israel had many things with which they stirred themselves to devotion—they had trumpets and harps and other stringed instruments, to whose sound they played joyfully before the Lord. Not so in the new covenant—I am Truth and I will be worshipped in truth. It is a joy to hear the organ, and it does not go against good customs to rejoice in it, but in My Mother's convent it ought not to be found. For only silence and solemn singing and the preaching of the Word of God must have a place there.(1)

No swelling organ music was to be heard under the lofty vaults of *blåa kyrkan*, only the singing of the convent people. It was therefore important to work out a divine office worthy of Our Lady. In the matter of writing down and translating the *Revelations* Prior Petrus of Alvastra was the right man. But if it was a question of music and singing it was to Prior Petrus of Skenninge that Bridget looked for assistance. They discussed the ritual together, and out of the fifty-two hymns and sequences which this contained in its final form, no fewer than nineteen were written and set to music by this master, who was skilled and competent in all spheres. Heaven listened well pleased to his voice —one day, after he had sung Mass before Bridget and some others, God spoke to her and said:

> Although only a few people were present, the host of heaven and the souls in purgatory rejoiced over this Mass. Tell him who writes hymns to My glory, not for the sake of fame and gold, but to praise and honour Me, that he shall not lose his reward, and I will receive him with the words: 'Behold, here comes the singer who did not sing for an earthly reward, but only for the sake of God.' Tell him, moreover, that he must not alter anything in the hymn that begins *Sponsae jungendo Filio*, but leave the verses as he has written them.(2)

In a hard spiritual conflict this faithful singer of God did indeed receive help from above, and in his infirmity he was comforted by being compared with Job and Lazarus. 'Tell him that he gains greater merit with me by sickness than by health.'

The whole of the Bridgettine ritual (*Cantus Sororum*, also called 'The Garden of the Virgin Mary') was to be the work of the Skänninge master, 'written and composed in the Holy Spirit by the most worthy Father, well pleasing to God, the Holy Master Peter, well pleasing to

God, confessor of Saint Bridget, to the honour and glory of the Blessed Virgin Mary.'(3)

Meanwhile the work was not finished yet. At Matins, the first of the seven times of prayer, there are three lessons (*lectiones*) of which the first is generally taken from the Bible, the other two from the writings of the Fathers of the Church. Bridget was not satisfied with this, however—as *everything* in her convent was to serve 'the honour and glory of the Virgin Mary.'

> But after Saint Bridget had lived for several years in Rome she did not know yet what lessons the nuns were to read in the convent which Christ had bidden her set up in Sweden. But now, while she was wrapt in prayer, Christ appeared to her and said: I will send you my angel, who will make known to you the words that must be read by the nuns at matins in that convent. He will dictate them to you himself, and you must write them down as he says them.(4)

From that moment the members of Bridget's household saw her go every morning to her oratory, carrying paper, pen and ink. Prepared in this way she awaited the coming of the angel of the Lord, and he came and stood very reverently at her side, with his face turned towards the altar in the church below. Standing in this position he dictated, clearly and distinctly in Bridget's mother tongue those lessons that are concerned with the gifts of grace bestowed upon the Blessed Virgin Mary from all eternity. With deep reverence she wrote them down day by day from the angel's mouth, and daily showed her spiritual father what she had written during the morning. But sometimes it happened that the angel did not come, and when her confessor asked on one of those days what she had written, she answered very humbly: 'Father, I have not written anything to-day. I waited a long time, but the angel did not come.'(5)

At length the work was finished. 'The robe for the Queen of Heaven is now cut out,' said the angel to Bridget—'it is for you now to make it up.' In this way arose that *Sermo Angelicus*, 'the utterance of the Angel,' which in the Roman edition of the *Revelationes* takes up not less than thirty-one folio pages of two columns, roughly speaking between 1,500 and 1,800 words. The inspiration was not always on the same level—the profane writer also has experience of days 'when the angel did not come.' But all the mediæval cult of Mary glows in words like these:

> The blessed body of Mary was like an exceeding pure vessel, her soul was like the brightest lamp, her spirit was like a fountain springing up to a

height and then falling down into a deep dale. For when the Virgin Mary came to years of discretion and she understood that the one true God was in heaven and that He had created all things, and most of all man to His own glory, and that he was an exceeding just judge, her wit and understanding rose up to the heights of heaven and sank down into the dale, which was her exceeding humble body. Without ceasing the understanding of the Blessed Virgin ascended to God's high heaven, embraced Him in faith and then descended to itself, tenderly embraced by His love. And by this love she kept a firm hold of this love with all her soul, and thus her body became subject to her soul for the service of God. As a lily is planted in the earth and is fastened to it with three roots, and makes lovely flowers grow, so the love of God was planted in Mary's body as in a good soil and took roots in it, and to the joy of God and the angels it bore the three fairest flowers, faith, hope and charity to mankind. And if any who were inclined to sin only beheld this lily, the flame of sin was on the instant quenched in him.(6)

Mary is the lily in God's garden—more closely defined: she is the *sword-lily*, the fleur-de-lis, the iris. Its leaves are like a sharp, two-edged blade. Mary is the flower above all flowers, she grew in the valley and rose up above all mountains. But the keen blade pierced her heart, such as old Simeon had foretold.(7)

Bridget's soul too, rose up like a fountain to God's kingdom and sank down again to the vale of tears of reality. For one day there was a loud knock at her door, and it was not an angel who was standing outside, but a messenger from Cardinal Beaufort. She had already once had a respite—at the last moment; she had had everything packed and ready to move. Two days before expiring of the lease a letter had come from the Cardinal, that she could be at ease, she could stay as long as she liked. But now it was serious—she had stayed *too* long! With her beautiful daughter she would now have to take refuge in one of the public hostels for pilgrims. The distinguished friends retreated—they had cares enough of their own, politically they were out of the game. Since the day when Bridget had sat begging at the door of San Lorenzo in Panisperna she had gone down socially—she was now *una contessa decaduta*, a noble lady who has come down in the world—no longer *principessa di Nericia* (Catherine of Siena calls her simply *contessa*).(8)

But there was a friend who did not forget Bridget in her hour of need, and that was Francesca Papazuri. She was the widow of a Roman nobleman—Petrus Jacobi Papazuri—and owned a house on Campo de' Fiori, not far from San Lorenzo in Damaso. She had taken part in the pilgrimage to Assisi, later she was to join in that to the Holy Land. Now she came and offered her Swedish friend and her *famiglia* houseroom. The house was not small—in the deed of gift which was drawn up later there is mention of a main building (*Palamagnum*) with gate and tower, and with large and small rooms, also a garden, three smaller houses joined on to the palace, as well as another house which is called turricella, the little tower.

Bridget entered in under her friend's roof with all her household. And when she went through the house with the Lady Papazuri and saw the whole, the palace, the tower, the side buildings, the garden, she suddenly became aware that she had seen it all before. 'Francesca,' she said, turning to her friend, 'when I was in Arras and watched by Ulf's sick-bed, a large house was shown to me in a vision, and a voice said to me: "In this house you are to die!" Francesca, it was your house that I saw!'(9)

But when Bridget was alone in her room she asked God why He had let her suffer all this fear and disquiet, when He had prepared a place for her. The answer was: 'So that you may know from experience what it is like to travel when one is a poor pilgrim, who must beg his way on the journey, and so that you may have compassion on such!'(10)

IV

It was in the year 1354 that Bridget moved into Francesca Papazuri's house. Ten years had passed since God 'drew her out of the nest'— now she felt as if she had found a new Ulfåsa. Here there was room enough to move about, there was a garden and orchard and vineyard, there were strong walls and a watch tower, and an iron-studded door which was bolted every evening with a substantial iron rod, a *catenaccio*. And Bridget needed plenty of room—her household (*famiglia* in Italian) consisted of not a few members, people from home came and took up their quarters with her—Karl's mother-in-law, the Lady Ingeborg Erik's daughter, married to Sir Ketil Glysing, stayed with her for five whole years, a priest named Nicholas, parish priest in Häradshammer, for three months.(1) A lady who had lain ill a long time in Bridget's house died there, and Bridget saw her soul before the judgment. A company of evil-looking policemen wanted to carry her off with them—'but immediately an exceeding fair maiden appeared and said to the policemen: 'What have you to do with her? She is of the family of my Son's new bride!' And the policemen fled.(2) Ingeborg Dannes' daughter, Juliana, was also for a long while a guest in the house. Besides these there were the servants—among them that abominable cook who had frightened Bridget with the false news about Karl's death, and the still worse servant who used to bring her the post, and who one day pulled out a knife and wanted to murder her.(3) Sir Magnus of Eka, who later became a priest, came to Rome after his wife's death and stayed with Bridget 'for about eighteen years' (also joined the pilgrimage to the Holy Land).(4) Finally there were the ecclesiastics—the young domestic chaplain, Gudmar Fredriksson and the two confessors, Master Petrus of Skänninge and Prior Petrus, who probably had to go home to Sweden now and then, but who always faithfully came back.

In Bridget's house it was good to die—in Bridget's house it was good to live. But outside the storm rose again—in that same year, 1354, Bridget was just in time to get indoors before the tempest broke.

For it was not 'peace, freedom and justice' that Cola di Rienzo had brought Rome. After the first enthusiasm had settled down the Romans saw that the tribune—who, by the way, now only bore the title bestowed upon him by the Pope: Senator of Rome—was no longer the same as before. The sedentary life of the years in prison had affected his physique—he had grown stout, his glance was dull, the mouth with the beautiful smile was hidden, according to the German fashion, by a big beard. He made his appearance only on horseback surrounded by a bodyguard of six hundred and fifty men, who had to be provided by the thirteen quarters of Rome. There were daily feasts in the Capitol, one banquet followed another and it was noticed that Cola drank freely. He was also changed mentally—he could often be seen plunged in deep melancholy, from which he would wake up to drink and unbridled gaiety. He felt that he had become a lonely man— the old friends and comrades in the fight of the first days of the movement kept far away from him; he took no interest in his family, during his long absence his wife had been unfaithful to him and had therefore been placed in a convent.

In order to quiet the discontent which Cola heard murmuring in the depths of the people he resolved to gain warlike honour. He determined to fight and conquer the Roman noblemen, first and foremost the Colonna family. In the middle of August, two weeks after entering the city, he resolved to attack the stronghold of the Colonnas. The two brothers from Perugia, Brettone and Arimbaldo, had entered his service, the supreme command he reserved for himself. But to carry on a war, as in our own times, three things are necessary: money, money and again money. But Cola had wasted on carousals the money which the Monreale brothers had advanced him. In Tivoli the mercenary troops had already mutinied. Cola had to return, his object unachieved—and found, when he came back to Rome a most unwelcome guest, Fra Monreale himself, who wished very much to know what had become of all his brothers' money. The great chieftain was ill-advised enough to speak disparagingly of Cola di Rienzo's strategic ability. Cola heard of it and took his revenge by inviting Monreale and his two brothers to one of the usual banquets. The three brothers were given the seats of honour. Cola made a speech to them and at a suitable moment they were arrested—the 'Nyköping banquet' in Italian! From the prison Monreale's path led to the scaffold—with an extreme sense of liturgical fitness Cola had fixed the day of execution on the feast celebrated by the Church of the beheading of John the Baptist (29 August). Brettone and Arimbaldo escaped with their lives but were kept in prison. Cola now boasted in public of having delivered Italy from 'the enemy of mankind No. 1'—which was true, in so far as the 'Great Company,' which had suddenly lost its leader, gave up the war against Milan, which it carried on for Venice. Cola himself took the field against the Colonna family and resumed the siege of Palestrina, which he was now able to finance with the money of the man who had been executed at his order. Meanwhile this unrighteous mammon also came to an end and Cola then had recourse to the most dangerous of all means: imposing a tax on salt and wine (in a later Italy *salee*, tobacco). The discontent had hitherto only been a murmur, a grumble, now it rose to a growl—was *that* what the Holy Spirit had inspired the tribune of the people to do? Any government could turn on the screw of the taxes—that did not require any particular heavenly support! In vain did Cola have one of his oldest friends, Pandolfuccio, who in 1347 had gained for him the goodwill of Florence, seized and executed on suspicion of having excited and increased the discontent of the people. Before the walls of Palestrina, as impregnable as ever, the troops growled: 'Money, money!' And in the neighbouring Montefiascone Cardinal Albornoz sat as immovable as a Spaniard at a bull-fight. In his despair Cola sent a message to him asking for help with money and soldiers—Albornoz answered by moving his headquarters some distance further away: from Montefiascone to Orvieto, the blood of the arena was not to be splashed on to *his* purple.

Then came 8 October. In the morning the rebellion broke out.

From the dingy quarters along the Tiber yelling crowds, armed with cross-bows and cudgels, marched towards the Capitol. Women and children joined the band, as they had done on 1 August, but now it was another shrill cry that came from the crowds: 'Down with Cola di Rienzo! Down with the enemy of the people who has imposed a tax! Long live the people! *Evviva il popolo, abbasso Cola di Rienzo!*'

Cola had arranged with his bodyguard that at a particular tolling of the bell of the Capitol they were to assemble at once. But before the bell could be touched the palace of the Senate was surrounded, and the rebels filled the square round the statue of Marcus Aurelius. Stones were hurled against the palace windows, the panes were smashed, behind a window a face appeared—Monreale's brother Brettone, who was a prisoner there. Waving his hand he called out to the people— *avanti, avanti.* . . .

Not till then did the bodyguard arrive—grasped the situation and went over to the attacking party. Brushwood and sticks were piled up before the palace gate, soon a lively fire was burning. Then the door of the balcony was opened, and up above the flames and the smoke Cola stepped out, clad in armour and with the banner of Rome in his right hand, the banner of Rome with the letters embroidered in gold, S.P.Q.R., those letters which the eagles of Rome in past centuries had brought from the rising of the sun to its setting, from the river to the outermost sea. . . . *Popolo di Roma!*—was still the cry uttered by the voice of the tribune of the people, but a howl from the multitude drowned his voice. Stones were hurled against him, an arrow struck the hand that was holding the banner, he had to go in.

And within he found only large empty rooms. In growing dread he went from room to room, called name after name—nobody! All had left him, all had fled! Perhaps *he*, too, could save himself, was there not a backdoor down in the tabularium out to Forum Romanum? Among these ruins Cola had dreamed the dreams of his youth about the departed glory of Rome, which was to rise again through him—was there to be a way to rescue for him now? But he would have to act quickly, quickly—away with the armour shining with gold—a pair of scissors quickly, two or three clips, away with the beard—in the kitchen there was plenty of soot in the fireplace after the last feast— the tribune of the people blackened his shaking hands and rubbed his face—in a corner he found an old cloak which he threw about his shoulders—and then away. . . .

But he did not get further than the courtyard of the palace—the gate had given way, and across burning beams, between smoke and flames, the attackers came surging in. For a moment he tried to act a part—pointing up to a window in the palace and screaming: 'He is up there!' But a man in the crowd had caught sight of the gold armlet that Cola always used to wear, and which in the confusion he had forgotten to take off—Cola was discovered! He understood that all was lost and did not try to defend himself.

Suddenly there was a great silence. There he stood in their midst, unarmed, his face besmirched, in a shabby cloak—the man of whom they had expected that he would establish the kingdom of the Holy Spirit! There he stood, his arms crossed upon his breast and looked at them with big, deep eyes—saying nothing, only looking at them, from one to another, and no one dared to touch him.

Minute passed after minute—Cola stood there, immovably facing the immovable multitude. Until at last a man forced his way through the throng, rushed at Cola and plunged a long butcher's knife in his breast. That broke the spell—all rushed upon the fallen man. A notary named Trejo split his skull, others planted their swords in his body, at last everyone wanted to join in the murder. And then the funeral procession began. The lifeless body was dragged through the streets of Rome by the legs, the head bumped against a stone and fell off, arms and legs were disfigured. At last the savage crowd reached Piazza San Marcello near Piazza Colonna, and here the ill-treated remains of the body were hung up—'like a slaughtered ox or cow hanging in a butcher's shop.' For two days and nights the body hung there, street boys threw stones at it. At an order from the Colonna family it was taken down and brought to the Augustus Mausoleum down by the Tiber. 'Here all the Jews of Rome assembled and lit a big fire of dry thistles. The body was thrown into this fire, and as Cola was a fat man the fire burned well. The Jews tended the fire and saw that it did not go out. And so the body was burned to ashes and the ashes were spread to all the winds of heaven.'(5)

V

On the same day that Cola di Rienzo's ashes were scattered to all the winds Charles IV crossed the Alps to go to Rome and be crowned. He had already been elected Emperor, but not until after the coronation in Saint Peter's was he 'römischer Kaiser deutscher Nation.' In a circular letter to the Italian republics he had announced his approaching arrival—Cola has answered it in expressions like those which Dante had applied to Charles' grandfather, Henry VII—Rome awaited her bridegroom with longing!

Cola was not to see the arrival of Charles—Bridget did. Now began the fulfilment of the promise made to her in Alvastra, when it was said to her: 'Go to Rome and stay there until you see the Pope and the Emperor.'(1)

Of the two it was the Emperor who came first. And he did not come as Emperor but as a prince of peace. His whole army consisted of three hundred horsemen, he had no other intention than that of reaching Rome and being crowned. On the way he was not received with any particular marks of distinction—Orvieto even closed its gates. On the way, however, several Tuscan noblemen joined his train, so that it was with an army of several thousand men that he pitched his camp outside the town, not far from Castel Sant' Angelo. His sojourn in Rome was only to be short—without an escort, dressed as a pilgrim, he set foot in Rome on 2 April 1355 and on the 5th, which was Easter Day, he was crowned in Saint Peter's by the Papal Legate, the Cardinal of Ostia, marched in triumph through the city to the Lateran and left Rome the same evening. On the way home he spent the night in Pisa, but the palace in which he had put up was surrounded and set on fire during the night by the Pisans because there was a rumour that the Emperor intended to restore to the neighbouring city of Lucca the freedom which Pisa had taken from it. The Royal couple escaped narrowly and Charles IV did not breathe freely until he was again out of the Italian nest of vipers. By his journey he had gained his object— he was henceforth the lawful Roman emperor 'deutscher Nation.' On this foundation he could build his policy. It did not affect him that Petrarch reproached him with his 'cowardly flight.' A long reign lay before him—from 1355 to 1378. And one of his first acts by the so-called 'Golden Bull' (of 1356), the first German constitutional law, was to make the election of the German emperor independent of the Pope's approval.(2) The long struggle between Emperor and Pope of the Middle Ages was ended.

During this short visit of the Emperor, which was, moreover, taken up with the ceremonies of coronation, it is not very probable that Bridget can have approached Charles IV in order, as the heavenly instruction said, 'to speak to him in My name and tell him the words that I will give you to say.' Nor is it likely that Charles would attach any importance to the letter which he had once received from her. She would

II   8

be able to see him riding from Saint Peter's to the Lateran, through Borgo Vecchio, across the bridge of Sant' Angelo, past the church of San Celso, across Piazza Colonna, past the Colosseum and along the Via San Giovanni. In his right hand the Emperor held a golden sceptre, in his left the orb of the realm; a baldacchino of silk interwoven with gold protected him from the April sun, already hot; the most distinguished citizens of Rome surrounded the slowly progressing steed, two of them holding the reins. Bridget and her family and other sightseers would be able to see the Emperor riding past without being able to come close to him. Now he rode into the palace—to pray in the chapel *Sancta Sanctorum*, it was said—then he came out again, mounted his horse and rode away with all his retinue out of the Via Tiburtina. Bridget's time of waiting was not over yet—not until 1368 was Charles IV to return.

It may have been during this time of waiting, after Bridget had seen her hope of a meeting with the Emperor disappointed, that she received a visitor, a monk, who wanted to prove to her 'out of his books' that the coming of Antichrist was drawing near. Bridget did not really doubt—she knew that this adversary of Christ was to be born of a woman 'who claimed to have an insight in spiritual things' (something like Madame Blavatsky). Only she did not believe that the time had yet come—the heathen had first to enter by the gate of faith and the Christians were to apostatize and become heretics, and persecution of the clergy was to break out in all countries.(3) At home in Sweden Bridget had already discussed the question with Master Matthias, and even Saint John the Apostle had appeared to her and confirmed the sensible answer of the learned theologian—'we know neither the day nor the hour.'(4) Bridget was never impressed by blustering talk—she knew what was often hidden under the eloquence. A very distinguished ecclesiastic—*religiosus magnae authoritatis*—pays her a visit; she sees that his heart 'is full of the filth of vain wisdom.' 'What did that windbag say to you?' the Blessed Virgin asks Bridget, after the learned master had gone. On another occasion it was Christ who inquired what 'this chatterbox' (*ille frater loquax*) has tried to make her believe, or what that 'sack of words' (*saccus verborum*) has made of a book he does not understand.(5)

In the midst of this external and internal confusion, however, she received a message with good news from home—Birger, her son, was on the way to Rome! After Cola's death and the coronation of Charles IV there was a period of peace—it was possible again to think of a journey. Cardinal Albornoz had completed the retaking of the papal state and returned to Avignon, where Innocent VI prepared a splendid reception of him; a carriage containing the keys of the conquered cities formed part of the triumphal procession. 'The great serpent,' Giovanni Visconti, was dead—Monreale's company had lost its leader and had given up its activity. It was a time for travelling and Birger set out from home to visit his famous mother.

For Bridget was famous. Birger received a proof of it when—after a stay in Rome (probably short, as he was a law man and had to return home to attend to the duties of his office) he discovered that he had not money enough for the journey home. It was then one no less than the Pope who supplied him with the necessary means. In a letter to the governor in Perugia, Geraldus, abbot of the Benedictine monastery of Marmoutier at Tours in France, Innocent writes: 'As it has come to our knowledge that our beloved son, Sir Birger from Sweden, and his sister, our beloved daughter Catherine, who are both living in Rome, are in difficulties, we command you this day to see that they are paid without delay, through a bank in Rome or another town, as a gift from us, four hundred gold florins.' The letter is dated 14 October 1355; at this time Birger must therefore have been in Rome on a visit to his mother and sister.(6)

And now Bridget could get real news about everything at home in Sweden.

VI

And so Bridget, Karin and Birger were sitting together round the evening fire in Francesca's house on Campo de' Fiori. When the day's work is over and the evening begins to be cold, as it does about the time of All Saints, an Italian family generally gathers in the kitchen to enjoy the fire on the hearth. The olive branches, which are far too fresh, perspire sap out of all their pores and burn but badly, now and then brushwood must be thrown on the fire to make it burst into flame. You sit and talk about the events of the day, perhaps there is an old granny who with a toothless mouth mumbles a song about Sant' Antonio—of how he stood preaching in a church in Italy, and at the same time he was in Portugal defending his brother who was to be unjustly condemned for murder. . . . Sant' Antonio simply proposed to the judge to examine the murdered man as a witness, which could very easily be done—Sant' Antonio and the judge with all the people after them went out to the churchyard where Sant' Antonio woke up the dead man, who settled the question by saying the real murderer's name. . . . Granny Ursula sings, the rest of us listen with a more or less sceptical smile. Then the fire burns down and the last embers are gathered up for the warming pan, a metal basin hung up in a wooden frame so that the bed-clothes do not come into contact with the burning hot metal. . . . With Italian lack of respect such a warming pan is called *un prete*—'a priest.' But if it is a man whose bed is to be warmed up he is asked if he wants a *monaca*, 'a nun.' . . . Perhaps the two names arose in Boccaccio's time—nowadays nobody thinks any longer about the meaning of the words—only a stranger feels that they are offensive (as I did on that cold night of the earthquake in Tagliacozzo in January 1915, when I was asked in the local albergo whether I wanted to have a *monaca* in my bed). . . .

Bridget, Karin and Birger were sitting with the rest of the family round the evening fire warming themselves. It was about the end of October, as yet no letter had come from Avignon in answer to Bridget's request for money—what would the answer be like? Would Bridget have to ask Francesca Papazuri for travelling money for Birger? But the Roman lady had already done so much for her Swedish friends—there was nothing to be done but to wait, always wait. . . . Meanwhile they could talk about Sweden. . . .

But there was not much joy in talking about Sweden. That crowned ass with a hare's heart is still sitting on his throne—Queen Blanca is the same frivolous and wanton woman that she was when Bridget shook the dust of Stockholm from off her feet—Duke Erik, Bridget's godson, has against all old law been ousted by his younger brother Haakon, who has become king in Norway—and in Vadstena, well, the ruins are still standing of the king's house which was pulled down, and the convent has not yet been built. One of Bridget's old friends, Sir Karl Näskonungson, had repented and given King Magnus his property in Källstad, a little to the south of Vadstena, with the express wish that the farm should belong to the convent—the king kept it for himself (and bestowed it later, together with the farms of Bjälbo and Sväm, and the nuns' convent in Skänninge. But Bridget did not know this yet!).(1) No, Magnus was no longer worthy to build a convent to the Mother of God—

he shall not build a house to the Lord like Solomon, he shall not be honoured like my beloved, Olav, and he shall not be crowned in heaven like my friend Erik, but he shall be made to feel my justice, because he did not know the time of grace, and my plough shall pass over his kingdom, until its inhabitants learn to pray for forgiveness.

Christ Himself had spoken thus to Bridget, and mysteriously He had added: 'There shall come one who shall build the convent, but who he is, and when he shall come, you shall not know yet.' The destroyed buildings would call down the wrath of God—'the stones shall cry to heaven for vengeance.'(2)

And—worst of all—Magnus had not repented of his unnatural vice. Bridget remembered that stormy night when she stood on the tower of the castle and looked down upon Stockholm. From the banqueting hall came the sound of gay singing and the music of stringed instruments—though it was late in the evening King Magnus and Queen Blanca were still sitting at table! But the storm was still howling, heavy clouds raced across the sky, at last came a coal-black cloud, looking like a dragon, and it opened its mouth and swallowed the moon.

'You shall know later what this means,' the Mother of God had said to her then. Eleven years had passed since then—and Magnus had persisted in his sin. In vain had the Blessed Virgin threatened him with a flogging—as many strokes as there was room for on him, until at last he begged for forgiveness.(3) And now, at last, had arisen from the depths that great dragon which was to swallow up both the moon and the sun, both Blanca and Magnus—that 'servant of the devil,' whom the king 'exalted above all others, and whom he loved with all his heart more than all others, nay, even more than himself, being glad to do his will in all things.'(4) Bengt Algotsson—for that was the man's name—had had a very rapid career: esquire in 1350, knight in 1351, counsellor of State in 1352 and now recently made duke over the south of Halland (the north-east belonged to Knud Porse and the Duchess Ingeborg). Bridget knew the family well, her eldest daughter Märta, who still brought her mother undesirable sons-in-law, married, after the death of Sigurd Ribbing, Bengt Algotsson's brother Knut. A couple of years were to pass ere Bridget's godson, Duke Erik (in 1356) dared to raise the banner of rebellion against his father's favourite.(5)

Bridget talked, Karin and Birger listened. Could their mother, then, not give a single good message for her son to take home to Sweden? Was the dragon to swallow both sun and moon and with its tail kill the people on the earth, so that nothing is left but vipers and creeping worms that eat up the fruits of the field? 'For that was how you saw it, dear Mother, that time eleven years ago, when you stood on the tower . . .'(6)

Birger asked, he and his sister listened with expectation. And then Bridget answered:

> The Mother of God has said to me: I am she to whom the angel said: 'Hail, full of grace!' And I therefore give grace to all who in their need cry to me to obtain it. And I will also help the kingdom in which you were born, if its inhabitants will be of one mind in striving to have a king who will guide the land to good deeds and seemly customs. The king who is now reigning shall lose the kingdom and all his house with him. But [Bridget lowered her voice] there is another born in the kingdom whom God has chosen to be king; he shall rule according to the counsel of the friends of God and to the true welfare of the country.(7)

Bridget ceased speaking. Birger and Karin looked at each other—they knew of whom she was thinking: of their brother's little son Karl, at home in Ulfåsa.

VII

If Saint Bridget had lived in the Rome of our times and had sat in the house on the Piazza Farnese, it is permissible to imagine that she would receive every morning after Mass an ample mail. She would almost certainly have subscribed to a Swedish newspaper, probably *Svenska Dagbladet*, an Italian one, perhaps *Giornale d'Italia* because of its articles on foreign politics, and of course *Osservatore Romano*. Besides the three newspapers the postman would every day bring her numerous letters from all the corners of the world with the most extraordinary stamps—*il postino*, who has a son who collects stamps begs for them, especially the rare ones. He has become slightly *blasé* in regard to the Swedish ones, they are always the same 20 or 15 *Öre*.* But the uncommon stamps, from Cyprus, from the Holy Land—he is very eager to get these. Bridget has correspondents everywhere—in Spain a bishop, in Cyprus a Dominican, in Jerusalem a Franciscan. What the papers and letters do not tell her she can hear on the wireless. And she has a telephone, perhaps even a private wire to the Holy Father—one cannot be always asking for an audience. . . .

But Bridget lived in the fourteenth century. It was but seldom that there was a letter from home, and before she could send an answer and the letter was received, what she had wanted to prevent had already happened. She had a greater possibility of achieving something in the world in which Providence had placed her, and where she had gradually

* 10 Öre = 1 penny.

come to feel at home. From Rome she looked towards the south, to the great kingdom of the Two Sicilies, about which she had heard so much, and where she understood there was work enough to do for God's cause. On the throne in Naples there was a young woman who was equally famed for her beauty and for her licentiousness—Giovanna, daughter of Charles of Anjou.

Since the Sicilian Vesper (1282), the kingdom of the Two Sicilies had been divided into two: the island of Sicily, where the Aragon family ruled, and the kingdom of Naples under the house of Anjou. During the whole of the fourteenth century an almost unbroken state of war prevailed between the two States, in which the see of Rome, because Sicily was properly speaking a papal fief, was on the side of Naples in the struggle against the Spanish usurpers.

During the Babylonian exile of the popes three monarchs wielded the sceptre in Naples: Charles the Lame (1285–1309), Robert the Wise (1309–43) and Giovanna (from 19 January 1343). Between Robert the Wise and the reigning Pope, John XXII, a state of tension gradually arose, as the king, in the strife between the strict and the moderate Franciscans, took the part of the former. When he learned that the Pope was preparing the bull *Cum inter nonnullos,* by which the doctrine of the absolute evangelical poverty was to be condemned, the learned king composed a treatise in which he requests the Pope not to go to such an extremity, as it would only cause dispute and awaken strife. When the bull came notwithstanding this (1323) a good while passed before it was published in the kingdom of Naples. And after Michael of Cesena had been dismissed as General of the Franciscan order and his writings condemned, the king's chaplains, Andrea da Galiano and Pietro da Cadeneto, used them as texts for sermons, and Queen Sancia decides in her testament that after her death the books are to be placed in security in the convent of the Poor Clares of Santa Chiara.(1)

King Robert of Anjou was above all a humanist. He collected a library of 7,000 manuscripts—the largest in Italy after that of the monks of Monte Cassino. For some time men like Petrarch and Boccaccio lived at his court—besides a whole number of learned men: the Calabrian Barlaam, who was Petrarch's tutor in Greek (in South Italy there were at that time still large districts in which the population had preserved the Byzantine language), the physician Nicola Roberto, the philosopher and astronomer Dionigi da Borgo San Sepolcro, a whole number of lesser spirits, whose names are now but names: Paolo da Perugia, Agostino Trionfi, Leone da Scala di Altamura, Niccolà d'Alunno di Alife, Matteo Spinelli. Naples was then what Florence was later to become under the Medici. Artists too, the best of the time, came at the call of King Robert: Masaccio, Giotto, Simone Martini, Pietro Cavallini. Petrarch could justly write of him: 'he was both intelligent and learned, a great theologian, a great philosopher, a great orator, the generous protector of literature, a wise and able politician, a beneficent and benevolent prince. In his time he had no equal.' And Boccaccio agreed with this in praise equally great: 'since the time of Solomon there has not lived so learned a prince.'(2)

It followed therefore, as a matter of course, that when Petrarch in March 1341 left his dear Vaucluse to go to Rome to be crowned with the laurel wreath at the Capitol, he sought out his friend and bene-factor of earlier times. For three days on end, from 2 to 4 April, the learned poet and the learned king spent the time in talks on philo-sophical and literary subjects; at parting the king took off his cloak and gave it to the poet—at the solemnity on the Capitol he was to wear a royal robe! At this parting young Boccaccio was present among many others, and at his side stood that Niccolà Acciaiuoli with whom Bridget was to become acquainted later, and in whose everlasting weal and woe she was to be so earnestly concerned.

King Robert's son, Charles, Duke of Calabria, was dead, only thirty-one years old, but leaving two daughters: Giovanna and Maria. In order to secure their future (and that of the kingdom) the king thought of getting them married into that branch of his own house that ruled in Hungary. The king there, Carobert or Robert, happened to have two sons: Louis and Andrew, and a betrothal was arranged between Giovanna and Louis, with the clause that if Louis died Andrew was to take his place, and if Giovanna died Maria was to take her place. This was altered, however, in 1333, to a double betrothal between Giovanna and Andrew, Maria and Louis. Giovanna's wedding took place in 1342 and she was then sixteen years old. Until she could take over the rule a guardian government nominated by her grand-father was to stand at her side. When King Robert lay on his deathbed in the following year he made the members of this government, and altogether all the great men of the kingdom take the oath of allegiance to Giovanna.

In the fourteenth century, however, an oath meant just as much as a treaty of friendship in the twentieth. King Robert's brothers, the Prince of Taranto and the Prince of Durazzo, were dead, but their widows were living. In spite of the engagement entered upon with

Louis of Hungary one of these ladies, the widow of the Prince of Durazzo, succeeded in getting her son Charles married to Princess Maria—in the event of Giovanna's marriage turning out childless her grandson would be able to make a claim on the throne. Naturally there was dissatisfaction in Hungary with this breach of faith and law; and in addition to this the young, vivacious and highly cultivated Giovanna —she was descended from the Counts of Provence and she had been brought up in *la gaya scienza*—could not become reconciled to the coarse and rustic manners of her Magyar husband, and carried her antipathy so far that she would not have him crowned as king. Neither Prince Andrew himself nor his father, the Hungarian king, however, were satisfied with the position of prince consort which Giovanna thought of giving her husband, and a complaint was sent to Avignon (in spite of all human frailty and even in Babylonian exile the Chair of Peter was still the court of appeal of Europe). In January 1345 Guillaume Lamy, Bishop of Chartres, arrived in Naples with the message from Clement VI that he, the Pope, had in a public consistory declared Andrew to be the rightful king, and that Giovanna had now to see that the coronation took place. The day fixed for this was 20 September, so that Giovanna had a respite of over six months.

September came and the royal couple spent the beautiful autumn days in their castle in Aversa (on the way to Caserta). In the evening of the 18th the king was about to go to bed when he was called from outside. He went out half dressed and in the darkness he was attacked and strangled. Giovanna left Aversa in haste and shut herself up in the fortified castle of Castelnuovo, which her father had engaged a French architect to build at the end of the preceding century. The castle is situated close to the harbour, with free access to the sea for one who wishes to flee.

Giovanna had good reason to think of flight. All Naples was well aware of the bad relations between the royal couple—all Naples murmured that it was the queen who had hired the murderers. *Is fecit cui prodest* says an old Roman proverb—'he has done it who has gained by it.' And could this murder have been more opportune for Giovanna if she had ordered it herself? The winter passed, and at Christmas time the queen gave birth to a son, to whom she gave the sonorous name of Charles Martel. She was allowed to nurse her child in peace. But when one of her sisters-in-law, Catherine de Courthenay, openly installed herself with her son Robert in the castle, and when it was rumoured that Giovanna had applied to the Pope for a dispensation to marry this far too closely related kinsman, scandal and bitterness broke out. It led to great demonstrations in front of the castle, and up against its crenellated walls could be heard the shriek, uttered with the full force of Neapolitan lungs: 'Down with the murderers! Down with the immoral queen! *Abbasso la putana Giovanna!*' At the same time a message came from Avignon that the king of Hungary had sent in a complaint against Giovanna for having broken her marriage vows and having had her husband murdered.

It availed Giovanna but little that after the death of the sister-in-law she refused to marry Robert. She did so only in the hope of being able to enter upon a new marriage with another of her cousins, Louis of Taranto. This time she did not wait for a papal dispensation—on 22 August 1347 she married Louis. It was Niccolà Acciaiuoli who had brought about this marriage; he had been young Louis' tutor and at the same time his mother's lover. Bridget was later to hear him cry in the flames of purgatory: 'Woe to me that I ever saw Louis and Giovanna!'(3)

Giovanna was still only twenty years old. Her grandfather, the wise King Robert, had discussed philosophy with Petrarch—her own favourite poet was Boccaccio, the lover of *Fiammetta* and the author of *Decameron*. He had written *Filocolo* for Fiammetta (the name given by the poet to his mistress, Maria d'Aquiro, King Robert's illegitimate daughter), he read aloud to Giovanna from the 'Hundred Novels.' Fillippa, the mistress of the young queen's household, had sat by listening and had smiled complacently. Beside them there was a certain 'Brother Robert,' a Rasputin figure, of whom Petrarch, in a letter to his friend Cardinal Colonna, gives the following portrait: 'he is small and stout, dressed in a ragged and greasy habit, bare-foot, walks with a stoop, not from age but because of hypocritical humility.' This man had won the confidence both of the dowager queen and of Giovanna, assumed the office of political adviser to the young queen, rejected all the justified complaints of the people, oppressed the poor, while all the time raking in money for himself. Petrarch must bitterly have deplored the result of this double influence—here Boccaccio, there Rasputin! 'I thought,' he writes, 'that it was only in Memphis, in Babylon, in the Mecca of the Saracens, that Christ was despised— now you, my beloved Naples, have also become like those cities. No piety, no faith, no honesty any more!' Petrarch sees Naples like a ship in a rough sea, and at the helm there is this Brother Robert (alas! he has even the same name as the late wise king!). 'Soon this great ship will founder, for the sailors are of the same kind as their master.'(4)

Petrarch's fear was not to prove unfounded. King Louis of Hungary's patience at length came to an end. Paying no heed to the admonitions of Clement VI to wait and see the turn of events he crossed the Alps to avenge the murder of his brother. Soon he will be standing before the gates of Naples. But before that Giovanna has taken ship (in January 1348) to go home to Provence, which is her inheritance from her father, and to go to the Pope in Avignon.

VIII

Bridget was at home in Sweden while all this happened. She was in Alvastra when Louis of Hungary under arms broke into Naples and had his rival, Charles of Durazzo, executed. She was there, too, when the great men of Naples rose up against the Hungarian usurper and his rule of force and drove him out (in June 1348). She was there when Giovanna, ten months later, came back and was welcomed with rejoicing by the same people who had cried death upon her and called her a harlot. The exiled queen had obtained money for the journey home by selling Avignon to the Pope, who was thus no longer living there as a tenant, and she came home acquitted of all guilt in the murder of King Andrew. 'It was like an evil spell—I could not endure my husband. But murder him, or have him murdered—No!'

If Bridget did not know all this when she was at home she would no doubt hear about it in Rome. The beautiful young queen of Naples was a standing subject of talk in the aristocratic and ecclesiastical circles frequented by Bridget. It was like the time at home when she heard the talk about Blanca. Ah yes, this Provence—this *gaya scienza*, so entirely the reverse of true wisdom!

The chastisement had come, however, upon Giovanna's Naples as upon Blanca's Sweden. The Black Death had ravaged there too, in Sicily alone 500,000 people died. Shortly after Giovanna had returned from Avignon she had to cancel a demand for taxes, for the simple reason that there was no one from whom a tax could be demanded.(1)

And not only was there the plague. In September 1349 the country was laid waste by a terrible earthquake which struck the towns of Aquila, Ascoli, Aversa, Sora, San Germano, Venafro. In the little Venafro alone seven hundred dead lay under the ruins. The large Benedictine monastery on Monte Cassino had fallen completely into ruins. In Naples the belfry of the cathedral fell. At the same time the country was devastated by the mercenary troops brought in by Louis of Hungary and led by the condottiere Betrand de La Motte, Fra Monreale (whom Cola di Rienzo was later to take into his service), a certain Stephen, Voivod of Transylvania, called *Lupo* by the Italians, besides the too well-known Werner of Urslingen, by the Italians called Guarniero. 'No citizen dared any longer go out to see to his property outside the town,' says a chronicle of the time. The records of those years are full of complaints of misdeeds, perpetrated by *malandrini* and *banditi*. In the little city of Agerula (near Amalfi) a band destroyed 200 houses, in another small city, Gragnano, 250 incendiary bandits came one early morning in May, dragged the still sleeping inhabitants naked out of their beds and along to the market place, where they put them to the sword and left them there. Out along the roads lay the corpses of women who had first been raped and then *spaccate nello ventre*, cut up alive in an attack of bestial sadism.(2) (The Mohammedans have preserved this custom; during my stay in Jerusalem in 1922 the newspapers reported a case of a Christian woman who had been assaulted and raped by Beduins, who had thereupon opened her body, filled it with flax, poured petrol over it and set it on fire.)

Some years were still to pass ere there was peace in the kingdom of Naples. Giovanna had for a time to flee to the fortress of Gaëta (where Pius IX was to seek shelter five hundred years later). At last peace came (1352) and on Whitsunday of the same year the coronation took place of Giovanna and Louis of Taranto. Bridget was then in Rome and the echo of the festivities must have reached her ears. The list of the invited guests was very long (whether they all came is another matter); at the head of it was of course King Louis of Hungary, with whom there was now peace. Then the following great lords: from Milan Cangrande della Scala and the Lady Isabella; Obizzo, Marchese d'Este; the lords of Padua and Parma; Malatesta and Galeotto Malatesta da Rimini; Rudolfo da Varano, Duke of Camerino; the Lords of Sanseverino, Sassoferrato, Faenza, Imola; Bernardino da Polenta from Ravenna. Florence was represented by an entire embassy, among whom were included Leonardo Strozzi and Giovanni Medici, Francesco de' Buondelmonti and Piero degli Albizzi. All who possessed a name were assembled in Naples. In the cathedral the Papal Nuncio, the Archbishop of Braga, crowned Giovanna and Louis king and queen of Naples. The ghost of the murdered king had been laid.(3)

IX

After Bridget had lived for many years in Rome it happened that while she was praying Christ appeared to her and said: 'I bid you go on pilgrimage to the holy places in the kingdom of the Two Sicilies, for many a saint lies buried there, who has loved Me with all his heart—among them My apostle Thomas. And when you come thither I will reveal to you certain mysteries.(1)

This marching order did not really come as any surprise to Bridget. In Arras, at Ulf's sick bed, where she had in spirit gazed into the lands to which she was to come later (and in Rome even Casa Papazuri), 'a most beautiful youth' had already led her to all the holy places of Italy, to those which as yet she only knew by name, but to which she was later to be allowed to make the journeys of a pilgrim. For it was not only Rome which had tombs of the apostles within its walls, but Saint Andrew lay buried in Amalfi, in Benevento Bartholomew, in Salerno Saint Matthew, in Ortona, on the shore of the Adriatic, Saint Thomas. Bari hid the relics of the great Saint Nicholas, and on the mount of Gargano stood the church of Saint Michael, built on the place where the archangel Michael had appeared—no Scandinavian pilgrim omitted to make a journey thither. The Normans had even at home erected an imitation of the shrine—Mont Saint Michel.

In Bridget's time the kingdom of the Two Sicilies—usually called 'the kingdom,' *il Reame*, comprised the island of Sicily and on the mainland the provinces of *Abruzzi* (with the towns of Aquila, Sulmona, Chieti, Ortona, Pescara), *Molise* (with Isernia), *Terra di Lavoro* (with Naples, Capua, Aquino, Fondi, Sora), *Calabria* (with Cosenza), *Capitanata* (Foggia, Lucera, Manfredonia), the principality of *Bari* (with the towns of Bari, Barletta, Bitonto), the principality of *Taranto* (with Taranto, Otranto and Brindisi), finally the province of *Basilicata* (with Potenza and Melfi). In the midst of this extensive kingdom lay, like a little papal enclave, the principality of *Benevent*.

First and above all, then, it was Ortona that Bridget had been told to visit—Ortona, where the apostle Thomas was buried. In 1258 his body had been brought thither from Edessa, where he had been laid to rest after his martyrdom—on the anniversary of this translation, 6 September, there was a great solemnity in Ortona, perhaps it was on that very day that Bridget intended to visit it.

For at home she had learned all about the saga of Saint Thomas. By profession he was a master builder, and it was in that capacity that he was invited to India to build a palace for Gundoforus, the king of the country. Together with the envoy of the Indian king, a certain Abbanes, Thomas set out from Cæsarea, where he had laboured hitherto, to the land of India, and on the way the two travellers came to a city where it happened that the king of the country was celebrating the marriage of his daughter. Thomas and Abbanes were invited to the wedding feast, and there Thomas heard, greatly wondering, a Hebrew maid singing to the guests and playing skilfully on the flute, and what the flute player sang was constantly the same: 'the God of the Jews is the true God, the God of the Jews is the true God!' No one but Thomas understood the words, but Thomas was so glad to hear his mother tongue that he quite forgot both to eat and drink. The king's butler, however, took great offence at this, and when he saw that the cup with the good wine still stood untouched in front of Thomas he was so scandalized that he gave the fastidious guest a smart blow in his face: 'Do you dare to refuse the king's wine!' Now perhaps Thomas ought to have obeyed his Master's commandment about turning the other cheek—but instead of that he was angry and shouted to the butler: 'Now just you listen to me—I will not rise from this table until I see a dog come in with your hand in its mouth!' It was the custom in that country never to drink wine unmixed, and soon after the scene with the unpleasant guest the butler had to go out to the well to fetch water. And while he stood there drawing up the bucket, it actually happened that a lion came into the courtyard and rushed upon the unhappy man. After the lion had taken his share it was the turn of the dogs—a whole pack of them fell upon the dead body and tore it in pieces—and thus it came about that one of the dogs (which had otherwise to be content with the bones that the guests threw under the table) came into the banqueting hall with the bloodstained hand in its mouth. Then they were all struck with terror, and threw themselves at the feet of Saint Thomas. And the Hebrew maid sang with a loud voice: 'the God of the Jews is the one true God!'

But the king begged Saint Thomas to bless the bridal bed of his daughter. And Thomas blessed it and said: 'May the Lord, the true God, bless these two young people with His right hand and grant them the flowers of ever-lasting life!' But when the apostle had gone out from the bedroom, behold, the bridegroom found in his hand a branch of a palm tree, and it was full of dates, and both he and his maiden ate thereof and then both fell asleep! But while they slept they both had a dream, and when they awoke they told one another the dream, and both had dreamed the same dream. They had both seen a fair king with a crown upon his head, and the king embraced them and said that his apostle Thomas had vowed them to everlasting life. And immediately Thomas came in to them through closed doors and spoke to them and preached to them of how great a virtue is chastity. The virtue of chastity overcomes all devils, it is the ornament of all joy, the victory of faith and the fruit of salvation which is always fresh. But of desires and the lust of the flesh come dishonour, uncleanness, infection, sin and vice. And while Thomas was speaking two angels of God came, who said: 'We are your guardian angels, and we counsel you to pay heed to Saint Thomas.' Then they received baptism with joy and promised to live in chastity. The name of the bride was Pelagia, she became a nun and died in martyrdom. And the name of the bridegroom was Dionysius, and he became a bishop of the city.

The legend now relates how Thomas travelled on and at length came to India. Here also he worked miracles, and among others he healed a great lady who was blind. The lady is a friend of the king's sister-in-law, Migdonia—she, too, became a Christian. At last even the queen follows the example of her two friends—'she received the Christian faith and would thereafter not go to bed with her husband if he did not become a Christian.' Now the king bids Thomas come to him and bids him 'turn again the will of the women to their husbands.' Thomas refuses, and when he goes uninjured out of a furnace into which he had been thrown, the Lady Migdonia's husband thinks that he can bring evil upon him by compelling him to honour and worship the image of the sun god. 'We cannot hurt Thomas so long as his God is of good will to him,' the angry husband reasons. 'But if he now worships our idols his God will be wrath upon him and help him no longer, and then we can be quit of him.' To everyone's surprise Thomas agrees to the proposal, kneels down before the image and prays. No one understands his prayer for he speaks in Hebrew, but soon they all see the effect—the image falls to pieces and turns to dust 'just as quickly as wax melts in fire.' 'Then the idol priests howled like wolves and their bishop cried that he would avenge his god and thrust a spear through the body of that man of God. But the Christians took Thomas' body and buried it and built a church over it. And from that day Christianity grew in the land. Then, two hundred and thirty years after the death of Our Lord, they moved his bones to Edessa . . . and in that place no heathen or Jew or heretic can live, and no robber or one who rules with violence can prosper. And the king of the country, Abgar, received a letter written by Our Lord Himself. And if the city is besieged a newly baptized child reads Our Lord's letter at the gate of the city, and straightway the enemies flee from this letter and from the power of Saint Thomas. And his feast is five nights before Christmas night.'(2)

Since the year 1258 the pilgrims therefore no longer needed to travel the long way to Edessa in Syria to venerate Saint Thomas. And Bridget, Karin and all the little family now go away from Rome, through Porta Sebastiano, out along the Appian Way. Cola di Rienzo had loved all the memories of the great periods in the history of Rome, Bridget passed them by with indifference, it may be that she did not even ask the permission of Master Petrus to look upon the tomb of Cæcilia Metella, later the fortified stronghold of the Gaetani family. She knew nothing about the romantic raptures of later times for the Campagna—it was not her figure that a painter was to depict, sitting in an attitude of classic dreaming on a broken column. But in the little chapel of *Domine quo vadis* she would, unaffected by all archæological criticism, kiss the stone bearing the imprint of the foot of Jesus on that occasion when He walked to Rome, and in answer to the fugitive Peter's question 'Lord, whither goest Thou?' answered: *Vado Romam, iterum crucifigi*, 'I go to Rome to be crucified again!' Perhaps she turned a little aside from the road to pray in the little Roman basilica of Sant' Urbano, dedicated to the bishop who had converted Saint Cæcilia's bridegroom Valerianus, and, a little further on, near the villa of the Quintiliæ, to linger by his grave. . . . In San Sebastiano Karin would certainly not omit to seek the protection of her favourite and heavenly saint.

It is difficult to follow in detail the route taken by Bridget to Ortona, and the difficulty is not lessened by the fact that she made the journey twice. Prior Petrus, who accompanied her on both occasions, says himself that he can no longer remember the names of all the places they visited. During the second of the two pilgrimages she made a halt at Sermoneta, a small town belonging to the Gaeta family—she lodged there with a nobleman of the curious name of Sculus. It may be that she also made a halt there the first time. Via Appia, which she followed, leads through the Pontine marshes, where Ninfa was still a living town, not a poetic ruin in a land ravaged by malaria.(3) Bridget may have passed by the Cistercian abbey of Fossanuova, where Saint Thomas Aquinas died in 1274, on the way to the Council in Lyons—it stands rather out of the way, like another Cistercian monastery of the thirteenth century, Valvisciolo, near Sermoneta. At Terracina she would come through the pass hewn in the rock by Trajan, and far out across the blue gulf at Gäeta she would be able to see the bluish Monte

Circeo—where lived the beautiful witch, Circe, who changed men into unclean animals; Bridget was soon to become acquainted with such another Circe—the young queen Giovanna of the kingdom of Sicily. . . .

Bridget reached Ortona, but at the apostle's grave she was only told that she had to come again.(4) Besides, the journey was made more difficult by illness—both Bridget and others of the company were ill (liver trouble and the like). And now came the season of Advent with its commandment of fasting—how was it to be kept? Bridget would not cause scandal by breaking the commandment. On the other hand. . . . The painful dilemma was solved by Christ Himself who revealed Himself to Bridget and said:

> Fish is very cold food, the weather is not warm. The road is rough and stony and you and the others are not well. I therefore say to you: 'Eat what is set before you' [the words to the disciples in the gospel of St. Luke x, 7]. 'I am above all rules of fasting, and what you eat now to the glory of God and needful refreshment shall not be counted to you as sin.'(5)

Bridget went back to Rome to keep Christmas. But she had set foot on the new field of her labours—the kingdom of Queen Giovanna.

X

First, however, there was an old reckoning to be made up—the reckoning with Sweden. And that meant the same as the reckoning with Magnus, with Magnus and his house. In a revelation which is apparently concerned with the people of Israel and their exodus from Egypt, Christ speaks to Bridget of 'that king' and 'that kingdom.' The king is Magnus, 'whom you have known,' the kingdom is Sweden.

The reproaches against Magnus are the usual ones—that he allows himself to be guided by bad advisers, that he is vacillating, that he will not obey those whose directions he ought to follow, and who had told him how he ought to behave. But there is really no cause for wonder at this—he is a chip of the old block, and Magnus comes of a bad stock and belongs to a race which has always provoked the wrath of God, and upon whom only the severest forms of chastisement have any effect.

And now Bridget tells Magnus from what kind of family he has come. There is not much to be proud of. First there was Birger Earl —an ambitious climber, a ruler who persecuted his enemies with cruelty. (In the convent of Sko, which Bridget visited with her mother, Bridget may have seen the grave of Holmger Knutsson, beheaded in

1248, and heard tell that miracles occurred at the grave.) But God was lenient with Birger Earl—he did do some good, and he was also a chastiser of the people because of their sins.

The next generation consists of Birger Earl's two sons, Valdemar and Magnus. They are characterized by two words—*incontinentia and injustitia,* immorality and injustice. Bridget is thinking of Valdemar Birgersson's scandalous love affair with his sister-in-law, Princess Jutta of Denmark, and she is thinking of his brother's social legislation, which earned for him the surname of *Ladulås* ('barndoor lock'), conferred upon him by grateful peasants, but which from Bridget's point of view was an unjust encroachment on the rights of the nobles and a traditional custom. It is added about Valdemar that God humbled him and deprived him of the crown, which happened after the battle of Hova in 1275, when, defeated by his brother, he had to give up his claim to the throne. The third generation comes to the time which is Bridget's own—the reign of King Birger Magnusson and the strife between him and his brothers, the dukes. In this strife between brothers the Finsta family were on the side of the dukes—and Bridget could not forget that she owed her life to Duke Erik. On the other hand she does not seem to have thought with much regret of the Nyköping banquet, and excuses everything with a few words about all the three brothers having sprung 'from a hard root.'

Then there is the fourth generation—Magnus Eriksson. There are severe remarks about him. He pretends to be pious and humble, but he is unjust in his judgments, and he is wasteful. There is still time for him to make amends, but if he does not at last alter his ways 'I will strike him with a scourge from the crown of his head to the sole of his foot, so that all who hear of it will be struck with terror at the justice of God.' Christ adds: 'He shall not trust in My having once called him My friend, but he must remember the pact that we made. If he had kept his word to Me I would have kept my word to him.'(1) Here it is a question of the pilgrimage to Rome—this time to Avignon—to which Bridget had urged him, and which Magnus really seems to have contemplated. Bridget had made the suggestion to him in the name of Mary—since it is Christ Himself who speaks to him through her.

I, the Son of God, advise the king to journey to the Pope and to pray humbly to him for the absolution of his sins. For he who sits in My chair in this world has the highest power to bind and loose in My name. And if the king follows this advice that I give him I will defend him against his enemies, pay all his debts, if he cannot do so himself [here it is in particular a question of the large sum for the ransom of Scania], and I will count every step he takes on this pilgrimage and in return I will give him everlasting life. But when the king comes to the Holy Father he must with all his heart humble himself and not hide or adorn anything.

Bridget has already the whole list of his sins ready—he has imposed new and heavy taxes upon the people, he has transgressed against the laws of the Church, he has promoted unworthy priests to ecclesiastical offices, etc., etc. Next, as a dutiful godmother, she has moreover given the king good advice for the journey. He must not, as certain of his courtiers have advised him to do, set out with great splendour, not take with him a great retinue, not throw alms about on the way to make an impression in the places to which he comes (the love of boasting of the old Northmen—as when Sigurd on his way to Jerusalem had his horse shod with gold, and when one of the shoes fell off at the ceremonious entry into Byzantium he contemptuously left it lying). He must take with him only a few and pious servants—and for the rest little Magnus must beware of robbers!(2)

This pilgrimage came to nothing. All Bridget's well-meant admonitions and all her good advice had no effect upon the reckless heart of her godson. Besides, she knew who stood between her and Magnus—it was Blanca! Like a dangerous thorn this French girl had forced her way into the king's heart and was about to become an obstacle on that road to perfection in which he ought to walk. She did not want to have any more children and had made the king take the vow of chastity which had such sinister results. She was beautiful—true! A rotten apple may also be good to look at, but it has a bad taste when you bite it. Jezebel was no doubt also a beauty but how did she end? The dogs devoured her body in the street!(3)

Bridget had been thinking of Magnus and Blanca one day out in Saint Agnes' church. And it seemed to her as if she saw a splendid chariot on four wheels, and in the chariot sat a woman in beautiful raiment. And Bridget had said to herself: 'What is such a creature but flesh and blood and filth and excrements, and what is there to be proud of?' Then Saint Agnes spoke to her and said:

If your guardian angel had not stood by you, you would no doubt also have sat in such a chariot. But now I will explain the four wheels to you. The first is called pride, so that one looks down upon and condemns others. The second is called presumption before God, so that one does not take much thought of one's sins. The third wheel is worldliness and wastefulness in order to be honoured and esteemed. The fourth is self-love and self-will so that one does not fear the judgment of God. The chariot is drawn by two horses—one is the hope of living long, the other the will to sin as long as one lives. But the coachman is the devil, and he drives the chariot straight into the abyss.

To this judgment on Blanca from the lips of Saint Agnes Prior Petrus added: 'She is a serpent and her tongue is sweet like the tongue of a harlot. Her heart is full of gall, her body of poison. Therefore the eggs that she lays are poisoned.'(4) The stern Cistercian now and then broke off his sojourn in Rome in order to go home to Alvastra(5)— —he would then probably hear news about the court in Stockholm. In one place Bridget speaks with contempt about a king who is 'a crowned ass,' because he submits to his beloved (*amasia*) striking him in the face when he does not smile kindly enough to her—he ought to have given her a good whipping!(6) Is this a chapter of the *chronique scandaleuse* of the court at Stockholm?

Which of the two women, Bridget or Blanca, is to gain the victory in the struggle for King Magnus' soul? In spite of everything Bridget cannot give him up. 'Charity beareth all things, believeth all things, endureth all things.' Once more the Blessed Virgin speaks in Bridget's soul about Magnus:

Now tell this king, for whom you are praying, that I, the mother of charity, warn him against shame and harm. For it would be shame if anyone changed a chest full of gold for an empty one. But the king is thinking of raising a servant of the devil to be his adviser, which would be a spiritual shame. I therefore swear by Jesus Christ my Son, that if the king does not—as prudent men have counselled him to do—rid himself of that servant of the devil, and not let him dispose of so much as a penny, I will torment and plague him from the crown of his head to the sole of his foot with aches and pains until he cries: 'Have mercy upon me, Mary, for I have incited thee to wrath against me.'(7)

Among the sins with which King Magnus has stirred up Mary's anger there was also the sin that he had not punished a nobleman who in his presence had blasphemed God. In the Middle Ages blasphemy was a crime incurring punishment by the secular authority. And he who failed to punish a blasphemer incurred the same judgment upon himself.(8)

But then was heard from on high a voice that said: 'Oh thou Mother of Mercy, look down in mercy upon the prayers of thy servant the king. Justice demands that he shall be plagued and tormented for his sins, but do thou pray for him that he may have grace to repent.' Then justice answered: 'The time is short, it will not be long enough to atone for the sins he has committed.'

The words are stern, are they the last words, then, about King Magnus? No, there is still the very last one. 'If anyone,' Bridget says with delicate discernment, 'speaks through a reed with three sound-holes and says: "Never more shall you hear my voice," he can still speak through the two others without contradicting himself.' Nor is it a letter that Bridget sends the king this last time, it is a *love song*. 'For now divine justice sings a beautiful song which concerns all, and whosoever hears this song and believes in it, and acts according to it by his deeds, shall find the way of salvation and everlasting life.'(9)

And Bridget's soul soars upward like an eagle, borne upon the storm of inspiration, and with the mighty beat of wings it reaches the realm of eternity. . . . It is not angels she beholds there, it is not saints, it is not even the Virgin Mary. What she sees is a vast hall, and in the middle of the hall is a desk, a *book rest* (as the old Swedish translator says) and on the book rest a *book*.

But to look at the book rest was like sun rays that are now red, now white, now shining like gold. The red colour was like a blushing rose, the white was like shining snow, the golden colour was like radiant sunshine. And all the three colours were blended in each other—when I saw the golden colour I saw also the white and the red, and when I saw the white colour I saw the two others in it, and so it was also when I saw the red colour, and yet the three colours were separate one from the other, and none was before or after another, and none was greater or less than another, but they were equal in all things and everywhere.

What Bridget saw, then, was simply the Holy Trinity, one God, Father, Son and Holy Ghost. She therefore says now, using the third person: 'When I looked upward I was not able to comprehend *His* length and breadth, when I looked down I could not comprehend *His* depth, it was all beyond understanding.'(10)

On this radiant book rest, then, lies the Book. In the Apocalypse it is said: 'And I saw in the right hand of him that sat on the throne a book written within and without, sealed with seven seals. . . . And no man in heaven nor in earth, neither under the earth, was able to open the book, neither to look on it' (Revelation of Saint John v, 1–3). The book that Bridget sees—'a book which shines like the brightest gold'—is open, and it is a book which does not need anyone to come and read in it, 'for every word in the book was not written with ink, but every word in the book was living and *spoke of itself*.'* That is the

---

* In the same way in the Apocalypse (Revelation of Saint John) it is the Altar that speaks: 'And I heard another out of the altar say' (xvi, 7).

book meant by Thomas of Celano when it is said in *Dies iræ: Liber scriptus proferetur, unde mundus judicetur,* 'Now the writing must be read, by which the world is judged.' And now the earlier vision of the Folkungs' three generations is extended and elaborated in a poetical form. In front of the book desk, which is a judgment seat, Bridget sees three Swedish kings—'one still living, the second dead and in hell, the third dead and in purgatory.' Bridget's eyes are turned, first and foremost, to the first of the kings, to him who is still living—for that is Magnus Eriksson. . . .

What she sees is strange and weird. King Magnus is sitting on his throne, with a crown upon his head, within a glass globe.* Above the glass globe hangs a sword which slowly draws nearer the globe—'like the weight in a clock.' That moment cannot be far distant when the sword—the sword of death—reaches the globe and crushes it. What will happen then? Bridget sees an angel standing on one side of the glass globe and a devil on the other. The devil is impatient—she hears him shout: 'How long is this to go on? The angel and I have been hunting this prey for a long time—which of us is to have it?'

Bridget does not see the sword of death striking the brittle shell that a human body is. But she has not much hope of a good end for King Magnus. She knows him far too well, alas! she knows that he is inconstant, now warm, now cold. 'When he falls into temptation he says to himself: "I know that I am offending God when I do what pleases me, but I cannot help it!" And then he sins knowingly and wilfully against his God, and because he sins knowingly and wilfully he comes under the power of the devil. Thereupon the king repents and goes to confession, escapes the devil and gets into the power of the angel. But if the king does not give up this inconstancy he will be in peril.'

It must be observed here that this exceedingly sinister revelation is not understood by all in the same way as it has been here. In the three kings Madame de Flavigny has even wanted to see a picture of Magnus Eriksson's soul in three different states—living, in purgatory, in hell—all meant as a threat to the king. 'See what awaits you if you do not in time . . .' There is little probability that this is a correct interpretation, and it is justly rejected by Swedish Bridgettine research, which is agreed that the king whom Bridget sees condemned to hell must be Magnus Eriksson's grandfather, Magnus Ladulås (1275–90).(11)

* Bridget may have been thinking of the king's seal; he sits in a circle on the throne, with orb and sceptre.

Bridget was born only thirteen years after the death of this king, and in her home in Finsta she must often have heard him spoken of. And no doubt not favourably, for—to use a modern expression—King Ladulås was a democrat. He sought the support of the people, not of the nobility. At the land law of 1279 (Alsnöstadgan) he earned his surname. It is said in it:

> Hitherto the bad custom has prevailed that all the men who take their ways in the kingdom, even though they may be ever so rich, do not shrink from entering the houses of the poor as guests, and there demand food without payment and there consume in a short while what the poor have laboured long to obtain.

This bad custom was now forbidden—the rhymed chronicle justly puts these words into the mouth of King Magnus:

> The poor call me barndoor lock,
> To rich and poor alike I gave peace,
> And bade them bolt the door of the barn
> And thereafter to fear no harm.

When the popular king died during a sojourn at Visingsö in Vättern grateful peasants carried his coffin on their shoulders all the long way to Stockholm. At Gråmunkholmen, in the present Riddarholm church, where he was buried with the Franciscans, there is still the Latin epitaph over him, in which he is called 'the prince who ruled with justice, the author and pattern of the law, the gentle King Magnus.'(12)

Rex mitis Magnus, 'the gentle King Magnus,' the title given him by the common people and the sons of Saint Francis. He had always been a close friend of the Franciscans, in his testament he left money for a journey to Assisi, which was to be made in his name and for the good of his soul. Soon there was even a rumour that he was a saint at whose tomb miracles occurred.(13)

Bridget did not believe in it, and she had reasons, for her fully valid, for it. On Candlemas Day in 1349, the year in which she left Sweden, she was at High Mass in the cathedral of Skara, and there (as related in Vol. I of this work, p. 257) she had a vision. After she had been to Holy Communion Mary and Jesus appeared to her, and Mary begged her Son to let the Sacrament take root in her heart, so that she might be transformed into Him. Thereupon the Blessed Virgin spoke of Bishop Brynolf who had recently died in the fame of sanctity, and for whom Bridget had a great veneration, but whose body lay buried here in contempt and dishonour. Brynolf had been like a sapphire which (according to the belief of the Middle Ages about precious stones) when worn in a ring keeps the body strong and healthy(14)—and this precious jewel now lay despised and forgotten in the dirt. And while this was the fate of the true saint, one who was unworthy was esteemed and honoured as if he was a holy man. It was easy to see that this was not the case—he had not 'lived in the imitation of the saints,' he did not rejoice in the thought of being able to shed his blood in God's cause, and he was either unmerciful or ill-advised in good works. If nevertheless he had come into the odour of sanctity it was because of false rumours, of the credulous ignorance of the common people and—not least—because certain ecclesiastics were interested in creating a saint.(15)

As Toni Schmid has correctly seen, Bridget cannot in this false saint have thought of any other than Magnus Ladulås. Now on the whole it is probably seldom that kings live like canonized saints. Besides, on the list of his sins Magnus had his broken promise of going on a crusade to Riga, to shed his blood there for the cause of Christ, and that, although otherwise a close-handed man, he had been generous when it was a case of his dear Franciscans. It is obvious that they were interested in spreading the fame of their benefactor for sanctity. Finally there was the fact that there had been open strife between the king and the powerful sons of Algot, to whom Bishop Brynjulf belonged. The situation had even been so critical that Brynjulf had been compelled to flee from his episcopal city of Skara to his friends, the Cistercians, in Alvastra; it was while he was lying out on Lake Vättern waiting for a fair wind that he had written his most beautiful office of a saint, that of Saint Helena of Skövde.(16)

'But whether this man is in hell or in purgatory it is not permitted to you to know, before the time to speak comes.'(17) Now the time to speak has come, and Bridget sees that King Magnus Ladulås is in hell. By his side stands a devil of a terrible appearance: 'his head was a dog's head, in his belly the navel was open and out of the opening flowed all kinds of coloured poison, on each foot he had strong and sharp claws.' It is the work of this devil to torment the king to confess his guilt. The king's confession says:

> I sought counsel of priests and learned men [not of the nobles] of how the kingdom fared. . . . And so that I could preserve the kingdom and defend it and preserve it from the onslaughts of enemies we had [the king and his advisers] to think of new ways of imposing taxes. For the old taxes and the estates of the crown and what belongs to the royal household were not

enough to rule and protect the kingdom. I therefore thought of new and unlawful taxes and impositions that wrought harm to many men of the kingdom, as also to many innocent wayfarers and merchants.

In the legislation of Magnus Ladulås there were many other things that did not please the great men, such as the new law of the right of the crown to what had before been considered the common property of all (commons, lands, fishery, etc.). It is well known that Magnus was often in economic difficulties and had several times to impose an extra tax. Concerning 'the innocent wayfarers and merchants' this means, of course, the prohibition against helping oneself from what belongs to the peasant.—Transgressing this prohibition incurred a fine of forty marks. 'When wayfarers,' Bridget complains, 'slept and thought that their gold was safely preserved in their purses they saw, when they awoke, that their money was in the king's coffers.' In the hostels set up here and there in the country one could only spend the night on payment to the host. The king was now punished for this 'fault' by the devil that was set the task of tormenting him by pouring poison over his hands—the hands with which he had seized 'the gold of wayfaring men.'

Bridget cannot deny, of course, that the king has been the benefactor of churches and convents. But has he done anything more than giving of his abundance? A man eats an apple—and throws away the peel to whoever will eat it. King Magnus has kept the juicy, delicious fruit for himself and cast a few alms to Our Lord. Bridget can say it another way—he has been like a man who owes twenty pounds in gold. But he does not want to part with the gold. So what does he do? He takes nineteen pounds in copper, gilds them with one pound of gold and gives them to the gullible creditor. That is how King Magnus has got out of his difficulty—he has followed the advice given him by the devil: 'Spend nineteen hours on your own will and desire and pleasure, then you will still have one hour to spare for repenting and mourning over your sins! And then, when you have confessed you can again do what you like, for the copper of your sinful deeds will always be gilded with the gold of repentance.' The king took this advice, and in this way he would be able to spend most of his time on his pleasures. (The devil wisely did not mention that a confession without the firm resolve to avoid sin is invalid.)

The king, then, lived as pleased him best. It was in vain that his good angel spoke to him and reminded him of the three great benefactions of God—'that He had drawn him from his mother's womb, that He had had patience with him throughout such a long life, and that with His passion He had saved him from everlasting death.' Magnus takes a sceptical view of these three great gifts of God. Bridget hears the devil whisper to him: 'After the joys of life come the horrors of death. He who lives long has much trouble and many tribulations. And who really *compelled* God to save men by his bitter death? Did King Magnus ask Him to do it? No, King Magnus did not. For if he had been permitted to choose he would rather live always on the earth than be parted from this fair world to enter into everlasting bliss.'

With this King Magnus has passed judgment upon himself. Everything is carried out justly, and it is put down to his credit that during his life he has done some good deeds. But he has already received his reward for them. He could take to wife that beautiful woman whom he desired (it was Hedwig, daughter of the Duke of Holstein); he had the gift of eloquence, was granted a good death and was honoured in remembrance (Bridget knew, of course, with what great honours Magnus Ladulås was laid to his last rest). This was his temporal reward, now he is to receive the everlasting one.

It is a sinister reward. For now the devil approaches him and greets him with the name of brother.

Oh brother [says the devil], come hither to me, not in love but in hate. I was the fairest of all the angels, and you were a mortal man. But because I would rather hate God than love Him, I fell as a man falls with the head down and the feet up. Now you have also recked little of God, and you shall therefore turn your head to my feet, and I shall take your feet into my mouth, so that we are joined together like two persons, of whom one has his sword in the heart of the other, and the other has his knife in the entrails of the former. You stab me with your anger and I will pierce you with my malice. I had a head, that is, understanding, and with it could honour God if I had willed, and you had feet, that is: strength to go to God and you would not. Therefore shall my terrible head swallow and devour your cold feet.

The dead king will now also assume a devilish form. Bridget sees him transformed: 'from the crown of his head to the sole of his foot he looks like an animal that has been skinned, and the eyes torn out, and the flesh looks as if it was corrupt.' And she hears him moaning: 'Woe is me, I have become like a newborn whelp that cannot see, and cannot find the paps of its mother. Woe is me, for in my blindness I see that I shall never see God.'

For now his brother in hell comes near to him and binds him with three cords. 'The first cord must be round the middle, so that my navel can be joined to yours, so that when I breathe you will suck my poison into you, and when you breathe I will draw your entrails into me. With the second cord I join your head and my feet, and with the third my head and your feet.' The punishment is terrible, but the devil proves to the dead king that it is just. As always in Bridget Satan himself is God's servant—he who executes his judgments. 'Oh brother,' he says to the king, showing him his claws,

> because you had eyes to find the way of life, and conscience to distinguish between good and evil, therefore shall two of my claws pierce your eyes, and the third shall go through your brain. You were also given two ears to hear the words of life and a mouth to speak what was good for the soul, but as you disdained to hear and to speak what was for the good of your soul, two of the claws on my other foot shall pierce into your ears and the third into your mouth. And all these claws of mine shall torment you so hard that everything that once seemed the sweetest to you when you sinned against God shall now be the bitterest.

> But when this had been said the king and the devil were joined together in the manner that has been said—the king's head and feet and navel with the devil's head and feet and navel. And thus joined together they were swept down into hell.(18)

XI

From the horror of hell Bridget now turns her eyes to purgatory, where the souls do indeed suffer but have not—as there—'abandoned hope.' And there she sees the third king. She sees him in the form of a newborn child, 'that cannot yet make any movement, only raise its glance.' At this king's side there is also a devil, as horrible as any on the pictures by Bosch or Höllenbreughel and thus described by Bridget: 'His head looked like a bellows with a long pipe, his arms were like two serpents, his knee like a press and each of his feet like a long hook.' But the dead king is not alone with this fearsome devil, 'at his side stands the most beautiful angel, ready to help.'

It is not the angel, however, but the devil who takes the lead. Sure of his right he turns to the book rest and states his case: And the list of sins that he reads out is a bad one. First a *Captatio benevolentiae*: 'Thou, oh Lord, art justice itself'—Thou wilt not fail to help a poor devil to his right. Then follows a quotation from the Bible, which in Lucifer's kingdom seems to be studied with greater zeal than by most Christians. He quotes from the Sermon on the Mount: 'Gather not up for yourselves treasures upon earth, where moth and rust doth corrupt, and where thieves break through and steal, but lay for yourselves treasures in heaven, where neither moth nor rust doth corrupt, and where thieves do not break through and steal,' in the sixth chapter of Saint Matthew. On this text, somewhat overlooked in Christian teaching, his Diabolical Reverence now preaches a sermon not very edifying for the late king.

> In this soul [he says] the place in which the treasures of heaven ought to lie is empty, but that place is full of worms and toads, that is, interpreted: of goods unjustly acquired. And although the king knew the commandment about loving his neighbour as himself he rejoiced in the goods he had unjustly taken from his fellow men, and recked not of their need, while he himself lived in abundance. He did what pleased him and took what he liked, and had but little care for right and justice. And this is the chief reason why he has come into my hands—but as to that there are many others!

The devil ceases for a moment—perhaps it is a rhetorical pause. But it is now the angel's turn to speak. There has been this peculiarity concerning him and the king whom he was appointed to guard, that from the very birth of the child he could not overcome his unwillingness to touch him—there was something loathsome about him. What he has to state in defence of the dead king is therefore not of much effect. 'He had the right faith,' says the angel, 'and he was afraid of God and hoped that his sins might at last be blotted out through contrition and confession.' He has not more to say. When the book chair calls upon him as well as the devil, ordering both of them to give their true opinion of the dead man, the counsel for the defence agrees with the prosecution. They are asked: 'What did this soul love when it was in the body and had the full use of its limbs?' Speaking as with one mouth they both answer: 'The children of the world and the good things of the world.' The next question is: 'What did this soul love when it fought the bitter fight of death?' And the answer comes: 'Itself. He thought only of his illness and the agony of his heart, he did not think of the passion of his Redeemer.' 'And at the extreme moment, when he was still fully conscious?' Only the angel can answer this. 'The soul thought, woe is me, I have sinned against my God! I grieve over this more than over my bodily pains. God grant that I may still have a little time to thank Him. Even if I should not get into heaven I would serve Him!'

With this disinterested act of love the soul is saved. Meanwhile it must first be punished, and through punishment chastened. And the punishment is terrible, as was the torture of the Middle Ages. The devil speaks: 'Because you came into my hands full of unjust mammon

I will now press you between my knees.' The king's head is now placed in this diabolical press and the devil presses so long that the brain comes out and is 'as thin as a leaf.' The next is that the devil applies his bellows. He puts the pipe in 'at the place where the virtues ought to be but which is empty.' The devil now blows so violently and fills the king with so much air that he simply bursts. Finally comes the punishment for the king's harshness against his subjects, who 'ought to have been his sons'—the devil embraces him with his arms that are like serpents, they both strangle and bite him.

The king cannot be spared this punishment. But now, when the devil continues and begins the same torments over again 'the angel stretches out his hands over the hands of the devil, so that the pains are lessened each time.' And the soul said nothing but lifted up his eyes to the angel after each torment and· let him understand that his presence was a relief, and that soon it would be saved. 'For even if a man has never loved God in his lifetime but at the last moment says: "Oh Lord God, I repent with my whole heart of having sinned against Thee. Grant that I may love Thee, and that I may do what is pleasing to Thee." Such a man will not come to hell.' So that, after all, the last word in existence is not justice but mercy.

It is not clear whom Bridget meant by this third king. It might be Duke Erik, who once saved her mother when she was pregnant with her when in peril on the sea. But Duke Erik never became king. Richard Steffen, who has carefully studied the revelation, suggests Magnus Smek's eldest son Erik, who was elected to be his father's successor, even before the death of the latter. Bridget held him over the font at baptism, she may even then have seen the angel and the devil at the side of the little one. That the angel could not touch the child because there was something unclean about it might be an allusion to the little one's origin, the bad inheritance from the progenitor and the father. King Erik died in 1359, the whole revelation must then be referred to the time about 1360. And after some hesitation Steffen does, in fact, suppose this. Otherwise he would have referred it to 1352 or 1353.

And he would have been right in this, for there is a great difficulty, not considered by him, in fixing the date at the later time. In the year 1356 young King Erik raised the banner of rebellion against none other than 'the devil's servant,' Bengt Algotsson. On 17 October of that year he issues a proclamation from Kalmar 'to bishops and priests, knight and esquires, merchants and all the common people of Sweden,' in which he complains bitterly of his enemy and the enemy of the crown, Bengt Algotsson, and calls to arms against him—and through him also to King Magnus. On Erik's side, among many other of the great men, was Bridget's son Karl, the law-man in Närike, and the feud ended, as is known, in Duke Bengt going into exile and his permanent castle of Varberg in Halland being seized. Not until the death of King Erik did Bengt Algotsson dare to return to Sweden, but at the castle of Rosenholm in Scania he was attacked by some great men of the Sparre family and killed (1360).(1)

It is highly improbable that an action which Bridget would have considered so meritorious as that of raising a rebellion of the nobles against 'that servant of the devil' would not have weighed heavily in the balance if the third king had really been Erik Magnusson. On the other hand, among the sins laid to his charge, his marriage, contracted as early as 1346, with Beatrix of Brandenburg, is not included. Bridget called it a 'playing with dolls' from which she did not expect anything good, because the bride was the granddaughter of the excommunicated Emperor Louis.(2) Besides, the punishment upon him is so terrible and—at the same time—so grotesque, that it is difficult to think of Bridget applying it to her godson. When at the time he was unjustly ousted in favour of his younger brother Haakon, who became king of the hereditary kingdom of Norway, while Erik had to be content with the elective kingdom of Sweden, no one was more scandalized than Bridget.(3) And now her godson was supposed to have come down to having been a quite ordinary selfish, average king, who is barely able to save himself from going the same way as his forefathers, Birger Earl and Magnus Ladulås! It is all the less probable as Bridget, in a revelation which is undoubtedly written after the death of Erik Magnusson—mentions him as one of the five kings, and gives him the beautiful name, taken from the Apocalypse, of *Agnus occisus*, 'a Lamb standing as it were slain.' * It is true that he was not 'without blemish,' but nevertheless by far the best of the five (the first was the well-known 'crowned ass').(4)

In looking for the third of the three kings then, in the revelations concerned, there is a name that suggests itself—that of Valdemar Birgersson, elder brother of Magnus Ladulås. Not much is known

---

* And I saw: and behold in the midst of the throne and of the four living creatures, and in the midst of the ancients, a Lamb standing as it were slain . . . worthy to receive power and divinity, and wisdom and strengthened honour and glory and benediction.' (Apocalypse (Revelation of St. John) v, 6, 12).

about this regent who ascended the throne immediately after the death of Birger Earl (1266), during the whole of his reign had to fight against his younger brother Magnus, and at last had to give up the throne (1275).(5) It was during his reign that the relics of Saint Erik were moved from Old Uppsala to the Gothic cathedral of Étienne Bonneuil in Östra Aros; the king was present himself at the solemnity. He had brought his wife from Denmark, Sofia, daughter of Erik Plovpenning. The Danish princess seems to have had a sharp tongue, she called her brother-in-law Magnus who (according to the words in the rhyme chronicle) was 'somewhat black and thin' the 'boiler smith,' she let her other brother-in-law, Erik, know that he was rather badly off, and gave him the nickname of 'Allsintet' (nothing at all). Valdemar himself, on the other hand, was 'fine and proud'— and that proved to be his misfortune. In Denmark the son of Erik Plovpenning's brother, Erik Glipping, had become king. His mother, Margaret Spraenghest, carried on the government during his minority, and as she feared that Erik Plovpenning's two unmarried daughters, Agnes and Jutta, would marry and their eventual sons make a claim to the crown of Denmark, she saw to it that both of them took the veil and in 1263 entered the convent of Saint Agnes in Roskilde. Agnes was only fifteen years old, she became prioress—Jutta was probably a year younger. But the handsome habit of the Dominican nuns weighed heavily upon both the two young princesses—'they were not made to be nuns.' They succeeded in fleeing and came over to their married sister in Sweden. The rhyme chronicle is able to relate something about them. It says about Jutta:

> At the time when she to Sweden came
> She was like an angel who from heaven had come.
> So proud was she and so lovely to see.
> To the king she became in truth so dear,
> That to her he came far too near.

Their relations could not remain hidden, and the queen

> With grief grew pale.
> Woe to me, my grief I shall never o'ercome,
> Woe to me that Jutta ever to Sweden came.(6)

An echo of this 'woe' is to be found in Heidenstam's beautiful poem: 'Jutta comes to the Folkungs.'

> The maiden was greeted, the maiden was kissed,
> And the stars shone over the hall,
> Now weeps the little maiden bitterly, hushed,
> Fallen, linden leaf, fallen!

But that which in the nineteenth century has become the music of poetry was in the fourteenth a sin demanding penitence. To atone for the breach of his marriage vows King Valdemar had to make a pilgrimage to Rome (in 1274), and on the journey home he may have travelled by way of Lyons where the Pope (Gregory X) was living that year. In order to gain the entire favour and support of the see of Peter, Valdemar even went so far as 'not admitting any other above him than the Roman Pontifex,' and that 'the realm of Sweden owed tax to the Roman Church.' In other words—'Peter's Pence,' which had hitherto come in voluntarily, were to be regarded as a feudal tax to the Holy See. This submissiveness did not help him, in the following year Magnus and his brother raised the banner of rebellion against him and their army came unawares upon the royal troops at Ramundaboda in the great forest country of Tiveden. The royal headquarters did not present exactly a warlike sight—the rhyme chronicle gives a drastic description. 'The king slept so long that the battle was over before he awoke. Some heard Mass, some sat and talked, some walked about, and some ate, the queen played at dice.' In the midst of this carelessness a man comes running from the battle, 'badly worn and in poor spirits' and advises the king to flee. The king follows this advice, afterwards tries several times to regain power, has to give up the throne, wanders about in Norway and Denmark, disowns his wife, takes a certain, otherwise unknown maiden Lucardis in marriage, and otherwise lives in a manner that causes scandal, ends as a prisoner of the State in the castle of Nyköping, where he dies in 1302.(7)

Now is there anything in the course of this very disedifying life that can be applied to Bridget's king in purgatory? As mentioned, we know too little about Valdemar Birgersson to be able to make a comparison in detail. But at any rate it can be said of him that he 'loved the body more than God' and that he thought but little of gathering treasures that rust and moth could not devour. And that he 'only did what pleased him and despised what was right and just.' His breach of his marriage vows and his later conduct against the lawful queen was proof enough of this. And that exactly 'was the chief occasion of his coming into my power,' says the devil. The king's repentance on his deathbed could also be applied to the penitent pilgrim going to Rome.

It is possible, then, that this great vision is like a triptych. Bridget here beheld three men of the house of the Folkungs—one on earth: Magnus Eriksson; one in hell: Magnus Ladulås; one in purgatory:

Valdemar Birgersson. One might have expected it to have been built up in a different order—first the earth, then purgatory, at last hell. But Bridget has not wished to finish with the trumpet of judgment. God 'willeth not the death of sinners, but that they may repent and live.' And the whole revelation therefore rings out with these words to Bridget:

> You shall know that it was the Mother of God who vouchsafed this vision to you. And this is the mercy which is promised to the kingdom of Sweden, that the people who live therein shall hear the words that come from the mouth of God. But that there are only few who receive and believe the heavenly words that are given to thee by God is not the fault of God, but of men with their cold hearts. The words of the Scriptures are not fulfilled through the first kings of this time, but there are times still to come when they shall be fulfilled.(8)

Bridget's love of Sweden believes all things, hopes all things, never wearies.

XII

In the year 1353 King Magnus had received as a loan from Pope Innocent VI the Peter's Pence collected in Sweden and Norway by Cardinal Jean de Guibert. It was no small sum—22,000 marks in silver is given in some sources, in others 25,000 (according to Montelius corresponding to a million and a half Swedish crowns). It was a short-term loan—on the next feast of Saint John at midsummer half the amount was already to be paid into the Pope's account with a bank in Bruges, the remainder in the autumn. Queen Blanca had been very active in arranging this loan (perhaps she and her family had connections with this bank) 'because of the distress prevailing in Sweden, Norway and Scania, and the dreadful wars that are still carried on, and that very probably may be expected very soon.' It was in the room in which she lived with the Grey Friars in Jönköping that the loan was arranged. A number of the great men of the kingdom were present and signed the bond as co-debtors and sureties.(1)

The loan was not repaid—not even the first instalment, to the merchants in Bruges. Innocent VI, however, treated his royal debtor with much forbearance—not until October 1355 did the Pope make his claim, but gave him a month's respite. When still no payment was made Innocent wrote, in February 1356, a kind letter to his 'dearest son,' the king, in which he expresses his firm conviction that the latter, when he learns the straitened circumstances of Innocent himself, will 'not only pay the debt but also think of giving generous help to his Mother, the Holy Roman Church.' Again the Pope is kept waiting—and not until May 1358 does the archbishop of Lund receive orders to institute excommunication—twenty-one Scandinavian archbishops and bishops carried it out, all over Sweden and Norway the bells tolled as though for a funeral. Candles were lit and again put out—as the light of grace was now put out in the soul of the excommunicated king. . . .(2)

The message of this excommunication reached Bridget in Rome and must have cut her to the heart. This was what her Magnus had come to then! And instead of submitting he was defiant, went to Mass as if nothing had happened, had the churches opened by force if a zealous bishop closed them to him. It was no wonder that the blessings of heaven had turned away from him. Bridget had been glad when, in 1341, he obtained Valdemar Atterdag's confirmation of the right to possess Scania, Blekinge and the island of Hven, which he had bought at a great price from Count Henry of Holstein, who had held a mortgage on the land. The Öre Sound had at last become the border between Goths and Danes, as Bridget had always wished.

And now? In the Franciscan convent in Visby a Grey Friar sat writing a book giving an account of the events of his time, and under the year 1360 he relates: 'When King Valdemar of Denmark had gained a victory over the Holsteiners and brought peace to the whole country, he harassed King Magnus, now with threats, now with promises, so that King Magnus gave him back without payment the whole of Scania with all the castles, without in the least having asked the councils of the kingdom. Moreover, he also agreed to letting him take Gothland if he could get it.'(3) This last accusation is unjust, on the contrary Magnus himself, in a letter to the citizens of Visby, had warned them against the danger threatening them from the Danish king. The letter is dated 1 May 1361 and not until July of the same year did King Valdemar carry out his attack on the rich capital of Gothland (so rich, it was said, that in it 'the pigs ate out of silver troughs'). Under the walls of Visby, on the so-called *Korsbetning* (Cross pasture), the old memorial cross is still standing, with its pathetic inscription: 'In the year 1361 on the Tuesday after Saint James's day (27 July), the Goth-landers fell into the hands of the Danes. Here they lie buried. Pray for them.'(4)

Scania lost, Gothland in the hands of the Danes—and King Magnus had still more on his list of sins. The old chronicle relates further:

'In the year 1361, when King Valdemar had taken Gothland and Öland (which lay on the road to Visby), the great men in the kingdom of Sweden rose up against King Magnus, in particular because his son, King Haakon, with his father's will, but against the promise given by the councils of the kingdom to the counts of Holstein, took Margaret, King Valdemar's daughter, to wife.' In 1359 the two royal children had already been betrothed—in vain had Bridget warned against it— she was not in favour of these early marriages, they seemed to her like 'playing with dolls.'(5) Had they not understood, then, who King Valdemar was, could they not see that now he was in Scania and in Gothland, encircling the country from the west and from the east with two sharp claws? A wolf in sheep's clothing is the Danish king, and what does the wolf do but seize, tear in pieces and swallow? And this is the wolf that has got the better of King Magnus, that crowned ass! Blanca is no doubt delighted with this fine marriage, 'but I tell her this, in God's name, that she need not look forward to having a grand- son of the seed of the wolf'!(6)

The great men at home in Sweden had done what they could to prevent this marriage—they had sought another bride for young King Haakon and found her in the Holstein count's sister, Elisabeth. The wedding took place in the summer of 1362 in Holstein, without the bridegroom being present personally (*per procura*) (King Valdemar the Victor was married in the same way to Queen Dagmar). The young countess Elisabeth, less fortunate than Queen Dagmar, did not reach the country in which an impatient bridegroom was curvetting his horse on the shore, the ship in which she was to sail to Sweden ran aground at Bornholm. And Bornholm belonged to the see of Lund, *i.e.*, to Denmark. The bishop of Lund, Sir Niels, was kind to the ship- wrecked princess, and while she was recovering from seasickness, Valdemar in great haste arranged a wedding in Copenhagen between Margaret and Haakon, whose parents had come across the Sound for the ceremony (April 1363). They got out of the difficulty with the jilted bride by studying the family registers and discovering that there were canonical impediments. Moreover, Haakon's betrothal to Margaret was just as binding as a solemnized marriage. The jilted princess entered a convent somewhere in Germany. But before King Magnus came back from Copenhagen he had finally and for ever given up all claim to Scania.(7)

Such were the tidings from Sweden, and they were not good. Was there not in all Sweden, then, a single person who could seize the sword of justice and carry the cause of God to victory against this king who had betrayed Sweden? Bridget had once had hopes of her godson Erik —her heart had leapt with joy when she received the news of his proclamation to the Swedish people from Kalmar on 17 October 1356. He had proudly called himself 'king of Svea and of the Goths and Lord of Scania'; he had made a complaint against his father that 'the crown was broken and divided and had lost houses and lands' which had been given away to the 'enemy of the king and the crown,' Bengt Algotsson. But Erik had soon been reconciled to his father; at the banquet of reconciliation in the spring of 1359 Queen Blanca herself waited upon the guests and poured out the wine, good French wine. But Erik died after having drunk of it—Blanca's wine had been poisoned!(8)

For a moment it had seemed as though Haakon would follow in the footsteps of his elder brother. In the same year that Valdemar Atterdag took Gothland 'King Haakon made common cause with the councillors of the kingdom and the great men and took his father prisoner on Saint Martin's day in the parish church of Kalmar and shut him up in a tower,' it is said in the annals of the Visby Grey Friars. And the year book of Sweden adds: 'It was the great men of the kingdom who drove on and incited him against his father, because the latter had let himself be cheated out of Scania, which the Swedes had bought at a great price.' But blood is thicker than water—'on Ascension Day (1362) King Haakon, moved to repentance, set his father free from prison. After being delivered from captivity Magnus was reconciled to his son in all matters.'(9)

But now the great men had to suffer for it, 'they had agreed to the imprisonment of the king'—they were driven out of the country and declared outlaws. Among them were Sir Niels, Bishop of Linköping, (not Nicolaus Hermanni, who did not become bishop till 1375), the High Constable Sir Niels Turesson, the mighty Bo Jonsson Grip, who was later to become constable, Sir Karl of Tofta, Sir Erikss Karlon and Bridget's son, Sir Karl of Ulfåsa. 'Banished by the king they came to Gothland, which was then under the kingdom of Denmark.' Bridget's eldest daughter, Märta, was also among the banished, as in her second marriage she was the wife of Knut, brother of Bengt Algotsson, also banished. She lived in Norway with her new husband and also enjoyed the favour of both King Haakon and Queen Blanca. Just as Blanca had been trained by Bridget, so Blanca's young daughter-in-law was to be trained by the Lady Bridget's daughter, and here 'she was made to taste the same rod,' says Margaret daughter of Klaus, like the Lady Märta's own Ingegerd, who later became abbess in Vadstena.(10)

Like great waves all these tidings swept over Bridget, and with the prophet she could say: My bowels shall sound like a harp.* She thought of the outlaws, of those who had had to flee to Gothland, and among them her son, the child of her heart and her tears, her own Karl. . . . What were the words that from the depths of her being rose to her lips, so that she had to utter them? She takes pen and ink and paper, she must write what the spirit tells. It is a message to four of the exiles in Gothland—above all to her own son Karl, then to Sir Karl of Tofta, married to the daughter of Bridget's brother Israel's daughter (among the great men he was selected to become governor of the realm if the child the Lady Beatrix expected proved to be a son), next probably also to Bo Jonsson Grip and Bishop Niels Markusson of Linköping. In the original manuscript, which is preserved in Stockholm, the four names are carefully erased, but a surmise may be permitted.(11)

Then the Mother of God speaks to these four:

I am she [she says] to whom the angel said: 'Hail, full of grace!' I therefore offer my grace to all who will accept it. I offer you my help to defend your kingdom against the enemies of God. I urge upon you so to work that the realm may have a king who may lead it to all good works and to seemly customs. I make known to you that the justice of God will take the kingdom from this king and his children. Another man, one born in Sweden, a man yet unknown, has been chosen by God to be king. He shall rule the kingdom according to the true counsels of the friends of God and to the real good of the land.

Bridget is thinking of her grandson, Karl Karlsson. And now she speaks like a commander giving orders to his soldiers before the battle:

Do according to the counsel that here is given to you. But keep it secret from both friends and foes, except if you find some about whom you feel that they will be on your side in fighting for the kingdom that it may find honour before God, that good morals may flourish, and the land which the crown has lost may be regained. One or several of you must make a beginning and go to King Magnus and say to him: 'We have somewhat of which to speak with you. It concerns your soul's salvation. We therefore beg of you to keep it secret, as if it was spoken in the confessional.' And then, when you are alone with the king, you shall speak openly and say: 'There is no one, neither in Sweden nor outside Sweden, who is of such bad repute as you, for it is said of you that you have commingling and intercourse with men, and it does not sound past believing, for there are certain men [Bengt

* Isaiah xvi, 11.

Algotsson and his predecessor] whom you love more than God or your own soul or your wife. Next, we do not know whether you are a Catholic or not, for you have been forbidden to come to the church, but you keep on going to church and hearing Mass as before. Thirdly and fourthly, you have wasted the land and estates of the Crown and have been a traitor to Scania and against the men who have served you and your subjects there, who served you and your son, and would serve you and your son, remaining under the crown of Sweden and fighting under Sweden's enemies. These you have now surrendered to their worst enemy, so that they can never be sure of their lives and goods so long as he lives.'

Bridget pauses in her writing for a moment—her thoughts grow more gentle. At length the four great men shall offer the king a possibility of remaining on the throne. They shall say this:

If you will do penance for your crimes and sins and regain what is lost we are willing to serve you. If you will not do so yourself, then give up the crown to your son and go away. Or stay at home, provided that your son promises under oath that he will recover what is lost, listen to the advice of his servants, and help the common people to obtain their rights. If not, another shall become king, for God has the same power over the young man as over the old one, and can banish the one as easily as the other.

But now wrath arises again in Bridget's soul—for if neither Magnus nor Haakon will listen? Then her four envoys shall shake the dust from off their feet. And in secret they shall seek out their friends and those of the nobility who may be thought to be of a like mind with them. They shall tell them openly what they have said to the king in secret—and declare that they will no longer serve a heretic or a traitor to his country, nor his son if he follows in his father's footsteps. 'And now choose yourselves a chieftain who can carry on a war on behalf of the Crown. If he is the right one, him whom my Son has chosen, he shall be established—if not, he shall be removed.'

One or two practical counsels—a matter of collecting 'money and the like,' for a war cannot be carried on without a well-filled war chest and plenty of provisions. If the king should think of flight no one must follow him. And then a last war cry: 'I will stir up your hearts and give you courage. And he who will not obey willingly shall be forced to do so!'(12)

XIII

Bridget's plan of rebellion against King Magnus must have been received in Sweden before the year 1365. That pamphlet of insurgence which the Swedish nobility wrote against King Magnus, and which is known under the title of *Libellus de Magno Erici Rege,* 'the book about King Magnus Eriksson,' is dated from the years 1365–71, and it contains (as Ingvar Andersson has pointed out) the most striking parallels to Bridget's letter. Among other things the accusation of unnatural eroticism is due to Bridget, as well as the reproaches of having betrayed Scania and surrendered it to Valdemar Atterdag's wolf's claws, which are identical. Likewise the accusation of not having obeyed the prohibition not to hear Mass.(1)

The rebellion really did come. King Magnus was driven into exile, a new king was elected. But *not* the king whom Bridget had wished and hoped for. The Visby chronicle is able to relate that 'the outlaws stayed over the winter in Gothland and later, just after Easter, they went to Vismar to Sir Albrecht, Duke of Magnopolis or Mecklenburg.* This duke was married to King Magnus' sister Euphemia, and by her had three sons: Albrecht, Henry and Magnus. Henry married King Valdemar's daughter, and her daughter married the Duke of Pomerania, whose son was Erik, king of Denmark, Sweden and Norway. Furthermore it happened that in 1363 the above-named duke, together with his eldest son, Junker Albrecht and the above-mentioned Swedish great men, came with an army to Stockholm and subdued Sweden to himself. . . . Meanwhile King Magnus gathered an army together in Norway and marched towards Stockholm. When the duke's knights and great men heard this they prepared to march against him by way of Västerås . . . and met King Magnus on the feast of Saint Lucius, pope and martyr, the fourth of March, in a meadow near Gata, where the duke's knights gained the victory. During the battle King Magnus was taken prisoner, while his son, Junker Haakon, barely escaped from the strife. Thereupon Junker Albrecht, son of the Duke of Mecklenburg, was chosen to be king of Sweden.'(2) 'Then the birds of prey perched high up on the hill tops, for the Germans ruled with violence over the kingdom for many years,' as we are told in the *Tänkiebok* of the convent of Vadstena (about 1365).

Neither were these tidings good for Bridget. If Valdemar Atterdag was a wolf, this new king's father, Duke Albrecht of Mecklenburg, was a fox. Bridget had been present at the wedding between him and Euphemia, King Magnus' sister (1336). The bride had been promised a very big dowry—5,000 marks in silver—and as the king's treasury

* *Magnopolis,* 'the great city,' *i.e.* Mecklenburg, from the German *mecklen,* Danish *mögle* in Mögeltonder, Old Norse *mikla* in Miklagaard. (And Scottish *muckle,* big.—Tr.)

was empty as usual, he had to mortgage, in 1339, his revenue from Scania and Falsterbo to his brother-in-law. Bridget had spoken vigorously against this transaction—it was like letting the fox get into the goose pen! The fox would not rest content with taking one of the geese, no, it would bite them all to death! Duke Albrecht would do just the same, once he had taken a bite of Swedish soil. The fox is sly, it pretends to be dead so that it may all the easier deceive simple fowls. It would therefore be better to set about paying the 5,000 marks, so that the towns in pawn should not come under foreign domination.(3)

King Magnus had not taken Bridget's advice. And he had been punished for it—he had lost his crown. But instead of him had now come 'a dangerous viper, begotten by a crafty fox and by a female viper.'(4) For was not Euphemia a daughter of the duchess Ingeborg of Halland, Knud Porse's mistress—and did not Bridget know what a viper this woman was?(5) Bridget had had the innate dread common to most women of every creeping thing, whether it be a viper, a snake, a slow-worm or merely an innocent lizard. Moreover she would have learned, through her study of natural history in *Physiologus*, the most sinister details about the family life of serpents.

When a little worm is born the mother lies down upon it at once, so that it is nearly choked. In order to protect itself from the heat from above the worm turns round against the cold ground and begins to suck and eat it. Then the mother pierces him in his tail, to make him pull it in, and in his head, to make him stretch it out and learn to twist himself. Next she takes him to a place where the sunshine is warm, and here she teaches him to use his sting, first against soft things that she lays before him, afterwards against stones and sticks and other hard things. And when her son has got so far she lets him run.

He has now learned all he needs to know!

But that is just the way in which Euphemia of Mecklenburg has brought up her son, the young snake. She warmed him under herself, that is to say, she taught him to love the world and the glory of the world. And at once he would begin to suck up soil, and the more earth he eats the more he wants to have. Then she pierced him in his head to make him learn to carry it high and to entice people to himself with good promises and fair words, and to be generous in order to be esteemed and honoured, and never to allow himself any rest, but always to work at gaining an honoured name. The ideal that Euphemia held up before her son is that of the great chieftain—'so did your father live and your house, and so must all brave and mighty men appear. Shame upon you if you would be holier than they, a dishonour if you would be humbler than they.' Her son must be a lordly man, beyond good and evil. He is therefore ruthless against 'poor and humble people who cannot make any resistance, and takes away their goods from them.' Others he robs of their lives, at last he causes a rebellion and arouses strife and war, nay, he even seizes that which is the highest of all—Holy Church. For the serpent's offspring has not much religion—'if it is decided that I am to be lost,' he says, 'I cannot alter it. If I am meant to be saved I shall be given time to repent.' God therefore pronounces His 'Woe, woe, upon him and upon his mother —That race shall not thrive, and she shall die in sorrow, and her name shall not be remembered. For the judgment is near, and the time is short.'(6)

Bridget was not to live to see the fulfilment of her prophecy. Albrecht of Mecklenburg survived her and died in 1389 as King of Sweden. She had therefore to give up the hope of seeing her grandson on the throne of Sweden. But Bridget knew of another road open to him—instead of the kingdom of Sweden he was to win a heavenly kingdom. Karl's son was to become a knight without blemish and reproach, and he was to be crowned with the crown prepared for the friends of God.

> Oh, my daughter, [says Christ to Bridget] there are women enough who boast that their sons are to live in the same abundance as the king. But there is no honour in imitating the affluence of the king. It is an honour, and a knight of honour is he who strives with all his might to give glory to God— he can glory in that. And he who is ready to suffer for God's sake what God wills that he should suffer, is God's knight and will be made a knight in heaven.(7)

Karl Karlsson, then, was to become a knight of God and a man of the Church. Margareta daughter of Klaus is able to relate that he 'was kept to school and study and was to have become a priest.' . . . But his mother (Katharina Erik's daughter Glysing) did not remain a widow more than six months, and took for a husband a German knight named Sir John Myltika. By the same Sir John Myltika she had two daughters. . . . Then Karlsson came home from his studies and saw the two young girls, his half-sisters. He said: 'Never shall these Garpisses' (a disparaging term for Germans) 'become my heirs.' After that he married, taking to wife the daughter of Sir Algot Magnusson— her name was the Lady Katharine. By her he had a daughter who was called after Saint Bridget. This same Karl Karlsson happened once to go to Vadstena as he often did. There was a wooden chapel there—it was before the church was built—into which he entered and prayed. Then Saint Bridget appeared to him and in her hand she had an hour-glass, which seemed to him to have almost run out. She spoke to him and said: 'Karl, do you see this glass? So nearly is the time of your life run out, and there is not more left than what you see. If you had obeyed God and had become a priest, as you were intended to be, and as it was God's will, you would have become the oldest man in my family and bishop in Linköping and a pillar of Holy Church.' He answered: 'Oh, dear Lady, pray for me, I would gladly try to be better.' Saint Bridget said: 'It is too late now, the time is past, and judgment has been given.' Then he turned to his servants and asked if they had heard or seen anything. They answered: 'We heard you speaking, but we saw no one, nor did we hear anyone speaking with you.' And in the same hour when this happened it seemed to many of the Sisters here within the convent, and to some of the Sisters outside as if the chapel was burning. And immediately, as he was standing there, he had a fit of trembling and then journeyed home to Ulfåsa and was laid on a sick-bed and received the sacraments of the Church, and then died and was taken to Vadstena and buried there. Bridget's grandson did not become King of Sweden nor Bishop of Linköping—he had to be content with being law-man in Närike like his father's brother, his father and grandfather before him.(8)

From her heaven Bridget also watched over her descendant, Karl Karlsson's daughter. She was named Bridget, but she did not live to be more than eight or nine years old. Her mother sent her to the Cistercian nuns in the convent of Vreta, 'so that she might there get book learning' and there she fell ill and was like to die, and the priest who was to shrive her was called to her. When the priest had gone Saint Bridget came and spoke to her, saying: 'Bridget, confess, for now you are going to die.' She answered: 'My dear lady, I have done so.' Saint Bridget said: 'Confess that when you were to have your cloak and your crown, you could not sleep at night for joy.' The little girl, like the little Ölgerd Brahe on her deathbed in Sko convent, had been clothed in the habit of a novice, that is, the mantle, the white cloak reaching down to the feet and a wreath, *corona*, of myrtle, rose-mary or the like as a sign that she was the bride of Christ.(9) In all innocence the little girl had looked forward to this feast—with which her stern great-grandmother reproaches her. 'Immediately she had the priest sent for and confessed as Saint Bridget had ordered her.' As a reward for this obedience the saint works the miracle that when the little girl, thirsting with fever, wants to have some strawberries, although it was 'between Christmas and Candlemas,' strawberries are found for her under the snow. Then little Bridget died and was carried to big Bridget's grave in Vadstena.

XIV

Bishop Thomas of Vexiö has come to Rome and has paid a visit to Bridget. They have talked about Sweden and what has happened lately, Duke Erik's rebellion, King Haakon's fight against his father and the reconciliation that followed, the banishment of the great men, the coming of the two Mecklenburgers to the country, the loss of Scania and Gothland. Bishop Thomas is anxious about what may happen further at home, and would rather leave to-day than to-morrow. Bridget wants to keep him back, would it not be better if he made a pilgrimage to Ortona, to the grave of his patron, Saint Thomas the apostle? Bridget is just intending to go there again, as she had been invited to do at her former visit. From Ortona the road continues to Saint Michael's Mount, to Bari with the grave of Saint Nicholas, and back by way of Benevento, Salerno, Naples, Amalfi, Rome. Everywhere there are saints' graves to be visited—in Ortona Saint Thomas, in Bari Saint Nicholas, in Salerno Saint Matthew the apostle, who wrote the Gospel, in Amalfi the apostle Saint Andrew, in Benevento the apostle Saint Bartholomew. The road to Ortona was known to Bridget from her former visit, besides, she could ask her way—Bridget now spoke both Latin and Italian. Bishop Thomas was not particularly pleased with the idea—he was not a good walker, and Bridget intended to walk as usual, but then the bishop could ride. . . .

When the ecclesiastical gentleman had said good-night, Bridget sat alone by the hearth and pondered. She had not failed to notice what was troubling this bishop—'he is like one who stands at the cross-roads and does not know which way to go. He stands between two roads, the way of joy the way of sorrow. But it seems hard to him to go the way that leads to perfect joy.'(1)

When he came to Rome Bishop Thomas Johannsson of the Malstad family had been bishop in Vexiö for over twenty years (since 1343). He was no longer a young man, death was not so far away (he died in 1375 or 1376). Doubtless he had often enough spoken in his sermons about the two ways—'that which is narrow in the beginning, but ends in joy, and that which is pleasing for a time but ends in the bottomless abyss.' Thus had he preached—but by himself he had thought that perhaps there was also a third way, an easy little short cut from the royal road of perdition to the narrow path of salvation. There are many who think like this—they say to themselves, we can still live a long time, and God's mercy is very great. This world that we happen to be living in is beautiful and created for our pleasure. It will be time enough to be pious when I grow old—then I will repent and go to confession and be saved. . . .

Bridget does not doubt that there is salvation for a penitent sinner. She is only afraid that there will not be any repentance at the last moment. Death will either come suddenly—or the sick person will be so tormented with pain that he cannot think of anything else. And thus it is seen that the short cut on which he relied is the longest way round. Nevertheless Bishop Thomas is thinking of walking in it. Bridget sees him standing at the parting of the ways—and it seems to her that she sees him taking out a book. It is not the journey book *— for there are only three leaves in it. The first leaf is one that Bishop Thomas likes to read, it is rose-coloured and on it is written about the riches and honour of the world. The second grieves him—it is black and the word *hell* is written on it. The third is white—on it ought to be written that the bishop fears God out of love of Him, but the writing is very indistinct. And then the bishop turns back to the first leaf—he enjoys reading that.

Bridget asked the advice of the Mother of God—what can be done for this man? How can he come to love God and despise the world? The answer is: by humility, mercy and good works. And one of the most precious works in the eyes of God is a pilgrimage—even the Mohammedans know that, that is why they go on pilgrimage to Mecca!

The next morning Bridget speaks to Bishop Thomas. 'It has been given to me by the Spirit, that it is of greater benefit to you to stay here than to depart, and that they who have departed earlier than you shall come home after you.' ('This did indeed happen'—Petrus Olai could add later—'for when the bishop came home he found the whole country in confusion, and they who had left before him were stopped on the way and came long after him.')(2)

Bishop Thomas allowed himself to be persuaded and joined the little group of pilgrims. Bridget, Karin, probably also Francesca Papazuri

* The breviary, which a Catholic priest reads, even when he is on a journey.

and Prior Petrus made the pilgrimage on foot, Master Petrus, with his lame leg, and the bishop were to ride. Bridget may have thought of reaching Bari for the feast of Saint Nicholas on 6 December. The journey did not begin very well—they had not much money, Bridget was anxious and afraid they might run short. Besides, it was late in the year—when the little pilgrim company came up to the Abruzzi they encountered not only the autumn but the winter. And one evening the dusk fell before they could get indoors. It seemed as if the little company of travellers had been warned against continuing the journey that evening, but Bridget was self-willed, she knew the road from previous journeys, and thought that they would be able to reach Ortona. So she did not listen to the well-meant advice. Prior Petrus tells about it in the process of canonization: 'We had to spend the night under the open sky (*sub Divo*, he says, using a classical expression), and the snow was high, and it was very cold—the horses also suffered much from the cold.' Some of the servants were sent on in advance as scouts, and did indeed find a small hut of osiers, in which the Lady Bridget and her escort spent the rest of the night with neither light nor fire. At last the day dawned and in the rosy light Christ appeared to Bridget and said: 'He who will not hear must feel. You would not believe those who told you that you could not reach Ortona that day, and now you have got what you deserved.'(3)

It was in doubt, however, and not in faith, that Bridget now came the second time to Ortona. From the legend of Saint Thomas, which she had read at home, she knew that his body had been subjected to a wandering existence down through the centuries—from India to Edessa, thence to Chios, finally in 1258 to Ortona, where he had rested since (in a shrine of onyx). Bridget now knelt before this shrine and heard Christ assure her that it contained, if not the whole of the apostle's body (part of it had remained in Meliapur) then at any rate 'more relics of him than any other place.' The shrine was precious, the church magnificent—and yet Bridget felt that Thomas was not duly honoured by those who ought to honour him. Who was it then, that did not give the apostle the honour due to him? Who but the king and queen of Naples! They had not been sparing in large gifts of alms and votive gifts. But what was the state of their morals, and their more or less illicit marriages? Bridget knew very well, as everyone in Rome knew, that Giovanna's various connections by marriage had at last been acknowledged by the Pope. But Giovanna had contracted them without caring the very least about the laws of the Church, and the matter 'would therefore, when the time came, be brought before the judgment seat of God, and there be judged.'

But Bridget had not heard anything about all this, and at her first visit to Ortona she had therefore been invited to come again. It was not until she was kneeling by the tomb that she was given the answer. Saint Thomas appeared to her. He knew how greatly Bridget revered the relics of the saints of God, and how glad she was to possess them. It happened once that she saved the relics of Saint Louis from profanation, on the occasion when Queen Blanca had carelessly placed them in one of the corridors of the royal castle. At home in East Gothland she heard that a young man from the village of Strå near Vadstena had sold a relic of the cross of Christ; she gets possession of it and has it encased in a costly setting.(4) Saint Thomas therefore appears to her and says that he will give her a present. 'And at the same instant a piece of Saint Thomas' bones came forth from the tomb, though no hand had touched it, and Saint Bridget received it with joy and preserved it with reverence.' Prior Petrus was present and saw this miracle; in the process of canonization he testifies to it, and the notary adds: 'the witness said that he had seen it himself.'(5)

Prior Petrus gave this testimony on 30 January 1380 before the papal commissaries delegated by Urban V, Bishop Thomas of Anagni and Bishop Paulus of Urbino. He was at that time close upon seventy-three, about ten years had passed since he had had that experience. His explanation is given after the usual taking of the oath, and there is no reason to doubt the excellent Prior's love of truth. As for the revelation that Bridget had had, in which Christ reproved her, he says very correctly that he had only heard her speak of it herself, he neither heard nor saw anything himself, although he was present himself in the wretched hostel. In the commentary (*Declaratio*) added by himself to the place in question in the *Revelationes* he says the same as in the process of canonization. Later in the Process he repeats almost word for word what he has said earlier.(6) But there are other witnesses than Prior Petrus. There is the Lady Bridget's chaplain, Magnus Petri, who 'served her for more than eighteen years'; his testimony does not differ much from that of Petrus Olai, and is given at about the same time (6.8.1379). Above all there is Bridget's own daughter Karin, whose description of the miracle is the most detailed. It is given on 31 August 1379 and reads as follows:

The witness said that she remembered very well that the Lady Bridget mentioned had been twice in the city of Ortona in the kingdom of Naples.

And the last time under Pope Urban V [that is, after 6.11.1362 and before 10.12.1370]. In the church where the body of the apostle St. Thomas is, the witness saw with her own eyes [*oculata fide*] that although the shrine of the saint with the remains of St. Thomas the apostle was well closed, without any hole or opening or cleft, there issued from it against and above the order of nature, a bone or piece of a bone, and the Lady Bridget mentioned took it into her hands with the greatest reverence and with the most beautiful words, and with tears she showed it from the altar to her confessors, and told them how she had desired to possess a relic of the said apostle, and at her first visit to this church had prayed for it, and how Saint Thomas had appeared to her and said: 'Return hither, and I will fulfil your wish.' And the witness said that present was also the Bishop of Vexiö and mentioned the Lady Bridget's confessors, namely, the Father Petrus Olai and Prior Petrus Olai of Alvastra monastery and the aforementioned Sir Magnus. And the witness said that everyone in Ortona spoke of it.(7)

However this experience is to be understood, Bridget felt that it was an initiation, 'it was as though her heart was aflame with spiritual joy, and she was near to falling into a swoon.'* Her prayer had been fulfilled—she had other and greater things to pray for, and they were also to be given her. With firm steps she guided her little company further along the road which Innocent III had made (or improved)—the road along the coast of Apulia down to the great seaports of Barletta, Bari, Otranto, Brindisi, whence the crusaders and merchants set sail for the country *altremare*, 'beyond the sea'—Syria and Palestine. Had Bridget perhaps already then felt longings awakening for embarking on one of the Venetian galleys and voyaging to the Holy Land?

But there was a great place of pilgrimage to visit first—Mount Saint Michael (*Monte Sant' Angelo*) on Monte Gàrgano, the mountain that shoots out into the Adriatic Sea like a spur on the Italian boot. The places to which the Christians of the Middle Ages made pilgrimages were indicated in three words: *Deus* (the Holy Land with the tomb of Christ in Jerusalem); *Homo* (the tombs of the apostles in Rome and in Compostella); *Angelus* (the shrine of Saint Michael on Monte Gàrgano).

The archangel Michael is first mentioned in the Holy Scriptures by the prophet Daniel. Here he is the guardian spirit of Israel, fighting with the guardian spirit of Persia and gaining the victory. On the last day, when the great tribulation comes, he will stand forth and protect the children of Israel. In the epistle of the apostle Judas Thaddeus, it is

---

* If this relic, acquired in an extraordinary way, was brought home to the convent in Vadstena, there must be a record about it in some register or other of Bridget's inventory.

described how the 'archangel Michael when contending with the devil he disputed about the body of Moses'—he is therefore present also at the last day of every human being and contends with the devil for the soul of the dying one.* He thus becomes the standard bearer in that host of angels that fights against 'the spiritual host of evil under heaven.' His very name, *Michael*, that is, 'Who is like God,' is a signal for war. He executes the judgment of heaven upon human beings—Gregory the Great saw him standing upon the summit of Hadrian's tomb and sheathing his sword—that sword of the plague which had devastated Rome. And the imperial mausoleum was given another name and was called Castel Sant' Angelo, the Angel's mount. *Signifer sanctus Michael* he is called in the Catholic liturgy—as God's holy standard bearer he is to lead the souls into the everlasting light. But besides the sword he also carries a pair of scales—in the fresco paintings in Danish churches of the Middle Ages he is shown engaged in weighing souls, a small naked figure kneels in one scale, its hands raised in prayer, a black devil keeps a tight hold of the other scale, so that it over-balances the other. In the Norse 'Draumkvæde' Michael is therefore called 'Soul Michael.' It is no wonder then, that people tried to gain his support by a pilgrimage to his shrine on Monte Gàrgano.

Of the origin of this shrine legend is able to relate: It was in the days of King Theodoric, and the city of Siponte (the present Manfredonia) was besieged by Odoacer and his Heruli. The surrender of the town seemed inevitable, but the bishop, Lorenzo Majorano, succeeded in gaining a truce of three days. The Sipontians spent these three days, not in repairing the walls, or in putting shafts on their arrows, but in invoking God's standard bearer, Saint Michael, for help against the barbarians of the North. And behold, on the third day the archangel appeared on the top of Monte Gàrgano with a drawn sword. And immediately a terrible storm arose, the earth trembled, the sea rose in high waves against the shore. The thunder rolled, flash upon flash of lightning struck Odoacer's army and the Sipontians went out to attack and put the enemy to flight. As a mark of thanksgiving the bishop resolved to raise a shrine to Saint Michael on the mountain. A runaway bull showed the way—high, high up it stood still outside a cave in a rock. And the archangel appeared to the bishop and said that there the chapel in his honour was to be built. Then Bishop Lorenzo and six other bishops walked in solemn procession up on the mountain. It was on 29 September, the sun was very hot, the road was steep and the

* Ep. of St. Jude, v, 9.

bishops were not young. Then seven eagles came and hovered over the bishops, shading them with their outspread wings. In this way they came up to the grotto, and who could describe their wonder when they found an altar raised, covered with a crimson cloth, above the altar a cross of clear rock crystal, and before the altar a footprint in the stone —'here the angel has stood' the seven bishops exclaim as with one voice—*hic steterunt pedes ejus.** . . . And every year, on 29 September, Mass is sung up here in honour of Saint Michael—'Holy Michael, archangel, defend us in the day of battle, that we be not lost on the day of judgment,' *Sancte Michael Archangelo, defende nos in proelio, ut non pereamus in tremendo judicio*. And out on the broad stone steps leading up to the shrine, the pilgrim cuts with his knife the outline of his foot in the step of the stairway and writes his name in it—he, too, will leave a footprint on the stairway that leads up to heaven. Saint Francis of Assisi did less than that—his reverence for the shrine was so great that he dared not even enter the grotto—at the entrance he was content to carve his mark in the stone—the letter Thau (T), with which he also signed the blessing of Brother Leone. This was indeed another kind of journey to Apulia than that of which he had dreamed in his ambitious youth, when he wanted to fight under the banner of Count Gentile di Manopello! One of his first disciples, Brother Egidio, made the same pilgrimage.†

A modern Christian, be he a Protestant or a Catholic, can scarcely imagine the significance attached by the Middle Ages to the angels, and especially to Saint Michael. Bridget wrote down the *Sermo angelicus* at dictation from the lips of an angel. A later woman saint, Francesca Romana, continually saw her guardian angel at her side. Joan of Arc was called upon and strengthened by Saint Michael for her great mission. *Va, fille de Dieu, va!* 'Go, thou child of God, go!' To this day a Catholic still mentions in the Confiteor blessed Michael the Archangel—he is to pray to God for the penitent sinner. For he is the angel of the Apocalypse of Saint John, who offers up the incense of prayer upon the altar of incense, so that the incense may ascend before the altar.‡ But to how many of the millions of Catholics, who every morning all over the earth receive Holy

---

* Psalm cxxxii, 7.

† Saint Francis of Assisi came to Monte Gàrgano in the year 1216. Brother Egidio was there twice, on his departure to the Holy Land, and on his return from it.

‡ The Apocalypse of St. John, viii, 3–4.

II

Communion from the millions of altars of the Catholic Church, is the Archangel Michael much more than a name? In Protestant Christianity all that remains of the nine choirs of angels (angels, archangels, virtues, powers, principalities, dominions, thrones, seraphim, cherubim), which Bridget's friend, the pious Brother Gerekinus was given grace to behold, are the Christmas angels (not always easy to distinguish from Christmas hobgoblins) and the angel Gabriel of Saint Luke's gospel, Chapter I, verses 26 to 35. . . .

To Saint Bridget and her fellow travellers the archangel Michael was as completely a real person as the Pope in Avignon or Queen Giovanna in Naples, and they now came to visit him or perhaps hear a word from his lips. From the coast of the Adriatic the road goes outside Monte Gàrgano, inwards across the flat, fertile country about Foggia—*le tavoliere delle Puglie*, square by square of luxuriant fields. Nowhere, perhaps, in Italy is the industrious, hardy, frugal Italian peasant more hardworking than here—after having first brought the harvest home many in earlier times crossed the sea to the Argentine, that they might in winter (which is summer there) gather in another crop and come home with money in their pockets so that they could purchase a small *podere*. (Did anybody say anything about 'lazy Italians'?)

The road goes round the southern slopes of Monte Gàrgano, past the little towns of San Marco in Lamis and San Giovanni Rotondo. (In the last-mentioned town the stigmatic Franciscan, Father Pio, lived about twenty years ago—and he may still be living there.) Then the ascent begins—the highest point of Monte Gàrgano is about 3,030 feet above the sea. At the present day a carriage road leads up to it, but it is not wise to make use of the motor bus—that is, if one believes what a modern Danish pilgrim has written about it. 'From that God-forsaken hole, Manfredonia, the motor bus leads up an extremely dangerous serpentine road up the mountain. . . . Women retch with giddiness and terror at the unprotected turns on the edge of a precipice.' It is wiser to be content with a horse-drawn vehicle—on the way you meet other vehicles of this kind, which with their brakes tightly turned, so that the wheels grind on the stones, scrunch down the mountain side. Perhaps a talk begins in a broad Apulian peasant dialect, closely related to the Neapolitan '*Da dove venit*,' 'Where do you come from?' If the answer is 'From *San Giovanni Rotondo*,' a new question follows: '*Avete visto Pad' Pi?*' 'Have you seen Padre Pio'? (the stigmatic). If this is also answered in the affirmative the interview is continued with a more intimate question: '*Vie siete confessat*'?' 'Did you go to confession?' The driver answers yes for all of us—but the interviewer is not yet satisfied. With his whip he points to a spectacled *professore* in the carriage: '*Anche lu*'?' 'Did he also?' 'Yes, he also went to confession to Padre Pio'—and we continue our journey.

For good reasons Bishop Thomas of Vexiö did not make use of the motor bus from that God-forsaken hole, Manfredonia, but at any rate he had a horse. And yet he did not make quicker progress than the others, quite the contrary. For all of a sudden his steed stumbled over some stone or other—the bishop fell from his horse and broke two ribs.(8)

But that was only on the way down the mountain. Before that he had been able, together with Bridget and the rest of the pious company, to kneel in the archangel's shrine. 'We stop on the top of the mountain in a town with dice-shaped houses limewashed in light colours round a tripartite Gothic façade with a huge tower,' writes the Danish pilgrim. 'Passing through the porch you come into a confusion of corridors and halls—a whole collection of buildings placed outside and round about the cave in the mountain. Many broad marble steps lead up to it; everywhere on the steps the pilgrims have scratched the outline of an open hand and on the palm and in the fingers they have cut their own names and the names of those dear to them. . . . Everywhere it is wet and cold, the heavy skirts of the women and the hobnailed boots of the men make a slushy sound when they walk up and down the steps which end in an enormous, dark and dripping wet mountain cave; there are altars under canopies of tin, gleaming from the falling drops, from the gleaming and dripping rock wall. Tapers are lit, in a little choir with a wooden floor and braziers (*fuoconi*); canons wearing fur capes and goloshes sing the Te Deum of matins, the tapers shine like red stars in the wet cold, and now that my eyes have grown used to it I see the marble figure of Saint Michael and with a great golden crown under the protecting baldacchino of the high altar. Small limbs of silver and primitive paintings of accidents on the sea and mountains hang on the walls, depicting the great *patrono* appearing as a protector in the clouds and warding off injury. The singing of matins being ended the soft soughing of the trees outside can be heard in the deep silence, the falling of drops from the roof of the cave sounds like little explosions; an old bent peasant is praying under groaning exertion. . . . In the light from the tapers I see the immovable holy Madonna profiles of young peasant girls, their faces resembling the countenances I can see on the half obliterated frescoes on the walls.'

The Danish pilgrim of the present day then recounts the old legend about the origin of the shrine and adds:

Whatever the legend is worth—at this very day large companies of the peasants of the Campania and Apulia still go there on pilgrimage as our Scandinavian forefathers did, prayers and Masses are offered there, confessions and acts of contrition are made, and in the wet cave row behind row thousands kneel at the communion rail, so that an archangel must rejoice. . . .*

In Bridget's time the pilgrimages were perhaps not so frequent as they had been earlier and became later.

For it seemed to her as if she saw a great company of angels hovering about the mountain, singing and saying: Blessed be Thou, our God, Thou who hast no beginning and no ending! Thou hast sent us for the consolation and help of men, and secretly we walk about among them. And in this place it has been Thy will to show us how great is our dignity, that men may learn to love Thee and to beseech our help. This shrine was long greatly honoured, but now it is despised by many, for the children of the earth keep closer to the evil spirits than to us. Then Bridget prayed: Oh Lord, my Creator and Redeemer, help men to refrain from their sins. But the Lord answered: they have grown so used to living in filth and will not be converted until they are flogged into it!(9)

Bishop Thomas succeeded, in spite of the two broken ribs, in getting down the mountain to Manfredonia. But there he had to take to his bed, and Bridget, as well as the others, wanted to go on to Bari. In the fourteenth century, too, Manfredonia seems to have been a 'God-forsaken hole'—the town had once been called Siponte and had been large and beautiful, but now everything was lying in ruins. Bridget tried to find an explanation of the reason for this disaster and in prayer she was enlightened; the town had been laid waste because of the sins of the inhabitants. A friend of God had once lived there, and in vain he had constantly preached penitence and conversion to the people. When that proved useless, and so many souls daily faced the death of sinners, he prayed to God rather to destroy the town. And this had come to pass.(10)

It is easy to understand that Bishop Thomas might not like to be left behind alone in this city of ruins. But he also understood very well

---

* Owing to the difficulties of the times I am debarred from making use of my own notes of my visit to Monte Gàrgano in 1927. I have, therefore, been glad to employ a description by Peter Schindler appearing in a Berlin newspaper on 18 September 1939.

that his fellow travellers could not prolong their stay for his sake in a town in whose churches there had formerly been so many relics to be venerated, but which were now all lying buried under the fallen arches. Besides, the times were unsettled—attacks by wandering robber bands might be expected at any time. He therefore sent for Bridget to come to his room and asked her to perform a miracle for him. 'Lay your hand upon my side where it hurts, and pray that I may be able to continue the journey.' Bridget refuses at first, she is only a sinner and not worthy to work wonders. 'But let us all pray, and then God will surely hear us for the sake of your faith.' And when they all rise from prayer Bridget touches the side of the injured bishop. 'May Our Lord Jesus Christ make you well!' And at once all pain left him, and the bishop stood up and went with the Lady Bridget on the whole journey.(11)

Barletta was the next station on the pilgrim journey. Here it was vouchsafed to Bridget to perform a miracle of a spiritual kind. In order to be sure of finding the way and not to get lost as they had done at Ortona, she had enlisted the services of a man acquainted with the locality to guide them on the journey. In some way or other a quarrel arose between this guide and the landlord of the inn where the pilgrims had sought quarters. Perhaps the guide had found the bill too high—anyhow it came to high words and to both parties drawing their swords. Greatly frightened Karin came rushing in to her mother. 'They are fighting out there in the inn parlour, they want to kill each other!' Bridget did not go out to make peace—she knew of better means, she began to pray at once. And then she saw that the air out there in the parlour was full of demons that incited the antagonists to strike. But she also saw an angel of God coming—was it Saint Michael himself?—and heard him shouting to the demons: 'Away with you, you have nothing to do with the bride of God and her escort.' And the angel kept the swords back, so that no blood was shed.(12) (Bridget would perhaps not have intervened on another occasion, when a chivalrous contest was fought for a wager on 13 February 1503, between thirteen Italians and thirteen Frenchmen to decide the fate of a town besieged by the French. On the French side Bayard, the knight without fear and reproach was the umpire, on the Italian Prospero Colonna, and the victory fell to the Italians. In this way a war could be ended in the sixteenth century.)

From Barletta the road again goes along the shore of the Adriatic Sea to Bari, and Bridget did not intend to go further south. At home in Uppsala her parents lay buried in the chapel dedicated to Saint Nicholas; here in Bari was the saint's own grave. Of all the holy men of early Christianity Saint Nicholas was one of those about whom the most legends had arisen. He was bishop in Myra in Asia Minor and died during a pilgrimage to Palestine on 6 December 352. Under Diocletian he had come near to martyrdom, but Constantine set him free. In the year 1087 there was a pious Italian merchant who stole his relics from Mohammedan Myra and brought them to Bari, where the great church of San Niccolò was built in honour of the saint. He worked many miracles while he lived—a French folk song relates about one of them the ballad of the three children who were killed by a wicked butcher, who made salt meat of them. Saint Nicholas hears of the evil deed, goes to this unchristian sausage-maker and demands to be taken to the salt meat barrel. He makes three signs of the Cross over it and the three children rise up, waken as though out of a dream—and not even a bad dream: *le premier dit: j'ai bien dormi, le deuxième: moi aussi*, and the third: *j'ai rêvé que j'étais au Paradis.* * Because of this miracle Saint Nicholas became the patron saint of children—and in South Germany he is still Father Christmas, who comes already on 6 December with his gifts, and puts them in the children's stockings before the hearth. On the other side of the Atlantic he is called Santa Claus. (And also in England.†) Santa Claus was the patron saint of children, but also of young girls. The Swedish legend relates about this:

> A neighbour of Saint Nicholas had become very poor, and therefore thought of giving up his three daughters to a life of dishonour so that he could make a living out of their shame. But Saint Nicholas came during the night and threw a lump of gold in through the window. The man thought it was an angel of God who had given the gold and gave away his eldest daughter in honourable marriage. Saint Nicholas did this a second and a third time and helped all the three sisters to get married. But the third time the man awoke at the sound of the gold falling, and ran out to see who had thrown it. And he fell down weeping at the feet of Saint Nicholas, but Nicholas forbade him to speak of it to anyone.(13)

Italian frescoes like to present this scene. You see the interior of a bedroom where the three young girls are sleeping in a bed broad enough for three. The window in their room is placed high up, but in the street an incredibly tall Saint Nicholas stands and throws gold coins in through the small window.

* The first says: 'I have slept well,' the second: 'So have I,' the third: 'I dreamt that I was in Paradise!'
† Translator's addition.

The holy man was also a good friend of sailors. He knew the Mediterranean well, having come by sea from Asia Minor to Bari. While he was still living he was already invoked by seamen when they were in distress—'then he would come and standing at the prow he would help them. They invoked him still more after his death—all through the Middle Ages he was the sailors' friend, and in Svendborg and other Danish towns there is therefore a church dedicated to Saint Nicholas. And he who by the saint's intercession had been saved from shipwreck, with skilful sailor's fingers made a small ship and hung it up in the church. . . .

While the earthly remains of Saint Nicholas were still lying in Myra, something strange already happened to his coffin—it exuded oil. It is said in the hymn to his honour that what Nature does not produce—oil from marble—happens here in a supernatural manner. In Bari, too, this marvel continued, and it was explained to Bridget in a revelation: in the arena of the world Saint Nicholas had been like an athlete of God, whose anointed limbs were always ready for fight. It was with this oil of humility and abstinence that the dry bones of the present time needed to be rubbed.(14)

While they were still in Bari Bishop Thomas of Vexiö, that somewhat troublesome fellow traveller, was again in a state of suffering. The ribs were healed, but now he was tormented by stone pains (kidney or gall). When the pilgrims had reached Benevento, the next stage of their journey beyond the Apennines, he had to go to bed, and a physician was sent for. (The route would probably be: back to Barletta, from there to Foggia and from Foggia to Benevento, perhaps with a stop in Ariano; mention is made of a Countess Francesca of Ariano, mother of Cardinal Elzear, as being among Bridget's Neapolitan friends).(15)

The physician's skill does not seem to have been of any use, for Bishop Thomas had again to invoke Bridget's supernatural aid, so that they could continue the journey. After passing Saint Bartholomew's grave the road led to Salerno, where the converted publican, Matthew, the author of the first Gospel, had found his last resting-place. Bridget knew him well, he was that good publican 'who when God called him, threw off the heavy burden of the world, and instead took upon him the light yoke of Christ.'(16) Kneeling in the crypt by the shrine of the saint, she prayed:

Blessed art thou, Saint Matthew apostle, thou wast a wise merchant who exchanged worldly goods for heavenly ones. Thou didst despise thyself and gained God, thou gavest up thy good position and madest thy vows to the hard life of an apostle. It is therefore just that thou art now with God.

And in Bridget's soul the apostle answered:

For the sake of this greeting I will now tell thee, first, what I was before my conversion, next in what manner I wrote the Gospel, finally what reward I have now received. As thou knowest, I held the office of publican. It is seldom that a publican does not take unjust gains, but I was firmly resolved not to deceive anyone, and all the time I longed to find a way of giving up my office and getting nearer to God. And then, when I hear the dear Lord Jesus Christ preach, the words with which He called me kindled a fire in my heart, and I cared no more about my riches and my position than if they had been straw. Far more did I love to weep and to rejoice that God had willed to call a man so little to be thought of as I, and so great a sinner, to conversion. And now, as I followed the Lord, I carefully kept in mind all His words, and thought of them day and night. Then after the passion and death of the Lord I wrote my Gospel from what I had seen and heard, had been present at—not to gain praise and honour thereby, but for the glory and honour of my Redeemer and for the good of my neighbour. And while I wrote my soul was burning with such ardour, that even had I willed to be silent I should have had to speak.

Such as the times afforded, there were, in the fourteenth century too, Bible critics with rationalist views. They draw attention to discrepancies in the different gospels—they would, says the old evangelist, 'rather dispute about the gospel than live according to it.' But the door to the kingdom of heaven is low, it is the lowly ones who can enter in at it, the haughty learned gentlemen who will not stoop have to remain standing outside. (Perhaps Bridget was thinking of these words when, some years later in Bethlehem, she went through the door of the church of the Nativity, for no one can enter in at it without stooping.) So much was Matthew able to tell about his life on earth. 'But about the reward which has now been bestowed upon me, I can only say that what the scriptures say is true; no heart can contain it, no tongue can utter it!'(17)

Thus spoke the old convert and evangelist to Bridget as she prayed. Did she see, when she came up from the crypt, the beautiful monument in the chancel, which Robert Guiscard had erected over the grave of Gregory VII? 'Because I have loved justice I die in exile.' These words of the great Pope might well find an echo in Bridget's soul. . . .

But now the pilgrim road came to an end. From ascetic and mystic Italy, 'Franciscan Italy,' Bridget and her escort had now descended to the land of Goethe and all English 'misses,' *wo die Zitronen blüh'n*. Before them lay the blue gulf, the rhythmic profile of Capri rose up in the horizon, smoke arose from Vesuvius and stood like the crown of a pine against the blue sky. When Bridget and her *famiglia* passed Nola on the way from Benevento her friend, Count Niccolà Orsini, joined them, he wanted to present Bridget in Naples to Lapa, the sister of the marshal of the kingdom, Niccolà Acciaiuoli—Lapa was married to another great Neapolitan, Manente Buondelmonte. Boccaccio was a friend of the house—he had dedicated his book, *De illustris mulieribus*, to Lapa's younger sister, Andrea. Bridget was again in the same surroundings as in Stockholm, only that they were on a larger scale. Queen Giovanna was a second Queen Blanca, and Niccolà Acciaiuoli —why, he soon proved to be an Italian edition of Bengt Algotsson! Had not Bridget on Saint Michael's Mount heard the complaint about those who, though they build a house to the Lord, reck but little about the commandments of the Holy Church? Bridget understood that her place was here 'to perform several errands in the name of God.' And what errand had she but that of the humble messenger who brings the message of the Lord? 'Ah, if only she could do something good for the benefit of her own soul and the glory of Our Lord Jesus Christ!' She resolved to stay in Naples. It proved to be a new time of waiting—close upon two years.(18)

XV

Bridget and her escort took up their quarters in the hostelry of the Knights of Malta, adjoining the little church of San Giovanni al Mare.(1) And there, in Naples, Bishop Thomas bids her farewell. It may be that he is not wholly displeased at getting away from further dangerous pilgrimages and getting home to his own good bishop's house in Vexiö. And then there would probably be a last evening when he and Bridget would sit by the fire together and talk. He who knows Italy and has lived with Italians knows that in an Italian house the hearth is the central point—as it was with the ancient Romans. After a cold winter day, a cool day in spring, you hear someone saying as you rise from the dinner table: *Andiamo al fuoco*, and in many families that means: 'Let us go into the kitchen!' For there, only there, a fire is burning, only there can you warm yourself. In many places the hearth is so deep and so wide that a narrow bench can stand on either side—on it sit old Granny Maria (mother's mother) and old Granny Ursula (father's mother) warming their wrinkled hands over the embers. But it is not always advisable to be so near the fire, now and then Rigo comes in with a big armful of olive twigs or dry vines which he has cut down (it is time now to *potare*, to do the pruning of both the olive tree and the vine), and the dry brushwood crackles, the flame darts up, the sparks fly up and catch on to the women's skirts and have to be brushed off quickly before they can burn a hole. . . .

Down in Southern Italy there is a little town called Casacalenda. It lies in the Neapolitan Apennines, in the province of Molise, a little more than ninety kilometres west of Monte Gàrgano. The nearest large town is Campobasso, which, notwithstanding its name, stands on a rather considerable height. But what are 2,100 feet here, where the summits of the High Apennines reach up to above 6,000? Then the hill of 2,100 is only low land!

It was in Casacalenda then, one evening in March 1927, and it was on one of my Bridgettine wanderings in unknown Italy. Casacalenda stands on a cliff top, the streets and market square have been hewn into the stone, the houses are of stone. It had rained all day, and it was still raining—we heard it pouring down outside—*lo scroscio dell' aqua*, according to the Italian onomatopoeic expression—*scroscio*—can't you hear how it pours? It rains like that on Mont' Alverna.

So there we sat round the fire—five people, of whom three were Italians, one a Frenchman, namely Frère Serafico from Brittany, and myself, Sor Giovanni. We two foreigners came from Campobasso, and in Campobasso we had met a Capuchin, Padre Paolino, who had shown us the town. 'Come home with me and make acquaintance with my mother and sister,' he said at last, 'It is only a short way further round, when you want to go to Monte Sant' Angelo after all.' This we did and we had spent two pleasant days with the *di Tommaso* family. On the Sunday we heard Padre Paolino preach to his fellow-countrymen—the big parish church had been full, the peasants standing on the grey stone flags, close together, in lambskin coats and with hobnail boots. It had rained on the Sunday, and now it was Monday, and it was still raining. The stone walls and stone floor were icy cold, the dampness settled on the walls. But in the large kitchen there was a huge, bright fire, and it was bright and warm there. 'And now you must sing to Sor Giovanni, Teresa,' said Padre Paolino to his sister—'the song about Santa Brigida.' I looked up surprised—my Capuchin friend's beard was full of smiles. 'We have not forgotten *la Principessa* * down here,' he said.

* 'The princess of Närke,' was the title by which Bridget was known in Italy. Ulf had been *law-man* in Närke. The word was translated by *principe*. Catherine of Siena called her *contessa*.

Then Teresa di Tommaso began to sing. She sang about Santa Brigida kneeling before the crucifix and intently contemplating the passion of Christ—'on her head she had a crown of thorns, in one hand she held a book in which she read, in the other a lighted taper.'* And what Brigida is reading in her book by the light of the taper is a contemplation of the passion of Christ. She sees Pilate 'on his balcony,' and at his side the Thorncrowned One. Pilate wants to release Jesus—'He is already half dead,' he says, 'besides, He is a just man and does not deserve punishment.' But six thousand Jews scream that Jesus must die, and then Pilate sends for the basin of water.

After this the walk to Golgotha begins. The disciples go with Jesus and on the way they say the rosary. They pity Him for His bleeding knees and for His lips that are swollen with the blows of the executioners' fists. 'And, oh God, how heavy is this cross!' But Jesus answers: 'There is only one thing that causes Me pain—it is, that at My side walks My sweet Mother weeping:

> *Una cosa sola mi dispiace*
> *Che appresso mi piange la mia madre dolce!* . . .

Teresa di Tommaso's voice broke a little as she sang these lines— Padre Paolino stooped forward and was very busy in throwing fresh fuel on the fire. I saw Frère Serafino's young face drawn as though on the verge of weeping. Then the singing went on and ended in a radiant promise: 'Blessed are they who sing this song or hear it sung, they will release a soul from purgatory with it. And a week before he is to die Santa Brigida will come and take him home.'(2)

There was a silence when Teresa ceased. Outside it was still raining heavily. Then a little bell began to ring outside in the night. Padre Paolino stood up with a little nod to the rest of us, made the sign of the Cross and began the hymn for the dead, *De profundis*.

XVI

Bishop Thomas left, and with him the widow of the Swedish great man Ulf Åbjörnsson Sparre, the Lady Kristina, Sigismund's daughter, also left. She had been waiting for an opportunity to go home and

---

* The Italian text of the song about Saint Bridget will be found in the Notes as I wrote them down from Teresa's dictation. 'The second hour,' according to old Italian reckoning, two hours after the bells have rung for sunset. The prayers for the dead are then said.

now joined the bishop and his escort. She had often spoken to Bridget about her departed husband—he had been one of the great men in the land. His first wife had been Margareta, daughter of the earl of the Orkney Islands, Erengisle Sunesson—he had been councillor of the realm, law-man in the Tio district, one of the three to whom King Magnus had entrusted the preparing of the Swedish land law. He had been a zealous opponent of Bengt Algotsson and had his reasons for it —his daughter Ingeborg had been disowned by the unscrupulous fortune hunter. The general opinion about him was that he was a good man, the fatherly friend of the poor.(1)

But God's judgment differs from the judgment of men. The Lady Kristina had prayed much for the soul of her husband—she had collected indulgences for him in all the churches in Rome. But her own soul was not at peace until she had questioned Bridget ; besides, they were related, her stepson Karl Ulfsson Sparre was married to Helena, the daughter of Bridget's brother Israel.

And Bridget had promised her kinswoman to pray for the soul of her husband. Kristina daughter of Sigismund did not stay long at home in Sweden, she returned to Rome and to Bridget and died in her house. Perhaps it was during this latter sojourn that the seeress told the anxious widow what she had seen in her nocturnal visions.

It seemed to her that a devil was standing with a soul in his hand— 'and the soul trembled like a heart that has just been taken out of the body,' a poor trembling heart. The devil has it in his hand, but it does not belong to him, he is only making a claim on it. He is so greedy to devour it, like a wild beast that is so hungry that it eats its own limbs. But first he must prove that he has a right to such a festive meal— 'hand over your proof of your claim,' says the judge. And the devil does not make him say that twice—he pulls out the dead man's list of sins—'it is quite a book,' he says with satisfaction. 'The book is in seven chapters,' he explains, 'each chapter is in fourteen pages, and on each page there are a thousand words, sometimes even more.' That makes, roughly, a manuscript of 100,000 words—yet the document is not to be read in its entirety, the devil will give only a brief résumé.

The title of the book, then, is *Disobedience* (against God and the Church). Chapter I: *Pride*, in the three forms of this vice: spiritual pride, pride of wealth, pride of belonging to a great family and of being of a handsome appearance. 'In this chapter there are countless words, which of course I need not tell you,' says the devil with a devout inclination towards the judge's seat. (Bridget's devil is always polite when he comes to court—'von Zeit zu Zeit seh' ich den Alten gern,' says his descendant Mephistopheles.)

The second chapter is entitled *Covetousness*—in this as in the preceding one there are three columns (the Swedish text has 'leaves.' But Bridget sees before her a manuscript with the text in three columns; though most mediæval manuscripts have only two). On the three leaves (or the three columns) there were 'countless words' about the dead man—that all his will and all his efforts were entirely directed towards gathering riches, making his name famous and bringing up his heirs to worldly honour and power.

The third chapter has a strange heading—it says *Envy*. Is it 'kungliga svenska avundsjukan' * that Bridget has in mind, traces of which Emilia Fogelklou has also wanted to find elsewhere in the *Revelations*?(2) It is in any case an envy which is allied with duplicity—out of envy the deceased, under the mask of friendship, gave his neighbour advice that was injurious to him.

Ulf Åbjörnsson had been reputed a good man, the friend of the poor. Nothing of the kind, says the devil—on the contrary, he was *niggardly*! Not only with money, but also with things that he knew might be of use or give pleasure to others—he kept everything for himself. This is written in the fourth chapter of three columns 'in countless words.'

The fifth chapter is concerned with *Sloth*: firstly, such purely corporal sloth of long midday sleep, secondly, spiritual sloth, so that he preferred light, merry thoughts to serious ones, and gay talk to pious prayers and godly conversation.

The sixth chapter is called *Anger*. It is short—there is not much to be said about an angry man. Though yes, other people get quite afraid of him when he gets really furious.

The seventh chapter deals with sins against the *sixth commandment*. Bridget was never afraid of calling a spade a spade—here, too, things are called by their true name. Ulf Åbjörnsson was faithful to his wife, it is true, but he treated her like a harlot and practised onanism upon her. (It is perhaps permitted to believe that here we find an echo of the Lady Kristina's complaints when the two widows sat together by the fire and talked about their married life.) In connection with this the devil brings the same accusation as that against Bridget's Ulf—Ulf Åbjörnsson also sat longer at table than necessary, ate and drank more than he needed and carried on all kinds of unseemly table talk. 'And

* The 'royal Swedish disease of grudging.'

now, O Judge, I have read my book to the end—award me this soul!'
You hear the assured victorious snap with which the devil closes the
indictment.

But now the Blessed Virgin appears and lays her cloak about the
trembling soul. 'He served me in three ways,' she says. 'He fasted on
the eve of my feasts, he read the office in my honour and led the singing
in the church.' Other saints appear and testify in the same way to the piety
of the deceased. And when the devil wants to look this up in his book,
he is compelled to see that all the seven chapters are erased—'you can
only see that something has been there,' he says. Notwithstanding
this the soul is left to him after all, but only to punish and purify it.
The punishment is severe enough—for the sins he committed with his
sight he is to see these sins in their shameful reality, he is to see the
devil in all his terrible hideousness, he is to see the woefulness and
punishment of the other souls. For the sins that he committed with his
ears he is to hear the horrible howls and shrieks of the spirits of the
abyss, and to bear their mocking. For the sins of feeling he is to burn
outside and inside, until everything is burnt out; he is to shiver in
terrible cold, because he was so cold to God, and he is to feel the hands
and claws of the devil upon his body.

More than this is not permitted to the Evil One, one or two of the
worst punishments are even mitigated at the intercession of the Blessed
Virgin. He is to be spared, for instance, the sight of the horrible faces
of the devils. But the suffering is to last a long, long time, even until
the day of judgment. And this is a punishment for his uncontrollable
will to life—'whoso desires to live here upon the earth until doomsday,
shall, even though he do not commit a mortal sin, suffer punishment
until doomsday.'(3)

Four years passed after Bridget had had this vision. Ulf Åbjörnsson
Sparre died in 1355, his widow had gone home with Bishop Thomas
ten years later; both at home and later, when she came back to Rome,
she had unweariedly continued to pray for her husband. And now
Bridget sees, not a devil, but an angel, who leads the cleansed and
purified soul up before the judge. And the judge speaks:

If there was a wagon full of ears of corn, and if many people, one after the
other, each took an ear, the wagon would at last be empty. In this manner
many loving deeds and many tears have come to me for this soul. And this
is therefore the judgment: he is to be led into that joy which no eye has
seen and no ear has heard, and which has never arisen in the heart of man.
For there is no heaven above and no earth below, but all is unutterable
height and inconceivable width and incomprehensible depth, and God

Himself is above all men, and around all men and in all, and rules all things, and supports everything and Himself is borne up by nothing.

And then Bridget saw Ulf Åbjörnsson's soul ascending to heaven like a star of exceeding brightness.(4)

XVII

Bishop Thomas had gone—the Lady Kristina had gone—Bridget could sit 'in loneliness by the evening fire and ponder over things' when all prayers had been said, when everyone had gone to bed, when quiet had come—the monastic *silentium*, which might not be broken until the next morning after matins.

Bishop Thomas had gone—Bridget's thoughts went with him on the way. She had told him that he could get home soon enough—there was no reason for haste. On his arrival at home he found the king imprisoned and the country in confusion.

The king—the country—Sweden. . . . It rises up before Bridget like a coast in the horizon—perhaps the long, low coast of Öland, when you are sailing into Kalmar. . . . What is the state of affairs in this kingdom, which she left now a good many years ago? Bishop Thomas has told her a great deal in the evening hours by the fire—severe visitations have passed over Sweden, but the inhabitants have not become converted, they have not grown humbler or more obedient to God—on the contrary! And Bridget hears a Voice—a deep, serious Voice—God the Father speaking to His Son!

'Oh, My Son, He says,

Thou who by Thy death hast saved the human race from hell, rise up and defend Thyself, for many men and women have driven Thee out of their hearts. Go therefore up to their city, lift its gates from off their hinges like Samson, attack the clergy, lay traps for the feet of the knights, make war upon the fine ladies, thrust down the mighty from their seats, let none of Thy enemies escape until they beg for forgiveness.(1)

Then God spoke to Bridget herself.

Hearken well to what I speak [says the Voice] and speak what thou hast heard. Let honour and dishonour be indifferent to thee—care not for those who praise thee, nor for those who blame thee. If thou art praised then take not pride therein, if thou art blamed, let it not anger thee. . . . I speak to thee, because it pleases Me, so that all may know how sin must be atoned for, punishment lessened, and the crown increased.(2)

The crown is to be increased—the crown of Sweden. Bridget cannot get away from this thought, that the territory of Sweden has been lessened—it is like a gnawing worm that leaves her no peace. And who is to blame but King Magnus? But the judgment upon him is drawing near and is gathering like a threatening thunder-storm. Once, when Bridget was sitting there in her loneliness, she had a vision—she saw heaven open, 'like a big house, where a judge was sitting in his seat of judgment'—and below heaven she saw a land lying stretched out, the land she knew so well—far too well—Sweden. . . .

But two persons were standing in front of the judge—one 'looked like a sad person,' and that was King Magnus Eriksson's guardian angel, the other 'looked like a happy person,' and that was his evil spirit, his devil. The sad angel had not much to say—the king had once been quite good, but he had turned away from his true friends who wished him well. The happy devil was all the more pleased—'You keep quiet,' he says to the angel, 'it is my turn to speak now.' And he relates how he had enticed the king to neglect his real duties, and did not even care that he was himself dissatisfied or deceived, if only his friends'—among these being Valdemar Atterdag—'could live in plenty.' A parody, that is, of genuine charity! But that time there was still hope. 'I will send the king some of my friends,' says the long-suffering judge, 'they shall warn him and show him the peril he is in.' ('But I will send some of my friends too,' says the devil with a mocking laugh.)

After this some time passes—some years even. Bridget's revelations reach home from Rome—in particular that one about the three kings before judgment might well make an impression on Magnus! But no— the devil has not been idle, when Bridget's envoys come to the king and deliver their message, he hisses at them as if he were actually a devil: 'Mind your own business! You can spare yourselves all your good advice, I am not a child any longer.' Then the king turned his back on God and his face to the enemy. And the devil receives permission from God to torment and plague the king—but not to take his soul. Magnus is again given a respite—of two whole years.(3)

But now the two years are ended, and the court is again sitting. Bridget is present at the judicial proceedings. The devil, as usual, is the State advocate—he knows every letter of the Christian moral code and knows which clauses the king has transgressed. God is love, says the devil, and God can therefore not dwell in the king's heart, in which only anger and envy have their dwelling. God is Truth itself, He can therefore have no dealings with a man who breaks his oath and betrays his country. And so on, and so on—the devil is an excellent advocate for a cause which is only indirectly his. He falls silent and the judge begins to speak.

'But then a wondrous change came over the judge, he seemed to shine like the sun, and in the sun could be seen three words: *Power, Truth, Justice.*' Then from this sun could now be heard a voice which examines all the sins of the accused and shows him all that has been done for him, and which he has despised. It is all Bridget's many good, useful counsels which are presented to him—now he was to beware of exaggerated piety; not to fast so much that he was unfitted to hold judicial proceedings and deal out justice to the poor as well as to the rich; nor to make himself unfit to sit in the court of justice by excessive use of the pleasures of the table. Further, how he was to serve God and pray to God, and on which days and times he was to sit in the council of the realm, and on which days he was to wear the crown, and that he was to seek advice about all things from the friends of God, and that he must never go against the law of Sweden and never impose any new tax, unless it was necessary for the defence of the realm and for crusades against the heathen. . . .

God said much more to him by Bridget, both when it was a matter of small things and when it concerned affairs of State. For instance, that he was not to keep more servants than he could afford—that he was to give presents with discretion—that he was to have patience with foolish and unbridled people and bear with them, but if that was no use he was to correct and punish them—he was not to leave to others what belonged to the king and the crown—he was to judge natives and foreigners with equal justice, honour the priests, gather the great men about him in affection, preserve the kingdom and the common people in peace. . . .

It had all been told Magnus in time—and what use had it been? It had been like talking reason to an ass—with true asinine obstinacy Magnus would go on walking on the edge of the abyss. (Everyone who has ridden on donkey-back in Italy knows this extraordinary obstinacy in a *somaro*—the animal *will* go on the extreme outside edge of the path, where the stones slip at every moment under its feet, and there are about six hundred feet to fall down the mountain side.) Moreover it is seen that the devil has been the king's guide—even in that which seemed to be good—the king's piety! Bridget hears the devil's hard and sharp voice. 'I egged him on to reading many and long psalms and prayers without thinking about what he was reading and without piety in his heart, and so he wasted his time to no purpose instead of sitting in court and hearing the complaints of the people.' Bridget's devil is not alone in bringing this complaint against King Magnus—in the pamphlet of the Swedish nobility against him it is said that 'from his youth he was used to hearing Masses, reading (prayers) and fasting, but not to give anyone his due.'(4) This kind of piety was in Bridget's view the most detestable of all—she was reminded of the place in the Bible about 'those who have the appearance of the fear of God but not its power.'

But the list of the king's sins is much longer, and the devil knows it by heart, better than the king's own conscience (but not better than Bridget). She sits there in court almost like an assistant judge—in any case she must nod in confirmation of point after point in the devil's _Libellus de Magno Erici Rege_. It was the devil who inspired the king with his unnatural predilection for Bengt Algotsson, it was he too, who incited the king to give up Scania to Valdemar Atterdag (whom the devil calls his 'sworn brother,' his bosom friend). (5) From this unlawful transaction followed war on land and sea, with the usual result of war: 'women are ravished, ships at sea are plundered, the means of grace of the Church are despised, harlotry is increased'—the devil's will, not the will of God, is done, as in hell, so on earth!

The spirit of darkness falls silent. Then judgment is given, and it is only a conditional judgment. 'The king's soul is not yet judged, it shall not be judged until he is at the point of death.'(6)

It is rather as though he were being excommunicated, as if his body (in the words of the apostle) is given up to Satan, so that the soul may be saved.* The devil is permitted to increase the evil in him, while at the same time God will lessen the good he still possesses (an extraordinary collaboration!) The consequence will be that he will be slighted by his former friends, his life threatened by his own people, he will be oppressed, exiled, so that he looks more like a vagrant than a crowned king.

Albrecht of Mecklenburg became the instrument for executing judgment upon King Magnus. One of Bridget's kinsmen, Karl Ulfsson Sparre, married to her brother Israel's daughter Helena, led King Albrecht's troops in the battle of the Gata forest (March 1365), where Magnus was taken prisoner and placed in the tower of the castle of Stockholm itself. King Albrecht did not prove himself generous to his mother's brother, for in a letter written in his captivity Magnus complains of 'the extreme distress of poverty and iron fetters,' and of

---

* I Cor. v, 5; I Tim. i, 20.

having always to lie bound. At last the great men had got the better of King Smek—they were therefore entirely on the Mecklenburger's side. It was Bridget's son Karl himself who in May 1367 subscribed the first big contribution, a whole year's income, to King Albrecht's loan for defence. Other great men followed Karl's example—it was the matter of fighting for Scania, the fight against Valdemar Atterdag! Bridget would probably, though it may have been with some hesitation—approve of her son's conduct. If it had to be, then rather the fox than the wolf!

Meanwhile Bridget would probably not always be able to follow the details in the game which Albrecht, Valdemar Atterdag, the great men and King Haakon were playing during those years about the land and kingdom of Sweden. Towards Christmas in 1369 her sons, Birger and Karl, came to Rome—Magnus was then still in prison, not until the peace treaty of 14 August 1371 was he set free at a ransom of 12,000 marks in silver (for which Bohus Castle was mortgaged), and on condition that he, like his son, gave up all claim to the crown of Sweden. He lived his last years partly in Norway, partly in the Swedish provinces which had been reserved for him and that were nearest to Norway (Värmland, Dalarne). He survived Bridget, though only by a year; on a sea voyage to Tönsberg, where he was to meet his son and daughter-in-law, he was drowned in Bömmelfjord, near Haugesund. 'The king's ship came into distress among the rocks at an island called Lyngholm. . . . Unwisely he jumped into the water, was pulled up by his servants and brought to land, but he died in an attack of cramp' (1 December 1374), says the year book of Visby. Blanca had died eleven years earlier—according to the Sealand chronicle it occurred in Copenhagen, during her son's wedding with Margrete, on the Sunday after Easter (9 April 1363).

Blanca is dead, but Magnus lives. He is in captivity, he is in exile, but he is living. Once more Bridget journeys to the regions beyond for his sake, and this time her spirit soars with mighty wing-strokes to the highest heavens. . . .

And after that I heard a voice like the voice of a herald, and it spoke in this wise: 'Oh all ye heavens and heavenly bodies, hearken well, and all ye spirits of the abyss who are in darkness, take heed, and all ye souls that are in the dark places, listen—for now the highest emperor intends to hold a court and to pass judgment on all the chieftains of the world.'

It is like hearing the trumpets in Berlioz' Requiem—the trumpets that sound more and more tremendous, and when you think that now

the climax has been reached, there is one that booms still mightier—
tuba mirum spargens sonum. . . .

'And immediately the eyes and ears of my spirit were opened to see
and hear in spirit. And I saw Abraham come with all the saints that
were born of his race. And all patriarchs and prophets came, and after
them I saw the four evangelists, and their figures were like the four
beasts with which they are wont to be painted on the walls here in the
world, but they were living, not dead.* Then I saw twelve thrones and
sitting on them the twelve apostles waiting for power to be given to
them.† After this I saw Adam and Eve and martyrs and fathers of the
Church and other saints that were descended from them. But not yet
did Christ appear as man, nor yet His blessed Mother, but they were
all waiting for them to come. The earth and the water also seemed to
be in expectation, and everything in them bowed humbly before the
seat of power.

'And thereupon I saw an altar standing upon the seat of power. And
on the altar there was a cup with wine and a loaf in the shape of a host.
Then I saw, down on the earth a church, and a priest clothed in his
Mass vesture, began the Mass. And when he had come to the words
with which the Bread is consecrated, it was to me as if the sun and
moon and all planets and all the heavens began to resound with
alternating voices and tones and singing. And all manner of singing
could be heard, and there were instruments without number, and the
singing and music were so sweet that it is impossible to utter or understand it. They who were in the light looked at the priest and bowed
down with awe, but they who were in darkness were afraid. But when
the priest had spoken the words over the Bread ‡ it seemed to me that
the Bread was sitting in the seat of power and yet remained in the hands
of the priest. And the Bread became a living Lamb and in the Lamb
appeared a countenance as of a Man, and round the Lamb a burning
flame of fire. But when I looked more closely there was a Virgin with
a crown upon her head beside the Lamb, and all the angels served
them, and the angels were as many as the motes in a sunbeam. . . .'

Bridget is present at High Mass in the cathedral of eternity. But
there now ascends towards the heavenly joy the plaint of the earth—
the dirge of the vale of tears of this world.

---

* Bridget is thinking of the symbols of the evangelists—the angel (Matthew),
the lion (Mark), the ox (Luke), the eagle (John).
  † To judge the twelve tribes of Israel (St. Luke xxii, 30).
  ‡ That is, the words: 'This is My Body . . .'

And then I heard from the earth the voices of countless thousands, crying and saying: 'Oh Lord God, just judge, let there be judgment upon our kings and chieftains, look upon our blood that is crying from the earth, and upon the sorrow and tears of our wives and children! Look down upon our wounds and our captivity, our hunger and our degradation, upon our homes which were burned down, upon our maidens and our wives who were ravished and dishonoured! Pay heed to all the injustice that kings and chieftains work against the Catholic Church, to all their false words and promises and treachery, and all the taxes they extort from us in violence and wrath. For they do not reckon much how many thousands are slain in war, if only they can extend their might.'

In our times, too, the same cry of woe rises from the blood-drenched earth. But Bridget hears more.

Thereupon it was as though countless thousands cried from the depths of hell and said: 'Oh Judge, we know that thou art the Lord of all things. Sit in judgment therefore on those chieftains of war whom we served on earth, for they plunged us deeper and deeper into hell than we should otherwise have come. We are not thy friends, but justice compels us to speak the truth and to accuse our masters. For they did not think us higher than dogs, and they cared not whether we loved thee or not. They are therefore worthy of coming to hell, for they led us into perdition, and we would willingly endure still harder punishment than we are suffering now, if only their torments may never end.

And they who were in purgatory spoke in the same way. . . . 'We complain of our masters who are still living upon the earth, for if they had done their duty and led us to what is good by word and example, we would not have suffered so hard or so long a punishment. Instead they incited us to sin and evil deeds . . .'

The threefold complaint about the kings and chieftains of the earth falls silent. It is now the inhabitants of heaven who all call down the judgment of God upon the princes of the earth. As on van Eyck's picture of the Adoration of the Lamb they sit round the throne of God in hierarchical order. The first to speak is the oldest and most venerable —Abraham. 'Above all the things that we hoped for and desired most,' says the father of the patriarchs, 'was this, that of our race should be born He, whom the chieftains of the world now refuse. We therefore pray for judgment upon them, for they despised Thy mercy and do not fear Thy justice.'

Then the prophets spoke and said: 'We foretold the coming of the Son of God, and that He should be born of a Virgin, and be betrayed and taken prisoner, and scourged and crowned with thorns, and then in the end die upon the cross, that sin might be atoned for and the kingdom of heaven opened. And because all that we said and foretold has now been fulfilled we pray for a judgment upon the chieftains of the earth, for they despise Him who died for love of them.'

Then the evangelists also spoke and said: 'We were witnesses that the Son of God fulfilled all that had been foretold about Him.' Next the apostles spoke and said: 'We are the assistant judges of God, and we sentence to perdition everyone who despises the commandments of God and the Sacrament of His Body.'

Only one voice in the gathering of the heavenly council is raised in defence of those who are so unanimously condemned, that of the Blessed Virgin. 'The Virgin, who sat beside the Lamb, said: "Oh, most gentle Lord, have mercy upon them!"' The answer is that which, with Bridget, is always an end of the matter: when everything has been heard—there is mercy to be found for every repentant sinner. But when kings and chieftains do not repent? And, in particular, when *King Magnus* does not repent?

Bridget dares not hope any longer. The great scene of judgment vanishes—all that remains is 'that Face which appeared in the Lamb'— that Face which, crowned with thorns and streaming with blood, was printed on Veronica's kerchief.

The Holy Face of God speaks to Magnus:

> I showed thee great mercy, for I made known to thee what thou shouldst do in thy rule and thy office, and how thou shouldst govern thyself in wisdom and seemliness. I enticed thee as a mother entices her child with tender words, and I admonished thee gently as a father admonishes his son. But thou didst obey the Devil, thou didst cast Me away from thee, as a mother casts away a stillborn child, whom she will not lay to her breast. Therefore shall all that is good in thee be taken from thee and be given to one who shall come after thee.(7)

There is no more any hope for King Magnus. Not even Mary has any word of consolation.

XVIII

Bridget was now over sixty and by this time she had lived a fairly long time in Italy. Besides knowing Latin, for use at audiences and on other solemn occasions, she spoke the language of the country. It is easy for Swedes, they have from home the rolling R, so sadly lacking in Danish (and in English). It would not happen to a Swedish tourist, as it did once in a *trattoria* to an English girl—she ordered *un piatto di carne* (a plate of meat) and was told that 'we do not eat dog in Italy' (*carne* pronounced without the r—*cane*, dog). From Bridget's lips the metallic

Italian language could ring as if spoken by a Roman woman. It may be that in Naples she would adopt some of the *lazzarone's* expressions. In any case she was so used to speaking Italian that when she bid her son welcome in Rome she involuntarily spoke to him in that language.(1)

Bridget's sojourn in Naples extended to rather more than two years: from July 1365 to October 1367.(2) Through Niccolà Orsini she had come into contact with more than one of the noble families in Naples—he may have offered her houseroom himself in his palace 'near Santa Maria Nova.'(3) The Countess Francesca may have made her a similar offer—she was the mother of that young Elzear who later became a cardinal, and who owed Bridget all his later spiritual development.(4) But, true to her pilgrim habits, Bridget took up her quarters at the guest house of the Knights of Malta at San Giovanni al Mare. (It was still standing there in 1903, and in the chapel is shown a crucifix before which Bridget had prayed.)(5)

The lady with whom Bridget became most intimate was Niccolà Acciaiuoli's sister Lapa, wife of a Buondelmonte. A miraculous healing was the immediate cause. The Lady Lapa's youngest son, Esau, was lying ill, severely attacked by tuberculosis, 'quite wasted and emaciated,' says Karin, who visited him in company with her mother. The physicians had given up the boy and Bridget was sent for. She came, 'touched the boy, made the sign of the Cross over his abdomen, and at once he recovered.'(6) After this the Lady Lapa became the friend of the Scandinavian saint and did everything she could to be of use to her. And Bridget requited the friendship with the only coin that she could give—like Saint Peter she could say, 'Silver and gold I have none, but the gifts of grace of the spirit and of miracles.' The Lady Lapa was soon to have a fresh proof of this. One day, when her brother was at the court to discuss matters of state with Queen Giovanna, Bridget came to Lapa with a serious look and presaged the approaching death of Messer Niccolà. The Lady Lapa was so alarmed that she immediately repaired to Castel dell' Ovo, had speech with her brother and found him perfectly well. Besides, Niccolà was at that time at the prime of life, not yet sixty—Lapa could go home reassured. But before sunset Messer Niccolà was lying on his sick-bed, and Bridget was sitting by his side together with the weeping Lapa. Ah, could the saint work a miracle now, as she had done with little Esau? . . .

But Bridget's soul was far away from the Palazzo Acciaiuoli, far away from Naples—she was in that great hall where she had her visions so often now, the hall in which the heavenly supreme court was sitting. She saw the hall, she saw the white-robed hosts of angels and saints, she saw the judgment seat, and a shining Sun sitting in it. Beside the Sun stood a woman with a crown upon her head—she too, was known to Bridget. 'And all of them praised God with hymns and psalms.'(7)

Niccolà died on 8 November 1366 and Bridget came to Naples in July of the preceding year. During that period she would have opportunity enough to form an opinion about him, both as a statesman and in private life. And now she was sitting by his deathbed and hearing a voice saying: 'Soul and body are not yet separated, he is still conscious.' He who says this seems to her to be 'an armed knight, courteous and wise in his speech.' But opposite him stands a policeman, gruesome to behold and as though inflamed with great wrath.

And now comes the usual judicial procedure and—also as usual, the 'blue man' seems to be right. Bridget sees 'countless devils darting up from hell like sparks from a furnace,' and she hears these devils make an entirely orthodox Catholic confession of faith. 'We know that Thou art and remainest for ever one God in three Persons, and that there is no other God but Thee. Thou art love itself, Thou art mercy, Thou art justice.' And these devils have not only faith, but also the knowledge of sin, so that they simply take God's part against themselves. 'Since we were inwardly inflamed with pride and envy and concupiscence, we were thrust down by Thy love, which was also justice, from heaven with the fire of our malice to the incomprehensible and dark abyss, which is now called hell.' The devils add some surprising words: 'Thy love did this.' There is no Promethean rebellion in these devils, no claim to be right against God, to fight in the army of *Lucifer*, the Light Bearer. The Middle Ages were acquainted with these Luciferians, the remote forerunners of the proud poets of Satan of the nineteenth century, from Byron to Carducci. But Bridget had evidently never heard tell of them, nor would she have understood them. God is God, the 'all powerful ruler' of the Eastern Church, *Pantokrator*, before whom one can only bow down humbly in the dust. The devils go so far as to say to God: 'If Thy Mother, the Blessed Virgin, whom Thou didst love so much, had committed a mortal sin, and not repented of it, wouldst Thou have sent her soul down to us in hell?' And now they demand the soul of Niccolà Acciaiuoli to be given up to them.

The dying man is now at the point of death, and Saint Michael, guardian of souls, blows his trumpet. 'Then all who heard it were silent, and there was a voice that said: "Oh all ye angels and souls, and spirits of the abyss, be silent and hearken, the Mother of God will speak to you." And immediately the Blessed Virgin appeared, and threw aside her cloak, and under one side of it could be seen a little church, and in it many monks were praying, and under the other side there were many friends of God, both men and women, and all of them cried with one voice: "Have mercy, merciful God!"'

Then the devils suspect that their cause, which they think is justified, is lost, and now they throw off the mask of piety and become sarcastic: 'Yes, thank you, we know all that, a few tears and a few idle promises, then God is not angry any longer!'(8) But the sentence is spoken from the seat of the Sun: 'For the sake of My friends and their prayers this soul shall at the moment of death be filled with perfect contrition, so that he shall not be taken to hell, but shall be purified with those who in purgatory suffer the severest punishment.' After having endured his punishment he shall have a humble place in heaven—yet, after all, a place!

Bridget recounted this vision to Prior Petrus, and asked him to translate it into Latin and to give the Lady Lapa a copy of it.(9) So with consolation in her heart she could make preparations to have her brother's body taken to the family burial place in the Carthusian monastery in Val d'Ema, which he had founded himself in 1342. His funeral would undoubtedly not have cost less than that of his son Lorenzo who was buried in the same place—a sum of 5,000 gold florins is mentioned.(10) The modern tourist, on whose programme an excursion to *la Certosa* is to be found just as inevitably as a visit to Fiesole, stands in the crypt of the monastery church full of admiration of the noble Gothic of Niccolà Acciaiuoli's tomb. Here he rests, here his son Lorenzo rests, here Lapa also found her last resting-place. But only very few are aware that the gentle figure of a woman on the monument, with a widow's cap on her head, and a rosary hanging down from her folded hands, represents the friend of Bridget of Vadstena. . . .

Can it be that Bridget told her everything that she still saw in her visions? For what she saw must have filled a loving sister's heart with horror. Bridget is in a dark and gruesome place where there is a burning furnace

and this furnace had nothing that could be burned but living souls. And above on this furnace appeared that soul which had been judged. The soul's feet were fastened to the furnace, and the soul stood erect like a human being. It did not stand on the highest place and not on the lowest but as it were on the side of the furnace. And the soul looked strange and terrible. The fire of the furnace seemed to draw up through the feet of the soul, as when water rises in a pipe, and the pressure was so great that glowing fire came out through all the pores. The ears were to look at like bellows in a foundry, they moved without ceasing and kept the brain in continual unrest. The eyes were in the back of the head and looked out backwards. The mouth was open, but the tongue was pulled out between the nostrils and hung down over the lips. The teeth were like iron spikes that were nailed into the gums. The arms were so long that they reached down to the ground. The hands held a ball of burning pitch. The soul had a hide that looked like the hide of an animal stretched over a human body, and was like a sheet upon which a man had expelled seed. And this sheet was so cold that everyone who saw it shuddered with horror. And from the sheet flowed matter as from boils and rotten blood, and it stank worse than any other stench in the world.

In this terrible picture Bridget sees Niccolà Acciaiuoli's soul. And now she hears the miserable soul lift up his voice in a fourfold woe.

Woe to me that I loved God so little and was so little grateful to Him for all His great goodness, and for the grace that He gave me! Woe to me that I did not fear the justice of God so much as I ought! Woe to me that I loved my sinful body's carnal pleasure! Woe to me for all my worldly riches and for my pride!

Then comes yet one more woe, the fifth, not for that for which most sinners must accuse themselves, but for something entirely personal: 'Woe to me that I ever saw Louis and Giovanna!'

In the life of every human being there are names that one would fain erase. Not names of one's enemies—one forgives them and hopes that they too will forgive. But names that once were like a wreath of flowers round one's temples—and now? 'The flowers with which thy desires wove wreaths of unlawful love, their heads are shaking against thee,' says the stern old Lutheran hymn. Those are the flowers, those are the names that one would cut out of one's life, but they are there, one will never be rid of them. And Niccolà Acciaiuoli would fain blot out of his memory that hour when, with a Boccaccio smile, he opened the door of Giovanna's bedroom for Louis of Taranto, although he knew that it was 'without the permission of the Pope and against the law of the Church.' On that occasion he had waved away, with the easy gesture of a courtier, the flaming sword of the angel keeping guard before the forbidden Paradise. And now—'Woe to me that I ever saw Louis and Giovanna!'

Bridget's glance glides slowly from Niccolà Acciaiuoli and the glowing furnace round the extensive region of purgatory, where there are also many mansions. First, there is the place directly over hell—in it were the hardest and most severe torments, the evil spirits were permitted to touch one, one is surrounded by venomous serpents and ravenous beasts, and there were at the same time heat and cold, and flames and darkness. But the soul is not to remain there—'the justice of God,' says Bridget, 'is like the master who sits at the melting-pot and cleanses the gold, which is the souls.' The souls are then taken to another place where the only suffering is a crushing feeling of hopeless want of power, and where all the souls anxiously listen up towards the world of sunshine above, as if there might not be one or another of those who are dear to them who might think of them and help them with a prayer or even refresh them with only a drop of holy water. (On the great altar in Vadstena there is a relief showing the souls sitting cowering in the grotto of a rock and waiting.) 'As one who is hungry is glad to get food, and one who is thirsty to get drink, a mourner to receive joy, one who is naked to be clothed, one who is sick to be put to bed, so are the souls glad and thankful for the good deeds done for them on the earth.' Finally the souls reach the third place—there is nothing to suffer there but the longing to see God. And most souls come to this place immediately after death.

But Niccolà Acciaiuoli's soul dwells in the deepest depths of the underworld. 'He is blinded by the darkness, he is in dread of the gruesome devils that he has to see,' and, most gruesome of all—he knows that judgment has been passed upon him, *but he does not know whether he is saved or not*. The devils shout and scream around him, so that he cannot hear a word, but they are not yet permitted to touch him—not yet. . . .

And then Bridget sees a consoling sight. A man appears, clad in a white alb and with a red stole round his neck—Saint Laurence! Saint Lars of the cathedral at home in Lund—San Lorenzo of San Damaso, of Panisperna, of San Lorenzo fuori le mura! Bridget feels hopeful— Saint Laurence has come to espouse the cause of Niccolà Acciaiuoli— 'for he honoured me and bestowed gifts upon me while he lived.' Saint Laurence will now see to it that the poor, distressed soul is brought to a better place in purgatory, where he will feel 'like a man who has been very seriously ill, but now all the pains are gone, he only feels very weak' (Bridget knows what this feeling is from her eight childbirths), 'and he is glad because he knows that he is not to die this time.'

But in order that a place may be found for Niccolà in this home of rest in the life beyond a high ransom must be paid. He cannot be released from prison until the last farthing is paid. Bridget writes down the conditions.

You heard [says Laurence] that five times his soul cried Woe. The first woe was because he had loved God so little. To save him from this woe, thirteen chalices for the altar must be given for his soul, that the blood of God in them may be offered up to the glory of God. The second woe was that he did not fear God. For this woe thirty God-fearing priests [the Latin text has a cautious reservation: 'thirty priests who are believed to be God-fearing'] shall each of them offer up thirty Masses, of which the nine are to be in honour of the holy martyrs, nine in honour of the confessors [*confessores*, saints who did not suffer martyrdom], nine for all the saints, one for the angels, one for the Blessed Virgin Mary, and one for the Holy Trinity. And these thirty priests must pray earnestly to God for the deceased, so that justice may be tempered by mercy.

The third woe was for his pride and parsimony. To make this good, you must take thirty poor persons and in humility wash their feet and give them food and money and clothes. And both they who wash and they who are washed shall pray to God, that by the merits of His humility when He washed the apostles' feet He will forgive the soul its pride and avarice.

The fourth woe was his profligate life. To make atonement for this it would be well if a maiden and a widow were to enter a convent, and another young maiden were to be given in marriage, for these are the three ways of living in the world according to the ordinances of God, and to all the three should be given so much goods that they would have enough for food and clothes.

The fifth woe was that he committed many sins that were a scandal to others, and that with all his might he tried to unite in marriage those two whom he named. And he put in order this union without the permission of the Pope, and against the lawful ordinances of the Church and the usage of Christian people. But this sin could be blotted out, if there were one who would go to the Pope and (without mentioning names) would tell him that there was one who had committed such a sin, and that he had indeed confessed it but died before he had done penance for it, but now this person would take upon himself to do penance on his behalf. And even if the Pope gave him no other penance than to say one Our Father, it would benefit his soul in purgatory and lessen his torment.(11)

XIX

From the abyss of purgatory Bridget had heard Niccolà Acciaiuoli's cry of woe—'Woe to me that I ever knew Louis and Giovanna!' He died on 8 November 1366—Louis had preceded him three years earlier, on 24 May. While he was still living Giovanna had deceived him with one of the higher officials of the court, the Grand Camerlengo Enrico Coracciolo, and a year after his death she entered into a third marriage, with the Spanish Infante James of Aragon—according to a contemporary chronicle 'the handsomest man of his time.' The wedding was celebrated with the usual splendour, but scarcely six months had passed before the young husband was seized with madness. When the attacks came on he thrashed the queen, hurled the worst terms of abuse at her, said that he was well aware that she had murdered King Andrew, and that she had men coming secretly to her at night. Bridget knew, of course, everything that all Naples knew, and she had found that it was a suitable moment to influence the wanton queen. The thrashings she had had to endure from her husband might be thought to have turned her mind to more serious things. So *la principessa di Nericia* took out her writing materials (she would most probably write these more personal communications with her own hand, she dictated only the revelations. Not everything was translated into Latin—a great deal which the editor of the *Revelationes*, Alphonsus of Jaen, found too open an attack on the queen's honour, was left out).(1) Bridget speaks in Christ's name.

'Write to the queen,' says the voice of God in her conscience, 'that she must make a true confession of all that she has done wrong since her youth, with a sincere will to repent and do better according to the advice of her confessor.' Confession comes first of all. 'Secondly, she must consider how she has lived in her married state, for she must give an account of all of it. Thirdly' (to the upright Bridget this point is one of the most important, upon which she always lays stress) 'thirdly, she must think of paying her debts and of restoring unjustly acquired lucre. And she must not think that she can give large alms instead—that is of no use so long as she keeps the lucre unjustly acquired.' The fourth commandment is also of a social nature— Giovanna must not levy new taxes, there are already enough of them, the groans of the poor taxpayers cry to heaven. (Giovanna is, spiritually, of the same race as the Portuguese queen, Berengaria.) Nor is a prescript lacking, of course (No. 5), about seeking advice of good and just persons (*e.g.* Bridget herself), as of appointing to the office of judges men who are impartial in their judgments, and who do not try to gain pecuniary advantage from their position, but are content with what is necessary for their means of living. This is the sixth commandment of Christ. The seventh is concerned with religion— Bridget's constant reference to the remembrance of the Passion and

Cross of Christ—Giovanna must bear it in mind now and then, it is good for the soul. But it is not enough to be pious in the oratory—faith without works is dead. Giovanna must therefore 'at certain times' (Bridget is probably thinking in particular of Holy Thursday) 'invite the poor, wash their feet and give them to eat. And she must have the same love for all her subjects, make peace between those who are at strife and help those who suffer injustice.' A following point is aimed at regulating the queen's munificence, not to overwhelm some with gifts and neglect others. In judicial procedure there must not be any consideration as to whether the accused is rich or poor—no respect of persons. And then there is point 10: Giovanna must think in good time about her successor who is to take over the kingdom after her death, 'for I foretell her that in spite of three marriages' (later there was even a fourth), 'she is not to see the fruit of them.' Bridget then goes into detail, the queen is not to paint her face, it is beautiful enough, she does not need any artificial make-up, etc., etc.

But at the end the tone grows sterner, it finishes with a serious warning. Giovanna has lived all her life 'more like a harlot than like a queen.' There has been enough of that. There must be an end to the worldliness at the court, the false women friends who think only of flattering her must be sent away. It is time to change her manner of living. If not—well, if not, Christ will judge her, she will be counted as an apostate, the scourge of God will chastise her with blows from head to foot, and she will stand in shame before all the angels and saints of God.(2)

This letter was not sent direct to the queen, but through the archbishop of Naples, Bernardo Montauro. He had heard the Scandinavian seeress mentioned and had sent her an inquiry about the state of some of his deceased relatives—whether they were in purgatory or not? She takes the opportunity afforded her to send him a lengthy communication. Firstly, as regards the dead, Bridget gives only an indirect answer—during a whole year the archbishop must have two Masses said for them every day, every day he must give a meal to two poor persons and every week he must give a lira in alms to the needy. Strictly speaking, it follows from this that the persons in question cannot be either in heaven or in hell—for in heaven they would not need help, and in hell it would be of no use. But Bridget does not say this in so many words.

On the other hand she takes occasion from the archbishop's inquiry to send him a number of good counsels, in fact, quite a life's programme. He is not to think lightly of her words because she is an unlearned woman—'a fair flame can come forth from a black furnace,' she says, with a memory of the smithy at home in Ulfåsa. And indeed the flame of zeal burns clear and bright in her letter.

First and foremost she admonishes the archbishop to do his duty in the supervision of his diocese. He must take heed to the apostolic admonition not to impose hands on one who is unworthy.* There are bad priests enough, he must not add to their number. Once a year he must assemble his suffragan bishops and all the priests of the arch-diocese, speak to them of their duties and examine their manner of living. Many ecclesiastics live in concubinage—when they say Mass Christ feels it as when Judas kissed Him. Bridget has heard it said that certain priests think that everything is permitted in the sexual sphere if only they keep from sexual intercourse with animals; they go to women, Bridget says, *propter Sodomise evitationem.*

Now follows a number of rules for the management of the arch-bishop's household. Not too large a domestic staff, keep an eye on the servants; keep them to what is good, be 'like a real father' to them.(3) Bridget goes so far in her housewifely care that she even gives direc-tions about the archbishop's wardrobe: not more than three sets of garments—and as to the silver: not more than for himself and for those who eat at his own table. The servants can quite well eat off pewter plates or wooden ones, and do not need to drink from silver cups, but can be satisfied with mugs of earthenware or glass. That was the way at Birger Persson's house, that was the rule at Ulfåsa—why should they be grander here among these people of the South? If there was too much silver the archbishop could give it to the poor—a Christian has always that way out of a difficulty! And now that we are on the subject of the service of the table, a little warning against luxury in food and drink is not out of the way—not too many courses, Your Excellency, and not too many refined French dishes!

Having finished with the dining-room Bridget goes out to the stables, and what does she see there? Each big horse is handsomer and more mettlesome than the other! They neigh, they stamp in their stalls, their well-groomed hide is as bright as satin! On such a steed a knight might sit, a champion of God, setting out to fight in a just cause, not a humble servant of the Lord. Bridget had once had a vision which she could not forget. She had seen a splendid train of ecclesiastical gentlemen, cardinals, bishops, prelates, all mounted high on splendid

* I Tim. v, 22.

steeds. And all these ecclesiastics spurred their horses and rode proudly away. Bridget stood watching this sight and could not help laughing. For astride each of these distinguished gentlemen there was a 'blue man,' a black devil! He sat astride the shoulders of the horsemen, so that his legs hung down in front on the rider's chest. And each time the ecclesiastic put the golden spur in the steed's side the devil grinned and pushed his two hoofs in the proud rider's chest. The devils had their fun out of it—and so had Bridget. She now told the archbishop this funny story, and finished the letter with a renewed reminder to keep a watchful eye on the sinners of the archdiocese, punishing them when possible, but if they were such exalted persons (*tyranni*) that he could not reach them with his crozier, then to admonish them without fear of those who can kill the body but not the soul.

We do not know whether Bernardo Montauro took this letter to heart. When Bridget returned to Naples later, on the way to the Holy Land, she found his successor, the Frenchman Bernard de Rodes, archbishop since 23 September 1368. She addressed a very severe letter to him, occasioned by the keeping of slaves by distinguished Neapolitans, after the Mohammedan fashion. He then summoned her to defend the genuineness of her revelations before an ecclesiastical court—but about this later.(4)

According to a local tradition Bridget and her escort would, after spending some time in the pilgrim hostel, have moved to the house of Niccolà Acciaiuoli's widow. The Swedish pilgrims could not, of course, live for two years on end in a guest house, and it is probable that Bridget, who in Rome had accepted the offer of Francesca Papazuri's house, would be glad to stay for some time with Lapa Buondelmonte. It is also easier to understand that in these surroundings she would be able to make certain valuable acquaintances—the future Cardinal Elzear de Sabran, with the great merchant Antonio de Carleto and several others.

It was young Elzear in whom Bridget was most interested. There was Provençal blood in his veins, his uncle was that Saint Elzear whose marriage to Saint Delphine was quite after Bridget's heart. In addition he was the son of the Countess Francesca of Ariano, who was an intimate friend of Bridget.(5) It was the Countess Francesca herself who presented her son to the Swedish seeress—he was just about to leave home to go to Bologna and begin his studies there. Young Elzear was a well-bred and moral young man, but in Naples he had come into contact with young men of different views, and what might not happen in the foreign university town? His mother wanted him very much to become a priest, Elzear was a devout young man who prayed a great deal and visited the sick. One of his Neapolitan friends found that he made too much of piety and advised him not to go further on the narrow road—'You can serve God just as well in marriage,' he declared. Another friend had no objection to Elzear wanting to study, but then it ought to be to reach a distinguished position, entertain on a big scale and keep many servants. . . .

The Countess Francesca, then, took her young son to her Swedish friend. 'Why, we know each other,' Bridget exclaimed at the first glance. 'It was you, my son, that I met at Canon Roberto's, when he was lying ill in his house by San Giovanni Maggiore.'(6)

On that occasion Bridget had already made so deep an impression on the devout young man that he had asked her unreservedly if she would not give him 'a rule of life, in teaching him how he could best serve God.' At the time Bridget had not given him any answer, she may have had enough to do with the sick canon who was suffering from a nervous breakdown brought on by overwork. But she had not forgotten this pious young man, who had asked, like the young man in the Gospel: 'What shall I do that I may inherit eternal life?' The words that were now spoken by her lips to Elzear were 'many and beautiful,' she promised always to think of him in her prayers, as if he were her own son.

And not only that—towards the end of the audience Master Petrus was called and asked to show the visitors out, and the Master then took young Elzear aside and pressed a sealed parchment into his hand— 'From the Lady Bridget.' When he had returned home and was alone he opened the letter with eager hands. Wonderful—Bridget had simply read his soul, and knew all about the struggle going on in it between the voice of God calling him and the enticing worldly calls of his friends. He had never himself spoken to anyone about those two friends, and he was certain that the friends had not mentioned the matter either to anyone—at any rate not to the Lady Bridget, whom they did not even know—and yet she knew all about it! With a feeling of awe Elzear read what the Blessed Virgin said to him by Bridget.

In the beginning [it said] a mighty king built a house for his daughter, whom he loved dearly, and he gave her into the care of a man to whom he said: 'My daughter has deadly enemies, you must protect her with all your might. And there are four things you must watch without ceasing and with the greatest care. The first is that no one may dig a way in under the foundation of the castle. The second is that no one may climb over the walls. The third is that no one may break through the walls of the castle. The fourth is that no enemy may enter in through the gates.'

This was the parable, now comes the interpretation. The king, of course, is God, the soul his daughter, the castle is the body. He who has to guard the castle is reason. The foundation of the fortress is the will to live entirely according to the will of God and to serve Him by word and deed. 'But they who try to undermine this foundation are they who come to you' (as the friends did) 'and say: "Live like a layman; take a seemly and fair, a distinguished and rich wife, so that you can be happy in having children and heirs, and not be harassed by the temptations of the flesh." Or it may be that they will speak like this: "If you are so set on being a priest, well then, study and see that you become a learned scholar, and get your share of the revenue of the Church, and then you will be honoured for your wisdom, and your wealth will obtain for you many worldly friends."'

In the Italy of the fourteenth century a particular gift of prophecy was probably not needed in order to know that such would be the alternative facing a young man of good family and with connections in the most exalted quarters (none less than Pope Urban V was Elzear's cousin). A wife with money—or a fat prebend—was not that the beaten track for a rich young man of the year 1350? Did Bridget believe, then, that marriage was a sin? Yes, when it draws a priest away from the care of that which belongs to the Lord. Does Bridget think that study is an evil? No, she says, when one studies with the object of being able better to defend the truth, to strengthen those who doubt, to guide the erring, to teach those who are in need of teaching. But these things do not require a big income or many servants, and if after all one does earn some money, there are plenty of poor people with whom one can share it. 'And in that way the watchman, that is reason, succeeds in driving away those who would undermine the foundations of the castle.'

In a similar way the other images of the parable are now interpreted. The battlements are love of one's neighbour, that is—

> you would rather endure all kinds of suffering than do harm to a single one of your Christian fellow-men, or cause them shame or pain, but cherish a brotherly love of all your fellow Christians according to the word of God. Oh, my friend, when you do this, you prove that you love God more than yourself, and then the watchman, who is Reason, can safely lie down to sleep, for then the enemy of your soul cannot climb over the wall.

This is the interpretation of the castle walls, 'which always stand around one, wherever one is,' like the longing for the everlasting joy of heaven, of hearing 'the sweet singing of birds, that praise God without ceasing,' and of taking part oneself in the everlasting Alleluia. He in whose heart this unearthly longing is always living is protected as though by strong walls.

For the enemy is outside, and he can undermine these walls. He tries to do so in two ways, through the ear and through the eye. Down by the harbour stands the Neapolitan *Cantastorie* entertaining his public with 'worldly songs and useless stories'; in the summer night the streets resound with the delightful strains of the mandoline and guitar; under the balcony can be heard the 'languishing songs of many musical instruments,' at court a *poeta laureatus* recites 'to the fame and praise of men'—*vanitas vanitatum*, all is vanity! The devil's other means of entry is through the eye—what does the world not offer of beautiful things, 'cunningly fashioned bronze, precious stones, splendid raiment, stately palaces, estates in the country with meadows and woods and lakes for fishing and gardens and vineyards and many other worldly goods'—such as Bridget had herself possessed. 'But if all this is ardently desired the walls are broken down'—there is no longer any desire for heaven. Must Elzear then, in the Franciscan manner, sell everything? Bridget does not demand so much; only that Elzear must be firmly resolved 'not to offend God by hankering after earthly goods'—he must not 'separate himself from fellowship with the comrades of Christ,' but what he has more than is needful he must put in the evangelical coffer, where it cannot be consumed by moth and rust. . . .

This programme is now worked out further in the second part of the parable—about the gates. The gates give admission to all that is needful for the maintenance of the body, and here Reason must stand in its excise office and take a toll of all that is imported, and if necessary reject the wares. It is Bridget's usual injunction about moderation in food and drink—not to treat oneself with dainties, but on the other hand not to eat too little, not to sleep too long, but neither to keep such long vigils that one is tired the day after and unfitted for work. Neither asceticism nor luxury, but the golden mean—in things of the soul too: if sorrows come to the gate Reason, together with his fellow servant, Piety, must receive them and prevent the soul from yielding to anger or despondency. Neither must joyful news give cause for too violent expression—'the grace of God shall subdue your joy so that it will be of most use to you.' Keep on the level, on the level—not (as one might expect it of Bridget) in the azure of ecstasy. . . .(7)

With this guiding thread in his hand young Elzear walked along the straight road of the Church. Bridget was yet to see him become a priest and doctor of theology. In the same year that Bridget died (1373) he became Bishop of Chieti (in the Abruzzi) and five years later Cardinal. On 18 July 1379 'the Most Reverend Father in Christ, the Lord Elzearius, by the grace of God Cardinal Priest of the Church of Sancta Balbina' gives his very personal testimony in the process of canonization of his spiritual mother. He has forgotten nothing of what happened then, it became decisive for his whole life. He also recounts a little incident which does not redound to his honour, but which he is honest enough not to keep back. He received then, on that occasion, the parchment on which Bridget had written—or caused to be written —what God had instructed her to say to the young student. (Karin cannot be right in her opinion that the letter was sent to him in Bologna.)(8) He received it and kept it carefully in a box. After some time he paid Bridget a visit, perhaps to bid her goodbye before leaving for the university, and she then asked him whether he had kept the letter in a safe place. Yes, certainly he had, it was lying at home in the box with his other papers. Or so he thought, but when he got home the letter was nowhere to be found. He turned everything in the house upside down, sought high and low—no, there was nothing to be done but to go to Master Petrus and tell him what had happened. The old priest listened with a frown to the young man's confession and gave him a very big penance for his carelessness in not having taken better care of such a precious document. By good fortune Master Petrus had kept the Swedish text so that he could give Elzear a fresh translation. 'But,' growled old Petrus of Skänninge, 'before you get it, young man, you must perform the penance that I now impose upon you. First you must give a meal to seven poor persons at your table, then you must give seven other poor persons a *carlino* (a Neapolitan coin) each, finally you must have seven Masses said in honour of the Blessed Virgin. When all that has been done you can come back again.' Elzear carried out everything to the least detail and Master Petrus gave him a fresh translation, 'but don't you go now and lose it again!'(9)

Elzear did not lose the letter from Bridget again and never forgot all the good lessons she had given him. He firmly believed in her prophetic gifts—when some ecclesiastical gentlemen of high rank laughed at Bridget's prophecy that the Pope and Emperor would come to Rome at the same time, and that she herself would be present, he defended her. He was present when the prophecy was fulfilled and stood by her side before Urban V. And when Urban had returned to

Avignon, notwithstanding Bridget's warnings, and there had met the death which she had foretold him, it was he who held the pen for her and in Christ's and her own name called Gregory XI to Rome. 'But because the said Lord Gregory despised what was said in this revelation, affliction and distress came upon him and the Church, which is known to all men.'(10)

As indicated above it was not only distinguished ladies and young noblemen in Naples who sought advice and guidance of Bridget, wealthy citizens also applied to her, like that Antonio de Carleto, who even, during Bridget's later (second) sojourn in Naples, sought her influence at the court of Queen Giovanna. It was one of the few cases in which Bridget acted without having consulted her confessor, and the result was as might have been expected—but this will be told later.(11)

Perhaps one of Bridget's most sinister revelations has its origin in the same time, at any rate it fits in well with the Neapolitan milieu. It is about three women, a mother, her daughter and her granddaughter. The mother is in hell, the daughter is still living on the earth, the granddaughter is in purgatory. The most terrible reproaches are heard from one to the other. The mother, who is in hell, speaks to her daughter:

Hearken to me, you poisonous snake of a woman—woe to me that I have been your mother! I laid you in the cradle of vanity and in the warm nest of worldliness—you grew up big in it. But now it is so that every time you look proudly around you and enjoy seeing men gathering about you to tell you how beautiful you are, it drips poison into my eyes, and my ears are filled as though with a terrible rushing wind. And every time you speak arrogant and vain words I have to swallow an exceeding bitter drink.

The granddaughter in purgatory also speaks to her mother.

Listen to me, you scorpion of a mother! [she cries]. You gave me three bad counsels: to love in a fleshly manner, in order to be loved according to the flesh—to be lavish with money in order to be honoured and esteemed—to clothe myself with beautiful and costly garments, a high headdress, a long veil, pearl-embroidered gloves, gilded shoes—but my breasts had to be shown. [Bridget declaims again and again against this fashion.] And when I came before judgment all my clothes fell off me, and I stood there, not only with a naked bosom, but naked from top to toe. And for very shame I could not remain standing there in God's palace, but the devils seized me and took me here to the place of torment. Mother [is the last scream of the erstwhile woman of the world and fêted beauty] Mother, woe to me that what I learned of you with joy I now weep over.

Prior Petrus had known these three women but he does not mention them. He knows, however, that the double accusation from hell and purgatory, made a deep impression on the third of the three who was still living on the earth. 'She entered a convent and lived there the rest of her days in great perfection.'(12)

Thus passed two years of Bridget's time in Naples. During one of the two years, in late autumn or towards Christmas, she made a pilgrimage to the nearby Amalfi, where the apostle Saint Andrew lies buried. Amalfi was one of the four seaports of Italy, the other three being Pisa, Genoa, and Venice. The Amalfians were industrious merchants and seamen—the compass (*sichtstenen*—sightstone—Bridget says) was invented here by Flavio Gioia—and they had offices in Constantinople, Saint Jean d'Acre, Beirut, Jaffa, Alexandria. From the oriental ports their ships brought home the spices and perfumes of the East, ivory, precious stones, pearls, dye-stuffs, Persian and Indian cloths and carpets. As an Italian historian has said:

> While the barons in Germany and France built castles and towers and oppressed the people, the Italian seaports took upon themselves the procuring of the treasures of the East . . . and the advantage of this trade to both Mohammedans and Christians would, little by little, have subdued the mutual hostility, if only the Crusades had not come.(13)

Besides being industrious traders the Amalfians were also pious people—both at home and abroad. In the year 1020 they already founded in Jerusalem the pilgrim hostel of Santa Maria Latina (in which Bridget, when her time came, was to take up her quarters). So also in Constantinople; in front of the hostel there was every year a big fair, where the traders had to pay two gold pieces for a stall. The Amalfian patrician Mauro established a hospital in Antioch, his son Pantaleone another in Constantinople. The Amalfians took no part in war, but they thought of the victims of war. It was an act of justice when the Latin king of Jerusalem, Guido of Lusignan, gave them the privilege of free trade in Saint Jean d'Acre 'for the good services you have rendered us and Christendom.'(14)

Amalfi itself was rich in churches and religious houses—the following churches are mentioned: San Germano, Sant' Antonio Abate, San Stefano, San Bartolommeo, San Martino, San Luca, San Pietro Apostolo, Santa Maria de flumine and many others. Among convents Santa Elena of the Cistercian nuns, of Benedictine nuns San Lorenzo, the Benedictine monastery of Santi Cirico e Giulitta, etc. In the midst of the town *il Duomo*, surrounded by a wreath of small churches: San

Giovanbattista, Sant' Erasmo, and, to a Franciscan tertiary like Bridget, perhaps the most interesting: *Sant' Antonio,* founded by the saint of Assisi himself, 'who with his companion Brother Bernardo de Quintevalle came hither in the year 1220 to pray at the tomb of the apostle Saint Andrew.'(15)

That was exactly what Bridget also wanted to do. For she had decided that at home in Vadstena the altar on the left of the high altar was to be dedicated to Andrew, 'who followed the Master and did not shrink from the shame of the Cross.'(16) In the Legend she had read about his last hours—how the wicked governor of the country in Achaia, Egeas, whose wife had become a Christian, first made twenty-one men stand and scourge Andrew and then stretch him upon a cross in the shape of the letter X.

> But as they were taking Andrew to his death the people gathered about him and cried: 'He is innocent!' But Andrew begged them not to hinder his death, and when he saw the cross raised up erect, he said: 'I greet thee, holy cross, which was sanctified by the body of Our Lord with drops of blood as though with precious gems. Receive me, as of a certainty He, who hung upon thee, was my Master!'(17)

Through the narrow streets, between closely shuttered houses, as in an oriental town, Bridget reaches the Duomo, which looks like a mosque. Perhaps an Amalfian had pointed out to her the place where the walls of the town against the sea had formerly been—the terrible storm of 25 November 1343 had swept them away and the ruins of the church of Santa Maria de' Turri could still be seen under the water —'but we were helped by the good Queen Giovanna, God bless her.' . . .(18)

In Bridget's mind there was but one thought, the apostle's tomb. She was not interested in the bronze doors, the work of a Byzantine artist, with the figures of Christ and His holy Mother inlaid in silver, she had seen something very like them at Monte Gàrgano and they were not what she had come to see. She did not notice the beautiful interior of the church, the play of light on the many-coloured windows, and that the church was rich in the mosaics of the triple nave, and the baptismal font made from a single piece of porphyry. But above the triumphal arch she would see the mighty figure of Christ and she would read the inscription: *In Patria pono justos et ipsos corono*—'I lead the just to their own land and crown them.' And down below in the crypt she may have been allowed to see the relics, and have been perhaps allowed to touch the skull on which the Saviour's hand had rested.

The visit to Amalfi took place shortly before Christmas, perhaps on the saint's feast day, 30 November. But it did not last long, Bridget was not feeling well and had also economic anxieties. She went back to Naples to keep Christmas.(19)

Then, in the next year, came the great, glad tidings for which Bridget had been waiting so long—the Pope had resolved to leave Avignon and go to Rome! On 30 April 1367 he left the city on the Rhône and an Italian fleet of six and twenty galleys put out from the harbour of Naples to fetch him from Marseilles. Five of them were from Venice, five from Genoa, five from Florence, two from Pisa, two from the Knights of Saint John of Rhodes, six were sent by Queen Giovanna, and one had been equipped by the nephew of Cardinal Albornoz himself.

BOOK VI

THE STRUGGLE WITH PETER

But when Cephas was come to Antioch, I
withstood him to the face.

Epistle of Saint Paul to the Galatians, ii, 11

I will not let thee go, except thou bless me.

Genesis xxxii, 26

I

In the morning of 19 May 1367 the papal fleet put out from the
harbour in Marseilles and set course for Genoa. From Genoa the
route lay alongside the Italian coast to Corneto, the port nearest to
Viterbo, where the Pope would go into residence for the summer.(1)

Corneto stands on a rock at some distance from the sea, and a
grass-grown beach stretches between the town and the blue Tyrrhenian
Sea. Here, on the morning of 4 June, there were busy preparations to
give the Pope a worthy reception. All the cities of Italy had sent
representatives hither—a great number of tents, flying the standards
of the different republics, had been pitched on the shore, a bridge had
been built so far out into the sea that the galleys could come alongside
it. People were crowding together on the beach and taking up positions.

Neither Bridget nor any of her *famiglia* seem to have been present.
It was a purely Italian reception, and perhaps that was the reason why
Urban was to be welcomed, not by a warrior and not by a politician,
but by a saint. From Siena Giovanni Colombini had come down to
Corneto with a company of his disciples, Colombini, the Tuscan San
Francesco, the merchant who like the saint of Assisi had sold everything to obtain the precious pearl of Holy Poverty, he and his brethren
stood there in the white habit of their Order, with olive branches in
their hands and crowns of olive leaves on their heads. When the papal
fleet appeared on the horizon the landing stage was cleared of all
intruders—only the Gésuati, Colombini and his disciples, were allowed
to remain standing. For it was a prince of peace who was coming—for
sixty years the Pope had failed Italy, and Italy had meanwhile torn
herself asunder in fighting, but now a new age was to begin, an age
of peace, an age of the olive branch. . . .

Driven by a brisk north wind the papal fleet speedily approaches
Corneto. The ship with sails of silk, carrying Urban, can soon be distinguished. A short while yet and the first galleys glide past the bridge
head, but without coming alongside. With lowered sails and backing
the oars with all their might they bring to and form a path of honour
for the Pope's ship. Up in Corneto all the bells begin to ring. Along
the shore men stand shoulder to shoulder and in towards the coast
head can be seen by head. The first row of spectators is pressed so far
forward that the waves run over their feet.

And so galley after galley glides past and swerves aside. Four men come carrying the baldacchino of gold-embroidered brocade under which the Pope is to walk. For now the Pope's ship is coming alongside—a galley with three rows of oars. A gangway is put out from the high poop, and a silken carpet is spread over it. Then the Pope's retinue begin to go ashore—the French noble guard, the officials of the papal court, the French cardinals, easily distinguished by their surly and discontented looks (five of them had stayed behind in Avignon). . . . And then, at last, comes the Pope, *il nostro dolce Cristo in terra* as Caterina of Siena was to say later, the pious little Benedictine Guillaume Grimoard de Grisac, who wears his common black habit beneath the gold and silk of the papal robe. . . .

But he had hardly appeared on the deck of the galley, hardly had he set foot on the gangway, than all the Gésuati begin to wave their olive branches and to take off their cloaks and spread them on the ground for him to walk on, and to shout again and again: 'Praised be Jesus Christ! Long live the Holy Father! Long live Urban!' And like a wild-fire the cry spreads to the land, all arms are waving, all hands stretched out, all swords are swung aloft, all banners are shaken, all mouths are shouting and up in Corneto all the bells are ringing as if they would fly out of their belfries. . . .

Then the Pope stops, smiling and with tears in his eyes—he had not expected that his coming to Italy would give so much joy. . . . Along his first walk under Italy's sun it was not barons and knights, not *gonfalieri* and *signori*, not nobles or rich merchants with golden chains resting upon velvet who stood there to welcome him, no, Italy sent her Pope a company of God's poor men to meet him. . . . There they were, in worn habits and with bare feet, looking overjoyed and waving their olive branches and crying to him, and throwing themselves on their knees and asking for his blessing. . . .

Then with a kind look Urban approaches Giovanni Colombini and asks who he and his followers are. And Colombini looks up from his kneeling position, happy and intrepid he looks into the wise and refined Benedictine face of the successor of Saint Peter and says frankly: 'We are the poor of Jesus Christ—we want to be also the poor of the Pope!' If a suspicion had arisen in Urban's mind that perhaps he was confronted with a disciple of Joachim di Fiore, he is reassured now. And as he steps over the old, worn cloaks of the Gésuati, his right hand raised, he blesses Colombini and his disciples, while the cry can without ceasing be heard about him: 'Long live Jesus Christ! Long live Urban!'(2)

II

Among those who stood on the beach to receive Urban Cardinal Albornoz was in the first row, and at his side the envoys from Rome, who gave the Pope the keys of Castel Sant' Angelo. Then Urban heard Mass beneath a silken tent and after Mass he proceeded to Viterbo, where he arrived on 9 June. There he met with a great grief—Cardinal Albornoz died (24 August). A great grief, and a great misfortune. For scarcely was the great statesman and warrior gone, than the work he had built up began to grow loose in the joints. In the month of September a rebellion already broke out in Viterbo—for the strange reason that the Pope's servants had washed a dog in a fountain from which people in Viterbo were used to fetch their water for drinking! 'Must *we* drink the water in which the Pope has washed his dog! Down with the Pope! Down with the Church!' The riots lasted for three days, four persons of the Pope's suite were killed, finally the military had to be sent for from Pisa and Florence to restore order. Possibly not only the washing of the dog, but also the haughty and arrogant manners of the French cardinals towards *ces Italiens* (in the twentieth century French travellers still looked a little *de haut en bas* at Italians) may have been a contributory cause of the rising. It was put down with severity—no less than seventeen of the guilty were hanged.

It was, therefore, not altogether as a prince of peace that Urban had come, nevertheless, everyone rejoiced when it was rumoured that he would soon make his entry into Rome.

Bridget departed from Naples, her great hope was to be fulfilled at last, for the Emperor Charles had announced that he would soon also be coming to Rome. With an eagerly beating heart Bridget would pack her trunks to return to her home on the Piazza Farnese. Nor would her return pass unnoticed. As soon as it was rumoured that she had come home people came to her as before to ask for help and advice and she was equally kind and helpful to everyone. There was poor Laurencia, for instance, who had fallen down from a stack of firing wood and had broken both legs—or was it her spine that was broken? No matter—*la Santa* was sent for, she laid her hand on the broken limbs, and Laurencia was restored to perfect health. Laurencia's little house on the Campo de' Fiori stood close to the Palazzo Orsini, and Monna Golizia was glad when she heard that Bridget had come back and had worked a miracle. For her own son of seven years old happened just then to be lying ill of a malignant typhus and dysentery. The physicians had given him up. Was little Gentile really to die, now at the very time when his father Messer Latino was away (in Viterbo or elsewhere outside Rome)? That must not happen, and Monna Golizia sent for her Swedish friend.

Bridget came. The Roman woman threw herself at her feet: 'Save my son!' Bridget begged to be allowed to be alone for a little while and was shown into a room by herself. Monna Golizia and her handmaidens listened outside the closed door, they heard the sound of long and earnest praying within. *É una santa*, they whispered to each other. Then the door was opened and Bridget came in: 'Where is the sick child?' With the same reverence and the same anxious hope with which a specialist in our own times is taken to a sick bed Monna Golizia shows her into the child's room. It was in August, the white fire of the Italian summer at its height showed between the slats. There he lay, hot with fever in spite of the shade and coolness of the room, poor little Gentile! It was said that once she had done what the prophet Elijah did with the widow's son in Zarephath—'and he stretched himself upon the child three times, and cried unto the Lord and said, O Lord my God, I pray thee, let this child's soul come into him again. And the Lord heard the voice of Elijah; and the soul of the child came into him again and he revived.' * But Bridget did something simpler—she only took off her cloak and spread it out over the boy, and said: 'Now you go to sleep, my child!' And to the mother: 'The child is not dead, it is sleeping.' The words of Jesus about the daughter of Jairus. That was all, and it was enough. For soon after *la Santa* had gone little Gentile awoke and cried in a clear and loud voice: 'Mother, I am well, give me my clothes, Mother, I want to get up!' Gentile and his mother often talked to each other later about this miracle, and then the boy always said: 'Was it not strange, that as soon as the Lady Bridget had spread her cloak over me I was not ill at all any longer!'

Messer Latino came home and found his son cured. Soon after, when he fell ill himself, he also begged Bridget to come. She came, and bending over him, she whispered in his ear: 'Be of good heart, it is not God's will that you should die!' And immediately the fever left him.(1)

Then the great day came when the Pope was to make his entry into Rome. He left Viterbo on 14 October 1367 and was at the gates

* I Kings xvii, 21-2.

of Rome on the 16th. The Margrave of Ferrara, Niccolà d'Este, followed him with an escort of a thousand men, at his side rode Rodolfo of Camerino carrying the banner of the Church. It was sixty years since a pope had been in Rome and all the people were out to see the stately procession. An eyewitness describes it. First came the Cardinals, eleven in number, with their escort and surrounded by five hundred mailclad soldiers. Next came the Pope on his white steed, various great gentlemen took it in turn to hold the horse by the bridle. Over the Pope's head waved *il Gonfalone di Santa Chiesa* with Peter's crossed keys, and after the Pope came an endless procession of archbishops, bishops, prelates and—finally—more than two thousand abbots, canons, monks and priests of all kinds, many of them on horseback, more of them on foot. Four hundred horsemen formed an escort. The procession slowly reached Saint Peter's, where the Pope said Mass and gave Benediction with plenary indulgence for all who were present.(2)

The Pope was in Rome—but barely had a roof over his head. In 1360 the Lateran palace was destroyed by fire and it had not been restored later. The Vatican, too, was in a ruinous state. In the papal accounts of 1367 to 1368 there are such modest items of expense as 100 florins for the repair of the balcony from which the Pope gives his blessing. Urban goes to his task with good courage—in the Vatican garden he has a vineyard laid out, of a Jew he buys tapestries for his private rooms, from another Jew materials for covering the walls of the audience room. He purchases a clock—as in our own times, too, the best clocks came from Switzerland. The Pope's clock is made in Basle, a canon from that town travels with it to Rome—price thirty florins.

Urban is active too in church matters. Sometimes concerning trifles—one item in the accounts is for 158 florins for having seven silver chalices gilded—sometimes there are also very great matters. In the chapel of the *Sancta Sanctorum* in the Lateran palace there was a casket containing two skulls, said to have belonged to the apostles Peter and Paul, and to have been preserved since the time of Leo III. Urban ordered the goldsmith Giovanni Baroncelli to make two busts of silver for these relics and decided to transfer them to the church of the Lateran. Above the high altar he had the beautiful Gothic marble ciborium built, which is there to this day—Barna of Siena and Giovanni Cosci of Florence adorned it with paintings. The rumour of this great gem quickly spread over the whole Catholic world— King Charles V of France sent two lilies of gold, adorned with precious stones, to place on the two busts of the apostles. On the day on which the two relics were translated to the Lateran church all Rome was present. All crowded about the high altar, where the Pope himself showed the relics to the people—at length his arms were so tired that two cardinals had to relieve him. One may venture to suppose that Bridget and her little *famiglia* were among the pious crowds.

In Corneto Urban had received the keys of Castel Sant' Angelo and with them the dominion over Rome. But the old fortress had to be repaired, in the single year of 1369 it cost the Pope 2,500 florins. He now gathered stores of provisions within its walls, he had seen in Viterbo how easily disturbances might arise. He provided himself with stores of food, *inter alia* of rice, almonds, sugar—and with wine (four hogsheads of good red wine, four of an inferior quality, four hogsheads of muscadel). For he expected guests and had to have something to offer them. . . .

And the guests came. The first was the king of a country with which Bridget was later to have much to do—that of Cyprus. He was succeeded (in May 1367) by Queen Giovanna, who came to thank him. She had that year received the *golden rose*, which the Pope consecrates every year on the fourth Sunday in Lent, and as a sign of special good-will sends to an eminent personage of royal rank. Finally the Emperor Charles had announced that he hoped to come to Rome to meet the Pope. He thought that he might possibly be ready to travel some time in the next autumn. . . .

And so that spring passed and the summer came to Rome, the hot Roman summer from which all who can flee away, out to the cool villa, to a *pranzo* under a roof of vine leaves and to a siesta within closed shutters—and the cicada singing outside in the burning sun. In the twentieth century the Pope still leaves Rome the day after the feast of Saint Peter and Saint Paul (29 June) and goes out to his summer residence of Castel Gandolfo.

The Castel Gandolfo of Urban V was Montefiascone, 633 metres above the sea, on the shore of the volcanic lake Lago di Bolsena with the town of Bolsena on the opposite shore. It was over there that the miracle had happened for the sake of which another Pope Urban had instituted the feast of Corpus Christi. And here in Montefiascone that grape which had cost the Bishop of Augsburg his life had ripened— the golden Est-Est. . . .

But in Rome there was one who did not think of having a vacation and did not go out to the country, and that was Bridget. One day a little dusty priest stood outside the door of the Pope's palace in Montefiascone and asked in bad Latin for an audience. It was Master Magnus Petri and he brought a letter from the Swedish saint.(3)

Bridget was not an unknown person to the Pope. Immediately after his coming to Rome she seems already to have sent him a letter—'and at the coming of the messenger his soul was spiritually comforted.' This letter has not been preserved for us. In the revelation which Magnus Petri records, the Son of God speaks to His bride about Urban and compares him to a ball of yarn wound round a spool of gold. He who has such a ball unwinds it until he finds the golden core. Urban, too, is of gold, but he is 'wound about with worldly cares.' A word of warning is therefore now given to him: 'Your time is short, Urban. Arise, therefore, and see how the souls that have been entrusted to you can be saved.' With the first letter Bridget must have sent the Pope the rule of her Order—'which rule came out from my mouth,' Christ declares. 'And in as much as you are vice-gerent here on earth,' He continues, 'I will that you shall establish and confirm it.' But not only this, Urban has also to grant Bridget 'that indulgence which is in the church of Saint Peter' (not Saint Peter's Church, but the church of Saint Peter *in vincoli*, where the chains of the apostle Peter are preserved)—the same indulgence which Saint Francis of Assisi obtained of Honorius III, and which Bridget herself had gained a year or two before in the Portiuncula chapel.

Bridget seems to have had her doubts concerning the last point. She knows that one does not get anything free from the papal chancery and she will not pay for this spiritual favour with money. When Saint Francis left the audience room in Perugia, after Honorius had granted him the desired indulgence, one of the Cardinals asked him in wonder, whether he did not want a document as proof of the matter. Francis answered that it was not necessary, Heaven was his witness! In the same way the words of Christ are now spoken to Bridget: 'And if you cannot get the Pope's letter and seal for this indulgence, let my blessing suffice. I will confirm and establish My words and all the saints shall be My witnesses. My Mother be to you a seal, My Father a surety, and the Holy Spirit shall comfort those who come to your convent.'(4) When Bridget's church was finished at last, the Sisters had a stone set into the wall by the gate which is called forgiveness of sins, and Christ's words are inscribed on this stone and can be read there to this very day.(5)

For in the midst of all her troubles with Queen Giovanna, the

Orsini family, French cardinals and Italian ecclesiastics, Bridget had not forgotten Vadstena. Among the Swedish pilgrims living for a time in her house in Rome, there was also a certain Johannes Petri, brother of Magnus Petri, who was domestic chaplain to Bridget.

> When this Jovan Pätterson [says the *Diarium Vazstenense*] was in Rome with Saint Bridget, the Lady Bridget said to him: 'My dear Johannes, when you get back to Sweden go to the farm of Vadstena. You must there have those houses built that are required, and you must stay there until, by the power of God, I can come thither to you. For a convent ought to be built there.' He answered: 'My Lady, I am married and have sons. I cannot become a monk.' But she said: 'You shall take your wife with you into the convent, but I will take care of your little ones. And you must go to Bishop Nicholas in Linköping' (*not* Nicholas Hermanni, who did not become a bishop until 1374), 'he is to give you the deeds of this place and is to support you on my behalf in everything.'

Jovan Pätterson then returned to Sweden (1369) and began to build eagerly and forcefully for five years. . . . And when some small houses were built he invited his wife and his mother, who were still living, to come with him to Vadstena. But they would not and said that they could not go into a convent. And he returned and laboured at his work. Later he went back to them to keep Christmas, and urged upon them to go with him. But when they refused and contradicted him he was almost angry and said: 'Deliver me from my duty to bring up the children, for you must know this of a surety, that I must keep my word to the Lady Bridget.' Then his mother said: 'Dearest son, be not so wrath. We are ready to go with you whithersoever you will. We only wanted to try if you were steadfast in this matter.' Bridget therefore has her way, the whole family goes to Vadstena, where, incidentally, the children and Jovan's mother die. From 1371 Jovan, together with Bridget's son Birger, supervises the building of the convent, plans the monks' garden, enters the monastery in 1384, at the same time that his wife (Karin, Brynulf's daughter) enters the convent of the Sisters. He dies at the age of ninety, after having been paralysed and almost unable to speak for the last eight years.(6)

Jovan Pätterson entered the monastery as a lay brother. Among the other lay brothers there was a cook (*Stekare*), a glazier and two tailors. One of these two, whose name was Petrus, had also in his way been made to feel the strength of Bridget's will. He had always been a pious man, including the long time before he went into the monastery, and by his work as a tailor he had earned a good sum of money which he wanted to spend on a pilgrimage—first to Rome and then to the Holy Land. One day, then, he stood outside the Casa Papazuri and knocked at the door. On the careful *Chi è*, 'Who is there?' coming from within, Petrus the tailor may not have known that he ought to answer *amici*, 'good friends.' It is more likely that he would answer 'Schwedisch,' for he must have learned a little German on his way through the 'great Fatherland.' In any case the door was opened and he was taken up to Bridget's room on the first floor. And there it turned out that he had come in the nick of time. It was on one of those very days when distress had knocked at Bridget's door—she had not even the smallest coin of the realm. What was more reasonable, then, than the worthy tailor lending her his hard earned savings intended for the pilgrimage to Jerusalem? They would be returned to him, Bridget wrote an order to her son Karl, to be cashed in Ulfåsa. Provided with that Petrus the tailor walked the long way back to Sweden, received the money he had disbursed and again set out on his journey to Jerusalem. Later he became a lay brother in Vadstena— 'never was he idle; either he was sewing or repairing the monks' clothes or he was digging in the garden or taking part in the divine service of the Order.'(7)

III

But the work now to be done by Bridget was to bend Urban to her will—which was God's will. She intended to seek an audience of him, and she would not come alone. Her two sons were to stand at her side —the Pope was to see that he had to do with people of distinction! 'When Sancta Bridget had lived for some years in Rome,' Margaret daughter of Klaus writes, 'Our Lord bade her let her sons come before the Pope in their knightly attire, as a witness for her of who she was; that those charges which God had laid upon her might be the better performed.' In the Middle Ages a journey to Rome was not looked upon as a particularly difficult undertaking—we hear again and again of Scandinavian pilgrims coming to Rome, going home and coming back again. Jovan Pätterson may have had messages and letters to take home when he came to Vadstena in 1369; at any rate in the autumn of the same year both Birger and Karl set out on a journey to Rome. It is possible that Bridget would have wished to have them with her earlier—for in October 1368 the Emperor decided to carry out his intention to go to Rome. Urban V went to meet him at Viterbo and then hastened ahead of his exalted guest to Monte Mario, where he welcomed him on 21 October. The Emperor Charles came with an escort of two thousand horsemen—when he saw the Pope he dismounted and himself led the Pope's steed by the bridle, until the procession reached Saint Peter's, where he served Mass as a deacon. On 1 November, the feast of All Saints, the solemn coronation took place—the Queen, Charles' fourth wife, also being crowned by the Pope. Bridget had indeed on an earlier occasion addressed a letter to Charles, when sending him the parable of the four banished virtues and the four evil maidens who had taken their place.(1) Now she could triumph over those who had laughed at her prophecy that the Pope and Emperor would come to Rome at the same time—the fame she had already grew when this prophecy was really fulfilled.(2) And in the name of the 'Emperor Christ' she now wrote to Charles:

I am the true light and it is I who have set you to be a light in the world, so that by your light all may be led to justice and the fear of God. I have let you rise to the imperial throne because thus it pleased Me to do. There is a woman here in Rome, with whom I speak the words of justice and mercy. Receive therefore what this woman has written down from My dictation (*de ore meo*) the contents of these books, and have a care that men fear My justice and hope for My mercy.

Part of Bridget's revelations must therefore have been sent with the letter—there was, in particular, a copy of the rule of the Order.

For you who have imperial power must know that I, who have power over all things, have dictated this monastic rule for nuns (*regulam monialum*) —[Bridget does not speak of any dual monastery]—and I have given this rule to the woman who is writing to you. Read it therefore with care and see to it that this rule, which I have myself dictated with My own mouth, is approved by My Vicar on earth, as I have approved it in heaven.(3)

The Emperor Charles stayed in Rome until early in 1369, but did not get time to do anything for Bridget, nor was he probably inclined to do so. She may have had an audience of him, this is, at any rate, the opinion of the Vadstena Diary.(4) But her only hope now rested on Urban. Some time after Birger and Karl had come to Rome, then, she

took them both with her and stepped forth before the Pope. Sir Birger was then wearing the garments reaching down to the ground and the belt that he usually wore every day. But Sir Karl had put on the knightly attire usually worn by those who love the world—with a silver belt, set with small bells, a chain across his chest and a necklace according to usage then, and he had on a cloak of ermine, and all the skins were stuffed, and when he walked or moved it looked as if the animals were alive and running about, some of them up and some down, and each animal had a gilt bell round its neck and a gold ring in its mouth.

The French Pope had seen many costumes just as strange in Avignon—men's fashions were extravagant in those times. Bridget presents her sons. 'You are your mother's son,' says the Pope kindly to the simply clad Birger. 'And you,' he turns to the popinjay, 'you are a child of the world!' All the three of them fall on their knees before the Pope—'absolve my sons from their sins,' Bridget begs. With a smile the Pope points to Karl's heavy silver belt with the bells—'it must be a real penance to wear that thing,' he says in jest, 'I do not need to impose any other penance upon him.' 'Holy Father,' Bridget insists, 'absolve him from his sins! I shall make him give up wearing that silly belt.'(5)

It would probably be after this audience that Bridget had the following vision:

> There was a person, to whom it seemed like being in a big chancel of a church. A big and shining sun appeared, and on either side of the sun there was as it were a pulpit, and a ray went out from the sun to each of these pulpits. From the pulpit on the left came a voice saying: 'Now has the Vice-gerent of Christ come back to the seat in which Peter, the chief of the apostles sat.' But from the right side came another voice that asked: 'But how can the Vice-gerent of Christ come into the church?' And now Bridget sees the ruinous church, the doors are hanging crooked, the hinges on which the doors should turn are rusty, or they have been twisted so that they do not fit any longer, the floor inside the church is full of deep holes, into which one can fall and be drowned, the roof is tightened with pitch and burns with a sulphurous flame, smoke is issuing from the burning roof [as when the Lateran church was burnt in 1361], a mist rises up from the pitfalls in the floor, the walls are blackened with soot, so that you cannot see any longer what colour they once had. No one who is a friend of God can be at home in a temple like this!

This is the vision—now comes the interpretation and it takes the form of a sharp criticism of Urban. The allegory is not quite clear—for the Pope is himself the ruinous door, the crooked doors that prevent him from going into the church. He leans towards the earthly and worldly things—it is time he straightened himself. He must give up all superfluous grandeur and display, all luxury in raiment, all gold and silver, all horses and everything else; he must keep only what is necessary and give the rest to the poor—'especially to those of whom he knows that they are the friends of God.' He must not have a big household of servants, though he is permitted to have a bodyguard. And then, when he has reformed his own mode of life he must take a hammer and tongs, and then set to work on the rusty or twisted hinges, which, with a Latin play upon words, signify the cardinals (*cardines*, hinges). He must try, first, to straighten them out with the tongs, that is, admonish them to live in a manner becoming the modest servants of the Lord. But if he does not succeed in using mild measures he must use the hammer. Then, when the hinges have been repaired, it is the turn of the floor in the church, that is, of the bishops and the parish clergy, 'whose avarice is bottomless, and from whose lives in arrogance and luxury a stench arises which almost stifles the angels in heaven and the friends of God on earth.' Here the Pope can do a great deal, both directly by keeping the bishops to a stricter mode of life, and indirectly by making the bishops watch over their ecclesiastical subordinates. And if there are some who will not obey, their prebend must be taken from them—'for it is better that no Mass is said than that unworthy hands touch the Body of Christ.'(6)

First and foremost the Pope was Bishop of Rome, and this bishopric of his, Bridget thought, needed his first care. She therefore undertook to tell him the state of things in the Eternal City. Bridget had friends at the papal court, as elsewhere, it was to one of them, perhaps the later Pope Gregory XI, Cardinal Beaufort, that she turned. He could then inform Urban what he found advisable.

For it was not a cheerful picture that Bridget sketched of the state of morals in Rome, from her experiences of close on twenty years. She begins with a short description of the material destruction which has passed over the churches of Rome—'the temples of many saints have neither roof nor door and have become privies for men and dogs.' But it is possible to make amends for this, Urban has already begun his work of restoration. The spiritual state of things is far worse, 'for many regulations given by the holy popes are now abolished and replaced by new abuses for the ruin of souls.' Bridget reviews these abuses one by one.

The Holy Church prescribed that those clerks who wished to be ordained priests were to lead a holy life, serve God in piety and by their works guide others on their way to the heavenly fatherland—and for this they received their wages. But against this custom the abuse has arisen, that the revenue of the Church is given to laymen, who will not take a lawful wife, because they bear the name of canons, but without shame they keep a concubine in their house during the day and in their bed in the night, and say shamelessly: 'We are not allowed to marry because we are clerics.' (This bad custom of giving clerical positions with their appurtenant incomes to laymen, was abolished at the French Revolution by the confiscation of the estates of the Church.) And like master, like man, both priests and ordained clerks (deacons and sub-deacons) keep mistresses, go out with them when they are in a state of advanced pregnancy, and as happy fathers they receive the jesting congratulations of their colleagues—'is it to be a boy or a girl?'

Such was the state of affairs among the secular clergy. Was it any better in the monasteries and convents? There was a time when that monk who kept the rule most strictly was the most honoured—Bridget had known such monks in Alvastra. In those times it was a joy to come on a visit to a monastery. But now—well, where is the Abbot? In one or another of his castles. Then you go into the church to hear the monks sing. Most of the choir stalls are empty, on many days there is no sung Mass at all. Here in Rome the common dormitory has been abolished—each monk has his own room, and in their rooms they receive the visits of good friends and of their illegitimate sons, whom they introduce to their friends: 'Look, this is my eldest.' Incidentally there is not much left of the monk's habit among these Roman religious, the habit hardly reaches to the knees, the sleeves, which were formerly wide and hung down a long way and in which there was room for a tablet and a pencil, are narrow now and closely buttoned up. The scapular (the broad apron that covers the habit back and front) is discarded by the monks when they go out, as if they were ashamed of wearing it. Many have a sword hanging at their side and a cuirass under their habit when they go out seeking adventures in the evening.

That was how matters stood among the Benedictines. Was it any better among the other Orders—Franciscans, Dominicans, Augustinians and the other mendicant Orders? Bridget knows them, and knows that there are many people who are said to be rich, yet who are poorer in money and silver spoons and other valuables than the so-called poor friars. And they boast that the habit of their Order is made of cloth that is just as fine as the Bishop's!

Yes, but the nuns then? the Benedictine nuns in the strictly enclosed convents? Bridget would rather not speak of these convents, they are simply disorderly houses, the doors are always open, priests and laymen go in and out of them both day and night.

Alas! there is a great deal more that Urban ought to know! It is concerned with ecclesiastical practice. The great Danish scald was unfortunately not altogether wrong when he sang: 'For a stiver, for a guilder, they offered heaven for sale.' It is true that it was forbidden by the law of the Church to take money for hearing confessions. Rich people, however, liked to show their gratitude to the priest by giving a smaller or greater alms. This grew into the habit of the priest expecting such alms, and when there were poor people who wanted to go to confession they had to come to an agreement with their confessor about a compensation. Bridget had even been scandalized at seeing the priest give absolution with one hand and slip money into his pocket with the other.(7)

Bridget further mentions a number of ecclesiastical laws that are transgressed. The Church orders, for instance, that every Christian, man or woman, must at least once a year receive Holy Communion. In Rome there is scarcely one in a hundred who does so, and those who do are priests, regulars and women (who are always more pious than the men). Christian marriage is also in a bad state—married couples leave each other, the man takes a mistress outside the house, or he has his wife and mistress living in the same house and rejoices—says Bridget, the realist, 'when he hears them in travail at the same time.'(8)

When the great commandments of the law are so badly kept it is not to be wondered at when people eat meat on Fridays or do not keep the law of fasting (there are some who fast during the day, but who have learned of the Mohammedans to make up for it by having a meal during the night). And as for keeping holy the day of rest, it is but so-so, if people do not work themselves they send their servants out to work, and so deprive them of the rest to which they are entitled. And Christians practise usury just as much as the Jews—often they are even worse! And although they are forbidden to associate with excommunicated persons,* this is disregarded by most people if the excommunicated one is a kinsman or a friend. In his time Saint Ambrose stood in the church door and forbade the great Emperor Theodosius to come in because he was excommunicated (Bridget had herself seen the church in Milan in which it happened). What priest has the courage now to do this or to refuse to bury the body of the excommunicated one in consecrated ground? It is therefore time that *one* should come who loves God above all things and his neighbour like himself—one who has courage to put things right and to fasten the doors on their hinges, 'for otherwise it is to be feared that the Catholic faith will soon have disappeared from the earth.'

First and above all it is the clergy who must be reformed, and on this point Bridget is inexorable. The priests' 'wenches,' as they are

---

* *Excommunicati vitandi, i.e.,* who ought to be avoided.

called in Sweden, 'who must be driven out—these accursed women-folk whom the priests keep and care well for, so that they can have their will with them.' But would marriage not be a solution? Here in Italy Bridget had met an archbishop who told her that if he were pope, he would allow all priests to marry, on the understanding that it would be more pleasing to God than if they lived in concubinage or lived a dissolute life, such as was now the case. Bridget does not mention the name of the archbishop in question, saying only that he was 'a friend of God, but in this matter he was not right.' Bridget is well aware that during the first Christian centuries the priests were married like the priests in the days of the Old Covenant. This was still a remnant of the old leaven, and it 'seemed to the host of heaven and to me [it is Mary who is speaking] very unseemly and hateful.' God therefore put it into the heart of a pope to ordain

> that Christian priests who have a charge so holy and of so much dignity, that they have to consecrate and handle the precious sacrament of the Body of Christ, may not by any means be defiled by the desire of the carnal pleasure of marriage. And those priests who do not live in the purity and continence of the flesh are accursed by God and worthy of losing their charge.

What if it happened that this archbishop became pope and used his power to set the priests free from their vow of chastity and tie them in the bonds of matrimony? Was it not told of the saintly Pope Gregory that at first he had ordered the priests to live in celibacy, but later came to another view? Bridget could not believe this of a man like Gregory. For she was convinced of this, that if a pope really permitted or even ordained clerical marriage, a terrible punishment would be his lot. She knew how certain great criminals were punished in Sweden—first their eyes were torn out, then lips, tongue, nose and ears were cut off, after that hands and feet chopped off, and when all the blood had run out and the body was quite cold and bloodless it was thrown 'to dogs and other savage beasts.' A corresponding spiritual punishment would fall upon the pope who dared to allow the priests to marry—'he was to lose spiritual sight and spiritual hearing, be robbed of all pious words and deeds, and after death he was to be cast into hell to be tormented for ever and to become the food of devils through all eternity.'(9)

As it happens to the souls that burn with zeal for the cause of God, or what they believe to be the cause of God, Bridget is here taking her own voice for the voice of God. If she had read Saint Thomas Aquinas (she probably knew enough Latin for that) she would have been taught that the celibacy of the Catholic clergy is not founded on a command-ment of God, is not *de jure divino*, but only an ecclesiastical ordinance, *de jure apostolico*, founded on the apostolic text (I Cor. vii, 22–33) that 'he that is without a wife is solicitous for the things that belong to the Lord, but he that is with a wife is solicitous for the things of the world.'(10) The great scholastic's definitions and *Quaestiones* and *articuli* would perhaps not have pleased Bridget, they would have seemed to her like the wisdom she usually compares to the hay and chaff chewed by asses. Nevertheless it is Thomas who is right. In a much less important field the following happened at the beginning of the present century: a newly elected pope desired an alteration in the ceremonial in force on a certain occasion. It was urged that one of his predecessors had decided upon the arrangement in question, and therefore . . . 'What one pope has ordained can be abolished by another,' was the answer, 'and *I* am pope now.' *Mi son el papa*, in good Venetian, for the newly elected pope was Pius X.

IV

When you have visitors you like to show them what the country around has to offer of beauty and interest. From Assisi, for instance, you make a trip to Perugia and its Museum, and to Montefalco with the frescoes of Benozzo Gozzoli. From Vadstena you go to Alvastra or to the Övralid of Verner von Heidenstam. Bridget would also like to show her sons something and thought of the shrines so dear to her out on the shores of the Adriatic—Monte Gàrgano and Bari. In order that the journey might be undertaken in a manner befitting her station, she even obtained a papal passport, made out to 'the Lady Bridget and her children Karl of Ulfasa' (so written in the Latin text—Latin not having the letter Å), 'Birger and Katherina, who are travelling from Rome to Saint Nicholas in Bari and to Sant' Angelo on Monte Gàrgano.' The passport is made out in Montefiascone on 13 June 1369 but the journey did not begin until 13 November of the same year.(1) Besides the passport Bridget received other signs of the Pope's good-will, such as permission to have Mass said in places that were under interdict. Magnus Petri took part in this pilgrimage, he had made the journey on an earlier occasion. To Karl and Birger everything was new, a little strange, perhaps, because they were Scandinavians. Bridget would have liked to extend the pilgrimage to other holy places as well, but the passport was made out only for Monte Gàrgano and Bari. It is possible, however, that nevertheless on this journey she visited the mountain monastery of the Benedictines high up on Montevergine and prayed there before the Byzantine Madonna.(2) She would have good reason to do so, as that great sinner, Louis of Taranto, was buried there in this remotely situated monastery church—only a year or two earlier his body had been taken thither from Naples.(3)

Sharing in this pilgrim journey there was a man who during the last years of Bridget's life was to be her best friend and firmest supporter, the Spaniard Alphonsus of Jaen in Andalusia. His full name was Alphonsus Pecha de Vadaterra; according to certain sources his father was said to have been an Italian from Siena. In 1368 he resigned his office as bishop and entered an Order, founded by his brother Pietro, of hermits living together like the Oriental desert hermits. Their patron saint was Saint Hieronymus, who is generally represented as sitting in his grotto at Bethlehem, engaged in translating the Hebrew Bible. The lion that guards him lies at his feet, on a nail hangs the cardinal's hat which he disdained. The Order which Pietro had founded was therefore called that of the Hieronymites—it was into this Order that Alphonsus entered.*

In Italy Alphonsus of course very soon came into the circles that knew the Swedish lady. It is only a hypothesis, but it is possible to imagine that on the pilgrimage to Assisi Bridget made the acquaintance of a group of hermits who lived on Monteluco near Spoleto, a mountain 2,400 feet high, in the forest of evergreen sessile oaks in which the hermits had settled, even in early times, in their huts or caves. Francis of Assisi had visited the mountain in 1218, and at the present day the grotto in which he prayed is still shown, and the spring which gushed forth at his prayer. Could Bridget pass by such a shrine? If she did not do so she must have met one of the hermits on the mountain; this agrees quite well with what is told by one of them—Andreas of Lucca—in the process of canonization, that he had stayed in Bridget's house in Rome, for even two entire weeks.(4) Several of these hermits, now living on Montefalco, were Spaniards, thus Brother Alphonsus of Gualdafaraia (a town in the diocese of Toledo), Brother Angelo and Brother Laurentius. It was through this Brother Laurentius or Lorenzo

---

* The famous monastery of the Escurial belonged to this Order, as also Belem near Lisbon.

that Alphonsus of Jaen first heard of Bridget. Alphonsus himself relates in the process of canonization that his fellow countrymen had talked to him about Bridget and Karin—that they were both very rich, but that they had given away everything to the poor, and had now for many years lived in Rome—and in other ways had spoken about these two remarkable women.(5) After this talk, which must have taken place on Montefalco, Alphonsus goes to Rome to seek Bridget and make her acquaintance—he relates himself how he went about in the streets and asked where she lived. He finds her, talks with her, comes back again and again, and henceforward he is her sworn friend and her help in need. As it happens, in the very year in which Urban comes to Rome, that both Bridget's Swedish confessors fall ill at the same time, it is Alphonsus who takes their place. He is also careful of her physical welfare—when they go on pilgrim wanderings together in Rome and he sees that Bridget, now close on seventy years old, cannot walk any further, he has something sweet for her in his pocket.(6)

Having completed their pilgrimage Birger and Karl go home to Sweden. Again there was a time of waiting—will Urban obey Christ's command and ratify the rule of the Order? On the return to Rome Bridget had been given a fresh proof of the power to work miracles that had been given her—in Sermoneta one of the maidservants had fallen ill and had a high fever. Karin was distressed at this delay in their plans, which also entailed large and unforeseen expenses, and therefore begged her 'almost in tears' to heal the sick maid. Bridget did so—she had dominion over demons. The sick maid rose and 'they gladly rode on, praising and glorifying God.'(7)

A collaboration now began in Rome between Bridget and the Spanish hermit, which was to endure until death and beyond death. Christ had already earlier compared Himself with the artist who wishes to carve an image and goes out to the forest to seek wood. He carries the wood home and carves an image with it as well as He can. Then His friends come to see His work of art, and they improve upon it by painting it with more beautiful colours. This is what has been done to the sayings that God has entrusted to Bridget—the confessors have perused them, and they have arranged them and beautified them according to the grace that has been given them.(8)

But what has happened now? Bridget has sent Urban the rule of the Order so that he might read it and approve it—and now it appears that the Latin of the two good Petruses is not of the best kind. Her friend, Count Niccolà Orsini, undertakes to inform Bridget about

this, there is nothing wrong with the content, but (it is found in the
Pope's entourage) the form is rather old-fashioned.(9) He offers to
write it all over again himself in a more modern style.

Bridget accepts the offer—but she is afraid. Perhaps the revelations,
then, are not well translated? Then she decides to entrust everything
to her new friend—a Spaniard is of course better qualified to write
good Latin than a Swede! 'Give up therefore all the books with my
revelations to the bishop who is now a hermit,' says the inward voice.
'He is to be my evangelist.' It was, indeed, Alphonsus who undertook
the final edition of the *Revelationes*.(10)

After Niccolà Orsini had read the proofs of the rule of the Order
and the regulations attached to it for the convent in Vadstena—for
papal approval was required for both—he took both documents in
person to Urban. As papal vice-gerent in Perugia, which he was at
that time,(11) he had free access to the Pope.

But what he gained was by no means what Bridget wished and
hoped for. She may not have known it (though it seems very improbable that she should be ignorant about it), but both the Lateran
Council in 1215 and the Council of Lyons in 1274 had emphatically
ordered all who would found a new Order to adopt one of the old,
tried rules. This ordinance had not affected Saint Francis of Assisi—his
rule received its first, papal confirmation in 1210. But Saint Dominic,
his contemporary, had to be content with the so-called Augustinian
rule, as had also other Orders founded at that time. But could this be
applied to a rule which Christ had dictated to Bridget *with His own
lips*?

Yet this was just what the Pope's answer meant. Full of expecta-
tions Bridget presented herself at Montefiascone, accompanied by
Alphonsus, whose title of former bishop ought to inspire respect. Her
friend, Niccolà Orsini, was also present at the audience and officiated
as interpreter; Urban spoke Latin *à la française*, and Bridget's accent may
have been a little too Scandinavian. She now learned that both the rule
and the constitutions for the convent of Vadstena had been examined
by several Masters of Theology, and that the Pope, in the opinion of
these learned gentlemen, had to advise Bridget to adopt the Augustinian rule, which he found was the most suitable one for her.(12) And
the *Regula Sancti Salvatoris*? Yes, that was also approved, but only as a
supplement to the Augustinian rule. But the convent then? Oh certainly
—Bridget is permitted to build a convent of nuns in Vadstena, and
next to it, a monastery. As for the ardently desired indulgence (the

Portiuncula indulgence) it could not be considered at all! The papal bull, dated 5 August 1370, was handed to Count Niccolà, and that was the end of the audience.(13) With a heart embittered Bridget left the papal castle. The bull was but a poor comfort—it was addressed to the archbishop in Uppsala, the bishops in Strängnäs and Vexiö, and there it could only be understood as a proof that she had suffered a defeat, or at the most had won only a half victory.

And there was still something else that she had understood—Urban wanted to go back to Avignon! On the evening after the audience she could not sleep. She got up from her bed during the hot Italian August night and sat down to her desk. The words came, there was a voice that spoke to her 'as though from a radiant sun,' and these were the words:

I am the Mother of God and the Mother of all those who are in the joys of heaven. . . . I am also a Mother to all those who are in purgatory, for they will for the sake of my prayers be assuaged from the torment which they must suffer for their sins in the name of justice. I am also the Mother of all just persons on the earth, and am ready to save all sinners who will repent, as a mother is ready to save her son from the hands of his enemies and save him from their drawn sword.

Among these sons there is one whom the Blessed Virgin will name in particular—

it is he who sits in the seat of God in this world—I will speak to you of the Pope whose name is Urbanus. To him the Holy Spirit gave the counsel that he should come to Rome to work justice and strengthen the Christian faith and renew the Holy Church. And as a mother leads her child whither she will, by showing him her breasts, so I led him to Rome by my prayers. But what does he do now? Now he turns his back on me and not his face and would leave me. And a false and evil spirit would entice him to do this. For it wearies him to do his duty, and he is longing for ease and comfort. He is longing for his own country, and his carnally minded friends urge him to depart, for they think more of his temporal welfare and conform more to his will than to the will of God and to what serves the glory of God and the everlasting good of the Pope.(14)

But woe to Urban if he follows the counsel of these bad friends and his own enervating longing for the castle by the Rhône and the sweetly gurgling Sorgue turning the wheels of the water mills!

If he should succeed in getting back to his own country he will be struck such a blow that his teeth will shake in his mouth. His sight will be darkened and all his limbs will tremble. . . . The friends of God will no longer include him in their prayers, and he will be called to account to God for what he did and what he did not do.

Bridget stayed in Montefiascone for three months while negotiations were going on, and Alphonsus stayed with her. But the Spaniard dared not bring Urban this last revelation. He went to Cardinal Pierre de Beaufort and tried to make him undertake the task but was refused. 'Then I will do it myself,' said Bridget. 'And though she might well be afraid to speak so boldly to so great a Lord, she feared neither death' (at the stake) 'nor any other peril,' writes Alphonsus, full of admiration.(15)

But Urban would not be kept back. On 16 September of the same year he again stepped on French soil. On 19 December of the same year he died and was buried 'among the great sinners in Avignon,' as Petrarch said.

V

Ten days after the death of Urban V the conclave already met in Avignon to elect his successor. In Rome Bridget waited anxiously for the result of the election. As for Urban and his everlasting destiny she had been reassured by a vision. The demoniac 'blue men' had approached him with instruments of torture in their hands—he was in terror of them, but they were not allowed to touch him. It stood him in good stead that he had worn the habit of the Order of Saint Benedict, and in the end the judgment upon him was pronounced that 'This soul is not among those who have to suffer the severest punishments in purgatory, but it is among those who daily come nearer to the face of God.'(1)

The conclave did not last long, it was even of unusually short duration. It met on 29 December 1370 and the new Pope was already announced in the person of Pierre Roger de Beaufort, who assumed the name of Gregory XI. (The popes of the fourteenth century knew nothing of that monotonous choice of a name which characterizes the last half century, in which one has seen Pius after Pius mount the Chair of Peter—Pius IX, Pius X, Pius XI, Pius XII. During Bridget's life a Clement followed a Benedict, a John came after Clement, then an Innocent, an Urban, a Gregory. Is the twentieth century not to see an Innocent XIV or a Gregory XVI—and would not a pope with the name of Urban (the Ninth) be a good expression of the peace made through the treaty of the Lateran in 1929 between the See of Peter and Mussolini's *Urbs*?)

Pierre Roger de Beaufort was only forty-two years old when he became Pope. His uncle, Clement VI, had made him a cardinal when he was nineteen. Far from taking part in the fashionable life of Avignon, the young prince of the Church went to the university in Perugia, where Pietro Baldo degli Ubaldi, one of the most famous jurists of the time, was then lecturing on civil and canon law. He returned as a scholar well grounded in all the subtleties of jurisprudence—Pietro Baldo was later to speak of 'my pupil, His Holiness!'

But would this man, whose learning was chiefly that of a studious scholar, and whose health, moreover, was frail, would he be able to achieve what Urban had failed to do: to bring back at last the Chair of Peter from the castle on the Rhône to the banks of the Tiber? At present it did not look much like it. Gregory was interested in the papal library and made purchases of costly manuscripts. He was interested in his residential city, acquired a new clock for the town hall and had the old bridge of Pont Saint Bénézet repaired. He also proved to be the stern guardian of orthodoxy—the Inquisition again set to work, the Waldenses being persecuted in the south of France, the Jews in Aragon. In Corsica the last of the Cathares, who had sought refuge among the wooded mountains of the island, in Germany the Béguines were persecuted, as also the wandering flagellants.

Meanwhile, would Gregory prove to be just as zealous in the department which Bridget had at heart—the *inner* reformation of the Church? For this could not well be delayed much longer. Bridget had read the book written by the Vice-chancellor of the Emperor Charles IV, the Archdeacon Milicz of Kremsier, when he was in the prison of the Inquisition in Rome, shortly before the coming of Urban, the book about Antichrist. According to the Bohemian reformer this adversary of Christ was to be born about the year 1366—his parents were said to be a woman who pretended to be of great piety and claimed great insight in spiritual things, and an ecclesiastic. Bridget agreed with Milicz that the last times were drawing near, just as she believed with Joachim of Fiore that it was now *the third period*. 'Ungodliness and pride are increasing, the Passion of Christ is despised and forgotten'— Christ has sent Bridget for the very reason that they who hear her words and act upon them may be saved. But she does not agree with the apocalyptic arithmetic of the Bohemian any more than with that of Joachim. God has reserved to Himself the knowledge of the time and the hour, besides, ungodliness and injustice shall grow and increase still more, many heathen shall come into the Church, the great apostasy shall come—'only *that* is the clear sign that now Antichrist is coming.'(2)

Night has not yet come—there is still time to work. Bridget had known Gregory XI while he was still only a cardinal—she had seen him at Montefiascone. Bridget is thirty years older than he—she might be his mother. What is he in relation to her but a child? A little, helpless child, lying naked on the ground, and unable to rise . . . And the little one is hungry, it is longing for food and it stretches up the little arms to mother and cries . . . and mother comes and takes up the poor, starving little mite and presses it to her warm breast and gives him her milk to drink . . . Gregory is a child—and Mary is his heavenly Mother. 'Write, Bridget,' says Mary, 'write to Gregory as you have written to Urban.'

And Bridget writes:

If Pope Gregory will come to Rome and will return to Italy to stay there and like a good shepherd will take upon himself the cause of the Church, then, like a good Mother I will lift him up from the earth, that is, I will set his soul free from all earthly desire and all worldly joy (which are displeasing to God) and I will give him joyful warmth at my breast, which is the love of God, and fill him with the milk of piety and prayer. And I will pray to my Son for him, that He will send His Holy Spirit to Gregory and pour it into the depths of his heart. And then he will not desire to live in this world for aught but to seek with all his might to add to the glory of God. Behold, now I have told him. For it *is* the will of God that he shall humbly bring back the Chair of Peter to Rome. And that he may not let himself be mocked or deceived by anyone I foretell him this: If he does not obey, he shall be made to feel the rod of justice, his days shall be shortened and he shall be called to judgment. And then the help of the worldly rulers shall not have power to help him, the skill of physicians shall not avail him, and the good air in his own land shall not be a relief to him, to lengthen his life. And even if he comes to Rome, but does *not* do what he has been commanded to do—[this was the case with Urban]—his days shall still be shortened, and the physicians shall not be able to do anything for him, and he shall not return to Avignon to regain his strength in the air of his own land, but he shall die.(3)

Bridget entrusted this communication to her friend Latino Orsini, and he rode with it on the long way to Avignon.

Gregory XI did not answer Bridget's letter. On the other hand he seems to have had an inquiry made to arrive at an understanding of the Swedish seeress's spiritual powers; in those times there were swarms of heretics and visionaries.(4) In Perugia the office of papal vice-gerent at that time was held by Gomez, nephew of the great Cardinal Albornoz.

He was later appointed governor of the duchy of Spoleto, with the right to bear the title of duke. His successor in Perugia was a French ecclesiastic, the Abbot Gerard from the monastery of Marmoutier near Tours; of his moral quality it is enough to mention that when a lady of the nobility in Perugia had been raped by his nephew and her family demanded the punishment of the miscreant, the ecclesiastical gentleman shrugged his shoulders and answered: 'Do you believe, then, that all Frenchmen are eunuchs?'(5)

At that time Niccolà Orsini was also in Perugia. Then one fine day he received a letter from Alphonsus of Jaen, in which the latter informed him that the Lady Bridget had written a fresh letter to Gregory XI, and now asked him—as lately she had asked Latino Orsini—to take the letter to Avignon. Alphonsus would travel up to Todi with the letter, so that Niccolà would not need to go to Rome. It is reasonable to suppose that Orsini would consult the two papal officials on the matter, and that they would then decide to accompany him to Todi. It was a favourable opportunity to learn of what kind of spirit Bridget was.

The four gentlemen (Gomez, Abbot Gerard, Orsini and Alphonsus) therefore met together one day in the year 1371 in the little Umbrian city, where the poet who had written the *Stabat mater* was born, and where he had closed his eyes on Christmas night in 1306, just when the choir of nuns began singing the *Gloria in excelsis* of the midnight Mass. The two Spaniards, Alphonsus and Gomez, would be glad to be able to speak their mother tongue. And then Alphonsus would take out Bridget's letter.

There were two copies of it. One was closed and sealed—can it have been with the seal of the Folkungs, with the lion rampant? The other was a duplicate, with which Niccolà Orsini was to make himself acquainted, in order that he might know what the message was that he brought. For the letter was so daring, Alphonsus thought, that the writer—perhaps the messenger too—might be in danger of being 'caught and executed.'(6)

Alphonsus took out the letter and read. It said as follows:

Holy Father. A person well known to you [that is, from meeting her in Montefiascone] was watching and praying. And while she prayed she felt her heart inflamed by the Holy Spirit, and she heard a voice that said to her: 'Write the words that you hear now, and send them to Pope Gregory.' But the voice was Mary's and the words were these:

'My Son has shown Pope Gregory a great grace, in making His most holy will known through me, as when it was made known in the previous

II 15

revelation. And this was done more for the sake of those prayers which ascended from the friends of God, than because he deserved it. But now I and his enemy the Devil have had a hard fight about him. For in the previous letter I admonished Pope Gregory to travel to Rome quickly, or at least to come to Italy, there to set up the Chair of Peter and to remain there until death. But the Devil and some of his counsellors advised him to delay the journey, and rather to stay where he was now, because there he has his kinsfolk and his friends and all manner of worldly comfort and joy.'

Through Abbot Gerard Pope Gregory had desired clear information, and this was to be given him so that there was to be no possibility of a mistake. Perhaps Alphonsus' voice trembled a little when he read the following to the exalted gentlemen:

This is God's will, that the Pope shall without delay come to Rome, or at least to Italy, and that he shall come now *in this month of March now coming or at least in the beginning of April*, if he desires at all to have me for his Mother in heaven. But if he proves himself disobedient I will not later do anything for him, and after death he must answer for not having willed to obey the commandment of God.

This was certainly plain speaking. And in as much as Bridget was well acquainted with the standing excuse of the Avignon popes for staying where they were, that it was on account of the political situation in France, there was a postscript to the letter. There would be no peace in France until the French people, by some work of piety had appeased God whom they had greatly offended by their immorality. Moreover, the Pope ought not to approve of those plans for a crusade cherished by certain members of the French chivalry—it was not in the least because of piety that these 'ungodly bands of the ungodly' wanted to go to the Holy Land, it was for the sake of robbing and plundering. And it pleased God just as much that money was collected for such a crusade as when the Jews collected gold to make the golden calf!

This was the message. And now something happened, which Alphonsus must have had to summon up all his courage to act upon. But Bridget had ordered it.

And so he gave the sealed letter to Niccolà Orsini. But he took the copy which he had read aloud and tore it into shreds and threw them at the feet of the three gentlemen. 'If Pope Gregory does not come to Rome at the appointed time everything that he now possesses in Italy shall be torn asunder and given to his enemies. And then he will not be able to regain it!'(7)

VI

Gomez was one of the two papal officials who had been struck most deeply by Bridget's words. His father's brother, the great cardinal, had consolidated the papal state—Gomez did not forget that day in Viterbo when his uncle stood before Urban V and had a carriage driven up, full of huge keys of wrought iron. Key after key was handed to him, and at each key he stated the name of the town whose gates it fitted. It was shortly before his death on 23 August 1367 in the castle of Buonriposo near Viterbo.(1)

Gomez and his cousin Blasco with his son Garcia came to Italy with their famous uncle and fought bravely in his army. By his defence in 1361 of the city of Bologna, which he governed in the name of the Pope, Gomez gained particular merit. He endeared himself there to the people, on leaving his office he was presented with the freedom of the city, with the right to be buried in one of the churches of the town, and as a memorial gift the elders of the city presented him with a skilfully made helmet, the crest of which was an angel, holding a sword in his right hand and a golden apple in his left—the guardian of justice. In the following year Gomez was sent by his uncle to Naples, and was entrusted with the honourable task of meeting Urban V in Marseilles; for this journey he had a ship built for himself. In thanks for his services Urban bestowed upon him in fief the city of Ascoli (in the marches of Ancona)—later he was appointed governor in the duchy of Spoleto. For some time he was governor in Perugia, just at the time when the message came from Alphonsus to Niccolà Orsini. The symbolic act with which the meeting closed made a deep impression upon him. Was the chief work of his uncle's life to be destroyed because of a pope's ill will and disobedience against the commandment of the Blessed Virgin? Gomez resolved to make the acquaintance of this remarkable seeress—his compatriot would no doubt introduce him? It was on purely personal matters that he wanted to consult her, for he had not always been that champion of justice that people in Bologna had believed him to be, there was, for instance, that affair of the little town of Piediluco in the Rieti valley, on the shore of the lake of the same name. His cousin Blasco and Garcia, the son of the latter, had been murdered there—but did that make it necessary to have the inhabitants of the town executed? And that was not the only occasion on which he went 'outside God's ways,' as the pious Giovanni di Pornacio was to say of him later.

Gomez was not to make the personal acquaintance of Bridget until 1373. But a correspondence began between the Spaniard and the Swedish saint, and two of Bridget's letters to Gomez have been preserved to us. 'Lord and son Alphonsus Bishop' had spoken to her about him as of a man of goodwill—'May God give you strength to persevere in this will until the end.' She therefore hopes that he will not take it amiss of her if she writes a few words to him now—'they may be a solace and consolation to him in the fight with the enemies of mankind.'

It is Alphonsus who writes this letter from Bridget's dictation.(2) This is, perhaps, a shorter form of a rough draft that he inserted in his edition of the revelations, with the heading: 'The Mother of God is speaking.'(3) The letter, on the other hand, is composed by Bridget herself, and it gives one an impression of how inspiration and composition worked together in her literary production. After the courteous introduction given above she writes:

> Dearest Lord, I have heard that you are a great and powerful man, that you have the right of judgment and power over other men, that you possess posts of honour and riches of this world, that you are of noble birth, and that, moreover, you have the human comfort of wife and children and kinsfolk, and that, moreover, God has bestowed upon you the grace that your heart is touched by the Holy Spirit. [It is probable that Gomez had talked with Alphonsus about his misdeeds and his repentance of them.] But therefore, oh my Lord, you must have exceeding care and be watchful, so that you may keep this grace of the Holy Spirit, and that the precious spiritual gifts of God may not be lessened for the sake of a vain and earthly good.

Now follow the maxims, the moral code, which Bridget never forgets to propose to those who approach her with prayers for guidance—the well-known commandments in her practical and social Christianity. In the first place Gomez must beware of passing unjust judgments—the warning notes of the 'draum kvad' * are still ringing in Bridget's ears. In the next place there is the matter of unjust lucre— that must be given back which has been unjustly acquired, and in future he must beware of this sin 'as of a deadly poison.' Gomez is the ruler of a province in the Pope's land—'he must rule according to the law, not levy new taxes or imposts, but have a care that the common people may wholly and entirely enjoy the rights given to them in former times by just lawgivers.' Here Bridget is speaking in Italy as if

* Vol. I, Book II, ch. xi, note 9.—Tr.

she was at home under her father's law. And she continues to speak like one who has known from her youth what is the duty of a Christian knight. She has just warned Gregory against giving his blessing to a crusade which is in reality only a robbers' expedition. She now clearly and sternly advises the condottiere Gomez against carrying on or leading, or taking part in a war, unless he knows that it is carried on 'for the protection and defence and help of others who are unjustly oppressed.'

This duty is so little to be evaded that not even for the sake of the Pope or the Church ought he to undertake an unjust war-like enterprise—still less submit to being persuaded to it 'by prayers or threats or for the sake of money or friendship.' He must beware of it—'as of the wrath of God.'(4)

Next comes advice with a view to the administration of the temporal goods which God has entrusted to Gomez—he must be content with what is sufficient for a suitable mode of life, and he must not hoard up money for his children or others in the family. He is married —good, then he must avoid all other women than his wife—and now that he has obtained this position as papal vice-gerent he must not seek for promotion or advancement, 'until we learn on what road the Pope intends to enter, and where he means to live.'

So far Bridget's advice is to Gomez, head of the army and head of the State. But she has also something to say to the man Gomez, and then her tone entirely alters, and she begins to address him by the familiar 'thou.' He has asked her himself to be considered as her son—and she complies with his wish. As an older woman in Italy can do it to a younger man, she calls him *figlio*. And the advice she now gives him is that of a good mother. He must 'confess his sins often and go to the Table of the Lord,' for 'as the child grows and thrives by its mother's milk, so will thy soul thrive and be strengthened in receiving the Body of the Lord.' And he must daily—as Bridget so earnestly insists— confess the Passion of Christ.

I counsel thee not to let any day pass without setting an hour apart and kept for this. Then must thou think, my son, of how our sweet Jesus was seized and bound, scourged, mocked and wounded, crowned with thorns, sentenced to death, crucified, pierced with nails, and how the bitterest vinegar and gall were poured out to Him, and He died a cruel death and was wounded with the lance to redeem thee—He, who is the king of glory and the Lord of lords. And when thou hast with a pious mind thought of all this, beseech Him humbly to increase the ardour of His love in thy heart and perfect thy desire for what is good according to the pleasure of His divine will. May He, who is praised for ever and ever, enlighten and rule and guide thee.

The letter is finished and now Bridget signs it. 'And that thou mayest believe this I have written my name with my own hand under this letter and have had it sealed with my seal as my custom is. Written in Rome on the seventh day of November' (1371).

It was in November, Advent was drawing near. The first Sunday in Advent was in that year 30 November. Then came Christmas, and was followed by the New Year. January was passing but there was no sign that Gregory would leave Avignon 'now in this month of March now coming or at least in the beginning of April.'

Then one day Bridget heard the voice of her heavenly Bridegroom saying to her: 'Leave Rome and go to Jerusalem.'(5)

BOOK VII

THE JOURNEY TO JERUSALEM

In the south Christ sits by the Urdar well.

EILIFR GUDRUNARSON

Et ils sont morts de chagrin, de ne pas mourir en Terre Sainte.

LOUIS LE CARDONNEL

I

'GLORY to God in the highest, and on earth peace to men of good will.' Christmas rings in these lines which Bridget dictates to Alphonsus one day in January 1372. They are written to Gomez Albornoz, from whom she has received the very best news. The previous letter, which he received in Perugia, had gone like an arrow through his heart and had pierced it with a dread of God. He had become a different man and had shown it outwardly too. Every Friday he was dressed in black, on Saturdays in white, on the other days of the week he wore a garment of Franciscan grey. And his piety was not only expressed in his clothes—twice a week he washed the feet of poor men and gave them alms, he prayed much in secret, and fasted besides, and in all things he was guided by his fellow Spaniard, the Franciscan Brother Corbius, whom he had chosen as his confessor, as well as one of the hermits on Monteluco, Andreas of Lucca.(1) Bridget might well sing out a 'Glory to God in the highest,' and dictate to Alphonsus that these good tidings which he had sent her in his letter were the best Christmas gift she could have.

> And I advise you now to keep in mind without ceasing the thought that the work you do in your office is done for God. It is for Christ, our high priest who is in heaven, that you must work, rather than for this Pope, and the friendship of God shall become dearer than all the gifts and benefits with which the Pope might reward you. . . . Moreover, I, unworthy person that I am, counsel you that if the Pope comes to Italy, you will remain in the office that is entrusted to you, so that the Lord Pope may receive faithful help from you, and that some greedy wolf may not come, who might offend God or not serve Him as faithfully as you. But if the Pope does not come to Italy, I counsel you that you will then also remain in your office a whole year and see what time may bring.

Bridget was known for being able to compose beautiful prayers, and Gomez had asked her to write one for him. She answers that she has but little time at the moment as she is preparing for her journey. 'But if God wills that I am to stop a while in Naples I will try to write one. Yet I advise you that you cannot say any better prayer than Our Father, which was given to us from the precious lips of Jesus Christ Himself.' Bridget now speaks of her journey—both her sons have again come to Rome, and she will take them, as well as her daughter, with her on her pilgrimage. Gomez is also to be with them in spirit—

'whithersoever I shall come I will take you with me enclosed in my heart as my son.' As soon as Bridget has come back from this journey across the sea (*oltremare*, as the Italian expression has it), Gomez shall be informed of it without delay. And in spite of what she said before she inserts in the letter—perhaps on a loose leaf, which Gomez can keep in his Missal—a prayer composed by herself. It was worded as follows:

> Oh Lord, my God, my Creator, my Redeemer, I, an unworthy sinner, beseech Thee, by Thy great and merciful miracle, whereby Thou dost change the Bread into Thy true Body, and the Wine with the Water [the few drops of water which the priest pours into the Wine in the chalice] into Thy Blood and to everlasting health-giving refreshment; bend my will entirely according to Thy will, so that in thought, word and deed I may always do what is pleasing to Thee. Amen.(2)

The letter concludes with polite greetings from 'my sons, my confessor and my daughter.' For Birger and Karl had again made the long journey to Rome so that they might go with their mother to the Holy Land, as they had two years earlier gone with her to Monte Gàrgano. Meeting them again had not been an occasion of mutual unalloyed rejoicing—an eyewitness relates of it in the process of canonization: 'Sir Karl, the Lady Bridget's son, came to Rome and stepped into the house where the said Lady Bridget was living. And he came into the parlour' (the text says *in sala seu tinello*, but *tinello* is a wine cellar, and Bridget would hardly receive her visitors there), 'and the Lady Bridget came out of her room, went up to her son, touched his chest and said *Questo cuore!* * And immediately after the Lady Bridget had said these words Sir Karl threw up so much blood that he could not say a word to his mother.' Karin was present too at this scene and wondered at seeing that Bridget 'went back to her room and did not seem to take much thought for her son.' A certain Cechus, who was also present, asked Karin for an explanation—she answered that there was something wrong with her brother's conscience, and that this rush of blood was a sign of it.(3) Nor was it to be long before death overtook Karl—he did not get any further than seeing *la bella Napoli*. . . .

'Now you must know,' Margaretha daughter of Klaus relates,(4) 'that when Saint Bridget journeyed to the Holy Sepulchre, three of her children were with her, to wit Sir Karl, Sir Birger and Saint Katherine, and besides these two servants and the holy Master Peter

---

* 'How is your heart?'

[of Skänninge] and the Prior of Alvastra, so that they were eight persons.' By the two servants Margaretha probably means the two Spanish women, Praxidis and Elvira, who bear witness in the process of canonization to having spent 'three months and a half' with Bridget in Jerusalem.(5) Alphonsus also took part in the pilgrimage —it was he who wrote the diary of the journey—as well as Magnus Petri, which brings the company up to more than eight. 'And then Our Lord revealed to Saint Bridget that they were all to come back, except one.' This one was Karl—but he was not to die in Jerusalem, nor was it, as Louis le Cardonnel said—'of grief at not dying in the Holy Land,' that his weak heart was broken. Bridget had not been wrong when she pointed to his breast and asked *Questo cuore*. . . .

For it was in Naples that he met his destiny.

The queen who ruled over the kingdom was named Joanna, and she was Bridget's very good friend and loved her much. Then Saint Bridget taught her sons how they were to step forth before the queen and greet her with courtesy after the manner of the country, with bowing and bending of the knee and kissing her feet. So now, when Sir Karl came up before the queen he greeted her with reverence as it was her due, and then he kissed her upon the lips. This awoke a great love for him in the queen and she would by no means allow him to depart, but said that she would keep him and have him for her husband. Saint Bridget said that it could by no means be allowed, because he had a wife still living in Sweden, but the queen said that she cared nought for this, but that it should be as she willed.

Karl never became Giovanna's husband, but he became her lover. For both of them it was a late summer's idyll, Giovanna was born in 1326, Karl was several years older. Did they perhaps spend a few weeks of guilty happiness out in Giovanna's castle in Aversa? The way out to it was well known to Bridget, and after the pilgrimage to Jerusalem she sought Giovanna there.(6) Or she may have been there the year before, to tear away her son from the embraces in which he met his death. In spite of everything she never broke off the connection with Giovanna—nor did Giovanna with her. On her return from Jerusalem Bridget even sent the queen a little gold cross which the latter wore day and night; after Bridget's death too, and when the young son of one of her good friends, the Marchesa of Monferrato, lay dangerously ill, the queen visited him, touched his feverish forehead with the cross and besought Bridget's help. And as if Bridget herself had been present the miracle happened—the boy recovered. The queen went home and wrote it in a letter to Karin in Rome; Magnus Petri saw the letter.(7)

But the living Bridget also worked wonders while she was waiting in Naples to get away to the Holy Land. It was particularly grave cases of hernia that she cured by her prayers, also malignant tumours. Often her personal presence was not necessary, nor was it the sick person himself who invoked her support. A Florentine merchant, who was on a business journey in the kingdom of the Two Sicilies, received in Salerno a letter from Naples, that his brother who lived there was very ill, and if he wanted to see him alive he would have to come at once. But there was quite a distance from Salerno to Naples—'perhaps I shall be too late in any case,' thought the Florentine and appealed to Bridget, about whom he had heard so much. The appeal was not made by letter but by prayer, addressed to the Lady Bridget of Ulfåsa, at the pilgrim hostel in the capital.

> But in the same night it seemed to the sick man that he was in a place where there was a great stretch of water, and on the other side of the water a lady was standing and saying to him: 'Come over here,' but he answered: 'I cannot, Madam, I am ill, I have a tumour here.' She said: 'Come all the same.' And then it was as if he went across the water and came to this lady, and at the same moment he awoke and was well.(8)

There may have been some people in Naples who would have been glad if the great *Santa* had stayed with them always. But Bridget had not been sent out only to work miracles for people in Naples—this conglomeration of Neapolitans, Sicilians, Provençals, Frenchmen, Greeks, Hungarians, Pisans, Siennese, Jews, Saracens, Spaniards, Dutchmen. Naples must often have seemed to her like the Babylon she had read about at home with Master Matthias in the Apocalypse of Saint John—when she passed the harbour she saw ships from the East lying there, either being moored or discharging their cargo—

> merchandise of gold and silver, and precious stones; and of pearls, and fine linen, and purple, and silk, and scarlet, and all sweet-smelling wood, and all manner of vessels of ivory, and all manner of vessels of precious stone, and of brass, and of iron and of marble, and cinnamon, and odours and ointment, and frankincense and wine and oil, and fine flour and wheat, and beasts, and sheep and horses, and chariots, and slaves and souls of men.*

Souls of men—yes, exactly! Bridget saw, everywhere in the fine houses that she frequented, that the servants were slaves—slaves that were bought and sold as if they were cattle. As to having a care and seeing to it that they were baptized, that was not even thought of—or if they were baptized no one thought of bringing them up in the

---

* Apocalypse (Rev. of St. John), xviii, 12, 13.

Christian faith, so that if they committed a sin they did not know how they could be restored to grace through confession and communion. The female slaves were treated the worst—they were either hired out to the public brothels so that they might there with their bodies earn money for their owners, or their masters kept them in the house as private harlots, for their own use, or for their guests.(9)

Bridget was eager to go away, the sooner the better, to the Holy Land, and thought once again of the house on the Campo de' Fiori in Rome. She saw Alphonsus busy packing a great many books—and said to him: 'Don't take more than one or two books, we shall not stay long in Jerusalem, but will be coming back to Rome.' 'Are you sure of that?' asked the Spaniard, who was secretly longing to stay in Rome and die there. Bridget answered yes. Karin was told the same: 'We shall all come back to Rome, all of us, except one who is very dear to me,' she added in a low voice.(10)

That one was Karl. He was not to come back from the Holy Land —for he was never to get there. With all the preparations for the journey they had now come to the end of January, Lent was drawing near, Ash Wednesday in that year fell on 10 February—and before that it was certain that there would be a Bacchantic carnival in Naples, a 'Shrove Tuesday' in an Italian form. At the castle Giovanna opened the ball with her Nordic *cavaliere servente*. The hectic passion of the consumptive would be on fire during these days of carnival—on the 24th of the same month Karl had to take to his bed not to rise again, and on 12 March he died—of a last hæmorrhage.

Bridget sat by her son's death-bed as she had sat by her husband's, just as immovable as then. Alphonsus of Jaen relates that he and other priests were near the dying man and read the last prayers for him— *Proficiscere, anima Christiana,* 'go forth, Christian soul.' But Bridget was sitting a little way off—'eight or ten paces,' and not even when her son drew his last breath did she stand up, 'nor could she be heard moaning or weeping, but she lifted up her hands to heaven and thanked God.' And when the Lady Giovanna, queen of Naples and Sicily, and many noble ladies and much people came mourning and weeping to carry her dead son to the nuns' church in Santa Croce, she stood like an unshakable pillar and did not weep or mourn like the others, but praised God and said: 'Go, my son, on your pilgrimage, with God's and my blessing' . . . and many wondered at it and spoke ill of her, but she only said: 'Let them speak ill of me; it is enough for me to do what God wills.'(11) Her good friend, Countess Francesca di Ariano, Elzear's mother, came on a visit of condolence and asked her if she did not grieve much over her son's death. 'No,' was the answer, 'not if I knew that he could become an emperor, would I wish him back to this misery.'(12)

She must have sat with the same stony face in the cathedral when the Archbishop, by Giovanna's wish, said the solemn Mass of requiem. Perhaps Giovanna knelt weeping by her side—Bridget did not shed a tear, but thanked God that her son had been torn from the arms of that beautiful sinner. Karl had died like a Christian—in this being in full agreement with the Italian principle: *non si vuol morire come una bestia*, 'one does not want to die like a beast.' And Giovanna—after all, she had done some good—here in Naples she built a church to the glory of *Madonna Incoronata*, the great patroness of Apulia, and next to it she erected a hostel for the poor. 'God is merciful,' Bridget hears her whisper, 'God is merciful!'—and how she weeps, nay sobs, so that her beautiful shoulders are shaken. Poor Giovanna! yes, God is merciful—but above all, He is just. And when Bridget gets home from the church she has a terrible vision. She sees Giovanna sitting in her gown, and on her head, instead of a crown, she has a wreath of willows, smeared with human dung and filth from the streets. She is sitting on a beam over the abyss, and the beam is about to fall. 'And a voice was heard, which said: "Look, what an ape!" The lower part of her body stinks, in her heart there is poison, she is a danger to herself and plunges others into misfortune. She is a brazen and seductive woman; she is looked upon as a great queen, but here you see what she really is.' A second vision follows this. Now Bridget sees Giovanna sitting on a golden throne, and on either side of her stands a footman holding a bowl in his hand. And the footman on the right says: 'Oh woman with the lion's heart, I bring you blood to drink.' And he on the left: 'Oh woman, I bring you fire, for your nature is a glowing coal.'

The vision, however, does not end here. An 'exceeding fair virgin' appears, and the footmen flee at sight of her. And the exceeding fair virgin—who is Mary—says: 'This woman lives dangerously. If she persists in doing her own will she will be of great harm to many, and of no good either to herself or others. But if she submits to the trials that will come upon her it will be of everlasting good to her.' Bridget hears the Son of God confirm this: 'This woman has done several things that pleased Me. And for the sake of My friends and their prayers for her, I will tell her how she is to avoid becoming a shame to men and suffering harm to her soul. Be it noted, if she obeys' (that is, the advice and the rules which Bridget has given her). 'If not, well, she must take her punishment!'(13)

Bridget and Giovanna were to meet yet once again.

II

Whoso wishes to make the holy journey to Jerusalem must prepare himself in the following manner. His purpose in making this journey must be that alone of visiting, contemplating in tears and adoring those most holy places, so that Jesus may forgive him his sins, and it must not be for the sake of seeing something of the world, or that he may say later: 'Yes, I have been there too, and I have also seen this and that.' Next he must prepare himself in the best manner by forgiving those who have offended him, restore unjustly gained goods and live in the fear of God, for without this first and needful preparation all his trouble will be in vain. Secondly, he must so order his affairs and make his testament that, if God should call him, no strife may arise among his heirs. Thirdly, he must take with him two purses, one full of patience, the other filled with two hundred Venetian ducats or at least one hundred and fifty—a hundred for the journey and fifty if sickness should overtake him.

It is true that the old pilgrim guide whom I quote here is about two hundred years younger than Bridget, but the conditions would probably be the same. Of the two hundred ducats the fifty or sixty would be for the voyage itself, the remainder for the food on board, for a horse in the Holy Land and for payment of all tributes to the 'Moors.' There are also several rules for what one has to take as provision on the journey—various remedies, *inter alia* arrowroot and certain spices which are good against sea-sickness. Also two small kegs, one containing wine, the other water. Various garments are also necessary, especially linen, so that one can always change—'to avoid lice and other vermin.' Then, when one has at last safely and happily reached the Holy Land, one must never stray away from the caravan, and never start a dispute about religion with the Saracens, as there is a great punishment for this. On the other hand one must always have an open purse, for tips must be given to everybody.(1)

Bridget had had her doubts as to whether she ought really to set out now on this dangerous journey—she felt old and feeble. But all doubts had to give way to the voice of Christ.

Am I not the Creator of all things in Nature? I am able to make ill whom I choose, and to strengthen others if it seems good to me. I will be with you and I will direct your road, and I will lead you thither and lead you back to Rome, and I will provide you more amply with what you need than ever before.(2)

Then there was no more cause for hesitation. It was on the feast of Saint Catherine of Alexandra (25 November 1371) that Bridget and her escort left Rome. Spring had come, in March 1372, before the departure from Naples took place. The old pilgrim guide advises the voyagers to take care to get a place amidships, 'especially if one's head is not able to stand the movement of the sea.'(3) Bridget did not make any effort to secure a good place in the first class—she wanted to lie in the hold like the other pilgrims. The voyage was not without danger, on the way between Sicily and Cyprus the ship ran on a reef, 'and both the sailors and the pilgrims were very frightened,' Alphonsus relates. Bridget showed no signs of fear, and when the ship was afloat again and the danger was over, he saw her lift up her hands to heaven. At his question as to what that might mean she answered that she thanked God because He had found her worthy of suffering something.(4)

On 14 April they reached Cyprus, where the pilgrims to Jerusalem made a halt to rest a little before they had again to defy the Mediterranean. In the account of his journey which Bernhard von Breidenbach, secretary to the Archbishop of Mainz, published a hundred years later, we read the following, which no doubt was also believed and recounted in Bridget's time:

On this island, according to what was said by them of old time, Noah's son lived here and began to cultivate the land. . . . It was also called Paphos: here stood that temple to Venus to which Paris took Helena. Here also was that beauty contest fought between Pallas, Juno and Venus. At the capital, Famagusta, there is a high mountain called the Mount of Venus, where she lived. . . . The island is full of pastures, fields, meadows and vineyards, and well adorned with fountains and other pleasing springs. The wine is good and very strong. The island is ill-famed, it is called 'a guest house or special chamber of all carnal pleasures.' Yet piety is also given its due—on the highest mountain of the island there is a church in which the cross of the Good Thief is preserved. And in Nicosia, in the church of Sancta Sophia, there is an imitation of the Holy Sepulchre in Jerusalem.(5)

Possibly Bridget made pilgrimages both to Sancta Sophia and to the cross of the Good Thief. That the island was 'a guest house of carnal pleasures' was soon to be made abundantly clear to her. But she was interested, first and foremost, in the political conditions. The island had been taken by Richard the Lion-hearted, who ceded it later to Guido of Lusignan. It was now an independent kingdom; King Peter I had been in Rome in 1367 to receive the Pope's congratulation on the occasion of his heroic fight against the Saracens. Two years later he was murdered; his two brothers, John of Antioch and Jacob, were said to have been in league with the murderers. His son was now reigning under the guardianship of his mother, Eleanor of Aragon.

Again Bridget met a queen who reminded her of Blanca at home. And like Blanca, like Giovanna, Eleanor was also full of reverence for the stern seeress. Bridget accepted the homage shown her—she even entered the royal castle as a guest, nay, she accompanied the queen to her country residence in Nicosia. Like Giovanna Eleanor laid her doubts before Bridget—ought she to have her son crowned already now? Ought she to punish her husband's murderers? Ought she to return to her own country, to Spain? Bridget did not answer these questions for the present, but attacked the matter from the root. She begged the queen to have the great men of the country and the people called to Nicosia—she would speak to them there. This was done. A young man from Genoa, the armour-bearer Karl Melanel (Malocello) who was staying in Cyprus at this time, and who was present at the meeting, relates that Bridget spoke first about the purpose of this journey, that is, to visit the Holy Sepulchre in Jerusalem, but that next she rebuked the people of Cyprus for 'the terrible and abominable sins which had always been and were still rife among them.' If they did not repent God's punishment would soon come upon them, but she, Bridget, offered to pray for them in the Holy Land, so that they might repent. The offer was only half accepted (perhaps the population, which mainly spoke Greek, did not understand Bridget's Latin). Many of them laughed and made merry over her; a Dominican, a certain Brother Simon, actually said: 'The woman is crazy!'(6) Among those who took the warning seriously was an elderly English warrior, William Williamson, who even joined the company of pilgrims and reached Jerusalem(7), as well as Queen Eleanor's confessor himself, the Franciscan, Martin of Aragon, to whom Bridget had sent a very serious letter about the perilous state of his soul. He, too, joined the company going to the Holy Land.(8)

This part of the voyage was good, but arrived in the harbour the pilgrims suffered shipwreck. The ship ran aground outside Jaffa—and there Alphonsus had to admit that Bridget had been right when she told him not to take too many books with him. Perhaps in order to save the ship the captain had all goods on board, all the pilgrims' luggage, thrown into the sea—including amongst it Alphonsus of

Jaen's belongings. How many of his dear books would not have been lying in the sea if he had not obeyed Bridget! Now the loss was not so great, though it was great enough. The ship, however, could not be saved, but went to the bottom. Boats came out from Jaffa to save the pilgrims. 'Everywhere could be heard 'shouts and screams and howling.' Bridget is fetched up 'from the hold below' and is taken on board a yawl; her Spanish maid Praxidis screams: 'We shall all be drowned!' Bridget calms her: 'We shall all be saved'—which was indeed the case.(9) Alphonsus bears witness to the incident in the beautiful picture of Bridget in the midst of the general tumult: 'she gave no sign of fear, did not shout nor weep, sat quite gently and peacefully (*tota suavis et pacifica*) in the boat, without any impatience and making no complaint about her belongings which had been thrown into the sea.'(10)

III

Bridget had been advised while in Cyprus that in the Holy Land she ought, as a matter of prudence, to blacken her face and dress in the Eastern costume. (At the present day tourists are still advised to exchange the Frankish hat for the headdress of the Beduins, the *kufieh*, fastened with a black horsehair cord bound with a silver thread—*agal*.) Bridget consulted her Lord and Master—the answer was in the negative: 'I, who preserved Sara from those who would seize her, will also preserve you.'(1) Yet of course she acted on the advice which the Franciscan pilgrims in Jerusalem gave all the pilgrims, including this: 'Let everyone beware of stepping or walking on the graves of the Mussulmans, for this they do not like or permit, but slay everyone who does it.'(2) Another problem was solved by the Blessed Virgin. Pilgrims of rank generally put up at the guest house of the Franciscans (at the present day called *Casa nuova*). But in order to set a good example Bridget was to be content with the ordinary pilgrim hostel, *Santa Maria Latina* (built by the Amalfians).(3)

While Bridget was in Cyprus she had not answered the questions put to her by Queen Eleanor. Now, in Jerusalem, the answers came, short and precise. Was the queen to go back to her own country? No —better stay where God had once placed her. Was she to marry again? No, she had been married enough; it would be better for her to mourn over the evil she had done. Ought she to punish her husband's murderers? No, vengeance is mine, says the Lord.

II   16

Then come the rules of life which Bridget never omitted to give those who asked her advice. Eleanor was to bring up her son well, give him good tutors who could teach him to rule justly and not levy hard taxes. He was to shun all flatterers and lip-servers, but gladly consult honest people, even if they were poor and not of high standing.

There was also advice for the queen herself—she ought to reform her costume, not to wear the fashionable, very narrow gowns that showed the shape of the breasts, not to use perfumes and other vanities.(4) She ought to read good books, in particular those about pious queens, she was not to be wasteful with presents and afterwards get into debt to pay for them. Then came the question which Queen Eleanor perhaps had most at heart—ought she to have her son, still under age, crowned? From her Swedish experiences Bridget answered: 'In the old times the kingdoms were well ruled,' she says, 'for a king was chosen who could and would, and who knew how to rule justly.' But now it is no longer like that—the rulers now living do not aim at anything but at filling their purse, and they devise all manner of tricks for pressing money out of people. (Had there not in Sweden been a Magnus Ladulås, whom Bridget reproached with just this fault?) The Holy Scripture says: 'Woe to thee O land, when thy king is a child.' * If, however, the young prince will take to heart the words that Bridget said in Nicosia and not follow in the steps of his forefathers, but put off his childhood and gather round him advisers who do not think of getting gifts from him, but think of his soul and his honour, then let him enter upon the road of kingship. If not his people will not get joy from him nor he from his people.(5)

It was now no longer the two Petruses alone who undertook the translation of Bridget's revelations. Since the incident at Montefiascone she had begun to have some doubt about their Latin. Karin relates in her testimony, that in Jerusalem *all three* confessors were engaged in the work, that is, the two Swedes and the Spaniard, of translating what her mother wrote in her own Swedish. Gradually it was Alphonsus who took the first place. There is, as it were, an undertone of the discontent of one who has been superseded, in Petrus Olai's words that at home in Sweden it was Master Matthias and himself who translated the revelations, but after Bridget had come to Rome and had met the Spaniard the latter was also taken into the work, though he did not understand the Swedish language.(6) Petrus Olai was in his time driven into the work by a supernatural drubbing, but about

* Eccles. x, 16.

Alphonsus it was said with far more refinement (and it was the Blessed Virgin who said it): 'He is to be like a man who carries a bunch of exceeding fair flowers, which are my words . . . And he is to shield them against wind and rain and heat. The wind is worldly talk, the rain is senusal pleasure, and the heat is the favour of the world.' In Bridget he is to behold his mother, his wife, his daughter, whom he is to teach and comfort and care for, and his sister, whom he is to warn and admonish if it should appear to be needful.(7)

Then Bridget and her escort left Jaffa and went up to Jerusalem. It was in May but the spring was long since over. In Palestine spring comes already in February, flowers rise in abundance from the earth— violets, both blue and yellow, pink mallows, dark blue chick-weed, tall, white-flowering myrtle, yellow ox-eye, violet asters, large bushy cinque-foil—'the flowers stand so high that you literally wade through them,' as it is said in the spring song of the Canticle. It is exactly that— an appearance, a revelation, which is soon to go down again under the earth from which it came up roseate. And then only the stony wilderness is left—the endless stony desert of Judaea.

> We tread in stones, we slip on stones, stones roll under us, stones rattle and slide under our feet, the road is bordered by stone fences, all the stony fields are surrounded by stone dykes, the few houses we pass are built of stone. And up above all this landscape of stone rise the great stone domes of the mountains—the bare, desolate, dull red, grey mountains, whose peaks are tinged with violet.

A pilgrim from the North saw the landscape like this in April 1922—Bridget and her caravan would not see anything different in May 1372.

In the little town of Rama they made their first stop. Joseph of Arimathea is said to have been born here—and what is it that is said in the Scriptures: 'A voice in Rama was heard, lamentation and great mourning; Rachel bewailing her children, and would not be comforted, because they are not'? The same Rama cry was heard many centuries later, during the murder of the children in Bethlehem. Did Bridget and her companions think of it, or did they think that here was the old Arimathea where Joseph was born, the just councillor who would not shed innocent blood, the artist who carved on a block of wood the picture of the Holy Face—*il Volto Santo*? In Rama there is a Greek convent with a large, beautiful church—under the high altar can be seen a stone with a hole in the middle—on this stone Saint George was executed, his blood ran down through the hole. Saint George was

one of Bridget's heavenly friends, the model of the Christian knight—
it may be that she would tarry in prayer at the place of his martyrdom?
On the journey home Bridget again made a halt in Rama—where she
converted the renegade, Turchimannos, a Christian who had gone
over to Mohammedanism.(8)

From Lydda the road is the old Roman road, by way of Beit-Nuba
to Nebi-Samuïl, the cone-shaped mountain that you see from Jerusalem
in the north-westerly horizon, and on whose summit a mosque contains the grave of the prophet Samuel. It was from the top of Nebi-
Samuïl that the crusaders and pilgrims for the first time caught sight
of the Holy City and threw themselves prostrate on their faces with
their arms outspread in the form of a cross. The pilgrims called it
Montjoie, the Mount of Joy, but Richard the Lion-hearted had to weep
on the mount of joy when the Duke of Burgundy by his treacherous
flight had prevented him from taking the city. Joinville relates how
one of the English warriors shouted to the king: 'Sire, Sire, come here
—here you can see Jerusalem.' But Richard Lion-heart would not see
anything; holding his steel gauntlet before his face he burst into tears
and cried: 'Dear Lord God, I pray to Thee, do not let me see Thy
Holy City, as I cannot in any wise deliver it from the hands of Thy
enemies.'(9)

IV

On 13 May Bridget walked in through the Jaffa Gate. She paid the
Mohammedan guard at the gate the nine ducats required to set foot in
El Quds, a holy city also to the Mussulmans. She had already then fixed
on her programme—it was to include only those places where Jesus
was born, had been baptized, had suffered and had died. The Lord
appeared to her and said: 'There are also other places where I have
been, but because of your weak health it must suffice for you to visit
those lying nearest. When therefore you come back from the Jordan
you must think of your journey home. For there are still several things
that you must write and send to the Pope.'(1) Bridget's mission was
not yet fulfilled, she was to carry on her struggle with Peter to the end.

Ever since Bridget had left Naples there was, however, a thought
which had constantly troubled her—a continual, distressing anxiety—
what was the state of her son Karl's soul? When she lay down in the
hold on the voyage and heard the waves striking against the side of the
ship so that she could not sleep, fear came upon her and settled like a
nightmare upon her breast—where is Karl now? He was to have come

with her to the Holy Land, together with his brother he was to have received the stroke of knighthood on the tomb of Christ—and if that illness from which he suffered was really a sickness to death, he ought to have been laid to rest in the valley of Jehosaphat and to have been among the first-fruits of the Resurrection on the Last Day. . . . And then it had all happened quite differently, it was in the arms of Giovanna that he had spent his last strength! 'Alas, Mary, you, whom he loved so much—did you think of him in his great need?'

And Mary heard Bridget's prayer. She came to her couch on the rocking ship, as she came once many years ago, when Bridget was to give birth to her eighth child. And Mary came to say that she had stood by Karl's death-bed 'as a woman stands by the bed of another woman and helps the child so that it is not choked in the narrow opening from which it has to come out, or drowned in the blood streaming about it. She is also watchful to see that the child is not murdered, if there are enemies of it in the house.' So did Mary too, and kept watch by the dying Karl, and as soon as his soul had come through the narrow pass of death, she took it into her care against the devils that came running at it and would swallow it.(2)

So much and not more than this Bridget was allowed to know, that Karl's soul was under Mary's cloak. With this she had to be content for the present. But only a few days passed before she was again caught away in spirit and saw the high court of heaven, that she had now come to know so well, and where Jesus sat on a throne with an emperor's crown upon His head, and surrounded by all His heavenly court.

And by His side stood His venerable Mother and hearkened to what was said. But before the Judge Karl's soul was 'like a naked child that has just been born, and that cannot yet rightly see.' On the right of the soul stands an angel, on the left a devil. And the devil is speaking—he invokes God's *justice*. There is no reason, he says, in 'this woman, your Mother,' coming here and presenting the soul that is now to be judged, and taking it under protection. Mary answers that she has a right to do so, for while Karl lived he often said a prayer which his mother had taught him, namely this one: 'Oh Mary, I rejoice when I think that you are dearer to God than all other creatures, and this joy is worth more to me than all earthly joys. And if it could be thought that you could lose only a single ray of your heavenly glory, and become but a single step further from God, I would rather, than that this should happen to you, suffer torment in hell everlastingly.'(3)

Seldom, perhaps, have the *Marienminne* of the Middle Ages been more forcibly expressed than in this prayer, which touched Mary's heart. The devil too, is overwhelmed—he had not imagined such unselfishness to be possible. *Non est mei juris*, he admits—'this soul is not under my jurisdiction.' And yet—and yet—ought he not, perhaps, to try applying to God Himself; the final judgment has not yet been passed? He does so with, as usual, a polite bow and scrape—'I know, Lord, that you are justice itself, and that you are just as fair to a poor devil as to an angel. Therefore *give* me this soul!' And behold, eternal justice does not give the devil a blank refusal, but begs him to state his claims. The devil asks for nothing better—he has a sack full of Karl's sins, and he has them all put down in a book.

And now begins a dialogue, to which Bridget listens in fear and trembling. As soon as Karl had come to years of discretion he gave himself up to worldly amusements and carnal pleasures, says the devil. That is true, answers the angel, but on the other hand his mother prayed very much for him, so that, every time he had sinned, he went at once to confession. The devil was not satisfied with this—he wanted to relate in detail some of Sir Karl's most serious sins. But suddenly something strange happened—he is seized with amnesia, he can no longer remember the sins! And not only that: the book in which he had written them down has disappeared, and he cannot remember any of the notes he had made in it. He may well shout and scream that he has been cheated now of the profit of his industry down through the years! Yes, says the angel, his mother's tears have done that. The devil has not his book any longer, but he still has the sack with all the sins that Karl may have confessed, but not done penance for—the devil will now punish him for them! The angel answers with delicate mockery: 'Yes, then, open the sack!' The devil does so and utters a scream, as if he had gone mad: 'I have been robbed, I have been robbed!' The sack is empty!

Bridget's tears have again been effective. The devil, however, does not give up yet—there are still Karl's pardonable small sins. The angel explains that they are blotted out because of his willingness to leave house and home, kinsfolk and friends, and to set out on a pilgrimage. Yes, but these sins are countless like the sand of the sea, the devil objects. 'Thousands and thousands again—I have them all on the tip of my tongue.' 'Put out your tongue and let us see,' is the answer. The devil does so, but he has no tongue any more! Bridget's good deeds have blotted out all transgressions and paralysed the accuser's tongue. Yet there is still a little for the evil spirit to mutter about—Karl has done something to which his mother has a particular objection: he has unjustly acquired some land and not restored it! The answer is that he has been very willing to make restitution of something he possessed unjustly, but death overtook him. And his heirs will fulfil his obligations.

Finally the devil brings up the sins of omission of the deceased—the good he *could* have done and did not do. Yes, says the angel, but to make up for that his mother has now for forty years worked deeds of mercy and has wept many thousand tears for Karl, that God might at last send him His Holy Spirit. Which did happen at last, for when he set out from home, it was his purpose and intention to fight against the infidels and to help in the work of restoring the Holy Land and the Lord's sepulchre to the Christians. After this the devil could not say anything more; with a roar he exlaims: 'Woe to me, I cannot do anything more—I cannot even remember what that man had done, nay, I cannot even remember his name! Cursed be that old sow, his mother, and all her tears!' But from the everlasting heights a clear and quiet voice says: 'Now he shall be called here *The Son of Tears*!'

'This revelation was consummated in the church of the Holy Sepulchre,' it is said in the old heading of this chapter in Bridget's *Revelationes*.(4)

V

It was on 13 May that Bridget came to Jerusalem. 'And immediately on the next day, which was a Friday, she went to the chapel on Golgotha, and there, Alphonsus of Jaen relates, had an exceeding fair vision of the Passion of Christ.'(1)

Bridget went to the chapel on Golgotha. In the large church, which the crusaders had raised above the holiest of all holy places, she did not go first to the tomb, the *empty tomb*. She looked for the place where the cross stood. The rock on which the Crucifixion took place is there to this day—a stairway with narrow steps leads up the wall of the rock—the pilgrims of a thousand years have worn it with their feet and hollowed its stones. Bridget walked up this stairway, Karin followed her, and all the others one by one—a Franciscan led them—'at the top there are two chapels: that directly opposite belongs to us Latins, that on the left belongs to the Greeks—and it was there the cross stood—in former times you could put down your hand down in the hole in front of the altar and feel the rock. . . .'

This is not the place for archæological discussions—Bridget and her escort had no doubts—there was the grave, and here was Golgotha.* She was sure of it, as she was sure that Mary had taken her child of sorrow under the cloak of her motherly mercy, and sure that it was Christ who spoke to her now and said:

> When you stepped into this church, which is dedicated to My Passion, you were cleansed of your sins, as if you had just been taken up from the font of baptism. And some of your kinsfolk who were in purgatory have for your sake been liberated and have entered into the glory of heaven. For all who come here with a good will to become better as well as they can, and not to fall back into sin, shall be forgiven all their sins, and receive grace to advance in what is good.(2)

Bridget knelt a long, long time before the altar on Golgotha—those who were nearest to her heard her weeping, her weeping was intense but controlled. At last she stooped down and with her lips touched the gold plate in the floor which covered the hole in the rock. One by one the others came and did likewise. In silence they stood up, silently they walked down the narrow steps of the steep stairway, Bridget leading the way. No one spoke. But when they had reached the foot of the stairway Bridget broke the silence—she turned to Alphonsus like one who is nearly fainting under a burden: 'I cannot bear any more.' She was quickly led to a seat in one of the many chapels nearest the church of the sepulchre—to that where the half of that pillar stands to which Christ was bound when He was scourged (the other half is in the church of Santa Prassede in Rome—Bridget had often prayed before it—it is in a little chapel on the left of the entrance from Via Santa Prassede).(3) They all stood anxiously round her—Karin, Francesca Papazuri, Master Peter, Petrus Olai, Alphonsus—perhaps the Spaniard found a piece of sugar in his pocket to restore her. At last she sighed deeply and then began to speak—in Swedish:

> When I was on Mount Calvary and wept bitterly I beheld my Lord naked and scourged taken by the Jews to be crucified, and they kept a strict guard over Him. I saw that a hole had been hewn in the rock and that the Jews were ready to carry out their fell purpose.† And Our Lord turned to me:

* See also Jorgensen: Jorsalafærd (Copenhagen 1921), I, pp. 47–51.

† According to St. Matthew's gospel (xxvii, 27–31) it was the 'soldiers of the governor,' *i.e.*, the Roman soldiers, who took Jesus into the hall 'to crucify Him.' Crucifixion was a *Roman* punishment, not a Jewish one. St. John's gospel (xix, 23) says: 'The soldiers therefore, when they had crucified Jesus.' But in the *last resort* it was of course the Jews who were guilty—Bridget probably wishes to express this.

'You who see this, mark that in this opening in the rock the cross was set fast in the hour of My Passion.'

And immediately I saw how the Jews made His cross fast in the hole on the mount, and with a hammer they knocked small pieces of wood fast round it, so that it could stand firm and not fall. Then, when the cross stood firm, they built as it were a stairway of wood up to the place where His feet had to be crucified, so that both He and the executioners could come up those steps and stand on them while they crucified Him. Then they walked up these steps and took Him up while they mocked and scorned Him, and He went with them of His own will and was like a meek lamb that is taken to its death. And now, as He stood up there on the steps, He stretched out His right arm, willingly and not forced, and opened His hand and laid it on the cross. And at once the cruel Jews pierced it with a nail in that very part of the hand where the bone is hardest.(4) And after that they dragged His left hand forcibly with ropes and crucified it in the same way. After this they stretched with exceeding force the whole of His body on the cross and laid one shin-bone over the other, and fastened the two feet thus joined together with two nails, and stretched His limbs so much that all the veins and nerves were burst. When this was done they put the crown of thorns, which they had taken away while they crucified Him, back on His head, and this crown pierced His holy head so severely that His eyes were filled with the blood flowing down, His ears were stopped up and His face and beard were covered and coloured with the rose-red blood. And then the executioners and soldiers took away the steps which they had set up, and the cross stood there, alone and high up and my Lord crucified upon it.

And now, as I looked at all this cruelty, overwhelmed with grief, I saw His sorrowful Mother, trembling and half dead, and her sisters and John comforting her, and they stood not far from the cross on its right side. And then a new pain pierced me, and it was as though I was pierced with an exceeding bitter sword. At length she rose, the sorrowful Mother, and looked up at her Son, and her sisters held her up, and she stood there like one living dead, pierced with the sword of grief. And when her Son saw her and the other friends standing there weeping, He commended her in a wailing voice to John. And it was plain to be seen from His bearing and to be heard from His voice that His heart was pierced with compassion for His Mother with the sharpest dart of grief.

And then His adorable and beautiful eyes seemed half dead, His mouth was open and bleeding, His face pale and perished, His whole body wan and pale and colourless because there was hardly any more blood. And the skin on His virginal body was so fine and thin that the least blow made a blue mark. Sometimes, when the pain became excessive, He tried to straighten Himself on the cross. Sometimes the pains passed from the limbs up the heart and gave Him terrible pain, thus making His martyrdom longer with intense suffering and exceeding bitterness. It was then, that overwhelmed with His great pain and near to death, He cried in a moaning voice to His Father: 'Oh Father, why hast Thou forsaken Me?' His lips were pale and His tongue bleeding. His stomach had fallen in and touched His back, as if it were hollow. And then He cried the second time in the greatest agony:

'Oh Father, into Thy hands I commend My spirit.' Then He lifted up His head for a moment, but it fell again at once, and so He gave up the ghost.

When His Mother saw this she trembled all over with exceeding great anguish, and she would have fallen to the ground if the other women had not held her up. At the same time His hands fell forward a little because of the weight of His body, which was only held up by the nails that fastened the feet. The fingers and hands and arms were stretched out more than before, the shoulders and the back being, as it were, pressed inwards to the cross.

Then the Jews who were standing by shouted to Mary and said: 'Mary, your Son is dead!' But others spoke words of scorn. Then from among the multitude one came running full of rage and thrust a spear into His side with such force as if he would thrust it right through His body. And when he drew out the spear much blood flowed from the wound, and the spear and part of the shaft were quite red and streaming with blood. When His Mother saw this it made her tremble and moan exceedingly, so that it could be understood that a sword was passing through her soul.

Now when all were gone some of the friends of the Lord took Him down from the cross, and His Mother took Him in her most holy arms and laid him upon her knees. And He was wounded all over and stained entirely with blood. His sorrowful Mother dried His whole body and all His wounds with a linen cloth and then they bore Him away in great grief and much weeping and laid Him in the grave.(5)

Everyone comes in his life whither in his inmost life he wishes to come. The little girl who had wept one night at home in Finsta over the Passion of Christ, now knelt, a woman of seventy, on Golgotha.

VI

When Bridget came back to the pilgrim hostel she asked for pen and ink, and sat down to her desk to write out what she had just beheld in spirit.(1) Afterwards it was handed to the confessors who were to translate it into Latin.

But she had hardly finished writing when she heard in her soul the voice of Christ.

The things you have seen now are what the princes of the world do not give a thought to. They do not think of making pilgrimages to the places where I was born and suffered—they prefer to go to races. The prelates of the Church also like worldly pleasures better than the contemplation of My Passion and death. I will therefore yet once again send you to them with My words; then, if they do not repent, they shall be judged like the soldiers who parted my garments among them and cast lots upon My vesture.(2)

Bridget's thoughts were drawn to Cyprus, to Famagusta. What had she not heard Christ say? 'This city is a Gomorrha, burning with the fire of lechery. Therefore shall its walls fall down and it shall be laid waste, its citizens shall go into exile, sighing with pain and torment, and its fall shall be spoken of in many lands, for I am wrath with it.' And as the city was, so was its ruler. On the ruler, John, Duke of Antioch, Bridget heard the following judgment: 'He shows shameless presumption, boasts of his excesses and does not think of what he ought to have done for his neighbour. . . . He shall therefore not have an easier death than his brother—rather a worse, if he does not repent.' Yet the Duke was a good man, he had a confessor. Bridget had talked with this confessor and found that he excused the Duke, saying that at heart he was a good man, and that he could not live in another way than he did. 'Such confessors,' Bridget exclaimed, 'are nothing but deceivers—they look like innocent sheep, but in reality they are foxes!'(3)

Bridget wanted to save Cyprus, as Abraham had wanted to save Sodom and Gomorrha. And with joy she seized the opportunity offered when Queen Eleanor's confessor, Brother Martin of Aragon, came to her one day to talk with her about the salvation of his soul. Brother Martin was a Franciscan, but hitherto his life had not been particularly Franciscan—Prior Petrus could relate of him that 'he possessed several garments, silver cups, books and various other objects for use and pleasure.'(4) His tutor had evidently not been *il Poverello* so much as that *frater Adversarius* whose corrupting influence Bridget had traced so clearly in Assisi. Like him Brother Martin had also attached importance to acquiring worldly learning and science with the object of 'attaining a high position in the Order, and getting saddle horses and silver and handsome clothes and costly jewels,' and if any-one reproached him with it he would answer that of course he had to live in a way befitting his position. And now Brother Martin had indeed obtained a good position as the queen's secretary and could procure for himself everything he desired.(5)

Brother Martin had lived in this manner until he met Bridget. The Swedish lady was only a sister in the Third Order of Saint Francis, but how strictly did she not keep her rule? And he? Brother Martin went to Bridget, and as her custom was she spoke plainly to him.

'There are two kinds of Franciscans,' she said, 'and they live in the same monastery. But they live according to two different rules—one rule is that which Christ revealed to Francis, the other is that which the Devil taught Brother Adversarius.' (Bridget never mentions Elias of Cortona, though it is of him she is thinking.) 'But after death they are to be separated—those who have followed the rule of Francis shall come to Francis in everlasting joy—those who have followed Brother Adversarius shall be condemned to everlasting torment in the abyss of hell—that is' (the constant addition) 'if they do not before their death humble themselves and repent.'

It may be that Brother Martin ventured on a small objection— 'after all, we do some good with the money we really ought not to have,' he may have suggested. But Bridget does not yield, she speaks in the name of Christ and with His authority. 'These and all other brethren, who are forbidden by the rule to possess anything, try in vain to reconcile Me by spending a part of their property on good works and pious purposes. It is dearer to Me that they keep to Holy Poverty as they have promised, than that they come and present Me with all the gold and silver and all the metal to be found in the world.'

Petrus Olai wrote down this revelation and handed it to Brother Martin. At the same time there was a pious soul who prayed very earnestly for the conversion of the erring disciple of Saint Francis. And the conversion came. Brother Martin made a heroic resolution— he would go back to Famagusta, sell all his books, his silver things and other superfluous possessions and then come back again to the Holy Land to live like a true Franciscan. He kept his word—'and now he is guardian of the monastery in Bethlehem,' says Alphonsus in 1379.(6)

Bridget took the opportunity of Brother Martin's return journey to give him a letter for Queen Eleanor. For the queen had devoutly asked Bridget for her intercession at the Holy Sepulchre. And Christ had revealed Himself to her and told her to write—'but' (here Bridget herself distinguishes plainly between what she has received from above and what is her own message) 'write it in your own name, not in mine,' Christ had said to her.

The letter therefore begins in a personal form—'the bride' (*i.e.* Bridget) 'writes to the King of Cyprus and the Duke of Antioch' (the king's uncle who, as the King was a minor, was at the head of the government). It contains, first the usual rules about going to confession and communion. Next Bridget gives rules for the carrying on of the government—'for the glory of God and the good of the subjects.' The regent, Prince John of Antioch and his brother Jacob (called *Jacqueto*, 'little Jacob') are accused of having been in league with the murderers of Peter I; perhaps that was why they were so anxious to make them harmless who had committed the murder. Bridget advised giving up the legal proceedings, it was more Christian to forgive. Besides, there were more important matters requiring attention. The army was to be made to live a Christian life (*vitam catholicam*). The soldiers were to be reconciled to those with whom they might be at enmity, to confess and go to communion, afterwards to live, 'either married, in widowhood, or in virginity.' In the Church, too, there were to be reforms, the parish priests were to examine whether there were, in their parishes, persons who caused public scandal by sinful living. If such is the case the parish priest shall first gently admonish them; if this is of no use he must report them to the bishop. In the case of persons of high rank the bishop, perhaps, has not the courage to say anything—in that case the secular power must intervene and 'with a mighty hand' punish these barefaced sinners, so that they, 'reformed by punishment, may obtain grace from God.'(7)

So much Bridget could say when she spoke on her own account. But then it happened that 'a person who was devout in prayer'—the usual paraphrase—'found herself caught away in spirit and found that she was in an incomprehensively and unutterably beautiful palace. And she saw Jesus Christ sitting among His saints on His emperor's throne, and He opened His adorable mouth and uttered the words that are written down here.'

O popule meus, quid fecit tibi? 'My people, my people, what have I done to thee?' these are the words in God's lament in the liturgy of Good Friday. An echo of them resounds in the cry heard by Bridget's ears alone, only her hand writes down: 'Oh people of Cyprus, who art so wrath upon Me, hear and think upon what I will say to thee now.' And God reminds this people of all His benefits towards it:

> I loved thee as a father his only begotten Son, whom he would bring up to great honour. I gave thee a land, where thou couldst find all that was needful for the wants of life, and I sent thee the warmth and light of the Holy Spirit, so that thou couldst understand the true Christian faith. I set thee in a place that one gives only to the faithful servant, namely among My enemies, so that by thy labour and thy fight against the infidels thou shouldst earn a more glorious crown in My kingdom. For a long while I have carried thee in My heart, and watched over thee as the apple of My eye in all perils and trials. And so long as thou didst keep My commandments and remain faithful to the Holy Church, there ascended countless souls of the kingdom of Cyprus to My heavenly kingdom to rejoice there for ever with Me.

But these times are no more. The people of Cyprus are not the same as in the century of the crusades. 'Now thou dost according to thy own will and followest thy own pleasure. Thou dost not fear Me, who am thy judge, thou lovest not Me who have redeemed thee by so bitter a death' (again and again with Bridget these two fundamental thoughts recur: fear of the just God, love of the suffering God).

Thou hast spit Me out of thy mouth as something that tastes ill, and I must share the chamber of thy heart with the Devil—nay, thou drivest Me out of thy gate as a thief or robber. And thou art not more afraid of sinning in My sight than the beasts without understanding when they mate. It is therefore a just judgment that thou art driven out of heaven where My friends are, and placed in the everlasting hell among My enemies. For this thou must know, that everyone who is like thee and will not repent, his soul shall go the same way as Lucifer because of his pride, and Judas who sold Me, because of his avarice, and Zimri, whom Phineas slew because of his whoredom lewdness. For he sinned with a woman against My law, therefore his soul was after death sent to hell.

That 'Bible in Swedish' which Bridget read was the Pentateuch in Master Matthias' translation. She alludes here to the account in the Book of Numbers of how the Israelites allow themselves to be seduced by the heathen women.

A man of the children of Israel came and brought to his brethren a Midianitish woman in the sight of Moses, and in the sight of all the congregation of the children of Israel. . . . And when Phineas, the son of Eleazar, a son of Aaron the priest, saw it he stood up and took a javelin in his hand. And he went after the man of Israel into the tent and thrust both of them through, the man of Israel and the woman through her belly. . . . Now the name of the Israelite that was slain, even that was slain with the Midianitish woman, was Zimri, the son of Salu.*

With the same stern mercilessness Bridget condemns the people of Cyprus; the punishment shall come upon it as upon Zimri if it does not repent.

I will destroy this generation and its seed upon the whole of Cyprus, I will spare none, neither poor nor rich, I will blot out this generation, so that no one shall remember any more that it has lived, and it shall be as if it had never been born into the world. And afterwards I will plant Me a new vineyard in Cyprus—a people who will keep My commandments and love Me with all their hearts.(8)

God spoke to Bridget as He had spoken to Moses in the days of the Old Covenant—the language of inexorable justice and slighted love. With this message Brother Martin went back to Cyprus.

---

* Book of Numbers xxv, 6–14.

VII

Bridget had only three items on her programme for her sojourn in the Holy Land: Jerusalem—Bethlehem—Jordan. She did not get to Galilee, did not see Nazareth, did not wander along the shore of the gentle Lake of Genesareth to Capharnaum, did not climb up on that Mount on which had once been spoken the words: 'Blessed are the meek, for they shall possess the land.' . . .

And how much there was to see in that holy city of Jerusalem alone! Here they were even shown the grave of Adam in the dark cave of the rock beneath the hill of Golgotha. Here he had been laid to rest by none less than King Solomon and through the cleft of the rock the redeeming blood of Christ flowed down to him. Bridget, however, does not seem to have attached much weight to these traditions, if she knew about them at all. It was the same about the different legends about the cross of Christ, concerning which she had read at home in Sweden: the cross was said to have been made from a tree planted by Adam himself; Solomon had cut it down and made a beam of it for his temple, but later the Jews had taken it and thrown it into the pool of Bethesda. It was for the sake of this beam that an angel descended every day and moved the water. Another tradition has it that the Jews had made a bridge of the beam, and the sheep were to pass over it when they came to the pool of Bethesda to be washed. 'But when Sibilla, queen of the land of the East, came to visit King Solomon, she dismounted from her horse, took off her shoes and kissed the beam. Later it came to the time when Our Lord was condemned to death, and then there was a mad Jew who cried that they should take the beam that lay over the sheep pond, and make a cross of it, because there was not in Jerusalem any cross more impure than that.'(1)

If Saint Bridget visited the pond, still existing in our times, but where in the days of the Old Covenant the sheep that were to be sacrificed in the Temple underwent the liturgical cleansing, it was for an entirely different reason. For here had stood by the pool of Bethesda that house where Mary was born—here Joachim and Anna had had their house and Mary the home of her childhood. This tradition was established in writing already in the seventh century—Saint Soppronius, Patriarch of Jerusalem, knows that 'by the sheep pond is the place where Anna gave birth to Mary, here the Queen of Heaven came into the world in the chamber of her fathers,' and here a church had already been raised to the glory of the Holy Virgin. One gate of the city in fact bears the name *Bab sitti Mirjam*, 'Our Lady's Gate.'(2) A grotto underneath the church is said to be the place where Mary was born.

Bridget knelt in this grotto, where the graves of Joachim and Ann were also shown her. She had always been in spiritual communion with the grandmother of Jesus. Once, when in Rome, she had gone out to San Paolo fuori le mura, a friendly sacristan had made her a gift of a relic of Saint Anna. When Bridget came home with it and was thinking of how she should preserve it, she saw in a vision the grandmother of Christ and heard her say: 'I am Anna, mother of all honourable married people in both the Old Covenant and in the New.' Bridget had moreover from the lips of Saint Anna learned a prayer uttered in the following words:

> Blessed be thou, Son of God and Son of the Virgin, who hast chosen thy mother from the marriage of Joachim and Anna. For the sake of Anna's prayers have mercy upon all who live in wedlock, that they may bear fruit to God, and guide all who strive after marriage that God may be honoured in them.(3)

A long time before, at home in Sweden, Bridget had already heard Mary praise her parents:

> The marriage of my father and my mother was so chaste that in all the world there has never been anything more chaste. They would not come together except to beget children according to the law. And when the angel had made known to them that of them should be born a virgin of whom should come the salvation of the world, they would rather die than come together in carnal love, and all sensual rapture was dead in them. . . . They came together at the bidding of an angel, but against their own will.(4)

This is Bridget's own ideal of a marriage as described here—marriage as it was in the garden of Eden, before the Fall: 'Love was to bear fruit in the womb of the woman without any voluptuous delight, and without any burden the woman was to bear the fruit of her womb and be delivered of her child without the pain.' After the expulsion from Paradise, however, the pleasure of the senses must be paid with suffering. This is not only Bridget's thought, in the whole of the Middle Ages the words of Genesis are thus understood: 'I will greatly multiply thy sorrow, and in sorrow shalt thou bring forth children.'(5)

Not until Mary was birth to come without pain, for she is the new Eve who has not sinned. Bridget hears her testimony of herself: 'The truth is this, that I was *conceived without sin*. . . . That hour, therefore, in which I was conceived, may well be called a golden hour, for then began the salvation of mankind, and darkness gave way to light.' This truth (of the immaculate conception of Mary), is, however, not known to many, one may even see pious people doubt it—'until the time shall come when the truth shall be revealed.'(6)

VIII

From the grotto by the pool of Bethesda, where Mary was born, Bridget's steps led to the grotto of the Nativity in Bethlehem. Sixteen years had passed since the Blessed Virgin had first promised Bridget this journey: 'For the sake of the great love that you bear me,' the Queen of Heaven had said, 'you shall come to Jerusalem as soon as it pleases my Son. And you shall also come to Bethlehem, and there I will show you how I gave birth to my son.'(1)

No promise could be dearer to Bridget. She was herself a mother, had given birth to eight children, as all other women bear them, in blood and anguish. She had been subjected to the stern laws of life— but this could not have been the lot of the blessed among women. Not in this way—but how?

Before the departure from Italy Bridget had already for a moment lifted a corner of the veil that concealed the mystery—that Mary had given birth to her Son while kneeling. Now she was to learn more.(2)

It is a walk of only an hour and a half from Jerusalem to Bethlehem, and Bridget and her company would probably make the journey on foot. It is a walk in the footsteps of the Patriarchs, for this is the way to Hebron and the grove of Mamre and to the cave of Machpelah— this is the road to Egypt, whither Israel went into exile, and by which Joseph returned. This is the road to Saba and Madian—at this very day a pilgrim still meets caravans of dromedaries striding solemnly along like those on which the wise men from the East came riding. On the way a halt is made on the hill from which you get the first view of Bethlehem—'here the wise men again saw the star of which they had lost sight in Jerusalem,' says the Franciscan who is one's guide. 'By this road on the right you go to Hebron. And the little mosque over there is built over Rachel's grave.'

Rachel's grave—Bridget knew Rachel from Master Matthias' translation of the Pentateuch, the five books of Moses. So it was here that Jacob buried the woman whom he loved most of all—the exceeding lovely one, whom Laban only gave him to wife after fourteen long years of service, and after he had first had to marry Leah with the inflamed eyes . . . When Jacob was lying on his death-bed far away in Egypt he did not think of Leah, but he thought of Rachel and spoke of her to his son Joseph. 'She died from me,' he said to his son,

> when I came from Padan—she died from me in the land of Chanaan in the very journey, when I had still some way to go to come to Ephrata, which is Bethlehem. . . . We were still some way from Ephrata when Rachel was in travail and her soul departed. And I erected a pillar over her sepulchre —this is the pillar of Rachel's monument to this day.*

Hundreds of years after Jacob and Rachel another couple came by the same road—Joseph and his affianced wife Mary. The apocryphal gospels describe how the holy couple draw near to Bethlehem, Mary riding, Joseph walking by her side. Mary says to Joseph: 'The time is drawing near when I must be delivered—we cannot get into the town in time—let us go into this grotto.' It is towards sunset, Joseph leaves Mary alone behind and hastens into Bethlehem for a midwife. He really finds one, in some of the apocrypha he finds two—but when he comes back with them Mary is already delivered. The women then take the liberty of rather intimate examinations and are convinced of Mary's virginity.(3) It is possible that Bridget knew these apocrypha and had rejected them.

But through the low door, where you have to stoop humbly, as if to get into heaven, she would enter Constantine's basilica, larger and more magnificent even than that which he built at the prayer of Helena, his mother, in Rome to preserve in it the relic of the Holy Cross. You advance between a double avenue of huge pillars—on two of them (but this Bridget did not know) there are paintings representing Saint Canute of Denmark, Saint Olaf of Norway.(4) From the central nave a stairway leads up to the high altar—it may be that a group of women from Bethlehem are just going up to it, clad in their costumes of the thirteenth century, with the same headdress (*le hennin*) as the ladies of the French nobility of the time of the crusades—a long white veil hangs down from it. Underneath the high altar is the underground chapel into which the grotto of the Nativity has been transformed— your feet fumble down some steps, after the light in the church the darkness feels like a bandage round your eyes. Then you see lamps shining before an altar—and beneath the altar a silver star, inlaid in the floor, and round the silver star an inscription: *Hic de Virgine Maria*

---

* Genesis xlviii, 7; xxxv, 16–20.

Jesus Christus natus est. 'Here Jesus Christ was born of the Virgin Mary.' All kneel down, Bridget in front. All bow down to the ground and kiss the silver star—Bridget first. And then she no longer sees either the silver star or the lamps—they are not there any more. But the grotto is there and it is the first Christmas night. . . .

I saw an exceeding fair maiden who was with child. She was clad in a white cloak and a robe that was so thin that her virginal body could clearly be seen. Her body was very swollen for the womb was full and she was about to be delivered. With her there was a very honourable old man, and they had an ox and an ass with them. And when they were come into the cave the old man tied the ox and the ass to the manger, then he went out and came in again with a lighted taper, which he set fast between the stones in the wall, and went out again not to be present at the birth. Then the maid took off her shoes, laid aside the white cloak that she wore, likewise the veil that she had on her head and laid them by her side. She was now clad only in the robe, and her hair, that was bright like gold, fell down over her shoulders. She took out two small pieces of linen and two very fine woollen cloths that she had with her to wrap the child in and two other small pieces of woollen stuff to bind about its head, and she laid it all by her side until the time should come when she would use them. When all things were now ready the maiden knelt down with great awe and began to pray. She turned her back to the manger, but lifted her face towards heaven and looked to the east. And with hands uplifted and her eyes towards heaven she knelt without moving, as it were enrapt in divine sweetness. And while she was thus absorbed in prayer I saw that which was in her womb move and in a moment she gave birth to her Son. And so much light went out from Him that the taper which the old man had brought no longer gave any light. . . .

But so sudden and instant was that movement of the infant that I could not see or distinguish how the birth came to pass. I saw at once the child lying on the ground, naked but very clean, there was no dirt or anything unclean upon it. . . . And immediately the maiden's body, which had newly been very swollen, contracted and her whole body was wonderfully beautiful and delicate. But when the maiden felt that she was delivered, she bent her head and folded her hands, and with great awe she adored the child and said to Him: 'Welcome, my God, my Lord and my Son!' But then the boy wept and trembled with cold on the hard floor, and stretched out His little hands to His Mother, and she took Him up and laid His cheek against hers and took Him to her breast with joy and great compassion. And she sat down on the floor and laid Him on her knees and began to swathe Him— first with the linen cloths and then with the woollen pieces and at last wound the whole about His little body, legs and arms in one swaddling cloth, and swathed His head in the two woollen pieces that she had brought with her. When all this was done the old man came in and threw himself upon his knees, adoring the child and weeping for joy. And in the virgin there was no weakness as in other women, when they are delivered, but she stood up with the child in her arms, and she and Joseph laid it in the manger and adored it with great joy. And then I heard wonderful sweet singing of many angels.(5)

Bridget had seen the birth of Christ, but she had not yet seen enough. Joseph wondered when he came back to the grotto, that Mary had been able to give birth without help. Bridget had heard unbelieving people assert that the birth of Christ had come to pass in a quite natural way—'in the ordinary manner'—'a delivery under concealment of birth had been heard of before!' 'The truth is,' says the Mother of Jesus, 'that my Son was born in the way that I have told you before, and thus as you have seen now.'(6)

But Bridget did not become actually clear about the 'how': she did not get further than the words in the Creed: 'born of the Virgin Mary,' Mother and Virgin.

In Bridget's Christmas gospel the shepherds and the wise men from the East also had their place, but not a very big one. 'The shepherds who watched over their flocks came to see the Child and adore it . . . and returned, praising and glorifying God for all that they had seen and heard.'(7) Bridget does not seem to have visited the little village of Beth-Sahur with the 'Shepherds' fields' near Bethlehem. About the 'Holy Three Kings' she is rather brief, only saying that the Jesus Child smiled at them.(8)

The relations between the Blessed Virgin and Bridget were like those between mother-in-law and daughter-in-law. Gradually, as Bridget grew older, the tender intimacy between the two grew greater and greater. Mary, daughter of Joachim, and Bridget, Birger's daughter, speak with one another as one mother with another. Bridget listens— the mother of Jesus tells her how beautiful Jesus was as a child—when people in Nazareth were sad they said: 'Let us go and see Mary's son, and they were glad merely at seeing Him. Mary had not much trouble in keeping Him clean—there was never any vermin upon Him, nor was there any in His hair.'(9) When he grew bigger He worked with His hands, and Bridget must not believe that if they were short of food in the house Jesus would work a little miracle to help their modest resources—no, He only urged them to have patience and said: 'Wait and see, God will be sure to help us.' And He was right, sometimes there were people who were better off and who helped with a small alms, but for the most part we lived by our work. And Jesus was the most obedient son—when Joseph said: 'Do this or that,' he did it at once. As He grew older His friends came on visits, they talked together about the Holy Scriptures and Jesus explained them to them. This was

soon rumoured in the town and Rabbis learned in the Scriptures came
—He discussed with them so that they had to wonder and they said
to each other: 'Well, well, Joseph's son teaches us!'

The apocryphal gospels recount similar features and in spite of the
Blessed Virgin's warning Bridget may, directly or indirectly, have
become acquainted with them. But from Mary's lips she hears a
description of the intimate beauty of Christ which is entirely Bridget's
own. It is a portrait of an ideal man drawn by her.

> He was above middle height, not stout but full bodied and well built. The
> hair of His head, His eyebrows and beard were brown, the beard as long
> as the breadth of a hand. The forehead was not projecting nor receding,
> but straight. The nose straight, neither too small nor too big, the eyes so
> clear that His enemies, too, were glad to look at them. The lips were not
> thick, but of a handsome red, the chin not projecting or too long, but
> fittingly big. His cheeks were round, the skin a clear pink, His carriage
> upright, and on the whole of His body there was not a mark, which is
> attested by those who saw Him naked, as when He was bound to the pillar.
> His countenance was so beautiful that none could see Him without taking
> comfort from it, and even those who were grieved with worldly grief
> (*mali a tristia sæculi*) felt glad so long as they looked at Him.(10)

What mother would not have been happy to have such a son? But
alas! Mary could never be really happy. It was a grief to her when
Herod had all the little children in Bethlehem murdered. It was a
greater grief when the old man, Simeon, foretold her in the Temple
that a sword would pierce her heart. Every day that passed the cross
came nearer—the cross on which her beautiful boy was to suffer.
'Why are you grieving?' He often asked her. 'Don't you know that I
must be about my Father's business?' Yes, yes, she knew it. But,
but . . .

> Oh Bridget, when I looked at my Son and considered how beautiful He
> was, my soul dripped with joy like a flower with dew. But when I looked
> at His hands and feet and thought of the prophet's words and knew that
> they would be pierced with nails, my eyes were filled with tears and it was
> as though a knife went through my heart. And when my Son saw that I
> wept, then He too, was sorrowful unto death, and thus my joy was always
> blended with sorrow. But when the hour was come that my Son was to
> suffer His enemies caught Him and struck Him on His cheeks and on His
> neck, and they did spit upon Him and mock Him.

It is the story of Christ's Passion being again unfolded—now it is
not Bridget who sees it, it is the Mother of the Lord herself who
recounts it.

Then He was taken to the pillar of torment, and He took off His vestments Himself, and He laid His hands upon the pillar Himself, and His enemies bound them fast without mercy. (The pillar of torment—the column to which Jesus was bound to be scourged.)

And as He stood there bound to the pillar He had no garments on at all, but was as naked as when He had come into the world and suffered shame that he had to endure this. Then all my Son's friends fled from Him, and His enemies surrounded Him and tore His body that was so pure and without blemish, and without any infection or sin. But I, who was standing near, fell down like one dead at the sound of the first blow. And when I came to myself I saw His body beaten and torn into the ribs, so that the ribs could be seen. And what was still more dreadful to see was that when the scourges were withdrawn His flesh was torn like the earth by a plough. And as my Son was now standing there, bleeding and wounded all over, so that there was not a whole spot left upon Him, there was one who took courage and asked: 'Will you kill Him, though He is not yet judged?' and cut through His bonds. Then they clothed my Son in His garments, and I saw there was blood in all the places where He had trod. And the executioners did not allow Him to put on all his garments but pushed Him and pulled Him, telling Him to hasten. He was taken away like a robber and He dried the blood from His eyes.

And so Mary followed her Son to Golgotha. 'But on the way to the place of torment some struck Him on the neck, some in the face, and the blows were so hard that although I could not see anything for the people I could plainly hear the sound of the blows. And when I came to the place of torment I saw everything made ready for His death.'

Mary tells Bridget all that she has seen—and not forgetting the detail that the nail was bored through the hand, 'where the bone was hardest and firmest.' She remembers the crown of thorns—

It pricked so hard that both my Son's eyes were filled with the blood that flowed down, and the ears were stopped up and His beard was thick with blood. And as He now stood there, so ill-used, bleeding and pierced, He saw me, standing there and weeping, and with His eyes full of blood, he looked at my sister's son John, and gave me into his care. And I heard some say that my Son was a robber, and others said that He was a deceiver, and that no one had deserved His punishment better than He. And hearing all this made me still more sorrowful. But when I heard the blow of the last nail being struck it grew dark before my eyes, my hands and feet shook and I fell to the ground like one dead.

But when I rose again I saw my Son hanging there so miserably, and I, His sorrowful Mother, could hardly stand up, and when He saw me He cried to His Father with a loud and tearful voice and said: 'Father, why hast Thou forsaken Me?' Then His eyes looked as if they were already dim, His cheeks were hollow, the mouth was open, His tongue was bleeding, His stomach was flat against His back, as if He had no entrails, His whole body was white from the great loss of blood, His hands and feet were stretched out hard, and the nails had made them as it were cross-shaped, His beard and hair were all over full of blood. So did my Son stand on the cross, wounded and blue and bleeding, only His heart was sound, for it was of the best and strongest nature, for from my flesh He had taken the very purest body of the very best health. His skin was so fine that even the slightest scratch made the blood come, and the veins could be seen through the skin. And because His nature was of the very best life and death strove a long while in His wounded body. For sometimes the pains from His torn body went up to the heart, which was the strongest part of Him, and sometimes the pains again darted into the limbs, and the death agony was long and bitter. And as my Son was suffering thus He looked down at His weeping friends who would rather have endured all His agony or burn for ever in hell, than see Him thus in agony. And the sorrow over the sorrow of His friends was more than all the other suffering in either His limbs or His heart, for He loved them exceedingly. But now when His fear and torment was becoming greater than he could endure, He cried to His Father and said: 'Father, into Thy hands I commend my spirit.' And when I, His Mother, heard this cry, all my limbs trembled in my heart's bitterest need, and afterwards, every time I thought of it, it was as if I heard those words again. But now, when death came, and His heart broke, all His limbs trembled, and His head rose up a little and then bowed down again. His mouth was open, His tongue full of blood, His fingers and arms shrank a little. His back fell hard in to the cross. Then someone said to me: 'Mary, your son is dead!' Others said: 'He is dead, but He shall surely rise from the dead!' Then they all went away, but one came and thrust a spear into His side. And when the spear was drawn out the point was red with blood, and it was to me, as if my own heart was cut asunder. Thereafter He was taken down from the cross, and I laid Him over my knees, and He looked like a leper. His eyes were glazed and full of blood, His mouth cold as snow, His beard like grass, His face shrunken, His arms had grown so stiff that they could not be bent further down than to the navel. As He hung on the cross, so I had Him upon my knees, and He was like a man who is a cripple in all his limbs. Then they laid Him in a clean linen shroud, and I closed His eyes and His mouth, for they were open. After that they laid Him in the sepulchre. Oh my daughter, how willingly would I not have gone into the grave with Him, if this had been His will. When this was done the good John came and took me home. Behind us we left the cross, standing high and alone.(11)

IX

From Mary's own lips Bridget had been convinced of Mary's immaculate conception. There was another dogma which had also caused her difficulties—the doctrine of Mary's assumption into heaven with soul and *body* (*Assumptio*). Bridget knew from home what the legend told about the death of the Blessed Virgin:

The apostles were watching over her in prayer and lit many candles and lamps. But in the third watch of the night Jesus came Himself with all His angels and all the holy patriarchs and prophets and all the host of heaven, and sweeter singing was heard than any ear had ever heard before. Jesus Himself commanded that His Mother's body should be buried in the valley of Jehosaphat. And Himself He took the soul to heaven. And a light shone round the dead body, so that the virgins who washed it could truly feel it with their hands but not see it with their eyes. And the light shone until the body was washed and clothed. Then Peter bade John go before the bier and Paul to help to carry it. The other apostles followed after. Sweetly they sang and so loudly that the Jews heard it and cried to each other that now the apostles were carrying Mary to the grave. And they took weapons and shouted that now the apostles were to be killed and Mary's bones were to be burned on a fire. The bishop over the Jews' land was quite beside himself, he laid hands on the bier and wanted to overthrow it. He was punished for his presumption for he became paralysed in his hands and could not get them away from the bier, it was as if they were nailed to it.

The chief priest, for it is he whom the legend calls a bishop of the Jews' land, now appeals in his need to Peter and begs him to let him get loose. Peter answers: 'We are busy with Our Lady and have no time to work miracles,' is touched, however, at length and liberates the high priest, who is then converted and becomes a Christian. All the other Jews become blind and cannot do any harm.

Afterwards the apostles laid the Mother of God in the grave in the valley of Jehosaphat and kept guard at the grave. But on the third day Our Lord Jesus Christ came to them and greeted them: 'Peace be unto you!' They answered: 'Glory be to Thee!' He said to them: 'What think ye that I shall do with My dear Mother?' They answered: 'It seems to us that in like manner as you rose yourself from the dead, so shall you also raise her from the dead and set her at your right hand.' Then Our Lord said: 'Arise, My dear Mother! Because you did never commit a sin you shall rise without any pain.' And the soul returned immediately to the body and she stood up and fared forth with her beloved Son and all the host of heaven to everlasting life.(1)

Thus had Bridget read and believed at home in Sweden. But now she had met, here in Bethlehem, one of these 'wind-bags' and chatter-boxes, against whom she had so much antipathy—one of those learned gentlemen who, instead of the kernel of the Word of God, chewed the chaff of worldly wisdom. And this eloquent gentleman had argued against the assumption of Mary into heaven, by referring to Saint Hieronymus—this great Father of the Church having written that he would rather doubt about the doctrine in question than maintain something that he could not prove from Holy Scripture. Hieronymus had lived here in Bethlehem for years; first he had learned Hebrew from a Rabbi, and after that, in his grotto beside the grotto of the Nativity (Bridget had visited it), he had translated, first the Old Testament, afterwards the New (it is the Latin translation of the Bible, known under the name of the *Vulgate*, which is still the official Bible of the Catholic Church).(2)

It was therefore a great authority to whom the 'wind-bag' appealed—it was not all learned idle talk. But Mary excused Hieronymus —he had not known any better. And now she herself told Bridget about her last days and about her death.

She survived her Son a long while—she had a strong and healthy body. Besides, it was God's will that she should remain a long while on the earth, so that her crown in heaven might be all the more beautiful. For every day was an agony to her—no matter whether she worked or ate, the passion and death of her Son were present to her. Every day she walked along the road by which He had walked— from the judgment seat of Pilate to the place of a skull and from Golgotha the few steps to the new tomb in the garden of Joseph of Arimathea. To this very day pilgrims still wander by the same road through the streets of Jerusalem to the church of the Holy Sepulchre. Bridget also walked daily on her *Via Crucis*—in her daughter Karin's prayer book, which has been brought from Vadstena to the Royal Library in Stockholm, the stations on this road of sorrow are written down, and at each station the prayer that is said, the hymn that is sung —from the mighty war song, *Vexilla Regis*, 'Forth comes the Standard of the King,' past Golgotha to the empty tomb and to the garden where Mary of Magdala was the first of them all to see the Risen One and to fall at His feet: *Rabboni!*(3)

The Blessed Virgin walked her *Via Crucis*, but did not allow grief to crush her—

I performed what I had to do, and went about as a human being among other human beings. . . . But when some years had passed after my Son's death, I began to long greatly to see Him again. And it was to me as though an angel of the Lord came to me and said: 'Your Son has sent me to make known to you that the time has now come when you are to come to Him and to have the crown which is prepared for you.' But I asked: 'Do you know the day or the hour when I have to depart hence?' The angel answered: 'When your friends come to lay you to rest.' Then the angel vanished, and I made ready for death by seeing once again all the places where my Son had suffered. And my soul was so filled with joy that it could no longer contain itself, and in this joy my soul was loosened from the body. . . . Thereafter my Son's friends came and buried my body in the valley of

Jehosaphat. Fifteen days did my body lie in the grave, then it was taken up into heaven, and the angels who bore me up were as great in number as the beams of dust in the sun.(4)

Bridget and her escort wandered to the Blessed Virgin's grave in in the valley of Jehosaphat—the other empty grave! Here the Benedictines built a church at the request of Geoffrey of Bouillon. A stairway with many steps leads down to a crypt—here is shown the sarcophagus in which the Blessed Virgin's body had rested. Midway on the stairway, in a chapel dedicated to Saint Joseph, Erik Ayegood's queen, Bodil, found her last resting-place—Bridget probably was not aware of it. Or could she have heard tell at home about the pious Danish queen who was said to have been born in Sweden—in Värmland there is a village named Bodilsäter, and above the western door of the church there is a relief representing a queen.(5)

But Bridget had no thought for anyone but Mary. She tells about it herself, in the first person, which she begins to use towards the close of her life instead of the earlier, impersonal: 'A person, who was watching and praying,' or: 'she who is standing near' (*illa quae astat*).

When I was in the valley of Jehosaphat and praying by the grave of the glorious Virgin, the same Virgin appeared to me, shining in great splendour, and she said to me: 'Hearken to what I will say to thee, my daughter. After my Son had ascended into heaven, I lived for fifteen years here in the world and a little more, as many days as there are years from the ascension of my Son into heaven until my death. And after my death I lay fifteen days in this grave and then I was taken up into heaven, but the garments in which I was laid to rest remained here in the grave. And now you must know that in heaven there are only two glorified bodies, my Son's and mine. But now you shall go back to the lands of the Christians and be converted every day to a better and better life, after you have seen the places where my Son and I lived and died and were buried.'(6)

Then Bridget said the prayer which the Blessed Virgin had taught her while she was still at home in Ulfåsa:

Blessed be Thou, O God, the Creator of all things, who hast deigned to descend into the womb of the Virgin Mary. Blessed be Thou, oh God, who didst not come to be a heaviness for the Virgin Mary, and hast deigned to receive of her a body without sin. Blessed be Thou, oh God, who camest to the Virgin with joy for her soul and who with joy for all her limbs camest forth from her free from sin. Blessed be Thou, oh God, who after Thy ascension into heaven often gavest her the joy of Thy visitations. Blessed be Thou, oh God, who didst take up the soul of Thy Mother, the Virgin Mary, into heaven and didst set her on Thy right hand high up above all angels. Have mercy upon me for the sake of her prayers.(7)

X

'In the south Christ sits by the well of Urd,' one of the old Icelandic scalds had sung, and by the well of Urd he meant—Jordan. Where the Norns had once sat Christ was now enthroned—He is therefore called 'the King of Jordan' in Snorre. All pilgrims to Jerusalem, to Jordan, to the river of baptism, all had to go, and those who could swam across the river, for it was over there, 'in Bethania beyond Jordan,' that John had baptized Jesus. Over there on the bank there was a thick growth of willow bushes, and those who went over 'made knots' of the flexible willow branches. It was these willow withes that, at home in the North, were used as the palms of Palm Sunday—and they who had made the pilgrimage to the Jordan were perhaps for that reason called 'palm pilgrims' (or had they plucked real palm branches in 'Abraham's Garden' by Jericho?). They took the palms home, carrying them 'between two shoulders.'(1)

Bridget, too, must needs go down to the Jordan. The road was not long but it was dangerous. King Baldwin of Jerusalem had in his time accompanied Sigurd, the Jerusalem pilgrim, thither with a great escort. Half-way down lies the place called *Locus sanguinum*—it was here that the man who went down from Jerusalem to Jericho fell among robbers (in our own times all kinds of things can happen on this road among the desolate mountains. Bridget, however, was not afraid—should she not be able to do the same that Saint Elin of Skövde had done two hundred years ago, or that Saint Ingrid of Skänninge had done exactly one hundred years earlier?)(2)

Bridget set out for the Jordan—to the well of Urd, to the waters of baptism. And on the way she came past a place where she felt almost on homely soil. The road to the Jordan first passes Bethphage, where Jesus mounted the ass to make His entry into Jerusalem; then you come to Bethany with the house of Martha and Mary Magdalen and the grave of Lazarus. How could Bridget help but be reminded of her silver wedding pilgrimage with Ulf to Saint Martha in Tarascon, to the grotto of Mary Magdalen and le Pilon on the summit of Sainte Baume? Her thoughts had often later, since that time, been engaged with the two sisters, they had been the symbols for her of the two forms of the religious life: contemplation and active love. That chapter of the *Revelationes* in which Bridget describes the quite different manner of life of the two sisters, almost has the effect of a preparatory work for the rule which she was to write for the convent in Vadstena.

Here as there it is worth while noticing how reasonable and lenient the stern Bridget is. If Mary finds it wearisome always to pray and contemplate she is to work with her hands. If that also wearies her she can pay a visit to a friend and have a talk—but on an edifying subject— or she can go and hear a good sermon. Necessary work must not be put aside for prayer. By the banks of the Jordan Bridget was to hear talk about one of the great ascetics of the Primitive Church—*Maria Ægypttiaca*—and about her works of penance. She had actually lived down there in the desert—perhaps many people confused her with Mary Magdalen. Bridget gave the asceticism of the desert Fathers a wide berth. 'Mary Magdalen,' says Bridget

> loved nothing more than God, would never displease Him, would always do His will. But that was no reason why she should eat anything poisonous, clothe herself in thorns or sleep on an ant-hill! Jesus Himself lived like other people, frugally and modestly, went to table in the name of God, was decently clad and slept in a bed. Of course, Mary Magdalen *could* have exercised the same penance as her Egyptian namesake, if she had understood that it was God's will—but then it was not.(3)

And yet, down there by the banks of the Jordan, Bridget was to meet the last great desert ascetic of the Old Covenant—he who was clothed with camel's hair, and whose food was locusts and wild honey. At an early age she had already thought of this forerunner of Jesus— and (she says herself) 'what you learn when you are young you do not forget when you are old.'(4) She had heard Jesus call the Baptist his 'very dearest friend' and praise him 'because nothing unclean entered into his mouth, and he took only what was needed of food.' As John had converted many by his preaching, so Jesus would now by Bridget bring many spiritual sons into the world. John had not been like a rush that is shaken by the wind, but 'like a reed full of sweetness and honey.'

Bridget then, was standing on the spot where that reed had grown. She stood there with Karin, with Birger, with the confessors, the handmaids, and it is permissible to think that Birger, at least, performed the ritual deed of swimming across the river and returning with a bunch of palms from the other side. Bridget stood watching the waters of the Jordan flowing past, down towards the Dead Sea. And she thought: 'This is like the world. Now it is flood time, now ebb. Now people are with us, now against us, we are never without fear and trouble. Therefore must he who will belong to God *go over the Jordan* like the prophet Elijah, for over there one can hear the voice of God.'(5) The important point is, not to give God *empty nuts*—John the Baptist never did this, for from his youth he had served God alone. The apostles, on the other hand, came with nuts that were only half full, for before they were called they had lived in an imperfect manner (and what was to be said about Peter, who had suddenly become so forgetful that he could not even remember his Master any more?).(6) Mary Magdalen, too, who had lived a long while in sin, offered God empty nuts among the full ones.(6)

On the way back to Jerusalem Bridget perhaps again made a halt at Bethany, by the house of the two sisters and by the grave of Lazarus. And she hears the voice of her Bridegroom, grave, almost stern, 'as I then awakened Lazarus from the tomb, so have I awakened your souls from sin.' It is therefore of importance to 'defend the risen soul against the Jews.' But who are these Jews? They are those, and they are many, who know how to speak loud words about spiritual things, but do not live according to their own words. 'Against these Jews I will defend you, from them I will protect you, so that you will not be seduced either by their words or by their works.'(7)

In the Holy Land, too, Bridget had met with these 'wind-bags' and talkers—they blow a good deal, but their windy talk does not cause any glow to burst into flame. One of them came to Bridget with a book that she must read—it was written in it that Peter and Paul had appeared to him and foretold him that he was to become both an emperor and pope at the same time! The Archangel Michael also appeared to him in the form of a merchant, and when he was in need of money he found on his pillow in the morning gold coins of an un-known stamp, which had been laid there by a friendly hand. Bridget made inquiries about the man—it turned out that he was a renegade monk who had gone to Jerusalem without the permission of his superiors, and who, in consequence, had been excommunicated. Moreover, Bridget knew from experience who that 'merchant' was, and advised the monk to beware of his gold coins—in any case he would never become emperor and pope at the same time.(8)

And so Bridget had completed the three pilgrimages for which she had come to the Holy Land. Notwithstanding her great admiration of John the Baptist she did not seek out Ain-Karim, the village in the Judæan mountains where he had been born. Besides, it was now late in the year, autumn was approaching with its storms. It was time to heed the marching order: 'Now depart to the lands of the Christians.'

From the valley of the Jordan the road ascends steeply towards

Jerusalem. Jesus and His apostles would have walked on this road in burning summer heat, and on the way they would rest and refresh themselves with a drink of water from the 'spring of the apostles.' It is before you get to Bethany. Here Bridget and her escort also made a halt. In the East water is a precious thing—at the present day the water seller can still be seen going through the streets of Jerusalem crying his wares—round the black, leather bag filled with water can be heard the rattle of a wreath of metal cups. By the Jordan Bridget would remember the Baptist; here by the spring she would meet the apostles, and the Blessed Virgin, Queen of the Apostles, would pro-mise her that they would all be her friends.

> Peter shall say to you: 'Open thy mouth, my daughter.' Paul, the strong fighter, shall clothe thee with the full armour of love. But John shall say: 'Sit on my knee, my daughter.' Peter is the firm faith in God's unshakable Church. Paul is the persevering patience in the work of the apostle. But to sit on the knee of the apostle John is to become like an obedient little child, who cares for nothing here on earth but to do the will of the heavenly father. *Contemne terrena, et eris clelestis.* Despise earthly things and thou wilt have the whole of heaven in thy heart!(9)

XI

There was still one thing left before Bridget could leave the Holy Land —in *Pulkrakyrkja* (this was the Scandinavian form of the Italian *San Sepolcro*) Birger was to be made a knight of the Holy Sepulchre. Bridget had, from her earliest years had a great predilection for the state of knighthood—she really came near to preferring the knights to the people of the monasteries and convents. To her the knight was *miles Christi,* the warrior of Christ, ready to give his life for the cause of justice and to shed his blood for the Faith. He orders his life according to the commandments of Christ, he represses the wicked and helps the humble in the community to obtain their rights, and he shall therefore enter into everlasting joy.(1) At the death-bed of such a knight Bridget sees in spirit the hosts of heaven approach the dying man and bring up his arms before God—the shield, which signifies his patience, the sword, which signifies his obedience, his helmet, his whole armour, nay, even his horse. Christ Himself is the head of the Christian knight's army—His title is 'Duke of Bethlehem,' the Cross His royal banner. He cries to His soldiers: 'Did I not go first into the war, was I not foremost in suffering? Why do you desert?' Christ's Passion is Christ's fight against the enemy of mankind—'He has won the great fight,

Satan is bound until the day of doom,' was to be sung later by the great Danish scald. He who has fought the good fight will on his death-bed be able to say: 'Blessed am I that I served God. Blessed am I that I was created.'(2) Saint Clare of Assisi said the same words when dying—the faithful knight and the self-denying nun are of the same worth in the eyes of God and receive the same everlasting reward.

Bridget is reminded of the time when Karl, the son nearest her heart, was made a knight. She sees the brilliant procession moving on its way to the church, the king's banner waving at the head. But at the churchyard gate it must remain behind. The gentlemen dismount and tether their horses at the churchyard fence, then they go into the church on foot, and there, on consecrated ground, they are met by the clergy, a train of men of pure lives in white copes, with candles and incense, with the processional cross at the head. They all go into the church, each one to his place, and Mass begins. But when the Mass has come to *Agnus Dei*—that is, just before Communion—the knight that is to be steps up before the altar and the king asks him: 'Will you be a knight?' 'I will.' 'Do you promise God and me that you will defend the faith of Holy Church and obey her bishops in all that belongs to God?' 'I promise it.' Then the king gives him the sword and says: 'Behold, I give you this sword so that you may defend the Faith and Holy Church, subdue God's enemies and defend God's friends.' Next the king gives him the shield and says: 'Behold, I give you this shield, so that you may protect yourself with it against God's enemies and protect the widows and fatherless.' Then the king lays his hand upon his neck and says: 'Behold, I lay upon you the yoke of obedience. Fulfil by your deeds what you have promised.' The new knight is then clothed in the cloak of knighthood, after which the Mass is continued and the priest gives the new knight Holy Communion. In spirit Bridget hears the words spoken by Christ to his new warrior: 'I will be in him, and he shall be in Me. I will kindle in him the fire of My love, so that he shall will nought but what I will, and fear none other than Me. And I will be with him whithersoever he goes.'(3)

These are the ceremonies at the initiation of a knight, such as everyone of those present could see and hear them. But one day, when Bridget was sitting peacefully studying Latin and was just busy with the grammatical difference between active and passive—she had been given the following sentence: *melius est prævenire qvam præveniri* (it is better to warn than to be warned)—just then John the Baptist appears to her, and she sees how the saints take part in the investiture of a knight.

The Baptist himself gives the newly created knight his underclothes, and they are not made of camel's hair but of soft material. They signify the love of God which makes the hardest breastplate easy to wear. The apostle Peter then comes with a coat of mail, made up of many small good deeds, Paul with a suit of armour, Mary provides a helmet, steel gauntlets and greaves, the war martyrs Saint George and Saint Mauritius a shield, the prophets of the Old Testament, and chief among them Elijah, a sword. All these single pieces in a knight's armour have a spiritual meaning. The five fingers of the steel gauntlet on the right hand, that which holds the sword, mean the five ways in which the knight is to exercise justice. The steel gauntlet on the left hand signifies prayer, and of its five fingers the first means faith in everything that the Catholic Church teaches, the second that one will not sin, and that one bitterly repents of past sins, the third is the prayer that all love according to the flesh may be transformed into love according to the spirit, the fourth that one will live here on earth only to glorify God, the fifth that one does not rely upon oneself but always fears God, and that every day and every hour one expects death.

Bridget goes so far in her allegorizing that she gives it a grotesque effect: The knight's horse, for instance, is *baptism*; the saddle on this horse is the Passion of Christ, from which baptism obtains its power; to keep in this saddle the knight must rest his feet in the stirrups of prayer. A golden harness, laid upon the horse, is made up of the seven gifts of the Holy Ghost.(4)

The knight's sword has, in particular, been the subject of Bridget's interpretation. It signifies *confession*, and must therefore have the following qualities: it must be well polished, which means that he who confesses must thoroughly examine his conscience; it must be bright, that is, that nothing must be hid, that everything is told; it must have a double edge, the will not to sin any more and the will to do penance for the sins committed; it must have a sharp point, which means a forcible repentance, with which the devil is killed; and so that one does not cut oneself on the blade of the sword there is a guard—it means that one must not fall into despair because of exaggerated repentance. But neither must one in presumptuous self-confidence neglect to confess again—and therefore the sword hangs in a strap at the wrist so that one does not lose it.(5)

In the church of the Holy Sepulchre there is not much room at the grave itself—only barely enough for the priest who is saying Mass and for him who serves it. It was the Guardian of the Franciscan convent on Mount Sion who said Mass one morning in the autumn of 1372, and it was Birger who served it. And when the sacred action had come to the place where the priest has to say *Agnus Dei*, 'O Lamb of God, who takest away the sins of the world,' the Guardian paused and turned to Birger. 'Qvid petis?' 'What do you want?' Outside in the forecourt Bridget knelt with Karin and the confessors and servants. And from within she heard her son's voice when he made his vow as knight of the Holy Sepulchre: 'I, Birger, Ulf's son, vow to God and to you, Reverend Father, that I will defend the Holy Church against her enemies, protect God's friends and do good towards widows and the fatherless, and if I do wrong in any action I subject myself to your chastisement, so that I may entirely fulfil God's will and yours.'

When this was done the priest clothed him in the habit of the Order, as a sign that he now had a superior whom he must obey. He put a sword into his hand and said: 'With this sword you must fight and slay the enemies of God.' He also handed him a shield and said: 'May this shield protect you from the arrows of your enemies, and may this shield break rather than that you may flee.' And the priest gave him the Body of Christ for the strengthening of his soul and body, and that he might never be parted from his God.(6)

Did Bridget's thoughts, in the midst of her joy over Birger, pass over to Karl? Could he not have stood there to-day by the side of his brother?

XII

Brother Martin of Aragon had brought Bridget's letter home to Cyprus, and having duly performed his mission, had returned to the Holy Land. He related that the letter had not made any particular impression on the court at Famagusta. Bridget, however, did not give up—what a letter had not been able to do, was now to be achieved through the living word. After a good crossing she arrived in Cyprus on 8 October—four days later young Peter the Second was to be crowned King of Jerusalem. (The house of Lusignan carried this title —which was now only a title.) Famagusta prepared itself for this festival, all the hostelries were crowded with distinguished guests.

But on the day before the coronation Bridget stood in the market-place and spoke. At her departure she had promised the people of Cyprus to pray for it in the Holy Land. She had kept her promise, she had prayed. Now she came to tell it what answer she had received to her prayers. It was on Golgotha itself that Christ had spoken to her. 'Dear Bridget,' He had said, 'you pray in vain for these people—they promise, it is true, to repent, but they fail to do so. Tell them, therefore, that if they do not repent in earnest, my revenge will soon strike them!'(1)

Bridget stood in the square in front of the castle and spoke. The Latin words probably had a Scandinavian accent—perhaps they did not all understand her. In the crowd that filled the square, most of whom had probably just come 'to see the lions,' there were not only Catholics—Latins, as Bridget had learnt to call them in Jerusalem— but also schismatic Greeks. Bridget had a special message for them.

Those Greeks who know that there is only one Christian faith, that is, the Catholic one, and only one Vice-gerent of Christ, namely the Bishop of Rome, yet who will not obey him as their rightful shepherd, will after death not find mercy with God. It is different with those who have never come to a knowledge of the Catholic Church, and who live a good and pious life according to the best dictates of their conscience—upon them God will have mercy. For the rest the Greeks must understand that the whole of their kingdom is on the point of falling, and that the Byzantine empire will perish before long.(2)

In the tumult of the festival preparations Bridget's words passed unheeded. Then the great day came. Among the numerous distinguished guests there was also a large embassy from the republic of Genoa. Somehow or other a dispute arose between Cypriots and members of the Genoese legation—it was probably a question of precedence in the procession and of places in the church. The result was that many Genoese were killed, many wounded—among the latter a relative of Bridget's Genoese friend Carlo of Malocello named Petrus. When Bridget heard this she understood that it was the beginning of the end—she begged Alphonsus to go to Queen Eleanor and tell her: 'This is the beginning of God's chastisement.' The chastisement came at once—the Genoese did not leave the attack unavenged. It is Carlo of Malocello who seven years later testifies to it in the process of canonization: 'It was not long before the Genoese sent a fleet and seized Famagusta with armed hands. Many of the inhabitants of Cyprus were killed, taken captive or imprisoned and their wives handed over to the mercenary troops as harlots.' The witness had himself seen distinguished Cypriots going about begging in the streets of Genoa.(3)

Bridget left Cyprus, the island where Venus was born. But before she left she sent Queen Eleanor a last warning. She would try once more to make her see reason. It is the same complaint as against Giovanna (and against Blanca in her time).

Your eyes desired to see what was beautiful, your ears gladly heard men singing your praises, your mouth was always ready to utter licentious talk and to speak ill of others. Your stomach was always filled with good things, you did not deny your belly anything. You adorned your body with fine clothes so that it might look still more beautiful. But My friends [it is Christ who is speaking] were standing outside, miserable, hungry, naked, and they cried to you but you would not listen to them, they entreated you to let them come in, and you had them turned away, nay, you laughed at them and had no pity on them. Everything that you did for your own sake was easy for you, but to do anything for Me was very hard for you. You took your ease, you treated with contempt the exercise of right and justice. You coveted all that the world finds beautiful, but you cared naught for Me, who am more beautiful than all beauty. And if I would deal with you as I ought, in justice, *this* would happen to you:

For the pride of your limbs you deserve to be shown to public contempt. Because of your lechery the flesh of your body ought to rot, the skin be full of boils, your eyes torn out, your mouth split up on both sides, your hands and feet chopped off. As a punishment of the contempt you have shown the poor you should be tormented so severely with hunger that you would begin to eat your own dung, and suffer such a thirst that you would drink your own urine. You would become so loathsome in the sight of men, whose favour you sought more than mine, that even your dearest friends would flee from you; you would stink in their nostrils like a carcase, so that they would rather hear that you were dead than that you were still living. Because you have taken the goods of others all your limbs should be cut one from another, and a very sharp saw should without ceasing saw through your flesh. For your great anger you would deserve that the devils should take you into their mouths and chew you like corn that is ground into flour, and without ceasing you would wish for death, but without being able to die, and constantly you would be crushed and constantly live on, for ever to endure the same punishment.

But God is not only just, He is also, and in particular, merciful. As always with Bridget the trumpets of the heavenly organ fall silent at last, and gently and soothingly sounds the *Vox coelestis*:

I am so just that I will not wrong even the Devil. But I am also ready to have mercy on every repentant sinner. Just as you have sinned hitherto with your limbs, so you must now do penance with all of them. Let your mouth refrain from all needless speech, your eyes look only at what it is needful to see, let your ears be closed to slander and detraction, your hands be open to give alms to the poor, your knees bow before them when you wash their feet, your body abstain from costly food which excites wantonness, and in your garments let there not be a single thread that speaks of vanity, but let everything be useful and necessary, nothing superfluous.(4)

When you have read outbursts like these of Bridget's fiery soul, you understand what happened once to Prior Petrus and his namesake Master Peter of Skänninge. It was during the first period in Rome, while Bridget and her escort were still staying in the Cardinal's palace next to San Lorenzo in Damaso. It was in the twilight, and the two ecclesiastics were sitting in a room directly above Bridget's apartment, and talking about the events of the day, mostly no doubt about her, who was now engaged in prayer in the room beneath them. And then something extraordinary happened—up through the floor a flame seemed to dart, and this flame darted up to the ceiling, went through the roof, then sank down between them and vanished.(5) The two priests looked at each other in silence—they understood that what they had seen was the flame from Bridget's soul.

XIII

Bridget and her escort shook the dust of Cyprus from off their feet and departed ere the punishing judgments could come. They may have had time for a prayer by the well where Saint Barnabas suffered martyrdom—the heathen threw him down into it, but he faithfully carried on his breast the holy Gospel, written by Matthew—the Gospel which he had preached together with Paul, both on his native island of Cyprus and in Pamphylia and in Antioch.*

The voyage from Cyprus was made in the wake of the Apostles— like Paul Bridget seems also to have landed in Syracuse, again like him, she may have 'tarried there three days.' She probably knew nothing about Archimedes and his circles, she did not visit the ruins of the Greek amphitheatre, and she did not—like Shelley—drink of the spring of Arethusa. But she would kneel in the catacombs by the church of San Giovanni. In those days there was not that gruesome exhibition of dead Capuchins which is now—as under the church in the Piazza Barberini in Rome—shown to tourists. But Bridget would pray in the catacomb chapel where Paul had said a Mass of thanksgiving for a sea voyage successfully ended. This is the tale of the local tradition. But of course, in Syracuse as elsewhere, in the places that Bridget came to, there would be a learned gentleman who would throw doubt on the

---

* Acts of the Apostles, ch. xiii. Later is quoted ch. xxviii, 12: 'And when we were come to Syracuse, we tarried there three days.'

pious traditions. Here it was a prior from a monastery on Mount Etna, he did not believe in either Saint Barnabas in the well or in the relics of Peter and Paul in the catacombs. Why should God have left them lying there so long, without anyone knowing it? Bridget referred to the forty years of Israel in the desert—a long time had to pass, too, before the bodies of the Apostles received the honour due to them. And the angels had always known where they were, and had shown them homage. There was always forgiveness of sins for the pious pilgrim, even at the graves of unknown saints! The sceptical prior listened to Bridget, he took her words to heart. Immediately after he had to go to Rome—'and there he heard, three nights running, a voice that cried to him: "Hasten, hasten, come, come!" But on the fourth day he fell ill, received the Sacraments and died.'(1)

Perhaps the plague was the cause of this sudden death. For the Black Death was raging again, the talk was of nothing else, that now so-and-so was taken ill, so-and-so was dead, 'sneezing and blaspheming God.' Bridget beheld all these poor souls before the Judge and heard His stern words to them: 'Why did you not repent? Did you not hear what I said?' Yes, the sinner had indeed heard it, but he had not troubled very much about it. 'Have you not heard, then, that I am a stern judge, why did you not fear to be condemned?' This, too, the sinner had heard, but he had closed his ears and choked up his heart. Now, when it was too late, his ears and his heart are opened at last— Bridget sees him thrown out of the court room and hears his despairing cry: 'When will my punishment end?' And a voice answers: 'When God no longer exists!'(2)

Bridget came back to Naples in February 1373 and found the capital, prepared by the plague, ready to hear her words. But first she had to be responsible to the ecclesiastical authority and to give an account of what spirit she spoke by and by whose authority. During her sojourn of a month in the Holy Land doubts had arisen about Bridget's mission. The Queen, in particular, had been troubled, and one day she asked Archbishop Bernard of Montauro to come up to the castle to discuss how the Swedish seeress was to be dealt with when she came back. An ecclesiastical commission was appointed—the archbishop presiding; among the other members there were three masters of theology, the Dominican, Nicholas Misquini, the Franciscan, Brother Leonard, and the Augustinian, Brother Francis of Foligno, besides two doctors of canonical law. Nicholas Misquini was Inquisitor for the kingdom of the Two Sicilies and later became a cardinal. In his testimony, given in

1380, he gives a vivid description of the commission's treatment of Bridget. The ecclesiastical gentlemen called upon her in the hostelry where she had put up, and found her lying in bed in a modest room, probably ill after the sea voyage. The archbishop took the lead— after a few pleasant words as an introduction and a greeting from the Queen, he asked whether anything had been revealed to Bridget in the Holy Land, and whether they might be allowed to know it. Bridget confirmed both questions and it was now decided that she was to speak in public, as at Famagusta. The archbishop, the three masters of theology, the two doctors of canon law, were to be present—besides a large number of persons invited, members of distinguished families.

Then the great day came. Bridget had written down the message which God had given her for the people of Naples, and the faithful Alphonsus had translated it into Latin. It is he, too, who now stands beside her, and it is he who at her request reads to the people what she has to say on God's behalf. She does not speak herself.(3)

First there is an introduction—the message that she has now to bring to the people of Naples she must not bring for the sake of gaining honour and praise, nor may she withhold it from fear of the scorn and contempt of men. For many years pious friends of God in Naples have prayed to God that the Neapolitans might repent—their prayers have been heard. He has therefore now sent His words by Bridget.

Like the first revelation she received so many years ago, this one also begins with the same majestic words: *Ego sum Creator omnium.* It is Bridget's fundamental idea, she therefore returns to it again and again—God is the Creator. 'I am the Creator of all things and Lord of all, of devils as well as of angels, and none shall escape my judgment.' But there was one of His creatures who rose up against Him—the Devil. The Devil's sin was threefold, it was pride, it was envy, it was self-will. So proud was he that he would be the master and God was to be his subject. So envious that he would have killed God so that he might sit on His throne. And so dear was his own will to him that he did not care about God's will if only he could fulfil his own. Because of these three sins he was thrust down from heaven, and from being an angel he became a devil.

Then God creates man and gives them His commandments—'so that they may be pleasing to me and displease the Devil.' Man sins— 'but because I loved man so much I came into the world and took bodily form of the Virgin, taught them personally by word and deed, the true way of salvation and opened heaven to them with my blood.'

Bridget has said this again and again, but she does not think she has said it enough. For again *God's Lament* rises in her soul: 'How do men treat Me now? They despise My commandments, they cast Me out of their hearts like the worst venom and poison, they spit Me out of their mouths like a rotten mouthful which is just as loathsome to them to see as if I were a stinking leper!'

The Devil, on the other hand—he is liked by men, to him they open their hearts, they follow his inspirations, gladly do his will. But the punishment will come—'because of their pride such people shall have everlasting disgrace, for their avarice the Devil shall fill them with his poison, so that in their souls there is no place that is not saturated with that devilish poison, because of the lechery with which they burned like unreasoning animals they shall never behold My face.'

Bridget now speaks of two sins that are particularly rife in Naples. The first is that the women paint their faces in order to look more beautiful than God has made them. The second is that men and women wear close-fitting costumes so that they may look more sensually enticing (a modern writer would say have more *sex appeal*). 'But of a surety they must know that so often as those women paint their faces, just so often will the presence of the Holy Spirit be diminished in their souls, and as often as they put on this immodest attire, just as often will the beauty of their souls be lessened.' They could not do this if they thought but for a moment of Christ's Passion. And now *Golgotha* again rises before Bridget's vision.

Oh you, who are not My friends [she hears the Saviour cry]. Why have you not thought of My suffering? Why were you heedless how I stood naked and bound to the pillar of shame and was scourged so cruelly, and how I hung naked on the cross, covered with wounds and clothed in blood? When you smear your faces you do not think of My visage that was all over blood, you do not see My eyes that were full of blood and tears, and My wan eyelids. You do not see before you My mouth, My ears, My beard which was stained with blood, nor My body and all its limbs that were so cruelly maltreated. You do not think of all the pain and torment that I had to suffer, and how I hung there, blue and bleeding for your sakes, and left by you to be mocked and despised by all, so that you might come to love Me, your God, and escape the snares of the devil in which you are caught.

But all these things are forgotten, unseen by your eyes and out of your minds. And you do as harlots do, and like the women who love the lust of the flesh but will not bear children. For when they feel that the child is living in their womb, they take a decoction of certain herbs so that they may have a miscarriage, and not miss the lust of their flesh, but still continue in their life of sin. So likewise do you, for as soon as you feel the inspiration of the Holy Spirit in your hearts, or you have heard a good sermon and would like to be better, you immediately kill the fetus conceived, saying that your sins cannot be so bad, and after all they were really so sweet. I stand at the door and knock, but you do not open to Me; however, if the devil comes, you open the door to him. Thus you are without Me, and I without you, for you are in the devil whose will you do, and whose incitements you follow.

This was the judgment. Perhaps Alphonsus paused here in his reading and looked at the archbishop, at the three masters of theology, the two doctors of canon law—and behind them the rest of the audience, ladies with painted faces and close-fitting bodices *ad ostentationem mamillarum* ('to show the breasts'), the knights in costly attire—will this be allowed to pass? But Bridget stands at his side, small and intrepid. And he reads on—'this was the judgment, now comes the message of mercy. "If any one will repent I will run to meet him, as the father to the prodigal son, and I will show mercy to him, and I shall be in him and he shall be in Me in everlasting joy."'

The last words are again threatening:

My justice shall come upon all those who harden themselves in their sin. The fisherman by the seashore throws out his hook and catches first one fish, then another. So shall I do to those who are not My friends. Soon I shall come and take them away from this world, where they feel so well pleased. In the hour when they least think of it I will take them away from this life and send them into everlasting death.(4)

Et mittam eos in mortem aeternam. The speech rang out with these words, and now the ecclesiastical examination began. 'In whose spirit and power do you say this to us?' asked the archbishop. Alphonsus was frightened, he saw already the prison of the Inquisition before him, torture and death at the stake. But Bridget stood intrepid, 'for she was filled with the love that drives out fear.' Nicholas Misquini could still, as a cardinal, remember how 'humbly and delicately and wisely' Bridget had explained to the archbishop in what manner Christ had revealed Himself to her. And then she spoke herself. Then she gave up her manuscript to the archbishop, and nothing untoward happened to Bridget.(5) The brilliant gathering of grand ladies and gentlemen went home, rather as though after a Lenten sermon by a famous preacher.

XIV

Bridget's fame was now established, her popularity greater than ever. She was sought by high and low, they begged for her intercession, for a miracle, sought her spiritual guidance, now and then also temporal protection—for Bridget knew the Queen. Very often it was ecclesiastics, even prelates of high rank, who came and asked Bridget for advice on spiritual matters. There was, for instance, the governor of the province of Mark of Ancona; he was a bishop, but had left his bishopric to occupy the greater position of papal vice-gerent. Had he been right in doing so? Bridget does not choose her words in giving her answer—or rather, she chooses the plainest ones. If anyone, she says, leaves his work as a bishop because of ambition or other worldly motives, he is to be likened to *a swine in clerical vestments*! She has a story to tell about it, and it was as follows:

> A great lord had invited his friends to a banquet. But when the banquet was ready and the king and his friends were already sitting at the table, a herd of swine came into the banqueting hall, dressed like ecclesiastics. The master of the house was forbearing enough not to drive out the grunting herd, but served them with the costly dishes standing on the table. But with loud screams the uninvited guests protested—hunc, hunc, hunc—we want pigs' food! Then the master of the house was angry and bade his servants drive out the animals so that they could get their usual food, 'for they are not worthy to eat of the food that I have prepared for my friends!'

But what is the papal vice-gerent really to learn from this parable? Bridget does not say. She concludes her letter with some advice in general terms—he must stay where he can do most good, whether it be as bishop or vice-gerent. And she finishes the letter with a pious curtsey: 'Excuse my writing such things to you; I am but an ignorant woman and a great sinner.'(1)

To the Archbishop of Naples she writes in a different strain, for it is not she herself who writes but the Queen of Heaven. 'I who speak to thee,' she hears Mary say,

> am in this world like the master of a garden. When the good master gardener sees bad weather coming he comes quickly and binds the young shoots and scions fast to the trunk, so that the storm cannot break them. So also do I, the Mother of Mercy, in the garden of this world. For when I see the Devil blow harmful despair and evil wrath into the hearts of men, I run quickly to my Son, and beg Him to send the Holy Spirit, that they may stand firm and not give way to the might of temptation, so that the Devil cannot break their souls and tear them up by the roots from the state of grace. But they who disdain to accept my Son's spiritual help, they will be bent by the

storm of temptation and torn up from the state of grace, and be led by the
Devil through inordinate desires into the everlasting darkness.

Mary falls silent, and now it is Bridget who speaks—'the person
whom you know so well.' 'You must know,' she writes to the
archbishop,

> that here in this city of Naples many terrible things happen. To-day, however,
> I will speak only of two sins that are common. The first is that many men
> and women run for advice and help to those accursed witches and sorceresses
> —some that they may have children, others to win the love of a man or
> woman, others again to know what the future will bring or to be healed
> of their diseases. But all who do this or who have dealings with such
> witcheries or sorceries, and all who harbour or shelter those who do this
> or trust in them are hated and accursed in the sight of God.

This is one the of great sins of Naples—it is a sin against God. The
other is a sin against one's neighbour. Bridget does not go about with
her eyes closed, and she has already earlier spoken of the scandal in a
Christian country of keeping slaves. In Sweden bondage had been
abolished, 'for Christ was sold and then redeemed all Christians.'(2)
Here, in Naples, the Christians were no better than the Mussulmans, in
keeping female slaves like harlots and overburdening the male slaves
with work, reviling them and beating them so that in despair more
than one of them committed suicide. These sins greatly displease God
and the whole of His heavenly host, for God loves all human beings,
He has created them all and has redeemed them all by His Passion and
His Cross.

'But you must also know'—Bridget says to the archbishop—

> that the master who buys pagans and infidels with the intention of making
> them Christians and bringing them up in the Christian faith and Christian
> virtues, and then setting them free, either while the master is still living
> or doing so by his testament, so that they do not become the property of his
> heirs—he who does this is greatly pleasing to God and will be rewarded by
> Him.(3)

This is the language of the North, spoken by Bridget—the *Christian*
North.

XV

Oh my God, it happens at times, that from a black furnace issues a fair
flame, with which many beautiful things may be wrought. Yet the black
furnace should not be praised for this, but He who bestows upon mankind
the perfect will to do what is good.(1)

With these words Bridget is thinking of herself. She had earlier
called herself 'a runner in the service of a great Lord.' In the East she
had seen 'the big, strong camels, carrying heavy burdens in the service
of their master' and had felt like an ant among all the great lords
around her.(2) Now she is still less—only a sooty forge in a smithy—
but the flame is clear and strong.

For what did she not have to hear in Naples? Gregory XI had not
come before the time fixed by Bridget—he was not thinking at all of
leaving Avignon. And why not? Yes, said Bridget's Neapolitan
friends, it was the king of France (Charles V, called the Wise) and the
French cardinals who were against it. And what was worse—the Pope
paid heed to the forecasts brought to him by various persons, and which
were all agreed that he was to stay in France. It was as in the days of
the prophet Jeremiah, Bridget thought, when the king of Israel listened
to the false prophets instead of listening to Jeremiah, and he was
punished by being taken captive and his people taken into bondage.
'But now, whether it be sages or interpreters of dreams or worldly-
minded friends of Pope Gregory'—said Christ to Bridget—'who
advise him not to set out, I am stronger than them all, and I will take
the Pope to Rome. But whether you are to see this or not, you are not
to learn this now.'(3)

Perhaps Bridget is not to see Gregory in Rome. But in a vision she
sees him stand before the throne of the heavenly Judge, and she hears
Him who sits on the throne speaking stern words to him.

Pope Gregory, hearken to what I will say to you and mark My words well.
What have you against Me? Why do you make bold to set yourself up
against Me? Your Curia is an enemy of My court here in heaven. Not only
do you rob Me of my sheep, but you take the goods of the Church and give
them to your worldly friends. I have made My will known to you through
the letters you have received from Rome [Bridget's two communications,
the first brought by Latino Orsini, the second by Niccolà Orsini]. Have you
perhaps even thanked Me for them? But I know the reason why you behave
like this—it is because the greatest pride prevails in the Curia. And not only
pride but insatiable avarice and the lechery and the abysmal simony that
are an abomination to Me. Countless are the souls that you steal from Me,
for you send nearly all who come to the Curia to the fire of hell; you do
not keep watch as you ought over the conduct of those who are under you
and do not correct them. But although I could condemn you for all this I
will be merciful and warn you yet once more, and advise you on what is
for the salvation of your soul—namely this: You must go to Rome as quickly
as you can, yet I leave it to yourself to choose the time. But the sooner you
come the more will the virtues and gifts of the Holy Spirit inflame your

soul—therefore come and do not delay. And do not come with the usual worldly splendour, but come in humility and love. And when you have come cleanse away all the vices of the Roman Curia. Pay no heed to your worldly-minded friends, do not fear, show yourself a man and begin to renew my Church which I have bought with My blood, so that it may be born again and return to its former state. For now it is rather to be reckoned as a brothel than as our Holy Mother, the Church.

It is as though one heard once more the voice of Joachim of Fiore and the voices from Monte Majella—the dream that failed with Cola di Rienzo. Then Bridget continues:

But this you shall know of a surety, that if you do not obey My will judgment will be passed upon you as upon a prelate who is degraded and deprived of his ecclesiastical vestments. Everything that has formerly been peace and honour to you shall then be damnation and shame. And every devil in hell shall have a piece of your soul and fill it with everlasting damnation.

The letter rings with promises of mercy if Gregory obeys—'then I will bless you and I will Myself clothe you in the papal vesture, and you shall be in Me and I in you, and you shall enter into everlasting glory.'(4) This letter too (written in February 1373) was sent to Avignon; it was Alphonsus of Jaen who undertook the dangerous mission and the long journey. He was not to return until after Bridget's death. Later she sent him one more letter which he was to deliver to Gregory—it will be mentioned presently. It may have been during this long sojourn at the papal court that Alphonsus found a vent for his feeling of scandal by composing that Mass in honour of 'Our Lady Simony,' which was found among his papers after his death. It is a bitter parody on the Mass in honour of the Blessed Virgin; the introduction is the same as in Bridget's *Revelationes* ('it seemed to a person who was not sleeping, but was keeping watch') and the content does not differ from what she says in the threatening letters to the various popes. Alphonsus, however, found it advisable not to include the Mass of Simony among the *Revelationes*.(5)

In spite of everything, however, Bridget did not agree at all with the extreme Franciscans. No pope could be more hated by these pugnacious sons of the peaceful Saint Francis than John XXII—it was he who had ended the lengthy dispute about Christ's poverty by declaring that the Saviour *had* had certain humble belongings. It is in Jerusalem that a Franciscan comes and consults Bridget—are the Spirituals right when they say that John XXII is in hell? Bridget lays the matter before the Blessed Virgin, who answers that in the first place Bridget need not know where the said pope is in the life beyond, nor with what list of sins he has been brought to judgment. (In most other cases Bridget is well informed on this matter.) In the next place, concerning the decree on the poverty of Christ—that it was in fact not so absolute as the Spirituals asserted—this decree contains nothing that deviates from the Catholic Faith, and is not heretical. Mary herself can bear witness to it—'for my Son had that vesture which I had woven for Him myself, and for which the soldiers cast lots.' And with the most desirable clearness the dividing line is now drawn between Bridget and the later reformers. 'You must know,' the Blessed Virgin says to her, 'that all those who say that the Pope is not the true Pope, and that the lawfully ordained priests are not true priests, and that the Mass they celebrate is not valid—all those who preach such doctrines are inspired by the devil.'(6) It is the office, not the person, that matters. Simoniacs and fornicators sit on the Chair of Peter—judge them not therefore according to their deeds but according to their preaching. Bridget's faith rests on this tenet.

Bridget was not to live to see Gregory XI return to the Eternal City, led by Catherine of Siena. Nor was she to experience the Great Schism and the cleavage in the Church in the sixteenth century. But beyond all of it, out in the furthest horizon of history, a vision stood before Bridget's eyes. 'I beheld from the Pope's palace in Rome to Castel Saint Angelo and from that to the Hospital of Santo Spirito and back again to Saint Peter's as it were a wide plain, and the plain was surrounded by a very strong wall. And I heard a voice that said: "The Pope who loves the Bride with the love of Christ and His holy friends shall live here with his counsellors and shall rule the Church of God in freedom and peace".'(7)

XVI

Bridget had made peace with Urban's soul, and there was one more with whom she became reconciled: Queen Giovanna. Away in the Holy Land Bridget had thought of the beautiful sinner—she had even brought home a gift for her, a little gold cross,(1) bought in the long bazaar street leading down to the square before the church of the Holy Sepulchre, where there is still in our own times a large number of booths with Byzantine icons and mother-of-pearl crosses from Bethlehem—the Russian pilgrims were the best customers in these shops. It is scarcely probable that Giovanna, in the absence of her pious friend, would seriously obey her admonition to lead a more modest life—she would paint her face and wear tight-fitting clothes that showed her beautiful figure. And yet—and yet Bridget could not give her up. There was something about these worldly women—Blanca, Eleanor, Giovanna—that attracted Bridget, could she not overcome their worldliness? And Giovanna—to her Bridget was Karl's mother, and she really knew so little about Karl and wanted to hear much more about him. It ended in her actually inviting Bridget to stay with her in the city of Aversa where she had a villa—it would be good for Bridget to have a little rest after the exertions of the Holy Land and the tiring sea voyage. Bridget accepted the invitation and stayed with her 'for several days.'(2)

During this visit Giovanna understood that her guest was short of money. Bridget travelled with a big escort and it is hardly likely that they all benefited by the Queen's hospitality. The hostel in Naples had to be paid and neither Birger nor his mother had the means required. Giovanna then offered to help—but could Bridget accept money from her son's mistress? In a revelation, however, Christ advises her to do so, 'You shall accept the Queen's gift with love and reverence, and you shall pray for her that she may come to the love of God. For it is written: no good deed will be forgotten by God.'(3)

It was of course soon rumoured in Naples that *la Santa* was staying out at Aversa as the Queen's guest, and seemed to be in great favour with her. And there were some who profited by it, among them the aforesaid Antonio di Carleto, who aspired to the post of director of the Customs. He applied to Bridget and she made a note of his name, as she always did in such cases, and promised to speak for him to the Queen.(4) It was one of the few cases in which Bridget acted without having first consulted God—and scarcely had she done so before she felt the peculiar smell of sulphur which told her that what she had done was displeasing to God. She went again to the Queen and asked her to let Messer Antonio stay in the position he had, and this was done.(5)

And so the saint bade the sinner farewell. Bridget was not to see Giovanna take the part of the anti-Pope Robert of Geneva, nor that she would be excommunicated by the rightful Pope, Urban VI. Another woman saint, Catherine of Siena, took Bridget's place and was not more successful. The Sienese saint would have gone to Giovanna in Naples together with her Scandinavian namesake, Karin of Vadstena, but Karin would not again look into the eyes that had spellbound her brother, and at the lips that had drawn up his last strength.(6) In 1379

Giovanna had given the anti-Pope, Clement VII, shelter in Naples, in 1381 she was struck by excommunication. For a time she wandered restlessly about in her kingdom, went on a pilgrimage to Monte Sant' Angelo, in whose church she was later to be buried, perhaps in the hope that the bishop of Siponte, Gian Pietro Gallo, who was the General of the Franciscan Order, and was in favour with Urban VI, would be able to raise the excommunication. Instead of this Charles of Durazzo was crowned king, had her taken prisoner and confined in his castle in Muro Lucano in South Italy. There she was first kept a prisoner for eight months and then, by order of the king, strangled in her bed (12 May 1382). On the night of her death she is said to have cried with a loud voice, so loud that it could be heard all over the country: 'I am innocent, I am innocent!' He who on dark nights, when the moon is not shining, passes the old castle, can still hear her screaming from the prison tower and crying for vengeance. And every year, on the night when she was killed, the bells in the adjacent convent ring of themselves for a burial, and dead priests sing in the church the requiem for the soul of Queen Giovanna.(7)

XVII

Bridget departed from Naples for the third and last time, but her memory lived long after her. In spite of everything she had not spoken to deaf ears. It can certainly be considered a result of her efforts against the keeping of slaves by Christians, that Queen Giovanna, directly after Bridget's departure, ransomed 'a Turkish woman' and sent her as a gift of friendship to the Swedish saint. It is said of this Turkish woman in the records of Vadstena: 'in her youth she was carried away by Christians from her country and taken to Naples, where she was given to the queen, who was named Johanna, and who immediately decided that she was to be given to Sancta Bridget who was then in Rome, and bestowed her upon the latter. But before she reached Rome Sancta Bridget was already dead.' Later the Turkish woman came to Vadstena and died there as Sister Caterina Magnus' daughter.(1)

At the last moment, almost on the gangway, Bridget worked a parting miracle. She had decided to make her journey home by way of Nola, where she had been before with her good friend Niccolà Orsini, not only for his sake, but to pray at the grave of Saint Paulinus —that pious bishop to whom the Christian world owes *the church bells* (which are therefore in Italian called *campane*; Nola being situated in

Campania). Alphonsus of Jaen had gone before, and one evening in the Palazzo Orsini—at the present day still one of the most beautiful buildings in Nola—Messer Niccolà placed before his ecclesiastical friend a ticklish matter which he was not able to deal with himself. It was concerned with one of his servants, a woman named Picciolella, the widow of a certain Spizzocchi. Picciolella was at an advanced age, not beautiful, and like her late husband, was of good repute. One day she had come to Messer Niccolà and had asked for permission to speak to him, and then she had told him a terrible story—she had intercourse every night with a devil! He was like a big, strong man, who came to her and took her by force. She could not see him, everything took place in the dark. She had had a suspicion of several of her neighbours, and through a third person she had begged them to cease these nocturnal visits, but they had all proved their alibi, and sworn that it was not they. Picciolella had then taken practical measures, had firmly secured all the doors, asked her women neighbours to keep watch with her— of no use. The women fell asleep and the devil turned up. Then she called in masculine help, of men who were to watch and keep the women awake—then the evil spirit came in with such noise and rumbling that they all fled and he was left alone with Picciolella. At last the poor widow had sought help of a priest—Messer Niccolà knew him well, he was the parish priest in Castrolauri, here in the diocese of Nola—he had given her a paper on which he had written some cabalistic flourishes, and told her to wear the paper in her hair. The devil had perhaps come less frequently than before, but anyhow he had come. 'Now the woman has come to me in her distress,' Messer Niccolà had said in conclusion, 'she believes me to be wiser than I really am. What is to be done, Father Alphonsus?'(2)

There was only one thing to be done, to send Picciolella to Bridget who was still in Naples. And Bridget knew what to do. As late as in the seventeenth century there were still in Sweden women who believed that they had carnal intercourse with the demon Lioten or Liothan— and at home in East Gothland Bridget had had to do with a woman who received nightly visits of an *incubus*.(3) She received Picciolella with kindness and asked her at once whether she had not used superstitious means. At first the Italian woman denied this, but then admitted it. 'Throw that rubbish away—a Christian must not be super- stitious,' said Bridget, and then sent her to confession and Communion. 'And she who had come to Naples in sorrow, went back to Nola with joy,' Niccolà Orsini concludes his testimony.(4)

In order to confirm Picciolella on the side of what was good Bridget gave her a girdle which she had brought with her from the Holy Land, besides three beads of her rosary, says Magnus Petri.(5) Alphonsus himself also relates this in 1379—moreover, he can remember that Picciolella wore the kerchief characteristic of the district (*il panicuelli*), nor had he forgotten the talk with Messer Niccolà, and the letter which the latter had written to him later on the case.(6)

It was no wonder, then, that after Bridget's departure, and still more after her departure from this earth, that the rumours continued to wreathe her memory with a halo. To the Neapolitan people she was already a saint—they did not wait for the canonization. There were pictures of her in two churches in Naples, Our Lady of Carmel and Sant' Eligio, flowers were taken to them and lighted tapers.(7) At last the archbishop found that there was occasion to institute an inquiry and entrusted it to the judge Carlo de Frisone. In the letter with which the archbishop authorizes him to carry out this commission, he speaks himself of the time when Bridget lived in Naples and 'gave Us and the people of Naples much good advice.' She was like a candle lit in the 'last days of this evil world,' and this candle ought now to be set in a candlestick. For two entire months Carlo de Frisone now carries on his inquiry; he visits all the persons who had, directly or indirectly, been in communication with Bridget, examines them and has their testimony written down by a notary accompanying him.

There was, for instance, Palmerio, the cloth dealer. He had not known Bridget himself, but his wife had, and once, when Palmerio had fallen very dangerously ill, she went to Bridget for help. Bridget prayed and the man recovered. Then there was Maria, married to a Spaniard—she had even (probably as a servant) been with *la Santa* in the Holy Land. When she came home from the pilgrimage she had the idea that her daughter was to enter a convent. The daughter refused and when Bridget was consulted she gave the answer: 'You will never see your daughter a nun, nor will she be married.' This was proved to be true, for the daughter was suddenly taken ill and died. Then there was a man whose wife had left him, she had gone home to her mother and had taken the furniture with her—Bridget prayed and the man received back both his wife and the furniture.

But all these cases were only trifles. The great proof of the impression Bridget had left behind her in Naples, and of the mighty power wielded by her memory, even after her death, and especially after her death, was given in the reconciliation effected by her between two contending families in Naples and recorded in the annals of the city. The houses of di Costanzo and Mormile, Neapolitan equals by birth of the Montagues and Capulets of Verona, had kept up a bloody feud since 1303. In vain had Queen Giovanna, the King of Hungary, nay, even the Pope himself, tried to mediate between them. In order to prevent further bloodshed Queen Giovanna had at last had the whole family of Mormile imprisoned, and in the prison the head of the family, whose name was Andriolo, fell ill of bubonic plague. When he felt that death was drawing near he sent for a priest. The latter admonished him that above all he would have to forgive his enemies, the family of di Costanzo—yes, he was quite willing to do this, if he regained his health! Now among the sick man's friends who came to visit him there was that Antonio di Carleto who had known Bridget—when she came back from the Holy Land she had given him a little gold cross like that which she had given to Queen Giovanna. Antonio always wore this cross on his person—now he took it out and touched the sick man with it. Scarcely had he done so, however, than Andriolo grew very restless, tossed from one side to the other of the bed and began to shout: 'I am damned, I am damned! I am damned because I did not honestly mean it when I promised the priest to make peace with my enemies. I am damned, I am damned!' Horror-stricken they all stood round the bed of the dying man, and the terrible cries continued a long while. Until the storm suddenly ceased, the cries stopped, the face that had been distorted by the terror of death grew gentle and smiling, and he could be heard whispering softly: 'Is it you, Lady Bridget?' Yes, it was Bridget, who came now when he was hanging over the abyss of perdition—it was she who came in the very last watch of the night, like Beatrice to Dante. It *was* Bridget, not in flesh and blood as he had seen her at Giovanna's court, but radiant in the light of eternity. And the threatening voice from the deep fell silent in the soul of the dying man, and he began to tell how he had seen the Lady Bridget, and that she had driven away the devil. 'And now,' he said to those standing round him, 'I want you to send for the whole family of di Costanzo. They must all come and then we will make peace.' And immediately the whole family of di Costanzo came, and with tears of joy they signed their names to this reconciliation 'in the name of the blessed Lady Bridget.' But Andriolo recovered and he had a picture painted of the Blessed Lady Bridget in the church of Our Lady of Carmel.(8)

When these lines were put on record (8 November 1376) only

three years had passed since Bridget's death. Andriolo Mormile still lived a long time; after the banishment of Giovanna he obtained a high position at the court of Carlo of Durazzo, became a wealthy man, who could lend Carlo of Durazzo's son Ladislaus a sum so considerable as 9,000 ducats, for which he received the royal castle of Castelnuovo as a mortgage. Later he even became viceroy of the province of the Abruzzi, with the right to exact toll at all the mountain passes in this part of the Apennines. At peace with God and his neighbour Messer Andriolo died in 1393 or thereabouts, and no doubt in his last hour he would think with gratitude of 'the blessed Lady Bridget.'(9)

BOOK VIII

'NUN AND MOTHER IN VADSTENA'

Amodo reputaberis non solum sponsa mea,
sed etiam monacha et mater in Watsteno.

Processus, p. 506

'Thou shalt not only be counted as my bride,
but also a nun and mother in Vadstena.'

Ego sum Brigida quae de Roma veni!
'I am Bridget, who have come back from
Rome!'

ONCE more Bridget was back in Francesca Papazuri's house on the Campo de' Fiori. She was again in Rome and it was the season of Lent. Easter of that year fell as late as 17 April, and on the hills of Rome and round the old churches flowers and blossoms showed that spring had already long since come. Once more, for the last time, leaning on her pilgrim staff, or on Karin's arm and followed by Prior Olaus, by the chaplain Magnus Petri or by Alphonsus (would she accept his sweets during Lent?) Bridget walked the old and loved way to the *churches of the stations.*

In Rome of the Middle Ages there was, for every day in Lent, a fixed church to which all the priests of the Roman parishes repaired to hold service. These churches were called—by a military expression— *stationes;* their names can be read in the Roman Missal. In modern Rome this custom has not yet fallen wholly into disuse. On the days of their station the churches concerned are adorned as for a feast. The pillars are draped with scarlet, the mosaic floor is strewn with twigs of box, and the acrid smell of the crushed leaves mingles with the sweet fragrance of incense from the altar, where the candles burn in clear golden flames while High Mass is sung.

Yet once more, for one last time, Bridget made these devotions. On Ash Wednesday the road led to Santa Maria in Cosmedin by the temple of Vesta, and then up the steep hill of the Aventine to Santa Sabina. Santa Sabina was the chief church of the Dominicans; in the adjoining monastery is shown the cell in which 'the holy men, Dominic, Francis and Angelus the Carmelite spent the nights conversing about the things that are of the kingdom of God.' Bridget would not be able to set foot in this cell, but in the garden she had stood in front of the orange tree which the Spaniard had planted with his own hands, and her thoughts may have gone home to Skara, to the Dominican monastery there, and to Brother Algot whose soul had ascended to heaven like a star.(1)

And every day in the long season of Lent leads the pilgrims to new holy places. To San Giorgio in Velabro, 'in the swamp' down by the Janus temple (which is no Janus temple, but the gate of honour built by the money-changers in Rome for Septimius Severus and his sons). On another day they went to San Gregorio Magno, where the home of the great Pope stood—Bridget can still remember when she was there for the first time, it was in the year of Jubilee, they stood in the room where the great Pope daily fed twelve poor people, there are twelve crosses hewn in the marble table. One day a thirteenth beggar appeared, Gregory fed also this unbidden guest, and it was an angel. . . . Day after day, morning after morning, Bridget paid her visits to these churches, wandering to Santa Pudenziana, to Santa Prassede (outside which she once found the Norwegian woman lying on the ground—'do you remember, Magnus Petri, that you helped me to drag her to the hospital?'), to San Sisto out on the Via Appia, to the old Porta Latina, where John the Apostle, under Domitian's persecution, was thrown into a vessel of boiling oil, but could not die. Was it here, perhaps, in the little church of San Giovanni *in oleo*, that Bridget heard the Blessed Virgin praise John—'you were nearer to me than the other apostles; you did not flee, but remained bravely standing by my side under the cross; my Son's Passion was of greater bitterness to you than to the others; you lived longer than the others, and your long life can be called a martyrdom.'(2)

During Lent Bridget did not take part in any worldliness, but she seems to have made an exception for Gomez Albornoz—she accepted an invitation to dine with him. She had never seen this spiritual son of hers, and now he had even let his family come to Rome from Soleto, so that Bridget might make the acquaintance of all of them. He put up at the papal palace adjoining Saint Peter's and at the festive table were not only Bridget and Karin but the three confessors, Magnus Petri and the whole *famiglia*. After the dinner Gomez had a private talk with Bridget and told her of his difficulties. Bridget gave him answers to everything but then said: 'Was there not anything more?' Yes, there *was* more—the Spanish soldier now admitted his most secret sins, and Bridget promised to pray for him. She did so and afterwards dictated a letter to Alphonsus, which he was to give to Gomez (we have not this letter).(3)

Soon after this letter Alphonsus must have gone to Avignon with the letter to Gregory. No effect of it could be traced. In Naples Niccolà Orsini's eldest son, Robert, had one day, with perhaps a rather youthfully supercilious air, said to Bridget that after all there was nobody who believed that Gregory XI could come to Rome—he was far too comfortable in Avignon! Bridget flared up: 'And I tell you, Robert, that the Pope *will come* to Rome and you will come to see it yourself!' Five years later Bridget's words were fulfilled—Robert

Orsini was not only present when the Pope rode from San Paolo into Rome, but it was he who led the Pope's steed by the bridle.(4)

In order to hasten the coming of this great day Bridget had once more, for the last time, to speak to Gregory's heart. She does so in a letter of July 1373 to her friend Alphonsus in Avignon. Gregory had a vacillating disposition, as Catherine of Siena was to learn later. He was not much inclined to set out for warlike Italy, where Bernabò Visconti was still fighting against him. The papal troops had now, under Amedeo of Savoy, won a great victory over the tyrant of Milan—ought the Pope to take advantage of this victory to make peace with Visconti? And how was he to deal with France, where Charles V had just deprived the ecclesiastical courts of the right to pass sentence in matters of inheritance?(5) Such were the doubts which Gregory had placed before Bridget.

Bridget cut these Gordian knots with the sword of the Gospel. The war between the Pope and Bernabò was an abomination to God, for many were the souls who perished because of it. It would be better for the Pope to be driven from his country than to take up arms and thereby become the cause of the loss of so many souls. The Pope must humble himself and seize every opportunity of making peace. As for the relations with France, the Pope will be informed about them when he comes to Italy, not before!

For this is the first and the last—*venire Romam*, to come to Rome. Bridget knows that a tug of war is going on about Gregory's soul. Many are pulling at one end of the rope—at the other only one, but Gregory must keep to this single one. 'And I will, therefore, that he must come to Rome now in this approaching spring. For he must know that he can do nothing dearer to me than coming to Italy.'(6)

It was a marching order from heaven. But Gregory did not obey.

II

Bridget was lying in bed and Mass was being said for her in her room. The visits to the churches in Rome were over, and the pilgrim wanderings to San Paolo, to San Lorenzo fuori le mura, to Sant' Agnese were ended. Ended, too, were the visits to Roman friends—one of the last she had seen was Latino Orsini, whom she wished to thank because, once when she was leaving Rome, he had escorted her part of the way. The visit had not passed off pleasantly—the saint had all the time held her hand before her nose and would not speak to Messer Latino. Master

Petrus was present and the Roman nobleman asked him what Bridget meant by her manner. 'She finds that you have a bad smell,' was the answer. Messer Latino could take a hint and confessed that he had dealt harshly with some of his vassals.(1)

Bridget did not visit anyone now any longer. She understood that the end was drawing near. And she wanted the holy sacrifice of the Body and Blood of the Son of God to be offered every morning in her cell. The faith in the real presence of Christ in the Sacrament of the Altar had been one of the corner stones in Bridget's piety. It was this faith that she proclaimed again and again to high and low, to King Magnus as well as to the peasants in Lödöse, who with the realism of peasants thought that a piece of bread was nothing but a piece of bread. Had she not herself seen in the consecrated Host as it were the figure of a Lamb, the Lamb that bore the sins of all the world, and in the Lamb as it were a Face, that Face before which all human souls are one day to stand to be judged?(2)

That was what Bridget had beheld—that was what Bridget had believed—that was what Bridget had taught. And now, when she was herself approaching that meeting with the visage of Christ—what was coming to pass now? It was as though she was again on the road between Alvastra and Vadstena. She beheld again the monk on the ladder, heard again his dry, creaking voice, again she heard his questions, his doubts—but no voice from heaven gave an answer. From her bed she heard Master Petrus saying the Holy Mass, heard his murmuring voice, that sank to a low whisper when he came to the moment of the consecration. Now he bowed his head deep down over the white Host—Bridget no longer heard anything, but she knew what he was saying: *Hoc est enim calix sanguinis mei.* . . . And then the wine in the chalice was the Blood of Christ. . . . Bridget saw the white, round wafer, saw the golden Chalice—but she saw nothing else—neither with the eyes of faith could she see anything else—there was only a small round disc of bread, there was only a golden cup with a little wine in it. . . . Jesus had vanished, His holy Body and Blood were no longer there. . . .

Then Bridget felt the ground sliding away under her, and it was as though she was falling into an abyss. And as she fell she heard the mocking voices of the abyss, the Devil's hard and scoffing voice:

Have you really believed that that piece of bread was God Himself? He would have been eaten up long ago! Besides, there are no sensible people who believe it! Look at the Jews, they are wise people—they do not believe

in that sort of hocus-pocus. Let us talk sense, Bridget. You see this host
with your own eyes, you hear the little crack it gives when the priest breaks
it like another piece of bread—do you really believe that you can break God
in two? Use your common-sense, believe what you can see and hear, and
stop imagining what is impossible!(3)

And as if these doubts of the faith which had sustained Bridget's
whole life were not enough, other temptations arose from the depths
of repressed urges. Her old acquaintance, the demon *Castrimargia* now
stole in upon the woman of seventy and conjured up before her
beautifully decked tables with great joints of roasted meats and wine
in silver cups such as those at home at Ulfåsa. And the happy years of
her married life revived in warm reality—Ulf and she were in their
room, they were playing the sweet games of love, he standing hidden
behind the hangings of the bed, while she lay waiting for his coming.
She had abandoned all of it, she had forsaken Ulf and let him live his
last years in a cold cell of the monastery of Alvastra, and she would not
wear the ring which he had given her on his death-bed. . . . And
the children, had she been a good mother to them, had she not left
them to their own devices, got rid of them as quickly as she could?
Bengt had sickened away in Alvastra, Ingeborg had died in Riseberga,
Cecilia had fled from the convent in Skenninge and had made more or
less unfortunate marriages. Karin—yes, but Karin was quite different,
but only after she had driven her love of Eggert out of her heart
because Bridget had willed it. And Karl, 'the son of tears,' would he
not have turned out quite differently if his mother had stayed at home
and had attended to his bringing up? Birger had given her joy—but
was it not because he was by nature a good child—had she, his mother,
really any merit in it? Bridget had set herself free of all of it to follow
her vocation—that which she believed came from God. Again and
again she had heard it ringing in her soul: 'Through you God will be
made known in the whole world!' Yes, but Bridget would also be
made known thereby—as God's envoy she had stood before popes and
cardinals, before kings and queens and had been honoured like a saint
during her lifetime. She had listened with complacency to Sister
Katherine's prophecy in Vårfruberga * Convent at home in Sweden:
'Even if you are scoffed at now, you shall be honoured later, and
generations in far future times shall praise your name.'(4)

From all corners of the world the storm raged about Bridget—
doubts, sensuality, pride, all the waves of the abyss roared about her.

* Vårfruberga—Our Lady's Mount.—Tr.

'Why must all these temptations torment me now?' she cried to heaven —'I have never felt them so strong before, neither in my youth nor during the time when I was married.' Mary answers: 'This comes upon you so that you may learn that without God's help you are nothing, and if my Son did not stand by you there would not be any sin which you could not commit.' And now the Blessed Virgin gives Bridget the same advice that every confessor gives every penitent that is tormented by temptations. 'The Devil,' she says,

> is like a scout who tries to find a way into the soul and to prevent men from praying. But do not be troubled about him. Whatever temptation may visit you do not cease praying—and if you cannot pray then try at any rate to do so, and the attempt will be counted as a deed fulfilled. And if impure thoughts torment you and you cannot drive them away although you try, they shall not be counted to you as a sin, if only you do not consent to them.(5)

Bridget followed this heavenly psychotherapy. Outwardly she preserved a perfect calm, no one suspected the storms raging in her soul. As late as in 1415 an English pilgrim (Margery Kempe), who visited the house on Campo de' Fiori, heard from Bridget's old servant, Katerina of Flanders, that her mistress 'had been gentle and kind to everyone and always shown a smiling face.'(6)

Perhaps this smiling face deceived the physicians—five days before Bridget's death they still said to each other that she would probably recover. The Blessed Virgin corrected this statement of the physicians— 'they don't know what they are saying'—Bridget no longer needed any earthly medical remedies. 'You ask me,' Mary says later, 'why this illness has lasted so long'—for Bridget had been ailing ever since Jerusalem. 'It is because my Son and I love you. Have you forgotten what my Son said to you in Jerusalem, that when you stepped into the church of the Holy Sepulchre all your sins were forgiven you, and you became like a child that has just been lifted up from the font of baptism? But He did *not* promise you that you should not continue to suffer.' Bridget is anxious about the work of her life—what will happen when she is no longer there herself? All her prophecies are far from being fulfilled. 'Remember what I told you in Stralsund,' Mary answers, and reminds Bridget of the promise which was already given her there on the threshold of exile: 'You shall not see all that you have written in the books of your heavenly revelations become reality, but for the sake of your goodwill you shall be counted a nun in Vadstena, and God will keep all His promises to you.'(7)

Then Christ Himself came and confirmed all His Mother's words, and the mists of doubt were dispelled. Again the Sacrament of the Altar shone like a sun before the eye of faith.

Five days before the death of the Lady Bridget Our Lord Jesus Christ came and stood before the altar in her room and spoke to her with a face of joy: 'I have done with you as the bridegroom does when he hides himself from the bride, so that she may desire him the more greatly. Therefore I did not visit you with my consolation during these latest times, for it was your time of trial. But now you have been tried and it is time for you to make ready. For now shall be fulfilled that which I have promised you, that you shall be clothed in the habit of a nun before my altar, and from henceforth you shall not only be called my bride, but shall also be called a nun and mother in Vadstena. For it is my pleasure that you shall rest now from your labour and I take your goodwill for the deeds. But you must know that your body must remain here in Rome, until it comes to the place which is prepared for it.'

At Bridget's bedside sits Petrus Olai with his writing tablet and takes down her words. Now he hears Christ's lament over Rome: '*Oh Roma mea*, Oh Rome, my Rome, the Pope despises you and does not count my words for anything. Therefore shall he no longer hear the sound of my music.'

Christ's music, that is Bridget—soon she will fall silent. But the revelations which have been given her shall not be forgotten, 'Tell the Prior' (Christ orders) 'that he must deliver everything to my friend the Bishop (Alphonsus). For a generation shall come which will receive my words with joy—another generation than this ungrateful one. And tell Alphonsus that among the last revelations he must put the very first great, general revelation that was given to you in Naples, for there shall be judgment upon all who do not return to me in humility.'(8) Once again, for the last time, the trumpet shall sound before the day of doom.

Then five days more passed, which Bridget spent in preparing herself for death. She was calm, as usual. Understanding and memory were not affected—'as if she were not ill at all, and as if she were not so near to death.' But Bridget was not deceived, she made the last preparations for the great journey. On the four last days still left her to live she no longer took any food, she only took a little water in her mouth to rinse it before Communion, nor would she change her linen.(9) Then one morning Petrus Olai came and gave her Extreme Unction.— The words were said over her, as they had been said over Ulf and over Karl: 'Lord Jesus, who hast spoken by Thy apostle James'—the apostle

James, Saint James of Compostella—in a few days it would be his feast, would he come and take her to the everlasting land of James? Bridget received the unction of blessing upon her eyes, ears, nostrils, mouth, hands and feet, that God might forgive her all that she had sinned by sight, by hearing, by desire, by speech, by the clasp of hands and by the steps of feet. . . .

After the Last Sacraments Bridget lay quiet, she did not expect that the power of the sacraments would restore her to life, as it had done with Ulf in Arras. But at midnight before the fifth day she sent for Karin and asked her to waken the others. About Karin's fate Bridget was not anxious—she had given her into the care of the Queen of Heaven. Karin had left her husband whom she loved more than herself, she had left her brothers and sisters, friends and kinsfolk, that she might help them in a spiritual wise; all her sins were therefore forgiven her, the kingdom of heaven was to be her inheritance, Jesus Christ her Bridegroom. 'Patience and silence,' were Bridget's last words to her daughter. After Karin came Birger—she may have repeated to him what she had already once in a letter admonished him to do:

Very dearest son, always have your Creator's and Redeemer's Passion in your heart; often be ready to receive His holy Body according to the counsel of your confessor. Where you hear that there are poor people help them as you are able—God will reward you for it. Pay well those who have worked for you and chastise your subjects with mildness. When you rise in the morning make the sign of the Cross over your face and heart and say: 'Jesus Nazarenus, King of the Jews, have mercy upon me.' When you hear Mass think of the sore Passion of Our Lord Almighty and your own sins. When you sit at table let your talk be seemly and godly, and beware of the custom of Sweden, for many do not leave the table until they are like grunting pigs. Be loath to mention the devil, but when you must speak or answer, make the sign of the Cross over your heart and say: 'Jesus Christ, Jesus Christ,' then you will find the right words. Fear God in all your works, and when you sit and have to pass judgment yourself, think with care of your words before you speak. Judge your neighbour as you have yourself to be judged by God. If anyone does you a wrong then take refuge in the law of Sweden. If you suffer wrong do not take revenge in anger, but give up your cause to Our Lord Jesus Christ—He will give you better help to gain your right than you can ever think. And with this I commend your life and soul to the Holy Trinity, and to the care of the Blessed Virgin and all the saints in heaven.(10)

Then, after Karin and Birger, came all the other members of the family—she appointed all of them to be present the next morning at Mass.(11) One of them was missing—Alphonsus. But he was acting as Bridget's messenger to Pope Gregory in Avignon.

Then came the last morning. Bridget's bed was made on the table in the middle of the room, at which she had so often sat writing. They were now all gathered round this hard bed—Karin, Birger, Master Peter of Skänninge, Prior Petrus of Alvastra, Sir Magnus Petri, Francesca Papazuri, the Spanish Elvira, Katerina of Flanders, the whole household. Some devout women from the neighbourhood had also slipped in quietly—the Lady Andrea Ottaviani, several of these old women who are always ready when they hear a bell ringing for Mass. At the altar at the foot of the bed stood Prior Petrus saying Mass—it was the feast of Saint Apollinaris, 23 July. In the Gospel for the day it is said: 'At that time Jesus said to His disciples: You are they who have continued with me in my temptations. And I dispose to you as my Father hath disposed to me, a kingdom: that you may eat and drink at my table in my kingdom and may sit upon thrones, judging the twelve tribes of Israel.' * Did Bridget hear the words? she too, had persevered through all temptations—she too, had been a judge in Israel. . . .

But when Prior Petrus lifted up the Sacred Host, the invitation to the heavenly banquet came to Bridget: 'You shall come to your convent, that is: you shall enter into the joy of your Lord. And your body shall be laid to rest in Vadstena.' The course was completed, the end was reached: *monacha et mater in Wadsteno!*

'Then Bridget looked up as if to give thanks to her Creator, and saying: "Lord, into Thy hands I commend my spirit," she fell asleep. It was in the year of the Lord one thousand three hundred and seventy-three, on the twenty-third day of July as day was breaking.'(12)

III

'Your body must remain here in Rome, until it comes to the place which is prepared for it'(1)—thus had Bridget heard the voice of Christ in her soul. Until the church which was to be built over her grave was ready, her inanimate remains were to stay in Rome. And what was more reasonable, then, that for her Roman resting-place she chose the convent of the Poor Clares, San Lorenzo in Panisperna? Here, in the time of her tribulations, she had sat on the steps among the other mendicants and begged—here she had come later as a dear and honoured guest. And now her body, clothed in the grey habit of the

* St. Luke xxii, 28–30.

tertiaries of Saint Francis, was taken thither. 'In order to avoid all demonstrations of honour and crowding of curious persons and people eager to make it an occasion of sight-seeing,' (2) she had ordained that the funeral was to take place at night. But she had reckoned without the enthusiasm of the Romans—for two entire days it was impossible to take the deceased out of the house, so great was the crowd on the stairs of people who wanted to see *la Santa* once more, to kiss her cold hands, to pray for her intercession. Not until 27 July could the translation to San Lorenzo in Panisperna take place. The body was laid in a wooden coffin which was covered with a costly cloth and tied round with cords—these cords were provided with the seals of the noblemen present, first of all the seals of Sir Birger and Latino Orsini. In the nuns' church, the crypt of the present church, there was in a chapel behind an iron grating an old heathen marble sarcophagus—into this the coffin was lowered.(3)

Here it remained a good while. Birger and Karin had promised their mother to take her with them home to Sweden—but first Alphonsus had to come back from Avignon. This faithful friend had not been present at Bridget's death-bed, he was at least to be allowed to pray by her coffin. Meanwhile, in the time of waiting, miracles flourished about the heathen sarcophagus with the naked *putti*. Among the nuns who kept vigil by the dead there was a certain Francesca Sabelli, who had been a particularly good friend of Bridget. Throughout two years she had been ill of a stomach complaint, and all the Sisters advised her not to go down in the cold church. But she was determined to do so, kneeling there on the marble floor, and weeping and sobbing she implored her dead friend to obtain better health for her, not to be restored to perfect health, but only so much that she could go to choir prayers in the church with the others, and to go about here and there in the house. And not only was Sister Francesca no worse after having sat on the marble floor a whole night—no, she was really better!(4)

Alphonsus did not come back from Avignon until the beginning of September, and now it was time to think of the journey home. But first there was something that had to be done, gruesome even for people in the Middle Ages—Bridget's bones had to be separated from the flesh, for only the bones had to be taken home. It was the domestic chaplain, Magnus Petri, to whom this task was entrusted—as his assistant he had one of Sir Birger's esquires named Peter Friis. Both of them came to the nuns in San Lorenzo in Panisperna provided with

razors and other edge-instruments, and asked for boiling water with
fragrant herbs.

> And then they opened the marble sarcophagus and found the coffin in it,
> bound and sealed as when it had been placed there. They loosened the cords
> and opened the coffin, and Master Magnus put his hands down to take up
> the body. And he found all the flesh consumed and the bones lying there
> without any flesh, as if ten years and not five weeks and a half had passed
> since the funeral. Only in the head was a little of the brain left. The cerements
> were not soiled or torn.(5)

From the bones taken out Magnus Petri gave one arm to the convent, as well as some smaller pieces of the skeleton—the arm is still
preserved in the sacristy of the church, enclosed in an arm of silver.
One of Bridget's cloaks was also given to the nuns. Then began the
journey northward—the whole company on horseback, including
Bridget. From the Roman authorities Birger and Karin had obtained
a passport for the journey—it is dated 13 November 1373 and was
issued by the Roman Senator (*i.e.* Governor) Fortunato Raynaldi of
Todi as well as the magistracy in Rome. The passport is very detailed
and gives an insight into the kind of baggage that the homeward-bound
Swedes took with them—they are mostly ecclesiastical articles, a portable altar with its equipment of chalice, cruets for wine and water, a
thurible, all of silver, a chasuble, ecclesiastical books, everything
necessary for saying Mass and the Divine Office, a large piece of silk
for making a chasuble, etc. It is emphasized in the passport that
Birger and Karin have a papal privilege to have Mass said everywhere
for themselves and their household—'for they are very spiritually
minded persons.'(6)

On 2 December Karin and Birger said good-bye to Francesca
Papazuri and went forth with the beloved and heavy burden out of
Porta del Popolo, to turn aside at Ponte Molle to the familiar Via
Flaminia. By the sides of the slowly striding mule that carried Bridget's
coffin rode Birger and Karin, Alphonsus of Jaen, Prior Petrus and Master
Peter, the Roman friends Niccolà Colonna and Petruccio Colonna. In
Spoleto Gomez Albornoz joined the cortège, in Foligno Corrado
Trinci. From Foligno the road passed across the plain, not far from the
field where Francis of Assisi had preached to the birds, up to Montefalco. Bishop Galhardus of Spoleto had made an appointment to meet
them here, that he might hear from eye-witnesses about Bridget's life
and miracles; it was the beginning of the process of canonization. The
meeting took place in the church of San Francesco, at that time not

yet adorned with the frescoes of Benozzo Gozzoli, and in the presence of a great gathering of ecclesiastical and secular notables the confessors now handed over to the officials chosen by Bishop Galhardus, the imperial notaries Egidio and Muzio, both of Montefalco, as also to Bartolomeo of Nocera, 'a fascicle of paper' in which Bridget's life and miraculous deeds were written down (the chief content of the fascicle was the biography written by the two Petruses). The Swedish travellers had no time to stay and submit to an oral examination, but Bishop Galhardus made them swear that what was written in the said little book was true, and that they had not been prompted by other feelings than by those of pure love of truth. It was on 14 December 1373.(7)

Before the Swedish travellers departed an incident in Montefalco itself occurred which was added to the list of Bridget's wondrous works. In Naples she had had, among her spiritual sons a former bishop, now a hermit, named Franciscus. When he heard of the funeral journey he proceeded to Montefalco to speak with Birger and Karin, but for some reason he was not received. Bridget herself, however, appeared to him while he was praying, embraced him and kissed him on both cheeks, and sent him to her children with the order that they were to receive him.(8)

From Montefalco you see Assisi over on the other side of the plain. But there was no time any longer for pilgrimages—and was it not the body of a saint that they had in their care? The Swedish travellers do not seem to have visited even the convent of the Augustinian nuns with the relics of Saint Clara of Montefalco—the heart bearing the imprint of the Cross and the instruments of the Passion.(9) In Montefalco they would probably bid their Roman friends farewell—or they would all accompany Gomez Albornoz home to Spoleto. Alphonsus, too, went back to Rome—not until six years later were he and Karin to meet again as witnesses in Bridget's process of canonization.(10) The Swedish travellers continued along the Via Flaminia by the mountain pass of *il Furio* through the Apennines out to Ancona.

IV

In Ancona a galley was waiting for the Swedish travellers to take them to Triest. On the way one of the maids named Mary fell ill—one night she suddenly fell out of bed and could not speak. Petrus Olai and Magnus both had a little medical knowledge but could not do anything. Karin knew what had to be done—in Bridget's name and with

Bridget's power she healed the sick girl—Mary got up and was again able to speak. Bright and well she could mount her horse and ride on with the others. Both the two priests and Karin tell the story themselves, but can only indicate that it was a place in Mark of Ancona, in a town whose name they cannot remember.(1)

The journey continued from Triest through Austria, Moravia, Poland and Prussia to Danzig. One wonders *where* the Swedish travellers would keep Christmas that year. Would they celebrate an Italian *Natale* with *il Bambino* or a South German Weihnacht with *das Christkind im Kripperl*? The little company of riders would not be able to make very long daily marches, so that Christmas would probably find them in Italy. The story of the crossing from Ancona to Triest is not mentioned at all in the original sources, and about the journey through Austria, Poland and Prussia there is only a remark that 'we deviated from our road to hear Mass at a convent in Poland called Claravallis.'(2) And then there is a story about an intended and planned attack on the travellers near Brünn in Moravia—a band of robber knights from the castle of Scherlach had lain in ambush on both sides of the road with the object of plundering the Swedish travellers. But Bridget managed as she had done at the time when young Orsini was lying in wait for her daughter on the road from Rome to San Lorenzo fuori le mura. The Swedish travellers came unharmed to the nearest town, Landskron, and put up at the hostel. In the evening some merchants arrived who had encountered the same robbers—one of the latter had related with vexation about the good booty they had missed—'we certainly heard footsteps and hoofbeats, but we could not see anything!'(3)

At Danzig the travellers reached the sea of homely regions, the Baltic. But their stay in the great Hanseatic city was to be a long one. From Marienburg in East Prussia the Grand Master of the Teutonic Knights, Winrick of Kniprode, came to do homage to the distinguished travellers—Karin spoke to him in her mother's spirit and power and reproached the order with having abandoned the monastic ideal. The stay in Danzig must have lasted several months, for not until the ice in the Gulf of Bothnia had at last been loosened could the Swedish travellers sail out of the harbour with the precious casket of relics on board. The crossing was stormy, for a time the sailors seemed to have mistaken their course. 'Then a star appeared, more radiant than the sun in its noontide splendour, and they followed the star and ran into the Söderköping, the seaport of East Gothland.'(4)

From Söderköping the road led over Halleby, Göthstad, Askebykloster and Vårdaberg to Linköping. It was by the old Eriksgata that Bridget advanced in victory. The bells were ringing from all the churches, and people came crowding up. It was in the last days of June (so long had the stay in Danzig lasted), everywhere the meadows were full of flowers and the fruit trees were covered with blossoms. Were there any who strewed flowers on the way?

Then the funeral cortège, which was a triumphal procession, entered Linköping. And who was standing there in the open portal of the cathedral—who was standing there in bishop's vestments but Niels Hermansson, Nicolaus Hermanni, once a tutor at Ulfåsa, once a teacher of Latin grammar for her who now came back in the fame of sainthood! Into the cathedral the procession advanced, and the coffin was placed before the high altar. Up from the choir rose the singing— the hymn in praise of Bridget:

> *Rosa, rorans bonitatem*
> *stella, stillans claritatem,*
> *Birgitta, vas gratiae!*

For several days Bridget's coffin was left standing in Linköping cathedral for Bridget had a word to say to Nicolaus Hermanni. Out of false piety Bishop Niels had resolved to retire from the complications of this world and to live solely for the salvation of his soul, 'with vigils in the night, fasting and prayer.' Karin showed him that this was not the way of duty.(5) More and more clearly was it seen— what Urban VI was to say later—that she had drunk of her mother's milk. In Rome she had already at Bridget's bier spoken words of rebuke to the elegant Roman women.(6)

Then the procession left Linköping and proceeded to Vadstena, everywhere meeting the homage of the multitude. Again and again a stop had to be made on the way—everyone wanted to touch the coffin with the holy bones and commend themselves to Bridget's intercession. Then Prior Petrus spoke to the people, telling them of all the wonders that had happened through Bridget, in Italy, in the Holy Land and now lately in Germany.(7) In order to be near the saint as long as possible people spent the night in the open air—it was in the summer.(8)

But it was not all enthusiasm—there were critics too, there were sceptics, there was infidelity. As, for instance, that nobleman who said contemptuously: 'How does that old hag and her bones concern me?' But the punishment was not long in coming—hardly had he uttered these insolent words when he was seized with the most extreme terror and ran into Saint Lars' church in Söderköping. Locking the door after him, and taking off his clothes he began to scourge himself till the blood flowed. Some of his friends came into the church through a window and with difficulty they made the poor man see reason—as a penance he walked barefoot from Söderköping to Vadstena.(9)

But one morning in July the funeral train reached Granby Hill, from which you get the first view of Vadstena. Down there lay the king's house, where the good Jovan Pätterson was probably at work building—Bridget had said to him herself in Rome that he was to stay there 'until with God's help I can come thither.' And now she had come.(10)

Down there lay Vadstena, and round about it lay East Gothland in the verdure of summer, and far out, over the summery blue of Lake Vättern, was the long bluish ridge of the Omberg—behind it lay Alvastra. From this land Bridget had set out—to this land she was coming back. In that same year of 1374 a new abbot had come to the monastery—his name was Jònis.(11) One cannot but think that he would be present with a company of his monks, both to welcome home Prior Petrus Olai and especially to greet her who had once been, and now was the world-famous guest of the monastery.

Half-way between Jovan Pätterson's half-finished building stood a small church built of wood—here the funeral train stopped. Birger and Karin unbound the coffin from the horse's back, Birger took it upon his shoulder and carried it in. When he had put it down before the high altar he took his sister's hand and said: 'Now I can hold up my head here, Karin. Often enough I have had to look down when I stood before my Lord, King Magnus and he said to me: "What has our kinswoman, your Mother, dreamt about in the night?" ' (12) 'It was on the Tuesday of the week after Saints Peter and Paul's day, namely 4 July.'(13)

Now in Vreta there was a woman who was sorely tormented by the devil. She was a great sinner and had often confessed, but every time the devil appeared to her and said contemptuously: 'Do you believe that a man can forgive sins? You belong to me and shall go down into hell with me.' Then in the night an exceedingly beautiful lady came to this woman and said: 'Tell the devil that God's mercy is open to everyone, go away and sin no more.' 'Who are you, lady?' asked the sinner. And the answer was: 'I am Bridget, who have come home from Rome.'(14)

V

But far away in Rome, in the house on the Campo de' Fiori, which had now grown so empty, Francesca Papazuri sat writing to her friend Lapa Buondelmonte, Niccolà Acciaiuoli's sister.

You have heard, Madam Lapa, I suppose, that the Lady Katerina, Sir Belinguerus [that is, Birger] and Brother Petrus from Sweden and all the rest of the family, have left Rome and gone home. It was on December 2nd. Before her death the Lady Bridget had ordered these her children to leave Rome and go to their own country, and there to build the convent, such as Christ had commanded. And now you must know that after this departure of theirs I have been very melancholy, and in all my life I have never borne so great a sorrow in my heart.(1)

NOTES

BOOK IV

I

(1) *Rev.* VIII, 48. *Cf.* Steffen, pp. 294-309 and Toni Schmid, pp. 63-70.

(2) 'The king ... was governed by others and he had the heart of a hare, and therefore he seemed to be sitting in the king's seat like a crowned ass' (*Upp.* III, 31. *Rev.* VIII, 24). Cf. *Extrav.* 78 about the five kings: *primus coronatus asinus.*

(3) *Extrav.* 67.

(4) *Rev.* III, 27.

(5) 'ad Romam peregrinando devenit ... habens semper secum ... duos seniores antiquos et maturos, virtuosos et expertos patres spirituales qui usque ad mortem ei secuti sunt.' (Prologus Alphonsi in lib. octavum, cap. 3). One of these two is 'monachus et prior Cisterciensis,' the other 'quidam presbyter de Suetia,' namely Master Petrus, who in Rome governed Bridget's house and gave her and her daughter lessons in Latin and singing.

About Gudmar Fredriksson, *Diarium* ad 1389; Magnus Petri, *Diarium* ad 1396; Silfverstolpe, p. 79, Magnus Petri (Tre Liljer) died 21.3.1396 in the monastery of Paradiso at Florence.

II

(1) Grimberg: *Svenska folkets underbara öden*, I (Stockholm 1938), pp. 379, 599.

(2) *Extrav.* 74; 27; 77.

(3) Emilia Fogelklou: *Ur fromhetslifvets svensk-historia*, II, 1, pp. 170-75.

(4) *Festschrift zum zwölfhundertjährigen Sankt Alto Jubiläum.* (Munich 1930), pp. 19-23 and S. Nordmark's interesting study in *Credo*, May-June 1941, from which I quote the following: 'At the Sisters' parlour, where they are permitted to speak with visitors, we also had the opportunity of seeing some ... very precious relics of Saint Bridget. Among these, precious above all others in our eyes, was Saint Bridget's pilgrim staff (which we were assured was made by Swedish hands). It can be seen through small glass-covered openings in the silver sheath bearing the Italian inscription: *Mazza di Santa Brigida.* Equally precious is the little wooden bowl from which Bridget drank on her pilgrim journeys. ... It is made of Swedish lowland birch, as an examination is said to have shown. On its inner side are carved the words which Bridget used to utter when she drank from it: IESU NAZ(ARENE) REX IUD(ÆORUM) MISERERE. ... The Italian inscription on the outside of the bowl: *Ciotola ove beveva Santa Brigida* (bowl from which Saint Bridget used to drink), also indicates, together

with the above-named Italian inscription on the pilgrim staff, that these objects came from Italy, probably from some former convent of the Order (*e.g.* Florence, Genoa or the hospice in Rome).' (*Credo*, May 1941, p. 20.) Cf. *Diarium*, 4.10.1416, in which it is said that Bishop Petrus of Roskilde 'offered to the convent of Maribo a bowl which formerly belonged to Saint Bridget.'

(5) Paul Riant: *Expéditions et pélerinages des Scandinaves en Terre Sainte* (Paris 1851), pp. 50-60, 81-5.

(6) Nils Ludvig Rasmussen: 'Birgittapenninger' (*Förnvännen*, 1942, p. 403).

(7) *Rev.* III, 7.

(8) Vielstedt: *Cola di Rienzo*, p. 321.

(9) *Rev.* III, 5.

III

(1) *Rev.* III, 8.

(2) The letter is preserved in the Royal Library in Stockholm, and a copy has been printed by Klemming, Vol. IV, pp. 192-6.

The Master's remarks state:

ad primum: magis eligo animam domini (episcopi) deo presentare spiritualiter.

ad secundum: quod nihil habeo proprium, et magis delector in paupertate qvam professus sum quam in omnibus divitiis mundi.

ad tercium: quod magis mihi placet simplex frater vocari quam pro vana et mundana gloria magister appellari.

Cf. *Rev.* III, 9.

(3) *Rev.* III, 8.

(4) *Rev.* III, 6.

(5) 'Iste . . . episcopus similis est testudini quae jacens in innata putredine trahit caput in terram. Sic iste jacet et delectatur in peccati abominatione, trahens animum ad terrena, non ad sempiterna' (*Rev.* III, 7).

(6) On the back of the first draft (of *Rev.* IV, 49) preserved in the Royal Library in Stockholm and written in Bridget's own handwriting, a later hand has written: 'Saint Bridget wrote these words with her own hand concerning the Pope and Cardinals.' (Klemming, Vol. IV, p. 181).

IV

(1) Ingeborg Dannes, *Rev.* VI, 102. *Processus,* p. 631. *Diarium* ad 1401. The process of canonization has her die in Milan; *Rev.* VI, 102, says that she lay ill in Rome; the *Vadstena Diary* that 'she was with Sancta Byrgitta in Rome and died there.'

Madame de Flavigny interprets the expression occurring in both sources: *maritus vero habebit desiderium suum,* to mean that Nicolaus Dannes bore ill will against *la malheureuse créature qui lui était unie* (p. 279). But why, then, did he try to keep her from the journey 'as much as he could' (*qvantum poterat*)?

(2) *Paradiso*, X, 125. See Peter Schindler: *Kølvand og Skinnestribe* (Copenhagen 1940), pp. 185–7.

(3) 'okeypis' (*i.e.* free) 'wine and drink' (Sverre Sten: *Ferd og Fest*, Oslo 1929, p. 126). The hospice lay a little to the south of Piacenza, between that town and Borgo San Domino. (Riant, *op. cit.*, p. 59.)

(4) Emile Mâle: *L'art religieux du XIIme siècle* (Paris 1922), pp. 253–7.

(5) J. Bédier: *Les Légendes épiques*, quoted by Mâle. See Vol. I of this work, p. 97. (Note on *il Volto Santo*), Vol. I, Book IV, Ch. XII, Footnote on Lueca.

(6) 'Distant women look fairest' (Sverre Sten, p. 107.)

(7) *Rev.* III, 27.

V

(1) *Rev.* II, 29.

(2) Henrik Schück: *Rom* (Stockholm 1912), p. 231.

(3) *Extravagantes* 65: 'Then you have four hours for reading your office and being occupied with other godly works and useful business.' The Latin text contains the same rule: 'habeatis quatuor horas pro orationibus legendis et pro aliis devotis et utilibus operibus perficiendis.'

(4) *Regula*, cap. 17.

(5) Afterwards you have two hours for eating and drinking in the evening, and for the modest recreation and relief of the body, and you have retirement until you go to bed.

(6) *Rev.* IV, 5.

VI

(1) 'non audiat amplius fistulam meam.' *Rev.* VII, 31.

(2) Ernst Benz: *Ecclesia spiritualis: Kirchenidee und Geschichtheologie der franziskanischen Reformation* (Sutttgart 1934), pp. 4–22, 40–48. Baldini's translation of Joachim's *Aforismi e Presagi* (Lanciano 1926), p. 25.

(3) It was Benz who first called attention to this likeness (*op. cit.*, pp. 78–9).

(4) Herbert Vielstedt: *Cola di Rienzo* (Berlin 1936), p. 62.

VII

(1) Vielstedt, *op. cit.*, pp. 142–3.

(2) Mollat: *Les Papes d'Avignon* (Paris 1912), p. 175.

(3) Benz, p. 390. Vielstedt, pp. 268 *seq.*

VIII

(1) *Indulgentie et stationi della Città di Roma.* (Rome), pp. 148–9.

(2) *Legender från Sverigs medeltid*, pp. 129–32.

(3) Johannes Jørgensen: *Romerske Helgenbilleder*, pp. 72–81.

IX

(1) *Processus,* p. 258.
(2) *Rev.* II, 7.
(3) *Rev.* IV, 13.
(4) *Processus,* p. 330.
(5) *Processus,* p. 436 (*circa* 1352).
(7) *Processus,* p. 193.
(8) *Processus,* pp. 235, 545.
(9) *Processus,* pp. 335–6.
(10) *Extrav.* 112.
(11) *Rev.* VI, 75.
(12) *Rev.* II, 30; IV, 122.
(13) *Rev.* IV, 124; VI, 90 (about Master Matthias).
(14) *Rev.* III, 27, 30; IV, 74.
(15) *Processus,* p. 546.
(16) *Processus,* pp. 445, 456.

X

(1) *Rev.* III, 10; IV, 78.
(2) Mollat, *op. cit.,* p. 81.
(3) *Rev.* III, 10, *Declaratio. Rev.* III, 11.
(4) *Rev.* III, 11. *Processus,* p. 515.
(5) *Rev.* VI, 115.
(6) *Rev.* VI, 71.
(7) *Rev.* III, 1.
(8) *Extrav.* 64.

XI

(1) *Rev.* III, 11.
(2) *Rev.* III, 10; VI, 70.

XII

(1) *Processus,* p. 491. *Extrav.* 97.
(2) *Extrav.* 105. *Processus,* pp. 525–6.
(3) *Rev.* III, 22, *Declaratio.*
(4) *Rev.* III, 21; VI, 8.

XIII

(1) *Vita Catharinæ,* capp. IV–V.
(2) *Rev.* VI, 118. *Vita Cath.* cap. V.
(3) *Processus,* pp. 323–4.
(4) *Rev.* IV, 34.
(5) *Rev.* IV, 34, *Declaratio.* Steffen, p. 58, note.
(6) *Rev.* IV, 35.
(7) *Processus,* p. 65. Steffen, p. 57, note, is of opinion that Petrus Olai must be mistaken in stating that Gustaf Turesson died in Montefiascone on the way home from Rome, for in a document of 1354 he is mentioned as

being alive. In the Process of 1377 Ingeborg, Magnus' daughter, says that she became a widow 'thirteen years ago'—that is, in 1364. She would then have lived in Rome with Bridget from 1364 to 1369.

(8) *Rev.* VI, 52.

XIV

(1) *Osservatore Romano*, 26.1.1933.
(2) *Rev.* IV, 81.
(3) *Rev.* IV, 81, *Declaratio*.
(4) *Rev.* IV, 16.
(5) Thus *Processus*, p. 544 and *Extrav.* 81. Not so *Rev.* I, 32, in which the same Sir Birger answered: 'The Devil sits in my heart and on my tongue—how can I do penance?' Likewise *Rev.* IV, 16, *Declaratio*: 'He went home, again became a tax-collector' and 'died miserably among strangers.' Both the Declaratio and the testimony in the Process are by Petrus Olai. Is he contradicting himself? Or were there two men of the same name holding the same position? It is scarcely probable.
(6) *See* Vol. I of the present work, p. 202.
(7) *Rev.* IV, 113, *Additio*.
(8) *Rev.* VI, 20.
(9) Edv. Ortved: *Cistercierordenen og dens Klostre i Norden*, II. (Copenhagen 1933), p. 239.

XV

(1) *Processus* pp. 15–16, 65.
(2) *Rev.* IV, 94.
(3) *Extrav.* 69.
(4) *Rev.* IV, 20.
(5) *Processus*, p. 324: 'elegi tibi statum aut matrimonii aut sancte castitatis et viduitatis.'
(6) *Legender från Sverigs medeltid*, p. 282.
(7) According to a later Swedish legend Karin was believed in her despair even to have run away from home, up to the nuns in San Lorenzo in Panisperna, whom she had visited together with her mother. It was when she came home that she was birched, 'so ungently that it was dreadful to see ... that the blood ran down all over her body.' (Grimberg I, pp. 418–19.)
(8) *Vita Cath.*, capp. V–VII.
(9) 'Vere, filia, tu bibisti de lacte matris tuae!' (*Vita Cath.*, in the Rome edition 1628 of *Revelationes*, II, p. 530.)

XVI

(1) *Extrav.* 8. *Processus*, p. 94.
(2) Vielstedt, *op. cit.*, pp. 274–5.
(3) Vielstedt, *op. cit.*, p. 282, then pp. 286–90.
(4) *Rev.* VIII, 51.
(5) *Rev.* IV, 45.
(6) *Rev.* IV, 71.

(7) *Diarium*, ad 12.3.1393, ad 5.12.1400.

(8) *Les Papes d'Avignon*, p. 89.

(9) *Rev.* I, 23, *Declaratio*.

(10) *Rev.* I, 28. It is strange that this description is to be found in *Book I* of *Revelationes*, which is mainly concerned with the time in Sweden. But both the fact that Saint Laurence occurs in it, and that the scorpion, with which Bridget did not become acquainted until she was in Italy, is mentioned, indicates the sojourn in Rome as the time of its being written. Can it be that Alphonsus placed it here for reasons of discretion?

(11) Mollat, p. 87.

(12) *Rev.* VI, 96 (Swedish translation, VI, 35).

XVII

(1) *Rev.* VI, 33.

(2) *Rev.* VI, 34.

(3) *Rev.* IV, 136. (Swed. IV, 133).

(4) Mollat, pp. 92–4.

(5) Ernst Benz, *op. cit.*, p. 403, Vielstedt, p. 334.

(6) *Extrav.* 8.

(7) *Rev.* III, 27.

(8) *Rev.* IV, 10.

(9) *Rev.* IV, 57.

(10) *Extrav.* 8.—'Ideo statuimus et mandamus easdem laudes, scilicet *Ave Maris Stella* . . . omni vespere futuris temporibus decantandas seu dicendas' (household rule for *Domus Sanctae Birgitta*, printed in the edition of *Revelationes*, Rome 1628, the last time in Vol. II, without page numbers).—The hymn *Ave Maris Stella* was not (as some of Bridget's modern biographers have thought) composed by Master Petrus. It existed before then—he only inserted it in the Bridgettine ritual composed by him. See *Jungfru Marie Örtagård*, ed. Robert Geete (Stockh. 1875), pp. LXXIII–LXXV, and also the *Register*, p. 299, where the pieces written by 'Master Peter' are marked by an asterisk, and *Ave Maris Stella* is not among them.—A passage in Master Petrus of Skenninge's *Vita* testifies to the tumultuous state of the Roman populace. He was sitting one day at the window in Bridget's house, engaged in translating one of her *Revelationes*, when a gust of wind came and carried away the paper —over to some Roman noblemen who were sitting on the flat roof of a house near by. They tried to catch it, but fortunately did not succeed in doing so, for it would almost certainly have had disastrous consequences for the authoress. (Silfverstolpe: *Klosterfolket i Vadstena*, p. 78, note 2.)

XVIII

(1) *Vita Catharinae*, cap. 8.

(2) *Processus*, p. 231 and p. 227.

(3) *Rev.* IV, 46.

(4) *Processus*, p. 359.

(5) *Vita Cath.*, cap. II. The source is Master Petrus.

(6) *Legender från Sverigs medeltid*, pp. 281–2.

XIX

(1) Madame de Flavigny places this pilgrimage as late as 1364. To this Steffen remarks that (it) 'seems scarcely probable that Bridget, who cherished such an ardent love of Saint Francis, would not have made a pilgrimage to his shrine before 1365'; he thinks that the pilgrimage may have been undertaken 'already about 1350.' According to the Process (p. 436) Francesca Papazuri would have been born in 1349. But may she not have made herself a little younger at the interrogation? Besides, she was already a widow when Bridget entered her house on the Campo de' Fiori in 1354.

(2) *Vita Cath.*, cap. 9.

(3) Johannes Jørgensen: 'I det Høje' (*Selected works*, pp. 101–2, 113). Angela of Foligno was born in 1248, died 4 January 1309.

(4) *Rev.* VII, 20.

(5) P. Egidio M. Giusti: *Le vetrate di San Francesco in Assisi* (Milan 1900, p. 99) about *de Maestri vetriari*, who made the windows in the basilica: *Forse il loro carattere, pieno di suavità mistica, rifuggiva del dramma doloroso della fine del mondo.*

(6) *Spec. perfectionis*, cap. 1. Johannes Jørgensen: *St. Francis of Assisi* (Longmans, 1912), p. 252.

(7) See Vol. I, Book II, Ch. XIV, par. 11, pp. 108–9. That the pilgrimage to *Sainte Baume* was not forgotten can be seen from the breviary that Karin possessed, in which a miniature exactly represents Mary Madgalene, carried up to *le Saint Pilon* by angels. She is wrapped in her golden hair and in a grey penitential habit. Underneath her there is a landscape with a river between green fields (MS. A 233, Stockh., fol. 16).

(8) *Extrav.* 90, *Rev.* VII, 3.—1348 il di 14 di agosto Bertrando Lagerio fù trasferito della chiesa di Ajaccio in Corsica a questa di Assisi per autorità del Pontefice Clemente VI. . . . In tempo di questo vescovo S. Brigida in compagnia della sua figlia, S. Caterina, circa l'anno 1350 fece il viaggio di Assisi e visitò la chiesa della Porziuncula dove ebbe una visione di S. Francesco. (*Storia di S. Rufino e dei vescovi di Assisi*, Assisi 1797.)

BOOK V

I

(1) C. Paludan-Müller: *Cola di Rienzo*, p. 143.—Herbert Vielstedt: *Cola di Rienzo* (Berlin 1936), pp. 337–52.

II

(1) *Processus*, pp. 443–4.

(2) *Vita Cath.*, cap. X.—*Medeltids legender*, pp. 280–81.

(3) *Rev.* VI, 46.

III

(1) *Extrav.* 10.

(2) *Rev.* IV, 32 with *Declaratio. Extrav.* 5.—This hymn is very correctly to be found among those ascribed to Master Petrus. (*Jungfru Mariae Örta-gård,*' Stockh. 1895, p. 301.)

(3) *Jungfru Maria Örta-gård,* pp. LXI, LXIX, LXXIII, LXXIV.

(4) *Sermo angelicus,* the prologue perhaps written by Alphonsus.

(5) The Prologue.

(6) *Sermo angelicus,* feria quinta, prima lectio.

(7) *Rev.* III, 30.

(8) *Extrav.* 107, 'quella contessa che mori a Roma' (Johannes Jørgensen: *Den hellige Katerina af Siena.* First edition, p. 138. English translation, p. 162.)

(9) *Revelationes,* Roma 1628, Vol. II, p. 553 verso. Collijn: 'Birgittinska Gestalter,' pp. 14–17. The deed of gift on the house is dated 8.1.1383 and is to be found reprinted in the above-named edition of *Revelationes,* pp. 554–6. In the Processus Francesca Papazuri mentions the earlier deed of gift: 'donacionem dicte Brigida *dum ipsa vivebat* de quadam domo sua magna ex hereditate sua posita in regione Arenulae.' (*Processus,* p. 442.)

(10) *Extrav.* 107.

IV

(1) *Processus,* p. 64. Silfverstolpe, *loc. cit.,* p. 105.

(2) 'Quid vobiscum cum anima ista quae est de familia novae sponsae filii mei?' (*Rev.* VI, 102).

(3) *Processus,* p. 332.

(4) *Processus,* p. 359.

(5) Rodacanacchi: *Cola di Rienzo;* Vielstedt, *loc. cit.,* pp. 366–8.

V

(1) *Extrav.* 8.

(2) Vielstedt, pp. 361–3. Rodocanacchi: *Histoire de Rome de 1354 à 1471* (Paris 1922), pp. 3–6.

(3) *Rev.* VI, 67.

(4) *Rev.* VI, 89.

(5) *Rev.* VI, 90; VI, 60; VI, 77; VI, 92.

(6) The letter was found by K. H. Karlsson in the archives of the Vatican (*see* Salomon Kraft: *Källstudier,* p. 143, note 4). It reads as follows:

Dilecto filio Goraldo, abbati monasterij Maiorismontis prope Turon, civitatem Perusium et nonnullas alias terras Romane ecclesie pronobis et ipsa ecclesia regenti, salutem etc. Cum, sicut audivimus, dilectus filius nobilis vir Brigerius, miles de Svetia, et dilecta in Christo filia nobilis mulier Caterina, ejus soror vidua, Rome commorantes, sint in aliquali indigentia constituti, statim receptis presentibus volumus et tue discrecioni percipiendo mandamus, quaternos (!) quadrigentos florinos auri eis in dicta Urbe vel alibi, suo procuratori ad hoc specialiter constituto, de mero nostro dono facias assignari. Datum Auinione II idus octobris anno tertio.

VI

(1) King Magnus' deeds of gift are of 18.5.1357 and 5.2.1358. (Kjellberg: *Vadstena*, Linköping 1917, p. 123.)
(2) *Extrav.* 26–7.
(3) *Extrav.* 69.
(4) *Rev.* VIII, 19.
(5) Andersson: *Källstudier*, p. 171, note 2.—That Bengt Algottsson was not the first to occupy the position of the king's favourite is seen from the indictment of the Swedish nobles against the king: 'the king again exalted another before and above all, by whom and in whom the previous infamy was revived.' (Ellen Jørgensen, 92.)
(6) *See* Vol. I, pp. 87–89.
(7) *Extrav.* 80. *Rev.* IV, 25. Steffen, pp. 287–9.

VII

(1) Mollat, pp. 181–2.
(2) 'uomo dotto per ingegno e studio, gran teologo, filosofo ed oratore, magnifico e magnanimo, protettore degli uomini di lettere, scaltro ed abile politico e principe benigno ed amorevole' (Petrarca: *Rev. Memor.* lib. II, *De ignorantia sui ipsius II*, p. 147), 'dopo Salomone non si era veduto sul trono alcun principe cosi dotto.' (Boccaccio: *De generatione deorum*, lib. XIV).
(3) *Rev.* IV, 7. Mollat, pp. 180–89.
(4) Ferdinando Russo: *Santa Brigida nella leggenda e nella storia* (Lanciano, 1913, pp. 121–5.)

VIII

(1) In a letter written home to Provence, shortly after she had come back to Naples, Giovanna relates:
'In tantum epidemialis pestis in istis regni nostri partibus nimis terribiliter contagii sui fimbrias dilatans per sex menses continuos incaluit, quod ex plurimis paucissimos faciens, nec etatem, nec sexum preteriens, fere in soli-tudinem loco redegit, et preter alia inconvenientia multa, quae, peccatis exigentibus secum traxit, tantam causavit difficultatem recolligendi et exigendi pecuniam, non existentibus qui solvant eandem, quod difficilius est nunc exigere unciam quam ante epidemiam recolligisse decem.' (Matteo Camera: *Memorie Storico-Diplomatiche dell' antica Città e Ducato di Amalfi*, Salerno 1876, I, p. 551.)
(2) 'die mercurij 17 presentis mensio maji (1346) accesserunt hora matu-tinali ad domos Guillielmi di Marino in Graniani (Gragnano) . . . ipsos nudos de lecto extraxerunt ad plateam publicam, ubi ipsos dire mortis gladio peri-merunt, dimittentes eorum corpora perforata in conspectu populi.' (*Ex regestis Johannae* I, ad 1345, noted Camera, I, p. 554—*spaccate nello ventre* Ferdinando Russo: *Santa Brigida*, Lanciano 1913, p. 156.)
(3) Camera, p. 558.

IX

(1) *Processus*, p. 483.

(2) *Legender från Sverigs medeltid*, pp. 211–217.—According to another tradition Saint Thomas the Apostle died in the town of Meliapur in India and in the cathedral of this town is shown his tomb with the following inscription: *Hic spectabili referente veteri traditione | corpus est humatum B. Thomas Apostoli | qui cum diceretur Didymus et unus est de duodecim | lancea transfixus in vicinia, vitam pro fide | effudit Magistri* A.D. 68. According to Saint Ephraim the Syrian the Apostle's body, however, was translated to Edessa and thence to Chios. From Chios some of the relics—the skull and some of the bones— were taken to Ortona.

(3) *Processus*, p. 333, p. 483, p. 331.

(4) *Processus*, p. 561.

(5) *Processus*, p. 483.

X

(1) *Rev.* VIII, 49.

(2) *Rev.* VIII, 52–3.

(3) *Rev.* VIII, 12; 10; 14.

(4) *Rev.* VIII, 15 (*Rev.* IV, 17).

(5) *Processus*, p. 526.

(6) *Rev.* IV, 84.

(7) *Rev.* VIII, 19.

(8) *Rev.* VIII, 21.

(9) *Rev.* VIII, 48.

(10) *Rev.* VIII, 48. On the *book rest* see also *Rev.* IV, 32 and IV, 50.

(11) Madame de Flavigny: *Sainte Brigitte*, p. 380.

(12) The inscription on the tombstone reads: *Svecia suspira, sublato principe plora, qui te protexit ac juris culmina rexit, conditus hic Regum flos et formmula legum, Rex mitis magnus.* (In Toni Schmid, p. 67.—Drawing in Sven Tunberg: *Sveriges historia till våra dagar*, II, Stockholm 1926, p. 137.)—In Olaus Petri it is said: 'And this name of Ladulås (barndoor lock) is an honest name, which gives King Magnus greater honour and praise than if he were called a Roman emperor. For there are not many in the world who can be called barndoor lock; barn breaker has always been more common in the world.' (Ewert Wrangel: *Svenska folket genom tiderne*, Vol. II, p. 20.)

(13) Toni Schmid, *op. cit.*, p. 66.

(14) *Saphirus membra conservans sana et corroborans infirma* (*Rev.* II, 30).

(15) *Extrav.* 108.

(16) Brilloth: *Svenska kyrkans historia*, II (Uppsala 1941), p. 169.

(17) *Rev.* II, 30.

(18) *Rev.* VIII, 48 (abridged).

XI

(1) Sven Tunberg, *Sveriges historia*, II, Stockholm 1926, pp. 240–41.

(2) *Rev.* VIII, 9. Engström, *op. cit.*, p. 25.

(3) Vol. I of the present work, pp. 184–85. *Rev.* IV, 3 (Latin); VIII, 41 (Swedish). *Cf.* Engström, *op. cit.*, p. 24, notes 63.

(4) *Extrav.* 78.
(5) Vol. I, p. 19.
(6) Grimberg, *op. cit.*, pp. 344–5.
(7) Sven Tunberg, pp. 110–17.
(8) *Rev.* VIII, 48 *in fine.*

XII

(1) Montelius, *op. cit.*, pp. 17–19.

(2) After Magnus had paid in a large sum in reduction of the debt the excommunication was raised, though only for a year. A similar respite was given in 1362 (Montelius, p. 13, note 1).

(3) Ellen Jørgensen: *Krøniker fra Valdemarstiden*, pp. 96–7 and p. 92, note 2.

(4) 'Anno Domini feria IIIa post Jacobi ante portas Wiisby in manibus danorum ceciderunt Gutenses hic sepulti. Orate pro eis.' Drawing of the Cross in Montelius, p. 43.

(5) *Rev.* VIII, 9.

(6) *Rev.* VIII, 16.

(7) Tunberg, p. 265.

(8) This accusation is advanced for the first time in the polemical pamphlet of the nobles against King Magnus. Erik's wife, Beatrix of Brandenburg, died in childbed shortly after her husband. She had to be delivered by Cæsarian section—the child 'was cut from her side,' as it is said in the ballad about Queen Dagmar. The son did not live even a day. (Ingvar Andersson: *Källstudier*, p. 171, note 2; p. 183. Engström: *Bo Jonsson Grip*, p. 27.)

(9) Ellen Jørgensen, pp. 97–8, 101.

(10) Johanne Skovgaard, p. 79.

(11) Sten Engström, p. 27.

(12) *Rev.* IV, 141, Swedish text. *Extrav.* 80. The original manuscript reproduced in Klemming. See the examination of the whole question in Toni Schmid, place quoted, pp. 150–66. There is in existence a Latin translation of the Swedish original (Toni Schmid, p. 154, reproduction). About Bishop Niels of Linköping it is said in the chronicle of the bishops of Linköping: 'Yet he stayed with King Magnus, who was banished to Norway. While the bishop lived he (the bishop) stayed in Norway and died at Båhus of grief.' (That is over King Magnus, who perished in 1374 at sea by an accident.—Tr.) (*Svenska medeltids dikter*, Stockholm, 1881–2, p. 496.)

XIII

(1) Ingvar Andersson: *Källstudier*, p. 160 (the parallel places between Bridget and *Libellus*).

(2) Ellen Jørgensen, *op. cit.*, pp. 97–8.

(3) *Rev.* VIII, 17.

(4) *Rev.* IV, 55.

(5) Sten Engström: *Bo Jonsson*, p. 23. I am not convinced that Ormungen was supposed to be one of Ingeborg's sons by Knud Porse. Engström, however, does admit that the expression 'Hugorm' may also have been applied

derivatively to Euphemia, the daughter.—*Cf.* Sten Engström: 'Ormungen och hans Moder' (*Personalhistorisk Tidsskrift,* 1930, pp. 1–6.)

(6) *Rev.* VI, with *Declaratio.*

(7) *Rev.* IV, 55.

(8) Johanne Skovgaard: *Den hellige Birgitta,* Copenhagen 1921, pp. 82–3. Karl Karlsson died 17.9.1398.

(9) Edw. Ortved: *Cistercierordenen i Norden,* II, Copenhagen 1933, p. 508, Johanne Skovgaard, p. 83.

XIV

(1) *Rev.* III, 12.

(2) *Rev.* III, 12, *Declaratio.*

(3) *Processus,* pp. 536, 561; *Rev.* VI, 107. Bridget quotes an Italian proverb: 'Whoso will not obey the mother will have to obey the stepmother.'

(4) *Processus,* p. 528.

(5) *Rev.* VII, 4. *Processus,* p. 495.

(6) *Processus,* pp. 472, 561.

(7) *Processus,* pp. 273, 333–4.

(8) *Processus,* p. 536.

(9) *Rev.* IV, 131.

(10) *Rev.* IV, 114.

(11) *Rev.* III, 12. *Declaratio. Processus,* p. 536.

(12) *Processus,* p. 536.

(13) *Legender från Sverigs medeltid,* pp. 160–68.

(14) *Rev.* VI, 103. The hymn on the feast of Saint Nicholas contains the lines: *Cujus tumba fert oleum, matres olivae nesciunt; quod natura non protulit, marmor sudando parturit.*

(15) *Processus,* p. 332.

(16) *Rev.* III, 1. In the fourth century Saint Matthew's relics had been taken from Brittany to Italy, but lay for several hundred years underneath the ruins of a devastated church. Camera, *Memorie,* p. 138.

(17) *Rev.* IV, 129. *Additio,* in which Amalfi is erroneously given instead of Salerno. Bishop Thomas does not seem to have gone to a physician in Salerno, which, incidentally, was famous for its medical faculty.

(18) *Processus,* p. 322. Bridget herself writes in a—later—letter to Monna Lapa: '*O si interim aliqvid boni facere possimus, quod nostre propinquum* [*i.e.* proficuum] *esset anime saluti.*' (Isak Collijn: *Birgittinska Gestalter,* Stockholm 1929, p. 19 and translated p. 10.)

XV

(1) F. Russo: *Santa Brigida* (Lanciano 1913), p. 55.

(2) *Santa Brigida inginocchioni stava
davanti al Cruciffisso non si partiva.
La Passione di Christo contemplava.
Una corona di spine in testa la teneva,
con una mano il libro leggeva,
in altro mano la torcia allumata.*

MEDITAZIONE DELLA SANTA:

Da cento fasci di spine fù fasciato
che parevan mille stelle matutine.
Andò per affacciarsi il povero meschino.
Presso si vede sei milia ladroni.
Si affaccia Pilato dal balacone,
dicendo: 'Sate-lu-i, sate-lu-i' [lasciate lo andare]
'che quisto è mezzo morto e mezzo vivo,
'è uomo giusto e non si può castigare!
'Non lu fate stare più in piedi la mattina,
'che nero si fece come un carbone!'
Un bacile d'acqua si fece calare,
e le sue mani si mise a lavare.

VIA CRUCIS

Ora ce ne andiamo abbasso a una via
dicendo Pater Noster e Ave Maria;
ora ce ne andiamo a monte per una costa,
dicendo Ave Maria e Pater Noster.
Ora ce ne andiamo in quel Calvario monte,
dicendo Ave Maria ad alta voce.

CRISTO PARLA:

'Ho le labbra squarciate e le ginocchie noce [addolorate],
'o Dio, quant' è pesante questa Croce!
'Una sola cosa mi dispiace
'Che appresso mi piange la mia madre dolce!'

CONCLUSIONE

Beati che lo dice e chi l'intende,
caccia un' alma santa del Purgatorio.
Chi la dice cinque volte il venardi
con cinque Paternoster e Avemari',
in ciel ci porta la Vergine Maria.
E otto giorni prima di morire,
Santa Brigida ci viene a visitare.

As will be seen from the last lines Bridget is understood to be a patron saint for a good death—'eight days before death Saint Bridget comes to visit us.' On Bridget's 'dödsmoderskap' ('mothership of death') see Emilia Fogelklou: *Bortom Birgitta* (Stockholm 1941), pp. 83–98.

XVI

(1) *Rev.* VI, 39. *Declaratio.*
(2) *Rev.* III, 31.
(3) 'Qvi vero voluntatem habet vivere usque in diem judicii, licet non peccat mortaliter, propter voluntatem tamen perpetue vivendi quam habet, tenetur habere poenam perpetuam usque ad judicium.' *Rev.* VI, 39.
(4) *Rev.* VI, 40.

XVII

(1) *Rev.* VIII, 55.

(2) *Rev.* VIII, 56.

(3) 'Post aliquos autem annos. . . .' Then: 'Duobus itaque annis peractis . . .'

(4) 'consuetudo Regis fuit a juventute audire missae, legere et jejunare, sed nullis facere justitiam' (Ingvar Andersson: *Källstudier*, p. 156, with the parallel place of *Rev.* VIII, 56).

(5) 'persuasi Regi . . . ut cuidam magno Principi alterius regni fratri meo adjurato, alienando donaret terras pertinentes coronae suae' (*Rev.* VIII, 56).

(6) 'in extremo puncto vocationis suae judicanda erit' (ibidem).

(7) *Rev.* VIII, 56. The parable about the angels like motes in the sun, also in *Rev.* VII, 30.

XVIII

(1) 'dixit ei, tangendo eum in pectore: *Questo cuore!*' (*Processus*, p. 436).

(2) *Processus*, p. 322: 'steterunt in eadem civitate (Neapoli) bene per duos annos.'

(3) 'dixit eam vidisse . . . in domo habitacionis sue prope sanctam Mariam Novam' (*Processus*, p. 227).

(4) *Processus*, pp. 322–3.

(5) 'vi era anche una hospedale per li povere pellegrini che venivano de Gerusalemme, et in questa cappella . . . si vede un Crucifisso depinto nel muro dove faceva oratione S. Brigida, vidua di Svetia' (Russo, *op. cit.*, pp. 271–2).

(6) *Processus*, pp. 331, 367.

(7) *Rev.* IV, 7.

(8) 'modica aqua et aër magnus placant iram Dei' (*Rev.* IV, 7).

(9) *Processus*, p. 330.

(10) Collijn, *op. cit.*, p. 7.

(11) *Rev.* IV, 8–9 (Swedish text IV, 8).

XIX

(1) 'alia quae ibi continentur, non ponuntur hic quia secreta sunt, quae pertinent ad statum et personam dictae Dominae Reginae' (heading of *Rev.* VII, 11, probably by Alphonsus).

(2) *Rev.* VII, 11.

(3) *Rev.* VII, 12.

(4) *Rev.* VIII, 28. *Processus*, p. 373.

(5) *Processus*, p. 249. Cf. *Proc.* p. 322: 'domina comitissa Ariani . . . erat multum amica et devota ipsius domine Brigide.'

(6) *Processus*, p. 251, Elzear only says that he had visited 'quendam infirmum jacentem juxta ecclesiam Sancti Johannis Majoris' and there met Bridget. It is Karin who relates that her mother healed a certain 'dominus Robertus, *canonicus sancti Johannis Majoris.*' (*Proc.* p. 232). Robertus later became a Cistercian.

(7) *Rev.* VII, 5.

(8) *Processus*, p. 323: 'quam revelacionem ipsa domine Brigida fecit conscribi et misit eidem domino Elziario ad Bononiam.'

(9) *Processus*, pp. 252–3.

(10) *Processus*, p. 267.

(11) *Processus*, p. 275; *Rev.* VII, 11 *in fine*.

(12) *Rev.* VII, 52. For an illustration of this gruesome revelation see Andreas Lindblom in 'Ord och bild,' 1915, p. 519.

(13) Matteo Camera: *Memorie storico-diplomatiche dell' antica Città e Ducato di Amalfi*, Vol. I (Salerno 1876), p. 293.

(14) Camera, *op. cit.* p. 200.

(15) Camera, p. 32.

(16) *Extravagantes*, 34.

(17) *Legender från Sverigs medeltid* (Stockholm 1917), pp. 32–3. A re-echo of the words in the office: 'tu exultans suscipias me discipulum Ejus qui pependit in te.'

(18) Camera, pp. 34–6.

(19) *Rev.* VI, 107. *Extravagantes* 99, where, meanwhile, she goes on the journey from Rome, and where the strange note is to be found that on this pilgrimage to Amalfi she 'propter infirmitatem varias transire non poterat nisi in Civitatem Bari.' For Bari does not lie on the way from Rome to Amalfi. Cf. *Processus*, pp. 331, 495; Steffen, *op. cit.*, pp. 313–14.

BOOK VI

I

(1) The exact itinerary was as follows: April 30th, departure from Avignon, arrival at Marseilles May 6th. Here the French Cardinals make a last attempt to keep back the Pope, but, as Gregory XI did later, he overcomes their resistance. May 19th departure from Marseilles, arrival in Toulon the same evening. May 20th Port Olive at Nice, May 22nd the first Italian port, *Albenga*, 23rd Genoa, where the Pope stays until the 28th, Pisa June 1st, Piombino June 2nd, Corneto June 4th, thence to Toscanella, where he spends the night. On June 9th he arrived in Viterbo; several of the French Cardinals went thither by land. (G. Mollat: *Les Papes d'Avignon*, Paris 1912, p. 113.)

(2) See my book *Den hellige Ild* (Udv. Værker, V., pp. 63–6). Giovanni Colombini died 31 July 1367.

II

(1) *Processus*, pp. 359-60, p. 271, p. 387, p. 455. Note the correct dating: 'anno quo felicis recordacionis dominus papa Urbanus Vtus primo venit Romam de mense Augusti ejusdem anni' (p. 359). It is the boy's father himself who gives his testimony in the Process.

(2) Rodocanacchi: *Histoire de Rome de 1354 à 1471*, Paris 1922, pp. 47–8.

(3) *Processus*, p. 260: 'ipsemet loquens' (that is, Magnus Petri) 'portavit unam visionem domino bone memorie domino Urbano papa quinto quam ipsa domina Brigida viderat de prefato domino Urbano.'

(4) *Rev.* IV, 137.

(5) The inscription on this so-called 'red' stone (it had probably once been painted over with red lead to protect it from the weather—now there is no trace of colour to be seen) reads: *et si non poteris habere litteram et gratiam papae et sigillum super concessione dictae indulgentiae, nisi præcedente pecunia, sufficit tibi gratia mea.*

(6) *Diarium*, ad 1405. Silfverstolpe: *Klosterfolket i Vadstena*, p. 107.

(7) Silfverstolpe, p. 107.

III

(1) *Rev.* IV, 45.

(2) 'habebant eam postea in maiorem et honorem,' says her daughter. (*Processus*, p. 329.)

(3) *Rev.* VIII, 51.

(4) 1367 'Blessed Bridget spoke in Rome with both the Pope and the Emperor.' (The year given is incorrect.)

(5) Johanne Skovgaard, pp. 79–80.

(6) *Rev.* IV, 49.

(7) 'dum penitarii oretenus absolvunt, non verecundantur manibus suis sibi pecuniam imbursare' (*Rev.* IV, 33).

(8) 'gaudentes qvod eas in eadem domo audiunt parturire (ibidem).'

(9) *Rev.* VII, 10.

(10) *Summa contra gentiles*, IIa IIae, quæstio, 88, artic. 11.

IV

(1) 'Viaticum pro Dna Birgitta ejusque liberis Carolo de Ulfasa, Birgero et Catherina, de Romana Curia recedentibus ad S. Nicolaum de Baro et locum S. Angeli de Monte Gargano, Siponte diæcesi.' (Celses *Bullarium*, cit. de Flavigny, p. 454, n. 1.)

The passport was issued in Montefiascone 13 June. The departure from Rome did not take place until 13 November.

(2) *Processus*, p. 227.

(3) 'Luigi detto Tarentino visse 15 anni marito di Giovanna . . . mori nel 1362, d'età anni 42, e fu il suo corpo da Napoli portato a Montevergine.' (Bacco Alemanno: *Il Regno di Napoli*. Napoli 1622, p. 219).—Is it this journey that is in question in *Extrav.* 99, where it is said that Bridget 'transire non poterat nisi in Civitate Baro'?

(4) 'conversatus fuit cum ea in Urbe per XV dies' (*Processus*, p. 211).

(5) *Processus*, p. 364. Isak Collijn (*Birgittinske Gestalter*, pp. 107–18) was the first to point out this connection.

(6) 'portabat interdum penes se secrete dum sic irent aliquantulum de zuccara, quam ipse domine Brigide in confortationem corporis, dum sic deficeret, administravit' (*Processus*, p. 367).

(7) *Vita* in Cod. Panisperna. (*Processus*, 635.)

(8) *Extravagantes* 49.

(9) 'plurimum discrepabant a stilo moderno Curie Romane' (*Processus*, p. 231).

(10) *Extravagantes* 99.

(11) *Processus*, p. 230.

(12) 'suadens tamen atque consulens ut regulam beati Augustini quae modo sibi revelato conformior videretur, assumeret.' (Højer: *Studier*, p. 60.)

(13) 'quam bullam . . . vidit, legit et in manibus propriis tenuit tempore prefati pape Urbani V[i] tunc existentis in Montefiascone' (*Processus* 321. It is Niccolà Orsini who is the subject of the discussion).

(14) *Rev.* IV, 138 Latin text; IV, 135 Swedish.

(15) *Processus*, p. 364, p. 372, p. 314.

V

(1) *Rev.* IV, 144.

(2) *Rev.* VI, 67.

(3) *Rev.* IV, 139.

(4) I understand in this way the words *Rev.* IV, 140: 'ipse Papa desiderat de voluntate Dei adhuc plenius certificare.' Gregory is not certain that it is really God who speaks through Bridget.

(5) Collijn, *op. cit.*, pp. 50–51.

(6) *Processus*, p. 372.

(7) *Rev.* IV, 140.

VI

(1) Collijn, *op. cit.*, pp. 42–57.

(2) *Processus*, p. 381.

(3) *Rev.* VII, 11. *Additio.*

(4) 'caveatis diligenter tamquam ab ira Dei quod nec propter ecclesiam seu papam nec propter instancias seu inimicias aut propter pecuniam seu aliquam familiaritatem nunquam sitis dux vel princeps aut cooperator alicuius belli seu guerre nisi pro certo sciveritis quod ex iusticia vos oporteat iuvare seu vindicare aut defendere alios seu auxiliari injuste oppressos.' (K. B. Westman: *Birgitta Studier* I, Uppsala 1911, p. 98.) The letters to Gomez translated into Swedish in Collijn, pp. 58–62, into Danish in Johanne Skovgaard, *Den hellige Birgitta*. Copenhagen 1921, pp. 152–138.

(5) When the bride of Christ was daily staying in Rome and one day was engaged in prayers, it seemed to her that Christ said the following to her: Prepare now to go on a pilgrimage to Jerusalem to repair to my grave and other holy places which are there, and you shall leave Rome on the day that I shall tell you. (*Rev.* VII, 6.) The Son of God spoke to His bride, saying: Go now, leave Rome and go to Jerusalem. (VII, 9.) According to the heading of *Rev.* VII, 6, it seems that the Blessed Virgin had urged upon Bridget to travel 'in die sancti Urbani martiris' (25 May 1371) but the departure did not take place until 'Die sancte Katerine eodem anno' (25 Nov. 1371). *See* in Collijn,

Acta, pp. 95-6, 636. On Mount Gargano Bridget's thoughts had already gone to Jerusalem: 'Quis locus sanctior est Hierusalem, ubi ego Deus impressi vestigia mea? Quis locus nunc despectior, qui ab infidelibus inhabitatur et conculeatur?' (*Rev.* IV, 104. *Additio.*) It is Christ who speaks.

BOOK VII

(1) *Processus*, p. 382.

(2) Westman, pp. 299-301; Johanne Skovgaard, pp. 156-67; Collijn, pp. 60-62.

(3) *Processus*, p. 436.

(4) Johanne Skovgaard, pp. 80-81.

(5) *Processus*, pp. 205, 208.

(6) *Processus*, p. 390.

(7) *Processus*, pp. 290, 349 (with wrong dating—it says *tempore domini Urbani V^u* for *VI^u*).

(8) *Processus*, p. 407.

(9) *Rev.* VII, 28.—On female slaves in the houses of wealthy Christians see Bongi: *Le schiave orientali in Italia* (Nuova Antologia II, 1866, pp. 215-46) and Zanelli: *Le schiave orientali a Firenze nei secoli XIV e XV.* (Firenze 1885). A sonnet by Antonio Pucci contains the lines: *La schiave comperata non à per matrimonio anello in dito, ma ella appaga a me l'appetito.*

(10) *Processus*, p. 379.

(11) *Processus*, pp. 370-71.

(12) *Processus*, p. 249.

(13) *Rev.* VII, 11.

II

(1) *Viaggio da Venezia al Santo Sepolcro ed al Monte Sinai, composta dal R. Padre F. Noè dell' Ordine di S. Francesco* (Treviso 1690), pp. 3-4.

(2) *Rev.* VII, 9 (Swedish text).

(3) *In Galea procura per tempo di aver il tuo alloggiamento a mezza galea, massime chi a triste capo per le agitazioni del mare* (Viaggio, p. 4). At the shipwreck in the harbour of Jaffa Bridget had to be brought up *de sentine galee* (*Processus*, p. 371).

(4) *Processus*, p. 371.

(5) Bernard von Breidenbach: *Opusculum sanctarum peregrinationum ad sepulchrum Christi* (Mainz 1486), fol. 19a-19b.

(6) *Processus*, pp. 429-30.

(7) *Processus*, pp. 431-2.

(8) *Processus*, pp. 327-38.

(9) *Processus*, p. 205.

(10) *Processus*, p. 371.

III

(1) *Rev.* VII, 16. Bridget is thinking of the story in the 20th chapter of Genesis.

(2) Breidenbach, fol. 21a.

(3) *Rev.* VII, 17. Camera: *Memorie*, pp. 231–2.—It was not until 1335 that the Franciscans obtained their convent in Jerusalem and became the guardians of the Holy Sepulchre, as they are to this day.

(4) 'deponat consuetudinem pudorosam mulierum, in strictis vestibus et ostensione mamillarum' (*Rev.* VII, 16).

(5) *Rev.* VII, 16: *de Regina Cypri.*

(6) *Processus*, p. 328: 'quam revelacionem ipsa domina Brigida statim . . . scripsit in vulgari Suenorum et dicti confessores sui transtulerunt eam in latino' (Karin's statement). P. 482: 'Revelaciones . . . quas habuerat in patria Swecie semper eas revelaverat magistro Mathie et isti (ipsi) teste loquenti (Petrus Olai) sed postquam venit Romam, revalavit eas dicto domino Petro et ipsi testi loquenti et domino Alfonso Yspano heremite . . . postquam habuit eius noticiam.'

(7) *Rev.* VII, 16: *de Episcopo Alphonso.*

(8) *Processus*, p. 637a.—On Rama: P. Noè, *op. cit.*, p. 22.

(9) Joinville: *Histoire de Saint Louis*, ch. CVIII.

IV

(1) *Processus*, p. 637a: 'sufficit vobis querere propinquiora propter infirmitatem vestram . . . Cum vero redieritis de Jordane, parate vos ad viam vestram quia adhuc sunt aliqua mittenda summis ponticifibus terre.'

(2) *Processus*, p. 386; *Rev.* VII, 1; *Extravagantes* 63.

(3) *Rev.* VII, 13: 'si possibile esset quod ipsa [Maria] in uno puncto minimo a dignitate in qua est, a Deo remotior fieri posset, ego magis mihi in permutationem eligerem in profundo Inferni eternaliter cruciari.' It is Karl who is speaking.

(4) The Devil is just as coarse in his speech as an Italian of the people, when railing at the Madonna: 'O quam maledicta est illa scrofa seu porca mater ejus.' *Rev.* VII, 13 *in fine.*

V

(1) *Processus*, p. 385.

(2) *Rev.* VII, 14.

(3) 'audivit eandem visionem ab ore ejus . . . in dicta ecclesia sancti Sepulcri prope capellam beate Marie, ubi est pars columne, ad quam Christus flagellatus fuit.' It is Alphonsus who testifies. (*Processus*, p. 385.)

(4) 'perforabant illam clavo per illam partem qua os solidior esset.' *Rev.* VII, 15. So that the nail was not driven in between the bones of the wrist, but through the bone itself; and this is one of the reasons for regarding as genuine the image of Christ on the shroud in Turin, where the mark of Christ's wound in His right hand is to be seen in this very place. *See* Pierre

Barbet: *Les cinq plaies du Christ* (Paris 1935), pp. 14–19. Giuseppe Enrie: *La Santa Sindone, rivelata della fotografia* (Torino 1933), pp. 67–9. Professor Knut Lundmark in Lund has dealt with the whole problem of the authenticity of the shroud of Christ—'at least just as much seems to me to speak for the genuineness of the shroud as against it,' he thinks. 'In addition to this the lofty, stern, impressive gravity of the noble face, the exalted peace while yet in death, and the suggestive, mystic impression radiating from it in spite of the imperfect delineation of the coarse material, speaks its mighty, convincing language to us.' (The image of Christ on Saint Veronica's napkin.) ('Kristusbilden på Svepduken,' *Östgota Correspondenten*, 19, XI, 1940).

(5) *Rev.* VII, 15; Swedish text VII, 16.

VI

(1) 'vidit dictam matrem suam scribentem eandem revelacionem in Jerusalem in hospitali Sancti Sepulcri' (*Processus*, p. 328). It is Karin's testimony.

(2) *Rev.* VII, 16.

(3) *Rev.* VII, 16. *Additio.*

(4) 'possidebat diversa vestimenta et vasa argentea, libros . . . et alia diversa jocalia et utensilia.' (*Processus*, p. 525.)

(5) *Rev.* VII, 20.

(6) *Processus*, pp. 383–4, *cf.* pp. 269, 327, 525. 'Alcuni registrano sotto il 1375 fr. Martino d'Aragona qual Provinciale di Terra Santa . . . il quale invece non fù che il Guardiano di Betlemme, d'ove per concessione pontifica ebbe facoltà di riedificare il convento.' *Serie Cronologica dei RR^{mi} Superiori di Terra Santa . . . compilata dal P. Girolamo Golubovich* (Jerusalem 1898), p. 16.

(7) *Rev.* VII, 18: 'emendati misericordiam Dei consequantur.' Bridget is thinking of a corporal chastisement—*cf.* Saint Luke XXIII, 22, where Pilate says: 'Emendatum ergo illum dimittam'—'I will chastise him therefore and let him go.'

(8) *Rev.* VII, 19 (Latin text); VIII, 23 (Swedish text).

VII

(1) *Ett fornsvensk legendarium*, ed. Stephens, Stockholm. 1847, pp. 88–96. *Legender från Sverigs Medeltid*, pp. 24–6.

(2) Gaetano M. Perrella: *I Luoghi Santi* (Piacenza 1936), pp. 36–8.

(3) *Rev.* VI, 104.

(4) *Rev.* I, 9; VI, 55: 'operata est ibi charitas divina plusquam voluptas carnis.'

(5) *Rev.* I, 26: 'Sanguis charitatis foecundaretur in corpore mulieris, absque aliqua turpi voluptate, et sic mulier fructifera fieret . . . infante concepto absque . . . voluptuosa delectatione . . . sic absque dolore portaret puerum et pareret.' Christ was conceived without Mary having felt 'kötsens orena lusta, hvilken år utan ful lukt'* it says in the Swedish translation of the chapter. In *Sermo*

---

* 'The impure lust of the flesh, which is not without a bad smell.'

Angelicus, cap. X, Bridget returns to the same thoughts—never on earth had there been a marriage like that of Joachim and Anna 'in omni divina charitate et honestate.'

(6) *Rev.* VI, 49: 'veritas est quod ego concepta fui sine peccato originali et non in peccato quia Filius meus et ego sicut nunquam peccavimus, ita nullum conjugium fuit, quod honestior esset quam illud de quo ego processi.' (Cf. *Rev.* V, 13. *Declaratio*: 'Maria vas vacuum . . . ab omni voluptate et peccato.' *Rev.* VI, 55, foretells that this truth of the faith will in due time be made known ('donec veritas claresceret in tempore præordinato'). As is well known, it was Pius IX who on 8 December 1854, defined the dogma of the Immaculate Conception.

VIII

(1) *Processus*, p. 96. *Rev.* VII, 1.

(2) *Rev.* VII, 21-2. Bridget's visit to Bethlehem fell between the 15th and 22nd August. *Processus*, p. 636: 'infra octavas assumptionis virginis Mariae.'

(3) The Blessed Virgin warns Bridget against the apocryphal gospels— *Rev.* VI, 52: 'non est tibi necesse scire.'

(4) Constantine's basilica was completed in the year 330. The pictures mentioned on two of the columns (the fourth and fifth on the right in the nave) —(see the photograph)—have during the most recent times been examined by Hans Kjær, Inspector of Museums, who has also had copies made which can be seen in the museum of Frederiksborg. They are not frescoes, they are executed by the so-called 'encaustic' method, with burnt-in wax colours. 'Saint Canute's picture is 1.40 metres high. The inscription at the head is on a blue background and consists of the words STS CHNUTUS REX DANORUM. The king stands with his right foot stretched out, he has a crown on his head and the halo of a saint. His right hand leans upon a lance, while the left holds a Norman shield, rounded above, pointed below. The king is wearing a white tunic reaching to the feet, over it a long reddish cloak. . . . The shield has ornaments in colours of gold and silver; the crown is a high, ring-shaped diadem with two rows of big precious stones. The picture of Saint Olaf is some- what higher, 1.63 metres, that is, almost lifesize. Like Saint Canute the royal saint is shown in a frontal position. In his right hand he holds a staff that looks like a sceptre; by earlier observers it has been believed to be a sceptre, but there cannot be any doubt that it is Saint Olaf's usual attribute: the axe. Saint Olaf also wears a diadem and has a halo. The inscription reads: STS OLAVUS REX NORVEGIE. The long tunic reaching to the feet has a wide border below, the shield is again a Norman shield . . . the bearing of the figures and their outline are unmistakable in character, simple and majestic—even now, in their faded state they correspond to the fundamental, solemn mood of the basilica. There can be no doubt about the dating . . . everything shows that the pictures were executed in the second half of the twelfth century.' (Hans Kjær, Inspector of Museums: 'Billeder af St Knud og St Oluf i Kristi Fødselskirke i Bethlehem,' *Berlingske Tidende*, 16.3.1932.)

(5) *Rev.* VII, 21. I have omitted the translation of certain details. ('vidi etiam pellem secundinam jacentem prope eum et valde nitidam'; [Maria]

'recepit cum digitis umbilicum ejus qui statim abscissus est.' Bridget knows
all this from experience.

(6) *Rev.* VII, 22.

(7) *Rev.* VII, 23. In the old Swedish translation the shepherds put offensive
questions to Mary and Joseph about the sex of the child—is it a boy or a girl?
They are shown that it is a boy, and they leave 'with much contentment and
joy.' In the Latin text the passage is left out.

(8) *Rev.* VII, 24. *Processus*, pp. 385–6. Saint Jerome relates that his female
disciple Eustochium had had a similar vision, but Alphonsus of Jaen is of the
opinion that Bridget's vision was a greater miracle 'quia [Birgitta] vidit
seriosius et clarius.' Mediæval works of art have presented the Nativity according
to Bridget's vision—Nicolaus of Nola already relates in his testimony (1380)
that he 'in ecclesia sancti Antonii . . . de Neapoli extra muros' had seen such
a presentation of the birth of Christ. (*Processus*, p. 253.) In Denmark we have
the old pilgrimage church at Ondløse near Holbæk. In the summer of 1918
some well-preserved fresco paintings were uncovered there, dating from
between 1450–1475, and among them a presentation of Christmas night. On
the picture it is particularly emphasized that the presentation is founded on
the *Revelationes*, for on the right you see a kneeling figure with a staff in her
hand and a bag over her shoulder. It is not a shepherd, for she is wearing a
woman's kerchief, and there is a halo round her head. 'This figure does not
belong to the usual picture of Christmas night. . . . It is *Saint Bridget* attired
like a pilgrim, kneeling by the crib in Bethlehem, where in the year 1370
[1372] she beheld in a vision that the Virgin Mary showed her what had come
to pass when she gave birth to her Son.' (Poul Nørlund: 'Den hellige Birgitta's
Vision.' A picture in Ondløse church in *Fra Nationalmusæets Arbejdsmark*, 1933,
p. 82). Dr. Nørlund quotes from the relevant passage of *Revelationes*, i.e.,
VII, 21, and continues: 'This is the scene that we see on the picture in Ondløse
church. The Infant Jesus lies in a huge radiant light, and Mary kneels before
Him in her robe; the shoes which she has taken off can be seen . . . in the front
of the picture, beside a piece of cloth, which is either a swaddling-cloth or
Mary's cloak.' A photograph of the fresco is to be found in the above-
mentioned Annual of 1931, p. 62. It was the Swedish art historian, Professor
Henrik Cornell, who was the first, in his book *The Iconography of the Nativity
of Christ* (1924), to point out clearly that we owe to Bridget's vision the
decisive change in the presentation of the birth of Christ which occurs at the
close of the fourteenth century. In his book about Matthias Grünewald (Bonn
1930) Heinrich Feurstein has pointed out very convincingly the Bridgettine
influence on the religious literature of the late Middle Ages (Martin von
Cochem), nay, even on Clemens Brentano's *Leiden Christi*, of the first half of
the nineteenth century.

(9) *Rev.* VI, 1. 'His body was also so clean that never did lice or other
uncleannesses come into His hair'; in the Latin text: 'quia vermis reverentiam
factori suo exhibebat.'

(10) 'Eamus ad Filium Mariae a quo possumus consolari.' (*Rev.* VI, 58.)

(11) *Rev.* VI, 57–8; *Rev.* I, 10; *Rev.* IV, 70. There is a great likeness
between these differing descriptions of the Passion of Christ; they are all the
fruit of a woman's and a mother's entering into the spirit of the drama of

Golgotha. In each individual account there are details not to be found in the
others—*Rev.* IV, 70, e.g. Mary's words, that so long as she lived on the earth
she could never forget her Son's voice when He cried: 'My God, My God,
why hast Thou forsaken Me?' Or little traits like this, that Jesus could not
see His Mother because His eyes were clotted with blood. Or that after death
His mouth was open so that it could be seen that it was full of blood. Bridget
lived through the whole of the terrible martyrdom. And she noticed every
little thing, for instance, that Jesus Himself helped to bind the loin cloth about
Him (IV, 70).

IX

(1) *Legender från Sverigs Medeltid*, pp. 12–14.

(2) Saint Jerome lived in Bethlehem from 386 until his death in 420. He
is one of the four great doctors of the Church, the others being Augustine,
Ambrose and Gregory the Great. Artists have pictured him either in a grotto,
half-naked, engaged in striking himself on his breast with a stone, or com-
fortably installed in his study, guarded by the lion which he had tamed. Above
him hangs on a nail the cardinal's hat which he had declined. The text alluded
to reads: 'quid horum' [the various traditions] 'verius censeatur, ambigimus,
melius tamen Deo cui nihil impossibile est, committimus quam aliquid temere
definire auctoritate nostra.'

(3) Karin of Vadstena's breviary is to be found in the Royal Library in
Stockholm (MS. A, 233); it is a parchment manuscript, 10 by 7 centimetres,
bound in leather, furnished with a clasp, on which there is a lion's head of bone.
The title page depicts the legend of *Sainte Baume*—Mary Magdalen, wrapped
in her golden hair, is borne by four angels up to *le Pilon*, a fifth angel supports
her feet. Below her can be seen a landscape with green trees and a river between
green fields. Round about the picture there is a floral frame of violets, colum-
bine, pinks, strawberries—the violet, according to Oscar Wieselgren of the
Royal Library, is the symbol of the confraternity of the Holy Sepulchre. The
book contains a calendar, the Office of Our Lady, the seven penitential Psalms,
the Litany of All Saints, the Office for the Dead (in the frame, *inter alia*, there
is an ass with pendulous teats and which is playing the lute!). On f. 87 then
begin *Orationes processionis fratrum minorum et peregrinorum factae ad singula loca
sancta in ecclesia Scti sepulcri et primo in capella beate Maria ad columnam*, f. 87b
the prayer which is said in the chapel named, that is, where the pillar of
scourging stands. The following stations are *ubi Christus apparuit beate Marie
Magdalene*—Christ's (legendary) prison—the place where He was deprived of
His garments—the place where He was crowned with thorns—Golgotha,
where Vexilla Regis is sung, the place where His body, when taken down
from the Cross, was laid upon Mary's knees—finally the grave. Next follow
(f. 97a–101b) the prayers said by the pilgrims in Bethlehem during the procession that takes place daily *et primo in altari ubi stella disparuit trium magorum*;
to this day is shown in the grotto of the Nativity the hole into which the star
of the Magi is said to have vanished. From this to the altar over the Crib
to the altar at which the Infant Jesus was circumcised. In her breviary Karin
would be able to experience again all her impressions of the Holy Land. The

manuscript is the work of French hands, but in spite of that she may well have bought it in Jerusalem. French illuminated manuscripts could be bought all over the world.

(4) *Rev.* VI, 60–62.

(5) Afzelius: Sagohäfder, II, 31 and 61, quoted by Paul Riant, *op. cit.*, p. 163.

(6) *Rev.* VII, 26.

(7) *Rev.* I, 8. As Bridget wonders that the Assumption of the Blessed Virgin was made known so late she receives the answer, that the belief in the Resurrection of Christ had to be established first in the minds of men 'quia corda hominum difficilia et dura erant ad credendum Ascensionem ejus—quanto magis si prædicata fuisset statim in initio fidei assumptio mea' (*Rev.* VI, 61).

X

(1) Riant, *op. cit.*, p. 18, n. 2. *Snorra Edda*, ed. Arne Magnussen, I, pp. 446, 450, 578.

(2) Riant, pp. 46, 88–9, 187, 233, 257–8, 359.

(3) *Rev.* VI, 65. *Rev.* IV, 108: 'non dederunt ei [corpori] venenum pro cibo, nec spinas pro indumento, nec jacuerunt in tumulo formicarum.' The rule for Mary and Martha, see *Rev.* VI, 65.

(4) *Rev.* I, 20. It is Christ Himself who applies this proverb to the Blessed Virgin. 'Proverbium antiquum est, quod illud quod juvenis discit in juventute, hoc retinet in senectute.'

(5) *Rev.* VI, 106. Bridget is thinking of the Second Book of Kings, Ch. 2.

(6) *Rev.* IV, 109 and *Rev.* IV, 5, where Peter himself says to Bridget: 'Have you not heard how *forgetful* I was?'

(7) *Rev.* IV, 72.

(8) *Rev.* IV, 68.

(9) *Rev.* IV, 18. See also *Rev.* VI, 93, where the Apostle Peter in a vision informs Bridget that it is he who has protected a woman who wanted to sin, but he contrived it so that she never found time or occasion for it, and when at last she had occasion she no longer had any inclination. At the hour of her death she saw Peter arrayed like a pope and the Peter Martyr the Dominican. The revelation is probably of Bridget's Swedish time, when she was in communication with the Dominicans.

XI

(1) *Rev.* II, 7.

(2) *Rev.* II, 11.

(3) *Rev.* II, 13. 'Hic miles creditur fuisse dominus Carolus filius Sanctae Birgittae,' says the old addition to the chapter. Cf. *Rev.* VIII, 32 and 35. I quote Bridget's own description.

(4) *Rev.* IV, 74.

(5) *Rev.* IV, 89. Other places where Bridget speaks of knights and noblemen are *Rev.* II, 8; II, 10; IV, 73; IV, 76; VI, 28. (Judgment upon a knight.)

(6) *Rev.* VIII, 32.—In the time of the Crusades, probably also in Bridget's time, there were three openings in the altar stone, through which could be seen the rock tomb itself.

XII

(1) *Processus*, p. 430 and pp. 372–3.

(2) *Rev.* VII, 19. Did Bridget foresee that the Turks would take Constantinople in 1430?

(3) *Processus*, p. 431.

(4) *Extravagantes* 75. I have hesitated between Eleanor and Giovanna as addressee. The text only says that it is sent *ad quamdam dominam.*—Cf. *Rev.* IV, 133: 'Qvid autem turpius esset quam quod aliquis nudus os suum in inferiora membra mitteret et comederet stercora sue et biberet urinam suam?'

(5) 'Item quando domina Brigida hospitabatur in sancto Laurentio in Damaso in Urbe, quodam die in crepusculo stabant dominus prior et predictus dominus Petrus ambo simul sedendo et loquendo in solario supra cameram predicte domine. Ipsa vero stabat in camera in oratione ad tunc quedam flamma ignis ascendit de camera et penetrans pavimentum solarij ascendit in altum et statim descendens cecidit in medio eorum, cum tamen non esset ignis materialis de quo ipsi satis mirati fuerunt.' (From a Sienese manuscript of the Process, in Isaak Collijn's edition, p. 641.)

XIII

(1) *Rev.* IV, 107. *Additio.* Cf. *Rev.* IV, 6, where Saint Paul complains that Saint Stephen is not sufficiently honoured, but is neglected 'et maxime ab his qui ei in nocte ac die tenerentur assistere. Hi enim portant ei vasa sua confracta et vacua, lutuosa et abominabilia.' Is Bridget thinking of the Brothers at San Lorenzo fuori le mura? Here Saint Stephen lies buried in the same sarcophagus as Saint Laurence. Perhaps Bridget found that the latter put the former in the shade, and after all, Stephen *was* the proto-martyr.

(2) *Rev.* VI, 28. *Responde mihi, ista audiente,* says the judge. Bridget is standing at his side and listening.

(3) Cardinal Misquini's testimony, *Processus*, p. 563. (Birgittam) 'invenerunt in camera sua et in satis humillimo loco jacentem.'—Alphonsus wrote down the revelation which Bridget then approved *manu sua et nomine proprio.* He read it aloud and delivered the manuscript to the archbishop. *Processus*, p. 363.

(4) *Rev.* VII, 27.

(5) *Processus*, pp. 325, 374, 563.

XIV

(1) *Rev.* VII, 29.

(2) The Uppland law. *See* Vol. I of the present work, p. 15.

(3) *Rev.* VII, 28. 'Illa persona, quam vos bene nostis.' In the whole chapter the archbishop is addressed with 'thou'—'hunc autem scias,' etc. The piece about keeping slaves is left out in the old Swedish translation, not being considered of any interest.

XV

(1) *Rev.* VII, 12.

(2) *Regula*, cap. 30. 'ego indigna persona inter tuos fideles servitores sum sicut minima formica inter fortes camelos qui magnas sarcinas portant ad Domini sui commodum.'

(3) *Rev.* IV, 141. Bridget is thinking of Jeremiah, 23rd chapter. This revelation was not sent to Gregory XI 'quia non fuit ei praceptum divinitus.'

(4) *Rev.* IV, 142.

(5) 'tam istud officium misse quam eciam . . . plures alie revelaciones facte sancte byrgitte reperte sunt in quaternis . . . domini Alphonsi episcopi et confessoris sancte matris nostre byrgitte . . . post mortem ejus' (Uppsala University Library MS. C., 86, in Toni Schmid: *Birgitta och hennes uppenbarelser*, Lund 1940, pp. 203–6). See Brilioth: *Svenska kyrkans historia*, II (Stockholm 1941), pp. 237–8.

(6) *Rev.* VII, 8; *Rev.* IV, 144.

(7) *Rev.* VI, 74. In this prophecy Pope Pius XI saw a prediction of the peace between the Vatican and the Italian State (the Lateran treaty of 11.2.1929).

XVI

(1) *Processus*, p. 290: 'parvula cruce aurea quam dicta domina Brigida tradiderat dicte domine regine.'

(2) *Processus*, p. 390: 'per aliquot dies.'

(3) *Processus*, p. 636: *Extravagantes* 110. The archbishop, too, helped Bridget, *Extravagantes* 111.

(4) *Processus*, p. 544: 'notabat illum verbum diligenter, ne oblivisceretur illud.'

(5) *Rev.* VII, 11.

(6) Johannes Jørgensen: *Den hellige Katerina af Siena*, Copenhagen 1915, pp. 303–5. (English edition pp. 366–7.)

(7) In a Neapolitan Canzone it is said:

> 'Quando non ci à la luna, s'ode un grido
> straziante di dolore,
> che parte dal Castello e va sul lido,
> e per tre volte si ripete e muore,
> quel grido parla chiaro, e vuol vendetta,
> e dice in ogni sera che l'aspetta.
> In ogni notte, in cui venne Ella uccisa,
> mandano le campane del convento
> rintocchi d'agonia,
> e ne la chiesa cantano i leviti,
> fra mortuarii riti,
> funebri salmodie.'

Giovanna was among the exalted persons who were most eager for Bridget's canonization; see her two letters of September and October 1378 to Urban VI. (*Processus*, pp. 54–5.)

Aversa, 12 kilometres from Naples on the road to Benevento.

Muro Lucano, 31 km. from Potenza.

XVII

(1) *Diarium*, ad 1414, 20th November. An Italian woman was also among the first Sisters—the diary mentions 'Margareta, John's daughter, with the surname of the Italian. She came from Rome at the time when Saint Bridget was borne away from it in the year of the Lord 1374'—and died in Vadstena, 22 October 1431.

(2) I make use of Messer Niccolà's letter to Alphonsus of Jaen, a first hand account, reprinted from a manuscript in the Panisperna convent. *Revelationes*, Roma 1628, II, pp. 494–6. In it there is Sir Niccolà's modest remark: 'credens me sapientiorem esse quam sim.'

(3) *Rev.* VI, 81. Torsten Fogelkvist *Karlfeldt* (Stockh. 1940), p. 213.

(4) *Processus*, pp. 234–5. Prior Petrus had seen this letter from Orsini to Alphonsus (*Processus*, p. 517).

(5) *Processus*, p. 273.

(6) *Processus*, p. 288: 'capite coperto velamine juxta ejusdem patrie morem.'

(7) The picture in Sant' Eligio was the gift of Maria, wife of the Spaniard Alphonsus (*Processus*, p. 167). A picture in San Gregorio Magno was the gift of a merchant named Candolus (p. 169). In his letter to Archbishop Birger, Karin mentions these pictures of her mother in Neapolitan churches (Andreas Lindblom: *Den heliga Birgitta*, Stockholm 1918, p. 9. The original in the Swedish National Archives, letters No. 28).

(8) *Processus*, pp. 164–74 = *Instrumentum Neapoli factum* in *Revelationes* 1628, II, pp. 484–90. Concerning Andriolo Mormile, *Processus*, pp. 171–3, 290–92 (Magnus Petri, from what he had heard from Andriolo's sister), pp. 408–10 (the sister's own testimony).

(9) Fernando Russo: *Santa Brigida* (Lanciano 1913), pp. 44–9.

BOOK VIII

I

(1) *Processus*, p. 513.

(2) *Rev.* IV, 23.

(3) *Processus*, pp. 268–9, 322.—Gomez d'Albornoz, cousin Blasco and Garcia, the son of the latter, who was killed in Piediluco in 1368, lie buried in the Franciscan church in Assisi, in the chapel of Sant' Antonio Abate.

(4) *Processus*, p. 518 ('dum de monasterio Sancti Pauli equitaret ut ingrederetur Romam, dominus Robertus primogenitus extitit deputatus, ut eundem papam dextraret'). The young man is so overwhelmed that he even says to the Pope: 'Now I know that the Lady Bridget has spoken the truth!' *Revelationes*, Roma 1628, p. 496.

(5) Mollat: *Les Papes d'Avignon*, p. 271.

(6) *Rev.* IV, 143.

II

(1) *Processus*, p. 359.

(2) *Rev.* VIII, 56: 'qualiter sponsa videbat Agnum et in eo faciem humanam in altari divinae Majestatis in coelo,' etc.

(3) IV, 61: 'Numquid credis tu fama quod haec cortella panis Deus est, diu denique consumptus esset, etiam si mons montium fuisset. Nullus quippe sapientium Judaeorum quibus a Deo data est sapientia, hoc credit.' IV, 63: 'consulo tibi, dimitte cogitare incredibilia et crede oculis tuis. Nonne tu vides et auribus ... audis sonum fractionis hostie materialis panis' (namely when the priest before Communion breaks the Host and lays a piece of It in the chalice with the wine).

(4) *Processus*, p. 482. ('Deus vult per te inmotesci mundo'), *Extrav.* 92. *Processus*, p. 502 ('nascituri predicabunt nomen ejus'). *Processus*, p. 488; *Extravagantes* 93.—On *Castrimargia* Extrav. 57 and Vol. I of the present work, pp. 230, 231.

(5) *Rev.* VI, 94 with *Additio*.

(6) 'Afterwards this creature spoke with Saint Bridget's maiden in Rome, but she could not understand what she said. Then she had a man who could understand her language, and that man told Saint Bridget's maiden what this creature [Margery] said and how she asked after Saint Bridget, her lady. Then the maiden said that her lady, Saint Bridget, was kind and meek to every creature and that she had a laughing face.' (*The Book of Margery Kempe*, 1436. A modern version by W. Butler-Bowdon. London 1936, p. 140.—Fredrik Paasche in *Svenska Dagbladet*, 22.12.1938.)

(7) *Extravagantes* 68 and 67.

(8) *Rev.* VII, 31. *Processus*, pp. 319–20 (Karin's testimony).

(9) *Processus*, p. 319: 'nunquam voluit sumere aliquem cibum corporalem nisi aquam cum qua lavit os suum et nunquam post illam diem voluit mutare linteamenta.'

(10) This letter from Bridget to her son Birger has only been preserved for us in Arvid Trolle's *lagbok* of the end of the fifteenth century and is printed by Klemming, V, pp. 140–41. Madame de Flavigny finds that its style differs much from the tone in *Revelationes*, but this very confidential and familiar style would seem to be a proof of its authenticity. I reproduce it here from Klemming's book:

'Saint Bridget wrote to her son, Sir Birger Ulfsson, lawman in Näricke, from Rome: Praise, honour and glory be to the Lord Jesus Christ, above all for the woeful pain He suffered on the gallows of the cross for our sins. Most dear son, if you desire to have the right love of God, your Creator and Redeemer, then bear ever His Passion in your heart, and prepare yourself often and in the fear of God to receive His holy Body according to the counsel of your confessor. Moreover, wherever you are, if you discover that there are poor people help them as you are able, God will reward you well. Moreover, you must pay well those who have worked for your sake, and chastise those under you justly with mildness and be zealous towards God in your service. When you rise in the morning commend your soul and your life to God and pray to Him to protect your thoughts, words and deeds, sign yourself with the cross before your face and before your heart and say: "Jesus Christ Nazarenus, King of the Jews, have mercy upon me." When you hear Mass, think of the infinite power of Our Lord, His bitter pain and your own sins. When you sit at table, carry on godly and seemly talk and beware of the habit of swearing. Many seldom leave the table until they are like grunting pigs in a common parish house. Do not willingly mention the devil. When you must speak or answer, make the sign of the cross upon your heart and say: "Jesus Christ, Jesus Christ, Jesus Christ." Then you will get the right words both for speaking and answering. If you fear God in all your deeds, and when you sit in judgment, then think with great care of your words before you utter them. Judge your neighbour (fellow Christian) in such a manner that you can answer for it before the stern judgment of God. If anyone does you a wrong then seek the law of Sweden. Do not take revenge in anger. If it be so that a wrong is done to you by those over you, then be content and leave your cause to Our Lord Jesus Christ, and do not doubt that He will help better to gain your right than you can think at any time. With this I commend you with body and soul to the Holy Trinity, to the Virgin Mary and to all the saints in heaven.'

(11) *Processus*, pp. 20–21. *Extravagantes* 69.

(12) *Processus*, p. 506: 'que quidem sacramenta ipse testis (Petrus Olia) dicte domine Birgitte amministravit.' Both Petrus Olai and Karin (p. 320) know that Bridget died 'in ipsa aurora'; and with both of them is to be found Christ's promise to Bridget that she was to be counted as 'Nun and Abbess in Vadstena.'

III

(1) *Processus*, p. 506.

(2) *Processus*, pp. 21–2, 264.

(3) *Processus*, p. 284: 'fecerunt funus inchludi in una capsa (Italian: cassa) lignea et ipsam capsam cooperiri panno et sigillis ipsius domini Birgeri militis et Latini de Ursinis de Urbe et aliorum quam plurium dominorum caute sigillari et in monumento lapideo recondi et sepeliri anno domini MCCCLXXIII die XXVII mensis julii ejusdem anni in monasterio Sancti Laurentii Panisperne infra cancellos ferreos ubi domina Brigida, dum vivebat, elegerat sepeliri.' (Thus Magnus Petri.) This sarcophagus is still to be found in the church of San Lorenzo in Panisperna: Isak Collijn has had a photograph taken of it. (*Birgittinska Gestalter*, p. 72.) The wooden coffin in which Bridget's body was brought home to Vadstena is preserved there in the chapel of the Sanctum Sanctorum, incorrectly called 'Bridget's oratory', in the convent of nuns. Until the solemn enshrining on 1 July 1393, two years after the canonization, Bridget's earthly remains reposed in a grave in the middle nave of the church— they were now laid in a silver shrine, which was solemnly borne up to the high altar by four bishops and deposited there. After her death on 24 March 1381, Karin was also given her grave in the church, her bones, however, were taken up later and in 1489 they were laid in a silver shrine like her mother's. The later fate of the relics in the stormy times following upon the Reformation of Gustavus Vasa have not been clearly set forth. There is, however, a probability that the two skulls which, with several other bones, are to be found in the saints' shrine adorned with the coat of arms of the Swedish nobility in the

chancel behind the high altar, may have belonged to Bridget and Karin. Some years ago both the wooden coffin and the bones were examined by Professor Carl M. Fürst. The coffin was found to be of Italian wood (stone-pine), and of the two skulls Fürst stated that one of them was that of a person of about 156 centimetres in height, the other of one of about 177 centimetres—the little Bridget and the tall Karin? (Andreas Lindblom: *Birgitta Utställningen*, Stockholm 1918, pp. 106–16. *See also* Carl M. Kjellberg: *Vadstena*, pp. 182–4.) A lady born in Vadstena, Madame Charleville Larsson, told me that in her childhood the shrine with the two skulls had stood open in the so-called 'image room'* (the former convent library) among other antiquities, and that the children went there and looked at the bones. Under the care of the 'Birgittastiftelse' (Birgitta Institution) everything has now been put in seemly order. (*See* Andreas Lindblom, *Vadstena*, Stockholm 1925, pp. 16–17.)—That Bridget was small of stature appears, *inter alia*, from *Extravagantes* 100: 'quædam domina mediocris staturæ,' who is Bridget.

(4) *Processus*, p. 342.

(5) *Processus*, pp. 284–5, 507.

(6) 'pannos laneos et lineos qvoddam cofanetum quod est altare cum calice, thuribulo et ampullis argenteis et cum quodam ymagine cum certis reliquiis sanctorum, libris ecclesiasticis, paramentis sacerdotalibus . . . cum quibusdam aliis ornamentis et rebus aptis ad missam et divina officia cele-brandum et certa privilegia papalia propter que . . . eis concessum quod . . . possunt pro se et corum familia . . . missas facere celebrari eo quod sunt persone totaliter spirituales.' (The original in the archives of the Swedish kingdom. A reproduction in Isak Collijn's *Birgittinska Gestalter*, p. 80.)—It is from Francesca Papazuri's letter to Lapa Buondelmonte that we know the day of departure, 2 December (Isak Collijn, p. 20: 'iverunt in patriam suam die secundo mensis decembris').

(7) *Processus*, pp. 71–3: 'quendam quaternum papireum; plura alia sciunt de vita dicte domine Brigide, sed propter eorum repentinum recessum ad partes Swecie ea scribere et et testificare, protunc non poterant.'—The text has several times erroneously Montefiascone for Montefalco.

(8) *Processus*, p. 104.

(9) Saint Clare of Montefalco, b. 1268, d. 1308. *See* her *Vita*, written *circa* 1315, edited by Faloci-Pulignani in *Archivio storico per le Marche e per l'Umbria*, I, pp. 583–635 and II, pp. 193–266.

(10) Karin's testimony given in Rome 31.8.1379, Alphonsus of Jaen's 16.9 in the same year (*Processus*, pp. 303, 363). According to *Vita Beatae Catherinae* 'duo de prioribus' accompanied the funeral cortège as far as Danzig. (Cap. XIII).

IV

(1) *Processus*, p. 285 (Magnus Petri), p. 344 (Karin), p. 550 (Petrus Olai). All three declare that it happened during the journey 'per Marchiam Anconi-tanam' and that it was 'in una civitate cujus nomine non recordatur.'

(2) *Processus*, p. 145.

* Old Swedish 'Celätes Kammere.'

(3) *Processus*, pp. 286–7, 345, 551.

(4) *Vita Beatae Catherinae*, cap. XIII.

(5) *Vita Beatae Catherinae*, cap. XIV.—The hymn *Rosa rorans* was composed by Nicolaus Hermanni. The first lines might be rendered in English something like this: 'Rose, thou whose dew is goodness—star, thou who dost shine out brightness—Birgitta, thou vessel of grace.'

(6) 'Qvibus . . . monita dabat salutis ut, perituri luxus seculi pompis postpositis, futurorum honorum desideriis ardentis inhiarent.'

(7) *Vita B. Catherinae*, cap. XIII, 'in Alemaniae, Italiae et Hispaniarum partibus' (Petrus Olai is probably thinking of Compostella) 'et in regionibus transmarinis.'

(8) *Processus*, p. 148.

(9) *Processus*, pp. 147–8.

(10) Jovan Pätterson was brother to Bridget's chaplain Magnus Petri. From 1371 it was he who directed the building of the convent in Vadstena. He entered the Order later and died nearly ninety years old (*Diarium* 18.9.1405). For eight years he had been paralysed and almost dumb, but was extolled by everyone for his angelic patience. (Silfverstolpe: *Klosterfolket i Vadstena*, p. 107.)

(11) Ortved: *Cistercierordenen i Norden*, p. 129.

(12) 'Samlinger utgifna af Svenska Fornskrift-Sälskapet.'

(13) *Diarium*.

(14) *Processus*, p. 558: 'Ego sum Brigida quae de Roma veni!'

V

(1) Isak Collijn: *Birgittinska Gestalter*, p. 20. 'Et sciatis quod de recessu eorum fui multum melancoliosa, in tantum quod postquam nata fui, non portavit tantum dolorem in corde meo.' Francesca intends to arrange the room in which Bridget died as a chapel and begs her friend to grant her an altar picture of the crucified Christ, His sorrowing Mother, John the Evangelist, John the Baptist, the Apostles Peter and Paul 'who embrace each other,' Saint James, Saint Catherine, Magdalene and Agnes—all Bridget's saints.

CHRONOLOGICAL SURVEY

1349 Bridget leaves Sweden.

1349 The Black Death devastates all Europe.

1350 Bridget in Rome. Visit to Farfa. Karin to Rome.

1350 Eggert von Kuren dies. Cola di Rienzo from Monte Majella via Rome to Prague.

1352 Bridget in Assisi.

1352 December 6, Clement VI dies. December 18, Innocent VI elected Pope.

1353

1353 Cardinal Albornoz to Italy.

1354 Bridget moves to the Campo de' Fiori.

1354 Cola di Rienzo's entry into Rome. He is murdered October 8.

1355 Birger Ulfsson in Rome.

1355 The Emperor Charles IV comes to Rome.

1356

1356 Duke Erik's rebellion against King Magnus.

1358

1358 King Magnus excommunicated.

1359

1359 Duke Erik dies.

1360

1360 Scania given up to Denmark.

1361

1361 Valdemar Atterdag takes Visby.

1362

1362 September 12, Innocent VI dies.
September 28, Urban V elected Pope.

1363

1363 Louis of Taranto dies. King Haakon of Norway betrothed to Margaret of Denmark. Queen Blanca dies.

1364

1364 Albrecht the Younger of Mecklenburg becomes King of Sweden.

1365 Bridget's first pilgrimage to Monte Gàrgano and Bari (July). Bridget comes to Naples.

1365 The battle of Gata. King Magnus taken prisoner.

1366 Bridget in Naples.

1366 November 8, Niccolà Acciaiuoli dies.

1367 Bridget leaves Naples. Is in Rome again (October).

1367 April 30, Urban V leaves Avignon, arrives in Italy June 4. August 24, Cardinal Albornoz dies. Urban V in Rome October 16.

1368

1369 Karl and Birger in Rome.
June 11, Papal pass to Monte Gargano and Bari. Second pilgrimage.

1370 August 5, Urban V's bull to Bridget.

1371 Karl and Birger again in Rome.
November 25. Departure from Rome to the Holy Land.

1372 March 12, Karl dies.
March. Departure from Naples.
May. Arrival at Jaffa.
May 13, Jerusalem.
August 15-22, Bethlehem.
October 8, Cyprus.

1373 February. Arrival in Naples.
Last letter to Gregory XI.
April 17, Easter in Rome.
July 23, Bridget dies.
November 13. Pass for the journey home.
December 2. Departure from Rome.
December 14, Montefalco.
Process of canonization begun.

1374 July 4, Funeral cortège arrives in Vadstena.

1375

1378 September 16, Master Petrus of Skenninge dies.

1381 March 24, Catherine of Vadstena dies.

1388 August 19, Alphonsus of Jaen dies.

1390 April 9, Prior Petrus Olai dies.

1391 May 2, Nicolaus Hermanni dies.
August 27, Birger dies.
October 7, Bridget's Canonization.

1368 October 21, Emperor Charles IV and Urban V in Rome.

1369 Jovan Pätterson returned from Rome to Vadstena.

1370 September 16, Urban V returns to France.
December 16, Urban V dies.
December 29, Gregory XI elected Pope.

1371 King Magnus liberated.
The building of the convent in Vadstena begun.

1372 Nicolaus Hermanni Bishop of Linköping.

1374 King Magnus dies.

1375 October 24, Valdemar Atterdag dies.

1378 March 27, Gregory XI dies.
April 8, Urban VI Pope.

PICTURES OF SAINT BRIDGET

Concerning the woodcut which I have used as a frontispiece see Isak Collijn: "Några sällsynta Birgitta Träsnit" (*Nordisk Tidskrift för Bok och Biblioteksväsen*, Stockholm 1927). The name *Mathis* below on the left is perhaps the name of the engraver, or it may be an allusion to Bridget's famous confessor Master Matthias.—About the next picture, "Birgitta as a pilgrim," see Nils Ludvig Rasmusson in the above-named periodical, Stockholm 1942, pp. 20–29.—The frequently occurring representations of Bridget in which she sits at a desk, and a ray of light from heaven reaches her (as in the Roman edition of 1628) are based on *Rev.* I, 34, where the Devil says to Christ: "Ego video quasi quoddam ardens descendere de te in eam, quod sic alligat cor ejus, ut nihil aliud cogitet vel diligat nisi te." On other pictures she is seen at prayer before a crucifix in San Paolo fuori le mura, which is said to have spoken to her; this crucifix is still to be seen in a chapel on the left of the high altar and in a niche in the wall there is a marble statue of the saint. Another crucifix which is said to have spoken to Bridget is in the church of Santa Maria in Montecelli, in Rome. (Information by letter from the author, Karin Gustaf's daughter von Horn.) A survey of Bridget's iconography in Vol. V of Klemming (Stockholm, 1883). See also I. Collijn: *Iconographia Birgittina typica* (Stockholm, 1915) and Isak Collijn och Andreas Lindblom: *Birgitta Utställningen* (Stockholm, 1918), pp. 169–174.

INDEX

ÅBJÖRNSSON Sparre, Ulf, seen by Bridget in a vision, 172–5; died (1355), 174; his widow, 171

Acciaiuoli, Lorenzo, 185

Acciaiuoli, Niccolà, 120; his death and judgment foreseen by Bridget, 183–8; dies (1366), 184; buried at Val d'Ema, 185

Agnes, St., Bridget's attachment to, 43; said to have taught her Latin, 44; reveals herself to Bridget in her church, 131–2.

Albornoz, Cardinal, welcomes Urban V at Corneto, dies (1367), 204

Albornoz, Gomez, Papal vice-gerent in Perugia, 224–5, 227; makes Bridget's acquaintance (1373) and receives two letters from her, 228–30, 232–3, 295; escorts Bridget's remains from Rome, 304 seqq.

Albrecht of Brandenburg, Duke, married to King Magnus' sister Euphemia (1336), 151–2; died as King of Sweden (1389), 153; instrument for executing judgment on King Magnus, 178

Algotsson, Bengt, his career, 117; 'the devil's servant', 141; denounced by King Erik, 148; killed (1360), 142

Algotsson, Knut, 117

Alphonsi, Ludovicus, a witness in the process of canonization, 67

Alphonsus of Jaen, first hears of Bridget, 219; her last spiritual director, 40; accompanies her on pilgrimage to Monte Gàrgano and Bari (1369), 218; undertakes final edition of the Revelationes and accompanies Bridget at her audience with Urban V at Montefiascone, 220; takes Bridget's letter for Gregory XI to Niccolà Orsini, 225–6; accompanies Bridget to the Holy Land, 234; at Karl's deathbed, 236; loses his belongings in the wreck off Jaffa, 240–1; takes first place as translator of the Revelations,

242; told by the Blessed Virgin how to regard Bridget, 243; reads Bridget's message to the Neapolitans, 278; takes Bridget's letter to Gregory XI, his Mass in honour of 'Our Lady Simony', 284; returns to Rome to pray by Bridget's coffin, 303; escorts her remains as far as Montefalco, 304–5; dies (1388), 16

Altopascio, 15

Amalfi, 198–9

Ammundsen, Sir Ingvald, brings Lady Gisla's bridal crown to Rome, 103

Ancona, Bridget's remains at, 305

Andreas of Lucca, 218, 232

Andrew, St., 198–9

Antichrist, 114, 223

Antioch, John, Duke of, 240, 251; accused of abetting the murder of Peter I, 252

Ariano, Countess Francesca of, 183; an intimate friend of Bridget, 192; visits her, 236–7

Arnaldo, Abbot of Farfa, 55, 56

Atterdag, Valdemar, King of Denmark, Bridget's bitterest enemy, 3; takes Scania, 146, Gothland and Öland (1361), 147

Aubert, Etienne, Pope Innocent VI, 79

Augustine, St., tomb of, visited by Bridget, 14

Ave Maris Stella, 316

Aversa, Bridget stays with Queen Giovanna at, 286

Bari, 166 *seqq.*

Barletta, 165

Bartold, Abbot of Varnhem, 67

Beatrix of Brandenburg, contracts marriage with Erik Magnusson (1346), 142; her death, 321

Beaufort, Cardinal Hugo de, brother of Clement VI, places his palace at Bridget's disposal, 19

Beaufort, Pierre Roger de, *see* Gregory XI

345